The RCN in retrospect,
1910-1968

DATE DUE

JAN 2 5 1993	
MAR 2 2 1999	
MAR 0 3 2002	
OCT 3 2002	

THE RCN IN RETROSPECT, 1910-1968

The

RCN in Retrospect,

1910-1968

edited by James A. Boutilier

The University of British Columbia Press
Vancouver and London

THE RCN IN RETROSPECT, 1910-1968

The RCN in Retrospect, 1910-1968
  ISBN 0-7748-0152-2
    1. Canada. Royal Canadian Navy—History—
Addresses, essays, lectures. 2. Canada—
History, Naval—20th century—Addresses,
essays, lectures. 3. World War, 1939-1945—
Naval operations, Canadian—Addresses, essays,
lectures. I. Boutilier, James A. 1939-
FC231.R392   359′.00971   C82-091038-4
F1028.5.R392

INTERNATIONAL STANDARD BOOK NUMBER 0-7748-0152-2

Printed in Canada

This book is dedicated to those who served.

A large number of organizations and individuals contributed generously to "The RCN in Retrospect" conference and to the publication of these proceedings. Institutions providing funds are listed below:

The Social Sciences and Humanities Research Council of Canada
The Leon and Thea Koerner Foundation
The Department of National Defence, Canada
The Ministry of the Provincial Secretary and Government Services of the Province of British Columbia
Halifax Industries Limited
Davie Shipbuilding Limited
The Naval Officers Associations of Canada
The Navy League of Canada
Burrard-Yarrows Corporation
Victoria Machinery Depot
The McLean Foundation

This book has also been assisted by the Government of British Columbia through the British Columbia Cultural Fund, the British Columbia Lottery Fund, and the British Columbia Heritage Trust.

CONTENTS

LIST OF ILLUSTRATIONS

CHARTS

ABBREVIATIONS

AMC	armed merchant cruiser
AS	anti-submarine
ASDIC	submarine detection equipment
ASROC	anti-submarine rocket-delivered torpedo system
ASW	anti-submarine warfare
ATP	Allied Tactical Publication
BAD	British Admiralty Delegation
BATM	British Admiralty Technical Mission
BdU	*Befehlshaber der U-boote* (U-boat headquarters)
BHP	brake horse power
CCNF	commodore commanding Newfoundland Force
CFR	Canadian Fleet Reserve
CGS	Canadian Government Ship
CID	Committee of Imperial Defence
CinC, CNA	commander-in-chief Canadian North West Atlantic
CINCLANT	commander-in-chief US Atlantic Fleet
CinCWA	commander-in-chief Western Approaches
CNAS	Canadian Naval Air Service
CNO	chief of Naval Operations
CNS	chief of the Naval Staff
CNTS	Canadian Naval Technical Services
COAC	commanding officer Atlantic Coast
COMINCH	comander-in-chief U.S. Fleet
COMNAVFE	commander Naval Forces Far East
CTF	commander Task Force
CTG	commander Task Group
CTU	commander Task Unit
DDE	destroyer escort
DDH	helicopter destroyer
DEW	Distant Early Warning (line)
DF	direction-finding
DNAD	Directorate of Naval Air Division
DNI	director of Naval Intelligence
DOH	Directorate of History
EASTOMP	Eastern Ocean Meeting Point
ECM	electric cypher machine

ECM	electronic counter-measures equipment
EPI	electronic position indicator (stations)
ERA	engine room artificer
FCR	fire control room
FIS	Foreign Intelligence Service
FONF	flag officer Newfoundland Force
FR	Fishermen's Reserve
HSD	higher submarine detector
HDWS	high definition warning surface radar
HEDA	high explosive direct action shells
HF/DF	high-frequency direction-finding
HHRSD	helicopter haul down and rapid securing device
HMCS	His/Her Majesty's Canadian Ship
LCVP	landing craft vehicle and personnel
LSI	landing ship infantry
ML	motor launch
MOD	Ministry of Defence
MOEF	Mid-Ocean Escort Force
MSTS	Military Sea Transport Services
MTB	motor torpedo boat
NATO	North Atlantic Treaty Organization
NBCD	nuclear biological and chemical defence and damage control
NCDO	Naval Central Drawing Office
NDHQ	National Defence Headquarters
NEDIT	Naval Engineering Design Investigation Team
NEF	Newfoundland Escort Force
NID	Naval Intelligence Division
NMCS	naval member Canadian Staff
NOIC	naval officer in charge
NORAD	North American Air Defence Command
NRC	National Research Council
NRE	Naval Research Establishment
NSCPA	Naval Stores Central Procurement Agency
NSHQ	Naval Service Headquarters
OIC	Operational Intelligence Centre

OPNAV	chief of Naval Operations
OPS	operations room
OSS	operation support ships
PC	patrol craft
RAN	Royal Australian Navy
RCNAS	Royal Canadian Naval Air Service
RCN/CCF	RCN Committee on Corrosion and Fouling
RCNR	Royal Canadian Naval Reserve
RCNVR	Royal Canadian Naval Volunteer Reserve
RDF	radio direction-finding
RFC	Royal Flying Corps
RMC	Royal Military College
RNAS	Royal Naval Air Service
RNCC	Royal Naval College of Canada
RNCVR	Royal Navy Canadian Volunteer Reserve
RNFAA	Royal Naval Fleet Air Arm
RNR	Royal Naval Reserve
RNVR	Royal Naval Volunteer Reserve
ROK	Republic of Korea
SACLANT	Supreme Allied Commander, Atlantic
SPENAVO	Special Naval Observer
SSF	Special Service Force
STR	Submarine Tracking Room
TACAN	tactical air navigation device
TF	Task Force
TU	Task Unit
UNTD	University Naval Training Division
VDS	variable depth sonar
VR	Volunteer Reserve
WLEF	Western Local Escort Force
WOMP	Western Ocean Meeting Point
WPL	Western hemisphere Defense Plan
WT	wireless telegraphy
Y-ARD	Yarrow-Admiralty Research Department

PREFACE AND ACKNOWLEDGEMENTS

The twentieth century has been a naval century, an age punctuated by the names of great commanders, warships and engagements: Togo and Nimitz, *Dreadnought* and *Bismarck*, Tsushima and Midway.

It has witnessed the rise and fall of mighty navies: The Royal Navy at its zenith in a moment of qualified glory; the Imperial Japanese Navy, triumphant and shattered; the United States Navy with its giant aircraft carriers and submarines patrolling the oceans of the world; and the Soviet Navy, aggressive, modern, and far-flung.

It has highlighted the value and versatility of sea power; protecting convoys in the Battle of the Atlantic; providing a springboard for invasion in Normandy and North Africa; destroying enemy shipping; and serving as a vehicle for contemporary gunboat diplomacy.

The Royal Canadian Navy was part of that great maritime tradition. It was shaped by and helped to shape this naval century. *The RCN in Retrospect* is a study of the commanders, warships, and engagements of Canada's navy. It traces the rise and fall of that gallant service, highlighting its various roles and remarkable accomplishments.

The chapters in *The RCN in Retrospect* are characterized by a mixture of sadness, pride, and admonition: sadness at the passing of a fighting force, pride in its achievements, and admonition to those who ignore the lessons of naval history.

The RCN in Retrospect is the result of a collective effort. I am greatly indebted to those who supported the idea of a conference on the history of

Canada's naval service and those who assisted me subsequently in the preparation of the proceedings for publication.

Without the support and enthusiasm of Colonel George Logan, the commandant of Royal Roads Military College, Commander Michael Morres, the vice-commandant, and Dr. William Rodney, the dean of Arts and head of the Department of History and Political Economy, "The RCN in Retrospect" conference, from which this book sprang, would not have been possible.

Captain Ed Zdancewicz and Mrs. Hélène Smith worked tirelessly to make the conference a success. I cannot thank them enough for their devotion and dedication. My thanks go as well to Ross Thomas and Chris Barrett of the College's audio-visual department for the excellent technical support they provided and also to the staff of the College who embraced the conference project so wholeheartedly. For their part, the authors allowed themselves to be harrassed and cajoled into writing their accounts, accepted editorial revisions with gentlemanly grace, fielded my enquiries with good humour, and made my work infinitely easier by their professionalism, patience, and commitment.

Supporting me at every stage were typists, proofreaders, mapmakers, and others. I would particularly like to thank Eileen Taylor who unhesitatingly worked overtime to type portions of the text, Eleanor Lowther for her craftsmanship in preparing the entire typescript, Rhonda Batchelor who helped so much with the editorial ground work, Susan Plumpton and Richard Niven, the director, Base Hydrographic Office, HMC Dockyard, Esquimalt, who prepared the maps of the Canadian Arctic, Danushya Hart who rendered indecipherable manuscript crisp and clean, Sergeant Marilyn Smith, the director of the Maritime Command Museum in Halifax, whose support was absolutely invaluable, Kathy Clark who wrestled good-naturedly with a daunting amount of correspondence, Captain Keith Cameron and Wally Yager of the Maritime Museum of British Columbia, who gave their professional advice freely and thoughtfully, the Canadian Forces Photo Units in Ottawa and Halifax, Joy Houston of the Public Archives of Canada, who tracked down so many photographs for me, Hal Lawrence who provided inspiration and an editor's eye, Derek Lukin Johnston of Vancouver whose wonderful enthusiasm gave me the necessary ginger when my spirits flagged, Fraser McKee, Skinny Hayes, Vernon Howland, and others of the Naval Officers Associations of Canada who worked so hard to raise funds for the conference and the book, Dr. W.A.B. Douglas, director of the Directorate of History, National Defence Headquarters, and his staff who were always extremely willing to help, Rear-Admiral Robert Murdoch, RCN (Ret'd.), for his constant encouragement, and Rear-Admirals Nigel Brodeur (ably assisted by his Staff Officer Lieutenant R.E. Burton), Robert Yanow, William Hughes, and John Tucker who did everything within their power to make the resources of the Department of National Defence available to me for the conference and publishing points.

Allan C. Harris, the managing editor of *Warship International*, and Commander W.R. Pettyjohn, USN, editor of *Naval War College Review*, generously granted permission for the reproduction of chapters 8 and 9, respectively.

I owe a great debt as well to the staff of UBC Press, to the director Tony Blicq who put his trust in *The RCN in Retrospect*, to Jane Fredeman and Brian Scrivener whose editorial assistance was tremendously valuable, and to all of the other staff members who supported me so ably.

I want to acknowledge the steadfast faith of my mother and father in my endeavours. Sadly, my mother did not live to see this volume completed. And lastly, I want to thank Bryony Wynne-Jones, whose encouragement, help, patience, and enthusiasm made this undertaking doubly worthwhile.

James A. Boutilier
Royal Roads Military College
Victoria
January 1982

INTRODUCTION

James A. Boutilier

This book is about one of the world's great navies, the Royal Canadian Navy. Its origins were humble. In 1910 the newly established RCN consisted of two aging, genteelly named cruisers, HMCS *Rainbow* and HMCS *Niobe*, and a handful of officers and men who looked to the Royal Navy for training and inspiration. Canadian naval operations during World War I were on a modest scale, with *Niobe* patrolling off New York and *Rainbow* transporting czarist bullion to Vancouver. There were no grand engagements, no Ypres, no Passchendaeles to excite the public imagination and secure for the RCN the patriotic support enjoyed by the Canadian army. Confined to the coasts and lacking a sentimental constituency in the towns and villages of the land, the Naval Service barely survived the penniless and pacific years between the wars. Undermined by public apathy, political uncertainty, and inter-service rivalry, Canada's derisively entitled "Five Trawler Navy" was reduced to a skeleton force. All that stood between it and extinction were a few second-hand RN destroyers and the dedication of its personnel.

World War II changed all that. The RCN became the third largest navy in the Allied cause. Its expansion was dramatic; its tasks, daunting. The war at sea was grim and unrelenting, the enemy skilful and tenacious. Doughty corvettes and salt-stained frigates plowed out of Halifax, Sydney, and St. John's to shepherd vital convoys to the United Kingdom. Canadian warships sailed to Murmansk, sank U-boats in the Caribbean, rescued refugees, transported theatrical Greek politicians, and bombarded the

Normandy coasts. But the war was not only at sea. Ashore, the RCN struggled to achieve operational autonomy; to free itself from the historic and strategic imperatives that had subordinated it, first to the RN and then, increasingly, to the USN.

When the war was over retrenchment and uncertainty weakened the Naval Service. The child of the Royal Navy, it was slow to bring about changes in keeping with postwar Canadian values. Mutinies and cutbacks blighted the RCN, but it recovered its fighting spirit during the Korean War. New and sophisticated destroyer-building programmes altered the navy's face during the 1950's and 1960's, while the emotional debate over the unification of Canada's armed forces rocked the navy to its foundations. The White Ensign—that symbol of RCN identity and association with the Commonwealth—was laid up in 1965 and three years later the Royal Canadian Navy ceased to be. The public remained largely unconcerned about the navy's plight. A maritime nation had displayed its indifference to the sea.

This book is the result of a conference entitled "The RCN in Retrospect," held at Royal Roads Military College in Victoria, British Columbia, in March 1980. I had four objectives in organizing that conference: to encourage historians to undertake research on the RCN, to encourage ex-RCN personnel to record their experiences, to bring these two groups together in dialogue, and—by way of this book—to re-introduce Canadians to their naval heritage.

The time seemed right. The RCN was scheduled to celebrate its seventieth anniversary in 1980, and more than a quarter of a century had elapsed since Gilbert Tucker had completed his history of Canada's naval service— a study to which each of us associated with this book owes a great debt. What is more, many of the principal actors in the RCN drama were passing from the stage. It seemed that we had reached a critical juncture: we were far enough away from the RCN to begin examining its history dispassionately, yet we were able, at the same time, to draw upon the recollections of some of its most important members.

The chapters of this book were written by historians, naval officers, and students of naval history. Their accounts vary in character and approach. Some are anecdotal, some archival. Some are exercises in diplomatic history; some are personal memoirs. The authors of these chapters discuss seven interrelated themes: the ways in which the RCN reflected and contributed to the national experience, the RCN's struggle for operational autonomy, the interplay of politics and naval policy, the roles of manpower and technology in RCN history, the navy's small-ship character, the spirit of Canada's naval service, and the importance of writing and revising Canadian naval history.

The RCN conference called forth, in the words of the naval historian

Philip Lundeberg, "striking examples of the constructive value and inevitability of sound historical revisionism, based on the availability of new evidence and the exploration of aspects earlier overlooked or deliberately ignored."

Rear-Admiral Nigel Brodeur of the Canadian Forces, for example, draws upon the private papers of his grandfather, Louis Philippe Brodeur, to shed new light on the origins of the RCN, while L.C. Audette, the last surviving member of the Mainguy Commission (convened to investigate mutinies in the RCN in 1949) draws not only upon his own recollections but also upon a vast body of commission evidence. These papers provide a re-evaluation of that commission's deliberations and of the state of Canada's immediate postwar navy.

Perhaps the most striking contributions to the historical record of the RCN are the chapters on the Battle of the Atlantic (1939-45) by Beesly, Milner, Lund, and Rohwer and Douglas. Lieutenant-Commander Patrick Beesly, RNVR (Ret'd.), was deputy head of the Admiralty's Submarine Tracking Room during much of World War II. He is thus uniquely qualified to comment upon the Battle, the links between the intelligence organizations in London, Ottawa, and Washington, and the hitherto largely secret roles of the Tracking Room and the Operational Intelligence Centre. He highlights the vital contribution made by "Special Intelligence" (the cryptanalysis of coded German message traffic) to the routing of convoys and the destruction of German U-boats.

Marc Milner examines the failure of historians to explain adequately the RCN's role in the crucial convoy battles of early 1943, while Commander W.G. Lund of the Canadian Forces analyses the nature of, and the lessons that can be derived from, coalition naval warfare.

Jürgen Rohwer and W.A.B. Douglas reveal, through comprehensive research in Allied and German documentation, the part played by the RCN in three great convoy battles in the North-Atlantic—SC 42, SC 107, and ONS 5. Their study illustrates "the value of re-examining events of the past in the light of new knowledge." On hearing their presentation, one of the participants in the RCN conference observed, "Now, for the first time, I understand what happened on that night in 1941." Confined to one corner of the convoy, he had been unable to grasp the magnitude and complexity of the struggle unfolding around him. The Rohwer/Douglas reconstructions are likely to be the most exacting analyses of RCN convoy operations available in naval literature for a long while to come.

The RCN was a national institution, reflecting and contributing to Canadian social and political life. Yet, when we examine the record, it appears that Canadians cared relatively little for their naval service. Brodeur highlights the reluctance of Canadian politicians prior to World War I to support the concept of a navy and refers to his grandfather's chagrin at the fact that the RCN failed to enjoy the favour it deserved. Barry Hunt describes how the Minister of the Naval Service, C.C. Ballantyne, "enraged and disgusted" by the apathy of his cabinet colleagues, ordered the RCN to be disbanded on 1 July 1920. His order was rescinded later, but the RCN limped through the 1920's and the 1930's in a dangerously neglected state, its annual budget slashed at one point to one-and-a-half million dollars.

The Battle of the Atlantic was Canada's sternest test and her greatest triumph. Yet the moment the war was over, the once proud service became a taxpayer's burden. During the 1950's and 1960's the RCN barely held its own for want of funds and public support, as Captain (NR) Michael Hadley describes in his chapter on public policy and the naval reserves. The naval reserves acted as a barometer reflecting the shifts in parliamentary and national attitudes towards defence in general and naval policy in particular. Unfortunately, the reserves have enjoyed a precarious existence and in the 1980's, with their slow moving, thirty-year-old ships and simulated convoy exercises, they appear to be "a paper force preparing for a paper war."

But the public and politicians were not the only ones to blame for the RCN's plight. The Naval Service itself was often sadly out of step with the times. As Rear-Admiral R.H. Leir, RCN (Ret'd.), Rear-Admiral P.W. Brock, RN (Ret'd.), and Rear-Admiral H.F. Pullen, RCN (Ret'd.) explain, the training of RCN midshipmen and junior officers took place in the Royal Navy between 1910 and 1951. As a consequence, young RCN officers absorbed the ethos of a foreign naval service, a world where officers were born to lead and men were born to be led. This "Big Ship Time" was invaluable, but it produced a fraternity of officers who tended to stand apart from the thousands of Royal Canadian Naval Volunteer Reserve officers who entered the navy during World War II. The RCNVR personnel seldom had long-term commitments to the service. The nation needed them, there was a job to be done, and they got on with it as well as they could, with little time for naval niceties. With their entry, the RCN became a force divided between the regulars and the reservists, between "the club" and the newcomers. Each group promoted unfair caricatures of the other. The former guarded their positions jealously, regarding the reservists as amateurs, while the latter perceived the regulars as privileged, blundering, or both.

When the war was over, the RCN suffered the dislocations associated with wholesale demobilization and the dismemberment of the fleet. There was a sense of uncertainty in the air. What would Canada's peacetime navy be like? And was there a role for a small navy in the atomic age, an age in which the awesome dimensions of warfare seemed to render traditional naval operations irrelevant? A significant number of officers failed to adjust easily to the new peacetime realities. The dichotomy in their ranks led to dissension, and their seniors failed to reduce the rivalry or to arrest the decline.

Not only was the officer corps divided, but it inhabited an increasingly anachronistic world, inimical, as Audette points out, to the interests of the RCN. The RN incubator had produced an artificial distance between officers and men "not wholly connected with the necessity of maintaining the essential differences of rank"; a distance that did not square with the egalitarian spirit of Canadian society. That spirit, which tended to level the distinctions between officers and men, had been masked by the exigencies of war, but reappeared in the postwar period. The Lower Deck were no longer prepared to endure the aloofness and insensitivity displayed by some of their officers. Moreover, the grievance procedures were cumbersome, and all around them the men saw officers resisting change. The result was a series of mutinies aboard HMC Ships *Magnificent, Crescent,* and *Athabaskan* in 1949, which revealed the need for fundamental reform in the RCN.

The Mainguy Commission, struck to investigate the mutinies, noted the need for an increased "Canadianization" of the navy, a suggestion in accord with the service's search for operational autonomy beyond the direct influence of the RN. Many of those interviewed by the commissioners considered that the RCN was merely "a pallid imitation . . . of the British navy" and was not sufficiently Canadian. Yet, the unification crisis of the mid-1960's, which Captain Keith Cameron, RCN (Ret'd.) describes, revealed that the RCN had failed to seize the opportunity offered by the mutinies to develop a Canadian identity and to create a constituency sympathetic to its interests. Consequently, the navy's "admirals were left in a time of crisis to plead for the retention of symbols, traditions, and a system to which the mass of the public could not relate."

The recorded history of the RCN may be regarded as a lament for a proud service. For, at the moment of achieving possibly its greatest degree of autonomy, the RCN was overwhelmed by the forces of nationalism and continentalism.

Throughout the nineteenth century the Royal Navy provided protection for Canada and her maritime interests. However, by 1900 Britain's naval and industrial supremacy was being challenged by Germany and the United States, and she turned to her colonies for assistance. Could they, she enquired, contribute to imperial naval defence? There were sound strategic and historical reasons for this request. Clearly, if the German High Seas Fleet was to be defeated in some future Trafalgar of the North Sea, colonial cruisers on the coasts of Nova Scotia and New South Wales could do little to affect the outcome. Concentration of naval power in home waters was the order of the day in the Royal Navy. The Admiralty hinted that it was time for the colonies to repay their outstanding debt to the Mother Country by contributing directly to the growth and maintenance of the Royal Navy's Grand Fleet.

Delegates to the various Colonial and Imperial Conferences on Defence prior to World War I wrestled with the problem of colonial contributions. In the 1902 conference Canada was the only nation that did not agree to help defray the expense of imperial naval defence despite the fact that naval protection, as Barry Gough notes, had cost her "not one penny" in the nineteenth century. The Canadians saw themselves as having two choices, both involving the sensitive issue of sovereignty: to contribute ships and money to the RN cause or to undertake defence of their own shores. Financial contributions were seen to contradict the fundamental principle of Canadian sovereignty. On the other hand, Canada was prepared to establish her own naval service and to co-operate with the imperial authorities so far as it was consistent with self-government. It was a stroke of political genius for Laurier and Brodeur to neutralize the naval issue by claiming that the Fishery Protection Service had constituted a near navy all along. Ironically, they built upon the idea of a naval militia that had been advanced in 1898 by the imperially minded Toronto branch of the Navy League, which had seen a local militia as a direct contribution to the empire's sea power. Some will argue that the ram bows and uniforms of the FPS did not a navy make, but the Canadian solution was an adroit one.

The Admiralty, however, was not prepared to let the matter of imperial defence drop. There was, as Barry Hunt points out, "an alarming disjunction between British ends and British imperial means" in the years following World War I. Imperial defence was seen "as a way of resolving the tension between compelling commitments and diminishing resources." A "unified, centrally directed and highly mobile imperial navy coupled with some kind of cost and burden-sharing arrangement with the dominions" would permit a financially straitened Britain to administer her empire and to face the twin challenges of the United States and Imperial Japanese navies.

The Canadian authorities were not blind to the advantages that accrued from close co-operation with the Royal Navy. The RCN adopted RN destroyer designs, as Captain (N) J.H.W. Knox of the Canadian Forces discusses, while the Senior Service remained alive to the fact that such vessels might fit smoothly into an imperial fleet at some later date. Over the years the RN provided technical expertise (indeed, the RCN's Engineering Branch was termed "a miniscule . . . adjunct of the RN"), trained RCN pilots, provided aircraft (as Lieutenant-Commander S.E. Soward, RCN [Ret'd.] describes), supplied intelligence, transferred aircraft carriers to RCN control, and stationed submarines in Canadian waters for RCN training purposes.

After the fall of France in June 1940, the situation in Europe was so grave that the Canadian government placed virtually its entire navy at Britain's disposal. Canada's first line of defence, Lund writes, "was recognized as being the English Channel and the fireproof-house mentality that had prevailed was swept away by fear approaching hysteria." It was under these circumstances that the RCN came to be seen as part of Britain's "negotiable assets" in her dealings with the United States. Accordingly, when the two powers divided the Atlantic into zones of strategic responsibility and the United States assumed control over the Western Atlantic in September 1941, Canada's naval service was relegated to the position of a "sub-command of the USN." The Canadian authorities were prepared to accept this arrangement on the grounds that they had a moral obligation to Britain, but when the Americans had to withdraw nearly all of their naval forces from the Atlantic following the Japanese attack on Pearl Harbour, the Canadians came to regard the command structure as "highly anomalous." By the end of 1942 Canada was providing 48 per cent of the escorts for convoy protection, yet "despite this preponderance of strength she had virtually no influence over the strategic direction" of her navy. Lund analyses the RCN's prolonged struggle to regain its operational autonomy in the North West Atlantic in the spring of 1943. But the liberation from American control was illusory, and the RCN began to drift inexorably into the USN's gravitational field.

A new set of political and military realities came to prevail after World War II. The North Atlantic Treaty Organization and its maritime wing, SACLANT, embraced the RCN once again as a sub-command. American naval influence or control also occurred elsewhere. Thus we find HMCS *Crusader* attached to an American Fast Carrier Group during the Korean War; the RCN relying increasingly on the USN for aircraft like Avengers and Banshees; the RCN icebreaker, HMCS *Labrador*, being transferred to the operational control of a USN Task Force in the Arctic; Canadian anti-submarine Tracker aircraft being designed to be interchangeable with American Trackers; and postwar RCN shipbuilding programmes drawing upon American technology as described in the chapters by Bovey, Soward, Leeming and Knox.

At the same time, the managerial revolution affecting the American defence establishment with its concern about cost effectiveness and the rationalization of military systems began to exert a profound influence over National Defence Headquarters in the early 1960's. This influence encouraged the unification experiment, which spelled the end of the RCN as a legal entity.

The authors in this book highlight the complex relationship between politics and naval policy. Laurier realized at the time of the Naval Service Act in 1910 what the political market would bear and created a navy of very modest proportions. Similarly, Hunt's analysis of the RN, RCN, and USN at the time of the Washington Naval Conference of 1921-22 reveals that "any acceptable solution to the imperial defence problem would be primarily political or diplomatic, and not military in nature." At the same time the meagre budget allocated to the RCN was seen as cheap and temporary and hence politically accceptable. That the Naval Service almost succumbed in the process and that the monies available were completely inconsistent with any sort of logical naval programme were other matters altogether. It was politics, not strategy, that more powerfully influenced naval policy. The same might be said of the command relationships in the first half of World War II with the RCN deferring to the needs of Britain and the United States, and the Canadians finding themselves unable to speak to the Americans except through the agency of the British Admiralty Delegation in Washington!

The story of the RCN is also one of men and machines. The fleet grew dramatically during World War II (from a handful of ships to a fleet of over 775 vessels within the space of six years). This growth was matched by the increase in the number of men and women in blue. A keen little force put to sea in 1939. Fewer than 1,700 of the 3,604 officers and men making up the RCN were on permanent active service. During the war over 107,000 Canadians donned naval uniform.

For every prewar officer and man, there were almost thirty times as many by war's end. This meant that there was only one trained person for every thirty new entries, a nearly fatal dilution under the circumstances. It is important to note that the RCN enjoyed no respite for training. There was no "Phoney War" and no Second Front in the Atlantic. As Milner points out, "the war and its insatiable demands for men and materials robbed the RCN of its opportunity to make expansion work." It is perhaps not surprising, therefore, that Canada's Allies were often scathing about the inexperienced amateurs that the RCN was obliged to send to sea. The dilemma defied solution. To keep men ashore for longer periods of training meant robbing the convoys of much-needed escort crews. To send men to sea in an untrained state meant courting disaster as the ill-fated convoy SC 107 revealed.

The Battle of the Atlantic was a battle of competing technologies and industries. Shipyard workers on both sides of the Atlantic worked feverishly to build and repair warships, while Allied and Axis scientists engaged in a grim game of innovation and application. Beesly highlights the enormous value of high-frequency direction-finding equipment ashore and afloat, which permitted the Allies to pinpoint German U-boats with ever increasing accuracy. Even more important was the penetration of German codes which gave the Allies complete intelligence mastery by 1943 and allowed them to exercise total command of the sea routes.

But the Germans were not the only ones with problems at sea. The RCN suffered from a severe equipment crisis which was exacerbated on occasion by national myopia. Canadian corvettes, for example, were fitted with unreliable short-range Canadian radar, and the Naval Staff was unwilling to install new radar sets because these were not Canadian. "The lack of modern anti-submarine warfare and navigational equipment aboard Canadian escorts," Milner notes, ". . . had a profound impact on [the RCN's] operational efficiency" during the Battle of the Atlantic. Moreover, these problems appeared at a time when the Germans were rendering the Allied task more difficult by introducing new and complex codes, more audacious tactics, improved torpedoes, and experimental, high-speed submarines.

In his second chapter, Knox relates how the RCN introduced innovations of its own in the years after the war, developing the St. Laurent-class destroyer, the first warship designed and built in Canada. Accompanying the St. Laurent and post-St. Laurent programmes were a series of major technological accomplishments in anti-submarine warfare, hydrofoil design, control systems, and engine design. The marriage of helicopter and destroyer led to a new generation of Canadian destroyer escorts, the helicopter destroyer (DDH), a vital element of which was the "Bear Trap," a Canadian designed and developed helicopter hauldown device that enabled helicopters to land safely on the decks of warships at sea.

Unlike armies, which must be largely self-contained, navies are able to function as sub-units of larger forces. This was the RCN's fate: to be a small-ship navy committed to an anti-submarine role in association with other fleets. Thus the big ships—the cruisers, the aircraft carriers, and the armed merchant cruisers, whose history Commander (R) F.M. McKee records—came and went, while the RCN remained an escort navy.

The Naval Service never realized its dream of a balanced fleet of large and small vessels. Laurier and Borden entertained the idea of such a fleet during the debate on the Naval Service Act, but their plan withered in the face of political controversy and indecision. Nine years later, in 1919, Admiral of the Fleet Viscount Jellicoe of Scapa advanced a similar proposal during his visit to Canada, but his scheme succumbed to economic pressures. Vice-Admiral P.W. Nelles, the chief of the Naval Staff, revived the concept in 1941, and the Cabinet War Committee agreed in September 1943 that the RCN should undertake the operation of aircraft carriers. Ironically, a proposal was made at the same time that small ships could be converted to carry submarine-hunting helicopters—a proposal that spelled the end of the balanced fleet dream.

Once the marriage of helicopter and destroyer was shown to be successful in the mid-1950's, the days of the aircraft carrier and RCN naval aviation were numbered. The new generation of DDH's was politically acceptable, inexpensive by capital ship standards, and relatively easy to man. Moreover, as Lund argues, they conferred upon the RCN an important degree of leverage in Allied naval circles. All of the historical evidence, he notes, suggests that "if Canada hopes to exert some influence on Washington in the direction of the maritime defence of [the North American] continent, . . . the maintenance of a strong anti-submarine force would be most advantageous."

But when all is said and done, the RCN's "heart of oak" was its spirit. We tend to forget too easily the dedication, courage, and fortitude of the men and women who served: those who endured hardship, boredom, and uncertainty; those who felt fear and elation; those who enjoyed pride and camaraderie in The Navy. They were the inheritors and promoters of the finest elements of a grand maritime tradition. When we examine the history of the RCN, we imagine the ill-fated Canadian midshipmen at Coronel, weary middle-watch men searching the darkness for the enemy, engine room artificers amid the roar of their reciprocating engines, and coal-smudged boy stokers. We envisage apprehensive new entries falling in beside the railway station at *Cornwallis*, make-do reservists, stoical merchant seamen consigned to their fate, and liberty men flocking through the dockyard gate. And we recall the warm darkness of the radar plot, the "old man" on the wing of the bridge, and generations of matelots trudging up Barrington Street in Halifax, the winter wind tugging at their great coats.

Tens of thousands of men and women gave their best, whether as subs, OD's, killicks, or admirals. Most of them remain unknown but a few loom larger—Kingsmill, Hose, Nelles, Grant, DeWolf, Lay, Brock, and Landymore. Supported by the many, they fought to keep the RCN alive, struggled to maintain its independence, led it during its greatest moments, and strove to prevent its demise.

Chapter I

THE ROYAL NAVY'S LEGACY TO
THE ROYAL CANADIAN NAVY IN THE PACIFIC,
1880-1914

Barry M. Gough

A significant and dramatic event in the history of the Royal Canadian Navy took place on 9 November 1910 when the naval base at Esquimalt, Vancouver Island, passed from British to Canadian authority. The event had long been anticipated. Five years earlier Britain had withdrawn her major naval units to face the threat of the German menace in home waters and was building massive capital ships of the Dreadnought and Invincible classes. At the same time she had resolved several outstanding points of dispute with the United States. Equally important, she had shored up her sagging defences in the Pacific by reorganizing her squadrons into a new Far Eastern Fleet and by signing a defensive alliance with the new Asiatic power, Japan, in 1902. Since the mid-1850's the Royal Navy had used Esquimalt as a base of operations, particularly for ships on the northern reaches of the most extensive of the navy's "foreign stations." But on that bleak November day two facts were patently clear to the assembled company: first, Britain had served her time in the immediate defence of British Columbia's interests and had other obligations more pressing; and, second, although Britain was not abandoning her responsibilities for the defence of the Empire as a whole, Canada was assuming, of her own volition, the duties of a senior partner in the emerging Empire-Commonwealth and a growing North American power with increasing interests in the Atlantic and Pacific.

The objects of this chapter are several: to review the diplomatic background to the transfer; to explain the relationship of Royal Navy fleet reorganization, new ship construction, and government fiscal stringencies to the changing role of Esquimalt and the Pacific squadron in the early years of the twentieth century; and, lastly, to describe how Canada acquired responsibility for maintaining Esquimalt and for contributing, through her own naval service and through other means, to the defence of the Dominion and the Empire.

On the occasion of the transfer, the Dominion of Canada was represented by George J. Desbarats, Quebec-born engineer who had become deputy minister and comptroller of the Naval Service of Canada seven months before. Interviewed in Victoria's Empress Hotel, Desbarats told reporters what was involved in the historic transaction:

> It has been intended that the Dominion government should have taken over the naval department at Esquimalt at an earlier date, but on looking into the matter it was discovered that up to one year ago it would have been impossible to legally give Canada that measure of full control at Esquimalt, which was the purpose of both the Admiralty and the Ottawa government, it being provided up to that date, that the British authorities should retain some measure of jurisdiction. Special legislation was passed at the last session of the British House of Commons and now nothing remains but the formal transfer from the Admiralty to the government of Canada.[1]

Desbarats' words were carefully couched. They implied that Canada had been more than willing to assume the burdens of responsibility but that the lack of necessary imperial legislation had delayed the transaction whereby the enthusiastic, young naval nation might have assumed her rightful place in imperial defence. The legislation he referred to was The Naval Establishments in British Possessions Act, 1909 (9 *Edward VII*, ch. 18) "to make better provision respecting Naval Establishments in British Possessions," effective 20 October 1909, fully a year before the transfer of Esquimalt was effected.[2] Under this statute the Imperial government possessed authority to vest any shore establishments in colonial authority by way of an order-in-council, subject to any conditions imposed at the time.

In accordance with these terms, Commander Gerald William Vivian, RN, the senior officer at Esquimalt, exchanged and signed the appropriate papers for the legal transaction. George Phillips, hitherto Admiralty agent at Esquimalt, continued as chief stores officer while the whole naval base became the responsibility of Commander J.D.D. Stewart, RN, commanding HMCS *Rainbow* (of which more later). Desbarats considered it unlikely that an increased clerical force would be needed at Esquimalt "for the reason that there is no immediate need that there should be." And, because there was only one warship on station, there was no necessity, he said, for maintaining the naval yard in a highly effective state; indeed, most of *Rainbow*'s repairs could be completed more economically in private yards.[3] Volunteers for the naval service would supply the crew. Naval cadets would be trained in Halifax for the cruisers *Rainbow* and *Niobe*. In short, Desbarats said that the naval base had been appropriately transferred after the mother country had cleared away legal obstacles, that Canada was assuming responsibility (given the limited needs of her ships) and that manpower requirements for officers and crew could be met.

The transfer coincided with the arrival of HMCS *Rainbow*, the first ship of the nascent Royal Canadian Navy to serve in the Pacific. This vessel, launched in 1891, was an obsolete light cruiser of the Apollo class and cost Canada £50,000. A ship with a heritage in names dating back to the Spanish Armada, she had been commissioned at Portsmouth on 4 August 1910 as an HMC ship and had a regular and reserve crew of roughly three hundred officers and men on two-year loan to Canada.[4] She arrived at Esquimalt on 7 November, fired a twenty-one gun salute to her new country, and prepared for the celebrations. "History was made at Esquimalt yesterday," the Victoria *Colonist* reported proudly and with certain vision, "HMCS *Rainbow* came; and a new navy was born. Canada's blue ensign flies for the first time on the Dominion's own fighting ship in the Pacific—the ocean of the future where some of the world's greatest problems will have to be worked out. Esquimalt began its recrudescence, the revival of its former glories."[5] "We are told in ancient literature that the first rainbow was set in the sky as a promise of things to come," the rival Victoria *Times* boastfully reported. "So may it be with His Majesty's ship. She is a training craft only, but she is the first fruits on this coast of Canadian naval policy, the necessary forerunner of the larger vesels which will add dignity to our name and prestige to our actions."[6] In addition to all of these expectations, the *Colonist* noted:

> The event [the *Rainbow*'s arrival] was one calculated to awaken thought in the minds of all who endeavoured to grasp its true significance. The *Rainbow* is not a fighting ship, but she is manned by fighting men, and her mission is to train men so as to make them fit to defend our country from invasion, protect our commerce on the seas and maintain the dignity of the Empire everywhere. Her coming is a proof that Canada has accepted a new responsibility in the discharge of which new burdens will have to be assumed. On this Western Frontier of Empire it is all important that there shall be a naval establishment that will count for something in the hour of stress.[7]

A number of distinguished personages came on board the cruiser for the celebrations. The proceedings, begun at 1430, were conducted by Senator William Templeman and by Desbarats, who had gone on board to take formal possession of the ship for Canada. Immediately afterwards the Lieutenant-Governor of British Columbia, Thomas W. Paterson, embarked, accompanied by his secretary, Mr. H.J. Muskett. Then the barracks' naval tug brought the rest of the party, including Richard (later Sir Richard) McBride, premier of the province, Henry Esson Young, provincial secretary and minister of education, D.M. Eberts, speaker of the legislative assembly, G.H. Barnard, member of parliament, Bishop A. Mac-Donald, Colonel R.L. Wadmore of the local artillery district, other army officers, including Lieutenant-Colonel A.W. (later Sir Arthur) Currie, Victoria's mayor, A.J. Morley, aldermen, several private citizens, and representatives of the Navy League.

Aft, under an awning spread over the quarterdeck, Templeman officially welcomed the *Rainbow*. "The arrival of the *Niobe* at Halifax and the *Rainbow* at Victoria," he said, "marks a new and important epoch in the history of Canada." In the nation's history, it ranked next to Confederation in its significance. Growing and progressive, Canada had relied on the mother country for defence too long, Templeman maintained. "Today," the report of his address stated, "he did not think there was a single patriotic man in Canada who would not say that Canada should find the men and money to better take part in the defence of her commerce and her homes." Support for the Empire would conquer indifference and divided opinion, he continued with resounding enthusiasm, and "out of this policy the Canadian navy had come into being. It was begun today and would be perfected until it was thoroughly effective." In Templeman's words, the *Rainbow*'s arrival signalled the birth of the RCN, and he concluded by welcoming Commander Stewart, and the officers and men of the *Rainbow* in the name of the government and people of Canada.[8]

By these events the Dominion of Canada, as yet adolescent in her defence policy, especially in terms of any commitment to provide forces for her own defence, had received the British imperial legacy. Since the late 1840's Britain had aimed at making colonies of settlement self-governing and self-defending;[9] she had not sought to abandon them. No secretary of state for the colonies had ever issued a statement describing overseas territories as "millstones around the neck" of the United Kingdom.[10] Rather, the evidence points to continued colonial expansion during the mid-Victorian age, and British Columbia is a case in point.[11] Faced with the possibility of American annexation, the British had established Vancouver Island as a colony in 1849 and British Columbia in 1858, and had united the two in 1866. Britain had also encouraged the confederation of British Columbia with Canada in 1871. In addition, she had guaranteed loans for the building of the Canadian Pacific Railway, which was completed to Pacific tidewater in 1885, with regular transcontinental service beginning in the following year.

Throughout all of this Britain would have preferred British Columbia to have been self-sustaining in defence matters. However, the Hudson's Bay Company, which held the charter to colonize Vancouver Island, sternly maintained that its posts were sufficient to guard against northern Indian incursions.[12] Besides, since the 1840's the ships of the Royal Navy had called in at the mouth of the Columbia River, in the Straits of Juan de Fuca and Georgia, and at Fort Rupert on the northeastern coast of Vancouver Island. During the 1850's British warships had come in increasing numbers—to guard against American annexation of the Queen Charlotte Islands, to punish Indian pirates and murderers on the west coast of Vancouver Island, to support Governor James Douglas's authority during the Fraser River gold rush, and to reinforce British claims to San Juan Island, adjacent to Vancouver Island's southeastern tip. Similarly, warships serving on other station duties had called at Esquimalt, as was the case with ships engaged against the Russians at Petropavlovsk, Kamchatka, in 1854 and 1855 during the Crimean War. Esquimalt had become the headquarters of the Pacific Station in 1862, and three years later the Admiralty had authorized "a small establishment . . . for the custody, etc., of stores and provisions for Her Majesty's Ships in the North Pacific." During the next thirty years, the navy at Esquimalt provided protection against American and Russian raids, though its main local duty was to support the extension of the British brand of law among coast Indians, by peaceful means if possible, by violent means if necessary.[13] In the 1860's the squadron consisted of some fifteen vessels, including a screw-frigate as flagship and several screw corvettes, sloops, gun vessels, and gunboats. By the 1880's this number had dwindled to half a dozen vessels. Meanwhile, Esquimalt had developed into a naval base serving British warships throughout the eastern Pacific and by 1887 possessed a drydock capable of holding the largest British warship in the Pacific. As the nineteenth century came to an end, the navy supported Victoria-based sealers going to the Bering Sea and provided them with protection against American interference.

Commanders of HM ships kept a watchful eye on affairs from the Bering Sea to Valparaiso, Chile, and from the shores of the Americas across to the station's western limits, at approximately the International Date Line. The British eyed the Hawaiian Islands jealously, fearing the acquisitiveness of the United States, but never took an active stance with respect to the archipelago. Thus by 1898 the formal American annexation of the Hawaiian Kingdom was completed, leaving only the Union Jack in the corner of the territorial flag as an ironic legacy to the fact that the Hawaiians had offered to cede the islands to Captain George Vancouver in 1794. Similarly, the British had not pressed their claims at Panama after the

Clayton-Bulwer Treaty of 1850. Consequently, the Americans were left to fortify their interests and, in 1914, to complete the transisthmian canal, transforming the Caribbean into an American lake and greatly increasing the mobility of United States naval units between the two oceans.[14]

Fortunately for Canada, the United States moved from enemy to ally, and for this reason alone the Royal Navy became largely redundant in local operations as a fighting force. The key to this happy shift was adroit British and American diplomacy in the last decade of the nineteenth and the first decade of the twentieth century. Though the two powers had reasons to pick any number of quarrels—over Venezuela, Panama, sealing, the Alaska boundary, or Hawaii—they shaped, out of necessity, a peaceful course (though not without some sabre rattling, especially by the Americans concerning Alaska). This course also allowed the United States unrestricted access to the eastern Pacific, a fact uncontested until the Japanese attack on Pearl Harbor in 1941 brought the stark realization to Americans and Canadians alike that they were not immune from foreign assault.

Nonetheless, the forging of the Anglo-American rapprochement was insufficient in itself to establish a balance of power in the Pacific. Although North America and the eastern Pacific might be neutralized as potential trouble spots for Britain, the Far East was a cockpit of world rivalries and tensions. China lay in chaos, while Germany, Russia, France, Britain, and Japan wrested concessions from her and seized territories of economic and strategic value. In 1902, fearing a possible French-Russian combination, Britain signed an alliance with Japan. Like Canada, Japan had feared that the Royal Navy would withdraw all forces and exacted a promise, written into the secret terms accompanying the treaty, that Britain would maintain a minimum force. Japan's local naval supremacy was ensured by her dramatic victories over the Russian fleet in 1904-5, which increased her influence in the Far East. When the Anglo-Japanese alliance was renewed in 1905, Japan possessed the capability of guarding the Far East while Britain concentrated her forces in home waters. Together the naval power of these island kingdoms was superior to any combination of potential enemy forces. Such an arrangement suited Britain admirably, so long as Japan posed no threat to British imperial territories within the Pacific rim. By 1909, however, the British regarded Japan as a real danger, and the security of British possessions was seen to exist only as long as the alliance lasted.[15] Eventually, Canada and her sister dominions, Australia and New Zealand, would force the abrogation of this alliance in 1921, fearing that it gave Japan a free hand in the Pacific at the expense of the United States (to which the dominions looked increasingly for security). In the interim, the alliance served its purpose.

British commanders-in-chief Pacific were scarcely aware of the great trend in diplomacy that was taking nearly two decades to complete. Thus

Rear-Admiral A.K. Bickford's sharp complaint to the lords-commissioners of the Admiralty in 1901 about the "dangerously weak state" of his squadron (a phrase he carelessly modified to "ridiculously small" the following year) brought a predictable rebuke from their lordships.[16] "Should diplomatic questions arise," Bickford explained in particular reference to Alaska and Panama, "we certainly are not in a position on this Station in any way to support our diplomacy but would probably on that account have to acquiesce in any demands which the United States might be pleased to put forward." Because the American squadron was increasing in size and Britain's was "dwindling," Esquimalt might be seized in wartime, stores and supplies taken, communications with Asia cut, Canadian Pacific and other steamers captured—all of this well before reinforcements could arrive—and British warships left with a base "nowhere nearer than China for their requirements." Bickford argued for strengthening the squadron and Esquimalt, but this view, which had been held by many of his predecessors, did not find support in the Admiralty.[17]

At this time Britain did not presume to maintain a balance of power in North America and had, like Sir Wilfrid Laurier, the prime minister of Canada, tacitly accepted the Monroe Doctrine of the United States hegemony within North America and upon adjacent seas. The United States Navy, particularly after the Spanish-American War of 1898, was the predominant naval power in the eastern Pacific. Indeed, in 1901 a lord of the Admiralty, Admiral Walter Kerr, complained of the limits of Britain's role as sovereign of the seas and self-appointed world policeman. "The very fact of the great naval superiority of the U.S. Squadron in the Pacific," he wrote, "should show us how impossible it is for us in view of the requirements elsewhere to maintain a Squadron in the Pacific capable of coping with it." "It is impossible," he concluded, "for this country, in view of the greater development of foreign navies to be a superior force everywhere."[18]

While these momentous diplomatic changes were taking place, the Royal Navy was undergoing major modifications in two aspects: units and the deployment of those units. Improvement in wireless telegraphy and submarine cables brought admirals on distant stations in closer touch with the Admiralty and made the deployment of ships more efficient. Similarly, in keeping with the emerging machine age and Admiralty decisions, such innovations as water-tube boilers, submarines, and all-big-gun ships of the Dreadnought type radically altered the old navy. Under the dramatic reforms of two great admirals of the fleet, Admiral Sir John (later Lord) Fisher and Sir Arthur Wilson, the navy was enlarged, improved, and modernized in the decade prior to World War I. Under Fisher in particular, the all-big-gun ship was developed and the fleets were concentrated in home waters.

These coterminous developments invite more detailed examination of the defence of British and Canadian interests in the eastern Pacific. In the sixty years previous to the transfer of Esquimalt to Canadian control, the British naval presence operating from there had invariably been exhibited in small naval units—frigates, corvettes, sloops, gunboats, and gun vessels. The commander-in-chief wore his flag in what might be described as a capital ship, but the squadron's role was one of exerting sloop and gunboat diplomacy. Once that role was completed and the diplomatic shifts effected, the navy could serve no specific use, except to remind British Columbians and other Canadians that their Pacific interests were being afforded security.

By 1905 Canadians were beginning to realize that the United States and Japan were useful allies and that the real danger lay in the relentless growth of the German High Seas Fleet. Perhaps the first to sense that danger was Admiral Fisher, who began to redistribute the British fleet in 1904 "to meet strategical ('and not sentimental') requirements."[19] He amalgamated the South American, West Indies, and Cape squadrons into one fleet, the Cape of Good Hope, and similarly, the China, Australian, East Indies and Pacific squadrons into the Far Eastern Fleet. In both cases effective cruisers were to be substituted for the motley assemblage of small vessels then on station, which were destined for sale or for the wreckers. The Pacific was allocated one unarmoured cruiser, first class, and two unarmoured cruisers, second class, to serve as a reserve in Asian waters. "All small vessels to be ruthlessly reduced," Fisher noted. "We have not yet got the right types of ships, but must make the best of what we have got."[20]

Fisher's rationale rested upon his understanding of what he called "Naval Necessities"—concentrating forces where they were most needed. "The principles on which peace time distribution of His Majesty's ships and the arrangement of their stations are based," the famous Admiralty (or Selborne) memorandum of December 1904 explained, "date from a period when the electric telegraph did not exist and when wind was the motive power." Now "new conditions have necessitated a review and readjustment of this distribution of ships and arrangement of stations."[21] These changes were effected to increase fighting efficiency, but they were also implemented to exact economies. By reducing units and bases the Admiralty estimated annual savings of £384,000, funds desperately needed for new ship construction.[22] With Esquimalt in Canadian hands, the Admiralty calculated, Britain would save £6,940 annually. Without a fleet to serve, Esquimalt was redundant. Such was the position of the Colonial Defence Committee of the British government, which mirrored Admiralty views. The committee's report said that formerly the navy had needed Esquimalt as a naval establishment and depot, the squadron's headquarters for the defence of Canada's Pacific shore. Now defence against the

United States was difficult, and, in any case, the Atlantic would be the main theatre in wartime. The navy from Hong Kong could guard against possible Russian threats, while Canada's trade in the Pacific was insufficient to require protection. For all these reasons, Britain should no longer retain Esquimalt as a "fortified port."[23]

In keeping with these policies, Britain proposed to abandon responsibility for the defence of Esquimalt and Halifax to Canada. This was not a decision thrust upon the Dominion precipitously; at the Colonial Conference of 1902 Canada had offered to undertake the full costs of garrisoning these bases. However, the Dominion remained reluctant to meet the costs of maintaining the naval bases, and for that reason a five-year delay developed in the formal transfer of Esquimalt from imperial to dominion control.[24] Meanwhile, the Admiralty ordered that 800 tons of explosives and 800 tons of naval stores be shipped to Hong Kong, the victualling yard and jail be closed, and the other stores be auctioned off.[25] This left only the dockyard and certain bunkering facilities in operation. Not least, in keeping with fleet reorganization, their lordships ordered the end of the Pacific Station. This was done when Commodore J.E.C. Goodrich, RN, struck his broad pennant at sunset on 1 March 1905, terminating a command dating from 1837.[26] The transfer of Esquimalt to Canadian control in 1910 was a necessary corollary taken for strategic and fiscal reasons and made possible by diplomatic shifts in the face of the emerging might of Germany, the United States, and Japan.

The Royal Canadian Navy was born in crisis. The question of how Canada should respond to the growth of the German High Seas Fleet was emphasized by the Anglo-German capital ship construction crisis of 1909. Two prospects presented themselves: a contribution of money or ships to the Admiralty, or Canada's own defence of ports and coasts in regular co-operation with the United Kingdom forces. Laurier maintained that the real question was one of political control. With typical respect for Canadian autonomy he told the House of Commons:

> The problem before us is the association of our small naval strength with the great organization of fleets of the mother country, so as to secure the highest efficiency and unity without sacrificing our right to the constitutional control of our own funds, and of any flotilla built and maintained at our own cost.[27]

Subsequently, the House resolved to approve the necessary expenditures to promote the speedy organization of a Canadian naval service "in co-operation with and in close relation to the imperial navy."[28] The service was to be run on the Admiralty model, as suggested by the 1907 Imperial

Conference on Military and Naval Defence, and "in full sympathy with the view that the naval supremacy of Britain is essential to the security of commerce, the safety of the empire and the peace of the world."[29]

Subsequent to the passing of the Naval Service Act on 4 May 1910, a Department of Naval Service was established under the minister of Marine and Fisheries, who was also the minister of the Naval Service. The command-in-chief of the forces remained vested in the Crown. A deputy minister and a director of the Naval Service were provided for, the former being the civilian head, the latter, a professional and preferably with a rank not lower than rear-admiral. A Naval Board was authorized to maintain a permanent force. The act also authorized a naval reserve, a volunteer force, and a naval college. In case of emergency, pursuant to section 23 of the act, the governor-in-council could place the naval service, in whole or in part (including any naval ships and officers and seamen), in the general service of the Royal Navy.[30]

Admiralty regulations served as the model for organization, training, and discipline and were to be authorized by the governor-in-council.[31] But the extent and form of Canada's contribution to her own naval defence and to that of the British Empire and its allies was by no means clear in 1910. At this time Britain was seeking commitments from the Empire, a "calling in of debts," which, owing to the Royal Navy's contribution to imperial protection during the century after Trafalgar, the United Kingdom expected due. Canada's defence contribution therefore became a major political question in the Dominion.[32]

What was the Royal Navy's legacy to the Royal Canadian Navy in the Pacific? A secret Admiralty memorandum of 1912 explained to the Canadian government:

> Mere statements of the cost of keeping certain ships near Canada, or of the expense of particular naval establishments in Canada are no measure of the value of the naval defence by which her territory and interests have been protected. The British Navy as a whole and the sea power which its supremacy ensures, and not the squadrons on the North American or Pacific Stations have given Canada the security she has enjoyed. The truth should never be darkened in detail.[33]

No more cogent statement representing the principles of British strategy in relationship to Canadian development can be found. Ships might provide local service but the overall power of the Royal Navy was the key to the security of British possessions overseas. The Admiralty, nonetheless, took pains to detail the cost of maintenance, personnel and property directly accruing to Canada in the fifty-year period after 1851 and estimated that £25-30 million had been spent on keeping ships in Canadian waters. "Apart from what is referred to in the foregoing observations," the memorandum concluded, "there is no record available of any *naval* expenditure properly attributable to the relations of the Mother Country to the Dominion of Canada." In other words, naval protection had cost Canada, whether as colonial territories or as a self-governing nation, not one penny in the nineteenth century.

When Canada reluctantly acquired full control over Esquimalt in 1910, she signified her reception of the Royal Navy's legacy to the Royal Canadian Navy in the Pacific. Canada continued to face problems of coastal defence and of protecting her seaborne commerce and her means of communication with other nations within the Pacific rim and farther afield. Russia, Japan, and the United States remained major powers with which Canada would have to deal as an ally or an enemy in the course of the next fifty years. How much Canada would contribute in the defence of her own interests would rest on political and financial considerations and, above all, on the necessity of dealing with the exigencies of war.

The Royal Navy had been the guardian of British colonial and Canadian national interests in the Pacific to 1910, but the assumption of that burden by Canada would be based on the demands of crisis-management in pursuit of national security and world order, rather than on any long-range plan for making the young nation a naval power. The pride, prestige, and traditions of the Royal Navy were inherited by the Royal Canadian Navy, but the new service had to face diplomatic requirements far different from Britain's splendid isolation during the Pax Britannica, an isolation which painfully came to an end in the period 1880-1910 and foreshadowed the great world crisis of 1914.

THE RECALL OF THE NAVY

Ah, you should have lived in the days of old,
When this was a naval port,
Full of the men with hearts so bold,
And ready for any sport—

Those were the days of right royal fun
And prosperity reigned supreme;
We ne'er gave a thought of the dark ones to come,
Never thought that 'twould end in a dream.

Fifty years of such times we Victorians have seen;
From now we depend on the fates,
For if England still wants us, we'll stay as we've been,
And we won't be annexed to the States.

These, and suchlike, are remarks we now hear,
Sad as they sound, they are true,
The Navy have gone, and with them good cheer;
Now the question is—what can we do?

Esquimalt—the harbour of which we're so proud,
Lies wasted and empty—forgot by the world,
Can nothing be done to lift off this cloud,
Can't the flag we all love once again be unfurled?

That colonials are loyal, we've had ample proof,
And they don't wait for England to call,
But went forward like men, and few held aloof;
They were ready to fight—and to fall.

Has England forgotten, or does she not care?
Or perhaps she thinks Canada's free
From attacks by the nations, who may think they dare
Show that they too can battle at sea.

England's statesmen at home, upon whom we depend,
Have ruled that these things should be so,
Is it wise, is it policy not to attend
To the wants of their sons as they grow?

Old England desert us!—oh, can it be true
That things should have come to this state?
Won't somebody help us and strive to undo
This awful—this terrible—fate?

Now Canada's sons, awake from your trance,
Take a leaf from the Commonwealth's numbers
Make a bid and leap, 'tis your very last chance,
And high time you arose from your slumbers.

*By Jim Strange, printed 20 April, 1905 (Victoria); copy in Provincial
Archives of British Columbia (NWp 821, S897).*

Chapter 2

L.P. BRODEUR AND THE ORIGINS OF
THE ROYAL CANADIAN NAVY

Nigel D. Brodeur

Louis Philippe Brodeur, the minister of Marine and Fisheries from 1906 to 1911, was also Canada's first minister of the Naval Service. He took up the latter appointment on 3 June 1910, one month after the Naval Service Act, establishing the Royal Canadian Navy, had received royal assent, and remained in office until 10 August 1911. A decade later, while serving as a justice of the Supreme Court, he learned that the Senate was trying unsuccessfully to obtain documents relating to naval matters for the period 1909-11. On visiting George J. Desbarats, the deputy minister of the Naval Service, Brodeur discovered that the department's information was very meagre indeed. He decided, therefore, to make his own records available to the inquiry. In the process he addressed the following observations to Senator Hewitt Bostock, the Liberal leader in the Senate, and to Desbarats, respectively:

> I hope that the Department will find advisable also to bring down the private documents above mentioned in order to give to the historians of the future all the facts and circumstances connected with the establishment of the Canadian Navy.[1]

and

> Il y a dans ces lettres et les autres documents qui les accompagnent des informations précieuses qui pourront servir plus tard à reconstituer

d'une manière parfaite l'histoire de cette question navale. Je crois de plus que ces pièces vont servir à populariser le service naval, qui, je regrette de le dire, ne paraît pas commander aujourd'hui autant de faveur qu'il le devrait.[2]

The L.P. Brodeur papers have now, more than a half a century later, been lodged in the Public Archives of Canada. An analysis of these papers, in keeping with his own desire that they serve "historians of the future," raises a number of important questions with respect to the origins of the Royal Canadian Navy.

Hitherto, the views of Gilbert Tucker, the author of the official history of the RCN, have prevailed on this subject. Tucker maintained in *The Naval Service of Canada* that the Canadian government paid little attention to naval defence until the Foster Resolution of 29 March 1909 called for the creation of a Canadian naval service. Prior to that time, he said,

the official attitude in Canada in regard to naval defence remained wholly negative, and at the colonial conferences the weight of the senior British dependency was heavy in the scales on which policy was weighed. To most Canadians the world of international power politics seemed too remote to call forth action, and only when an unusually obvious and apparent imminent threat appeared [in the form of the menacing growth of the German High Seas Fleet prior to World War I] . . . was positive action taken.[3]

Yet Tucker acknowledges, and the papers confirm, that as one of the Canadian representatives at the 1909 Imperial Conference on Defence in London, L.P. Brodeur observed:

even before 1907, and as a consequence of the statements which were made at the [Colonial] Conference [on Defence] of 1902, we started immediately the nucleus of a Navy. We bought a cruiser which we put on the Atlantic coast, which was not a very large one it is true, but which was a beginning tending to show our desire and our wish to carry out the idea which had been announced at the Conference of 1902.[4]

Was then the Naval Service Act of 1910 the beginning of the Naval Service of Canada? Or can it be more appropriately described by Churchill's phrase, "the end of the beginning"?[5] Did the act institutionalize a shadow RCN already in existence? This chapter examines these questions for the period 1902-11 and chronicles a number of little known aspects of the naval service in those early years.

It would be illogical, if not irresponsible, to view Canada's early naval history in isolation from contemporary developments in the Department of Marine and Fisheries. If we are to look anywhere for the origins of the RCN prior to the Naval Service Act, it will be here. L.P. Brodeur headed both departments, and his full title was minister of Marine and Fisheries and the Naval Service. Moreover, by 1910, his deputy minister, Desbarats, and his director, Rear-Admiral Charles (later Sir Charles) Kingsmill, had spent their previous two years as deputy minister of Marine and Fisheries and director of the Marine Service, respectively.

The Department of Marine and Fisheries was the largest department in the Canadian government by 1904. Its responsibilities were manifold:

> Sea-Coast and Inland Fisheries, Trinity Houses, Trinity Boards, Pilots, Decayed Pilots' Funds, Beacons, Buoys, Lights and Light-houses and their maintenance, Harbours, Ports, Piers, Wharfs, Steamers and Vessels belonging to the Government of Canada, harbour commissioners, harbour masters, classification of vessels, examination and granting of certificates of masters and mates, and others in the merchant service, shipping masters and shipping officers, inspection of steamboats and boards of steamboat inspection, enquiries into causes of shipwrecks, establishment, regulation and maintenance of marine and seamen's hospitals and care of distressed seamen, and generally such matters as refer to the marine and navigation of Canada.[6]

These responsibilities were further increased in the same year when the government decided to make the Department of Marine and Fisheries responsible for the St. Lawrence ship channel—previously administered by the Department of Public Works—and for the exercise of sovereignty over the Canadian Arctic.

The latter decision led the minister of Marine and Fisheries to commission Captain Joseph E. Bernier, a renowned Canadian mariner, to explore the Canadian Arctic and take possession of the lands therein in the name of the Government of Canada. Bernier conducted three voyages in northern waters in his vessel, the *Arctic*, between 1904 and 1911. Unfortunately, public attention, following Bernier's 1906-7 voyage, became focused not on his considerable achievements but on the costs of the voyage, the quantities of victuals, rum, medicines, and stores carried, and the alleged failure to secure these through competitive contract.

In order to discharge its marine responsibilities the Department of Marine and Fisheries operated a fisheries protection fleet consisting of eight armed cruisers and a marine fleet consisting of six icebreakers and some eighteen other vessels over eighty feet in length (Appendix). In addition, the department operated thirteen Marconi marine radio stations on the east coast of Canada. The scope of its responsibilities with respect to fisheries can be inferred from the fact that nearly 83,000 persons were engaged in fishing in 1905 and total fisheries employment was 114,000 or 5.2 per cent of the overall labour force.

The heavy responsibilities shouldered by the Department of Marine and Fisheries and the broader challenges preoccupying the Canadian government in those early years left little, if any, time, energy, or resources to create a navy. But the Fishery Protection Service contained some of the ingredients for the nucleus of a navy, and the 1902 Colonial Conference on Defence seems to have provided the stimulus to create that nucleus.

The Prime Minister, Sir Wilfrid Laurier, was accompanied to the 1902 conference, by his newly appointed Minister of Marine and Fisheries, Raymond Prefontaine. Following the conference, Prefontaine, together with his Commander Marine Services, Osprey George Valentine Spain undertook to implement the government's intentions. The Canadian Government Ship (CGS) *Canada* was purchased in 1904 as the newest and largest of the fisheries protection vessels, and in the same year a bill, entitled "An Act Constituting the Naval Militia of Canada," was prepared by O.G.V. Spain for first reading, along with a proposal to establish a Canadian naval military academy.

CGS *Canada* was not the first Canadian fisheries protection cruiser. The Canadian government had built or bought eight armed vesels for that purpose between 1891 and 1904. The first, *Constance*, was 116 feet in length, and was built of iron and wood in 1891 at the Polson Works in Owen Sound; the second, *Curlew*, was also 116 feet in length, and was bought from Polson's in 1892; the following year *Petrel*, a 116-foot vessel of steel construction, was also purchased from Polson's. The government then bought a 127-foot wooden fisheries protection vessel in 1896, the schooner *Osprey* built in Shelburne, Nova Scotia. In 1903, *Kestrel*, another wooden fisheries cruiser 126 feet in length, was bought from A. Wallace Builders in Vancouver, British Columbia. Then, in 1904, CGS *Vigilant*, a 175-foot steel vessel described as the first modern warship to be built in Canada, was purchased from Polson Iron Works in Toronto. Another fisheries protection cruiser bought in 1904 was the *Falcon*, but unfortunately there is no information available on the character or location of her construction. CGS *Canada* was the largest of the Canadian government fisheries protection cruisers. She was 200 feet in length, of steel construction, and was built by Vickers Barrow in England. Early photographs of some of these cruisers show that they were indeed small warships with ram bows and cannons. This was especially true of *Vigilant* and *Canada*, and this fact, together with the timing of their acquisition and the appearance of the uniforms worn by personnel in those ships (which even included

"Half-Whites"), gives credence to L.P. Brodeur's statement that Canada started the "nucleus of a navy" after the 1902 conference. Additional evidence is provided in a memorandum of 28 January 1907, from O.G.V. Spain to the deputy minister of Marine and Fisheries:

> The Cruiser *Canada* which is manned and armed in all respects as a man-of-war, was built in England and brought out in 1904; in 1905 she was sent on a training cruise to the West Indies, carrying a large number of young fishermen as recruits; this according to the late Minister's idea, was proposed to be the beginning of the Naval Militia. On the return of this ship from her instructional cruise, the men who had already been trained were distributed amongst the other ships; fresh men taken on; and instruction continued. The material that we have in the Canadian Naval Militia is probably the best in the world.[7]

Notwithstanding the proceedings of Canadian government ships, there was little attention paid to or money made available for the building of a navy in the period 1902-9. This is not to suggest, however, that there was not a concerned interest in naval matters in certain segments of the Canadian government and the public. There certainly was an extensive communication and liaison established between the Toronto and Victoria branches of the Navy League and the ministers of Marine and Fisheries.

The Navy League of Canada had been active for many years, and in 1898 the Toronto branch had presented a memorial to the governor general proposing the creation of a Canadian naval reserve. In fact, it was proposed that an initial Canadian naval force of five thousand men be raised to supplement the militia of Canada; that it be governed by regulations "similar to those of the Admiralty as far as local conditions permit"; that for training purposes Canada "procure from the Home authorities suitable vessels for such crews of instructors as may be necessary paying a reasonable sum for their use"; and that "the fishermen of Canada might do their training in the winter months in a warmer latitude."[8]

The individual who deserves much of the credit for these proposals and for encouraging Prefontaine and Brodeur to create a Canadian navy was the honorary secretary of the Toronto branch of the Navy League, H.J. Wickham. Until his death in 1909, he maintained a close contact with Brodeur and was instrumental in arranging meetings with influential persons in England and in Canada.

It was Wickham who urged Prefontaine to hold conversations with the Navy League of England in 1905, and it would appear that the minister of Marine and Fisheries acceded to his request.[9] However, before he could return to Canada, Prefontaine died in France. His death, the delay in appointing a successor, the time required for his successor to familiarize himself with such a large department, the problems which that successor inherited, and the economic and political preoccupations of the ensuing years probably had more effect in delaying the establishment of a naval service in Canada than any other considerations.

Laurier assumed the position of minister of Marine and Fisheries for two months, until February 1906, when he was able to appoint a successor to the post, his protégé and close personal friend, Louis Philippe Brodeur. Born at Beloeil, Quebec, in 1862, the son of Toussaint Brodeur (one of the rebels of 1837), L.P. Brodeur was educated at the College of St. Hyacinthe and at Laval University before being called to the Quebec bar in 1884. He was elected to the House of Commons for the County of Rouville seven years later and represented that constituency until the fall of the Laurier administration in 1911. He was appointed deputy speaker of the House of Commons in 1896, immediately after Laurier's accession to power, and was elected speaker of the House in 1901. In January 1904 he was appointed minister of Inland Revenue, and in his first session in that capacity he introduced and passed the bill against the American Tobacco Trust. In August 1905 he joined W.S. Fielding, the minister of Finance, and Sir Richard Cartwright, the minister of Trade and Commerce, in the 1905 Tariff Commission to revive Canada's industrial and agricultural trade. The commissioners' extensive hearings took them from coast to coast and lasted until February 1906, at which time Brodeur was appointed minister of Marine and Fisheries and became Laurier's Liberal leader for Montreal and the surrounding area. A physically impressive and fearless man, possessing great magnetism and charm, Brodeur was respected for his integrity, patriotism and wisdom. Laurier nicknamed him "mon sage."

Two months after he assumed responsibility for the Ministry of Marine and Fisheries, Brodeur introduced a bill to reorganize the Harbour Commission of Montreal, a sorely needed measure which, together with the deepening of the St. Lawrence channel and the improvement of its navigation facilities, occupied much of his attention that year and the next. In April 1906, his department came under severe criticism as a result of a commissioner's report into the disastrous wreck of the American steamer *Valencia* in British Columbia waters on 23 January 1906. The incident, in which 126 lives were lost, necessitated a thorough review of ship inspection procedures and the construction of five new Marconi marine radio stations on the west coast of Vancouver Island. The following month, in May 1906, his department came under attack again for the costs entailed in outfitting Bernier's *Arctic*, and a committee of inquiry was appointed to investigate the department's procurement of supplies for that expedition. At the same time Brodeur became engaged in the planning of the Hudson Bay Railway project.

Plate 1. Before the formation of the RCN in 1910 Canada relied upon the Royal Navy to defend her coastline. Here, HMS *Cormorant* enters the drydock at Esquimalt, 20 July 1887. (Maritime Command Museum, Halifax [MCM])

Plate 2. Personnel of the Royal Navy on route march, Esquimalt, ca. 1900-1905. (Public Archives Canada [PAC]—PA 115388)

Plate 3. Officers, midshipmen, and crew of HMCS *Niobe*, "Diadem"-class cruiser which was the RCN's first warship based in Halifax. Shown are Midshipmen V.G. Brodeur (right) and C.T. Beard (left of officer with sword) and Stoker J.O. Cossette (standing, sixth from left) who later achieved flag rank as rear-admiral. (Maritime Division, Nova Scotia Museum—MP 31.7.49)

Plate 4. Stokers on board HMCS *Niobe*. (Maritime Division, Nova Scotia Museum—MP 31.7.48)

Plate 5. HMCS *Rainbow* (right) an "Apollo"-class cruiser, was the RCN's first Pacific warship. Shown here with HMS *Shearwater*, Esquimalt, 17 November 1910. (PAC—PA 115365)

Plate 6. HMCS *Niobe* served until 1915, when she was paid off as a depot ship in Halifax. (MCM)

Plate 7. CGS *Canada*, largest of the Canadian government fisheries protection cruisers in the Department of Marine and Fisheries fleet, which was a precursor of the RCN. (Directorate of History, National Defence Headquarters [DOH, NDHQ]—CN 3740) (insert) Louis P. Brodeur, minister of Marine and Fisheries, 1906-11, and minister of the Naval Service, 1910-11. (PAC—PA 30853)

Plate 8. Original RCN cadets training on CGS *Canada. Back row (from left)*: C.T. Beard, P.B. German, V.G. Brodeur, Wright; *middle*: Fortier, C. Stewart, Woods; *front*: H.T. Bate, P.W. Nelles, J.A. Barron, (N.D. Brodeur collection, MCM)

It would appear that Brodeur's attention was fully occupied by these matters and that it was not until December 1906 that he was able to devote some time to naval matters. In this context he resumed an extensive correspondence with the Navy League which was to continue throughout his term in office.

This correspondence highlighted the respective positions of the branches of the Navy League of Canada on the naval question. The champion of the Victoria-Esquimalt branch was Clive Phillipps-Wolley, a poet, demagogue, imperialist, and advocate of Canadian contributions to the Royal Navy. At a meeting in the City Hall, Victoria, British Columbia, on 14 May 1907, Phillipps-Wolley concluded an emotional oration with the following resolution:

> That it is the duty of the Navy League and of every patriotic Canadian independent of party, to press in every way for a substantial contribution to that Imperial Navy, upon which the very existence of Canada as a portion of the Empire depends, and that this meeting believes that a plebiscite of the people of Canada (independent of party) would support this resolution.[10]

The resolution was carried unanimously and with enthusiasm.

On the other hand, the position of the Toronto branch of the Navy League was reflected in the annual report of its executive committee for the year 1907:

> This Branch of the Navy League has, since its formation in 1895, consistently opposed a direct cash contribution by Canada towards the upkeep of the Royal Navy. We hold that Canadian money should be spent in Canada, making naval preparation go hand-in-hand with the development of a truly Canadian maritime policy, the encouragement of Canadian shipbuilding, the proper equipment of Canadian national ports, and the employment of our maritime population, than whom no finer seamen exist.[11]

Subsequently, the Toronto branch sponsored a $400 prize for the best essay on the subject "Shall Canada Have a Navy of Her Own?" The winner was a Mrs. W. Hewes Oliphant of Toronto, whose analysis included the statement:

> Upon the whole, it seems impossible to reject the conclusion that Canada should, for Canadian reasons, have a navy; having regard to the functions of a naval equipment, our geographical and trade conditions and our relations, actual and possible, to the outside world.[12]

Apparently Brodeur attached considerable importance to the Navy League correspondence since he took it with him to the 1907 Colonial Conference on Defence. It is easy to infer from Tucker's account of the conference that Laurier and his minister of Marine and Fisheries were opposed, in principle, to the formation of a Canadian navy at that time. What seems more likely, however, is that they went to the conference with memories of the position taken by the British government and the Admiralty in the Colonial Conference of 1902. Concerted attempts had been made then to discourage the formation of individual colonial navies and to encourage the colonies to make contributions towards maintaining the Royal Navy.

The general tenor of the 1902 talks had revealed that "the conditions and circumstances of the several Colonies were so different that further discussion with a view to framing a general resolution [on imperial defence was] not likely to lead to any practical results."[13] As a consequence, the colonial representatives held separate private meetings with the First Lord of the Admiralty, and all of them, save the Canadians, had agreed to help in some way to defray the Royal Navy's imperial defence costs.[14]

The First Lord of the Admiralty, Lord Tweedmouth, inaugurated discussions on naval defence at the 1907 conference by advancing a number of positions: that the Royal Navy had served the country and empire well; that, therefore, the colonies should have faith in the British government and the Admiralty "who have the charge of strategical questions"; that the sea linked them all for commerce and defence; that there was "one sea, one empire and one navy"; that though the Navy welcomed further contributions they did not wish to insist on contributions being sent only in the form of money; that colonial governments could assist by providing smaller vessels for local service in imperial squadrons and by maintaining dockyards, coal, and storing facilities for the imperial squadrons; that the Admiralty was prepared to make arrangements with the individual colonies; and that they welcomed contributions and would spend the money wisely.[15]

On the completion of his presentation Lord Tweedmouth called upon Alfred Deakin of Australia and Sir Joseph Ward of New Zealand to express their views on the issues raised. They, in turn, were followed by L.P. Brodeur for Canada. Brodeur's statement leaves little doubt of the fact that he and Laurier were annoyed by what they considered to be the misinformation tabled by the Admiralty. He pointed out that Canada's situation was different from that of the other colonies and that consequently she should not be treated in the same manner. He further argued that Canada had taken on full responsibility for fisheries protection (protection which had cost the Dominion more than $3 million since 1885), operated wireless installations on both coasts which had previously been maintained by the

Admiralty, trained Canadian seamen in naval matters and assumed responsibility for hydrographic work and for the dockyard in Halifax. These were costly services, he noted, and yet the Admiralty, which had included such services in its own cost estimates, had entirely failed to acknowledge them in its calculations as a Canadian contribution to imperial defence.[16]

The British position became somewhat more conciliatory by the thirteenth day of the conference. Lord Tweedmouth, after announcing that he had talked with a number of the prime ministers and their colleagues, observed:

> With regard to Canada, I think I may say there has perhaps been some exaggeration in the idea that Canada does not do anything for the Empire in this matter. I think not sufficient account has been taken of the work they have done in taking up the protection of fisheries. They are very anxious to extend that work, and they have now taken over the dockyards at Halifax and Esquimalt, which I hope the Dominion will keep up and improve. I think that is really a very considerable contribution towards the general upkeep of our naval interests. There is at present no proposition from Canada to make any change at all, and I think it is proposed that matters shall go on very much as they have gone on, except that the Canadian representatives announced that they are anxious to do all that they can to expand the interests in the navy throughout the Dominion, and in that way think that they will be really giving a great help to the Empire as a whole.[17]

Later the same day Brodeur had an opportunity to respond to Lord Tweedmouth's statement:

> There was a discussion in previous years to the effect that we should contribute something directly to the British Navy. I may say with regard to that, there is only one mind in Canada on that question. . . . I think perhaps I might mention what . . . [Sir Charles Tupper] said in regard to that. He said: "It is known that from the outset I felt the interests of Canada and the true interests of the Empire to be opposed to the demand for Colonial contributions to the Imperial Navy" and "I maintain that Canada has discharged that duty in the manner most conducive to Imperial interests." So it shows that both sides of politics in Canada agree with the policy which has been going on for some years there. He adds also . . . that "Canada protects her fisheries by her own cruisers, and when the Imperial Government expressed a wish to be relieved of the expense of maintaining the strategic points the harbours of Halifax and Esquimalt the Canadian Government at once

relieved them of that large expenditure amounting to £185,000 per annum." Negotiations are now going on for taking over the Naval stations there. I do not know exactly what will be the amount by which the Admiralty will be relieved but I think it is a somewhat larger amount. . . . Since the matter has been brought before this Conference, I might say that Parliament has voted a large sum of money for the purpose of purchasing another cruiser and putting that cruiser on the Pacific Coast for the protection of our fisheries. . . .

We are very glad to see that Lord Tweedmouth has recognized that in this matter it should be left almost entirely up to the Colonies. I may say, in conclusion, that we will be very glad to work in co-operation with the Imperial authorities, and under the advice of an Imperial Officer, so far as it is consistent with self government.[18]

The message was clear; the Canadian government considered that it had already assumed a reasonable share of the naval expenditures through the costs of the Fisheries Protection Service and the various works which it had undertaken: those which were new and those which had been carried out by the Admiralty previously. It was also clear that financial contributions were perceived to be contradictory to the fundamental principle of Canadian sovereignty and that this was unanimously agreed upon by all political parties in Canada.

Four months after Brodeur's return from England, a Civil Service Commission report was tabled in the House. It contained serious allegations of patronage and wrongdoing in the Department of Marine and Fisheries. The Opposition launched a vigorous attack against Brodeur's administration, and in March 1908 he was obliged to call for a special commission to investigate his department. The Cassels Commission was formed for this purpose on 1 April 1908.

It was generally recognized that the minister of Marine and Fisheries had inherited a variety of difficult problems in his department; that his prolonged absence in 1907 (at the conference and subsequently negotiating shipping votes and trades treaties in England and France) had limited his opportunities to deal with them; and that he was a man of great personal integrity who by his own account was working fifteen hours a day to bring about much-needed changes. Nonetheless, he came under strong and continuous public and private censure throughout 1907. In the process, distorted reports in the more radical papers of both the French and English press fanned racial and religious bigotry and aroused divisions which would later have a considerable impact on the naval question.

Laurier dissolved Parliament on 17 September 1908 and scheduled a national election for 16 October. Brodeur was federal Liberal leader for the province of Quebec as well as being responsible for the district of Montreal. He campaigned arduously on behalf of Laurier and his fellow Liberals throughout the province and won his own seat, Rouville, by acclamation. The election returned the Laurier administration.

Recognizing the challenges which faced the Laurier administration and the Department of Marine and Fisheries in the period from 1906 to the beginning of 1909, it is hardly surprising that naval matters enjoyed a low priority. It is not known which vessel Brodeur was referring to in the conference of 1907 when he said that Canada proposed to buy a new cruiser at a cost of $500,000. There would appear to have been no such vessel built.

Whether as a result of the Cassels Commission or other circumstances, some key changes took place in the Department of Marine and Fisheries in the latter part of 1908. George J. Desbarats, who had been director of the Canadian government shipyard in Sorel since 1901, replaced François Goudreau as deputy minister, and O.G.V. Spain was replaced by Rear-Admiral Sir Charles Kingsmill. Kingsmill had retired from the Royal Navy to return to Canada and accept the post of director of the Marine Service in the Department of Marine and Fisheries. Supported by this capable team and exonerated by the Cassels Commission, Brodeur was able to turn his attention to the matter of establishing a naval service and of transferring the remaining Admiralty properties at Halifax and Esquimalt to Canadian government control.

At the same time he continued to maintain contact with the Toronto branch of the Navy League and with its Secretary, H.J. Wickham. In one reply to Wickham, Brodeur said he was glad to learn that the League had always been opposed to a direct contribution to the Royal Navy but pointed out that certain branches of the League in Canada had declared themselves in favour of such a step. He repeated Canada's intention of constructing another cruiser larger than CGS *Canada* for service on the Pacific Ocean in the near future and noted that the government planned to maintain the same military training and discipline on board her as that on the *Canada*. All the fleet engaged in protecting Canadian fisheries, he observed, would be governed by the rules of naval discipline; vacancies would be filled as far as possible by promotion according to merit and seniority; and Canada would establish a naval reserve on a basis which would command the confidence and support of the Canadian people.[19] Wickham continued his efforts on behalf of a Canadian navy even after he retired from the League and returned to England. He informed Brodeur in May 1909 that Admiral Lord Charles Beresford, the commander-in-chief Channel Fleet, was an ally to the Canadian cause and was "in full and active sympathy with principles that naval preparation on the part of the self-governing dominions should proceed along national lines." Wickham went on to predict the Canadian position in the 1909 Imperial Conference on Defence:

> Believe me that when you get to close quarters with this subject . . . a plan will be found whereby Canada and the others may provide naval forces of their own, under their own control, and so organized, trained, etc. (both as to men and ships and other material) so as to be, when occasion requires, interchangeable with the Royal Navy and capable of forming one weapon with that service with the consent of Canada should an emergency arise making concerted action necessary.[20]

There seems to be little doubt that the Navy League, and Wickham in particular, exerted considerable influence behind the scenes in persuading the Canadian government to establish a Canadian navy.[21] In contrast to Phillipps-Wolley's critical (and somewhat cunning) letters to Brodeur, Wickham continued to provide helpful advice and assistance to the minister of Marine and Fisheries and was probably responsible for the invitation from the Committee of the Navy League in England to Brodeur to become a vice-president of the League, an honour which the latter respectfully declined, pointing out that he was already contributing his support to Navy League branches in Canada.[22]

Commencing in 1909, and possibly as a consequence of his association with Brodeur during the Quebec Tercentenary in 1908, the Governor General of Canada, the fifth Earl Grey, began to take a wider interest in naval matters. The L.P. Brodeur papers reveal a considerable correspondence between the two men which continued until Grey's retirement and the fall of the Laurier administration in 1911.[23]

Grey wrote to Brodeur on 29 April 1909 to enclose a part of a letter from Sir Charles Parsons (the inventor of the steam turbine) and to say that he (Grey) was disappointed that Parsons could not find time to pay a visit to Ottawa. Grey added that since the German scare had focused Canada's attention on naval construction, Sir Charles's visit would have been opportune, particularly in view of the fact that the British had adopted the turbine as the power plant for their revolutionary new battleship, HMS *Dreadnought*, in 1906.

Brodeur acknowledged Grey's letter and in preparation for the 1909 Imperial Conference on Defence set about to obtain information from the United States Navy on the types and costs of warship construction for the American, British, Argentinian, and Brazilian navies. He corresponded with H.B. Jayne, the proprietor of the *Pacific Marine Review*, received information from Admiral W.L. Capps, chief constructor of the USN, and secured tables from the US Naval Intelligence Bureau showing the comparative sea strength of the world's navies.[24]

Brodeur received a proposal from the British shipbuilder Sir B.C. Browne in July 1909 with respect to the need to commence naval shipbuilding in Canada. Brown wrote prophetically:

> Confining our attention to Destroyers or small Cruisers, there would be no difficulty in being ready to build the Hulls in Canada in a very short time, and the same appliances would be perfectly suitable for commercial work.
>
> As regards Engines, the case is a little more complicated, because whereas necessarily all the engines for War Vessels are turbines, these have not yet made any great way in the Mercantile Marine, though we hope they will do so rapidly, but it may be hoped that before long this work could also be done on the spot.
>
> As regards Ordnance Works, we have no actual experience, but we believe that to start such Works as could meet the whole of Canada's requirements would run into a very large amount of capital indeed, whereas to start Works that could make field guns or small marine guns, and execute all repair work and make ammunition, would probably not cost more than one-tenth part of the money.
>
> There is no reason why Works should not be started at more than one place, provided the Government could give suitable encouragement to private enterprise.
>
> Canada does not appear, on the face of it, as though it would be a likely place from which one would ever develop a trade building War vessels for other countries.[25]

The Imperial Conference on Naval and Military Defence opened at the Foreign Office in Whitehall on 20 July 1909, with H.H. Asquith, prime minister of Great Britain, presiding. Asquith recapitulated the conclusion of the 1902 conference, listing the individual cash contributions made by the colonies and mentioning Canada's intention of establishing a local naval force in lieu of a contribution. He mentioned the failure of the 1907 conference to reach a consensus on naval defence and expressed concern over Germany's naval re-arming, especially over her battleship programme; described his government's intention of building eight new Dreadnought-class battleships; and hinted at divisions of opinion in Britain over the adequacy of the naval programme. He acknowledged New Zealand's offer to bear the cost of one or, if necessary, two battleships. He recounted the resolution passed in the Canadian House of Commons on 29

March which recognized "the duty of Canada, as the country increased in numbers and wealth, to assume in a larger measure the responsibilities of national defence, and approving of any necessary expenditure designed to promote the speedy organization of a Canadian naval service in co-operation with and in close relation to the Imperial Navy." He followed this by reporting Australia's intention to offer an Australian dreadnought to the Empire.

Asquith then turned to a discussion of Admiralty statistics on individual dominion naval expenditures. A new variation had appeared by this time—a comparison of defence expenditure and trade (seaborne exports and imports). Once again Canadians were shown to be misers, but the comparison was not entirely fair since Canada's overland trade with the United States had not been excluded for the purposes of the calculation. Asquith acknowledged this fact, but his remarks failed to erase the negative impression that the figures created.

The statements attributed to L.P. Brodeur in Tucker's work do not reflect what he actually said in his principal speech and are, in fact, misleading. Moreover, they appear to have been abstracted from a document other than the actual proceedings (which, contrary to the footnote in *The Naval Service of Canada*, contain the major speeches by Borden and Brodeur on pages 40 to 44). In any event the official history appears to have overlooked the important comment that "as a consequence of the statements which were made at the Conference of 1902, we started immediately the nucleus of a Navy"; as well as other significant points.

On the sixth and last day of the conference the chairman, Lord Crewe, secretary of state for the colonies, introduced a draft resolution for discussion:

> This Conference, whilst recognizing that the provision made for defence in His Majesty's self-governing Dominions beyond the seas is primarily designed for local purposes, and is subject to the conditions imposed by the Legislature of each Dominion, desires to declare its full acceptance of the principle that the whole of the military and naval forces in the British Dominions should be so organized as to render each . . . force capable of performing the most efficient service in any emergency which might threaten the integrity of the Empire.[26]

The Canadian delegates had been forewarned. Five days earlier, on 14 August, Brodeur had sent the text of the resolution to Laurier in a telegram with a suggested amendment, adding the words, "in which the overseas Dominions elect to play their part." He queried Laurier, "Crewe suggesting following Resolution—what should we do?"

Laurier's reply arrived on 17 August: "Represent to Crewe how impolitic it would be to depart from terms of Resolution of last session." It can be reasoned from this that Laurier, having successfully obtained all the unanimity he could hope for in the Foster Resolution of 29 March, had no desire to see a new Commons debate arise out of the 1909 conference.

As had happened in 1907, no joint resolution on naval defence emerged from the 1909 conference. However, in this instance Canada was not alone in opposing such a resolution; most of the delegates considered the discussions at the 1909 conference to be extremely sensitive. As a consequence, Lord Crewe took extraordinary measures with respect to the conference documentation. Specially prepared *Confidential Proceedings* and *Papers Relating to the Conference*, in a form suitable for eventual publication, were forwarded to Lord Grey; but the actual record of proceedings at the conference was kept secret.[27] This explains why the accounts of the 1909 conference in *The Naval Service of Canada* differ from the actual proceedings.

Moreover, an exchange of correspondence between Brodeur and Laurier reveals that there was a behind-the-scenes "gentleman's agreement" at the conference respecting Canadian naval policy.[28] It appears that Reginald McKenna, the First Lord of the Admiralty, was prepared to abandon the pursuit of naval contributions where Canada was concerned. He was prepared to agree to a Canadian navy, but was not prepared to let this be known either inside or outside the Admiralty (whose records of the discussions would no doubt show that Canada had opposed and altered the Admiralty proposal). Canada could have her navy, but the Canadian government would have to bear the public responsibility for opposing the British government and the Admiralty. Laurier's reply to Brodeur's letter shows that he accurately foresaw the political storms ahead:

> Je viens de recevoir votre lettre et le mémoire du programme adopté à la conférence. Le paragraphe II va nous causer quelques tracasseries, c'est-à-dire que les Tories vont s'en emparer pour nous accuser d'avoir bloqué l'Amirauté. Je dois ajouter cependant que cette attaque ne m'effraie nullement.[29]

Brodeur's letter also stated that McKenna had consented to lend Canada one or two cruisers and that, as Laurier knew, Canada should be building one immediately for fisheries protection in British Columbia. (This arrangement tends to confirm that the new cruiser planned and funded prior to the 1907 conference was never built and that its place was taken, ultimately, by HMCS *Rainbow* in 1910.)

When the post-conference discussions on implementation had been concluded between Brodeur, Kingsmill, the Admiralty, and potential shipbuilders, the Canadian naval programme was expected to consist of one Boadicea-class cruiser, four Bristol-class cruisers and six River-class destroyers.[30] *Niobe*, a large Diadem-class cruiser, and *Rainbow*, a smaller cruiser, were procured, and the remainder of the vessels were to be built in Canada. When Brodeur reached Quebec he announced that "Canada must have a navy of her own. . . . Our ships we shall have to build and I am convinced that we shall be able to build them with our own men, our own materials and on our own soil.[31]

It is not intended at this point to review the naval debates prior to the arrival of HMCS *Niobe* in Halifax on 21 October 1910, the 105th anniversary of Trafalgar. The Brodeur papers contain considerable material covering that period, some of it tending to contradict the official record and popular impressions concerning the degree to which Canadians supported the navy. However, a full treatment is clearly beyond the scope of this chapter. Instead, the intention is to examine three issues which arose in 1910-11, about which very little is known: the flag, jurisdiction, and language issues.

As previously noted, Lord Grey began to take an interest in naval matters from 1909 onwards. Indeed, his concern about the flag and jurisdiction issues resulted in over thirty separate letters, memoranda, and messages between Grey, Brodeur, and the colonial secretary between 26 October 1910 and 16 March 1911. That correspondence leaves little doubt that the Admiralty was reluctant to give Canada full sovereignty over her own warships. The formal transfer of HMCS *Niobe* did not occur until 12 November 1910, three weeks after her arrival in Halifax, and then only after two messages from Lord Grey to the colonial secretary. The Canadian White Ensign, a white ensign with a green maple leaf centred on the cross of St. George (quite likely devised by Grey and approved by Laurier and his ministers), was not accepted by the Admiralty. Then, notwithstanding Lord Grey's express desire to sail to the West Indies in *Niobe* in the spring of 1911 and his message that a cruise was essential to provide training for her crew, the Colonial Office and the Admiralty refused to allow *Niobe* and *Rainbow* to steam beyond the three-mile territorial limit until the whole question of the "status of Dominion navies" was resolved, a question which was a key issue in the 1911 Imperial Conference on Defence.

The frustrations of those days are evident from the last exchange of correspondence between Lord Grey and L.P. Brodeur, found in the latter's papers. The former wrote to the minister of the Naval Service on 14 March 1911 with respect to the jurisdictional problem:

It is fair to remember that the officers and men of the 'Niobe' have in the main been lent by the Admiralty to the Canadian Government and that the Admiralty have done all in their power to meet our convenience. In these circumstances I feel sure that you will agree with me that we ought not to press upon them a course of action which in their view will be productive of the gravest inconvenience to them. The naval authorities in England regard this matter, which may seem a simple one, as one of grave moment and difficulty, but we may hope that the result of Mr. Smith's mission may be to find a solution satisfactory to all parties.[32]

Brodeur replied two days later:

When it was decided at the Conference of 1909 that a Canadian Navy should be established, I thought that this Navy would be permitted to go outside territorial waters. Otherwise it would have been obvious, as you state, that no Navy could exist under such restrictions. If they had told me at that time that the existence of the Navy should depend on some restrictions of that kind, I would certainly have never favoured its establishment in the country. Then was the time to raise the question, instead of letting the Canadian Government go on with the establishment of a Navy, acquire vessels, and then be told: "You will have to remain within the three-mile limit." Nothing of the kind was then said or mentioned. Now they state that we cannot go outside the territorial waters without passing automatically under their own rules and regulations.

I do not see why they would not trust Canada in the management and control of her Navy. Do they fear some illegal acts on our part? We have had for years and years a Fisheries Protection Service which has come constantly into contact with foreign vessels. We have seized some of those vessels at different intervals, but we never did anything which brought the Imperial Authorities into serious difficulties. I am not even aware of any difficulties which have happened in that connection. Having taken part in the Conference of 1909, and having strongly urged on my Colleagues the principle of a Canadian Navy, I am personally in a very awkward situation, and if there was no fear on my part that the idea of a Canadian Navy would be jeopardized, I would have to take some steps which otherwise would not conform with the obligations that a Minister has to fulfill in the discharge of his duties.[33]

While Grey and Brodeur were debating the jurisdictional problem, R.C. Smith, an eminent Liberal lawyer and Canadian parliamentarian, was engaged in protracted negotiations with the Admiralty in preparation for the 1911 Imperial Conference on Defence. He wrote to Brodeur with respect to two of the more contentious issues which he and their lordships of the Admiralty were attempting to resolve: the question of Canadian warships

v:siting foreign ports and the matter of the relative status of RN and RCN
ships operating in company.

> [Their lordships] very strongly protest that their position upon this
> question [of visiting foreign ports] is not prompted by any attempt or
> desire to curtail our liberty or to control our ships, the rule is that the
> Admiralty never sends a ship to a foreign port without consulting the
> Foreign Office, as relations might be strained or some reason might
> exist why a ship should not be sent to such or such port. They ask that
> we should do just what the Admiralty does. . . .
>   They are willing to give up their contention as to strict territorial
> jurisdiction, but they suggest that as each fleet has what is called its
> "station," there should be constituted the Canadian Atlantic station
> and the Canadian Pacific station say (merely suggestive and not
> authoritative) from 40[°W] on the Atlantic to 160[°W] on the Pacific
> and north of 30[°N]. This would take in Bermuda and a great part of
> the U.S. coast, and would adjoin the West Indian station. They would
> agree not to send ships into the Canadian stations without your
> concurrence.

With respect to the status of RCN and RN ships together, Smith concluded, "We have fought rings round upon this. It is of course a very
delicate and difficult question."[34]
   By the time that Laurier, Frederick Borden, and Brodeur arrived for the
1911 conference, much had been accomplished. It remained for Brodeur
and Graham Greene, the capable and highly respected secretary of the
Admiralty, to negotiate a final position at the conference. It was agreed that
Canada would enjoy exclusive control over her Naval Service and that
Canadian Atlantic and Pacific Stations would be established. Moreover,
specific wartime and peacetime command relationships between the RCN
and the RN were defined.[35]
   The third issue, that of the use of the French language, was a purely
national problem. In August 1910, Brodeur received a copy of the proposed
"Regulations for Entry of Naval Cadets," which had been prepared by
Commander D. Roper, RN, and Paymaster P.J. Ling, RN (Rear-Admiral
Kingsmill's chief of staff and naval secretary respectively). These regulations were accompanied by a memorandum in which the officers argued
that "it [was] not desirable that candidates should be permitted to take the
[entrance] examination in French."[36]
   Brodeur wrote the following minute in reply:

> It should not be forgotten that Canada is a bilingual country and that
> French and English are on the same footing. It follows that the instruc-

tion in national establishments should be conducted in both languages. The instructors who are to be appointed should be fairly conversant with French and English. If the rule suggested in the above memo were adopted it would mean that the French speaking young men could not enter the service. I am sure that this is not the end aimed at by the officers who prepared it. I fully realize that the use of two languages is creating inconvenience but that is not sufficient to prevent the true spirit of the constitution being carried out. I would request the Chief of Staff and the Secretary to reconsider the matter with the hope that they will realize themselves the impossibility of carrying out their suggestion.[37]

Brodeur returned the minuted memorandum to his deputy, Desbarats, under a covering letter (written in French) in which he expressed concern over such restrictions and commented on the likely loss of popular support for the naval service.[38] Desbarats forwarded the memorandum to Roper and Ling directing them to have the entrance examination held in both languages. They, in turn, replied that they could not modify their previous position; that any attempt to combine the two languages would be detrimental to the service; and that the entrance examinations after November 1911 should be in English only, thereby giving parents of French-speaking candidates a period of grace in which to have their sons educated in English prior to that time.[39]

On receiving this second memorandum Brodeur wrote to Desbarats to express his regret at their attitude and stubbornness. He concluded that he saw no reason to alter his position on the entrance examinations or on the requirement for the instructors to know both languages—not in order to give the courses in both languages but to be able to assist French-speaking students in cases where their knowledge of English was insufficient to enable them to understand explanations given by the instructors.[40]

It is perhaps just as well that these three issues—the flag, jurisdiction, and bilingualism—were not made public in 1910 and 1911 for they had the potential to destroy the naval service of Canada. In retrospect, it seems most unfortunate that the efforts toward a distinctive ensign, greater autonomy, and a partial form of bilingualism did not succeed. Throughout most of its history, including World War II, the RCN was perceived to be more British than Canadian by most French-Canadians, a perception which later spread to English-Canadians as well during the dawning of the new Canadian nationalism in the 1960's. As a consequence, the RCN forfeited much of its potential to attract and retain the popular support of all Canadians. Today, as in 1921, the words of Louis Philippe Brodeur are, sadly, all too familiar, "le service naval, qui, je regrette de le dire, ne paraît pas commander aujourd'hui autant de faveur qu'il le devrait."

It is vitally important for Canadians to remember what an achievement it was to create their own naval service for, once lost, it cannot be readily restored.

Chapter 3

COMMANDER E.A.E. NIXON AND
THE ROYAL NAVAL COLLEGE OF CANADA,
1910-1922

P. Willet Brock

The Royal Canadian Navy and the Royal Naval College of Canada were established as a result of the Imperial Conference on Naval and Military Defence held in London in 1909. The British government sought to secure assistance to meet the threat of the German High Seas Fleet which was being developed by Admiral Tirpitz. Elements of the Empire were invited to contribute ships or money directly to the Royal Navy or to create individual navies capable of working with it.

New Zealand, Newfoundland (which was still a British dependency), and South Africa, amongst others, offered contributions, while Canada and Australia opted for their own navies. Despite opposition from the Conservatives, who favoured a gift of ships, and from many of his own followers in Quebec, who had no enthusiasm for any form of naval defence, the Canadian Prime Minister, Sir Wilfrid Laurier, introduced a Naval Service Act which received the formality of royal assent on 4 May 1910. This act provided for the establishment of a college to train naval cadets.

The Royal Naval College of Canada (RNCC), as it was entitled in October 1910, had the ambitious object of imparting "a complete education in all branches of naval science, tactics, and strategy."[1] Entry was open to young Canadians from fourteen to sixteen years of age, of good health and character, who had successfully completed a competitive examination. They were enrolled on a two-year course, followed by a year in a Royal

Navy training squadron in order to qualify them as sub-lieutenants. Before an examination could be held, however, six midshipmen were inducted on Trafalgar Day 1910. They were to receive preliminary training in CGS *Canada* before being lent to the Royal Navy. These cadets included Percy Walker Nelles, who was later to become chief of the Naval Staff, and V.G. Brodeur, son of the minister of the Naval Service, who was also to reach flag rank. The Civil Service Commission announced the first competitive examination for entry to the RNCC in November. Two hundred inquiries were received. Thirty-four candidates sat, and twenty-one were accepted for training. Little did they realize what lean and even tragic years lay ahead of them.

Laurier's government was heavily defeated in September 1911. Whatever its merits, Sir Robert Borden's victory was a blow to the RCN, and his proposed contribution of capital ships to the Royal Navy was rejected by the Liberal majority in the Senate. Somewhat surprisingly, the RNCC survived: an achievement all the more remarkable in view of enrolments which averaged only ten cadets per year (and bottomed at six in 1915), the elimination of the obligation on the part of graduates to enter the RCN, and the broadening and extension of curriculum from two years to three in order to permit entry into the second year of some universities.

In August 1914 HMS *Good Hope*, later the flagship of Rear-Admiral Sir Christopher Cradock's South American Station, called at Halifax to take on coal. Midshipmen M. Cann, W.A. Palmer, A.W. Silver and J.V.W. Hatheway, who had just passed out from the RNCC, were sent on board to fill vacancies created by an Admiralty clerk's error. Within three months these young men were dead. The *Good Hope*, reduced to a flaming hulk, exploded and went down with all hands on 1 November following a disastrously unequal encounter with Admiral Graf von Spee's Pacific Squadron off the Chilean coast. They were Canada's first service casualties of the war.

I did not become involved with the RCN until two and a half years later. My good friend Charles Carrington, best known as Kipling's authorized biographer, used to say than when he started writing his recollections of life as a subaltern in World War I his diaries revealed that for half a century he had been dining out on events that had never happened.

Fortunately, I kept diaries as a cadet, and those, supplemented by material from the college journal, *Sea Breezes*, have allowed me to recreate my days as a midshipman. I blush now for some of the views I expressed then, but they were what I thought when I was green.

My interest in a naval career stemmed from the influence of two people; my father, who since his post-graduate days at Heidelberg at the turn of the century had fully expected that Germany would go to war when she was ready, and a cousin who used to make beautiful warship models for me.

However, I had no idea of how to set about becoming a naval officer until one morning when I happened to see a notice about the RNCC at King Edward High School in Vancouver.

I sat the examination in May 1917 and became one of twenty cadets who entered the college in August. Nine of us came from Ontario, five from Quebec, four from the Maritimes, and two from British Columbia. Very few ever came from the Prairies, and Roman Catholics were scarcer still. In fact, we mustered seventeen Anglicans and three Methodists in all. At fourteen to sixteen years of age we were older than English cadets at Osborne but younger than those from the English public schools who had recently been introduced in the Royal Navy as a secondary intake.

The site selected for the college was the old naval hospital at the north end of the Halifax dockyard. The setting was not particularly salubrious, but the structure with a single-storey extension on the northern side which made the ground plan a T-shape, afforded us reasonable accommodation. The lower floor provided senior and junior gunrooms, a large messroom for all cadets, and a wardroom for officers and instructional staff. The officers' cabins and junior and senior cadet dormitories were located on the second floor, while the basement served as the lower deck for the ship's company. The annex held a large study which accommodated all cadets for examinations, general lectures and evening "prep." Its other half, known as the quarterdeck, was used for divisions, evening quarters, cadets' defaulters (known as "8:40" because that was the time when they were seen), and sometimes as a gymnasium or for a dance. In addition, we had access to the engineering workshops in the dockyard, the playing fields of the Admiralty House grounds, and to the cruiser HMCS *Niobe*, which was, by this time, a depot ship secured alongside a jetty just below the college.

We were allowed time to "sling our 'ammicks" (to use an English able seaman's phrase) on our first day and to realize our remarkable lowliness. During the forenoon we were examined medically and measured for our uniforms. There was a swimming test after lunch, and then we were taken around Halifax harbour by George Helier Kinch, an ex-Royal Navy warrant officer of the highest calibre. He pointed out the sights to us—the big liners like the *Olympic* and *Calgarian*, now used as transports and dazzle-painted to confuse U-boat captains, and also the auxiliaries and cruisers employed as ocean escorts to protect convoys from surface raiders. In the evening the senior cadets explained what was required of us in such matters as always running past their gunroom, entering the messroom after them, leaving them all the seats in the bootroom, standing to attention when summoned to their gunroom, running errands, and the like.

I should say quite firmly that although we occasionally muttered about our treatment, grumbling has always been a seaman's custom. The general tone was perfectly healthy. We had nothing approaching the hazing, known as "recruiting" at the Royal Military College in Kingston, or its equivalent in the fleet which had, on occasion, led to the court-martial of the sub-lieutenant of the gunroom.

The senior and by far the most impressive member of the college staff was Commander Edward Atcherley Eckersall Nixon. He was born in 1878 and became a naval cadet in January 1892. After service in the Channel Fleet and in the flagship of the China Station, he was promoted to sub-lieutenant and specialized in navigation. Nixon served in a variety of ships and stations and then became first lieutenant and navigator of the battleship HMS *Swiftsure* in the Mediterranean. He retired at his own request in order to come to Canada where he was appointed to HMCS *Niobe*, as lieutenant (navigator), RCN, for the RNCC, on 6 September 1910. Contrary to what Tucker suggests in *The Naval Service of Canada*, Commander Nixon was not the college's first commanding officer; rather it was Commander Edward H. Martin, who had retired from the RN in 1909 and been appointed to command both the dockyard and the college. Nixon was posted to the RNCC as the first lieutenant and soon acquired the nickname "Jimmy" from the lower deck expression for a first lieutenant, "Jimmy-the-One." He was promoted to the rank of commander, RCN, on 1 August 1915 and took charge of the college.

Like the complements of the elderly cruisers HMCS *Niobe* and HMCS *Rainbow* (purchased for sea training), nearly all of the college staff had to be secured from the Royal Navy, either on loan or by transfer following retirement. In view of the iron rule imposed on that service by the First Sea Lord, Admiral Sir John Fisher, we never lacked volunteers. The Director of Studies was Instructor Commander Basil Shakespeare Hartley, a devoted mathematician whose only fault was that he sometimes soared well above our heads. He was assisted by two instructor lieutenants, RCN. There was also Engineer Lieutenant-Commander Howley, who had been lamed in the sinking of HMS *Irresistible* in the Dardanelles in 1915. He, too, was on loan from the RN and was supported by Engineer Lieutenant A.D.M. Curry, RCN. The warrant officers transferred from the RN included two boatswains, George William Brooker and Mr. Kinch, as well as the Chief Artificer Engineer Joseph Kelly. Marie Joseph Romeo Oscar Cossette, who started as a temporary warrant writer RCN, was later to rise to the rank of paymaster rear-admiral. In the meantime he contributed some amusing cartoons of college life to *Sea Breezes*.

Three civilian instructors joined the staff when the curriculum was broadened: Messrs. Richardson, Hatcher, and J.J. Penny. In addition, we had a remarkable part-timer in the person of Archibald MacMechan, who appeared each Friday in Study 8 to instruct all three terms in naval history. His lectures, given at dictation speed, were to be taken down verbatim. We "new kids" had to start where the others had left off, and so for some years we knew infinitely more about the Second Anglo-Dutch War (1664-67) than any earlier period of British naval history.

We began each day at 0615 and "cleaned" into flannels for boatwork or gym after a cup of cocoa. At the conclusion of our exercise period we washed, and shaved if necessary, and plunged into a cold bath. I remember the cadet captain standing over us to ensure that we immersed ourselves completely. Breakfast was followed by "defaulters" at 0840 and divisions at 0900, at which time we were inspected by the commander. Studies, interrupted by a break for a glass of milk, commenced shortly after the inspection and continued until 1300.

In accordance with Admiral Sir John Fisher's belief that seamen and engineer officers should be interchangeable, much of our time was devoted to engineering, including workshop training. This started with an ordeal known as "chipping." Chipping involved squaring off a large rough plate of mild steel with a cold chisel and a hammer, a procedure well described in an English cadet ditty from Dartmouth:

> Blistered thumb and bleeding finger,
> Scars that come and mean to linger,
> Sights to shame the chicken-hearted
> All proclaim that chipping's started.
> Useless now to grouse and grizzle
> That a cow could hit a chisel.
> Try to make the hammer kiss it—
> I will stake a bob you miss it!

This was exactly my experience: despite "Joe" Kelly's cry "Look at the point man, look at the point! Hanimal hinstinct will make the 'ammer 'it!,'" my animal instinct was clearly lacking.

Work resumed after lunch from 1400 to 1600, when we had milk and biscuits before taking exercise, usually in boats or on the football field. The order was reversed in winter so that we might exercise during the daylight. Supper came at 1900 and was followed at 2000 by an hour of study known as "prep" in Study 8. We were then given five minutes to undress and two minutes to say our prayers while kneeling before the seachests at the foot of our cots. Then we turned in by order of the cadet captain. We were all dog-tired, and there was very little risk at this stage of Satan finding mischief for idle hands.

Work stopped at 1300 on Wednesdays and Saturdays but there was always organized sport. On Saturdays we were allowed to "go ashore," as we religiously called it, with seventy-five cents pocket money (from our parents' pockets, issued to us in a ceremony known rather wryly as "payment") until 2100. We had leave from 1300 on Sundays, and fortunately most of us found friends who "showed willing" to give us tea or supper.

We enjoyed a cruise in the college schooner *Diana* twice during the term for the purposes of practical navigation and pilotage. Other variations laid on by Commander Nixon to alleviate the monotony included an afternoon walk around Bedford Basin to Dartmouth, a distance of sixteen or seventeen miles, cutter competitions with two stretches under oars and two under sail, occasional visits to one of His Majesty's ships awaiting her next wartime convoy, and anything unusual that offered.

Six months after I enrolled the unusual was indeed offered. It was Thursday morning 6 December 1917. Our term-end examinations were due to start, and after breakfast most of us were in Study 8 doing some last-minute cramming. At about quarter to nine one of the cadets noticed a ship on fire in the harbour and we left our books to watch.

It was the French freighter SS *Mont Blanc*. Loaded with explosives and proceeding up the harbour to join a convoy for the Atlantic crossing, she had collided with the outward bound Norwegian steamer, the SS *Imo*, chartered for Belgian relief. The collision in the Narrows between Halifax Harbour and Bedford Basin resulted from a combination of errors and led to extended litigation. Eventually, the House of Lords decided that the masters and pilots of both ships had been to blame since they had ignored an elementary rule of the road summed up for young seamen in the jingle:

> In danger with no room to turn,
> Ease her—stop her—go astern.

The *Mont Blanc* was rammed. Unhappily, she was carrying a deckload of inflammable benzine above her cargo of TNT and picric acid. When this caught fire it provided the detonator for disaster.

We watched her burning, spellbound. Then the warning gong sounded for us to square ourselves off for divisions, and we "new kids" retired to our gunroom on the landward side of the college. Three minutes later the *Mont Blanc* blew up.

The explosion was the greatest man-made explosion on earth to that date. Many supposed that there had, in fact, been two explosions, because the first effect was felt through the earth rather than the air. People at a distance ran to their windows only to be caught in a blizzard of flying glass. The outside walls of the college stood up, but the partition walls were badly damaged. One cadet was driven through the gunroom window while the rest of us staggered through a shower of plaster and rubble to the green outside. We cowered there with rivets and pieces of iron plate falling all around us. Later we saw that a large piece of boiler plate had come through the roof of Study 8, where we would otherwise have been. A gigantic cloud of smoke, visible for miles, rose over the harbour. Buildings were devastated for fifteen hundred yards around the explosion and there were many fires.

Although we juniors escaped for the most part with minor cuts, the senior terms and the officers who were on the harbour side of the college received many serious injuries. Commander Nixon and several others were badly cut, while two cadets each lost the sight of one eye. Chief Petty Officer King was taken to a mortuary, where he remained for two days before he could demonstrate that he was still alive. When the injured had received what treatment was available, the rest of us began to recover our gear. However, at this stage we were warned that a magazine just north of us might explode and that we should evacuate the area. Many of us fetched up on Citadel Hill, a vantage point from which we could survey the scene below. Most of the ships and craft in the harbour seemed to be under way, while visibility northward was obscured by smoke and flame.

Once the word was passed that the danger was over, we returned to the college, where we were told to finish our packing and find a billet with friends. That evening a heavy snowfall hindered rescue and rehabilitation efforts, and not until Monday were we able to depart by train on our Christmas leave.

When we reassembled it was not two weeks later in Halifax but two months later in Kingston at the Royal Military College. Shortened war-time courses there allowed us to be bedded in separate cabins, and we had the further good fortune of having a gymnasium at our disposal. Moreover, the Ontario winter gave us opportunities for winter sports, including tobogganing on the slope below Fort Henry, ice hockey on the RMC rink and skating for miles on Lake Ontario. In the spring and summer we had sailing in various craft, pulling in our cutters (that had been brought up from Halifax), and one or two cruises in a handsome steam yacht which had been acquired for the naval service. This was also the time when we had cricket—a game I never learned to consider as much more than an organized waste of time.

There were, of course, more serious concerns than cricket. One of our biggest complaints was the food, which was apparently put out to con-tract. It did not compare at all in quantity or quality with what we had been used to from the naval cooks and stewards in Halifax. More serious still was the location of the college. A naval training institution one thousand miles from the sea seemed hardly appropriate, and while we did not resent being called "water babies" (we replied in kind) we did feel out of place and rather like "Johnnies-come-lately" in Kingston. When the four seniors in A Class departed for service with the Royal Navy's Grand Fleet, and Lieuten-ant Percy Nelles was replaced as first lieutenant by Lieutenant J.E.W. Oland, it was decided to shift the RNCC to Esquimalt naval base on Vancouver Island.

Delays seem to be inevitable in wartime, and it was nearly three months later, on 21 September 1918, before we reassembled on the Pacific Coast. The new college buildings were not complete, so for nearly four weeks we were accommodated in HMCS *Rainbow*. Our first so-called recreation was clearing some rough ground for a tennis court. A number of cadets came down with Spanish influenza during this period, but our general level of fitness spared us any fatalities. While the flu was a nuisance, we were soon to be rewarded. A premature report of an armistice gave us a holiday on 7 November, one which was repeated on 11 November when Germany finally did capitulate.

The senior term left us in February 1919. They were the last to have taken the shortened two-and-one-half-year wartime course. Out of their original number of fourteen, one had joined the army, one was discharged, and one had failed his final exams. Of the others, only four were still in the RCN twenty years later when World War II broke out.

Three cadet captains, George M. Mitchell, Arthur N. Budden and George C. Myers, were appointed when we became A Class, and in March 1919 Lieutenant George C. Jones, a future chief of the Naval Staff, relieved Oland as first lieutenant. Shortly thereafter the Director of the Naval Service, Vice-Admiral Sir Charles Kingsmill, visited the college informally on 6 May. He was accompanied by Lieutenant John M. Grant, who remained behind as a welcome addition to the college staff. Years later, as Captain Grant, he became the first commanding officer of HMCS *Royal Roads*, a wartime training establishment for Royal Canadian Naval Volunteer Reserve sub-lieutenants.

When we rejoined on 10 September, with a new C Class of seventeen that included one of my brothers, we had a succession of distinguished visitors. His Royal Highness the Prince of Wales arrived in the battle cruiser HMS *Renown*, escorted by a squadron of light cruisers. He inspected the college buildings, after which the whole establishment at Esquimalt fell in on the lawn outside the sick bay. The Prince presented Lieutenant Oland with a Distinguished Service Cross, earned in the destroyer HMS *Marvel* in December 1917, and granted us a whole holiday instead of the half-holiday that had been recommended to him. Quite clearly the prince was twice as important as Canada's Governor General, the Duke of Devonshire, for when the duke visited us in October we received only a half-day's holiday. A week later, Admiral of the Fleet Viscount Jellicoe of Scapa arrived in the battle cruiser HMS *New Zealand* during the course of a global tour to advise India and the dominions on postwar imperial naval policy.

Apart from his array of stripes and decorations, my first impressions seem to have been of his large nose and small stature. But his kindly and generous nature soon showed through. After a thorough inspection of the college, Jellicoe told us that he had seen many gymnastic displays but that, weight for age, he had never seen a better one than ours. He reported most favourably on the ex-cadets he had met during the war and added: "They can tell you the one essential quality in war, a quality in which I have never known a Canadian to be lacking, and that is of determination"; a remark which Commander Nixon was later to endorse when he observed that he had always been able to "rely on cadets to back [him] up in an emergency."

Our last six months at the college, from January to June 1920, were overshadowed by doubts about the future of navies in general and of the Royal Canadian Navy in particular. The cost of "the Kaiser's War" in men and money had made governments more than ready to pin their hopes on the League of Nations, and so Lord Jellicoe's recommendations for the reorganization of the Canadian Naval Service fell on stony ground in Ottawa.

The Government of Canada announced on 25 March 1920 that the RCN would henceforth consist of one light cruiser and two destroyers, surplus to the needs of the Royal Navy. Shore establishments would be reduced, but the RNCC would remain. Two H-class submarines, CH 14 and CH 15, acquired the year before, were to be paid off. As cadets, poised on the brink of our careers, we could only await further decisions.

On our return from Easter leave in April we learned that Captain Walter Hose was to become the new director of the Naval Service. Vice-Admiral Sir Charles Kingsmill paid us a farewell visit at the end of May. He was entertained informally and treated to a concert by the cadets, including a review written by one of my term, entitled "Hullo Esquimalt!" The admiral seemed to enjoy it despite such irreverent lyrics as

There was a ship in Esquimalt,
The *Rainbow* was her name.
She was obsolete ten years ago,
And now she's just the same.

The admiral's farewell inspection took place at the beginning of June. After expressing sympathy for the uncertain circumstances in which we found ourselves, he produced a cup presented by the Minister of the Naval Service, C.C. Ballantyne. On it was inscribed the name of the cadet judged to have shown the highest degree of athletic ability combined with good fellowship. I correctly predicted that the recipient would be Cadet Captain, Frederick L.S. Pickard.

Our passing-out examination, set by an English board, lasted from 11 to 23 June. On our last evening the commander addressed us class by class. The newcomers, C Class, he suggested, needed to buck up a bit; B Class showed great promise; and (I proudly quote) "For my old friends, A Class, I have nothing but praise. They have worked hard and well." Despite these generous words, the omens were not good. We still had no information on how many naval vacancies might be offered, and all Commander Nixon could do was to ask our preferences should we qualify. As the examination papers had to go by ship to England to be marked we had to wait until mid-August for news. When we received the results, we learned that Pickard and I had been accepted as seamen, while Arthur C.M. Davy and Seymour C. Crowell had been selected to be engineers. No one, it seems, had volunteered to be a paymaster. The four of us sailed from Quebec a month later for midshipman's training in the Royal Navy.

I, of course, was not present for the last two years of the RNCC. As a consequence I have had to rely mainly on *Sea Breezes* and what I heard from my brother in the last term in order to complete this story of the Royal Naval College of Canada.

Fifteen new cadets joined the college on 10 September 1920. Led by the new senior term, RNCC maintained a high reputation in Victoria rugby circles and continued to have plenty of exercise in other fields. The new Canadian Squadron commissioned in England early in November. The captain of the destroyer HMCS *Patrician* was our former first lieutenant, Lieutenant George C. Jones, RCN, the first RNCC graduate to command a major warship. The squadron reached Halifax in time for Christmas, and three months later, on 9 March 1921, it arrived at Esquimalt where it received a warm welcome.

As in 1920, the RCN was prepared to accept six cadets as midshipmen, two in each specialization. All the vacancies were filled. The seamen were Harry DeWolf, a future CNS, and Horatio Nelson Lay, who also reached flag rank. Cadets John G. Knowlton and William W. Porteous attained the higher levels in engineering, but one of the paymasters fell out and the other, Francis R.W. Nixon, was lost in the Atlantic.

Unhappily, the Liberal government, which had taken office the previous December, announced its decision on 16 May 1921 to reduce the RCN to one destroyer on either coast and to close the college. No cadets from the senior term were to be accepted for entry, though, as things turned out, one member, K.F. Adams, was entered later and reached flag rank following the RCN's remarkable expansion during World War II. On the closing of the college, *Sea Breezes* remarked, "The success of the College is mainly due to the unsparing efforts of Commander Nixon and his able staff, and it is with the deepest regret that we say good-bye."

Commander Nixon was, without a doubt, the driving force behind the college. I remember him as slightly below average height, well-knit, with iron-gray hair, a slightly sardonic expression and a masterly command of language; I recall him describing a beginner on a football field as "the personification of misapplied energy." Except when dealing with a flagrant offender his bark was generally worse than his bite. He took a genuine interest in all cadets and knew much more about us than we realized at the time. Nixon was always well aware of what went on around him. He made regular visits to every cadet in sick bay. He frequently refereed our internal matches, attended all of our external ones, and emphasized sportsmanship and unselfish play at all times.

As I hope I have shown, Nixon was outspoken when he felt that we had lived up to his expectations on an important occasion. It is only since rereading my journals that I have realized how well he sought to avoid monotony in our routine and how closely he monitored our social activities and general development. I have been forever indebted to him for his talk to my class on our last evening in Esquimalt. He made three main points. The first was on the value of continence, on principle as well as to avoid venereal disease. The second was the warning that the effect of strong drink varied with circumstances. The rule he laid down, with examples, was to be most cautious on those occasions when you felt most in need of stimulus. And the third contradicted the American army dictum for success, namely: keep your mouth shut, your bowels open, never volunteer, and get a signed receipt for everything. Nixon's advice was: *always* volunteer. The reason he gave was that with normal youngsters nervousness stems from inexperience, and thus we should seek experience whenever the opportunity arose. This advice was to prove invaluable.

Commander Nixon died of pneumonia on 10 November 1924, at the age of forty-six, from a cold caught while refereeing a rugby game in the rain at Shawnigan School. We do not often hear of a broken heart these days, but there are grounds for thinking that the unceremonious closing of the RNCC was a contributing factor to his death.

Admiral Sir Michael Denny, another great man to whom I am deeply indebted, once told me that he regarded the expansion of the Royal Canadian Navy as the finest Allied naval achievement of Hitler's war. Without discounting the contribution of members of the Royal Canadian Naval Volunteer Reserve, whom I saw in action and admired on more than one operation, I submit that Canadian naval development could not have proceeded so successfully without the officers who had seen the RCN through the lean days and who owed so very much to Commander Nixon.

Chapter 4

THE ROAD TO WASHINGTON: CANADA AND EMPIRE NAVAL DEFENCE, 1918-1921

Barry D. Hunt

In the years immediately following World War I, the concept of "imperial defence" acquired a sharpened focus and renewed strategic significance. Foremost were indications of an alarming disjunction between British imperial ends and British imperial means. Whatever the suspicions of particular dominion nationalists, this reality underlay the British Admiralty's attempts to resurrect its controversial proposal for some kind of Empire naval defence structure based on centralized operational control and on specific role- and cost-sharing agreements. However, the unity of purpose so evident in wartime Commonwealth relations could not be sustained in the early postwar period, and attempts to create a single Empire navy proved impossible so long as the Commonwealth relationship itself remained unsettled. Events in the early 1920's revealed that a common foreign policy for the Empire-Commonwealth was a political impossibility, and this realization bore directly on all prospects for sound naval policy formulation.

Contrary to what has been conventional wisdom among Canadian historians until fairly recently, this failure to extend Empire solidarity into the postwar world was less a result of the various dominions' preoccupations with status in or outside of the Commonwealth as it was a consequence of the need for closer Empire-United States relations.[1] It represented a victory for those who favoured Anglo-American conciliation, or some form of "Atlantic Concord," and who therefore saw the solution to the complex issue of international naval arms competition as primarily a matter of diplomatic initiatives.[2]

By war's end, British-U.S. differences on the question of international maritime law governing belligerent and neutral rights had brought relations between the two Allies to a state of open tension. Since 1915-16, President Woodrow Wilson's persistent criticisms of British blockade practices and the American government's decision to implement its "navy second to none" building programme had minimized chances for any special relationship. Even the internment of Germany's High Seas Fleet in November 1918, and its subsequent scuttling in June 1919, did little to lessen their mutual mistrust. These antagonisms came to a head at the Paris peace talks where the "Freedom of the Seas" question (the second of Wilson's Fourteen Points) threatened all chances of the Anglo-American co-operation which many deemed essential to a European peace settlement and to the future of the League of Nations. The possibility of a new naval arms race, this time between the victors, was avoided only when Prime Minister David Lloyd George successfully arranged postponement of discussions on Point Two in return for Britain's acceptance of the Monroe Doctrine amendment to the League Covenant. The underlying causes of Anglo-American naval and commercial rivalry remained nonetheless unresolved and a source of future conflict.

Canada's leadership on behalf of an Anglo-American accord at the Washington naval disarmament talks in 1921-22 was, in the words of one recent analysis, her "single most important endeavour towards the end of her own national security" in the entire interwar period:

> In effect, London had to be persuaded that the price to be paid for the termination of the naval building race with the United States (and for improved Anglo-American relations) was the abandonment of her Japanese Alliance [which dated back to 1902]. . . . This major exercise in Canadian persuasiveness was conducted by Arthur Meighen at the Imperial Conference in London in June and July 1921.[3]

But this Canadian initiative necessarily involved the contradiction or ignoring of other options, not the least of which were those offered by established professional naval advice. The arrangements worked out ultimately at the 1921 London and Washington conferences, for international naval limitations and the abrogation of the Anglo-Japanese alliance, were concessions to American objectives and the demands of Canadian nationalism. Moreover, these arrangements entailed a collective shutting of eyes to strategic realities, especially with respect to the Pacific and a thereafter isolated Japan. The Washington agreements actually increased the need for an Empire fleet or, at the very least, for centralization of planning and

operational control. But the Canadian government drew quite different
conclusions, and in very quick order reduced what remained of its sea-
going naval service to a severely restricted reserve force with two destroyers,
HMC Ships *Patrician* and *Patriot*, and a few trawlers.

The early postwar period presented the Admiralty with some unusual
problems in terms of working out peacetime policy norms. Historically,
British governments had always faced a serious dilemma when they
attempted to establish some reasonable concordance between their foreign
policy and their decidedly limited military capacities. So it was after 1918,
though with important shifts in emphasis, when defence of the Empire and
its sea routes once more became the first priority. The peace treaties and
League mandates would swell the Empire to its maximum territorial
limits. But these new territories brought new risks and a dangerous extension of defence liabilities in the Middle East and Asia, where the stirrings of
colonial nationalisms and revolution compounded already uncertain circumstances.[4] Japan's emergence as an indigenous great power in the Far
East posed again the question of safeguarding Britain's interests in Asia.
This could be achieved either through Japanese sufferance and a reaffirma-
tion of the prewar Anglo-Japanese Treaty or, more directly, through a
build-up of Royal Navy strength in the Pacific.

Following Germany's defeat in 1918 and Russia's collapse into revolution and civil war (1917-20), Britain's other principal naval rival was
the United States. America's potential for outpacing Britain in naval
construction demanded careful reassessments of trans-Atlantic relations,
since any intentions of meeting this challenge to British naval pre-
eminence had to be tempered by an awareness of how much the mood and
nature of British defence politics had changed since the armistice. Lloyd
George's coalition government was committed to restoring civilian ascendancy and "treasury control" in every branch of government. However
sincerely he embraced the League of Nations' commitments to the new
peace through international discussion and world disarmament, domestic
political stability and social reconstruction implied defence spending cuts,
not new construction and expansion. This was the central issue of postwar
Empire defence policy: could Britain adjust to these domestic political
realities and, at the same time, protect that sprawl of territories, trade
routes, interests, and obligations which were the real basis of her international existence? Did the preservation of British prestige and pre-eminence
demand a renewed commitment to naval primacy or new departures in the
direction of naval limitations? Both First Sea Lords in these years, Admirals Sir Rosslyn Wemyss (10 January 1918 to 1 November 1919) and Sir
David Beatty (1 November 1919 to 30 July 1927), would face the frustrations
of developing general naval policy for a government which, until the

Washington conference of 1921, was paradoxically committed to both alternatives at the same time.

One particularly startling feature of these early years was the degree to which British naval primacy was undermined by factors largely beyond the Royal Navy's control and unconnected with any perceptible decline in efficiency or expertise. As of 11 November 1918, the RN stood at its zenith as the most powerful maritime fighting force in the world. Its strength in operational vessels almost equalled those of all other navies combined. Compared to Britain's seventy capital ships, France and Italy had thirty each. The United States had thirty-nine capital ships with four building and a further four planned. Japan possessed fourteen with two building. But these ratios were soon altered by the cancellation of wartime building programmes and the laying-up and scrapping of outdated ships. By 1921 the RN could only claim parity to any single navy (the so-called One-Power Standard) and superiority to the European powers combined.[5]

Following the official demise of the Grand Fleet in December 1918, RN capital ship dispositions showed a continuing emphasis on European waters. With almost two-thirds of its battleships scrapped or placed in reserve, the remainder were formed into four battle squadrons—the first and second assigned to the Atlantic Fleet, the third to the Home Fleet, and the fourth to the Mediterranean. Economy measures necessitated the suppression of the Home Fleet, which was placed on reserve, leaving the Atlantic Fleet to cover all waters from the Arctic south to the Cape Verde Islands, west to Greenland and east to include the Baltic and North seas. The China Station, covering almost a quarter of the earth's circumference, was left without any capital ships. By 1921 this was the responsibility of the 5th Light Cruiser Squadron, a dozen submarines and a few sloops and gunboats, based in Hong Kong.

Prior to 1914, geography, finances, superiority in quality and numbers, and the provisions of the Anglo-Japanese Treaty had justified such a disproportionate weighting. Concentration in European waters had been directed at the German High Seas Fleet, though it had still permitted worldwide domination by strictly controlling Europe's access to the rest of the world. Overseas bases and lines of communication could be then entrusted to auxiliary squadrons and the local navies of the various dominions. This had been the basis of Admiralty policy in proposing its Fleet Unit Schemes at the 1907 and 1909 conferences and was directed specifically towards covering British deficiencies in the Pacific. But control of world shipping through fleet concentration in the North Sea rested on two assumptions: first, the importance of Europe (Germany) as the central strategic pivot; and second, the lack of any serious rival to the Royal Navy outside of Europe. By 1918-19, neither assumption held. While neither

Japan nor the United States would soon achieve the near-monopoly of control over the world's oceans once exerted by Britain, the danger was that both new major naval powers would compete to fill the vacuum created by the relative decline in the Royal Navy's power. The essential difference then between Britain's prewar and postwar situations was that extra-European priorities had once again posed the dilemma of imperial interests and obligations that far exceeded her military capabilities. With the shift of the Empire's most vulnerable points to the western Pacific, "imperial defence" assumed larger proportions and scope as a means of resolving this tension between competing commitments and diminishing resources. It was this unsettling reality that prompted the Admiralty's decision to resurrect its prewar demands for a unified, centrally directed, and highly mobile imperial navy, and its persistence, even after 1921 and 1923, in calling for some kind of cost- and burden-sharing arrangement with the dominions.

Postwar naval defence arrangements had been first discussed by the Imperial War Conference in March 1917, on which occasion the Admiralty was severely criticized by the Australasian representatives. Sir Joseph Ward of New Zealand, noting that there had been no positive direction on naval policy since 1909, accused the Admiralty of defaulting on its promises to maintain adequate force levels in the Pacific. This failure to build up fleet units for the Australian, East Indies, and China Stations as agreed at the 1909 conference was seen as a breach of good faith that left the Pacific dominions dangerously exposed.[6] Ward therefore urged their lordships to consider a new scheme for the Empire's postwar security and pressed for a decision for either a single imperial fleet or separate dominion navies. Canada's Sir Robert Borden supported Ward's appeal in general terms but baulked at his reference to "the importance of maintaining the unity of strategic direction of the whole Navy for the Empire." After considerable debate, Borden eventually secured the agreement of both Ward and New Zealand's Prime Minister, William F. Massey, to a modified resolution (Number Four, 30 March 1917) which directed the Admiralty to produce a new plan based on a thorough study of the Empire's strategic needs and not merely upon whatever contributions the dominions might offer. Borden was determined that delineation of these needs should not derive from any preconceived notions, especially one of centralized "strategic direction." Moreover, there was insufficient opportunity for the Admiralty, already preoccupied with fighting the war, to come up with a balanced assessment of future requirements. More to the point, in Borden's mind, their recommendations would have to recognize the principle that "co-operation in Imperial Defence should carry with it the right to an effective voice in determining the foreign policy of the Empire."

The Admiralty's response, the work of a committee chaired by Admiral

Wemyss, was finished in May 1918 and tabled at the Imperial War Conference the following month.[7] It called for a single Empire navy and an "Imperial Naval Authority" which would deal with

> all questions of naval strategy, and subjects connected with the provision, equipment, efficiency, organisation and utilisation of the Navy as a fighting force; promotions and appointments; principles of training; the formulation of requirements on which the annual estimates would be prepared.

The precise form and status of this central authority could not be specified, pending the outcome of the projected Constitutional Conference which, under Resolution 9 of the 1917 War Conference, would define all such Commonwealth connections. Wemyss was aware of the political and constitutional difficulties this must involve. For the moment, however, he was more concerned to set out the strategic logic of centralized seapower as demonstrated by wartime experience. He ruled out monetary contributions and control their own expenditures. A proposed imperial naval staff would also offer career opportunities for dominion officers on a basis of full equality with their British colleagues.

Predictably, the dominion prime ministers were not impressed. They challenged Wemyss's arguments by pointing out how efficiently the dominion navies, particularly the Australian, had co-operated under the Admiralty's wartime direction. Still, they did not reject the idea out of hand; instead, they agreed that should the dominion navies expand to any extent, the possibility of creating "some supreme naval authority" would warrant further consideration. As to the merits of a single imperial fleet, Borden led the prime ministers of Australia, New Zealand, and South Africa in declaring for "standardization" of the dominion navies as the next best choice. "The Prime Ministers," Professor R.A. Preston has suggested, "had asserted that in naval organisation as elsewhere the Empire must follow the principle of association rather than of integration, that is to say of commonwealth defence co-operation rather than imperial defence."[8] But, in rejecting unlimited commitments to British controls, the prime ministers had no intention of refusing British advice or assistance. Their joint response of 15 August 1918 emphasized the need for their separate navies to develop along common lines, and, to that end, the prime ministers agreed to "welcome visits from a highly qualified representative of the Admiralty."[9] This then was the basis on which Admiral of the Fleet Viscount Jellicoe of Scapa was dispatched on his famous Empire Naval ters agreed to "welcome visits from a highly qualified representative of the Admiralty."[9] This then was the basis on which Admiral of the Fleet Viscount Jellicoe of Scapa was dispatched on his famous Empire Naval

Mission to advise each of the dominions in turn on their separate naval defence needs.

The Admiralty accepted this rebuff to the 17 May memorandum, but was not enthusiastic about the Empire tour idea. Jellicoe's instructions consequently were drawn up to make it obvious that he went out at the dominions' request and not as an Admiralty spokesman. His terms of reference as approved by the War Cabinet on 23 December authorized him to

> advise the Dominion authorities whether in the light of the experience of the War, the scheme of naval organisation which has been adopted or may be in contemplation requires reconsideration, either from the point of view of the efficiency of that organisation for meeting local needs, or from that of ensuring the greatest possible homogeneity and co-operation between all the Naval Forces of the Empire. . . .
>
> Should Dominion authorities desire to consider how far it is possible for the Dominion to take a more effective share in the naval defence of the Empire, he will give assistance from the naval point of view in drawing up a scheme for consideration.[10]

But encouragement of local discussions of naval affairs and promotion of common development standards, as the First Lord, Eric Geddes, suggested to his cabinet colleagues, might also serve the Admiralty's interests; Empire standardization could in the long run "assist the realisation of many of the objects underlying the Admiralty Memorandum."[11] Otherwise, Jellicoe's role was to be purely advisory, and he was not expected to raise broad strategic questions. He was permitted to see the reports of the Admiralty's Postwar Reconstruction Committee, but firm directions on wider policy questions had to await the results of the Committee of Imperial Defence (CID) deliberations which were begun in May 1919 and completed that summer.[12]

The Admiralty's submission to this latter CID study ("Imperial Naval Defence and the Naval Situation in the Far East") which was despatched to Jellicoe, who was then in Canada and nearing the end of his mission, gave reluctant recognition to the dominions' desires for separate navies each with their own budgets.[13] These dominion fleets could be assigned to protect local coastal trade and assist in the control of imperial communications. However, the memorandum continued: "The requirements of sound strategy can . . . only be met if every ship is available for war service in any part of the world, and the general plan of campaign is directed by one central authority." This centralization of command assumed the eventual creation of an "Imperial Council" to handle all foreign and defence policy matters and dominion representation on the Naval Staff "with a view to co-ordinating the higher strategy of Imperial Defence, and the institution of a definite system of co-operation between the Naval, General, and Air Staffs." The Admiralty, convinced that dominion opposition to the Wemyss memorandum of May 1918 had not involved a categorical denial of a future need for a "supreme naval authority," once more advanced the notion of a single navy. If Jellicoe was expected to encourage this point of view, the suggestion came too late. In the end, he failed in that aspect of his mission, in part because of continuing dominion opposition, but more immediately because of Lord Beatty's appointment as First Sea Lord in November 1919. Before moving to that event some explanation of Jellicoe's own thinking is merited.

In light of the circumstances of 1919-20, a good deal of what Jellicoe recommended was economically and politically unrealistic. However, his strategic premises were sound and would influence naval planning for years to come. Central to his analysis was the explicit recognition that the Empire's strategic centre had shifted to the Pacific, where Japan was the only possible source of danger. He dismissed the possibility of any American threat, at least "in the near future," but felt it unwise to count on U.S. naval assistance in time of difficulty. From his talks with Indian and Australian officials, and his own knowledge of recent events in the Pacific, including information about Japanese naval strength projections for the next few years, he concluded that "sooner or later a fleet of a certain definite strength would be required either in the Pacific or in the vicinity" and that "the whole Empire Navy would need to bear a definite relative strength to that of Japan."[14] His reading of Japan's options suggested that she must first seize a series of advanced bases in the area of New Guinea or the Dutch East Indies as a prelude to invading Australia and, at the same time, forestall possible counter moves by attacking British holdings in Asia, including Hong Kong and Singapore. Given Britain's inability to pre-position major naval reinforcements from European waters before the outbreak of hostilities, he concluded that the first requirement in the Pacific was a powerful British-Australian-New Zealand fleet commanded by a British admiral and based on greatly expanded facilities at Singapore. This Far Eastern Fleet was to be a sizable one, including eight battleships, eight battle cruisers (incidentally matching the Hara government's eight battleship-eight battle cruiser fleet programme approved by the Japanese Diet in July 1920), four aircraft carriers, ten light cruisers, forty destroyers, thirty submarines and other auxiliaries, all to be paid for on a fixed shares basis by Britain (75 per cent), Australia (20 per cent) and New Zealand (5 per cent), with Canada opting in as she saw fit.

The Admiralty's response to this scheme was to shelve the reports as quietly as possible; a statement appended to the 1920 Naval Estimates simply acknowledged their receipt with the comment that they were being "studied by the Naval Staff." In fact, Wemyss was furious with his former superior and, before leaving office as First Sea Lord, had urged that Jellicoe be reprimanded for exceeding his instructions by independently assessing the Japanese threat and formulating an overall plan to deal with it.[15] Ironically, CID and Naval Staff studies largely substantiated Jellicoe's disturbing conclusions, though not his Far Eastern Fleet solution. By early 1920, they were urging instead the case for "some satisfactory understanding with Japan." The worst situation the Empire could face, the Naval Staff warned, would be any double threat of a crisis in Europe combined with Japanese "aggressive action in the Pacific at a time when . . . reinforcements capable of dealing with the whole of Japan's main forces could not be immediately spared."[16]

By then, too, Admiralty interest in these Pacific dimensions of its problems was overshadowed by the changed personality equation that followed Beatty's appointment as First Sea Lord and the march of events which forced him to accept the One-Power Standard as the best compromise between the navy's minimum needs and the demands of domestic budgetary politics. Beatty's determination to preserve British naval supremacy through renewed battleship construction entailed some policy inconsistencies and important concessions, not the least of which was acquiescence to spending cuts elsewhere, such as personnel and overseas bases and fuel reserves. Moreover, it was not strategic but technical arguments of avoiding obsolescence that Beatty and his advisers employed to back their case for eight new post-Jutland capital ships. Unfortunately, even these arguments were difficult to sustain, especially in the wake of the Jutland controversy, which helped stir up doubts about the value of battleships and the wisdom of renewed building.

By late 1920, widespread public and professional criticism resulted in the appointment of a special shipbuilding committee of the CID (the Bonar Law Enquiry) whose findings, though unfavourable to the critics of the battleship, did not fully endorse the case for an extensive programme of building new ones. Instead, the committee recommended the replacement of eight prewar battleships with only four battle cruisers of the "super-Hood" design.[17] These were capital ships of 48,000 tons displacement carrying nine 16-inch guns and a complement of over seventeen hundred men. By October 1921, immediately prior to the Washington disarmament talks, orders for only two of these had been placed. This limited new construction called into question the Royal Navy's ability to lay effective claim to even the One-Power Standard. As a result, two other considerations became vital to the Admiralty's chances; first, a now obvious need for more direct dominion support and, second, some reasonable accommodation with Japan.

The 1921 Imperial Conference therefore became a critical turning point in the evolution of postwar Empire defence arrangements, for it was there that these separate strands of naval pre-eminence, Commonwealth co-operation and renewal of the Anglo-Japanese Treaty came together as a single policy thread. The Jellicoe plan (except the recommendation to expand Singapore) was not discussed. Instead, the dominion delegates endorsed the One-Power Standard and naval parity with the United States as a "minimum standard" for the Empire's security. With this much achieved, the Admiralty then pressed its case for a centralized navy and renewal of the Anglo-Japanese Treaty. Failure in either instance would expose the loopholes in Beatty's compromise position.

Canada's position going into the 1921 Imperial Conference was any-thing but settled; indeed, decisions for a permanent naval policy had been deliberately put off, pending the outcome of these talks. By then, however, Prime Minister Arthur Meighen would try to avoid the question alto-gether. For over a year his government had known that long-range com-mitments involving naval expansion would be politically unacceptable for the foreseeable future. All this came about in the wake of Jellicoe's dominion tour, which had revealed a good deal of public indifference to imperial defence matters. Anxious not to have such a response translated into active opposition, the Unionist coalition government preferred to delay controversial decisions on the principle that in the absence of a clear advantage for doing otherwise, procrastination was the safest bet.

In practice, very little by way of a constructive naval policy had been undertaken since the armistice. The wartime Naval Service of some 5,400 personnel and 123 vessels was reduced by the spring of 1919 to what C.C. Ballantyne, the minister of Marine and Fisheries and of the Naval Service, described as "the vanishing point."[18] When the estimates for that year were reduced to $600,000, the Naval Staff concluded that the prudent course would be to reduce what remained "as far as possible to the minimum with a view to making a fresh start after the report from Lord Jellicoe had been presented."[19] Some preliminary consideration was given to the transfer of surplus RN ships so that, by early 1919, Borden was able to express his "deep appreciation" for a British offer of two submarines (CH 14 and CH 15 acquired in June).[20] In April, while at the Paris peace talks and without consulting his colleagues in Ottawa, Borden also broached the question of Canada taking over a fleet unit of more surplus ships including, perhaps, a battleship, some cruisers, and supporting destroyers. The Admiralty quite rightly questioned the value of such transfers to the small Canadian establishment, although, as Captain Dudley Pound, the director of Plans, suggested, some transfers might help to stimulate local interest in the development of a "useful" Dominion naval policy.[21] In November the British cabinet approved the transfer of one cruiser (HMS *Glasgow*), but otherwise the Admiralty, like the Canadian Naval Staff, preferred to await Jellicoe's findings.

In reality, the times were not propitious for any serious consideration of naval affairs in Canada. Borden's Union government was clearly nearing the limits of its wartime mandate. Borden's deteriorating health forced him into prolonged convalescence, and, until July 1920 when Meighen took over as prime minister, his steadying influence was absent from the deliberations of his ministers. Many of these senior men were no less worn out, including Ballantyne who was ill throughout much of this period. As a Liberal who had entered the coalition in 1917 and whose name was intimately associated with the controversial Canadian merchant marine, his political future was perhaps more uncertain than that of his Conservative colleagues. Still, neither they nor many of their Liberal and Progressive opponents were prepared to risk tenuous claims on the future for the contentious, but still secondary, issue of naval expansion. In the words of one senior naval officer, these were "discouraging" times:

> The party wrangle as to what policy should be followed is perhaps normal enough, but when it took the shape of a scathing—you might say scurrilous—ridicule for years in the press and in parliament, against the navy itself, which was trying its best, making bricks without straw, to maintain the highest efficiency possible, and which could not defend itself, it was indeed discouraging.[22]

Against this background, the Naval Staff in Ottawa set out to write a series of thirty-seven studies covering most aspects of Canada's naval needs. By modern staff work standards, these "Occasional Papers" seem amateurish and unjustifiably optimistic, if not naive. Yet, considering the severely limited resources of the embryonic staff—in February 1919 its principal officers were formed into the Naval Committee consisting of the deputy minister and the comptroller of the Naval Service (George J. Desbarats), the director of the Naval Service (Vice-Admiral Sir Charles Kingsmill), and his assistant (Commander R.M.T. Stephens, RN (Ret'd.))—and the fact that few senior government officials had ever tested or trusted its advisory skills, the wonder is that any studies of value were produced at all. Much earlier, Loring Christie of the Department of External Affairs expressed what was probably a common attitude in Ottawa when he suggested that the Naval Staff had never "once had a policy or opinion" of its own; admittedly, he added, the government had never expected it should.[23] By November 1919, when Jellicoe arrived, twenty-three of the occasional papers were finished, some of which were shown to Jellicoe.

Of these studies, Occasional Paper no. 2, entitled "Proposals for Canadian Naval Expansion," was the most important.[24] It envisioned a progressive four-phase development: phase 1, provision of base facilities for imperial ships; phase 2, the provision of additional forces for local defence; phase 3, the addition of a "small service" on the fleet unit model; and phase 4, the building of a fully complemented Canadian fleet together with supporting repair and building facilities. The final and most ambitious phase was to be completed in two seven-year building programmes which, by 1934, would result in a Canadian fleet of eighteen patrol craft (anti-submarine/escort boats), twelve destroyers, seven cruisers, six submarines, and three parent ships, to be manned by 8,500 officers and men at a total estimated cost of just under $58 million. Capital ships were rejected as being beyond the resources of Canadian shipyards and the numbers of senior officers to command them. Whichever alternative the government decided on, the Naval Committee urged the absolute necessity of a permanent and settled policy:

> ... a certain sized Naval Service should be aimed at in say 15 or 20 years, the whole scheme being sealed by a special Act of Parliament. .... It is not too much to say that a navy founded on the above principle, even though of very small size, would be far more efficient than a numerically larger navy constructed on some haphazard principle.

The paper was discussed by the Naval Committee in early June, but although endorsed by Ballantyne as a "good basis for future development,"[25] it did not lead to the firm decisions suggested. Not one was made prior to Jellicoe's arrival. However, the paper was handed to Jellicoe and figured centrally in his report to the Canadian authorities.

Jellicoe's two-week progress from the west coast to the east, and then to Ottawa, occasioned no exceptional outbursts of opinion for all that some nationalist editorials warned of the dangers to Canadian autonomy which his visit raised. He was fêted by various branches of the Navy League of Canada, who hosted many of the gatherings which he addressed. Jellicoe's treatment by the national and local press was friendly and polite, but restrained. Most commentaries concentrated on social pleasantries but were generally indifferent to the broader reasons for his presence. Official Ottawa's inertia on the naval question therefore came as no surprise to him. In private talks with Borden and some of his ministers, and with William Lyon Mackenzie King, leader of the Opposition, it became obvious that most wanted to postpone and preferably avoid any decision or commitment. Only Ballantyne was prepared to run the risks which his colleagues preferred to keep at arm's length. In a letter to the First Lord, Walter Long, Jellicoe wrote that

Mr. Ballantyne, who is very much in earnest, is concerned that unless the matter is settled now, before I leave Canada, nothing will be done for several years. He tells me distinctly that unless a serious start is made now, he intends to wipe out completely the present Canadian Naval Service, as being a pure waste of money. He is right.[26]

Jellicoe's three-volume report was placed before the Unionist cabinet on 22 December 1919, shortly before his own departure for home.[27] Volume one, which was eventually distributed to all members of Parliament, contained a broad discussion of the Empire Naval Mission and matters generally affecting Canadian naval organization and administration. The second volume dealt with specific aspects of local defence, naval yards, fuel reserves, and air forces. The third covered the current world situation and possible enemies of the Empire. The latter volumes were withheld as secret documents and never released to public view. Leaning heavily on the ideas and data provided in the occasional papers, Jellicoe recommended four methods for a Canadian contribution. The first two provided for a local defence capability only, while the latter two assumed that some contribution to imperial defence was wanted. Annual costs were estimated at 1, 2, 3.5, and 5 million pounds sterling, respectively. His other recommendations, for the creation of a separate naval ministry and a navy board analogous to the Admiralty Board in London and for improvements in recruiting, training and discipline, bear the stamp of his own experience of wartime reforms in British staff procedures and organization. The Canadian Naval Staff had pinned its hopes on Jellicoe's visit and had looked to him to lay the groundwork for a permanent government commitment to the RCN. Jellicoe reciprocated that trust by backing and using their arguments. However, even his most modest scheme far exceeded the limits of what the Unionist cabinet would tolerate. Three months elapsed between the submission of the report and its release to Parliament on 10 March 1920. In the interim it became the focus of a crisis of confidence within the inner cabinet.

In Borden's absence the ministers were unwilling to support even a reduced version of Jellicoe's Plan (estimated annual cost $4-5 million). They resorted to the highly unorthodox expedient of putting Ballantyne's proposal of acceptance to the plan to a vote of the parliamentary caucus. According to the acting Prime Minister, Sir George Foster, Ballantyne agreed to argue his own case while his cabinet colleagues said nothing either way. Whatever this reveals about Ballantyne's political judgment, the principle of cabinet solidarity was not a factor in what transpired. In Foster's words, some senior ministers "broke faith" and spoke out against Ballantyne's plan; the caucus, as a result, "knocked it sky high."[28] Enraged and disgusted, Ballantyne returned to his office and, at some point over the next two days, ordered Vice-Admiral Kingsmill to disband the entire naval service as of 1 July 1920.[29] As Foster reported to Borden, " 'Then the mouse was in the soup sure.' " A week of confusion followed until, after more discussion, another compromise was reached by which, with caucus approval, it was agreed:

(a) To give the Minister a free hand to reorganize by notice of discontinuance of present staff. (b) Accept two destroyers and one cruiser from G.[reat] B.[ritain] to replace the *Rainbow* and *Niobe* for training and protection purposes. (c) Keep the [cadet training] College. (d) Defer permanent navy policy for the present.[30]

This plan was acceptable for two reasons only; it was cheap, and it was temporary. The budget of $2 million annually for the next two years entailed no heavy capital outlay. The ships in question, the British destroyers HMS *Patrician* and HMS *Patriot*, and the cruiser HMS *Aurora* (instead of the originally offered HMS *Glasgow*), were gifts which Jellicoe had been urging the Canadians to accept.[31] When these arrangements were announced to the House on 25 March 1920, the government emphasized their interim nature: a firm decision for a "permanent naval policy for Canada" had yet to be made and would now be put off entirely until after the Imperial Conference met.[32]

Ballantyne's earlier fears, that unless something positive was decided upon, and quickly, nothing ever would be, were proved correct in the long run. In reporting these results to Borden, he put on as brave a face as he could by referring to our now "small but energetic and absolutely efficient" naval service.[33] But he did nothing himself to guide the plan through the House. That was left to N.W. Rowell and Arthur Meighen, who carefully avoided lengthy or unpleasant, and therefore dangerous, partisan debate. Later events would show that Ballantyne's compromise was in effect a commitment to permanency for the RCN. However small, there was a naval establishment, which, under the leadership of Captain Walter Hose (who replaced Kingsmill in 1921), survived to act as the nucleus for wartime expansion. The point here is that despite Ballantyne's failure to get a settled policy, the Naval Staff under Hose persisted in its belief that Jellicoe's plans would be implemented eventually. This was made obvious in Occasional Paper no. 32, dated 4 June 1921, and entitled "Canadian Naval Programme: Alternative Schemes," which was drawn up in preparation for the 1921 Imperial Conference in London. It assumed that the case for a Canadian navy was now beyond dispute, that the existing organization was but a "tentative force" pending future decisions concerning its actual size and composition, and that Jellicoe's four-phase scheme was the only sensible course to follow.[34]

But Arthur Meighen, who had succeeded Borden as prime minister the previous summer, was resolved not to discuss the Jellicoe plan in London, or anywhere else for that matter. He made this clear to the Colonial Office in the months leading up to the Imperial Conference and during the Canadian Commons' discussions of the conference agenda when he quite deliberately gave the impression that naval defence carried a much lower priority in British eyes than was actually the case. Even Borden had warned the House that the times were "altogether inopportune for considering the problems of Imperial defence."[35] A crucial autumn election was in the offing, and it was preferable to emphasize how thoroughly naval costs had been trimmed so that, as Meighen himself later suggested, "no man can make the question of defence an issue."[36] This was sound politics. It should be emphasized, however, that at no point in cabinet, caucus, or in the Commons discussions were the strategic dimensions of the issue even raised. No judgment was ever rendered by the government on Jellicoe's main arguments. Nor were they ever fully adjudicated by the Canadian Naval Staff, who now found their hopes for the future straddling the two stools of domestic and external Empire politics. This is not to suggest that Meighen's stance later in London was determined exclusively by domestic considerations; they did dictate, however, that any acceptable solution to the imperial defence problem would be primarily political or diplomatic, and not military in nature.

Meighen therefore approached the London talks determined to avoid the issue of naval defence co-operation altogether. Prompted by Loring Christie, who had been Borden's chief adviser on international affairs, he sought to turn imperial policy towards abrogation of the Anglo-Japanese Treaty (due to expire on 13 July 1921) and the calling of a "Conference of Pacific Powers . . . for the purpose of adjusting Pacific and Far Eastern questions."[37] Claiming a "very special" and "predominant" position for Canada's understanding of the American situation, he urged consideration of an early approach by Borden to the Washington authorities. This departure, especially as it seemed to imply an independent Canadian initiative, now underscored the inconsistencies in the British plans for somehow accommodating American feelings to the One-Power Standard and a renewed Anglo-Japanese arrangement. Unwilling to have his hands tied before all the dominions' opinions were in, Lloyd George preferred to delay all decisions on these naval and diplomatic options until the conference met in July.

At the conference itself the Anglo-Japanese Treaty dominated every other issue, and Meighen found himself ranged against the foreign secretary, Admiralty, War Office, and the other dominions, and most especially Prime Minister William M. Hughes of Australia, who challenged the Canadians' exaggerated claims to speak for and shape Empire policies as they affected relations with the United States. Above all, Hughes questioned the value of U.S. friendship unsupported by an unqualified guarantee of aid in time of war:

> What does he offer us? Something we can grasp? What is the substantial alternative to the renewal of the Treaty? The answer is, that there is none. If Australia were asked whether she preferred America or Japan as an ally, her choice would be America. But that choice is not offered her. As against the substance she is offered the shadow.[38]

Backed by New Zealand and India, Hughes supported the British proposals to renew the treaty. The result was an impasse which would be resolved only by the timely arrival of President Warren G. Harding's invitation to attend the Washington talks and by assurances from Lloyd George that should these talks fail to produce a modified or extended treaty which included the United States the original alliance would be renewed.[39]

This deadlock overshadowed the Imperial Conference's other important deliberations, including the definition of Empire constitutional relationships, the co-ordination of foreign policy, of League matters, and of immigration policy. On the question of naval co-operation, agreement was possible only to the extent of a statement that "The method and expense of such cooperation are matters for the final determination of the several Parliaments concerned, and that any recommendations thereon should be deferred until after the coming conference on disarmament."[40] No consensus was reached on specific naval standards or suggestions for dominion contributions for new capital ships and fuel storage facilities at Singapore. Even endorsement of the One-Power Standard was limited to an ambiguous resolution which described that measurement of Empire naval security as "equality in fighting strength with any other Naval Power."[41] Like everything else, more precise definition of that "equality" was set aside until after the Washington meetings.

Meighen had undoubtedly played an innovative leadership role in forcing the pace of these events towards Washington and the decision to convene there, in November 1921, an international conference on the Pacific and naval arms limitations. Canada's part in the complicated manoeuvrings that ensued, though no less significant, was comparatively less visible as her representative, Borden, kept a watching brief to ensure that the initiatives for closer Empire-U.S. relations should not founder on the rocks of expert naval dissension or obstruction. As a civilian member of the British Empire delegation and representative of a nation for whom, in his words, the naval aspects of the issue did not appear "to involve any special Canadian interests,"[42] Borden played no direct part in the negotiations that resulted in the Five-Power Treaty on naval reductions. He did draw upon his very considerable personal prestige and friendships within the British and American delegations to ensure that professional naval opposition to U.S. Secretary of State Charles Hughes's proposals for total tonnage limitations ratios and a moratorium on battleship construction did not wreck the general atmosphere for a wider accord on the vital problem of the Pacific.[43] In this respect, Borden's most important intercessions came in support of A.S. Balfour's initiatives to replace the Anglo-Japanese Treaty with a four-power agreement (Britain, Japan, the U.S., and France) which, though not involving military obligations, did commit the signatories to the principles of preserving the status quo in the Pacific and settlement of future disputes by international negotiation.

From the Canadian perspective, the signing of the Four-Power Pact on 13 December 1921 was an unquestioned victory, the culmination of Borden's and Meighen's commitment to bring the United States more actively into the world arena alongside Great Britain. But it was a short-lived triumph. An Atlantic entente was not created; nor was Empire cohesion fostered. America's subsequent drift into deeper isolationism would lay bare a good deal more than just the flaws in Canadian diplomatic idealism. This included some worrisome implications of the Washington agreement's more serious strategic defects: in particular, the "non-fortificiation" clauses of the Naval Limitation Treaty, which provided that the powers would not arm or fortify their island bases in the Pacific west of Pearl Harbor and east of Singapore. Without such bases, neither the U.S. Navy nor the Royal Navy could realistically contemplate fleet operations of any extended size or duration. Virtually by default, Japan would become supreme in Asian waters. Moreover, in material terms any future thoughts of a Jellicoe-style Empire fleet were nullified as Britain was committed to a standard of naval "adequacy" based not on any assessment of defined imperial strategic needs but on mere numerical "parity" with the United States. That these concessions were accepted in flat contradiction of expert naval advice on both sides of the Atlantic was a major cost of that victory for innovative diplomacy.

Nor was this a case of judgment with hindsight. Even as the Washington talks were winding down, the Naval Staff in London began its assessment of their impact, which indicated a clear realization that Japan had won most of the advantages. The Admiralty's opinion was that the U.S. Navy was no longer an important factor "so far as effective interference with Japan in the western basin of the Pacific is concerned."[44] This placed an even greater premium on dominion co-operation, standardization, contributions to oil reserves and the build-up of Singapore. "Naval Defence," they warned, "can only be assured by adequate naval forces, capable of offensive and defensive action, which in turn can only be maintained by fuelling and base facilities." Looking ahead to the 1923 Imperial Conference, the Admiralty went on to reaffirm these needs, especially for cruisers, whose numbers were not restricted by the limitation agreement and whose cost (in anticipation of Canadian objections) could best be minimized within an imperial fleet.

Canada, not surprisingly, drew very different conclusions from the Washington experience. In his lengthy official report and his private correspondence, Borden assured the new Liberal government in Ottawa that the agreements imposed "no duty or obligation upon Canada except to restrict naval armament she would otherwise be at liberty to undertake."[45] This was welcome news to Mackenzie King, who only a few days before becoming prime minister had confided to his diary a personal commitment to expose and "clean up" the "expenditures and waste" of the defence establishment generally.[46] Within weeks, Commodore Walter Hose and his staff were confronted with new estimates which, arbitrarily slashed to $1.5 million, left few options other than the skeleton reserve force announced in May.[47] The road to what Arthur Meighen derisively called Canada's "Five Trawler Navy" was heartsickeningly short, but it was one well posted and marked by his own government's surveyors.

Chapter 5

THE ROYAL CANADIAN NAVY BETWEEN THE WARS, 1922-39

Hugh Francis Pullen

While the Washington Conference on Naval Disarmament (1921-22) was in progress, the Conservative government of Arthur Meighen was succeeded in December 1921 by a Liberal administration under William Lyon Mackenzie King. This boded ill for the armed forces, as they soon discovered: the times did not favour sailors, soldiers, and airmen. Canada had just come through World War I, and there was little public support for national defence. What is more, Mackenzie King had a great personal distaste for anything to do with military matters and was eager to find ways of curtailing expenditure on national defence. The Washington Conference gave him his opportunity so far as the Royal Canadian Navy was concerned: the naval estimates for 1922-23 were slashed from $2.5 million to $1.5 million, and the director of the Naval Service was told to make do with what was left.

In May 1922 George P. Graham, minister of National Defence, announced the government's naval policy. He observed that countries of the world were trying to reduce armaments as far as possible without sacrificing their national dignity. Canada had certain obligations both internationally and to the Empire, and one of these was to maintain a naval service of some kind. His recommendations were that the five warships (HMC Ships *Aurora, Patriot, Patrician*, and the submarines CH 14 and CH 15) be paid off and that the Royal Canadian Navy be reduced dramatically. A naval reserve force of fifteen hundred officers and ratings should be organized. All this, he remarked, "would be more in keeping with the protection of our coasts than it would be in harmony with high-sea fighting, because the fleet as now constituted is for action on the sea, and not for the protection of our harbours and coasts as we understand that protection."[1] This was an incredible statement coming as it did from a presumably intelligent man in high office. Graham lived to see what happened to Canada's navy between 1939 and 1942, and one cannot help wondering what he thought about the RCN's accomplishments.

As a result of the new policy, four RN officers serving on loan to Canada were retained, while the remainder were returned to the United Kingdom. The Youth Training Establishment at Halifax was closed, and the dock-yards at Halifax and Esquimalt were reduced to repair and storing status. The naval barracks at the two bases were to be used as training centres for the reserves. The Royal Naval College of Canada was closed in June 1922. I remember when this piece of news was given to us on the quarterdeck of the college by the commanding officer, Commander E.A.E. Nixon. He announced quite coldly that as a result of government policy the college would close permanently at the end of the summer term. "Turn forward, double march," he barked, and that was that. The disposal of HMC Ships was later modified so that one destroyer and two minesweepers were retained in commission on each coast for training purposes. By the end of 1928 HMCS *Aurora* and the two submarines had been disposed of. The result was a minute sea-going navy, with HMC Ships *Patriot*, *Ypres*, and *Festubert* stationed at Halifax, and HMC Ships *Patrician*, *Armentières*, and *Thiepval* at Esquimalt. By July 1922 the total complement was down to 402 officers and ratings.

Concerned officials at Naval Service Headquarters in Ottawa realized that, to prevent the Navy's position from being undermined further, a concerted effort would have to be made to present the case for an effective standing Navy to the public. The naval secretary at that time, Paymaster Commander J.A.E. Woodhouse, RN, left the following account of the logic by which the Service arrived at the course of action it was to take in the years between the wars:

The deciding considerations were:
(a) If a Dominion is to spend money on the Navy, its people must be convinced a Navy is necessary.
(b) In Canada a large majority of the people live far from the sea and do not visualize the necessity for safe sea communications.
(c) The first necessity therefore is to educate the people.
(d) The most effective method of educating the people is to bring the Navy to their doors, into the lives of families and friends.
(e) A small Navy is of no value as an educative measure as its personnel live in the neighbourhood of the naval base; but a reserve force distributed across Canada would bring the Navy home to a great number of

inland people; would be the only means of doing so within the appro-
priation available; would form a useful field of recruiting for the RCN;
would give the Director of the Naval Service opportunity to visit the
Reserve Centres throughout the country and address Chambers of
Commerce, Rotarian Clubs, etc., on the elements of Naval Defence;
would provide in the Reserve Centres a subject for articles in the press;
would be the first step in the conversion of Quebec.[2]

This plan was accepted by the government, and from it came the formation of the Canadian Naval Reserve Forces. The first of these was the Royal
Canadian Naval Reserve, which was authorized by Privy Council order
(P.C.) 80 of 15 January 1923. The RCNR was originally organized with
nine port divisions, but was soon reduced to five at Charlottetown,
Halifax, Quebec, Montreal, and Vancouver. At each of these ports a regis-
trar was appointed to look after the interests of the officers and ratings
belonging to his port division. He was also the link between the RCN and
the RCNR. Candidates for entry had to be British subjects, living in
Canada, physically fit, of good character and willing to serve at sea or
wherever required. Normally they had to follow the sea in a civilian
capacity. The authorized complement was 70 officers and 430 ratings. By
31 March 1924 there were 24 officers and 81 ratings enrolled. Recruiting
was suspended in 1925 when the strength was 36 officers and 110 ratings. In
due course it was resumed, and by 31 March 1939 there were 67 officers and
199 ratings.
    The second reserve element was the Royal Canadian Naval Volunteer
Reserve (RCNVR), which was authorized by P.C. 139 of 31 January 1923.
On the same day P.C. 140 cancelled the authority for the Royal Naval
Canadian Volunteer Reserve, which had been established in May 1914,
largely as the result of public initiative. The authorized complement of the
RCNVR was 70 officers and 930 ratings organized into companies of 100,
and half companies of fifty in the following cities: Calgary, Charlottetown,
Edmonton, Halifax, Hamilton, Montreal, Ottawa, Quebec, Regina, Saint
John, Saskatoon, Toronto, Vancouver, and Winnipeg.[3]
    To join the RCNVR, applicants had to be British subjects between the
ages of eighteen and thirty-two and be physically fit. They signed on for
three years and had to agree to serve whenever required. They were obliged
to perform at least thirty drills annually in their particular headquarters, as
well as carry out two weeks of training each year at Halifax or Esquimalt.
Each rating was paid twenty-five cents per drill; the officers were not paid.
While doing his annual training, each officer or rating was paid in accordance with the RCN scale for his rank or rating and specialist qualification.
    Once the order-in-council had been passed, Naval Service Headquarters

moved swiftly, and on 14 March 1924 the Montreal English-Speaking Company was formed under the command of Lieutenant Frank Meade, RCNVR. The French-Speaking Company was commanded by Acting-Lieutenant Alexandre Brodeur, RCNVR. These were the first companies to be organized. With the formation of the Charlottetown Half Company on 14 September 1924, under the command of Lieutenant George H. Buntain, RCNVR, there were twelve companies and half companies spread across Canada. Recruiting for the RCNVR was brisk: by 31 March 1924 there were fifty officers and 764 ratings enrolled. Vancouver and Prince Rupert commissioned in 1924, followed the next year by Halifax. There were no further increases until 1934 when the RCNVR was established at Port Arthur, followed in 1938 by London and in 1939 by Kingston and Windsor.[4] The strength of the RCNVR companies, which came to be known as "divisions," was 113 officers and 1,292 ratings by 31 March 1939.

I am indebted to Captain Vernon W. Howland, RCN, (Ret'd.) for the following "Recollections of the RCNVR," the reserve force which he joined in Toronto in 1937.

At the beginning of 1937 I wrote a letter to the Commanding Officer of the Toronto Division RCNVR saying I would like to join as an officer if I was eligible. I received a reply from the Chief Petty Officer Instructor telling me to report to the "Naval Barracks" on Lakeshore Boulevard any Wednesday evening (which was their drill night). I reported in early February, and turned out for every drill night and every other activity of the Division from then until called up for active service on 1 September 1939.

We bought all our own uniforms including cap, greatcoat, burberry, regular "No. 5's," frock coat, sword, mess kit and at least two suits of white "No. 10's." Not all these uniforms were compulsory by regulations, but officers were expected to outfit themselves properly if they were accepted into the Navy. This was a tall order for many of us who were relatively impecunious young men, but we solved our problem by ordering secondhand blue uniforms from Moss Brothers in London.

Recruiting was never a problem. The Division always had a "probationers division" of twenty-five to forty men in civilian clothes waiting vacancies so they could join up. There were occasionally one or two gentlemen attending drills in the hope of being accepted as officers.

Most of the officers of the Division spent many hours of each week working at the barracks on various projects or on social occasions. The barracks was also used by the men for social occasions and the chiefs and petty officers had a fine mess which was the equal of the wardroom. It must be emphasized that all this was done with virtually NO MONEY. No one got paid, no money was available for the bits and pieces needed to build training aids. The officers reached into their already thin wallets and the chiefs and petty officers "liberated" bits and pieces from places of employment. There was tremendous enthusiasm for the navy and great pride in belonging to the RCNVR. We *were* the navy in Toronto. For many of us, young unmarried men like myself, the "Naval Barracks" was the centre of our life outside working hours. If you belonged to the RCNVR you didn't have time or money left for other activities!

It all came to an end on 1 September 1939 when our call-up telegrams started to arrive from Ottawa. The Naval Reserve has been different ever since.[5]

This was the means by which Commodore Walter Hose, RCN, who had succeeded Vice-Admiral Sir Charles Kingsmill as director of the Naval Service on 1 January 1921, hoped to spread the navy across Canada and bring it forcibly to the attention of a great many citizens. It was one of the wisest moves ever made in the history of Canada's sea service and was to pay great dividends between 1939 and 1945.

In 1922 the government established the Department of National Defence, combining the Departments of Militia and Defence, the Naval Service, and the Air Force. As a result of this amalgamation the Defence Council was formed by adding a naval member and an air force member to the old Militia Council. Its duties were to advise the minister on matters relating to national defence. The formation of this new department led to a tendency for the army to dominate the other two services. The senior army officer at headquarters became chief of staff, Department of National Defence, and inspector general of the militia, navy, and air force. The director of the Naval Service resisted every attempt by the chief of staff to interfere with the navy or to advise the minister regarding it. In March 1922, as a result of a 60 per cent reduction in the air force estimates, the Canadian Air force became a directorate of the General Staff. This left the RCN as the only opponent to complete army control of the three armed services; Commodore Hose was immovable and refused to give way to the policies of the chief of staff. This unfortunate situation continued until Chief of Staff Major-General J.H. MacBrien retired in 1926. The office of chief of staff was abolished in May 1927, while the title of director of the Naval Service was changed to chief of the Naval Staff in March 1928.

The early 1920's were grim years for the RCN. It required a great deal of courage and fortitude to continue to serve Canada in the navy in the face of apparent government indifference and public apathy. The only encouraging sign was the response to the RCNVR and the eagerness displayed by

Plate 9. Royal Naval College of Canada, founded in 1910 to provide "a complete education in all branches of naval science, tactics, and strategy," was first situated in the old naval hospital at the north end of Halifax dockyard. (MCM—RCN-5914) (insert) Commander E.A.E. Nixon, RCN, second commanding officer, after Commander E.H. Martin, of the RNCC. (P. Nixon collection)

Plate 10. Royal Naval College of Canada, 1st term cadets, entered January 1911. *Rear*: J.B. Lowrie, W.A. Palmer, W.M. Maitland-Dougall, J.E.W. Oland, L.J.M. Gauvreau. *Centre*: R.C. Watson, L.W. Murray, R.I. Agnew, J.V.W. Hatheway, G.C. Jones, D.B. Moffatt, R.F. Lawson, H.R. Tingley, G.A. Worth, H.I.F. Hibbard. *Front*: H.A. David, J.M. Grant, M. Cann, C.W. Reid, A.W. Silver. (Royal Roads Military College)

Plate 11. Vice-Admiral Sir Charles E. Kingsmill, RCN, first director of the Naval Service, 1910-21. (Maritime Museum of B.C. [MMBC]

Plate 12. Charles C. Ballantyne, Arthur Meighen's minister of Marine and Fisheries and of the Naval Service, 1917-21. (PAC—C-8656)

Plate 13. Commander Walter Hose, RCN, succeeded Kingsmill as director of the Naval Service on 1 January 1921, a post he retained until 1934. (MMBC—P1031)

Plate 14. Vice-Admiral Percy W. Nelles, RCN, the first Canadian Chief of the Naval Staff, 1934-44. (MMBC—P4929g)

Plate 15. J.L. Ralston (right), minister of National Defence, 1926-30, and G.J. Desbarats, deputy minister and comptroller of the Naval Service, 1910-22 and deputy minister of National Defence, 1924-32. Ottawa, 4 January 1930. (PAC—PA 62522)

Come along Canadians!
Men are wanted
to help Britannia "Rule the Waves"

Get overseas at once by joining

the Royal Naval Canadian Volunteer Reserve
OVERSEAS DIVISION.

Y $1.10 a day and upwards—Free Kit—Separation allowance as in C. E. F.
No experience necessary—Candidates must be sons
of natural born British subjects—Ages 18 to 38.

*EXPERIENCED MEN FROM 18 TO 45 MAY ENLIST FOR SERVICE IN
THE CANADIAN NAVAL PATROLS TO GUARD CANADIAN COASTS.*

Apply at the Nearest Naval Recruiting Station

or to the Naval Recruiting Secretary, Ottawa.   A1-3-17

Plate 16. World War I recruiting poster for the Royal Naval Canadian Volunteer Reserve. The Reserve was formed in May 1914. (MCM—CN 6233)

Plate 17. Personnel of the RNCVR outside the Legislative Buildings, Victoria, B.C., 1914. (PAC—PA 115374)

Plate 18. Officers and men of the RNCVR manning trawlers and drifters carrying out St. Lawrence and Atlantic patrols, Quebec City, taken 1917-18. (PAC—PA 115373)

Plate 19. The trawler HMCS *Armentières* served intermittently as a training ship and examination vessel, 1918-46. (Maritime Division, Nova Scotia Museum)

Plate 20. HMCS *Aurora* (foreground), "Arethusa"-class light cruiser, one of five RCN warships paid off in post-World War I retrenchment. Also shown are the destroyers *Patrician* and *Patriot*. (PAC—PA 115369)

Plate 21. Canada's two World War I submarines, CC1 and CC2. Purchased by Premier Sir Richard McBride, they constituted British Columbia's own navy for two days before being transferred to the RCN. (MMBC)

Plate 22. HMC Ships *Saguenay* I (foreground) and *Skeena* I, the first warships built to Canadian specifications, with *Champlain* (ex-HMS *Torbay*) (rear) entering Halifax harbour, 8 July 1931. (DOH, NDHQ—PMR 80-646)

Plate 23. Winnipeg Company, RCNVR, church party, 5 May 1932. (DOH, NDHQ—PMR 80-647)

Plate 24. HMCS *Skeena* I crew members Lieutenant-Commander F.L. Houghton and Petty Officer Priske, RCN, with members of the British railway staff, San Salvador, January 1932. *Skeena* rescued British nationals during an uprising in El Salvador. (PAC—PA 115345)

Plate 25. HMCS *Saguenay* I entering Willemstad, Curaçao, Netherlands Antilles, 1934. Between the wars, RCN ships joined Royal Navy ships for exercises in the Caribbean. (Department of National Defence [DND])

Plate 26. HMCS *Fraser* I, ex-HMS *Cresent*, "C"-class destroyer, commissioned into the RCN 17 February 1937, was stationed on the West Coast until the outbreak of World War II. (MCM—E2294)

Plate 27. Presentation by George VI to Lieutenant J.C. Hibbard, RCN, of the King's Colours, Beacon Hill Park, Victoria, on the eve of war, 30 May 1939. (MMBC—P3703)

those who joined it. The RCN had shrunk to 67 officers and 385 ratings by 31 March 1924. At the same time personnel were still being sent to England for courses that could not be given in Canada. The authorized complement for the RCN was increased to 70 officers and 446 ratings by 31 March 1925.

In early 1924 a decision was made at Naval Service Headquarters to start entering cadets into the RCN. The last entry had been four graduates from the Royal Naval College of Canada who joined the service in 1921. As far as I know, letters were sent to those first and second-year cadets discharged from the RNCC when it was closed in 1922. I was the only member of my term (1920) to join. With three of the 1921 term we were entered as cadets RCN and sent to join HMS *Thunderer* at Devonport in September 1924. She was the Special Entry Cadet Training Ship until 1926, being followed by HM Ships *Erebus* (1927-32), *Frobisher* (1933-36), *Vindictive* (1937-39) and *Erebus* (1940-41). Cadet training was continued in the Royal Canadian Naval College when it was commissioned on 21 October 1942. Eighty-five RCN cadets were trained by this Special Entry scheme between 1924 and 1939. In the summer of 1932 twenty-three cadets from the Royal Military College of Kingston did eight weeks training at Halifax. The idea was to prepare these young men for entry as cadets RCN. This system of training RMC cadets was continued each summer until the outbreak of war in September 1939.

The general condition of HMCS *Patriot* was such that by 1926 she was reduced to a reserve status during the winter, at seven days notice for steam. It was during this period that Admiralty House in Halifax became the Officers' Mess and work was started on the joint naval and military magazine on the Dartmouth shores of Bedford Basin. *Patriot* was finally paid off into reserve at the end of October 1927; moreover, the government had decided to build two destroyers to replace *Patriot* and *Patrician*, which were worn out. In the meantime the Admiralty was asked to provide replacements, which they did with HMS *Torbay* (HMCS *Champlain*) and HMS *Toreador* (HMCS *Vancouver*). These two ships were commissioned at Portsmouth on 1 March 1928 and sailed for Canada, *Champlain* arriving at Halifax on 12 May 1928, and *Vancouver* at Esquimalt on 24 May 1928. During that same year *Aurora* and the two submarines CH 14 and CH 15 were sold for scrap, while *Patrician* was paid off into reserve.

The old naval hospital at Halifax which had housed the Royal Naval College of Canada and which had, after being repaired, become the Youth Training Establishment from 1920 to 1922, was transformed into the Royal Canadian Naval Barracks (HMCS *Stadacona*) at this time. In addition to providing living quarters for ratings, it accommodated the signal and WT school, schoolrooms, a canteen, and offices for the senior naval officer. Two houses nearby provided accommodation for the chief and petty officers, while a third became the naval medical quarters.

During 1929 the authorized complement of the RCN was increased to 104 officers and 792 ratings to provide crews for the two new destroyers and the larger training staffs required to deal with the increased number of RCN and reserve ratings. The new complement was not to be recruited until the new ships were commissioned in the spring of 1931. By 31 March 1930 there were 83 officers and 709 ratings in the RCN, of whom 27 officers were serving in the Royal Navy. By 1932 the complement of ratings was full, although there were only 86 officers, 8 of whom were Royal Navy.

Contracts for the two new destroyers were awarded to Messrs. Thornycroft in January 1929. The ships were to be similar to the Admiralty A-class with certain Canadian improvements. They were to be strengthened for ice, to have steam heating installed, and to be fitted with scuppers on the upper deck. HMCS *Saguenay* was launched on 11 July 1930 and commissioned at Portsmouth on May 22 1931. HMCS *Skeena* was launched on 10 October 1930 and commissioned at Portsmouth on 10 June 1931. Both ships sailed on 23 June, arriving at Halifax in thick fog on 3 July 1931, the first men-of-war to be authorized by a Canadian government. *Skeena* sailed on 8 July for the West Coast, arriving at Esquimalt on 7 August 1931. In 1930, when these two ships were being built, the chief of the Naval Staff recommended that the minimum naval force required by Canada in peacetime was one flotilla leader, five destroyers, and four minesweepers. This minimum level was not reached until late in 1938.

The chief of the General Staff in 1931 was Major-General A.G.L. McNaughton, who had very definite ideas on the matter of national defence. He considered that the Department of National Defence should be reorganized and that the position of chief of staff, Department of National Defence, should be revived and given to the most eligible officer of any of the three services. As the army was the largest, the odds were that it would be held by a soldier. McNaughton got no support from either Commodore Hose or his successor, Captain Percy W. Nelles, RCN, and the proposal was dropped.

On 22 January 1932 HMC Ships *Skeena* and *Vancouver* were on passage to the Panama Canal. A wireless message addressed to Naval Service Headquarters from the commander-in-chief North America and West Indies Squadron was intercepted by *Skeena*. It stated that the British Foreign Office had reported that British lives and property in the Republic of El Salvador were in danger owing to the possibility of a communist-inspired uprising and asked if *Skeena* and *Vancouver* could be diverted to the ports of Acajutla and La Libertad respectively. *Skeena* altered course for Acajutla and ordered *Vancouver* to La Libertad. These actions were approved by Naval Service Headquarters. *Skeena* arrived at Acajutla at noon on 23 January 1932 and embarked five ladies, the wives of British officials of the local railway company. They were to remain onboard for eight days until the danger of any trouble was past.[6]

Commodore Hose waged his final battle on behalf of the RCN in 1933. The depression was making itself felt, and the Department of National Defence was being pressed to reduce its expenditures. McNaughton said that if there were not enough funds to maintain a really efficient army, navy and air force, one of the three services would have to go; he maintained that the navy was the least necessary and stated that it should be sacrificed. The Treasury Board suggested that the naval estimates for 1933-34, which were $2.422 million be cut to $0.422 million, but the chief of the Naval Staff objected so vigorously that this extraordinary proposal was dropped.

Commodore Hose retired as CNS on 1 January 1934, having served in the Royal Canadian Navy since June 1911. It was as a result of his enthusiasm, drive, and determination that Canada had a navy which had grown steadily in strength and numbers since the early 1920's. His greatest contribution was the formation of the naval reserves, especially the RCNVR which was to be the mainstay of the wartime navy. He retired with the rank of rear-admiral and was succeeded by Captain Percy W. Nelles, RCN, the first Canadian to become chief of the Naval Staff, who was promoted to commodore first class.

In November 1934, as a result of the threat presented by the bellicose policies of the German Chancellor, Adolf Hitler, Naval Service Headquarters recommended that the force of six destroyers and four minesweepers be increased by the taking up of twelve auxiliary vessels in the event of war. In their opinion, this force would be the minimum for the security of one coast alone.

In accordance with the terms of the London Naval Treaty of 1930, HMC Ships *Champlain* and *Vancouver* were paid off and sold for scrap by the end of 1936. Early in 1935 Naval Service Headquarters had conducted negotiations with the Admiralty about the transfer of two C-class destroyers to the RCN to replace them. HM Ships *Crescent* and *Cygnet* were recommended and were purchased for $978,527 each. They were similar to *Saguenay* and *Skeena*, having been built in 1931. Both ships were commissioned at Chatham on 17 February 1937, *Crescent* being renamed HMCS *Fraser,* and *Cygnet,* HMCS *St. Laurent.* They sailed from Portland on 12 March 1937 by way of the Azores for Barbados, where they joined HMC Ships *Saguenay* and *Skeena.* HMCS *St. Laurent* in company with these two ships arrived at Halifax on 8 April 1937. HMCS *Fraser* proceeded to Esquimalt, arriving on 3 May 1937.

HMC Ships *Ypres* and *Festubert* had been paid off into reserve at Halifax and in 1937 were being refitted as gate vessels. A contract for

$57,508 was placed for the building of an auxiliary three-masted schooner to be used as a training vessel. This was to be HMCS *Venture*, which was commissioned for service on the East Coast in October 1937. The RCNVR Supplementary Reserve, a list of men with special qualifications or experience useful to the navy in wartime who did no training but were available to be called up, was also formed that year.

In early 1938 contracts were let for the building of four Basset-class minesweepers. They were commissioned later on that year as HMC Ships *Gaspé, Fundy, Nootka* (renamed *Nanoose* on 1 April 1943), and *Comox*. Arrangements were also made with the Admiralty to acquire the two remaining C-class destroyers, HMS *Crusader*, and HMS *Comet*. Purchased for $1,635,000, they were commissioned at Chatham on 15 June 1938 as HMC Ships *Ottawa* and *Restigouche* respectively. They sailed from Portland on 6 September 1938, arriving at Gaspé one week later. In due course they sailed for the West Coast, arriving at Esquimalt on 7 November 1938. The RCN had now achieved its stated objective of six destroyers and four modern minesweepers.

The Canadian Fleet Reserve (CFR), with a complement of 500, was authorized during 1938. It was made up of ratings who had served at least seven years in the RCN and had been honourably discharged. At the same time, a Fishermen's Reserve (FR) was organized on the West Coast with an authorized complement of 200. The officers and ratings of this force were to carry out their annual one-month training period in their own vessels during the off season. The main object of the FR was to conduct coastal patrols. HMCS *Skidegate*, a fishing vessel, was commissioned on 25 July 1938 for duty with the Fishermen's Reserve. During this year the auxiliary ketch HMCS *Glencairn* was presented to the RCN for naval reserve training.

In January 1939 the Western Division of HMC Ships, *Ottawa*, with Captain (D[estroyers]) George C. Jones, RCN, *Restigouche, Fraser*, and *St. Laurent*, sailed from Esquimalt for spring exercises in the Caribbean. There they rendezvoused with the East Coast subdivision of HMC Ships *Saguenay* and *Skeena* and carried out exercises with HM ships of the North America and West Indies Squadron. This was the only occasion when all six Canadian destroyers were able to train in company.

On Good Friday, 7 April 1939, the Western Division was at Balboa, homeward bound for Esquimalt. On that day Mussolini invaded Albania and brought the threat of a European war closer. The four first lieutenants of the Western Division held a meeting at which it was decided to make certain preparations for war once the coming royal visit was over and summer leave had been completed. War orders were to be brought up to date, non-essential gear was to be landed, identity discs and gas masks were to be drawn from the dockyard, and any other steps taken that seemed appropriate. This pre-planning was to pay dividends when the time came to prepare for war.

May 1939 saw the royal visit to Canada of King George VI and Queen Elizabeth. The East Coast subdivision met the RMS *Empress of Australia* near Cape Ray and escorted her to Quebec. HMCS *Skeena* provided passage for Their Majesties from Pictou to Charlottetown and return, escorted by HMCS *Saguenay*. Both ships also provided the escort when the King and Queen sailed from Halifax on 15 June 1939 in the RMS *Empress of Britain*. The crowning glory for the RCN in this royal visit was the Presentation of the King's Colour to the Royal Canadian Navy by the King at Beacon Hill Park in Victoria, British Columbia, on 30 May 1939. The West Coast division provided the escort to Vancouver and Victoria to the CPSS *Princess Marguerite* and the CNSS *Prince Rupert*.

In August 1939 arrangements were made with the Admiralty to purchase HMS *Kempenfelt*, the flotilla leader of the C-class destroyers. She was commissioned on 19 October 1939 as HMCS *Assiniboine* and arrived at Halifax on 17 November 1939.

After the royal visit and some well-earned summer leave were over, the four destroyers settled down to some intensive training on the West Coast. The ships were to remain in the Gulf of Georgia and not allow themselves to be trapped in some inlet by fog. The only divisional torpedo attack ever carried out by HMC ships was that against HMCS *Armentières* as the centre of the target line. Thirty-two torpedoes were fired, the target was "hit" and all torpedoes were recovered! At the end of August 1939, with the international situation deteriorating rapidly, HMC Ships *Ottawa, Fraser,* and *St. Laurent* were at anchor in Vancouver harbour. It had been planned that all ships be at Esquimalt to carry out their full calibre firings, but the minister of National Defence ruled otherwise. *Restigouche* was at Esquimalt for some minor repairs, while the crew of *Ottawa* was busy issuing identity discs, fitting gas masks, and filling lewis gun magazines.

On Friday morning, 1 September 1939, the commanding officers of *Fraser* and *St. Laurent* were sent for by the captain (D) in *Ottawa*. After some discussion they returned to their ships, and in a few minutes both vessels were the scene of considerable activity. Smoke poured from the funnels, awnings were furled, boats hoisted and booms and gangways were secured for sea. Roughly two hours and forty-five minutes after receiving their orders, HMC Ships *Fraser* and *St. Laurent* sailed for Halifax with despatch. They arrived in time for HMCS *St. Laurent* to form part of the escort for Convoy HX 1 which sailed from Halifax on 16 September 1939. It says much for the efficiency of both ships, especially in their boiler and engine rooms, that they were able to make this long sea passage, chiefly in tropical waters, so quickly. In fact it is a record which has yet to be broken.

Ottawa sailed for Esquimalt early on Saturday, 2 September 1939. At noon orders were received to "Prepare for War." By 1600 that day both *Ottawa* and *Restigouche* were reported ready. Much had been achieved already through careful planning and foresight.

At 1713 on Friday, 1 September, the following signal had been received from Naval Service Headquarters. It read:

"IMMEDIATE."

"From; NSHQ [Naval Service Headquarters]
To   C. [Commander-in-Charge] Esquimalt 812, C. [Commander-in-Charge] Halifax 613, (R) Admiralty, S.O. [Staff Officer] (I) Kingston [Jamaica], C in A.&W.I. [Commander-in-Chief America and West Indies (Station)] 685.
R.C.N. Has been placed on active service today 1st September. Reserves are being called up as necessary.

1254

And so Canada's sea services went to war. From a low ebb following World War I, they had been rebuilt into an effective fighting force (see Table 1 p. 73 and the accompanying chart.) By September 1939 the mobilized strength of the RCN, RCNR, and RCNVR was 397 officers and 2,276 ratings. By the time the war was over some six years later, the Royal Canadian Navy was the third largest navy in the Allied cause, but that is another story.

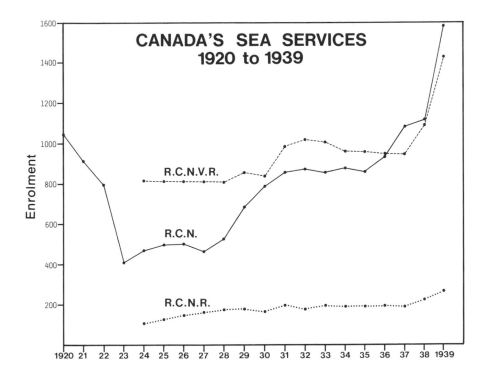

TABLE 1: RCN COMPLEMENT, INCLUDING RESERVES, SELECTED YEARS, 1918-39

		RCNa	RCNVR	RCNR	Total
15/2/1918	officers	275	427 b	8 c	710
	ratings	323	4417 b		4740
31/2/1924	officers	67	50	24	141
	ratings	385	764	81	1230
31/3/1937	officers	106	68	44	218
	ratings	977	879	144	2000·
31/3/1938	officers	114	106	54	274
	ratings	1196	1081	170	2447
31/3/1939	officers	129	113	67	309
	ratings	1456	1292	199	2947

a) Includes RCN personnel serving in RN.
b) RNCVR before 31 January 1923.
c) RNR members.

Source: *Annual Report of the Department of National Defence* (Chief of the Naval Staff) for the years listed.

Chapter 6

"BIG SHIP TIME": THE FORMATIVE YEARS OF RCN OFFICERS SERVING IN RN CAPITAL SHIPS

Richard H. Leir

In the fifty years of Canadian midshipmen training in the big ships of the Royal Navy, the dates 1 November 1914 and 24 May 1941 stand out as milestones. On the former date, at Coronel, HMS *Good Hope* blew up, taking with her four midshipmen—Cann, Hatheway, Palmer and Silver—the first Canadian casualties of World War I. In the Denmark Straits, on the latter date, HMS *Hood* exploded, killing three Canadian midshipmen, T.N.K. Beard, F.F.L. Jones, and S.J.B. Norman—the last RCN midshipmen casualties of World War II.[1] These two events largely encompass the time when all Canadian permanent force naval officers were required to serve in major units of the British fleet, peace or war notwithstanding. This period of training and indoctrination was commonly called "big ship time," with service performed by those in the rank of midshipman and, in some cases, by cadets.

A midshipman, as the term implies, was neither an officer nor a rating, but something between the two. Historically, it was a title used for "young gentlemen" in training at sea to qualify for service as commissioned officers. Until about 1720 midshipmen were, in theory, volunteers accepted aboard ship with a letter of service which led them to be called "king's letter boys." Traffrail and Bartimeus, the two prolific writers of sea stories of the nineteenth century, popularized the term "snotty" as a title for midshipmen. This term, originally one of endearment for twelve-year-old boys, did not sit well on the average nineteen-year-old Canadian with a five o'clock shadow, particularly when dropped from the condescending tongue of a baby-faced English lieutenant. But "snotty" describes very well indeed the condition of this naval aspirant: a king's letter boy shut up in the gun rooms of those huge engines of war, guided by a headmaster called the "snotty's nurse," taught seafaring academics in a steel-bound classroom by one or two commissioned school masters, and ruled by a school prefect called the sub of the gunroom. It was all very much a uniformed extension of the British public school system. The midshipman was an embryo in a very carefully supervised English naval incubator—the very womb of the British navy and the source of the Royal naval ethic.

"Get them young, treat them young, and you will have them forever," has been the axiom for the professions, whether cabinetmaker, medical intern, or articled student of law. It referred to the traditional method of cradling the aspirant, of developing the professional ethic, and of learning the practical skills. A midshipman's big ship time in the Royal Navy was one of character-moulding and training that had been refined for over two hundred years—a distillation of decades of experience in the production of dedicated, skilled, and disciplined seagoing officers. Officers were trained to man and lead one of the greatest instruments of imperial power in world history.

From 1910 to 1951 the Canadian government stocked this powerful incubator with young men selected from Tofino to Tatamagouche: young men to officer an unwanted naval service, the commissioned ranks of which seldom exceeded half the company of one of those big ships.

On 29 March 1909 George (later Sir George) Foster introduced a resolution in the Canadian House of Commons:

> That in the opinion of this House, in view of her great and varied resources, of her geographical position and national environments and that spirit of self help and self respect which alone befits a strong and growing people, Canada should no longer delay in assuming her proper share of the responsibility and financial burden incident to the suitable protection of her exposed coastlines and great sea ports.[2]

From this Foster Resolution came the Naval Service Act of 1910 and a naval service for Canada. But the service was a sickly creature. A country is unfortunate when the basic principles of its defence policy are included in the field of political party strife. The greater part of the history of the Royal Canadian Navy, from its inception in 1910 to unification in 1968, was one of a precarious existence through political contention. An army or an air force is generally rooted in the home soil, but a navy, particularly in this period, by its very existence forced its creators into the international arena. The milieu in which it operated focused the government's attention on offshore and foreign policies. Thus parliamentary debates on the birth and development of the Canadian navy called into question the Dominion's relations with England and the young nation's status within the Empire. The Naval Aid Bill of 1912 set in motion one of the longest, most implacable, and most famous debates since Confederation.[3] The debate hinged on whether to contribute money to build ships for the Royal Navy (Conservative), build a Canadian navy (Liberal), or do neither (Quebec). It was silenced by World War I with no decision having been made. The matter was not taken up in the postwar years, as concerns about disarmament dominated the 1920's and early 1930's, threatening the existence of the small Canadian military forces and culminating in the near demise of the RCN in 1933.

The tenuous nature of Canada's navy and the Admiralty's policy of one navy for the Empire predicated a training system that was interchangeable between the two services. The Canadians could be absorbed into the Royal Navy at any time should their careers in the RCN be terminated by political action. This policy was encouraged by the Canadian government to the extent that the administration and disciplinary detail of the King's or Queen's Regulations and Admiralty Instructions, and the Royal Naval Discipline Act governed the Canadian navy until well after World War II.

Such an uncertain climate made it very difficult for the naval service to offer a stable and promising future to a young Canadian. Yet, over the thirty years from 1910 to 1939 small numbers of aspirants came forward looking for naval careers. In which of the two navies these careers were to be was often in doubt. More often than not the young men came from a militarily oriented family of British extraction whose vision of the navy meant the Royal Navy and who might use the RCN as a back door to that service.

In 1933, in a small town in the Okanagan Valley of British Columbia, a twelve-year-old lad strongly stated his desire to join the Royal Navy. Without further enquiry, his father sent for the entrance examination for the Royal Naval College, Dartmouth, England. It was a disappointed pair who acknowledged the huge academic gap which existed between the Penticton Junior High School and the average English public school. There was no hope of joining *the* navy. There was no local knowledge of the Royal Canadian Navy until some mention was made of it in the Vancouver newspapers on the matter of its demise. An inquiry in Ottawa by Grote Stirling, member of Parliament for the Yale electoral district, confirmed that the service still existed and provided the necessary information on entrance and training for the boy. Current wisdom had it that the Canadian navy was second-best; however, since all training was done in the Royal Navy, one might enter into the real navy by this route.[4] There was considerable comfort to be had from the knowledge that, should the

RCN vanish by political magic, the young Canadian officer might continue his career in the Royal Navy.

The first naval institution in the country was the Royal Naval College of Canada at Halifax, an offshoot of the Royal Naval College, HMS *Osborne*, and later the RNC, Dartmouth. The RNCC was established in 1910 and was commanded and manned by Royal Naval personnel. Ten years later Admiral of the Fleet Viscount Jellicoe of Scapa suggested that it be renamed the Royal Canadian Naval College, but this was never done, and it closed its doors the following year. For the next two decades Canadian naval cadets were sent to England for training and indoctrination. They were between seventeen and twenty years old, had obtained a provincial matriculation, and successfully passed a civil service entrance examination and service interview. The civil service exam was a selection device to overcome the varying provincial educational standards and to choose from a short list of candidates for the limited intake of the 1930's. The successful applicants joined the Royal Navy's special entry system with other young men from the English public schools and from similar backgrounds in Australia, New Zealand, and India. The cadets spent twelve to sixteen months in the training ships HMS *Erebus* and HMS *Frobisher* before going to sea as midshipmen. A Canadian officer normally spent about five of his first years' service with the Royal Navy, a sizable proportion of the formative period of a young man's life.

When the Royal Canadian Naval College re-opened in October 1942 at HMCS *Royal Roads* in Esquimalt, British Columbia, this training was reduced to three and one-half years. Canadian midshipmen's big ship time ceased in 1951, and the technical training of acting sub-lieutenants commenced in Canada four years later.

It is not the object of this chapter to discuss the merits of the Canadian policy of casting its naval service in the British naval image for so long a period, nor whether the immersion in and absorption of the Royal Navy ethic was suitable character training for Canadian naval officers. Unlike the Canadian army and air force, the navy continued to train a key group of officers in the Royal Navy throughout World War II in the traditional way. Had the service returned to its prewar size, this cadre would have sufficed, but the need to expand the postwar officer corps with a larger number of wartime home-trained officers produced a peculiar schism in the wardrooms of the fleet. Cadet/midshipmen training came to be considered "the club" in the RCN. Initiation to the club was via big ship time in the Royal Navy.

The remainder of this chapter is devoted to a description of Royal Navy training and indoctrination for midshipmen. What follows is a series of vignettes recalled from the lost journal of a Canadian midshipman serving in the battleship HMS *Prince of Wales* during 1941. These experiences are typical of a midshipman's big ship wartime service in the Royal Canadian Navy.

    As service in the cadet training ship drew to a close, their lordships of the Admiralty asked the new midshipman what class of big ship he would like to serve in. This unexpected courtesy elicited considerable discussion among the ten Canadian cadets of the graduating term. Some felt that smaller ships were better, and asked for "D"-class cruisers knowing that they were stationed in the Far East Station and that there would be leave in Canada for those who went to join them. But this midshipman wanted to serve with the biggest guns and asked for the largest and newest, a "King George V"-class battleship. For the only time in his long career he got what he asked for: HMS *Prince of Wales*. But alas, as the great day approached, she was bombed in her building berth and her commissioning was delayed. He got instead a one-month "pier head jump" into the battleship HMS *Nelson*.[5]

    It was getting late on a cold November evening when the launch from HMS *Nelson* came alongside the old depot ship *Dunlace Castle* at Scapa Flow, the great naval base in the Orkney Islands. It had been a long train journey the length of the British Isles and some hours since the young midshipman had disembarked from the Thurso Ferry after a very rough passage across the Pentland Firth. Nonetheless, he was bubbling with excitement and anticipation at boarding his first ship. As he climbed the long ship's ladder up the high steel side he made frantic efforts to remember the correct procedure for an officer joining his ship. He stood alone for some time on the great quarterdeck looking about for the officer of the watch until rescued by a midshipman, who led him off through a labyrinth of passageways to the gunroom. He had not spoken a word of his carefully memorized joining procedure. The gunroom was crowded as this ship carried more than thirty midshipmen, but none took much notice of the new arrival save the one other Canadian midshipman. Hearty greetings were exchanged, for they had been to school together on the West Coast.

    His Gieves tin trunk had been delivered to the "chest flat," but as there were no spare chests for the transient, the midshipman was obliged to live out of his metal box and sling his hammock in a nearby passageway. As instructed he reported to the senior midshipman for his duties—understudying others in various parts of the huge ship seemed to be his principal occupation. However, as the junior midshipman aboard, one very special duty fell to him, that of running a bath for the senior sub-lieutenant at 1800 hours sharp, except when the great man had a dog watch, "then add or subtract fifteen minutes, snotty!"

The seven RN and one RCN midshipmen looked down into the dry dock at Birkenhead at the scurry of activity around the port side aft of the huge hull of the battleship HMS *Prince of Wales.* Great steel blocks shaped like squares of chocolate two feet on an edge and fifteen inches thick littered the bottom of the dock. This was her side armour plate being "buttoned back on" after structural repairs had been made to her bomb-damaged frame. The group of young gentlemen, now old hands of some two months experience, reported on board to find themselves the sum total of the ship's gunroom. There were eight midshipmen in quarters designed for twenty or more—there were even bunks in the chest flat—but the young men were soon ordered out of these luxuries by the sub of the gunroom. As midshipmen they must sleep in hammocks like the ratings; only officers slept in bunks. Throughout the short life of the ship the gunroom never held more than twelve midshipmen, with one Canadian in a ship's company of fifteen hundred.

The senior lieutenant-commander, usually passed over for promotion to commander, was known as the first lieutenant and was usually designated "snotty's nurse." Some took great interest in the training of the young gentlemen, while others found it a bore and an unwanted additional duty. The snotty's nurse in this ship was of the latter mind. One of the few survivors of the battleship HMS *Royal Oak,* he always seemed vague and distant to the midshipmen. On the other hand, the senior sub-lieutenant or sub of the gunroom was *keen,* too keen by half in the opinion of the midshipmen.

The battleship was commissioned soon after the eight mids arrived and settled into their duties. In harbour, four kept watches on the quarterdeck while four operated the ship's boats. These two major duties were alternated about every two months. At sea, four kept watch on the bridge while four were closed up in the weapons control systems. These sea and harbour watches were superimposed on a schedule of formal classroom instruction. In addition, each midshipman had a permanent fighting or action station and was attached to a division of men usually made up of the crews of his action station. Finally, midshipmen were assigned positions about the ship for special manoeuvres, such as entering and leaving harbour, fuelling at sea, or launching and recovering aircraft, where they could learn or be instructed in the special skills of these activities.

The Canadian's action station was in the foremost 14-inch gun turret in surface action. He was also officer of the quarters of the eight-barrelled "pom-pom" on the turret roof in anti-aircraft action, part of the fo'c's'le or foredeck crew for special manoeuvres, and attached to the fo'c's'le division of about two hundred men for personnel administration. The equipment on this part of the ship was massive. Her anchors weighed ten tons; each link of its steel cable weighed thirty pounds. There were eight-inch towing wires, four-inch berthing wires, two huge electric cable windlasses, and forty-pound carpenter stoppers. But there was lots of manpower and room to handle the gear, for she had a long graceful fo'c's'le and a huge beam to carry the great gun turrets and armour.

"Snotty, go aft and tell the commander that I think we have gone aground." The battleship was being manoeuvred by tugs in a January fog downstream from Birkenhead. Her destination was the safer dockyard at Rosyth in Scotland. Only two of her four screws were fitted; the other two great bronze wheels were lashed on the quarterdeck.

The midshipman jumped off the huge bollard, where he had been with the fo'c's'le officer staring down into the murky waters, and fled down the long deck. He nipped into the great armoured superstructure tower, up four decks of iron ladders, and panted to a stop in front of the brass hat and shining telescope. The square face went red, the tongue lashed, and the midshipman flew up another set of ladders with his bad news to the captain. Cold looks and a further message in a voice of disdain sent the young gentleman back to the brass hat and telescope. More invective and some curt advice for the fo'c's'le officer propelled the snotty back up the long foredeck, completing the "chain of command." Messengers of the gods are not a happy breed, but this was a common duty for midshipmen, and it provided ideal exposure to the art of the pungent phrase delivered in telling and measured tones.

A warship bridge or compass platform does not expand, as one would expect, in direct proportion to the size of the vessel. Thus the bridges of large destroyers, cruisers, or battleships were more or less the same size. The battleship's bridge looked ridiculously small for the size of the ship and, unlike most current warships, was fully enclosed, electrically heated, and armoured against flak. Two officers and a midshipman stood watch on the compass platform at sea in war. The principal control officer, usually a lieutenant-commander had the duty to fight the ship, if surprise attack occurred, with the weapon systems that were manned by the cruising watch; the officer of the watch had the standard duties of ship safety, navigation, and ship routine; and the midshipman had duties which were somewhat ill-defined. Primarily he was there to learn the duties of officer of the watch, but he had a number of menial tasks: writing up the log, chivvying up the lookouts, and most important, making the kye. Kye was a cocoa concoction made of unsweetened black chocolate, sugar, and canned milk melted into a thick dark semi-liquid. Hot and sweet, it was the British equivalent of the ubiquitous American cup of coffee. A midshipman of the watch was judged by his kye, and he had to know his watchkeeping team's tastes of thick or thin, sweet or bland, light or dark. Wherever a kye cup was placed, it left an indelible brown ring—on charts, signal files, and ship's logs—much to the chagrin of the navigating officer, who held all midshipmen responsible for the condition of his precious charts and logs.

"How about some kye, snotty?" and "What's that smell of burning?" The officer of the watch's remark was directed into the darkness of the compass platform at the midshipman of the watch. In the silence of the middle watch, the midshipman had been dozing on his feet, leaning unnoticed against one of the electric radiators. He came to and scuttled to the back of the bridge to an enclosed cabinet and commenced the ceremony of making the "pusser's cocoa." In the dim red light he perceived a neat ten-inch square burned into the side panel of his beautiful calf-length greatcoat. The greatcoat was the most expensive item in his uniform inventory: replacement would be comparatively simple; meeting the staggering cost would not. Like all his fellow officers, he was firmly in the clutches of Mr. Gieves, the famous London naval tailor. This one-sided partnership was formed very early and would last the whole of his naval career.

Back in Penticton, British Columbia, hard on the heels of the official brown envelope announcing his acceptance into the RCN, had come another official-looking document from Mr. Gieves. It demanded, on a comprehensive form, the exact measurements of the new cadet and gave a list of the complete kit and instructions as to how his parents would pay for it. The parents complied with these instructions believing them to be an official Admiralty order. Upon arrival in London the new cadet was fitted-out, then posed for a portrait photograph which was sent to his proud parents, and the cost was added to the cadet's account. It was a very smooth and efficient marriage. Although the original uniforms and equipment were provided by the parents, the upkeep came from the midshipman's pocket. This usually came in the form of a monthly allotment to Mr. Gieves of one or two pounds—10 to 20 per cent of his pay. Mr. Gieves had his measurements and the best naval intelligence system of the war. He seemed to know where all the Royal and Commonwealth warships were operating and who was serving in their gunroom and wardrooms. A short note to these excellent outfitters brought forth any item of clothing or adornment of the best quality. Vital warship stores and mail might go astray and be lost forever, but packages and statements of account from Mr. Gieves always seemed to arrive aboard anywhere in the world.[6]

Second only to Mr. Gieves in the efficient clothing of a midshipman was the firm of Collars Limited. Starched white collars, detachable from a white shirt, were mandatory dress for midshipmen. Whereas the shirt could and did remain unwashed for many days unnoticed, a soiled collar brought an instant rebuke. Four or five dozen collars were required in order to maintain this rigid standard of dress. These came in one-dozen lots in stout cardboard boxes already labelled and postage prepaid. When the collars were soiled, they were dispatched by mail to a remarkably efficient laundry somewhere in England known as Collars Limited. It was said to be run by retired Maltese stewards. Frayed or broken articles were replaced as part of the service which ran at about four cents per collar. These packages also appeared to arrive aboard with greater regularity than news from home.

" 'A' turret's gunhouse, magazine and shellroom crew, close up to the drill." The shrill bosun's call and the bosun's slow west-country accent sounded through the schoolroom, and the midshipman closed his navigation books and left his messmates to the drone of the "schoolie" lieutenant-commander to join the drilling of the gun crews of his surface action station. This was the largest gun turret afloat anywhere in the world, weighing as much as a modern destroyer and taking about the same number of crew to man it. Four 100-ton, 14-inch rifles were set in a steel barn of a gunhouse which had 12-inch armour plate on the sides and face and 8-inch plate on the roof. The whole swivelled in a cylindrical armoured barbette that reached down to the 15-inch armoured side belt around the magazines and shell rooms. Each gun was served by a mechanical cage which ran down six decks on wire cables to the magazines and shellroom. Each cage carried a 1-ton shell and two 4-foot silk bags of cordite propellant. The great breech block, like a very thick bank vault door, opened electrically, and the breech was automatically cooled by a fine spray of water after each round. The cage lined up behind the barrel; a mechanical chain-rammer pushed the shell firmly in with enough force to seat the metal driving band on the skin of the projectile into the rifling of the gun. Then it gently pushed the two silk bags of propellant in behind it. The cage was lowered for reloading, the breech block was closed, and the gun was elevated from the level loading position sufficiently to hit the target. All these and many other mechanical movements had to unfold automatically in the correct sequence. They were controlled by 120 mechanical interlocks to prevent a gun smash of prodigious proportions. This gun turret was the *raison d'etre* for man's largest mechanical war machine, and it represented the epitome of the age of the gun.

At the right hand of the gunhouse in a small steel cabinet sat the officer of the turret and beside him a midshipman. With the aid of an armoured periscope, the latter's duties were to "spot" the huge white splashes that climbed slowly to the height of 100 feet around the target, as each projectile struck the water. These white sheets of water were seen as over or short, left or right of the target at a distance of fifteen miles from his turret position. With the aid of a simple mechanical computer in the cabinet and the 30-foot range-finder across the back of the turret, the two officers could fight the turret independently of the main fire-control system. This was the midshipman's surface action station, and, somewhat like a submariner, he viewed the outside world through a periscope, surrounded by thick cold steel. The roar and bang of the huge machinery in that barn-like structure could all but mute the shuddering crump of a broadside. It would be felt rather than heard even out on the exposed decks. Two 1-ton shells could be hurled twenty miles by each of the four guns every minute; the midshipman would never again control such awesome fire power.

Seamanship was the prime subject in the midshipman's curriculum. At the end of his big ship time he would be required to face a seamanship board, held in another ship before a strange body of officers. It was the first of a series of exams for the rank of lieutenant. The subject embraced a wide range of shipboard knowledge: the organization of the domestic and watchkeeping life of the crew; the construction, stability, and maintenance of the hull with its system of water pumps for flooding and the control of fire; the operation of all the standing and running rigging and of the anchor and ground tackle; and the use and handling of sail and motor boats. In addition, the midshipman was expected to have mastered the conventional subjects of knots, splices, pilotage, and ship handling, all to the cadence of a specialized naval language, rich in vigour, vividness and humour.

The art of seafaring was a subject that a sailor never stopped learning, and some of the early lessons came hard. The *Admiralty Manual of Seamanship* states that "A coxswain must be careful never to let his boat get between the ship and the mooring buoy"—sober advice for a young midshipman.

A stiff March wind was blowing through the islands of Scapa Flow as the battleship approached her mooring buoy in the darkness. The ten-ton bower anchor had been removed from its hawse pipe and "catted" so that it hung from the foredeck level, its huge crown within two feet of the water. Through the empty hawse pipe, the great anchor cable hung with a forty-pound mooring shackle buttoned on to its last link. Swinging out on its davits near midships, a thirty-two-foot wooden cutter of twelve oars and no engine hung close to the water. The midshipman in command gripped the tiller and looked up the towering steel side, straining to hear, above the wind and the roar of the boiler room exhaust fans, the next order from the boat's officer.

"Slip." The cutter with its fourteen-man crew and two "buoy jumpers" dropped with a great splash to be towed forward by a rope passing through the eyes of the ship and pulled by fifteen men on the fo'c's'le deck. Its destination was a fat Admiralty pattern buoy, fifteen feet long by eight feet in diameter. Again, "slip," this time ordered by the midshipman in the boat, and the towrope was let go. The timing was right, for the boat's momentum would carry them to the buoy without having to get out the cumbersome oars. Time was short, for the battleship was coming downwind fast on both buoy and cutter. The two buoy jumpers scrambled up the steel curve of the buoy from their place in the bow of the boat now alongside the far side of the buoy. They snapped a great hook on the end of a four-inch steel wire rope to the ring of the buoy. But as the ship began to override the buoy, the wire pulled taut, the buoy rotated, sweeping the cutter around and pinning it against the crown of the catted anchor. Forty-thousand tons inched down on the buoy and the imprisoned boat. The massive anchor swung inwards under the flare of the battleship's bow, its crown creeping up the cutter's side now cracking and groaning under the strain.

"Now sur, we must all get under the thwarts." The quiet west-country drawl of the veteran petty officer gave the midshipman beside him his cue, and the order was given to the crew. Even as they pressed down on the boat's bottom, the huge anchor splintered through the wooden side, swinging across the boat above their heads. At that moment a sixteen-year-old seaman leaped up in panic for the buoy. The great pendulum caught him against the buoy, crushing out his life with a short sharp sigh. The petty officer scooped the body into the boat as it fell back with the return swing of the anchor. The battleship backed off the buoy, and the battered boat swung clear. High above them a white smudge of a face and a flashlight ordered "All right snotty, get back aft for hoisting." It took half an hour with the six remaining oars to manoeuvre the waterlogged boat and its frightened crew to the davits for hoisting. As the boat swung up to deck level the brass hat and telescope standing in the murk said quietly, "If you are all right, snotty, go and shift into dry clothing and report back to me." Then the petty officer gripped the young gentleman's oil-skinned elbow. "Come on, sur, we'll get warmed up." A tot of pusser's rum from the petty officers' mess brought peace to a quaking stomach and some strength for the subsequent inquiry.

"This is the hew pee and will be your air defence station, sur. No one aboard has seen her fired, but I'm told she's Mr. Churchill's secret weapon." The chief gunner's mate and the midshipman were standing on the turret roof looking at a steel reproduction of the common outhouse, complete with a small glass window but no crescent moon carved in the door. Welded to each side of the structure were twenty-four tubes at a fixed elevation of seventy degrees. The whole was mounted on a turntable and could be trained from beam to beam, by the single occupant of the throne inside. In each three-inch tube lay the predecessor of the inter-continental ballistic missile, a three-foot rocket which contained a parachute attached to 1,000 feet of piano wire ending in a large grenade. This was the weapon—the unrifled projectile, or UP. The control system was situated in the highest manned position on the forward superstructure. There sat a small steel tea cup from the floor of which rose a six-foot steel fence post. Mounted on the top of the post were the butts of two double-barrelled shotguns, each complete with twin triggers and set shoulder-width apart. Between the butts was an open ring-sight fixed at an elevation of seventy degrees. Sight and gun butts could be trained from beam to beam, the movement being transmitted to the weapon which followed the sight. Each of the four triggers fired twelve rockets. This was the midshipman's air defence station—command and control of a two-man missile defence system, at the height of the gun age!

The UP was the brainchild of Sir Winston Churchill and was designed to be a static defence against the Stuka dive bomber. Its modus operandi was simple. The dive bomber, with its single 500-pound bomb, dove on its target at the fixed angle of seventy degrees. Once committed to the dive, it could not take avoiding action without throwing off its aim. The UP controller simply laid his sight on the approaching aircraft and fired his missile salvos at the moment the plane tipped into its dive. A curtain of piano wire, armed with lethal grenades and suspended from parachutes, was thrown up in the path of the oncoming aircraft.

The system had been a great success in the defence of the city of Dover, bringing down many enemy aircraft. Rumour had it that Churchill had insisted that his pet weapon be fitted in his latest battleship as she completed her building. Thus the UP replaced the original eight-barrelled pom-pom which had been planned for the class.

"UP fire when ready." The order from the air defence officer rang in the midshipman's headphones; his great moment had come. The battleship was exercising in the Flow, steaming slowly with two escorting destroyers. The target, in a clear April sky, was a yellow smoke-burst put up by one of her guns. The yellow blob sailed into the ring sight and, like a good son of the West, the midshipman let 'em have it with both hands. No one was quite prepared for the subsequent blinding flash and smoke as twenty-four missiles screamed into the air. The midshipman was delighted to see the parachutes blossom all about the smoke target—a virtual wire fence in the sky.

Moments later a signal lamp clattered angrily from the bridge of the port escorting destroyer. "WT aerials destroyed by wire, stop. Live grenade on my quarterdeck, stop. Permission to return to harbour, ends." Due to irregular burning of the propellant, or mutual interference, two of the missiles had careened off at right angles over the destroyer!

"Snotty, you will take charge of a paint party and clean up that filthy mess *your* rockets made of my paint work." And filthy it was, with acres of paint on the turret top and the bridge superstructure black and blistered. The missiles were never fired again, and the eight-barrelled pom-pom was returned to its planned position some two months later.

Included in the "care and feeding" of midshipmen was a measure of exposure to social functions, so that the young gentlemen would fit smoothly into all social occasions as they represented their country and the navy around the world. The Canadian was not exempt.

"Done any hunting, Canada?" The question came from the gun turret officer now in his native Scotland. "Oh yes, sir," replied the midshipman thinking of his few victories over deer and even a bighorn sheep once, high in the interior of British Columbia. "Well, you will be coming home with me to a hunt ball next Friday, and we'll do some hunting on Saturday." This was an order as much as an invitation, for the lieutenant was the midshipman's divisional officer, and like the best of the Royal Navy officers he took a keen interest in "his mid."

A short train ride north from Edinburgh brought the two to a quaint granite station; then they travelled by car to a modest country house. It was an enjoyable time; scotch, drambuie, and highland dancing made up a very energetic evening. The young gentleman was not allowed to stand and watch but was scooped into the whirling groups where his slight knowledge of square dancing and a good deal of scotch made for a joyful and unique experience. It was a heady mixture to wake up from.

"I expect a young fellow from the West will need a strong horse," said the host as the two stood in the stable yard early next morning. The lieutenant wore jodhpurs, hacking jacket, and ratcatcher, while the midshipman was dressed in grey flannels, Canadian windbreaker, and field-training boots! Mustering all of his little trail-riding knowledge of horsemanship he climbed up the huge mare and into a "pancake" saddle— no horn, and short thin stirrups. He was hunting; or, more correctly, the horse was hunting and the rider was following. At the first wail of the horn she was off with the leaders over the low stone walls of that countryside. They managed two jumps in company, but at the third, she jogged a bit left, and he went right and into the soft earth. She waited impatiently for him to remount, then tried to make up for lost time. They parted company once more before the midshipman noticed the very young and old taking the gates through the walls rather than jumping over them. He persuaded the reluctant mare to join those sensible riders. "No, snotty, that is shooting. This is hunting. We really must educate you colonials."

"Now you two snots will have breakfast with the captain on Tuesday morning, be bright and cheerful so that the rest of the ship's company won't suffer," said the sub of the gunroom. Why breakfast? Why not tea or lunch? No amount of research has uncovered the origin of this peculiar, but common, practice in the Royal Navy. It has been touted as a terrifying experience by some midshipmen, but it was not on this particular occasion, for the captain of the battleship had an easy charm. He had been a first-class athlete and a navy squash and tennis champion as well as being a very keen fisherman.

At seven o'clock in the morning the two midshipmen were ushered into what seemed to be palatial quarters. A smart steward showed them to the breakfast table set with immaculate napery. They sat in silence, then quite suddenly the captain appeared with a signal log in his hand. He viewed the two for a moment saying, "Ah! midshipmen for breakfast," as though they were on the menu, then added, "Our resident Canadian, too." A silence fell as they attacked their meal, then "Where in Canada is your home? Ah, let's see, where is that? Oh, on the Pacific side. How's the fishing there?" The midshipman sprang into the silence with his best story of landing, at age eleven, with the aid of an uncle, a sixty-two pound Tyee salmon which was about the same weight as the boy at the time. "A sixty-two pound salmon, snotty?" choked this accomplished fisherman in disbelief. "Oh, ah! really. . . !" The midshipman addressed his egg in embarrassed silence. Later, as the two clattered down the ladders to the gunroom, the breakfast companion remarked, "What a fish story you spun the old man, I didn't believe it either, you black troops certainly try it on."

RPC Dinner 1900 WSB—the message read from HMS *Hood*.[7] The three Canadian midshipmen in the flagship of the battleship squadron were "pushing the boat out" to their fellow countrymen in the ships around the anchorage at Scapa Flow.

In due course, HMS *Hood*'s big steam picket boat came alongside. This was the last of the steam picket boats in the fleet and the pride of her ship. The tall brass funnel gave off a heat haze, warming the backs of the midshipmen as they stood behind a brass-bound dodger, one at the helm, the other at the engine room telegraph. Below and behind them, from a small engine room hatch, the stoker petty officer thrust his head, ignoring the telegraph orders. He gauged the movement of the boat, making his own engine adjustments to bring her smartly alongside. Beneath him the beautiful miniature triple-expansion steam engine glowed in all its brassy splendor. Each midshipman cast an envious glance as they stepped into the commodious cabin beautifully decorated with coachwork and smelling of polished mahogany. This was the real picket boat of the stories from Traffrail and Bartimeus. She even had a fitting for a 6-pounder gun in her bows.

Most gunrooms had two levels of society, the junior and the senior midshipmen. One graduated to the senior level after about one year's service, stepping into the shoes of the term that left at the end of their big ship time. Thus, each year a new group of midshipmen joined the gunroom. A Saturday night mess dinner usually excluded most junior midshipmen to make room for those who had been invited on board. So it was on this night that some fifteen hosts sat down with their guests. The sub of the gunroom was always mess president and ruled the dinner with an iron hand. He was a paragon of naval etiquette, and his duty was to teach the young gentlemen. This he did, with many strange punishments for misconduct during the meal: one could take one's dinner off the imitation mantlepiece; sit cross-legged on the deck; or hang inverted from the overhead pipes. But all returned to their places for the round of port and toasts. Then out "dogs-of-war," and the guests were obliged to climb out of a big brass scuttle in the ship's side, hang by their fingertips to the upper deck, work their way along to the next scuttle and return inboard. Many physical games followed, such as "where are you Moriarity?" in which two blindfolded contestants crawled about the deck searching for each other by sound while armed with rolled-up newspaper clubs. Trials of strength and liquid consumption were standard postprandial fare, each visiting midshipman representing his ship and feeling honour bound to guard its reputation.

These physical contests could ruin one's best uniform and evening shirt. The problem was solved somewhat by recourse to "Australian Rig." Doffing the monkey jacket revealed a special gunroom mess dinner shirt. The fighting garment consisted of two starched cuffs, no sleeves and a cut-out dicky front and collar, the remainder of the torso being bare. It was altogether ideal for gunroom games.

It was calm and dark on this May evening as the midshipman's boat pulled away from the long graceful hull of the flagship, her tall tripod main mast outlined against the stars of a rare clear Scapa night.

"I'll get you over when we all get back," the midshipman had said to his three hosts on parting; for the battle squadron had come to immediate notice for sea.

The midshipman had been at his action station in the big gun turret since midnight, but now, just before six in the morning, the enemy came into the periscope sight. First their two sets of battletops, then the handsome rakish hulls of the German warships with their ripple of gun flashes. His guns-ready lamp winked on, the fire gong tinkled, and the turret rocked as the first broadside let go. HMS *Hood* on the port bow was out of his line of vision, but two small alterations to port by the battleship brought her almost into view. The midshipman's attention was on "spotting" the great white shell splashes when suddenly an orange reflection grew across his sight, followed by tumbling, burning debris and a great falling tripod mast. Jerking the periscope a little to his left he saw the *Hood*'s long graceful foredeck canted up out of a towering pall of smoke. The great ship vanished in a maelstrom, sweeping her three young Canadian midshipmen down into the still darkness. Then the warning rattler for his fall of shot sounded, jarring his attention back to the enemy and the job at hand.

Admiralty Form S. 519 (revised March 1927), "Journal for the Use of Midshipmen," has the following notes on its cover:

1. The Journal is to be kept during the whole of a Midshipman's seatime.
2. The Officer detailed to supervise instruction of Midshipmen will

see that the Journals are kept in accordance with these instructions. He will initial the Journal at least once a month and will see that they are written up from time to time during the month not immediately before they are called in for inspection.

3.   The Captain will have the Journals produced for his inspection from time to time.

4.   (i) The objects of keeping a Journal are to train Midshipmen in—
        (a) The power of observation
        (b) The power of expression
        (c) The habit of orderliness

5.   The Journal is to be produced at the examination in seamanship for the rank of Lieutenant when marks to a maximum of fifty will be awarded for it.

The heavy green line-bound ledger was the drudge of a midshipman's life, particularly if he did not possess the gift of penmanship. The Admiralty charged the young gentleman four shillings and sixpence for this burden, half a day's pay after pension deductions. Many dreary hours were spent by the midshipman trying to match the writing skills of the graduates of the British public school system. He was never able to close this gap in his education, and thus his journal became a record of tart remarks written in pencil by the snotty's nurse. This officer was something of a literary man, known to write verse. Such exhortations appeared as "this is a journal, not a signal pad; make your writing flow" or an ink-blotched page "more thought, less ink" or again "more and better sketches, please."

Sketches or diagrams were required twice a month. Line diagrams of ship's equipment and hull layout were acceptable, but the captain and the snotty's nurse came to expect interesting and even artistic pen sketches. To those in the gunroom who had such skills the journal was a ticket to the good life. The less accomplished would pay well for a supply of sketches. The currency, as with most transactions in the gunroom, was the midshipman's wine bill—ten shillings a month for juniors, fifteen for seniors. No spirits were allowed, only wine and beer, with the latter not often available because of the difficulty of storage. So, sherry was the gunroom drink. At four cents a glass, the average consumption was about two a day if you didn't entertain a guest. Duty watches and journal sketches were bought and sold with this medium of exchange.

Situated below the gunroom, abaft the heavy side armour and on the waterline, was the midshipman's chest flat. This space, with its row of neat four-drawer chests and rack of lashed hammocks, was the young gentleman's dormitory and dressing room. All his clothes and possessions had to fit into the chest.

An 8-inch shell from an enemy cruiser drilled a neat hole at the waterline in the unarmoured side plating, passing through the chest flat and exploding in the wardroom wine store next door. The blast reduced the two spaces to a shambles, and the sea, slopping into the shell-hole, reduced the remains to a soggy pulp. The midshipman's hated journal perished along with two sketches, unused, but dearly paid for.

"Away the first motor boat. Starboard crew, man your boat." Whether in the schoolroom, his hammock, or at meals, the midshipman of the boat's crew dropped everything, donned oilskins, and reported to the officer of the watch for his running instructions. Once they were received, he went forward to the boat boom. Thrusting out from each side of the ship was a pair of tree-sized wooden spars to which the boats were attached by painters when not in use. In a good chop, a standard condition in Scapa Flow, the midshipman had to run out along the spar and make his way down a rope ladder which was loosely secured to the bow and which thrashed wildly as the boat surged in the swell. It was a common sight to see a figure in heavy-weather gear dangling by his hands from the boom, his sea booted feet vainly seeking the rungs of the whipping rope ladder.

Boat running, as it was called, was one of the major harbour duties of the big ship midshipman. Current wisdom held that there was no better training for young gentlemen than lots of boatwork, and, as these big ships seldom went alongside, there was always much to-ing and fro-ing to be done from the anchorage. The number and variety of harbour boats differed from one class of capital ships to another. This new battleship carried two forty-five-foot, triple diesel, fast picket boats and a pair of thirty-five-foot fast motor boats—one for the captain and one for the admiral. The latter two boats were never manned by midshipmen, as they were too beautifully kept to be misused by amateurs.

On a normal day, one picket boat and one launch were on duty, each with a pair of crews doing a twenty-four-hour, day-on, day-off routine. It could be a long day if traffic was heavy, as it usually was when it came to satisfying the transportation needs of a community of fifteen hundred souls.

To the midshipman, it was an interesting and varied duty. He got away from the great hierarchy of the ship to his own small command where he could do a little thinking of his own. "A ship is known by her boats" goes an old naval maxim, and no amount of funnel grime and salt from the North Sea patrols would lower the peacetime standards of this ship's boats, according to the boats' officer. Thus the midshipman came in for considerable tongue-lashings, from above and below, as the amount of "scrubbing out" and making the boat look "tiddly" rose in direct proportion to the ship's operational commitments.

Tact became an abiding necessity for the mid of the boat. Tact was certainly required in handling a launch full of rowdy, belligerent liberty men coming off canteen steps at closing time and in handling superior would-be passengers from the officers' landing, wishing to use the boat as a personal ferry service to every ship in the anchorage. Tact was also needed to deal with the endless advice by officer passengers who felt they were god's gift to boat handling. To bring a forty-five-foot boat to rest, at a three-foot-square platform, suspended on the end of a long flight of steps down a wall of steel, in choppy weather, took skill and judgment. Like the act of love, when it was done successfully it was a wonderful experience; when it was not, one was surely told about it.

The three battleships were hastily making ready for sea on a dark night when a message from the depot ship stated that there was mail awaiting collection. The sailing of the squadron would be delayed to allow the mail to be picked up. A picket boat left each ship to rush over the four miles in order to collect this valuable cargo. The course was strewn with other ships at anchor, strings of anti-torpedo nets and unlighted buoys as a strict blackout was enforced. Once loaded with better than sixty bags of mail, the return trip became a race between the three boats. The midshipman had the furthest to go but the fastest boat, and he pushed the three throttles through the gate. Suddenly, a two-foot-round buoy marking the end of an anti-torpedo net flashed under the planing bows. He had cut a corner too closely. The large boat leaped up, skidded sideways with a terrific impact on the hard chine bottom. The starboard engine screamed and stopped. The double-skinned mahogany hull was punctured, and the boat took on water. Using cotton waste the coxswain stemmed the in-rushing sea, holding the wad in place with both hands. By steaming very slowly, and with the midshipman pumping by hand, the boat just made her ship.

The rest of the squadron had sailed before the waterlogged boat with its wet cargo came alongside under the waiting crane and was hoisted. As he climbed down from his boat now on the deck the midshipman was confronted by the brass hat and telescope. "Snotty, you will relieve the mast head lookout, until further orders." It was a long, cold night.

Quarterdeck watchkeeping in harbour was the other major duty of a midshipman. He was to do whatever the officer of the watch wished him to do. His general instructions were to run the ship's routine. The ship's routine was the metronome that kept in time the multitude of activities that take place in the large community of a battleship: when to get up, when to eat, when and where to work, when to keep watch, and when to clean up the living spaces. Then there was the boat routine: send in the mail; get these stores aboard or that party ashore. A quartermaster with a bosun's call stopped or started all of these functions by first whistling for attention over a loudspeaker system, then pronouncing the activity in one of the many peculiar accents that comprise English in the British Isles. In addition, the midshipman was a general messenger for senior officers, since he was always available and could be reached by phone from anywhere in the ship. The mid of the watch was usually seen rushing up and down ladders, inside or outside the ship, with his badge of office, a battered telescope. This instrument, usually common gunroom property, had long since lost its capacity to allow clear vision, and was even known to be converted for carrying cigarettes and chocolate bars.

Nothing disturbed the smooth operation of the ship's routine more than the coming and going of senior officers. During the ceremonies of meet and greet, and of parting, all activities on the quarterdeck came to a halt, and the routine was delayed. Most visits by the brass were prearranged and could therefore be written into the routine. On these occasions the captain and commander were always informed by the mid of the watch when the visitors' boat appeared to be approaching. However, the midshipman in the visiting boat would often play hide-and-seek, to see how close he could get to the gangway without being spotted by the team on the quarterdeck. Unable to see from both sides of the huge deck at once, the young gentleman put in many miles not to be caught out by a cunning fellow midshipman from a rival ship. When this did occur the verbal blast from the officer of the watch usually started with "Where the hell have you been Snotty?"

The United States Navy cruiser had been secured alongside the battleship on an August morning as she lay at anchor in Placentia Bay, Newfoundland. There was above-average activity on the quarterdeck. Wooden ramps had been laid about the ship so that the President of the United States, Franklin Roosevelt, could be wheeled aboard to meet with the British Prime Minister, Winston Churchill. The midshipman had the afternoon watch when a personal note for the captain was delivered to the quarterdeck gangway from an accompanying Canadian destroyer. The mid of the watch was instructed to deliver it in person. The captain was taking tea with the president and the prime minister in the wardroom when the midshipman stepped discreetly in to pass the white envelope. At this moment there was a lull in the polite conversation, and the captain suddenly said, "Ah, Mr. President, may I introduce our captive North American?" The midshipman shook a firm hand. "Where are you from son?" asked the great man. Then, "Oh, great fishing country out there," when he heard the midshipman's answer. "Do you go after those big salmon?" The midshipman looked at the captain, and then replied that he had, but confined the next few minutes of fishing conversation with the president to the Kokanee of the Okanagan River.

Returning to his place of duty on the quarterdeck, the midshipman was greeted with the usual "Where the hell have you been, Snotty?" It seemed the moment to abide by the old naval adage of "Never explain, never complain."

Second only to his journal in the list of midshipman's penances came the navigation sight book. Mark St. Hilair was the patron saint of this activity and cosine-haversine formula his scourge. A midshipman was required to keep a sight book in which he recorded a designated number of astro-navigation sights taken and worked out at sea. Each sight was checked and signed by the schoolie, and the sight book was presented at the navigation examination for the rank of lieutenant. Before the advent of the computer and precomputed tables, the solution of each spherical triangle to obtain a fix from a heavenly body was found by simple mathematical tables. This was the Mark St. Hilair system—a cumbersome and time-consuming formulation requiring much interpolation of six-figure numbers from tomes called *Inman's Tables* and the *Nautical Almanac*. The work called for much addition and subtraction, and there was a great deal of room for foolish errors. The soporific effect of this exercise on a watch-weary midshipman in the stuffy schoolroom of a heaving warship was often overpowering. In addition, the correct conjunction of heavenly bodies, cloud cover, and off-watch time never seemed to occur in the North Atlantic, and the sight book remained unfilled as the time flew by. A clever young gentleman might steal the ship's position from the chart on the bridge, and work his sight backwards to come up with a suitable angle of elevation for an unseen star or planet. But this took more than an average knowledge of the science of astro-navigation, and the schoolie was a clever detective, always on the alert for such forgeries.

As the battleship rolled down the west coast of Africa and across the Indian Ocean, in her high-speed run to the Far East, the sun and stars shone constantly, and the horizon was a hard straight line. The sight book filled to the satisfaction of the schoolmaster and the relief of the midshipman.

Exhausted and oil-soaked survivors were packed everywhere on the destroyer's upper deck. A big leading seaman moved among them dispensing rum and brandy, rum for the men, brandy for the officers! Without his officer's cap, and in oil-soaked tropical rig, the midshipman had none of the distinguishing marks of an officer. "Are you an officer?" the grizzled Florence Nightingale enquired. "I'm a midshipman," choked the young gentleman, leaving the question unanswered. "Oh, you get rum," and down it went on top of the oil fuel. It dwelt a moment inside, then the whole horrid mess came up at the rush.

HMS *Prince of Wales* had gone, the victim of a Japanese aerial attack. She turned her acres of red bottom with the four bright bronze propellers momentarily to the blue Malayan sky, then plunged down taking the journal and sight book with her. How would he get another set of sights? What of the fifty marks for his journal? These pressing problems, together with his aching stomach, were the total concerns of the midshipman on that tenth day of December 1941.

In retrospect, it seems that the system of early training of Canadian naval officers described in this chapter had become archaic by the outbreak of World War II. By that time the existence of the RCN had become secure, and a home-grown officer could expect a full-time career serving in the Royal Canadian Navy. With the outbreak of hostilities, the other Canadian military services took immediate steps to produce useful combat officers in Canada, giving little thought to the long-range aspects of their respective permanent officer corps. After discontinuing big ship time with the RN in 1951 the RCN continued its own midshipman service until 1955. But try as it might the RCN was unable to create an environment in their cruisers and aircraft carriers similar to that which had prevailed in RN capital ships. Big ships became scarce in both navies, producing too many midshipmen and too few gunrooms. The need for higher education robbed the system of young men in those critical formative years between the ages of seventeen and twenty-one. The navy was unable to "get 'em young and keep 'em young" in a carefully controlled incubator. So midshipman service became a casualty of the small ship navy and higher education. The naval aspirant went from cadet to commission, foregoing a professional apprenticeship.

With the demise of big ship time went an unparalleled system of training and exposure of an embryo officer to the very critical relationship between officers and ratings. Living, learning, and fighting as a sort of "non-person" in the military hierarchy, the midshipman existed between the two worlds of the officer and the man, with a window into each. He could observe, at close range, the interaction of these worlds and develop, at an early age, the skills required to bind them together.

Chapter 7

AN ENGINEER'S OUTLINE OF RCN HISTORY: PART I

J.H.W. Knox

Naval engineering encompasses all the technical activities which define, develop, provide, operate, and support the fleet. A history of naval engineering in the RCN must concern itself with the succession of ship acquisitions, the use and maintenance of materiel, and the men who performed the engineering: the naval architects, marine and combat systems engineers and technicians—naval and civilian. Although this chapter is not a definitive history of RCN naval engineering, it, together with Chapter 18, provides a chronology of major events—principally the acquisition of ships.

The introduction of the Naval Service Act of 1910 brought forward a number of alternatives for the acquisition of a Canadian fleet. These included serious proposals for the construction of cruisers, destroyers, and lesser vessels in Canada.[1] Sir Wilfrid Laurier's government put forward one such proposal which called for the construction of four "Bristol"-class cruisers and six "River"-class destroyers in a Canadian shipyard in the remarkably short period of six years. Warship construction entailed the establishment of suitable building yards, since none existed in Canada, and the acceptance of higher costs compared with purchase from United Kingdom yards. Fortunately, the Admiralty had agreed, before the Naval Service Act was debated, to provide not only specifications and plans but also overseers and the benefit of the Admiralty's unrivalled experience in warship construction.

Laurier had earlier rejected a more cautious approach. This would have seen the first two ships of each type built in British yards while Canadian shipyard workers gained on-the-job experience in warship construction. At the same time, British shipyard workers were to have been attached to the Canadian yard in which the next ships were constructed with a progressively increased content of Canadian equipment. There is an interesting parallel between this scheme and the "Tribal"-class destroyer building programme of the 1940's in that both had "lead ships" constructed in the United Kingdom followed by the construction of the remainder in Canada.

Following the passage of the Naval Service Act, the Laurier government pursued a more ambitious proposal and had discussions with nineteen firms, including three in Canada—Collingwood Shipbuilding Co., Polson Iron Works, and the British Columbia Marine Railway Co. Six firms produced tenders, while a seventh mistakenly tendered on the basis of construction in Britain. The mean of the tenders for construction in Canada was $12.4 million, slightly less than one and a half times the British amount.

When Laurier was voted out of office a year and a half later, the contract negotiations for the warship building programme were still incomplete. His successor, Sir Robert Borden, wasted little time in arresting the domestic building plan. Having taken office in October 1911 and having consulted with Sir William White, a former director of naval construction at the Admiralty, Borden announced that the tenders for the projected warships would not be accepted and that all the deposits would be returned.

Although he quickly concluded that he did not want Laurier's programme, Borden took much longer deciding what his own would be. He accepted White's advice that Canada's naval effort be centred on armed merchant cruisers, defended bases useful to the Royal Navy, and arrangements for training naval personnel. White also recommended the gift of funds to Britain for the construction of battleships if Canada wanted to help meet the German naval threat. Borden, however, failed to act on these recommendations or to develop an alternative naval policy. Thus, when World War I broke out, Canada had only the merest skeleton of a navy despite five years of brave words, grandiose plans, and parliamentary rhetoric.

We may very well ask what would have happened to naval engineering in Canada if Laurier's plans for the establishment of a domestic Canadian warship building industry had come to fruition. Quite possibly, if Canada's naval industrial development had taken place during World War I, the nation might have been able to contribute significantly to the Allied naval effort. Certainly, when the explosion in shipbuilding activity did take place in Canada during World War II, it set the stage for more ambitious naval programmes in the Cold War era.

In the event, the Naval Service of Canada had distinctly modest beginnings. Two Royal Navy cruisers, *Niobe* and *Rainbow*, were transferred to the RCN in 1910, with the major portion of their ships' companies, and these vessels remained the sole elements of the fleet until the stimulus of World War I revived some Canadian interest and activity in naval expansion. Serving in *Niobe* and *Rainbow* were the RCN's earliest naval engineers. The first officer to join the Naval Service was Acting Engineer Sub-Lieutenant A.D.M. Curry. He was appointed to *Rainbow* on 10 August 1910, six days after the ship's commissioning in Portsmouth. Although a seaman officer, Acting Sub-Lieutenant E.G. Hallewell, was appointed to *Niobe* on that same day, that ship did not commission until the following month. Hallewell was joined in *Niobe* on her commission by Acting Engineer Sub-Lieutenant H.J. Napier-Hemy.

When *Niobe* reached Halifax, these pioneers were joined by Acting Engineer Sub-Lieutenants G.P. Clarke, A. Hollingsworth, F. Jefferson, and S.N. de Quetteville. The fate of this group was varied: Hollingsworth's naval career ended before World War I began; de Quetteville was killed in action on 31 May 1916 while serving in HMS *Indefatigable* at the Battle of Jutland; Napier-Hemy appears to have been released as "medically unfit" in the early 1920's after a colourful career which included service at Jutland in HMS *Colossus*; Clarke died in 1930 while still serving in the rank of engineer commander, having been appointed engineer overseer for the building of HMC ships *Skeena* and *Saguenay*; Curry and Jefferson having served throughout World War II, both retired in the rank of engineer captain.

In addition to these early pioneers, HMC Ships *Niobe* and *Rainbow* brought to Canada a number of engineers who elected to stay with the Naval Service on the completion of their loan service, and who were to have a remarkable influence on RCN engineering. Included in their ranks were Engineer Lieutenant John F. Bell, Artificer Engineer R.H. Wood, and Engine Room Artificers Richard "Dickie" Pearson and G.L. Stephens. Pearson, who had Royal Navy submarine experience, played a key role in the commissioning of Canada's World War I submarines, CC 1 and CC 2. Later, having retired from the RCN, he became a civil servant and ably assisted the senior naval engineer in Ottawa. Bell returned to the RN but came out of retirement in 1940, took up a position as assistant director of Naval Engineering Development in Naval Service Headquarters, and retired again from that position as an engineer captain toward the end of World War II. Wood was seconded from *Rainbow* in 1910 to become chief engineer, Esquimalt dockyard. He retired in July 1920 and as a civilian became manager of Halifax dockyard, retiring from that position in the mid-1930's. Stephens, having been promoted from engine room artificer (ERA) to artificer engineer in October 1912, rose steadily through the ranks to become the first technical officer to reach flag rank. This he achieved while serving as chief of Naval Engineering and Construction; once again as an ERA but this time as an engineer rear-admiral. From February 1941 until his retirement five years later, Stephens was responsible for the technical control and execution of all activities involved in the massive materiel expansion of the RCN during World War II. These responsibilities included naval shipbuilding and repair, the development of technical services, and the training of personnel to man both the shore support facilities and the technical departments of the fleet.

The first cadet-entry to the engineering ranks was A.C.M. Davy, who entered the Royal Naval College of Canada in August 1917. He served throughout World War II as director of Shipbuilding and completed his service in the rank of commodore (E[ngineering]) as engineer-in-chief during the construction of the St. Laurent-class destroyer escorts. (1949-56).

Another pioneer deserving mention is T.C. Phillips. First appointed as engineer lieutenant on loan from the Royal Navy to HMCS *Niobe* in February 1917, he was promoted and appointed consulting naval engineer at Naval Service Headquarters from August 1918. Promoted to engineer commander and transferred to the RCN in February 1923, he remained in the position of consulting naval engineer (from 1932 director of Naval Engineering) in headquarters until 1933. He spent his final three years of active service as chief engineer at Esquimalt dockyard, being promoted engineer captain, RCN, (the first to reach that rank) on his retirement in 1936.

Naval construction in Canada during World War I included twenty-four submarines, forty-eight trawlers, one hundred drifters, and five hundred and fifty anti-submarine launches. Of these only twelve trawlers were to Canadian account. The Italian and Russian governments ordered eight and six submarines respectively. The remaining vessels were to Admiralty account, although many of them were operated by the Naval Service as part of its East Coast Patrol. The trawlers were 136-ton ships with a speed of ten knots mounting a 12-pounder gun and depth charges. Built by Polson in Toronto and Canadian Vickers in Montreal at an average cost of $191,000, they were the first vessels to be constructed expressly for the Naval Service. The trawlers and drifters entered service in 1918. Four of the former, *Armentières*, *Festubert*, *Thiepval*, and *Ypres*, remained in RCN service after the war, the first two until the end of World War II.

The submarine construction activity was unexpected, since such vessels had been dismissed at the 1909 Imperial Conference on Defence as too complex for dominion building programmes. The Naval Service's sudden acquisition of the American-built submarines CC 1 and CC 2 in August 1914, and their successful manning with largely novice crews, provided inspiration to Canadian Vickers Ltd.[2] Under the direction of the Electric Boat Co. of Groton, Connecticut, Canadian Vickers assembled twenty-four

"H"-class submarines in short order, fitting American machinery and equipment into Canadian hulls. The first six left Montreal in the summer of 1915 only a few months after the start of construction. They were the first vessels of their kind to make a trans-Atlantic passage under their own power.

One of the first demands made on the ships' companies of *Niobe* and *Rainbow* was to assist in bringing the dockyards at Halifax and Esquimalt, which had languished since the departure of permanent Royal Navy units in the previous decade, up to operating condition. Subsequently, during War I, activity in the two dockyards picked up. They serviced not only the units based in them but, more importantly, visiting RN ships. Esquimalt dockyard provided the operations base for *Rainbow* until she was paid off as a depot ship in May 1917 and for the submarines CC 1 and CC 2, from their hasty acquisition until their transfer to the East Coast in June 1917. In May 1915, HMS *Kent* underwent battle repairs and a general refit in Esquimalt following the Battle of the Falkland Islands and her encounter with the German cruiser SMS *Dresden*. Halifax dockyard was busier than Esquimalt, supporting *Niobe* until she was paid off as a depot ship in September 1915, meeting the requirements of the RN Fourth Cruiser Squadron and, from 1915, supporting the Canadian East Coast Patrol, which exceeded a hundred vessels by war's end. From July 1917 onwards, Halifax became the assembly point for East Coast and trans-Atlantic convoys whose escorts placed further demands on the dockyard. In December of that year the famous Halifax explosion, involving the steamers SS *Imo* and SS *Mont Blanc*, damaged every building in the yard, including the Royal Naval College of Canada. Restoration was a gradual process, and months elapsed before the dockyard was back to normal.

Canada was considering her postwar naval requirements as early as the Imperial War Conference in May 1918. Borden recognized that imperial contributions were no longer appropriate and that any Canadian navy would have to be a separate entity. The Naval Staff recommended a long term plan extending over fifteen to twenty years with a programme of naval construction as a central feature. Admiral of the Fleet Viscount Jellicoe of Scapa visited Canada in 1919, at the government's invitation, to advise on naval matters. His recommendations included alternatives ranging in size from two "fleet units" down to a local defence flotilla. Concurrently, the Admiralty was divesting itself of surplus warships, and Canada modestly requested one Bristol-class light cruiser and two destroyers; a significant stipulation was that these vessels should be oil fired. The Admiralty agreed, and HMC Ships *Aurora*, *Patriot*, and *Patrician* arrived in Halifax before the end of 1920. Nearly two years earlier two submarines, CH 14 and CH 15, built in the United States to Admiralty account and sisters to the twenty-four H-class submarines that had been built in Canada, had been accepted into the RCN. They had been offered by the Admiralty as surplus even before reaching U.K. waters. Their acquisition, however, did not increase the RCN's submarine strength as the first Canadian submarines, CC 1 and CC 2, were sold in 1920.

With the arrival of peace in 1918, the RCN, in which 9,600 had served during the war, was drastically reduced in size. A ceiling of 500 naval personnel was authorized in May 1919. This was further reduced the following year when the total naval and civilian strength was adjusted by a process of wholesale dismissal and re-engagement from 1,303 to 521. This was the strength needed to man the recently acquired RN vessels and left very little for the RNCC (now transferred to Esquimalt) and the two dockyards. The navy reached its lowest ebb two years later: HMCS *Aurora* and the two submarines were paid off, and the naval college was closed. The RCN was reduced ignominiously to two rather tired destroyers and a skeleton shore organization while Halifax dockyard almost ceased to exist. *Patriot* and *Patrician* were clearly worn out by 1927, and the government, accepting the necessity of replacing them, was persuaded that Canada should have new ships built to order. Pending delivery of the two new vessels, two refitted destroyers, HMC Ships *Champlain* and *Vancouver*, were acquired on loan from the Admiralty as interim replacements for the destroyers destined for the breaker's yard.

The design selected for the new Canadian ships was, not surprisingly, British and was representative of the Admiralty's most modern postwar plans. These had been developed in two prototypes in which the builders had been invited to incorporate certain features of their own with a view to evolving a standard type for construction. The prototypes, HM Ships *Amazon* and *Ambuscade*, entered service in early 1927. The Admiralty ordered two, eight-ship flotillas, the "A" and "B" flotillas, of the resultant standard design for completion in 1930-31. The Canadian ships, to be developed from the Admiralty design but with Canadian variations, were ordered from Thornycrofts. The official Thornycroft company history tells the story of the design variations:

> The Canadian destroyers HMCS *Saguenay* and *Skeena* were ordered in March 1929 after severe competition with the principal British and Canadian firms. The selected design was a special one that had been prepared by Thornycrofts, who were entirely responsible for all the speed and other guarantees. This design was preferred to the Standard Admiralty type for which the firm had also tendered. At the same time the ships had to be generally similar to the British "Beagle" or "B" class, as they might have to operate in a common flotilla. In order to ensure that the lines were the best possible, . . . complete tests were made at the Teddington tank of the National Physical Laboratory. . . .

To meet the . . . exacting Canadian conditions, many interesting features were introduced, such as strengthened bows and forward plating as a protection against ice. They were also given exceptionally good metacentric height, as it was calculated that at times there might be 50 or 60 tons of snow and ice on the upper decks and rigging . . . [S]team heating was provided . . . to maintain a comfortable internal temperature in sub-zero . . . conditions. At the same time . . . good ventilation was . . . essential in view of the boats frequently having to pass through the Panama Canal and work from a base in the West Indies. Many improvements were introduced, as the Canadian Naval authorities were much more receptive to new ideas than the Admiralty. The bridges were exceptionally wide and partially streamlined. The bows were well flared, and this, in conjunction with special bridge screens, resulted in a very dry foredeck. Other features included steel masts, automatic electric fresh and salt water services, a high-speed motor boat and. . .other innovations. In fact so many improvements were introduced that on arrival at Portsmouth for working-up after delivery the ships were promptly dubbed the "Rolls Royce destroyers."[3]

Saguenay and *Skeena*, the first warships built to specific Canadian order, commissioned on 22 May and 10 June 1931.

In August 1930 the chief of the Naval Staff proposed to the Defence Council that the fleet should be expanded in due course to include one flotilla leader, five destroyers, and four minesweepers. There was no suggestion, however, of domestic construction. Since the fleet consisted at that time of two destroyers which were due to be replaced by two others under construction, this proposal represented a substantial increase in Canada's naval strength. Less than three years later, in June 1933, the CNS was required to defend his service estimates against a savage and potentially fatal cut from $2.422 million to $0.422 million. Fortunately, he won the day. In November 1934, the target for fleet strength was increased by the addition of twelve auxiliary vessels to be taken over from other government departments in the event of war. In the 1935-36 estimates there was, for the first time in three years, an increase in the funds approved. The Admiralty agreed to transfer two "C" flotilla destroyers to the RCN in 1935 to replace HMC Ships *Champlain* and *Vancouver*, which were to be disposed of under the terms of the London Treaty. HMCS *St. Laurent* (ex-HMS *Cygnet*) and HMCS *Fraser* (ex-HMS *Crescent*) were commissioned on 17 February 1937. As early as 1936 the Naval Staff considered the ultimate fleet objective to be nine destroyers on each coast. In September of that year the Joint Staff Committee recommended a five-year acquisition plan which included in the first year the purchase of one destroyer and the laying down in Canada of four minesweepers. A second destroyer would be purchased in the third

year. A second five-year plan was intended to produce two more destroyers
and four more minesweepers, thereby bringing a total of eight ships of each
type into service. The government adopted these recommendations in
1937.

A significant event occurred in October 1937 when the auxiliary train-
ing schooner HMCS *Venture* was commissioned. This was the first
Canadian-built vessel to be commissioned into the RCN since the end of
World War I. In January and February of the following year orders were
placed for the first four warships to be built in Canada for the Department
of National Defence. These were the 460-ton, coal-burning minesweepers
Fundy, Gaspé, Comox, and *Nootka* (later *Nanoose*), built, respectively, by
Collingwood, Morton, Burrard, and Yarrows to the Royal Navy's "Basset"
trawler design with modifications for ice-strengthening. Coal had been
selected to foster the use of indigenous Canadian fuel. Fortunately, this
choice was not to be repeated.

The second pair of destroyers, which had formed the RN's half-flotilla
of the C-class, HMCS *Restigouche* (ex-HMS *Comet*) and HMCS *Ottawa*
(ex-HMS *Crusader*), were commissioned into the RCN at Chatham on 15
June 1938. In the same month the Joint Staff Committee recommended the
purchase of a flotilla leader as well as the construction in Canada of two
motor torpedo boats and two anti-submarine vessels in order that Canadian industry might gain some experience building these types. The ultimate objective was the construction of sixteen motor torpedo boats and
eight anti-submarine vessels. In addition, the Joint Staff Committee
recommended the purchase of one or more cruisers as soon as sufficient
personnel were available for manning.

In April 1939 the minister of National Defence announced the government's intention to purchase a flotilla leader and to construct new facilities
at Halifax and Esquimalt. He foresaw a fleet of eighteen destroyers, eighteen anti-submarine vessels, sixteen minesweepers, eight motor torpedo
boats, one destroyer depot ship, and one motor torpedo boat depot ship. He
also proposed that the strength of the RCN should be raised from 1,965
officers and men to 6,000 and that subsidiary bases should be developed at
Sydney, Nova Scotia, and Prince Rupert, British Columbia. The RN
Tribal design was selected for the new destroyers. This choice was preferred
because their armament of eight 4.7-inch guns made these ships a reasonable match not only for armed merchant cruisers and submarines but even
for cruisers. The Admiralty-type flotilla leader HMCS *Assiniboine* (ex-
HMS *Kempenfelt*) was purchased for the RCN in August 1939 and commissioned on 19 October.

A Canadian Manufacturers Association mission had visited Britain in
August 1939 to investigate war production. Thanks to their efforts, the
Naval Staff became aware of the work being done by William Reed of

Smith's Dock Co. in developing for the Admiralty what was later to become the corvette design. The first details about corvettes were relayed by telephone on 13 September from the National Research Council to the then director of Naval Engineering, Engineer Commander A.D.M. Curry. The same mission also brought back information about the Admiralty's "Bangor"-class minesweepers. These two types were to provide the materiel on which the Canadian wartime shipbuilding industry cut its teeth and on which the RCN based its early and rapid growth.

The cabinet gave approval in principle to Canada's first wartime shipbuilding programme on 19 September. This two-year programme called for the construction of four destroyers, forty anti-submarine escorts, twenty-eight minesweepers, thirty-two motor torpedo boats, two "Black Swan"-class sloops, and the conversion of three "Prince" ships into armed merchant cruisers. The Black Swans were a late addition in response to an Admiralty request.

Further examination of the requirements for construction of Tribals in Canada showed that substantial technical assistance and materiel would have to come from the United Kingdom at a time when the Admiralty was preoccupied with enlarging its own fleet and was reluctant to spare resources of any type. British shipyards were also fully engaged. Interestingly, the Royal Australian Navy was successful in arranging for the construction of Tribals in Australia at this time, the first being ordered from Cockatoo Docks and Engineering, Sydney, and laid down on 15 November 1939. The RAN, of course, was more than three times the size of the RCN at this stage, and ships up to the complexity of sloops had been constructed in Australian yards for some years.

The same problems that stymied the construction of Tribals in Canada also faced sloop construction, and both types were dropped from the domestic plan temporarily. In the winter of 1939-40 the Admiralty recognized the crucial importance of escort ships. Accordingly, the Canadians offered to augment British naval construction by building corvettes in Canada if the Admiralty would agree to construct Tribals for the RCN in the United Kingdom. Ten corvettes for the Admiralty were laid down in Canada in early 1940 and on 5 April a Canadian order for two Tribals was placed with Vickers-Armstrongs's Tyne yard.

In October 1939 the building programme of the previous month was revised to produce four destroyers, forty escorts, twenty-eight minesweepers, and thirty-two motor torpedo boats. Thereafter, in each of the next two years, a further two destroyers, ten escorts, ten minesweepers, and sixteen motor torpedo boats were to be added. In the same month Lambert, German and Milne of Montreal were contracted to prepare plans for the Prince ship conversions. The ships were taken in hand: *Prince Robert* and *Prince David* at Burrard and Halifax Shipyards, respectively, on 9 February 1940; *Prince Henry* at Canadian Vickers on 15 May. *Prince Robert* commissioned in July, the other two in December.

In December 1939 the War Supply Board, having been asked to investigate Canadian industrial capacity for building corvettes and Bangors, reported that thirty of either type could be built in 1940 and sixty in 1941. Tenders were invited, and on 7 February 1940 the Privy Council approved a programme for the delivery of ninety ships by the end of 1941 at a cost of $54.25 million. Sixty-four corvettes (twenty-eight for delivery before the end of 1940, the remainder for delivery in 1941), of which ten were to Admiralty account, and twenty-eight Bangors were ordered between February and August 1940. The last ten Bangors were to be equipped with diesel rather than reciprocating steam engines. In fact, only fourteen corvettes were delivered before the close of navigation in 1940, ten for the Admiralty and four for the RCN. The first to commission was HMS *Windflower* on 26 October 1940. Only three RN ships and one RCN vessel, HMCS *Collingwood*, were actually in operation or en route to the United Kingdom by year-end. However, by January 1942, all but one of the sixty-four corvettes had been completed.

Many new yards were brought into steel ship and naval construction work as a result of wartime programmes, and the transition was not without its difficulties. Some of the problems were the result of design changes, some of materiel and equipment supply, and some of shipyard production arrangements. The problems in engining the diesel Bangors are illustrative: the 1000 brake horse power Sultzer engines were manufactured by Dominion Engineering from drawings produced by the designer in Switzerland. The drawings were obtained via Gibraltar where they were delayed for some time by contraband control and on receipt in Canada had to be changed from metric to imperial dimensions for manufacture. The first engines were ordered for delivery in nine months—they took sixteen months, and the last of twenty was delivered twenty-one months after ordering. As a result, no diesel-powered Bangor minesweeper was available before the freeze-up in 1941.

The initial Canadian building programmes had been heavily dependent not only on British drawings and specifications but on British materiel of all sorts. The Department of Munitions and Supply had been set up in April 1940 incorporating the Shipbuilding Division of the former War Supply Board as a branch of the new department.[4] Meetings were held under the auspices of the new department to determine the likely domestic sources for everything from high-tensile steel plate and machinery to armament and electrical equipment. The minister, C.D. Howe, advised that a government-owned company was to be established to develop and manufacture optical and scientific instruments. This company would also consider naval equipment. At the same time, the British authorities recognized the need to draw to an increasing extent on North American sources. Thus the Supply Mission in Ottawa was enlarged with the arrival of the British Admiralty Technical Mission (BATM) in August 1940.[5]

The BATM's principal function was to arrange for the development of sources of supply in Canada to meet Admiralty requirements. It had been determined earlier, by both the Supply Mission and Canadian naval agencies, that British naval practice was so dissimilar to Canadian commercial practice that firms would have to be educated first in new standards and processes. For this purpose the technical officers of the BATM made frequent visits to their Canadian suppliers. Thanks in large measure to the efforts of these technical representatives, who numbered some two thousand at peak strength, the picture changed in a matter of months from one in which production for Admiralty and Canadian purposes demanded a substantial measure of British manufactured materiel and equipment to one in which the dependency was reduced to specialized small-quantity items. Included in the lengthy list of items manufactured in Canada for Allied naval use were such varied items as the Admiralty Fire Control Clock (AFCC: a gunnery control computer), magnetic compasses, ASDIC (sonar: submarine detection equipment), RDF (radar), and a range of naval guns and mountings. The Canadian radar was designated RXC and was similar to the Admiralty Type 271. Guns included 4-inch Mark XVI, 4-inch, high angle, Mark XIX twin, 4-inch Mark II, 12-pounder, 2-pounder, the Vickers .5-inch naval machine gun, 20-mm oerlikon twin Mark XII and XIIA mountings and naval rocket mountings. The 4-inch Mark XXI had been planned for manufacture in Canada, but the contract was not let. The quantities manufactured were substantial. An order was placed on 27 September 1941 for 432, 4-inch Mark XIX guns. A further order for 362 of the same gun was placed less than a year later on 28 May 1942. An order for 643 twin 20-mm oerlikon power-operated mountings was placed in March 1943. Although it did not enter production, a quadruple power-operated oerlikon mounting underwent trials by John Inglis Ltd. in June of the same year.

A substantial scientific effort was mustered to support Canadian naval operations and warship production.[6] During World War I, R.W. Boyle had worked on ultra-sonics and the acoustic detection of submarines and had kept this interest alive at the National Research Council (NRC) between the wars. Stimulated by Dr. Boyle's enthusiasm, G.S. Field established an acoustics laboratory at NRC in 1930. In February 1940 the RCN requested G.H. Henderson and J.H.L. Johnstone of Dalhousie University, Halifax, to assist in the development of magnetic mine counter-measures. A laboratory was established for this purpose at Dalhousie, and space was provided for the work in Halifax dockyard. Techniques were developed from this work firstly for de-gaussing and later for de-perming of ships (processes designed to reduce a vessel's magnetic field and hence vulnerability to magnetic mines). In October 1940 the NRC Optics Section developed solutions to problems in quartz crystal processing which were central to the manufacture of sonar. In addition, the NRC Acoustics Laboratory invented an instrument for checking the efficiency of quartz crystals. These scientific efforts came to fruition in the manufacture of a large number of sonar sets. The first Canadian manufactured sonar was produced in July 1941. By 1943, 2,600 sets had been produced involving some 175 firms in all.

The number of shipyards and the personnel engaged therein increased many-fold as a result of the demands of wartime naval and merchant shipbuilding and ship repairing. The Canadian shipbuilding industry produced 4,336 tons of shipping and employed fewer than four thousand men in 1935. At their peak, in mid-summer 1943, Canadian shipyards employed 73,000. At that time there were eleven major building yards and four outfitting yards handling warships. In the six years from September 1939 to September 1945 Canadian yards produced 403 merchant ships with a gross tonnage of 3,784,500 plus 550 naval vessels of some 750,000 tons.

In August 1940 contracts were placed for a further ten Bangors and corvettes, the latter to be provided with water-tube boilers in lieu of the more easily manufactured, but less efficient, cylindrical variety which had been used in earlier construction. The first Canadian Tribals were laid down the following month on the Tyne: HMCS *Iroquois* (as *Athabaskan* I) on 19 September and HMCS *Athabaskan* I (as *Iroquois*) presumably on the same or at an earlier date. Bomb damage during construction delayed completion of the lead ship and prompted an exchange of names prior to launching on 31 September and 15 November 1941.

The Admiralty had agreed by October 1940 that if contractors were willing and able to do so, the specifications and working drawings for the Tribals and their machinery might be supplied to the Canadian authorities with a view to constructing this class of ship in Canada. Messrs. Vickers-Armstrongs and Parsons, who had already been contracted to build Tribals for the RCN in Britain, both agreed. Prime Minister W.L. Mackenzie King and J.L. Ralston, the minister of National Defence, were persuaded to prevail upon the British authorities, including the prime minister, for the provision of technical assistance in the form of constructors and overseers. Mr. Churchill, however, displayed an understandable reluctance. On 18 December, he made the following observation in his reply to Mackenzie King:

> I think, however, that it might be feasible, and would certainly be of the greatest assistance to the common cause, if you could undertake to build, say, a flotilla of destroyers to the latest American design, obtaining technical help from USA. It would probably also be possible to

obtain from the same source much of the special equipment for the ships. This is usually a bottleneck here and provision from the USA would save shipping space.[7]

Since none of the Canadian-built Tribals was completed in time to see service in World War II, it is easy to argue in retrospect that the adoption of Churchill's proposal would have been a sound course. It would have anticipated the conversion from British to North American standards and practices in design, manufacture, and equipment which came with the postwar construction programmes. Presumably the American design would have been the "Fletcher" class, the first of which was laid down on 3 March 1941 at Bath Iron Works, although the slightly smaller Bristol and Benson classes were still in production. These ships mounted 5-inch guns in single mountings with totally enclosed gun houses, which, unlike the Tribals 4.7-inch twin shielded mounting, had a good anti-aircraft capability. The earlier classes were also fitted with two sets of quintuple torpedo tubes in contrast to the Tribals' single quadruple set. In addition, the endurance of the American design was substantially better than the British. Most significantly, the construction times achieved in American yards, thanks in part to an uninterrupted supply of equipment, were impressively short. On the other hand, domestic Canadian sources of supply, and hence the Canadian industrial base, might not have developed with American destroyer designs as they were forced to do with the British ones.

The Canadian authorities were advised on 7 January 1941 that the Admiralty approved the construction of destroyers to British design in Canada and would provide the necessary help. An earlier Canadian suggestion that this help be provided on a contractor-to-contractor rather than navy-to-navy basis was also agreed to. Later that month, with the assistance of the BATM, Halifax Shipyards and Vickers-Armstrongs were identified as the two collaborating shipbuilders, while John Inglis was designated the turbine manufacturer. Both Curry, now engineer-in-chief, and his successor (from February 1941), Captain (E) G.L. Stephens, preferred to produce simpler vessels than destroyers in Canada, particularly as they had just received information about the twin-screw corvette or frigate. In May the BATM, through the director of Shipbuilding, recommended the adoption of the British "Intermediate" destroyer design over the Tribal. Throughout these exchanges the CNS stuck to the selection of the Tribal as the destroyer with the greatest possible size, armament, and radius of action. British designs were regarded as best for operations in conjunction with a British fleet. A second pair of British-built Tribals was ordered from Vickers-Armstrongs in April 1941; in June, Halifax Shipyards received an order for the first pair of Canadian-built destroyers. Inglis expressed no particular concern over the technical challenge involved in building the main propulsion machinery but later observed that a decision on the number of ships to be built in Canada, whether two or four, would determine whether the auxiliary machinery should be procured outside Canada or from largely Canadian sources.

Meanwhile, escort production was moving apace. In February 1941 the last ten Bangors were placed in contract to make a total programme of forty-eight for the RCN. A further twelve were built to Admiralty account, six of which were loaned to the RCN. In March, ten more corvettes were ordered, being the first of the "Revised Flower" design.

In December 1940, the first word of the twin-screw corvette (the "frigate") was received in Canada. In addition to the frigate design, the Admiralty had developed an improved minesweeper, the "Algerine." Each of these designs represented substantial advances over earlier corvette and Bangor designs; moreover, increased capability had been achieved without major technical complications. However, the BATM anticipated the Canadian authorities in placing orders for the new classes in Canada, and this, plus the demands on shipyards for merchant ship construction, was to delay the placing of orders for the RCN. The British order in the summer of 1941 was for ten frigates, fifteen Algerines, fifteen revised corvettes and sixteen "Western Isles" trawlers. This building programme was funded by the United States under Mutual Aid, and the United States Navy retained two frigates and eight corvettes for its own purposes. Despite the delay which they placed on RCN construction, the BATM orders helped to develop Canadian shipyard and manufacturing capability, not least because BATM technical advisers and consultants were able to transfer current British expertise to Canadian industry.

The USN, recognizing its own desperate need for convoy escorts and the merits of the Admiralty's frigate design, arranged for large teams of shipyard design and production engineers to visit Canadian frigate yards and glean all of the information they could. This provided the basis on which the American PF programme of frigates was developed in rapid and prolific order.

The Naval Service approved the building of thirty frigates and ten Algerines in October 1941. The intention was to construct frigates to the exclusion of corvettes. However, the coast and river yards' capacity for the larger vessels was limited, while the Great Lakes yards had capacity to spare but were prevented from building frigates because of the limitations of the St. Lawrence locks. Consequently, a further thirty-eight corvettes were contracted before the middle of 1942, although the last eleven were cancelled when a general cut-back in escort building occurred in December 1943. In the second half of 1942 orders were placed for a further seven frigates and eighteen Algerines for the RCN. Sixteen of the latter were eventually exchanged with the Admiralty for sixteen British-built corvettes, twelve being of the "Castle" design. Once again it was the BATM which, in March 1943, placed the first Castle-class orders in Canada. In the same month orders were placed for sixty-four RCN frigates. Subsequently, all of the Castle class and forty-one of the frigate orders were cancelled.

Construction of wooden warships included motor torpedo boats (MTB), motor launches (ML), and minesweepers. The twelve 70-foot Scott-Paine MTB's built by Canadian Power Boat were ordered in June 1940, delivered rather more than a year later and turned over to the Admiralty for use in the Mediterranean. Eighty-eight ML's of the 69-ton "Fairmile B" type were constructed, including eight for the USN. Most of them were built in small Great Lakes yards which had obtained experience in light-weight construction requirements while building pleasure craft. Although the first twenty-four ML's were ordered in April 1941, only nine were deliverable before freeze-up that year. The magnetic mine had been the stimulus for the design of wooden minesweepers. Two classes were built in Canada, the first 105-foot (109-foot, 4-inch overall) and 228 tons displacement, the second 126-foot (140-foot overall) and 360 tons. The first orders for sixteen of the 105-foot vessels were placed by the BATM early in 1941. These utilized all of the available space in the East Coast yards, so an order for the first two RCN vessels was placed on the Ile d'Orléans; a second Canadian order for eight vessels was placed in British Columbia yards in early 1942. The BATM also ordered twenty-four larger vessels from yards in the Maritimes in mid-1943. The RCN sought to fulfil its own requirement for sixteen, 126-foot craft by placing ten orders with the Great Lakes ML builders, followed by two in the Maritimes and four in British Columbia. The Maritime and five of the Great Lakes orders were subsequently cancelled, and, as it turned out, the first vessels were not delivered until August 1945, while the last arrived in March 1946. All nine of those built for the RCN were turned over to the USSR on delivery.

A study of the various World War II Allied escort vessel programmes was published by the United States Naval Institute Press in 1977. It notes, *inter alia*, that "the shipbuilding effort made in Canada was probably the most remarkable even of the three great naval powers, and delivery delays can take nothing away from the fantastic achievement."[8] And further that:

> The planning and production of [the RCN River class of seventy frigates] is one of the more fascinating stories of the [Allied] escort building programmes. On the face of it, this was simply a carry-on from the RN "River" class building program in the UK. But it was a magnificent achievement for the Canadian yards to switch from the much simpler "Flower" class corvette program to these . . . sophisticated frigates, and if the Canadian ships are examined closely a number of significant improvements can be found over the UK-built ships.[9]

Warships built in Canada during World War II included seventy frigates (eight for the RN), 123 corvettes (seventeen for the RN and eight for the USN), sixty-two Algerines (fifty for the RN), fifty steam Bangors (twelve for the RN), ten diesel Bangors, sixteen Western Isles trawlers for the RN, twelve MTB's, eighty-eight Fairmile B ML's (eight for the USN), thirty 126-foot minesweepers (twenty-one for the RN) and forty-two 105-foot motor minesweepers (thirty-two for the RN) and twenty-six Transport Ferries for the RN.[10] In addition, nineteen escort aircraft carriers were modified and completed in Canada for the Royal Navy.

These building programmes were clearly the spectacular engineering accomplishment of World War II. However, the development of support facilities on both coasts and the repair, modification, and improvement of ships and equipment under chaotic conditions represented an achievement of equal importance.

While the first twelve months of war on the East Coast were relatively quiet in comparison with later activity, the demands on the shore support facilities grew substantially. The East Coast destroyer fleet had doubled in size shortly after the outbreak of hostilities when the West Coast units arrived. A substantial and heterogeneous collection of vessels, co-opted from other uses, was pressed into service with the navy, while Halifax became the terminus of the trans-Atlantic convoys and a base for the convoy escorts, large and small, from a variety of Allied navies. The fall of France in June 1940 raised the prospect of large Allied naval forces being based in Canada and provided a stimulus for the expansion and diversification of shore facilities. Late in the same year it was realized that the large increase in the number of escorts using East Coast facilities, including the addition of seven "Town"-class destroyers to the Canadian fleet, required an increase in docking capacity. This was provided by a number of newly opened subsidiary bases in Nova Scotia as well as at Halifax. Marine railways were ordered for Halifax, Sydney, and Shelburne (all 3,000 ton capacity), Pictou (2,000 ton), and Liverpool and Lunenburg (both 1,400 ton). In addition, 200-ton railways were built in Halifax, Sydney, Shelburne, and Gaspé. In January 1941, as the first of the new escort vessels began arriving, Engineer Captain F.H. Jefferson, chief engineer in Halifax since 1934, identified the major changes that were needed to transform Halifax dockyard into the major repair base it had to become. That same month the USN started constructing the base it had acquired at Argentia, Newfoundland, in partial exchange for the Town-class destroyers. In February HMS *Forth*, a submarine depot ship, was stationed at Halifax to provide accommodation for Royal Navy personnel and to supplement hard-pressed repair facilities. A 24,000-ton floating dock was ordered for Halifax in June to be leased to Halifax Shipyards. The following year the Naval Armament Depot was relocated on the Dartmouth side of Halifax harbour in order to relieve the pressure for space on the Halifax waterfront. It became apparent by early 1943 that, despite additional plant, the East Coast repair facilities, catering as they did for both naval and merchant ships, had become saturated.

In May 1941 the Admiralty, recognizing the increasing operational range of U-boats, decided to base escort forces in St. John's, Newfoundland. In response to a Canadian offer to concentrate all available RCN escorts in the Newfoundland area, the Admiralty requested that a Canadian be appointed commodore commanding Newfoundland Force (CCNF). Suitable naval facilities were almost non-existent to begin with in the small and land-locked harbour at St. John's. Consequently, a joint RN-RCN effort was organized to develop the facilities necessary to support operations and provide running repairs for the escort force. HMS *Forth* moved to St. John's in June 1941, and a second depot ship, HMS *Greenwich*, arrived in September. Facilities were developed over a three-year period to support a large escort force and its personnel. Workshops (manned predominantly by naval personnel), stores depots, and an armament depot were constructed rapidly and placed in operation as the demand for running repairs increased. Beginning in mid-1942, supplementary facilities including workshops for running repairs and a 3,000-ton marine railway were developed at Bay Bulls, eighteen miles south of St. John's. By June 1943, sixty destroyers, corvettes and minesweepers were based on St. John's; six months later the number was seventy-four, and at war's end, eighty-nine. St. John's, or Newfyjohn as it was known, was largely a Canadian-manned base principally supporting RCN escorts. Royal Navy escorts depended chiefly upon the USN facilities at Argentia, which operated to an ever-increasing extent to support RN ships as USN escorts were diverted from the North West Atlantic to other theatres. From mid-1943 onwards Argentia was used almost exclusively by RN vessels.

The USN had also developed escort repair facilities at Londonderry in their characteristically rapid fashion. This was fortuitous for the three Canadian escort groups operating from that area since the USN supported the RCN in Northern Ireland just as they supported the RN in Newfoundland. Canadian warships represented more than half those using the USN base by March 1943, and by the end of that year a total of eighty-eight USN, sixty-four RCN, and twenty-four RN ships had been taken in hand for repairs.

It was also in March 1943 that a decision was taken by Canadian and Admiralty officials to double the repair capacity at St. John's. This included provision for a floating dock of 1,800-ton capacity to supplement the hopelessly overworked drydock. Less than a year later this expansion was curtailed substantially as the submarine war moved eastward.

It was officially recognized by the middle of 1943 that the crucial naval engineering problem was not the production of new escorts but the repair, refitting, and especially the modernization of the existing fleet of escorts. The East Coast naval bases were plagued by an acute shortage of skilled civilian labour, and the commercial facilities were overloaded by the requirement to complete newly constructed ships, which had been delivered from the builders' yards, as well as to provide urgent repairs to merchant ships. Older corvettes were being improved by extensions to their forecastles, accommodation changes, radar installations, and the addition of the anti-submarine mortar "Hedgehog." Naval personnel, despite the long training they required, were used in large numbers as work parties and shop labour from 1942 in Halifax and from late 1943 in Sydney and Shelburne when the decision was taken to man up these last two as major refit bases.

Plans for Canada's postwar fleet had been maturing for some time before V-J Day. The impending cessation of hostilities in the Atlantic and the expected shift of effort to a very different naval war in the Pacific provided a strategic basis on which a balanced postwar Canadian fleet might be constructed. Such a fleet was intended to include aircraft carriers, cruisers, and modern fleet destroyers as well as convoy and coastal escorts. In fact, the pursuit of the Tribal requirement, which had begun before the war and persisted throughout it, was aimed at a general naval capability. This was certainly not a prime Canadian objective in World War II, at least so far as the Atlantic Theatre was concerned. The balanced fleet objective was a logical successor to the objective which both Laurier and Borden had in mind during the debate on the Naval Service Act in 1910. This had been a "fleet unit" comprised of armoured and unarmoured cruisers, destroyers, and submarines. Jellicoe had recommended to the Canadian government a comparable naval force a decade later, preferably with the inclusion of battle cruisers and aircraft carriers. The objective of 1910 had withered in the face of political controversy and indecision. Jellicoe's proposal of 1919 succumbed to economic pressures. The Naval Staff had undoubtedly dreamed for more than three decades of a balanced fleet, and now, at last, after five years of war, it was in sight. Had the Pacific War continued, the Canadian fleet might have been expected to reach substantial proportions: two light fleet-carriers with Canadian squadrons embarked; two cruisers; six Tribals, eight "Crescent"- and two Intermediate-class destroyers; HMCS *Prince Robert*; a large number of frigates; the twelve Algerines; and assorted auxiliary and small craft.

A balanced fleet of modern ships represented a major shift from the heavy predominance of relatively small and simple escorts. The shift entailed a move to more complex types of ship with a multiplicity of equipment and systems. The equipment and systems were themselves more complex and sophisticated involving remote power controlled gun mountings and turrets, elaborate fire control, and action information radars. They also included air control, steam turbine propulsion, multiple power generation and distribution systems, not to mention the wholly new range of devices and skills associated with naval aviation and the operation of carriers. Furthermore, these technological changes demanded organizational changes among the personnel using and maintaining the equipment.

The acquisition of a balanced fleet and the changes in organization of technical personnel were in mid-flight when Japan surrendered in August 1945. The rapid demobilization which followed interrupted fleet development but gave impetus to the organizational changes. These had, of necessity, to be clearly and quickly spelled out, particularly if large numbers of Royal Canadian Naval Volunteer Reserve experts were to be persuaded to remain with the RCN. The three-year period immediately after the war was one of consolidation and adjustment. River- and Town-class destroyers, virtually all of the corvettes, the large majority of frigates, the steam Bangors, half of the Algerines, and huge numbers of auxiliaries and small craft were disposed of. Naval manpower had fallen from nearly one hundred thousand to approximately five thousand by 1947. It was stretched to the limit to man the first light fleet-carrier, commissioned six months after the war, and the two cruisers (often manned on an alternating basis), four destroyers and as many frigates which comprised the immediate postwar active fleet.

The domestic Tribal programme came to fruition with the delivery of four ships between September 1945 and January 1948. Having docked the British-built *Iroquois* in Halifax Shipyards in March 1943, the Canadian builders were able to obtain a detailed view of the British product and to determine, among other changes, where additional stiffening was needed to improve the hull integrity of the Canadian-built ships. The weapons outfit of the first two domestic Tribals followed closely that of their British-built predecessors. The second pair was a marked improvement, particularly in their anti-aircraft capability, being modified to carry the latest British Weapons-class armament: four twin 4-inch with the Mark VI radar director. However, in recognition of the submarine threat, HMCS *Cayuga* was back in dockyard hands within a year of delivery to receive two "Squid" anti-submarine mortar mountings in lieu of X and Y gun mountings, sonar modifications, and, because of Canadian expectations of habitability, a new laundry. This was the first of a steady succession of modifications and conversions to these destroyers which continued throughout the decade.

In 1948 the RCN also acquired the aircraft carrier, HMCS *Magnificent*, and contracted in January 1949 for the construction of HMCS *Labrador*, a modified USN "Wind"-class icebreaker. The former, known affectionately as "Maggie," replaced *Warrior* as the second light fleet-carrier to be loaned to the RCN. It had been possible to incorporate in her a modest

Plate 28. As war approached, Canada's shipbuilding programme accelerated. HMCS *Nanoose* (formerly *Nootka* I), a modified "Basset"-class minesweeper launched 26 September 1938, was one of the first four men-of-war built in Canada in time of peace. (MCM—Canadian Forces photo S-3933)

Plate 29. HMCS *Shawinigan*, a Flower-class corvette, under construction at the shipyards of Geo. T. Davie & Sons, Lauzon, P.Q., 1941. (PAC—C-6571)

Plate 30. Launching the corvette HMCS *Moose Jaw*, Collingwood Shipyards, Collingwood, Ontario, 10 April 1941. (PAC—PA 37449)

Plate 31. Frigate building at Yarrow Shipyard, Esquimalt, B.C., 28 April 1943. (PAC—PA 116336)

Plate 32. View south from Jetty No. 3, HMC Dockyard, Halifax, Nova Scotia, 3 August 1944. Left to right in background are HMC Ships *Charlottetown* (K244), *Kokanee* (K419), and *Lasalle* (K519). (PAC—PA 115367)

Plate 33. Ships riding at anchor in Bedford Basin, N.S., prior to forming up for a North Atlantic convoy. (DOH, NDHQ)

Plate 34. HMCS *Saint John,* River-class frigate, served 1943-45. The vessels shown on this page and opposite illustrate the growth and diversity of Canada's wartime navy. (MCM)

Plate 35. HMCS *Ontario* (ex-HMS *Minotaur*) "Swiftsure"-class cruiser, served 1945-58. (MCM)

Plate 36. HMCS *Ottawa* I (ex-HMS *Crusader*) River-class destroyer, served from 1938 until 14 September 1942, when she was torpedoed and sunk in the North Atlantic by U-91. (MCM—Canadian Forces photo H-205)

Plate 37. HMCS *Sackville*, Flower-class corvette, served 1941-46. She is now stationed at the Bedford Institute of Oceanography, Halifax, and is the last surviving corvette. (MCM—CN-3557)

Plate 38. HMCS *Prince David*, one of the "Princes Three"—ex-Canadian National steamships which were, at the time of their conversion to naval use, the largest vessels in the RCN. (MCM—PD-653)

Plate 39. HMCS *Prince Henry* was converted with *Prince David* as a landing ship infantry (LSI). Both served as transports in the Normandy landings. (MCM—F-1901)

Plate 40. CN Steamship *Prince Robert* carrying their Majesties King George VI and Queen Elizabeth from Victoria to Vancouver in the fast time of 3 hours, 32 minutes, June 1939. (MMBC—P244)

Plate 41. HMCS *Prince Robert*, here seen after her second conversion as an anti-aircraft cruiser, helped protect Allied convoys from German air attack. (MMBC)

Plate 42. Rear-Admiral V.G. Brodeur, RCN, naval member Canadian Staff, Washington, during World War II. (MCM)

Plate 43. Rear-Admiral L.W. Murray, RCN, helped shape RCN convoy operations in the Battle of the Atlantic. (MCM)

Plate 44. Vice-Admiral G.C. Jones, RCN, who became chief of the Naval Staff in 1944 and held the appointment until 1946. (MMBC—P1041b)

Plate 45. Commanding officers of RCN destroyers who later attained flag rank, Plymouth, England, 2 June 1940. *Left to right*: Lieutenant-Commanders H.G. Dewolf, H.N. Lay, J.C. Hibbard. (PAC—PA 115303)

number of improvements in thermal insulation, steam heating and messing arrangements, to better suit her for Canadian operations. HMCS *Labrador* reflected Canada's interests in the Arctic and was the first instance of warship construction in Canada to North American standards and specifications. Her construction provided Canadian naval engineers and shipbuilders with vital experience for the shipbuilding programmes that lay ahead.

During this period of immediate postwar consolidation, a great deal of thought was given to the lessons of the war and the requirements of the Canadian fleet. Anti-submarine warfare, but under radically altered conditions, was the most likely form of naval war for Canada in the future. This was suggested by several factors: the advent of nuclear weapons; the potential advantage to the submarine of the snorkel and high-powered propulsion plants (such as the hydrogen peroxide system developed by the Germans in Type XXI and XXIII submarines); and the Cold War confrontation between the USSR and the Western Allies. However, one lesson was clear: Canada need not and should not be dependent on others for future warships and their equipment. Canadian industry had come of age and had demonstrated its ability to produce virtually the full range of materiel needed for warships at least up to the size and complexity of destroyers. The dangers of depending on non-Canadian and particularly overseas sources of materiel had been amply demonstrated when Canadians struggled to get their wartime shipbuilding programmes underway. It was also apparent that the designs and specifications for Canadian manufacture should adhere to Canadian standards wherever possible if domestic industrial capability was to be properly utilized. What was needed was a warship design capability, the one element still outstanding if self-sufficient warship production was to be achieved in Canada. How naval engineers met that challenge is the story of the RCN's postwar shipbuilding and reconversion programmes described in Chapter 18.

Chapter 8

PRINCES THREE: CANADA'S USE OF ARMED MERCHANT CRUISERS DURING WORLD WAR II

Fraser M. McKee

The Prince-class ships of the Royal Canadian Navy—armed merchant cruisers (AMC), landing ships infantry (LSI), and auxiliary anti-aircraft cruisers (AAC)—were a conundrum and a paradox. They were the three largest vessels in the Canadian navy for several years during World War II, and yet their activities are relatively little known today. By the end of the war, they had completely changed their original naval design and were as well known to soldiers as to sailors. In five years of hostilities, only one of them was engaged in a battle as such, yet the three of them cost the Germans almost eighteen thousand tons of shipping.

The three ships, *Prince David, Prince Henry,* and *Prince Robert,* were ordered on one contract in 1929 by the Canadian National Railways' subsidiary, CN Steamships, from Cammell Laird and Company of Birkenhead, England, "as Sir Henry Thornton's last extravagance."[1] They formed part of his costly plan to create a comprehensive service from his position as first president of the newly organized government railway. They were specifically designed to succeed five older Prince ships that the CNR and its predecessors had operated on the West Coast of Canada since 1910. In addition, they were to compete with the Canadian Pacific Railway Company's Princess ships operating between Vancouver, Victoria, Seattle, and Alaska. They cost over $2 million each, a huge sum at the time of their delivery in the summer of 1930. The Depression affected their prewar life markedly, and criticism of their cost contributed directly to Sir Henry's resignation in 1932.

They were actually small luxury liners, designed by A.T. Wall and Co. of Liverpool, with accommodation for some 334 first-class and 70 third-class passengers in three decks, plus cargo space forward. Each was 385-feet overall, by 57-feet moulded breadth, and 20-feet, 2-inches moulded depth. Their trial draft was 16-feet, 6-inches aft, with a displacement of 5,579 tons, 6,893 tons gross and 3,072 tons net. It is interesting to note that in 1946, even after two major wartime conversions, de-stored draft was still 16-feet, 6-inches. They were powered by twin-screw Parsons reaction three-stage single-reduction geared turbines, giving 19,300 IHP at 267 RPM, or 14,500 SHP, driving them at up to 22.25 knots on trials. Each was provided with six Yarrow water-tube five-drum super-heat main boilers, plus two Scottish marine three-burner auxiliary boilers. Their endurance or range was 6,000 miles at economical speed, though it was closer to 3,500 miles at their normal operating speeds of about twenty knots. Despite their royal soubriquet, *David* and *Robert* were named after CN vice-presidents, while *Henry* was named after Thornton himself.

Prince Henry was launched on 17 January 1930, *Prince David* on 12 February, and *Prince Robert* on 3 April, as Cammell Laird ships numbers 964, 965 and 966. They were fairly high ships, with a small enclosed upper wheelhouse; a full width open bridge passed across the front of this wheelhouse, duplicating a similar arrangement on the lifeboat deck below. This deck gave a rather cluttered appearance by today's standards, with three tall dark funnels, six large and many small cowl ventilators, and six lifeboats per side. Two antennae-like booms jutted toward the bow from the forward face of the deckhouse over No. 1 hold. As each port had wooden jetties of different heights, "shell doors" were let into the hull at each deck, and an internal elevator for two cars transferred vehicles from deck to deck. The ships were fitted out elegantly for extended cruising, with ornate woodwork in the cabins and saloons. They were turned over to locally signed-on crews in mid-1930, within six months of their launching. One problem occurred as a result of their high flared bows which "effectively removed many of the roofs on the CN dockside sheds when the ships approached the jetties at too broad an angle."[2]

When *Prince David* and *Prince Robert* arrived on the West Coast in the summer of 1930, they were put on the Vancouver-Victoria-Seattle daily service. *Prince Henry* arrived on 21 June and left on her first Vancouver-Alaskan cruise on 3 July. The three ships led a somewhat varied if shaky existence, as the Depression eliminated the necessity for using all of the vessels on the Alaska run. *Prince Henry* and *Prince Robert* made extended cruises on East Coast charter from Boston and New York to Bermuda, South America, and Hawaii.

Prince Robert followed her consorts to Boston, Bermuda, and the West Indies in 1932 but then returned to serve, as intended, on the Alaska cruises.

These were eleven-day, 2,047-mile return trips to Skagway ("The Gateway to the Klondike"), calling at the forestry and fishing towns of Prince Rupert, Sitka, Ketchikan, and Juneau, via the Inland Passage. The sea at Skagway was normally frozen from November to February, so the *Robert* was usually laid up for overhaul. The *Prince Henry* was chartered out to Clarke Steamship Co. of Montreal in 1938, renamed the *North Star*, and put in service on their Montreal-Maritimes-West Indies trade until the war broke out.

By the late 1930's the Canadian chief of the Naval Staff was examining the shipping requirements for a war he knew would come. He had opposed the sale of the Prince ships outside of Canada during the lean Depression years on the grounds that they had wartime potential as armed merchant cruisers. The Admiralty had deposited defensive equipment in Canada between the wars in order to arm fast liners as AMC's in the event of hostilities. The first was to be the *Letitia*, and the RCN volunteered to arm its own AMC's if the Admiralty would release twelve 6-inch guns.

With the sailing of convoy HX 7 from Halifax on 31 October 1939, AMC's began to undertake the protection of fast convoys. It was customary for unusually large or valuable convoys to be escorted by battleships, while cruisers and AMC's shepherded less important ones, assisting destroyers in providing protection against surface raiders.

It is hardly surprising, under the circumstances, that the Princes came to mind even though their conversion to AMC's promised to be a sizeable task. The minister of defence had the authority to requisition ships, and he notified the Admiralty on 9 September that the three ships were available for wartime use. Ten days later the War Cabinet approved a shipbuilding programme of $10 million, which included the conversion of the Princes. The Admiralty replied that two of the vessels could be fitted out with the RN equipment stored in Canada, but they expressed concern at the Princes' limited range, low water supply, and moderate top speed. Consequently, they advised the RCN not to convert the third ship at that time. The two vessels selected were those still in CN service, *Prince David* and *Prince Robert*.

Proceedings were instituted in mid-October 1939 to requisition the two ships on a charter-hire basis. It was soon apparent that the alterations would be substantial and that reconditioning after the war would be expensive. Thus the chief of the Naval Staff recommended on 8 December that the ships be purchased outright and retained in the RCN after the war. The Treasury Board allocated $1.2 million for the Princes, but negotiations dragged on between CN and the navy in a surprisingly desultory way, considering that the war was four months old and German raiders were known to be at large. The two vessels were finally acquired late in January 1940.

The navy recommended that the *North Star* be purchased as well, since war-suited ships were scarce. She was transferred to the RCN at Halifax on 11 March 1940 and renamed *Prince Henry*. The final prices agreed upon after prolonged negotiation were $700,000 each for *Prince David* and *Prince Robert*, and just over $800,000 for *Prince Henry*.

Plans were prepared by Messrs. Lambert, German and Milne for the conversion of the Princes to AMC's, and tenders were called for. Table 1 indicates the arrangements made and the appropriate conversion dates.

TABLE 1

Ship	Contractor	Start Date	Planned Delivery
Prince David	Halifax Shipyards	9 Feb. 1940	August
Prince Robert	Burrard Dry Dock, Vancouver	9 Feb. 1940	July
Prince Henry	Canadian Vickers, Montreal	15 May 1940	September

Ship	Contract Prices		Recommissioned
	Original	Actual	
Prince David	$583,400	$763,000	28 Dec. 1940
Prince Robert	$654,790	$755,300	31 July 1940
Prince Henry	$530,000	$815,000	4 Dec. 1940

Although *Prince Robert* was essentially complete by the end of July, *Prince David* and *Prince Henry* were in much poorer condition, particularly in terms of their hulls and machinery. The top two decks were cut away during the conversion and a light cruiser superstructure fitted, thereby removing the boat-deck cabins and lounges. Accommodation was revised, the hull and decks stiffened in places, and a small amount of watertight subdivision added. However, there was a basic weakness in their design as warships, in that there were still large cargo and accommodation compartments extending across their hulls with open access. A torpedo in their forward holds or in their large undivided engine rooms would probably have been disastrous.

Each of the ships was equipped with four 6-inch guns, one on each of the two decks forward, and two similarly mounted aft. Two 3-inch guns were fitted on the upper deck amidships, plus some light anti-aircraft machine guns. Two depth charge chutes were added at the stern, although anti-submarine detection equipment was not supplied. The guns provided from the Admiralty store were as much as forty-five years old, and although serviceable, they lacked any semblance of range and fire control equipment; the 6-inch weapons had been manufactured as early as 1896 and had been fitted in the wing casemates of "King Edward"-class battleships, launched in 1905 and 1906. As these guns had been designed to train over only a small arc, which had now to be extended to about 300 degrees, training was sluggish. The 3-inch guns were slightly newer. They dated from 1916 and had been designed for light cruisers. Still, no matter how ancient, this firepower made the Princes the most powerful RCN units until the acquisition of the cruisers HMS *Uganda* (HMCS *Quebec*) and HMS *Minotaur* (HMCS *Ontario*) late in the war. Under full load, the draft of the AMC's was now 21-feet, 1-inch aft, and a notable feature was the replacement of their three tall funnels with two shorter oval ones. This gave the ships a rather more handsome and belligerent appearance, appropriate to their new role, and even made them resemble a small version of a Hawkins-class cruiser, a fact which was to pay dividends at least once.

On 31 July 1940 *Prince Robert* recommissioned as HMCS with pennant number F56 at Esquimalt, under the command of Commander C.T. Beard, RCN, with a crew of 241. The navy was concerned about the number of German ships which had taken refuge on the outbreak of the war in western Mexican and South American ports. Some of these ships were known to be preparing to sail, possibly for Japan. The knowledge that at least six armed merchant raiders were at large in the Pacific, Indian, and South Atlantic Oceans caused even greater anxiety. Only a small British squadron of light cruisers and some destroyers were available to meet this threat. Consequently, the *Robert*'s completion was hastened, and in early September it was agreed that she would reinforce the blockading ships off the coast of Mexico. She went to sea for one trial 6-inch shoot on 11 September and sailed southward the following day "in a very unready state," with only stores embarked.[3] She was just in time for one of the more famous Canadian naval exploits of the war—a capture at sea.

While on night patrol off Manzanillo, Mexico, on 25 September, her lookouts sighted a large ship setting out to sea. As Beard had planned, HMCS *Prince Robert* lay close to the land, unobserved, until the other ship was clear of the port. The merchantman was tracked visually from a mile astern until both of the vessels were in international waters. Then *Prince Robert* went to full ahead to close. Still unseen, she came churning up on the port quarter, illuminated the other by searchlight and ordered the vessel to stop. Her prey was the 8,000-ton *Weser*, a re-supply ship for the raider *Orion*, then at large. Thus *Weser* was a doubly worthwhile catch, and her capture gave the AMC's crew a tremendous fillip. Although prepared for scuttling, *Weser* was boarded so quickly that there was no time to open the sea cocks. She was seized and steamed to Esquimalt under the control of a small prize crew. Once there, she was overhauled, renamed *Vancouver Island* and used for regular service until sunk by a U-boat in the Atlantic a year later. She proved to be the only large undamaged prize taken by the Prince ships. Prize money was awarded for her at the end of the war, but it was turned over to the Naval Benevolent Fund rather than being distributed, much to the sorrow of the potential recipients, particularly as this marked the end of the centuries-old custom of naval prize money.

Prince Robert continued patrolling without further incident from southern California to the Straits of Magellan, until mid-January 1941, when she went to Australia to provide trans-Pacific troop convoy protection for Australian and New Zealand personnel coming to Canada.

Meanwhile, on 4 December 1940, *Prince Henry* had commissioned as F70 at Montreal, under the command of Captain R.I. Agnew, RCN; to be followed by *Prince David* as F89 on 28 December at Halifax, under Captain W.B. Armit, RCNR. The advance party had been standing by *Prince Henry* since August, but her conversion had been delayed by corvette construction at Vickers. In fact, when it came time for her to sail she was frozen in and had to be broken out twice by icebreakers before she could clear Sorel and proceed to Halifax. By mid-January both ships were in Bermuda for "working up" in company with another AMC, the *Queen of Bermuda*, and the battleship HMS *Duke of York*.

It took a while to learn the idiosyncrasies of the equipment. During *Prince Henry*'s first 6-inch shoot, the target tug disappeared behind four spouts of water, and the ship received the urgent lamp signal "Fire at the Target Not at the Tug!" During the night firing, the opening salvo switched on all the running lights and in the ensuing efforts to get them off again someone became entangled in the siren lanyard and set it wailing. Pandemonium!

Prince David remained on the East Coast as a convoy escort. Early one day in the spring of 1941, while the ship was steaming alone and closed up at dawn action stations, the executive officer, Commander W.B. Shedden, RCNVR, was called forward to the bridge by Captain Armit, who handed over his binoculars with the query "Do you see that?" referring to the horizon ahead. Commander Shedden could see the heavy upper mast and fighting top of a major warship approaching them. Knowing that there were no friendly forces in the vicinity, Captain Armit asked, "What do you think we should do?" "I don't know what you are going to do," said Shedden, "but I'm going aft to my action station, because the first place they are going to fire at is this bridge!" The ship's course was altered hastily and she steamed off in the opposite direction at almost twenty-three knots. Fortunately the other ship also decided that discretion was the better part of valour and she turned away to the north. Neutral American aircraft reported later that she was a German pocket battleship, apparently deterred by the *Prince*'s superficial resemblance to an 8-inch cruiser.

Prince Henry returned to the Pacific and relieved an RN cruiser on the offshore patrol of the South American coast. In February 1941, she was off the Peruvian port of Callao, where the two German vessels, *Hermonthis* and *München*, were obviously preparing to set sail, and two more, *Leipzig* and *Monserrate*, were making ready. Naval intelligence kept the ship fully informed of their condition, and on 16 March Captain Agnew took the *Henry* into Callao for the permitted twenty-four hours, ostensibly for supplies, but really to see what was happening at first hand. The British consul knew that the enemy ships were fully stored, fuelled, wired for instant demolition, and ready to depart at any time. Captain Agnew sailed at once, maintaining an out-of-sight patrol in order to encourage the Germans into thinking that the blockade had been relaxed and that they should make a break. At 1830 on 31 March, a message was received from Radio Lima that the *Hermonthis* and *München* had requested permission to sail. This they did at 1930, when *Prince Henry* was sixty miles to the south, nearly three hours steaming away. She turned north and it is a credit to those involved in plotting her closing course that it was correct to within five degrees and that the estimated speed was exact.

At 0630 on 1 April, *München* was sighted heading north, then altering to the west. Fifteen minutes later, at six miles range, *Prince Henry* ordered "Stop Instantly or I Will Open Fire," and shortly thereafter fired one shot cross the freighter's bows. *München* slowed at once, but smoke and flames were seen issuing from the after end of her superstructure. In fact the shot and the appearance of flames so nearly coincided that the captain was moved to remark sourly to the officer of 'A' gun, "Now look what you've done!"

As *Prince Henry* drew alongside, it was apparent that the freighter, engulfed in smoke and flames, could not be saved. As her boats were obviously evacuating the ship's company in a rehearsed manner, Captain Agnew steamed south to seek the fleeing *Hermonthis*, with whom the *München* had been heard to communicate. Four hours later, at 1225, she was sighted to the southwest, but like her compatriot she fired demolition charges and lowered her boats.

Agnew hoped that she could be saved and *Prince Henry*'s boats were sent away to round up some of the Germans and take them back on board to fight the fires and flooding. The *Henry* was taken alongside on the weather beam despite a moderate sea surging between the hulls. The salvage party, under Commander A.C. Wurtele, managed to shut the seacocks and all hands turned to fire-fighting. But *Hermonthis'* generator compartment had been flooded and this prevented the use of her pumps while the rolling of the two ships broke *Prince Henry*'s hoses. The fire in one hold was still uncontrolled after four hours and could not be smothered because the hatches were damaged. *Prince Henry* recovered her party at 1700, cast off, rounded up the German boats, and sank the furiously burning ship with 6-inch gunfire.

She turned north again to look for *München*'s crew, but discovered that they had been taken prisoner by the Peruvian cruiser *Almirante Grau* and that the freighter had been sunk. The *Prince Henry* continued on off-shore patrol for another three weeks and then proceeded to Esquimalt where *Hermonthis'* crew was put ashore. She patrolled the West Coast of Canada for some time, went to Bermuda and thence to St. John's, Newfoundland, to act as a temporary depot ship for the Newfoundland Escort Force. It was "a most depressing period, moored like a hulk . . . while the captain and most of the crew left the ship."[4] After only a short time she sailed with a maintenance crew for Halifax. She must have been the only warship to enter that heavily defended port throughout the war without being challenged and without flying any identifying pennants. The "gate" in the anti-submarine nets opened automatically, and she proceeded past the Port War Signal Station and alongside without instructions and without a report from her acting commanding officer.

Meanwhile, *Prince Robert*, after a refit at Esquimalt, undertook the armed escort of the transport *Awatea* carrying Canadian troops to Hong Kong. She embarked 4 officers and 105 other ranks of the Royal Rifles while *Awatea* carried the balance and the Winnipeg Grenadiers. The total contingent, Force "C," consisted of 96 officers, 1,877 other ranks, 2 Auxiliary Service Supervisors and 1 stowaway, who fortunately made the round trip as the whole force was lost when Hong Kong fell to the Japanese a month later.

The two ships sailed on the night of 27 October 1941, via Honolulu and Manila, where HMS *Danae* was added to the escort. They reached Hong Kong on 16 November, and *Prince Robert* sailed for home a week later, passing through Honolulu on 3 December, without any inkling of the large Japanese fleet bearing down on the Hawaiian Islands from the north. Although she picked up some mystifying signals, she saw nothing of Vice-Admiral Nagumo's Pearl Harbour strike force and returned to Esquimalt unscathed.

Following her sojourn in Halifax, *Prince Henry* was sent to Puerto Rico and placed under the control of Rear-Admiral J.H. Hoover, USN, commander of the Caribbean Sea Frontier, on 19 January 1942. There were two old four-stack American destroyers and a new Dutch gunnery training ship, *Van Kinsbergen*, in the force. The Canadians and the Dutch were horrified by the casual way the Americans used their wireless sets, and the Dutch refused to reply to *any* messages while at sea. *Prince Henry* remained at San Juan briefly before being banished to Charlotte Amalie, St. Thomas, as her sailors, unaccustomed to the cheap rum, had overwhelmed the Puerto Rican town for the first couple of days. She attempted to rescue the torpedoed tanker *Lihue* on 22 February when the crew, who had already been picked up, refused to return on board. A party was put aboard the stricken vessel and managed to raise steam, but the weather deteriorated so badly the next day that the ship had to be stopped. *Prince Henry* left the area to continue her patrol, and an effort was made by the minesweeper USS *Partridge* to tow *Lihue* stern first with a sweep wire. However, the holds continued to fill, and as the boiler room bulkhead threatened to collapse, the crew abandoned ship in *Prince Henry*'s whaler. Shortly thereafter *Lihue* sank, another success for the Germans and *Prince Henry*'s third loss.

German submarines were active in the Caribbean now, and *Prince Henry* was a vulnerable target, lacking as she did ASDIC and adequate watertight subdivision. But the authorities appeared unconcerned about these realities. At one stage she evacuated a berth in Port Castries for the SS *Lady Hawkins*, which was torpedoed alongside the following day by a U-boat that fired a salvo through the harbour mouth. Commander Tenth Fleet C&R's (convoy and routing) operational orders from New York tended to be informal and included such gems as: "My dear [Captain] Edwards: I would like you to proceed to French Guiana"; and enclosed was an aviation chart, being the only one available, with no water depths or sea marks thereon.[5] *Prince Henry* got herself into shallow water on more than one occasion and was only able to extricate herself by sounding ahead with hand lead and line from a motor cutter, in a fashion reminiscent of Captain Cook. On 3 April *Prince Henry*, guided by a Catalina flying boat, rescued the survivors of the sunken SS *Delvalle*, picking up forty-four people from a raft. The *Delvalle*'s captain had seen a submarine the night before and feeling that his ship was doomed he had rehearsed evacuation and arranged to take all of the ship's cash in a bag so that he could purchase supplies for his passengers and crew.

On 20 April 1942, *Prince Henry* sailed for Esquimalt where all three ships were reunited by May 7 to face the Japanese threat. They were taken in hand by the dockyard for some modernization—plastic bridge armour, elementary ASDIC's, and several 20-mm oerlikon guns. In addition, their duties were outlined at last. They were to:

1. guard the focal points for shipping in the northeast Pacific, particularly off British Columbia;

2. patrol sheltered waters where enemy vessels might hide along the coast;
3. reassure the public by their presence;
4. satisfy American demands for a Canadian naval force in the area;
5. make credible threats designed to keep the enemy away.
What the Prince ships were supposed to do in the face of a major warship attack was never spelled out.

Whatever the shortcomings of this programme, it was successful, and for three and one-half years no enemy patrol was detected off the coast of British Columbia except for a lone Japanese submarine that shelled Estevan lighthouse. *Prince David* was even employed in a propaganda movie, "The Commandos Strike at Dawn!"

When Japanese forces seized the Aleutian Islands of Kiska and Attu in June 1942, the three Prince ships and two corvettes, HMCS *Dawson* and HMCS *Vancouver*, were ordered to co-operate with American forces being transported to Kodiak, a base which was to serve as a springboard for the projected recovery of the islands. The Princes sailed for Dutch Harbor on 20 August, the two corvettes preceding them. When Captain J.C.I. Edwards asked for berthing instructions, he was chastened with the reply "Berth with the other corvettes."

Their escort duties continued for two months over some three hundred and fifty miles of open sea between the mainland and the outer islands. Although enemy forces were in the neighbourhood, none were encountered, and the ships had only to endure the usual foul conditions in that corner of the misnamed Pacific—sudden gales, erratic currents, uncharted shoals, and dense fog. Second only to these tribulations was the American army officer, who, while demonstrating his new automatic rifle in the wardroom, let off a blast "scattering the afternoon tea drinkers, penetrating the deckhead, and irretrievably damaging pots in the wardroom galley above.[6] It was all very taxing, particularly when standard brands of liquor ran out and had to be supplemented by such exotic mixtures as cherry brandy and Coca-Cola. The ships were popular nonetheless. They had acquired a striptease movie in Hollywood from one of Basil Rathbone's friends which was tremendously popular in the monastic environment of Alaska! After helping tow a ship off Dry Spruce Island, the ships turned south in mid-November to resume their British Columbia coastal patrols.

By this stage in the war the ships could no longer serve as effective AMC's against new types of enemy armed vessels. There was increasing concern that the Japanese might operate major warships off the West Coast. The Princes could neither defend their charges effectively nor fight their way clear from such opposition. Moreover, and somewhat surprisingly for ex-liners, these ships had a jerky and rapid roll that made them poor gun platforms, particularly as they had no sophisticated gunnery control. At the same time, the navy had agreed to provide vessels for

combined operations and these would have to come by way of new construction or conversion. So the decision was made to convert at least two of
the Princes to Landing Ship Infantry (Medium). One was also to be fitted
as a headquarters ship and both were to carry a flotilla of small landing
craft. The conversions were approved early in 1943, and *Prince Henry* and
Prince David were taken in hand by Burrard Dry Dock on 30 April and 1
May respectively.

As all three ships could not be used as LSI's, it was decided to rearm
Prince Robert as an auxiliary anti-aircraft cruiser, to provide convoys with
protection from German air attack. She was taken out of service at Esquimalt on 2 January 1943 for modification. From this point on the careers of
the *Robert* and the two LSI's differ so widely that they must be treated
separately.

Refitted for anti-aircraft duties, *Prince Robert* recommissioned on 7
June 1943, under Captain A.M. Hope, RCN. She was armed with ten
4-inch twin high-angle/low-angle dual-purpose guns, eight 2-pounder
pom-poms, and twelve oerlikons. She was also provided with four depth
charge throwers, making her one of the most powerful anti-aircraft ships
of her size afloat.

She put to sea on 29 July bound for the United Kingdom via Panama
and Bermuda. Several modifications were made to her gunnery systems
while she was in Bermuda, and it was not until 20 October that she was
ready to sail from England in support of fast troop convoys returning from
Gibraltar. U-boats were now making attacks in concert with long-range
aircraft, many of which were equipped with glider bombs capable of being
homed in on their targets from distances of up to six miles. Consequently,
the run past the Bay of Biscay had become one of the most dangerous of the
war. *Prince Robert* went into action for the first time on 21 October, in
support of a convoy under extensive air attack and harassed by U-boats,
three of which had already been sunk. Her position was on the convoy's
port quarter, providing anti-aircraft cover. At one point she managed to
drive off two glider-bomb-equipped Heinkels with gunfire while a bomb
from the third went wide. Only one ship was lost, and her complement was
rescued.

From that point on, *Prince Robert* was engaged as an A/A escort on
convoys from the U.K. to Naples. Even when she was in harbour she was
called upon to supplement the local A/A batteries whenever a raid took
place. She was tied in by land telephone line from her mooring buoy or
jetty to the local control for this purpose, and her weary ship's company
seldom received a stand down. She arrived in Plymouth for the last time on
13 September 1944, having sailed as an escort to seventeen convoys during
one hundred and thirty days at sea.

As danger from aircraft in the European sea theatre had decreased following the Normandy invasion, it was decided to prepare *Prince Robert* for the Pacific war, to meet commitments that the Canadian government had made to the Admiralty earlier in 1944. She set off on a twenty-three day voyage back to Esquimalt where she paid off for a short refit on 20 December in preparation for her new role.

She commissioned again on 4 June 1945 at Vancouver, under Captain W.B. Creery, RCN, and sailed on 4 July for Sydney, Australia, via San Francisco—in San Francisco her four twin oerlikon mounts were replaced with four heavier bofors. On 15 August, as the surrender of Japan was being announced, she sailed independently for Hong Kong to assist in the control of the area and in the repatriation of prisoners. The problems of re-occupation were exacerbated by the reluctance of the Americans to assist the British in recovering their colonial territory. With this delicate issue still unresolved, Admiral Sir Bruce Fraser, commander-in-chief of the British Pacific Fleet, sent Rear-Admiral C.H.J. Harcourt, RN, to Hong Kong in HMS *Swiftsure*, together with the carriers *Venerable* and *Indomitable*, the cruiser *Euryalus, Prince Robert*, fourteen destroyers, minesweepers, a hospital ship, and the 8th submarine flotilla. *Prince Robert* was the fifth ship to enter the roadstead, and after a very cautious examination of the western dock area at slow speed, she approached the Kowloon dockyard on the mainland shore.

Landing parties had been formed from the ship's company and given intensive training during the passage. They consisted of a company headquarters and two platoons under Lieutenant J.W. Whittall. At 1330 on 30 August *Prince Robert* secured alongside Holt's Wharf and, well within signalling view of the powerful armament of the flagship anchored in the harbour, landed her party, "to the accompaniment of shrieks of joy from the Chinese onlookers."[7] Further up the same wharf a small coastal steamer and a barge were being loaded with loot and salt by Japanese soldiers, all of whom were armed. The landing party soon put a stop to these activities but then had to clear the dock area, rail yard, and station of Chinese looters who were taking advantage of the loss of Japanese authority. It was not until the following evening that HMS *Anson* could land a large party of Royal Marines to relieve *Prince Robert*'s men. It was by no means certain that the enemy garrison would heed the general surrender, and anxious days followed, firstly in disarming the vastly superior numbers of Japanese and then in policing the exuberant population. The official surrender of the Hong Kong area took place on 16 September with Captain Creery as one of the delegates for Canada. The only casualty had been a commissioned gunner who had shot himself in the leg accidentally.

Prince Robert's landing party were the first troops to enter Sham Shui Po prison camp, where 370 Canadians, imprisoned for three-and-one-half-years and wondering if they had been forgotten, gave vent to wild demonstrations of enthusiasm when they caught sight of Canada flashes on the naval uniforms. It was a wonderful occasion which lifted the hearts of liberators and liberated alike. Contrary to popular belief, the prisoners were in unexpectedly good shape, the high standard of morale, discipline, cheeerfulness, and general physical condition being noted by the relieving force. There was practically nothing left for *Prince Robert* to do after the first few days, apart from mounting some security guards and helping transfer some ex-prisoners from the notorious Stanley Camp on an off-shore island to the troopship *Empress of Australia*. And so, on 26 September, *Prince Robert* was detached from the British Pacific Fleet and sailed for home, via Subic Bay and Manila in the Philippines, where fifty-nine former prisoners were embarked.

The ship slipped from her mooring at Manila at 2200 on 29 September (narrowly avoiding a typhoon in the process) and arrived at Esquimalt, via Pearl Harbor, at 1037 on 20 October. It was her final task. She experienced a few "open houses" and was paid off on 10 December 1945, being transferred to the War Assets Corporation for disposal in January 1946. She had steamed some 21,900 miles during her last commission alone.

We must return now to mid-1943 to follow the fortunes of the other two armed merchant cruisers, in hand at Burrard Dry Dock Vancouver, for conversion to landing ships. Each was to be equipped to carry eight 20-ton, box-like landing craft, four per side, slung in solid quadrantal davits along the upper deck. The old 6-inch guns were removed, and each ship was equipped with two twin 4-inch high-angle/low-angle mountings, two single bofors, and ten oerlikons, essential for anti-aircraft protection. Captain T.D. Kelly, RCNR, who had been the executive officer of one of the ships, was retained to supervise their fitting out. He had a relatively free hand as there were few precedents and the navy's plans were changed frequently as the conversions proceeded. One problem that he was obliged to wrestle with was the necessity of carrying large quantities of gasoline aboard for the landing craft. Drawing on his prewar experience with oil tankers, he devised the idea of floating the gasoline on water and pumping the fuel up into the landing craft by forcing water into the storage tanks. The water did not mix with the fuel and ensured that the tanks and lines were always full—of gasoline or water—so that no dangerous fumes collected. The accommodation area was cleared out to provide for an enlarged sick bay in anticipation of casualties in the new role, an elaborate signal command installation was established, more ship's messing space provided, a much larger wardroom (to hold up to 90 officers and a full-sized grand piano) allowed, and accommodation organized for 550 army personnel. In addition, bunks were installed. This was an unusual arrangement in assault ships, where the men usually slept on folding cots, but it was a blessing in rough weather.

The complement of each vessel was raised to 31 officers and 322 men, including the landing craft crews. These additions created the usual manning problems as the RCN was already committed to manning 30 large landing craft for the forthcoming invasion. Consequently, in view of the reduced threat to the West Coast of Canada, it was agreed that the army would assume full responsibility for any combined operations vessels there, and that the Princes and their landing craft would be manned from the trained crews made available thereby.

Prince David recommissioned on 20 December 1943, under Captain Kelly (her final commanding officer), and *Prince Henry*, under Captain V.S. Godfrey, RCN, on 6 January 1944. They left Esquimalt shortly thereafter, but they were by no means ready for the fray. They could not be darkened, as many of the deadlights did not fit over the portholes properly; some of the scuttles leaked when closed because the gaskets were the wrong size; the radar broke down during passage; and the bilges had to be pumped continuously. This sorry state of affairs was not entirely the dockyard's fault. They had been pressed to complete the refit as quickly as possible, since the Admiralty had informed Naval Service Headquarters in Ottawa that if the two ships did not arrive in the United Kingdom by mid-February, they could not be integrated into the invasion armada.

After transiting the Panama, *Prince David* embarked 437 American soldiers for passage from New York to the Clyde while *Prince Henry* was diverted to Bermuda to repatriate 250 British school children who had been evacuated from England at the time of the blitz. Although his passengers were a source of concern to Captain Godfrey and despite a storm encountered off Scotland, the trip was treated as a lark by the children. On arrival, the two ships were taken in hand by John Browns of Clydebank for a final fitting out with oerlikons, radar, and communications equipment in preparation for "Neptune," the sea phase of the Normandy landings.

Both ships sailed south in mid-April to Cowes, Isle of Wight, for sea training. Captain Godfrey was full of praise for the ability of the captains of the various merchant ships that took part in the pre-invasion exercises.

As the Senior Officer of all the [landing ships] composing one of the forces, I was responsible for their deployment on D-Day. I exercised them continuously at all kinds of maneuvers in the Channel from the time of our arrival until June. It was interesting and exciting but extremely difficult to exercise these troopships in equal speed maneuvers due to [their] different sizes, shapes and speeds, ranging from the 16,000 ton *Llangibby Castle* to small cross-channel steamers of a few hundred tons. However, we became pretty good, and deployment on D-Day itself went off perfectly. It was amazing how some of the larger ships were able to keep station on a line of bearing, observing that they were not fitted with engine revolution telegraphs.[8]

During this period the Princes picked up their landing craft. *Prince David* carried the 529th Flotilla, with Lieutenant R.G. Buckingham, RCNVR, as flotilla officer, and six boats commanded by volunteer reserve lieutenants and one RCN leading seaman. She also carried two Royal Navy landing craft, with Royal Marines embarked for initial fire support and frogmen for beach obstacle clearance. *Prince Henry* embarked the 528th Flotilla, with Lieutenant J.C. Davie, RCNVR, as commanding officer, and eight boats commanded by a motley group of RCNVR lieutenants, sub-lieutenants, leading seamen, and an able seaman.

May was given over to practical training with the troops, both ships embarking their complements on 30 April. This was the last of a series of exercises which tested loading and landing arrangements as well as sea-sickness remedies for the soldiers. On 24 May King George VI reviewed the invasion fleet in Southampton Water. The final troop movements had been completed ashore, the area sealed off, and briefings held in the regiments. At last, on 2 June, *Prince David* and *Prince Henry* embarked their forces for the assault and anchored downstream in the Solent.

The shipborne allocation of troops was complicated. Not all members of a regiment were to be carried in a single vessel in order to avoid the loss of a complete unit. In reviewing the invasion plans, one derives the impression of very considerable fatalism. Terrific losses were anticipated and difficulties were encountered adjusting the plans when these losses failed to materialize.

Prince David embarked 418 troops, 132 of whom were "A" Company of Le Régiment de la Chaudière from Lévis, Quebec, forming part of the 8th Infantry Brigade Reserve. The balance of *Prince David*'s complement were support troops, to be lifted ashore by tank landing craft, on the cheerful supposition that none of the ship's landing craft would have survived the initial beaching. Sadly, this was nearly true in *David*'s case. She also embarked the Royal Marines who were to be landed forty minutes behind the assault waves for beach duties.

Prince Henry embarked 147 of the Canadian Scottish from Victoria and 128 other support troops, forming, with their parent units, the reserve for the 7th Infantry Brigade. Everyone was in high spirits and interest was intense because of the unpredictable weather. Of the seven-thousand ship invasion flotilla, the smaller and slower craft sailed first, aiming at the "Piccadilly Circus" concentration point in mid-Channel, from whence they proceeded down the marked "lanes" swept through the mine-fields the night before to Normandy. At 2140 on 5 June, *Prince David* and *Prince Henry* weighed and proceeded around the Isle of Wight and into the dark and stormy Channel. They were bound for landing areas northwest of Caen, between Asnelles and the mouth of the Orne River, on "Mike" and "Nan" beaches in the British "JUNO" sector, east of the Americans.

In addition to her troop-carrying role, *Prince Henry* was also the senior officer of Force J1, twenty-two merchantmen destined for the "JUNO" beaches. *Prince David* was senior officer of a subdivision of Force J2, all part of Force J, under Commodore G.N. Oliver, RN, in HMS *Hilary*.

After advancing up-channel in the dark, the two Princes separated at the entrance to their respective swept channels; *Prince David* passed up lane eight, led by HMCS *Sioux*, while *Prince Henry* entered lane seven astern of HMCS *Algonquin*, the destroyers forming part of a thirteen-ship support bombardment group. The larger Prince ships were able to offer a more comfortable passage for their troops than the leading battalions enjoyed in their smaller and less seaworthy assault craft. The long weeks of ship-handling practice paid off now as the fully darkened Princes swept past the long columns of slower landing craft so that all of the vessels—in their milling thousands—arrived at their pre-assigned locations in the murky dawn just as planned. It was a staggeringly impressive sight.

Reveille was at 0430 and by 0535 on 6 June *Prince David* was anchored seven miles off "JUNO" beach, three hundred yards from her next ahead. Due to the pre-invasion sea and air bombardment, it was difficult to make out details ashore because of dust and smoke. By 0617 the first Royal Navy armed landing craft had slipped to deliver a party of marines ashore for obstacle removal and fire support. The second craft was away at 0637, followed by the six Canadian landing craft. It could hardly be said to have been a successful landing! Both RN craft hit mines or obstacles and sank, high seas having obscured the German anti-invasion devices. The crews managed to stumble ashore but without much of their gear. Landing craft number 1375 had been detailed off as duty boat for the senior officer and so was not involved in the assault. She was kept busy running messages, picking up wounded, and generally acting as a beach ferry for several days.

Only landing craft number 1151 was undamaged by mid-morning; all of the others had hit underwater obstacles or mines or been damaged by mortar fire. Number 1138 had beached safely, but half-submerged in the heavy surf, she was washed back onto a mine and sunk. However, most of the troops were put ashore safely by 0830 with the assistance of the tank landing craft, although many of the men were wet and lacked their heavier equipment. The Chaudières were still waiting to land at 1400, delayed while the Queen's Own Rifles fought their way inland past fortified blockhouses. Even so the French Canadians reached their D-Day objectives by 1600. By noon, number 1151 had embarked all the stranded landing craft crews for *Prince David*, but on her way out, weaving amongst the obstacles and wrecked craft, she was forced onto one of them by a lumbering in-bound tank landing craft and sunk. All of the personnel were rescued and ferried out to the mother ship which had failed to recover any landing craft that day. Later, *Prince David*, having accepted fifty-eight wounded and two dead on board, sailed for Southampton. She moved to Cowes on the eighth, where, owing to prodigal planning and few losses, she lay until the seventeenth. She made two more trips to Normandy between then and early July, after which she sailed to Barry Docks, Cardiff, to have her boilers cleaned.

Prince Henry's D-Day was rather more successful. Boat number 1372 was lowered first as duty boat for the senior officer just after 0545. Then the others were lowered to upper deck level, where the Canadian Scottish of the first wave (provided by the ship's galley staff with two hard-boiled eggs and a cheese sandwich each to supplement their field rations) were piped into their boats. The landing craft were lowered, slipped, assembled into "beaching flights" of the three sub-flotillas, and dispatched shoreward. The Scottish started landing at 0827, only forty-five minutes behind the assault regiments, and were all ashore within five minutes. Only landing craft 856 hit an obstacle, while 1021 collided with a tank landing craft. Nevertheless, both beached successfully and put their men ashore or onto stranded landing craft, from whence they managed to gain the beach under heavy mortar and machine gun fire. In addition to their normal small arms, the Scottish carried bicycles so that they could push inland and seize key bridges before they were blown up by the Germans. The landings went off successfully without major casualties.

All of the landing craft, except the duty boat, were hoisted back aboard by 1230, having landed the balance of the Scottish and support troops. At one point the duty boat had her bow damaged by mortar fire. She returned to the *Henry* for welding repairs, was on her way within the hour, and stayed off the beach for several more days. *Prince Henry*, having taken on fifty-six wounded and the survivors of several sunken craft, returned to Cowes at night with a nine-ship convoy. They arrived at the Isle of Wight in the dark, and with no word from the control ashore, Captain Godfrey told the others to anchor independently while he sought out a cramped berth at the western end of the island. Godfrey was later informed that the officer in charge of the anchorage had acted on the assumption that most of the ships involved in the initial landings would be sunk and that all of the available billets should be assigned to vessels being used for the build-up. It was rather a shame to spoil such organization by surviving. *Prince Henry* took over a group of landing craft and some Americans for "UTAH" beach during the reinforcement phase. She had serious problems this time because she was forced to operate in the vicinity of merchantmen that were unaccustomed to steaming on a line of bearing in the swept channels. Several of the U.S. ships were lost, particularly at night, in the flanking minefields. Subsequently, *Prince Henry* joined *Prince David* for ten days at anchor, made one more Normandy run from Portland on 18 June, three in July, and then sailed into Southampton for boiler cleaning.

Both ships sailed for Gibraltar and Naples on 24 July, arriving on the thirty-first for immediate inclusion in "Operation Dragoon," the invasion of southern France by the U.S. 7th Army, with supporting troops from Canada, France, and Britain. The overall naval command was vested in Vice-Admiral H.K. Hewitt, USN, while the "Sitka-Romeo" Force, responsible for overwhelming island strong points near the coast was commanded by Rear-Admiral T.E. Chandler, USN, who flew his flag temporarily in *Prince Henry*.

The Princes were involved in two attacking forces, subsidiary to the main landings. "Bravo Unit," under Captain G.E. Maynard, USN, with *Prince Henry*, and the transports *Barray, Greene, Roper, Osmond, Ingram* and five motor torpedo boats, was to capture the offshore Iles d'Hyères, Ile de Port Cros, and Ile du Levant, in order to neutralize the three-gun, 164-mm batteries on the eastern flank of the assault five hours before the main landings near Toulon. In addition to Rear-Admiral Chandler, *Prince Henry* carried 36 officers and 243 men of the Canadian-U.S. 1st Special Service Force (SSF), 2nd Regiment. *Prince David* was to be headquarters ship of "Romeo Unit," under Captain S.H. Morris, RN, comprising herself, *Princess Beatrix, Prince Albert*, and four U.S. motor torpedo boats. *Prince David* carried 283 French commandos of Le 1er Commando Français de l'Afrique du Nord, a unit which included two singularly pretty English girls as nurses and drivers. This force was to take the gun batteries at Cap Nègre on the mainland. Both ships were provided with new landing craft, and the area was scouted from the submarine HMS *Untiring* at the end of July.

The commandos were embarked from the beaches at Agropoli, Italy, by landing craft on 11 August for training exercises on the Pontine Island of Ponza. As is so often the case, the trial assault at night went poorly, and it took the 1st SSF four hours to clear the top of the chalky cliffs alone. Fortunately, they were higher and tougher than those at Iles d'Hyères. After the exercise, the troops were taken to Propriano Bay, Corsica, for two days relaxation. Then, fully rested, the force sailed on the fourteenth for the Riviera and "Dragoon."

Prince Henry was three miles off Levant before midnight and lowered her landing craft by 2345. They motored quietly in toward the island, towing some of the commandos in inflated rubber boats. These troops were released a thousand yards off the beach and left to paddle the rest of the way. Once ashore they were to seize the headlands and cover the follow-up from the landing craft. Each island was defended by roughly a company of German coast defence forces, and most of the defences faced the mainland to the north. There was an underground defence system of pillboxes but no movable artillery on Levant. Port Cros was to prove a particularly tough position to crack as the German troops were of high morale and based their defence on a series of impregnable Napoleonic stone fortresses which were linked by tunnels.

The men were ashore on Levant by 0130; by 1100 the fighting was over as the SSF had been able to penetrate the German defences. It was only then that they discovered that the guns *Untiring* had sighted were wooden dummies, manned by straw-filled men. Port Cros was a different case, and there were a good many wounded to be ferried out to *Prince Henry*, where the U.S. 43rd General Hospital was embarked. The fortresses resisted stubborn attacks by bazooka, small arms, and even 8-inch shellfire from the cruiser USS *Augusta*, whose rounds bounced off the tremendous walls without denting them. Sixteen Marauder dive bombers attacked with 5-inch rockets, also without results. On 16 August, Fort Lestissac fell to the 1st SSF, who made a frontal attack on the entrance with bazookas. It took four days to clear the island, and the task was completed only after HMS *Ramillies* put twelve 15-inch shells into the last fortress. She opened fire at 1300 and forty-five minutes later the Germans surrendered.

Meanwhile, *Prince David* arrived off Cap Nègre, and by 0130 on 15 August, six-and-one-half hours before the main army landings, the French commandos were put ashore. They silenced the coastal batteries and cleared the way for the balance of some seven hundred men who were landed to cut the main Toulon road. After the landing craft had returned with wounded and been hoisted aboard, the Princes weighed anchor at 1600 and sailed for Corsica. The ships made two more reinforcing trips to the French coast later, carrying in all 2,941 troops, mostly Ghoums from French North Africa. The Ghoums were so intrigued by *Prince David*'s flush toilets, the first that they had ever seen, that the chief engine room artificer was forced to shut off the water supply in order to prevent the urinals from becoming plugged with their washing.

By early September the Germans were being harried by Greek irregulars in that war-weary country and were evacuating the Aegean Islands. Thus, on 14 September, *Prince David* sailed with a powerful force, carrying 530 troops of the 9th British Commando to take and, if necessary, occupy the island of Kithera. The men swept ashore in their landing craft at night but met no resistance, being enthusiastically welcomed instead by the Greeks. *Prince David* sailed the next day for Taranto and on 8 October went to the Greek island of Páros in the Cyclades to loan her landing craft to the commandos for a series of local inner-island attacks and reoccupations in the Aegean. She was back in Taranto by the tenth.

Prince Henry, meanwhile, had been running short ferry trips from Taranto to the Adriatic coast of Italy, taking troops and landing craft to more convenient staging points for landings in Northern Greece and Yugoslavia. The situation in Greece was worsening alarmingly as the communists and royalists had begun fighting one another. It was decided, therefore, to lift the 46th British and the 4th Indian Divisions into Greece to establish a responsible government in Athens. On 14 October, M. Papandreou (the Greek prime minister-designate) and his provisional government, along with American, British, and French missions, boarded *Prince David* at Taranto. *Prince Henry* embarked 408 army personnel, including a parachute brigade headquarters staff. The whole force of seven landing ships, cruisers, carriers, and three minesweeping flotillas sailed on the fifteenth.

In preparation for the return of Papandreou's party, *Prince David* dropped her landing craft near Póros Island in the Gulf of Saranikós on the ninth. She did so in order to examine the passage leading into the port of Piraeus and to test the reaction of those ashore. As no firing developed, these small craft proceeded up the gulf, following the minesweepers. The first landing craft entered Piraeus at dawn on the fifteenth and received such a tumultuous welcome that they were nearly swamped. It turned out that the Germans had left for the north only a few days before.

The temperamental prime minister (he resigned several times between Taranto and Póros) transferred with his staff to the ancient Greek cruiser *Averoff* off Póros. The cruiser followed *Prince David* through the mine fields to the port where the liberation government and troops were landed. In the next few weeks both Princes made several trips between Taranto and Piraeus, carrying troops and returning Greeks. *Prince Henry* took troops to Salonica, in Macedonia, and in November took Greeks to the islands, rescuing a sorry lot of Italian prisoners of war in the process, and in general acted as a coastal ferry, just as she had done in the halcyon days before the war on the West Coast of Canada. When the populace at Preveza became embroiled in fighting on Christmas Day 1944, *Prince Henry* evacuated a crowd of fourteen hundred (including goats, sheep, arms, and baggage), in heavy seas and high winds, to Corfu. Two more trips were made; on the twenty-seventh for seventeen hundred and on the twenty-ninth for thirteen hundred. The evacuees were extremely excitable and completely unfamiliar with getting into and out of small boats while the sea was running: all of this in a ship designed to carry only five hundred and fifty troops! *Prince Henry* finished off by carrying ex-Italian and Russian prisoners of war to Taranto and 247 New Zealanders to Alexandria, on the first leg of their journey home.

Prince David hit a mine on 10 October but was able to limp into Salamis Bay. She had been following a "Hunt"-class destroyer up a swept channel ten miles from Piraeus when a mine detonated against her port side, immediately forward of her 4-inch magazine and next to her fuel and fresh water tanks. It blew a six by ten-foot hole in her plating and buckled her keel upwards. As there was no change in the ship's trim, she got underway again and continued to Piraeus. The minesweeping control officer was

most incensed when Captain Kelly objected to finding a mine in a sup-
posedly cleared channel! She transferred her landing craft to *Prince Henry*'s control and, after effecting makeshift repairs, went to Ferryville, Tuni-
sia, for docking. The large patch which was fitted to her hull fell off a few
days after her release from the dockyard while she was on her way to
Gibraltar.

On 18 November 1944, the Admiralty requested that the two vessels be
transferred on loan to the RN if the RCN could not man them for use in
southeast Asian operations. Thus, at the beginning of 1945, with the Greek
situation stabilizing, *Prince David* sailed directly to Esquimalt for refit.
She was transferred to the RN in June but was never taken over or renamed
by the British because of the termination of the Pacific War. She was laid
up instead at Lynn Creek, North Vancouver, where she was joined by her
erstwhile sister ship, *Prince Robert*, at the end of the year.

As a result of the same negotiations, *Prince Henry* reached Gibraltar in
March, 1945, escorted a home-bound convoy to the U.K. and was paid off as
a Canadian ship at London's East India Docks on 15 April since the RCN
had informed the Admiralty that they could no longer man her. Thus, as
HMS *Prince Henry*, and with an RN crew, she sailed for Wilhelmshaven as
an accommodation and headquarters ship late in 1945. *Prince Henry* never
returned to Canada. After her naval stint, she was transferred to the British
Ministry of Transport for $500,000 and her name changed to SS *Empire
Parkston*. Under the management of the General Steam Navigation Company she continued to serve the armed forces as she was put to trooping
duties between Harwich and the Hook of Holland. Apart from a new paint
job and the removal of the landing craft, her appearance was changed very
little. In fact, a curious cycle had been completed, for it was on this same
run to Holland in the early years of the century that her originator, Henry
Thornton, had gained his shipping experience working with railway
ferries. But by the end of 1961, she was over thirty years old and too
uneconomical to refit or retain. Instead, she was sold to a firm of Italian
shipbreakers at Spezia and broken up in February 1962.

At the end of 1945 *Prince David* and *Prince Robert* lay together at Lynn
Creek while the War Assets Branch of the government searched for buyers.
The CNR's president, R.C. Vaughan, investigated the practicality of
repurchasing them but decided that the costs of conversion were prohibi-
tive. A purchaser was finally found for both ships in the Charlton Steam
Shipping Co., the English-based subsidiary of a group of Greek companies. They bought *Prince David* on 7 January 1946 and *Prince Robert* eleven
days later for $375,000 each, renamed them *Charlton Monarch* and *Charl-
ton Sovereign* respectively and sailed them to Europe. After a refit, the
Prince David (no other name seems fitting after so long a tenure) made
trips from the U.K. to Europe, Africa, and South America in the general

immigrant and package cargo trade. She lasted less than six years and was sold and broken up in 1951 at Swansea. *Prince Robert*, on the other hand, made runs from Europe to the Far East. She was sold in the 1950's to the Italian firm of Fratelli Grimaldi Sicula Oceanica S.A., renamed *Lucania*, and traded in the Mediterranean and to the West Indies. Finally, she too outlived her usefulness and was broken up at Vado, near Leghorn, in 1962.

From the small wooden jetties of the Alaska ports, to the minor opulence of prewar West Indies cruises, the hell-fire of convoy battles, the smoke and uproar of D-Day, and the monotony of freighting service, the Princes Three travelled the oceans of the world. Their crews and commanding officers remember them affectionately, despite their rapid roll as AMC's, and all who served in them are quite prepared to reminisce about the Princes with rarely a critical word. Cammell Laird would well be proud of these three fine ships. Their kind are unlikely to be seen again.

Chapter 9

THE ROYAL CANADIAN NAVY'S QUEST FOR AUTONOMY IN THE NORTH WEST ATLANTIC: 1941-43

W.G.D. Lund

The Royal Canadian Navy assumed responsibility for the protection and control of shipping in the North West Atlantic on 30 April 1943. This event marked the successful conclusion of a campaign by the RCN to gain control of its rapidly expanding sea power and to assert autonomy in an area that was of primary national interest. The Mackenzie King government had stated in 1941 that it was "not prepared to place the strategical direction of the Royal Canadian Navy [in the Western Atlantic] unreservedly under the will of the United States."[1] Yet, when Great Britain signed the American-British Conversations-1 Agreement (ABC-1) with the United States on behalf of the British Commonwealth in March of that year, the RCN was considered merely a sub-command of the United States Navy. It was only the persistence and dedication of a few senior naval officers, struggling against this subordination, that allowed the RCN to achieve autonomy in the North West Atlantic and to fulfil Mackenzie King's hopes.

On 14 September 1939, an order-in-council was issued that directed Canada's six destroyers "to co-operate to the fullest extent with the forces of the Royal Navy."[2] These ships (*Ottawa, Fraser, St. Laurent, Restigouche, Saguenay,* and *Skeena*: a seventh, HMCS *Assiniboine*—ex-HMS *Kempenfelt*— was on her way out from England to join the RCN at the time), in addition to five minesweepers, constituted the main strength of the RCN, and the intent of the order was to assist in the war effort but to avoid placing Canada's small navy completely under Admiralty control. This measure reflected Mackenzie King's prewar policy of maintaining the greatest measure of autonomy possible in defence arrangements with Great Britain.

A change occurred in early 1940 when the Naval Council received approval from the Cabinet War Committee to place all of the Canadian destroyers under the Admiralty's operational control.[3] This action, prompted by a request from Britain, was recommended by the Naval Council for two reasons: first, the Admiralty were better able to take a worldwide view of naval dispositions and ensure that every ship was profitably employed; second, it was pointed out that these dispositions would probably be to Canada's advantage.

As the strategic situation deteriorated in Europe, further changes were made in command relationships. On 23 May 1940 an urgent request was received from the Admiralty for RCN destroyers to assist in the protection of the British Isles against a possible invasion.[4] With the Germans ensconced on the Atlantic seabord after the fall of France in June and with Britain under the threat of invasion, there was no question of the Canadian government taking a stand on the question of autonomy, a fact which even Mackenzie King was prepared to acknowledge.[5] "To co-operate to the fullest extent" took on quite a different meaning in October 1940. Naval Service Headquarters and the Canadian government placed virtually the entire navy at Great Britain's disposal and the commanding officer Atlantic Coast (COAC) was left with only a handful of ships.[6] The Cabinet War Committee viewed the situation as an "extreme emergency"; Britain's survival was at stake.[7] There was a strong feeling that if Britain fell Canada would be the next target for Nazi aggression. Canada's first line of defence was recognized as being the English Channel and the fireproof-house mentality that had prevailed was swept away by a fear approaching hysteria. It was under these circumstances that Great Britain gained control of Canada's naval resources and was able to treat them as part of her negotiable assets when she entered into ABC-1 with the United States.

The acquisition of ports on the Bay of Biscay enabled the Germans to extend their submarine operations further westward. By the end of 1940 Germany's strategy of starving Britain into submission by blockading sea commerce through unlimited submarine warfare became evident, and the long struggle by Commonwealth forces to maintain the vital lines of communications began. The RCN eventually dedicated nearly its entire resources to this struggle, which came to be known as the Battle of the Atlantic. Rear-Admiral L.W. Murray, RCN, recalled that the prime minister had been appalled when the SS *Athenia* was sunk by a U-boat.[8] Murray subsequently observed:

> We were able to impress upon [Mackenzie King] that this type of anti-submarine war was one our small Canadian navy was best [suited] to compete in. We got his approval for anything that could be done and there was never anything to stand in our way.[9]

The government's favourable attitude toward the policy of concentrating on anti-submarine warfare (ASW) complemented Rear-Admiral Percy W. Nelles's ambition to expand the Royal Canadian Navy. Nelles, the chief of the Naval Staff, was intent on building a force of modern destroyers which would form the basis of a peacetime navy on a much larger scale than before the war.[10] Therefore, when the Admiralty extended an invitation to Nelles to establish an escort force based on Newfoundland, he seized the opportunity.[11] In July 1941 the Newfoundland Escort Force (NEF) was created. Command of the force, which was based in St. John's was given to then Commodore L.W. Murray, with the title commodore commanding Newfoundland Force (CCNF). The Admiralty returned the destroyers which had been on loan to serve as the nucleus of the NEF; these were supplemented by a squadron of Canadian-built corvettes which had been working up in Halifax.

The establishment of the NEF enhanced Canada's military presence in Newfoundland (a point which found favour with the Cabinet War Committee) and extended her naval operations to mid-Atlantic.[12] Moreover, the force had a distinctive task which quickly developed as Canada's most important contribution to the war at sea. Neither the significance of the undertaking nor the resources required to execute it were fully realized at the time. It was impossible to foresee the developments which were to take place in the Battle of the Atlantic and how vital that theatre would become to the Allied effort. Admiral Nelles's original commitment to the NEF was forty-eight destroyers and corvettes.[13] Between May 1941 and October 1943 this commitment was more than doubled as Canada built more corvettes and recruited more crews. By the end of 1942 Canada was providing 48 per cent of the escorts for convoy protection. Yet, despite this preponderance of strength, she had virtually no influence over the strategic direction of these resources.

In January 1941 plenary meetings had been held in Washington between the British chiefs of staff and the U.S. joint chiefs of staff to discuss future military co-operation. Canada was neither consulted on her views nor directly represented during these talks.[14] The meetings resulted in a document, entitled ABC-1, dated 27 March 1941, which was submitted to the American and British governments for approval.[15] ABC-1 set forth the principles which would guide the military collaboration of the United States and the British Commonwealth should the former be obliged to enter the war.[16]

The provisions outlining command and staff relationships proved unsatisfactory to Canada,[17] a fact which was to have a considerable bearing on Canadian-American co-operation and on Canada's role in the war. Specifically, ABC-1 divided the Atlantic Ocean into eastern and western zones of strategic responsibility. In the event of the United States entering the war, "the High Commands of the United States and the United Kingdom" were to "collaborate continuously in the formulation and execution of strategic policies and plans . . . [governing] the control of the war."[18] It also stated that the United States would take responsibility for the strategic direction of British forces, including the RCN, in the Western Atlantic with the exception of "the waters and territories in which Canada assumes responsibility for the strategic direction of military forces, as may be defined in United States-Canada joint agreements."[19]

While the ABC-1 talks were in progress Mackenzie King raised objections privately through Great Britain's high commissioner on the subject of the proposed command relationships,[20] objections which were ignored, and Canada was presented with a *fait accompli* when the United States assumed strategic control of the Western Atlantic in September 1941. Although Canada was not bound to accept this situation from a constitutional standpoint, she was morally obligated to do so as Britain's ally. Nevertheless, this state of affairs disturbed many Royal Canadian Navy officers and provided some of the motivation for the subsequent establishment of a command independent of interference from both the United States and Great Britain.[21]

Concurrently with ABC-1, negotiations were carried out by members of the Permanent Joint Board on Defence, which had been established to act as the co-ordinating agency for any Canada-United States defence ventures. The Joint Board's task was to formulate a plan, entitled ABC-22, to complement what eventually became ABC-1. The negotiations were the scene of hard bargaining. Canada resisted American proposals for an agreement that would bring Canadian territory and forces, and also Newfoundland, under U.S. control for the purposes of ABC-22. The position adopted by the Canadian Chiefs of Staff Committee and supported by the Cabinet War Committee was that the improved strategic situation rendered the invasion of Great Britain unlikely and, therefore, that the circumstances in which ABC-22 would be brought into effect were "offensive."[22] Under threatening circumstances Canada was willing to accept direction from the United States because of the latter's preponderance of resources. However, now that it appeared that the United States would be brought into the war for the purpose of assisting in the destruction of the enemy in Europe, Canada was unwilling to give unqualified strategic control over her armed forces to the United States.

The Canadian chiefs of staff had their way and "command by co-operation" was established as the basis for the command relationship.[23] But for some time it was a hollow victory. Colonel S.W. Dzuiban has suggested that the U.S. War Department blocked repeated efforts by Canada to set up a military mission in Washington as a *quid pro quo* on the command relationship issue.[24] This denial of recognition of Canada as an equal partner on the operational level resulted in the RCN being relegated to the position of a sub-command of the United States Navy under the terms of ABC-1, and Canada's naval service was obliged to communicate through the Admiralty delegation in Washington on all matters of strategic policy.[25]

The Canadian chiefs of staff pressed the government to have the command relationships in ABC-1 altered when it was submitted to Canada for consideration in May 1941. Having evaded the snare laid by the Americans in ABC-22, the chiefs of staff were concerned that an acceptance of the ABC-1 report would place the armed forces in the very position that they had been trying to avoid.[26] The government agreed with the chiefs of staff, but the prime minister's efforts, referred to above, to have ABC-1 altered were ignored by Great Britain. The Department of External Affairs also attempted to lay Canada's case before the United States government through the United States naval attaché in Ottawa. Mackenzie King's reluctance to place the RCN unreservedly under the control of the United States was made clear. This had not been done with respect to the United Kingdom at the beginning of the war and would not be done now. However, Canada did not press the matter too far for fear of sabotaging the agreement. Consequently, Naval Service Headquarters was obliged to accept American control of its ships in the Atlantic after the Argentia Conference held 10-15 August 1941, even before the United States entered the war.

During the latter part of the summer, the USN began to come into the Battle of the Atlantic.[27] On 26 July 1941, the USN Western Hemisphere Defense Plan No. 4 (WPL-51), with the exception of Task B which provided for the escorting of ships under the flags of nations other than the United States, was brought into effect.[28] Between 26 July and mid-September, the USN began to work itself into the Commonwealth's convoy escort organization in the North Atlantic. British withdrawal was discussed by Roosevelt and Churchill at the Argential Conference. Admiral Sir Percy Noble, RN, commander-in-chief Western Approaches (CinCWA), and Admiral Ernest King, commander-in-chief U.S. Atlantic Fleet (CIN-CLANT), set mid-September as the date for the assumption by the United States Navy of strategic direction and responsibility in the Western Atlantic.[29] Canada was not consulted as to the date of the British withdrawal, although she had assumed responsibility for the anti-submarine escorts in that ocean area. However, on 23 August 1941 the U.S. naval attaché in Ottawa proposed to the chief of the Naval Staff that conversations begin between representatives of CINCLANT and NSHQ to determine what tasks would be carried out by their respective navies under ABC-1 and ABC-22.[30]

As a result of these conversations, the RCN accepted responsibility for escorting slow convoys, originating in Sydney, Nova Scotia, (designated SC) to the Mid-Ocean Meeting Point (MOMP) south of Iceland and slow westbound convoys (designated ONS) originating in the United Kingdom, on the return leg.[31] The CCNF's responsibility was to be restricted to control of SC convoys under CINCLANT's "broad supervision."[32] CINCLANT decided initially that the USN would only escort fast convoys originating in Halifax (designated HX) but would assume escort duties for some portion of SC convoys when it had gained experience.[33] On 11 September 1941, Task B of WPL-51 was executed, and on 16 September, the USN began to escort its first trans-Atlantic convoy, HX 150. On 25 September, all RN units were withdrawn from the Western Atlantic, and the command relationships in ABC-1 came into effect officially.

As of 13 September, CCNF and COAC passed under the strategic direction of CINCLANT. This occurred by virtue of Naval Service Headquarter's acceptance of an invitation from Admiral King to put the Royal Canadian Navy's convoy escort forces under one controlling authority.[34] This agreement, with regard to strategic control of naval forces, had been tailored to ABC-1.[35] Although the United States had not declared war when WPL-51 was brought into effect, neither the Admiralty nor NSHQ disputed the USN's assumption of control—American assistance was welcome under any terms. It was only after the United States entered the war that the Admiralty and then NSHQ raised the question of the strategic direction of convoy escorts in the Western Atlantic.[36] The reason, as we shall see, was that demands made by the Pacific and other theatres, which were not anticipated in ABC-1, reduced the number of anti-submarine escorts that the United States could contribute to the Battle of the Atlantic to an almost negligible quantity.

The United States was catapulted into the war by the Japanese attack on Pearl Harbor on 7 December 1941. Up to that moment nothing had occurred to test the definition of command relationships as set down in ABC-1 and ABC-22. On that day the U.S. secretary of the Navy ordered the commanding officer Atlantic Coast and the commodore commanding Newfoundland Force to take belligerent action against Japan before Canada had declared war against that country. CCNF, Commodore Murray, queried NSHQ on the signal: "In the interest of co-operation, and because the particular matter has very little immediate interest for NEF, this signal is being relayed to the ships of the NEF." Murray then asked for direction on that and any subsequent signals, remarking that he thought such instructions should come from either the Canadian or British authorities. Minutes appended to the letter after it was received in NSHQ indicate an uncertainty as to exactly what Commodore Murray's position was. The naval secretary under the direction of the Naval Council replied to Murray's query, "While the NEF is under the strategic direction of the U.S. Navy, this particular signal referred to dealt with policy and was therefore properly outside the scope of 'strategic direction.' "[37] The Naval Council insisted that the matter be forgotten since it would do more harm than good to make an issue of it. What the correspondence revealed was that the USN considered the COAC and the CCNF to be under its direct control in all matters of strategy and that the RCN would be prepared, rather apathetically, to accept this control in early 1942.

The USN's performance turned out to be considerably less than had been intended and the RCN's considerably more. The ships provided under ABC-1 included three battleships, five cruisers, forty-eight anti-submarine escorts (all destroyers), and forty-seven seaplanes. The contribution under WPL-51 was even more impressive and included three aircraft carriers. The Canadian contribution under the latter scheme was to be five destroyers and fifteen corvettes,[38] the policy still being to send as many escorts as possible to European waters.[39] When WPL-51 went into effect, American participation was limited to protection of HX eastbound and ON fast westbound convoys, while Canada increased her forces to eight destroyers and twenty-five corvettes. When the United States entered the war, all of the American destroyers were withdrawn immediately for service in other theatres, and by February 1942, there were only two United States Coast Guard cutters available for duty as convoy escorts.[40]

The withdrawal of the USN from the organization for the protection of trans-Atlantic shipping once again necessitated close co-operation between the two Commonwealth navies. In fact, it was obvious by late January 1942, that the American admiral, Rear-Admiral Arthur L. Bristol, Jr., (commander Task Force 24 [CTF24] with headquarters at Argentia, Newfoundland), whose responsibility it was to direct the control and protection of shipping in the North West Atlantic, was superfluous in the organization for operational control of escorts as he had no ships of his own.[41]

This fact was implicit in a signal from the Admiralty to the commander-in-chief U.S. Fleet (COMINCH) on 29 January 1942, which raised the question of the strategic direction of trans-Atlantic escorts. It proposed that trans-Atlantic escorts be controlled by the commander-in-chief Western Approaches. Admiral King, now COMINCH, rejected the proposal, stating that the system was working efficiently and that the United States should retain strategic control of the Western Atlantic. The First Sea Lord was not prepared to press the matter at the time, but he felt that the dual control scheme would not work and that he would need to re-open the question if the operational situation demanded.[42] Naval Service Headquarters was content to sit out this battle and stated that COAC and the flag officer Newfoundland Force (FONF, replacing CCNF) would continue to provide the maximum number of ships possible.[43]

By August 1942, the main action of the Battle of the Atlantic was concentrated in the mid-North Atlantic. It was there, in the Greenland "air gap," beyond the protective cover of Allied aircraft, that the Canadian and British escorts bore the full weight of the battle.[44] By this time many Canadian naval officers, who had either been in the midst of the fighting or who had held important positions on the staff of COAC or FONF, were beginning to fill vital positions in Ottawa. These officers, and a number who had been at NSHQ for some time, discovered an unwillingness at the higher levels to assert Canada's claim for more strategic responsibility in the control of the RCN.[45] Therefore, wheels were set in motion at lower levels to overcome this inertia.

A significant occurrence with regard to the command relationships issue was the establishment in July 1942 of a Canadian service mission in Washington. This mission, called the Canadian Joint Staff, was set up after a year of arduous negotiations with the U.S. State Department; the Americans were anxious to "avoid the establishment of any undesirable precedent" which would encourage other small allies to press for military missions.[46] The Canadian Joint Staff was actually established using the Permanent Joint Board on Defence as a guise. The Canadian chiefs of staff hoped that the Canadian Joint Staff would provide a link with the U.S. joint chiefs of staff on operational policy decisions involving their forces, particularly the Royal Canadian Navy.[47] The Permanent Joint Board on Defence had never been intended to fulfil this function. However, the terms of reference of the Canadian Joint Staff were ill-defined, and individual members were left to make what they could out of their mission.

Rear-Admiral V.G. Brodeur, RCN, was appointed as the naval member of the Canadian Joint Staff. A man of strong personality, he was a Canadian nationalist, a proud naval officer, and, to a great extent, anti-British.[48] Though he does not appear to have been selected for any of these attributes, it was for these reasons that he set out to assert Canada's position in councils between the RN and the USN when the RCN's interests were involved.[49]

Up to this point the commanding officer Atlantic Coast and the flag officer Newfoundland Force were considered sub-commands of the USN operating under the direct control of CTF 24. NSHQ and the two commands were normally included in joint negotiations on escort and convoy organization between the Royal Navy and the United States Navy. But in many cases NSHQ was not consulted when major strategic decisions were made concerning the actual employment of ships and other resources. This, to a great extent, was the fault of the British Admiralty Delegation in Washington, which was only too ready to keep Ottawa out of the picture. Consequently, the USN found itself dealing with NSHQ, sometimes with the British Admiralty Delegation, and sometimes with Admiral Brodeur after he was appointed naval member Canadian Joint Staff (NMCS). This was the situation that Brodeur sought to correct. He was determined to establish his office as the only link between NSHQ and the U.S. joint chiefs and to see to it that the British Admiralty Delegation no longer spoke for the RCN.

The first reports from the Canadian Joint Staff to the Canadian chiefs of staff confirmed that Canada had been left out of important decisions which concerned her forces.[50] Admiral Brodeur's first report to the CNS, Admiral Nelles, disclosed that Admiral King believed that there was collusion between NSHQ and the British Admiralty Delegation. This alleged collusion was seen as an indication that the RCN did not recognize King's strategic control in certain areas outside the Canadian Coastal Zone. Moreover, Brodeur explained, there was a rumour afoot that Canada and Great Britain were trying to cut out COMINCH completely. Brodeur suggested that the cause of the complaint was the too frequent use of the "old boy" network between the RN and the RCN, a network which the USN did not recognize as a *bona fide* channel of communications. He concluded: "This kind of private arrangement will never obtain for us the confidence nor consideration of the USN. It is most strongly recommended that such personal contact be stopped before we are completely ignored due to this kind of personal intrigue."[51]

Another significant event occurred in September when Rear-Admiral R.M. Brainard, USN, succeeded Rear-Admiral Bristol as CTF 24.[52] Brainard was a competent officer "with whom," remarked Admiral Murray, "we had nothing but the best and pleasantest relations."[53] However, signals sent during September and October indicate that Admiral Brainard was not above criticizing the RCN's materiel readiness and operational procedures.[54] These criticisms were accepted with good grace, but they were a source of embarassment to the RCN, coming as they did from a foreign commander.[55] These comments reached NSHQ just as the Director of Trade, Captain E. Brand, RCN, was receiving correspondence from the Naval Control Service Officer, Sydney, criticizing the inefficiency of CTF 24's staff in convoy control and the USN's "know-it-all" attitude with respect to learning from Canadian experience.[56]

By piecing together the evidence, one can see that the important departments at NSHQ, namely Operations, Plans, and Trade, were receiving a

Plate 46. Two of Canada's seven destroyers sent to assist the Royal Navy in the early days of World War II. View from the HMCS *Assiniboine* I (ex-HMS *Kempenfelt*) of HMCS *Saguenay* I off Halifax, 28 September 1940. (PAC—PA 104309)

Plate 47. Draft of new entries arriving at HMCS *Cornwallis*, Deep Brook, N.S., 16 June 1943. (PAC—PA 115372)

Plate 48. Castle-class corvette HMCS *Bowmanville* leaving St. John's, Newfoundland, base for the Newfoundland Escort Force protecting shipping in the North Atlantic. (PAC—PA 115210)

Plate 49. Three Flower-class corvettes of the Royal Canadian Navy, awaiting convoy duty in St. John's, Nfld., November 1943. *Left to right:* HMC Ships *Orillia, Trillium,* and *Calgary* (Revised Flower). (PAC—PA 107932)

Plate 50. A pause from convoy duty in the wardroom of HMCS *Ottawa* I, October 1940. *Left to right:* Lt. (E) E.N. Clarke, RCN; Lt. A.G. Boulton, RCNVR; S/Lt. E.W. Jones, RCNVR; Lt. (E) G.F. Winterburn, RCNR; Gunner (T) P.D. Budge, RCN; Lt. P.E. Haddon, RCN; Pay Lt. V.W. Howland, RCNVR. (H. Lawrence collection)

Plate 51. Rough weather in the North Atlantic made convoy operations a stern test. HMCS *Eyebright*, Flower-class corvette, in heavy seas. (MCM)

Plate 52. HMCS *Matapedia* (foreground), St. John's, Nfld., iced up after winter run, 2 March 1943. (PAC—PA 115344)

series of little annoyances concerning Canada's subordinate position in a theatre where her contribution was predominant. Discussions on the subject of establishing an independent command began on an informal basis between Captains H.N. Lay and H.G. DeWolf, who were the directors of Operations and Plans, respectively. This was the beginning of the autonomy campaign. Captain Lay wrote to various officers in the operational commands to solicit their views, and strong support was received from all quarters.[57]

By early November a very frustrated Admiral Brodeur was beginning to find his position in Washington untenable. On 26 October he had written to the chief of the Naval Staff that "the USN is 'undoubtedly baffled by our present way of dealing with them . . .' and that the British Admiralty Delegation was making a point of keeping him out of the picture with regard to matters of concern to the Royal Canadian Navy." Brodeur asserted that for this reason, "there is no doubt that the USN is under the impression that the RCN is partly under the control of the Admiralty.[58]

A few days later the Admiralty Delegation bypassed Admiral Brodeur and NSHQ once again on a matter concerning British strategic and materiel requirements which included Canadian necessities. It appears that the secretary of the Navy had posed a query which the delegation answered without consulting Brodeur. Brodeur found this out only when the Americans circulated the British reply to the Canadian Joint Staff.[59] Brodeur wrote a strongly worded appreciation to the CNS, which he said "was not meant to be a criticism" but which outlined all of his grievances regarding the British Admiralty Delegation's policy of ignoring Canada. He cited several incidents, including one involving operations which could have had serious repercussions. Brodeur summed up the Royal Navy's attitude concisely when he remarked:

> This appreciation could go back to 1907 and all its political complications concerning the relations between the RCN and the Admiralty, but as the situation still seems to be very much the same as it was then, only recent facts will be related because they indicate that regardless of all decisions reached at previous Colonial and Imperial Conferences, the Admiralty still looks upon the RCN as the naval child to be seen and heard when no outsider [the USN] is looking on or listening in.[60]

This letter put the CNS in the right frame of mind to counter a move by the British Admiralty Delegation and CINCLANT to limit distribution, to the Canadian Coastal Zone, of information on U-boat positions from NSHQ's highly developed high-frequency direction-finding (HF/DF) system.[61] This system located U-boat concentrations by using bearings obtained on U-boat high-frequency radio transmissions by a number of listening stations and a triangulation process. HF/DF information was used mainly by Canadian anti-submarine escort groups operating in the Western Atlantic. The British Admiralty Delegation, obviously in collusion with COMINCH's staff, politely raised the question of the promulgation of information in one signal,[62] then followed it up with another proposing that NSHQ greatly curtail their distribution. It was also proposed that COMINCH be the sole authority for promulgating such information. NSHQ's terse reply stated flatly that the RCN would not be pushed aside on the matter and that their system was far more efficient than the USN's. The Admiralty Delegation's reply pleaded that duplication of effort prompted the proposal, and they defended the USN's efficiency.[63]

The chief of the Naval Staff followed up his signal to the British Admiralty Delegation with a letter to Admiral King which he asked Captain Lay to draft. Lay had approached Nelles on the question of command relationships, and the latter had asked him "to put it all down on paper and I'll look at it."[64] Lay was in the process of drafting a detailed memorandum when the HF/DF information dispute presented an opportunity to raise the matter of command relationships with the United States Navy.

The letter to King, which proved to be the opening salvo of a campaign to have the command structure revised, reviewed the entire HF/DF issue and suggested that had Admiral Brodeur been consulted, the matter could have been cleared up in Washington. Nelles pointed out that it was the USN and the Admiralty who had asked the RCN to establish the system in the first place. He went on to review Canada's contribution to the Battle of the Atlantic and to emphasize the fact that her ships had made up 48 per cent of the escort forces while the Americans had provided only 2 per cent. Nelles's letter also drew attention to the similarities between the RCN and the RN, which were bearing the brunt of the battle, and the dissimilarity of the USN to them both. Mentioned as well was Canada's contribution in ships to the Operation Torch (North African) landings and the loan of anti-submarine escorts to the USN when it found itself hard pressed in June 1942. The letter concluded: "I hope you will agree that in all matters of common policy the RCN have done their best to co-operate with the two Services [USN and RN] and have placed the general strategic needs of the United Nations ahead of their purely Canadian coastal needs." Then Nelles proposed that a conference be held to discuss "the question of general operational control of all Trade Convoy Escorts."[65]

The letter went forward over Nelles's signature, but the thoughts were those of Captain Lay. Lay followed up the letter with a very long memorandum to the CNS which reviewed all of the agreements to which Canada subscribed or had been committed to by the British. He observed that regardless of what might have been intended, the Canadian ships on the

East Coast were, for all practical purposes, under the direct control of the USN.

> In spite of the RCN's efforts to co-operate fully with the U.S. Naval authorities in the general prosecution of "the Battle of the Atlantic" the attitude of the C in C U.S. Fleet had been considerably difficult. Other U.S. Naval authorities have taken their cue from him. The general attitude appears to be that they consider the RCN as purely a small part of their own fleet and have from time to time issued orders either directly or indirectly to RCN authorities or ships without in any way consulting NSHQ first.[66]

Captain Lay's recommendation was that Canada press for assumption of responsibility of the operational control of all escort forces and convoys in the Western Atlantic. He cited commander Task Force 24's unnecessary role which made effective co-operation between British and Canadian anti-submarine forces difficult. He also highlighted Canada's major contribution to the Battle of the Atlantic. Lay recognized that Admiral King would no doubt offer considerable resistance to a command reorganization and suggested that it would be best to have the matter discussed at a conference on the international level. Although he did not suggest that the Admiralty's help be solicited, he probably thought that the RN would support the proposal in a round table conference.

Naval Service Headquarters developed their campaign at every opportunity during the rest of December 1942 and January 1943. In this period the hottest action in the U-boat war was in the North West Atlantic, a fact which emphasized Canada's role and importance. Impetus was provided for the campaign when Admiral Brodeur intercepted a signal from CTF 24 to COMINCH and CinCWA which criticized the operational efficiency of Canadian escort groups.[67] Then, without consulting the NSHQ, the Admiralty suggested to COMINCH that alterations be made in the type of ships in Canadian escort groups.[68] Apparently these alterations had been discussed unofficially at a conference in Ottawa on 20 November 1942, but at Admiral King's request there had been no official agenda. The CNS also received a reply from his letter to Admiral King. COMINCH reluctantly agreed to a conference at some time in the future but maintained that an additional authority would only complicate the situation.[69] Obviously, King did not realize that the Canadians intended to remove CTF 24 from the scene.

While the situation fermented, Captain Lay worked on Canada's proposals to be tabled at the projected conference.[70] He also visited the COAC, which was now Admiral Murray, to sound out his views on the matter. Murray agreed that it was time for both the COAC and FONF to be removed from USN control. Murray's reasons were those of operational efficiency: he obviously considered CTF 24 to be superfluous. Moreover, he objected to having to report to an authority which had yet to prove itself any better at anti-submarine warfare than the Canadians.[71]

In early January, Nelles reacted quickly to the unauthorized transfer of Canadian destroyers by commander Task Force 24 between escort groups. The CNS chastised CTF 24 by signal for not requesting NSHQ's permission. CTF 24 replied that he was only following the directions of the Admiralty and COMINCH and stated, "To maintain [the] desired degree of flexibility it is expected that it will be necessary to make further similar changes from time to time without reference to other operational authorities."[72] Nelles realized, of course, that flexibility was essential, but by asserting NSHQ's claim he hoped to gain a purchase on Admiral King which would force the elimination of CTF 24 and bring about his replacement by a Canadian authority.

CTF 24's action was the last bit of ammunition Nelles required, and he moved over to the offensive by informing Admiral King that Canadian escorts could not be transferred between groups or commands without Naval Service Headquarters' authority. He followed up this announcement with a letter outlining recent grievances and pressed once again for a conference to discuss command relationships.[73] Then he wrote to Admirals Murray and Brodeur and to Commodore H.E. Reid, FONF, asking for their official opinions on his letter to Admiral King. He also instructed the operational commanders to continue co-operating with CTF 24 but added, "you are responsible only to NSHQ for the administration of these RCN ships and no change is to be made in their dispositions without NSHQ concurrence."[74] This effectively relieved Murray and Reid of the embarrassment of having to tilt with Brainard and ensured that the USN would have to deal through Ottawa. Nelles had effectively added yet another authority to the play and caught a strong purchase on the USN while remaining within the terms of ABC-1 and ABC-22.[75] The spirit of those agreements, of course, had never been defined.

Admiral King may have found this altercation tiresome, for he left the reply to Nelles's signal and letter to his Chief of Staff, Admiral R.S. Edwards.[76] Edwards asked Nelles to explain his policy with regard to the transfer of destroyers and to outline Canada's objections to the present procedure. Nelles, spurred on by yet another attempt by CTF 24 to execute an unauthorized transfer, indicated that his headquarters had taken charge of all RCN ships in the Western Atlantic and would decide in which command they would serve.[77] Then the CNS, hoping to imply that CTF 24 did not understand the operation of the escort cycle, asked the Admiralty to explain it to him.[78] This was the first time the Admiralty had been brought into the picture, and it was obviously intended that their lordships emphasize that the escort organization was really a function of the Commonwealth navies and that CTF 24 was an unnecessary authority.

By the end of January Nelles had received replies from his letters to Brodeur, Murray, and Reid. Murray was adamant that Canada should be given responsibility for the protection of sea communications in the North West Atlantic, including the organization of both escorts and convoys. However, it was his opinion that "the broader naval strategy must be left to the U.S. Navy because they have the potential force of the U.S. battle fleet behind them."[79] Brodeur's reply was premised on the view that the USN's policy had been to avoid consulting the RCN representative on important matters affecting the two services.[80] He stated that if the USN had dealt with him in the same way it had done with the British Admiralty Delegation, then it would have raised NSHQ to the same status as the Admiralty. Brodeur believed that the United States and Great Britain were trying to keep policy decisions their own preserve and that only a redefinition of the terms of ABC-1 and other agreements and operating instructions would correct this.

Nelles's point finally struck home. On 1 February, Admiral King ordered CTF 24 not to conduct transfers of either Canadian or British ships between commands without NSHQ's authority. King also wrote a conciliatory note to Nelles. He pointed out, quite correctly, that the issue could have been avoided if NSHQ had raised objection to his initial message authorizing the transfers. Apparently, Nelles's staff had missed the signal. The CNS replied that he had not raised an objection in order "to avoid confusing the issue at a time when it appeared essential to take immediate action to counter the U-boat threat."[81] This was a lame excuse, however, since his obstructionist tactics during December and January had caused the very sort of confusion that he said he was trying to avoid. Nevertheless, no harm had been done, and Nelles won his point, for Admiral King agreed to a firm date for a conference on command relationships. King made his intentions known to all concerned in a signal announcing "that at the request of the NSHQ" there would be a conference on 1 March 1943.[82]

With concurrence having been wrested from Admiral King, Nelles completed details on the Canadian proposals.[83] It was felt that Canada's argument would be stronger if a commander-in-chief for the North West Atlantic was created prior to the conference. Plans to make the commanding officer Atlantic Coast fit this title were drawn up, but they could not be put into effect in time. It was also considered essential that all anti-submarine aircraft, which included Canadian, British, and American forces, be brought under Admiral Murray's control. By the third week in February, Canada's proposals had received the concurrence of the Naval Board.[84]

The Atlantic Convoy Conference opened on 1 March 1943 in Washington as scheduled. Admiral Brodeur headed the Canadian delegation which included Captains Lay, DeWolf, E.S. Brand, and W.B. Creery (the chief of staff to the commanding officer Atlantic Coast). Admiral King commenced by remarking that he did not believe in mixed forces, a comment which implied that Canada would be given sole responsibility in the North West Atlantic.[85] When King was finished, he turned the conference over to Admiral Edwards and did not participate further. Admiral Sir Percy Noble, who had recently been appointed to head the British Admiralty Delegation, spoke on behalf of the RN.[86] Then Admiral Brodeur made his opening statement, declaring that the main Canadian purpose in the conference was "to clarify and improve the present complicated chain of Command in existence in the North West Atlantic." He remarked that he was sorry that the subject of operational control was not contained in the proposed agenda and that he wanted it included. Thereupon he tabled Canada's three main proposals:

(1) A North Atlantic area to be established and defined as the area north of 40°N. In this area control of convoys and anti-submarine warfare to be exercised solely by British and Canadian authorities (except within U.S. sea frontiers).
(2) The present COAC to become commander in chief North West Atlantic and to have general direction of all surface and air forces employed in anti-submarine warfare in the North West Atlantic.
(3) Control of convoys, U-boat information, diversion of convoys to be exercised by NSHQ and commander in chief North West Atlantic to be similar to that by Admiralty and CinCWA in the North Atlantic.[87]

Brodeur stated that Canada's strong reasons for asking this were based on several concerns: her large contributions in escorts and escort aircraft and sea and air bases; her three years of experience in the very specialized field of anti-submarine operations; and her large programme of naval and air development from the beginning of the war. He concluded by intimating that if these proposals were not accepted, then Ottawa would continue to force the issue. Here we see Brodeur's nationalism coming through strongly:

And finally I wish to express this most important fact about Canada which appears to be little understood, that is, that all Canadian armed forces are under the control of one, only one, higher authority which is the Canadian government and only by the latter's consent can any armed forces be moved from Canada or from one theatre of war to another and if all sub-committees of the conference studying the present agenda will remember that important factor, a great deal of time will be saved and many misunderstandings avoided.[88]

On the completion of Admiral Brodeur's remarks, Admiral Edwards moved quickly to explain that owing to an administrative error the Canadian delegation had not received a revised agenda which had as its first item operational control of escorts in the North West Atlantic.[89] The conference broke up shortly thereafter into sub-committees to discuss specific subjects assigned to them from the agenda.

The discussions went well for Canada in the Committee on Command Relationships, and the outcome was never in doubt. On 6 March Admiral Brodeur was able to report to the CNS that unanimous agreement had been reached on Canada's proposals.[90] The committee, Brodeur noted, would recommend that Canada be given control of all surface and anti-submarine escorts in the area west of 47°W and north of 40°N. In addition, the United Kingdom and Canada would control all convoys between the British Isles and North America, including those originating at New York. Brodeur observed that the committee was using the term "commander in chief, Canadian North West Atlantic (CinC, CNA)" as the new title for COAC.[91]

The conference concluded on 12 March, and its recommendations were forwarded to the respective governments for approval. The proposed date for the transfer of command was set as 31 March. Captain Lay wrote to Captain R.E.S. Bidwell (chief of staff to the flag officer Newfoundland Force), "The RCN got practically everything which they asked for at the conference, and from that point of view it was extremely satisfactory."[92] Captain Lay had every reason to be satisfied for all the evidence indicates that he was the originator and driving force behind NSHQ's campaign. He was the first to press Nelles on the matter, and once the CNS had been persuaded it was simply a matter of applying constant pressure on the USN. Lay drafted all Nelles's correspondence and messages to the U.S. naval authorities on the matter and co-ordinated the drawing up of Canada's proposals within NSHQ. He based Canada's argument on the RCN's major contribution to the Battle of the Atlantic because he knew he could win on those grounds.[93]

Admiral Brodeur also played an important part in the campaign. He had alerted Nelles to the fact that Canada's voice was not being heard when naval matters were being discussed in Great Britain and the United States. Brodeur was not a man to be bypassed; he and Lay pressed Nelles almost simultaneously. Nelles was an officer who would support a good idea; a man of decision, once he was committed to a course of action, he would see it through to the end.[94] He persisted in his contest with King until the American admiral gave in. With obvious satisfaction Nelles reported his success to the Cabinet War Committee stating, "This new arrangement would place a much heavier responsibility on the Canadian Navy. It was, however, regarded as a satisfactory solution to an important and difficult problem."[95]

Interestingly, the RCN had achieved what the Mackenzie King government could not do: to assert Canadian autonomy in the military sphere. Moreover, all the evidence suggests that the inspiration and motivation behind the campaign developed at the senior level of the officer corps. Throughout the campaign the Minister of National Defence for Naval Services, Angus L. MacDonald, remained an interested observer and nothing more. He and Nelles kept the Cabinet War Committee informed of what had transpired, but there is no evidence that suggests the committee influenced the Naval Board in its course of action.[96]

While the concurrence of the governments was awaited on the recommendations arising from the Atlantic Convoy Conference, preparations moved ahead in Halifax to set up the new facilities that Admiral Murray would require to direct operations. The RCN had the experience required for the job, but the facilities, particularly communications, were inadequate. The truth of the matter was that the change of command was to be effected before Halifax was materially ready to accept it.[97] No mention of this fact was made outside of Canada since it would have proved extremely embarrassing after the vigorous agitation to be given responsibility.

It was confirmed that the new title of COAC would be CinC, CNA.[98] However, because of Admiral King's reluctance to transfer control to the RCN, the change of command did not take place until 30 April 1943. Shortly after the Atlantic Convoy Conference, Admiral King proposed that Admiral Murray be appointed as deputy to Admiral Brainard, to learn the ropes so to speak, and that subsequently Brainard be left as a permanent adviser to Murray.[99] The latter proposal was passed through Admiral Brodeur, who informed Nelles of its contents:

> The USN felt if any serious thinking [sinkings?] took place while we were in command that the world would say [the] USN passed the command to Canada and took a less risky area for [the] USN knowing heavy sinkings would occur and they certainly did not wish to give that impression in what takes place in the Northern North Atlantic.[100]

Nelles consulted Murray by teletype on King's two proposals. Murray said that he thought Nelles should turn King down politely by signal on both proposals and also should instruct Brodeur to intimate to the Americans "that Canadian authorities are willing to accept responsibility for this [heavier sinkings] and we could not possibly accuse the U.S. authorities of leaving us in the lurch through removal of their control, any more than we did at any time since they withdrew their escort forces thirteen months ago."[101]

Nelles replied to King that Murray could be appointed as deputy to Brainard but that the latter's services as an adviser would not be required and that Murray was prepared to take over command as of 31 March 1943.[102] These replies were courteous but firm and indicated clearly that the RCN was willing to take on the responsibility. Nelles did not include Murray's suggestion that the withdrawal of American escort forces in early 1942 had left Canada in the lurch.

King answered Nelles's signals by a personal letter which he said he hoped the CNS would take in the spirit in which it was written—"that of stark realism applied to a situation in which our only wish is to be helpful." King said he viewed with satisfaction that U.S.-U.K. convoys in the North West Atlantic would now be handled by the Canadian navy. "However, we consider it a fact that your people have as yet little opportunity to conduct the work involved on the scale required."[103] Then he suggested that Admiral Brainard be left in his post until 30 April so that the Canadians could avail themselves of his services; thereafter, he could assume an advisory status. It appears that Admiral King was completely out of touch with the realities of the situation in the North West Atlantic and blatantly ignorant of the scope of the RCN's participation in escort work since September 1939.

Nelles transmitted King's letter to Murray, whose reaction could have been predicted. Murray suggested a reply on the grounds that King had been "very blunt in his statement that they do not think we are capable of handling the job and it may be necessary to be blunt in return."[104] Murray pointed out the three-and-one-half years of experience of the RCN as compared to the one year of the USN in convoy escort work. Murray added it was he who had taught Bristol and then Brainard the system for convoy organization and escort protection. Moreover, Brainard's staff had nothing like the experience of his own either at sea or running the escort organization. Murray's final point was that since the withdrawal of U.S. escort forces from the North Atlantic, the training, operation, administration, and tactics of escorts, with a few minor exceptions, had been under RCN control with "nominal supervision" from CTF 24.

Had Nelles been as blunt in his reply to King as Murray had suggested, there would probably have been serious repercussions.[105] Nelles also sent a personal signal to the First Sea Lord, Admiral Sir Dudley Pound, outlining King's suggestions and asking for Pound's view. Pound agreed that the proposals arising from the Atlantic Convoy Conference should be implemented as soon as possible. He suggested, not knowing the whole story, that the Americans were probably only trying to be helpful with their offer of Brainard's services. He observed that "possibly acceptance of their offer would help the RCN's future relations with the USN." Nelles decided to accept King's proposal to leave Brainard in command until 30 April and informed King in a short signal to that effect. Accordingly, King set that date for the official change of command.[106]

If Admiral King had ever felt reluctant to part with command, he must have experienced chagrin when he received a letter which originated in the office of the director of Naval Intelligence in NSHQ. The subject of the letter was a news release which was to herald the change of command.[107] The release greatly exaggerated the Royal Canadian Navy's new responsibility, made no mention at all of USN involvement, and, in fact, gave the impression that the Americans had disappeared from the scene completely. As the release had been sent to the USN for approval and expressed an opinion that King wanted to suppress, he set down what he thought was wrong with it and sent a detailed list of corrections to the director of Naval Intelligence.[108] NSHQ made some amendments to the release, and the story appeared in papers in Canada and Great Britain, but not in the United States, on 1 May 1943.

On 18 April Admiral Murray paid an official visit to Admiral Brainard and a formal "turnover" agreement was signed.[109] CinC, CNA's signal of acceptance of responsibility was sincere yet filled with meaning:

> I accept the torch as from 1200Z April 30th and hope to carry it as successfully as it has been carried since Admiral Bristol received it from my hand in September 1941. It has been a personal pleasure to serve under your direction and in co-operation with your staff whose excellent understanding of our problems has made our task a simple one.[110]

The key words are "our task." The RCN had never relinquished the role of the protection of shipping, and the USN never played more than a token role in the northwestern theatre of the Battle of the Atlantic. This is the meaning that is implicit in the signal. The Battle of the Atlantic was fought essentially by the British and Canadian navies and air forces, although invaluable assistance was received from the United States anti-submarine aircraft and "hunter/killer" groups during April and May 1943 when the battle was at its peak.

A number of conclusions can be drawn from this study of command relationships between the RCN and its British and American Allies. First, it seems to confirm Clausewitz's suggestion that the pattern of relationships between large and small powers in wartime with respect to political influence is not so much a function of military strength as it is a reflection of the state of military tension within the war. In the early stages of World War II, Canada was willing to suppress national aspirations for the protection of the predominant British and American military force and for the good of the alliance. It was only when the crisis started to fade that the RCN began to press the more delicate question of command relationships to the point where it became a contentious issue.

It can also be concluded that the interaction between the RCN and the USN during the Battle of the Atlantic established the present pattern of command relationships for the maritime defence of North America. Existing defence agreements allocate areas of operational responsibility to Canada. These areas adjoining the east and west coasts of Canada are of primary national interest and are under the control, respectively, of the commander Maritime Command and his deputy. However, these officers are under the broad strategic direction of NATO or American authorities on matters of joint defence.

A very interesting facet of this study is that it shows that strong nationalist tendencies existed in the RCN during the early 1940's. Although the navy reflected the RN in dress, training, and ships, it had a distinctive Canadian personality. This personality emerged when the navy came of age in 1942; the RCN could now stand alone on the strength of its demonstrated ability on the field of battle and on its numbers. A strong national pride in the RCN and a dedication to anti-submarine warfare, which is a distinctively Canadian area of specialization, has prevailed to the present day.

Possibly the most important conclusion that can be drawn from this study is that it was through its commitment to anti-submarine warfare that Canada was able to gain some measure of control in the Battle of the Atlantic, which was a major theatre of the war. No other small power enjoyed such a position. There is a strong submarine threat directed against North America today from the same strategic area. If Canada hopes to exert some influence in Washington on the direction of the maritime defence of this continent, the historical evidence suggests that the maintenance of a strong anti-submarine force would be most advantageous.

Chapter 10

ROYAL CANADIAN NAVY PARTICIPATION IN
THE BATTLE OF THE ATLANTIC CRISIS OF 1943

Marc Milner

It is generally conceded that the Royal Canadian Navy made a vital contribution to the Allied victory in the Battle of the Atlantic, September 1939 to
May 1945. Yet no attempt has been made to explain the role of the service in
the final crisis of 1943, when the German U-boat wolfpack campaign
against the main North Atlantic convoy routes was finally and decisively
beaten. This apparent oversight is disturbing, particularly since historians
assure us that the RCN was a major participant in the struggle. However,
this gap in our knowledge of RCN operations with the Mid-Ocean Escort
Force (MOEF) may stem not from neglect but perhaps from a conspiracy of
silence—early 1943 was a very trying time for the RCN. The ability of
Canadian escorts to carry on operations in the mid-Atlantic had been
brought into question by the convoy battles of late 1942; mounting losses to
Canadian-escorted convoys led the British to propose, in early December,
that the RCN component of the MOEF be withdrawn until such time as its
training could be improved. The Naval Staff in Ottawa reacted bitterly to
this proposal in light of the British allegation that poor training was
largely at fault. However, as the Canadians mustered their case the disastrous battle of convoy ONS 154, in which the RCN escort proved incapable
of preventing the loss of fifteen ships, eliminated all hopes of successfully
challenging the British. In early 1943 Canada's MOEF escorts were quietly
transferred to a British command, and the role of the RCN in the North
Atlantic over the following months was much reduced. In short, Canada's
most prestigious naval commitment collapsed as the battle reached its

climax. With it fell all chance of active participation in the great destruction of the wolfpacks in April and May, 1943, a goal towards which the RCN's unbending efforts, the source of its ultimate shortcomings, had been directed.

While the role of the Royal Canadian Navy in the Battle of the Atlantic is of immense importance to the battle generally, and to the history of the RCN in particular, the record of the Canadian service—its problems, accomplishments, and failings—has not been analysed thoroughly. There are two predominant themes in the existing literature. Canadian historians quite rightly lay emphasis on the size of the Canadian forces committed. Indeed, in naval terms alone, by early 1943 no less than 48 per cent of the escorts assigned to the main North Atlantic convoys were Canadian.[1] This theme, heavily laced with the pride of accomplishment, colours the works of the official historians Gilbert Tucker and Joseph Schull.[2] Unfortunately, Tucker's penchant for detail and analysis is not found in Schull's operational history. In fairness to Schull, detailed analysis was not his mandate. His history is really a survey of notable RCN adventures, enjoyable anecdotes designed more to foster a national following for the navy than to satisfy historians; it does not place peculiarly Canadian problems and achievements in fighting the Battle of the Atlantic in context. Schull's account of the ten month period from July 1942 to May 1943, about which so much has been written, is a case in point.

That period was one of sharp contrasts for the Battle of the Atlantic. The U-boat campaign had gained momentum all through the latter half of 1942, and in November Allied shipping losses reached 807,754 tons, a new wartime high.[3] Foul weather in December and January gave the Allies some respite, but the increasing number of U-boats being deployed in the mid-ocean made it painfully clear that the worst was yet to come. Only good intelligence kept losses down in February 1943, but when the Germans changed their codes in early March, the wolfpacks achieved their greatest successes of the war. During the first three weeks of that month 22 per cent of all the ships sailing in the main trans-Atlantic convoys failed to reach their destination. The British, in desperation, considered abandoning the convoy system, a desperate move indeed since there was no viable alternative. The situation was only restored by the timely repenetration of the German U-boat cypher, "Triton," later in the month. In April and May the combination of excellent intelligence, recently arrived support groups, and extended aircover dealt a death blow to the German wolfpack campaign and eliminated the serious threat to the main North Atlantic convoys for the rest of the war.

If the RCN was a major participant in this phase of the battle, as both Tucker and Schull would have us believe, that cannot be gathered from the history of the operations in which neither large scale participation nor

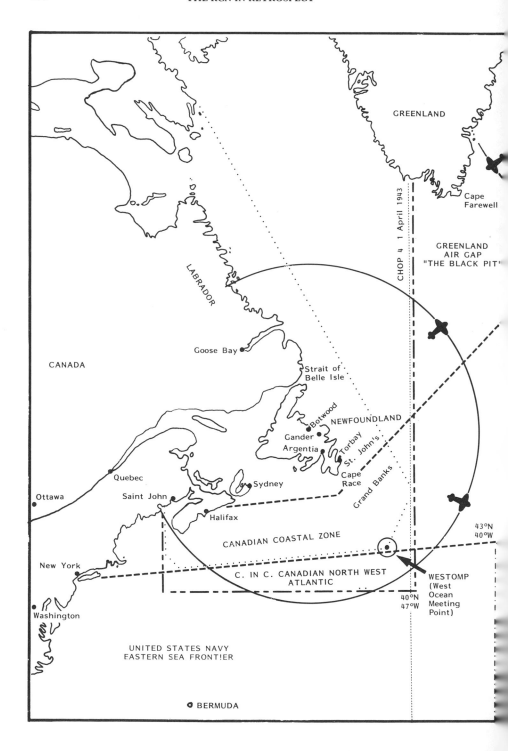

GREENLAND

Cape
Farewell

CHOP 4 1 April 1943

GREENLAND
AIR GAP
"THE BLACK PIT"

LABRADOR

CANADA

Goose Bay

Strait of
Belle Isle

Botwood

NEWFOUNDLAND

Gander

Torbay

Argentia

St. John's

Cape
Race

Grand Banks

Quebec

Sydney

Ottawa

Saint John

Halifax

43°N
40°W

CANADIAN COASTAL ZONE

New York

C. IN C. CANADIAN NORTH WEST
ATLANTIC

WESTOMP
(West
Ocean
Meeting
Point)

40°N
47°W

Washington

UNITED STATES NAVY
EASTERN SEA FRONTIER

BERMUDA

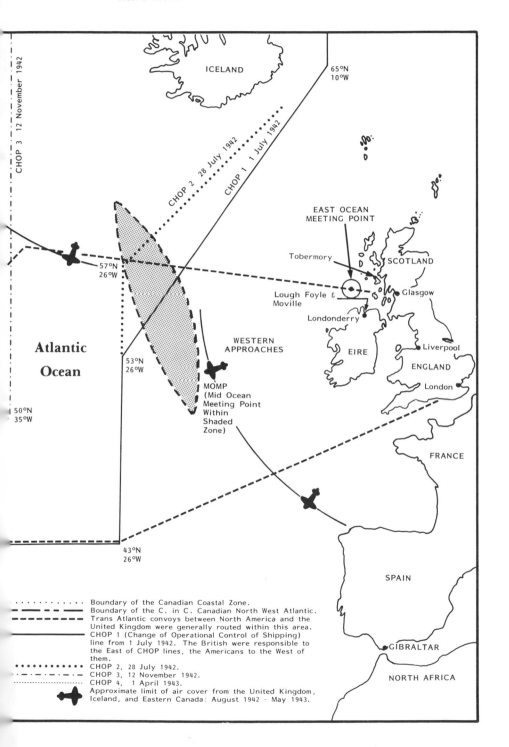

CHOP 3 12 November 1942

ICELAND

65°N
10°W

CHOP 2 28 July 1942
CHOP 1 1 July 1942

EAST OCEAN
MEETING POINT

Tobermory
SCOTLAND

Lough Foyle &
Moville
Glasgow

Londonderry

57°N
26°W

Atlantic

Ocean

53°N
26°W

WESTERN
APPROACHES
EIRE
Liverpool

ENGLAND

London

MOMP
(Mid Ocean
Meeting Point
Within
Shaded
Zone)

50°N
35°W

FRANCE

43°N
26°W

SPAIN

GIBRALTAR

NORTH AFRICA

· · · · · · · · · · · ·   Boundary of the Canadian Coastal Zone.
— · — · — · — · —   Boundary of the C. in C. Canadian North West Atlantic.
— — — — — — —   Trans Atlantic convoys between North America and the
United Kingdom were generally routed within this area.
————————   CHOP 1 (Change of Operational Control of Shipping)
line from 1 July 1942. The British were responsible to
the East of CHOP lines, the Americans to the West of
them.
• • • • • • • • • • • •   CHOP 2, 28 July 1942.
· — · — · — · — · —   CHOP 3, 12 November 1942.
· · · · · · · · · · · · · · · · ·   CHOP 4, 1 April 1943.
Approximate limit of air cover from the United Kingdom,
Iceland, and Eastern Canada: August 1942 - May 1943.

successes are documented. In fact, Tucker, whose interest in operations at sea in volume two of *The Naval Service of Canada* was peripheral, mentions without qualification that a disproportionate number of Canadian escorts were in refit in early 1943. While he states that four RCN escort groups doing "coastal" work were to be assigned to the MOEF in the months of March and April 1943,[4] he does not disclose which coast, nor does he account for the four groups apparently already assigned to MOEF.[5] Unfortunately, it is not clear if Tucker intended to sort out these unexplained remarks in his unpublished third volume. Certainly Schull did not.

In the section of Schull's *The Far Distant Ships* dealing with this period, the small role of the Royal Canadian Navy in the crisis of 1943 is apparent.[6] Schull recounts at length the RCN convoy battles of 1942 but says little of the first five months of 1943. At a time when other historians focus on the exploits of embattled escorts and support groups, Schull writes in general terms about the course of events at sea. His main stress is on the establishment of the Canadian North West Atlantic Command, in itself no mean achievement. Yet, he almost suggests that there was really nothing left to say about Canadian operations in early 1943, despite the fact that the battle was passing through its most crucial phase.

That the Canadian side of the story of these months has been inadequately told is clear from its lack of impact on foreign accounts. General accounts of the Battle of the Atlantic treat the RCN tersely. Reference to the Canadians is usually limited to one or two paragraphs that note the rapid expansion from six prewar destroyers in 1939 to over two hundred warships of all types by the end of 1942 and comment on the fact that the expansion caused some problems.[7] It may be expected that chauvinism among the larger powers would deny the RCN a proper place in the history proportionate to its actual role. In fact, the fault lies with the Canadians, who have simply not put their own house in order, for from the outset, the inadequacies of the operational history left the field open for others to speculate and hypothesize on the merits of Canada's contribution. Nowhere is this more apparent than in the works of Captain Donald Macintyre.[8] Macintyre wrote several books about the Battle of the Atlantic, all of which were published after the official Canadian histories in the early 1950's. It is obvious that Macintyre was unimpressed by the RCN. His vehement attack on the RCN, in the first five pages of chapter seven in *U-Boat Killer*, is the most damning criticism of the Royal Canadian Navy in print.[9] The gist of the Macintyre thesis is simply that Canada's wartime fleet expanded too quickly and as a result was utterly inefficient. Macintyre suggests that the RCN should have swallowed its national pride and contributed men and ships directly to the Royal Navy, where the cadre of experienced personnel would have softened the effects of expansion. The very things which

Plate 53. View from HMCS *Chambly* of the 1st Corvette Flotilla en route to St. John's, Nfld., 24 May 1941. *Chambly*, with *Moose Jaw*, came to the defence of convoy SC 42. (PAC—Pa 11535)

Plate 54. Fog often led to dispersal of convoys, but it also hampered pursuing U-boats, as convoy ONS 5 illustrated. (PAC—PA 115352)

Plate 55. Oiling at sea was necessary for continuous operation of escorts. Heaving hose aboard a destroyer in the Atlantic, 7 November 1942. (PAC—PA 116335)

Plate 56. Signalman Jack Scott of HMCS *Sherbrooke* on duty while HMCS *Barrie* oils from tanker. (PAC—PA 115354)

Plate 57. Air cover for convoys was provided by Very Long Range Liberator bombers, which spanned the formerly unprotected Greenland air gap. (DOH, NDHQ)

Plate 58. HMCS *Battleford*, like many corvettes, served throughout the war with a number of escort groups, including NEF, C.1, W.3, and W.4. (PAC—PA 115381)

Plate 59. HMCS *Barrie* saw service during the war with MOEF and escort groups W.1 and W.8 (PAC—PA 115357)

Canadians regard highly about their World War II achievement—its tremendous growth and subsequent participation in important tasks—are the very things which Macintyre abhors.

One may ascribe Macintyre's opinions to the British attitude towards "colonials." Indeed, the opinion that Canadians were rowdy, ill-disciplined frontiersmen was widely held by the British. Even Admiral Sir Max Horton's biographer, Rear-Admiral W.S. Chalmers, RN, who was generally sympathetic to the Canadians, equated the makeshift nature of the wartime RCN and its conduct at sea to the frontier spirit.[10] Clearly, the British never appreciated the RCN's desire to assert itself as an independent service. Nor did the British outgrow their first impressions of Canada's expanded navy, which were formulated during the winter of 1941-42 in the western Atlantic. At no other period in the war was the overall efficiency and appearance of the RCN at so low an ebb. The first construction programme of sixty-four corvettes was being hurriedly commissioned, while the debilitating effects of bad weather and an ever-expanding war meant that the navy was literally learning on the job.

The most startling example of Canadian shortcomings in the latter half of 1941 was the disastrous passage of convoy SC 42 in September of that year (see pp. 193-207). But it was not the spectacular failures which left the lingering impressions. It was the day-to-day exposure of professional servicemen to these fledgling "warships." The senior officer of the escort of convoy SC 45, for example, found his Canadian escorts more trying than the U-boat threat. In his report of proceedings, he noted laconically that the Canadian corvettes were sloppy and reckless signallers (particularly at night) and concluded that their convoy discipline was "not good."[11] A memorandum submitted to Commodore L.W. Murray, RCN, the commodore commanding Newfoundland Force (CCNF), in November observed, "RCN corvettes have been given so little chance of becoming efficient that they are almost more of a liability than an asset."[12] And if they were of questionable value in a defensive role, they were of equally dubious value as a threat to the enemy. Referring to the latter quality, captain (D[estroyers]), Newfoundland, wrote in September 1941, "At present most escorts are equipped with one weapon of approximate precision—the ram."[13]

As many British officers were exposed to this trying phase of Canadian naval expansion, the RCN suffered from the RN's suspicion and doubt about its merits. John Costello and Terry Hughes, in *The Battle of the Atlantic*, adopted the Macintyre thesis in their characteristically brief passage about the RCN.[14] As in other general works, salutary remarks about the tremendous growth of the Royal Canadian Navy form the basis of their comments on the performance of the RCN which follow. Wartime expansion has been equated with inefficiency in a way which suggests that the

Canadians knew little of, or cared less about, the finer points of anti-submarine warfare and trade escort.

Fortunately, Canadians can take some solace from the Americans who, in general, tend to look more favourably on the RCN. The idea that Canadians should have submerged their identity in some form of Commonwealth navy never emerges from American literature. Although at least one American writer, Patrick Abbazia, author of *Mr. Roosevelt's Navy*, describes the RCN as ill-disciplined and rather misguided, his criticism is based on different grounds. The Canadians, Abbazia claims, were inefficient because they lacked the necessary mechanical aptitude to keep their escorts in fighting trim.[15] Though this is clearly part of the myth that the Americans were naturally more mechanically minded than the British, or, in this case, near-British, the criticism is not without foundation. Certainly United States Navy officers serving with MOEF felt this way, with good reason, and it is likely that Abbazia derived his opinions from them.

Nonetheless, on the whole Americans have treated the RCN rather better than the British have. This is certainly true of writers who were themselves serving officers. Though perhaps it is not fair to let the British case rest with Macintyre's heavily subjective appreciation, the general sense of his stand is typical. Captain Stephen Roskill simply avoided the issue of operational efficiency in the RCN, as though he felt constrained by his position as the official historian of the Royal Navy.[16] No such sentiment need have inhibited his American counterpart. Perhaps the feeling that they shared a similar experience with the Canadians may have tempered American opinion. Certainly neither Admiral Samuel Morison, in his official history,[17] nor Captain J.M. Waters, in *Bloody Winter*,[18] voice strong condemnations of the Royal Canadian Navy. On the contrary, both find reason to praise the Canadians for doing a good job under very trying circumstances. Even Abbazia inadvertently suggests the link between problems of inefficiency, which were seen to be peculiarly Canadian, and those which affected American forces in the same zone of operations. In the winter of 1941-42 —even before it had undergone wartime expansion—the USN found it difficult to maintain a professional service on the Newfoundland to Iceland run.[19] Even the British, Abbazia observes, were forced to neglect their professional appearance to allow more time for shore leave.[20]

The RCN had some very serious problems, more serious perhaps than the operational history would have us believe. In *50 North*, Alan Easton pointed to the weakness of the RCN's manning policy,[21] and more recently James Lamb has argued that the policy was "the biggest impediment to operational efficiency."[22] Their point is well made, for it is clear that the long term benefits of a wide distribution of experienced personnel were achieved only at the expense of efficiency initially. The Naval Staff appreciated this problem but insisted that quantity, not quality, was the immediate goal.[23] The lack of modern ASW and navigational equipment aboard Canadian escorts also had a profound impact on operational efficiency. It was said of Canadian escorts that they lagged behind their British counterparts in the fitting of new equipment by as much as a year.[24] Not one RCN escort, for example, had been fitted with the anti-submarine mortar "Hedgehog," by the autumn of 1942, and of the Canadian ships in the MOEF only one was fitted with high-frequency direction-finding and four with modern radar. In addition, only one of the Canadian corvettes of the MOEF, HMCS *Eyebright*, was modernized. The remainder continued to operate with wet and cramped living conditions as well as with outdated bridges and navigational equipment.

While Tucker mentioned what is now known as the equipment crisis in his second volume,[25] most historians seem to have overlooked this most important piece of Canadian naval history, or at best dismissed a work on shore establishments as having no application to the study of operations at sea. Certainly there are no subsequent references to Tucker's discussion of equipment in any of the general texts. It was not until 1970, and the publication of C.P. Stacey's *Arms, Men and Governments*, that the issue of equipment and RCN operational efficiency was "resurrected" in the literature.[26] This theme was further developed by W.A.B. Douglas and B. Greenhous in *Out of The Shadows*. They suggested that the poor showing of the RCN during the crisis of 1943 was a direct result of the equipment crisis.[27]

In fact, the crisis of 1943 was more complex than Douglas and Greenhous imply. On 7 January 1943 the War Committee of the Canadian cabinet agreed to the temporary transfer of four escort groups then operating with the MOEF to the RN's commander-in-chief Western Approaches, whose area of jurisdiction encompassed the waters immediately west of the British Isles.[28] Ostensibly, this was to permit a reorganization of the Atlantic escort systems designed to facilitate the movement of oil convoys direct from the Caribbean to the United Kingdom. But this was only a half-truth. Certainly, there was an oil crisis of considerable proportions in Britain as a result of the Operation Torch landings in North Africa in November 1942. However, the real reason why the Canadians were involved in this shuffling of escort groups, and why they were now to switch their base of operations from St. John's, Newfoundland, to the eastern Atlantic, was the apparent alarming decline in the operational efficiency of the "C" groups, the Canadian formations in the MOEF, over the previous few months.[29]

In December 1942, after three years of war during which the RCN had experienced as much of the Atlantic battle as any service, a British suggestion that Canadian escorts be withdrawn from the most important theatre in the Atlantic was greeted by the Naval Staff as a breach of faith. They could blame overextended commitments in support of the USN and the RN

for their difficulties in 1942. Problems had begun when the RCN committed unprepared escorts, recently commissioned from the first construction
programme, to the newly established Newfoundland Escort Force. The
Naval Staff's estimation of the size of the force that it could dispatch to St.
John's quickly had been cautious. Nonetheless, the old axiom that any
escort was better than none prevailed. As one senior RCN officer wrote
later, "they were only sent to sea in this condition on the urgent request of
the Admiralty."[30] In any event, the NEF was intended to be simply an
interim measure, designed to fill the Western Atlantic gap until the United
States assumed such responsibilities.

The participation of the USN in the escort of fast convoys between
Newfoundland and Iceland, which commenced in September 1941, lifted
some of the burden from the NEF. Along with the continued influx of
newly commissioned Canadian corvettes, this gave the NEF a measure of
flexibility in terms of ship numbers which Commodore Murray, now flag
officer Newfoundland Force, planned to channel into training programmes
in early December.[31] Unfortunately, his plans to make qualitative improvements to the Canadian escort forces came to naught. With the bombing of
Pearl Harbor on 7 December 1941 and the hurried withdrawal of all but a
token USN force, the RCN was left holding the proverbial bag, and Murray's plans evaporated before the increasing demands of operations.

Once RCN escorts were fully committed to operations, events passed
beyond the control of the service, and mid-ocean operations became a severe
impediment to orderly expansion. Not only did they rob the RCN of much
needed surplus escort time to make material improvements to the ships and
upgrade the training of crews but also, aside from giving men sea experience, they denied it the opportunity to master techniques of anti-
submarine warfare. The operational burden also caused the escort group
system, upon which so much ultimately depended, to collapse. The British
had learned, at some cost, that good teamwork, depending on the permanent group composition of escort groups, was the very basis of convoy
defence. The lesson had not been lost on the RCN, and initially the NEF
was organized into groups with this concern in mind. However, by
December 1941, attempts to keep the same escorts together in distinctive
groups had been abandoned by the NEF in the face of increasing operational demands.

The continued expansion of the war during 1942, and the extension of
the convoy routes that this involved, reduced the leverage that the navy
might have expected from its growing fleet. The Canadians were forced to
expand operations nearer home, partly to provide escorts for shipping
along the American coast which the Americans were incapable of protecting. As the year wore on, commitments grew. Canadian-based escorts
operated as far south as New York, six corvettes were lent to the commander

Eastern Sea Frontier, USN, and in August seventeen corvettes were made available at British request for support of the North African landings. All navies were hard pressed during 1942, and it was only natural that the RCN should have done its utmost. However, it was the least able to absorb extended commitments and consequently suffered the greatest for its selflessness.

The effect of all this on "C" groups was devastating. Both the men and the ships of Canada's MOEF commitment were nearly exhausted by the autumn of 1942 (indeed the same can be said of the whole RCN escort fleet). Despite Admiral Murray's protests, group strength was reduced to meet the growing need elsewhere. Murray also complained that his groups were short in destroyer complements, while most of the destroyers he had were old and unreliable.[32] In addition, virtually all of the escorts in "C" groups, the RN escorts excepted, were seriously behind in the fitting of modern equipment.[33]

By November Murray's warning that heavy losses would befall convoys escorted by the much weakened "C" groups came true. Early in the month convoy SC 107, with C.4 as its escort, was severely mauled as it passed through the Greenland air gap beyond the protective range of Allied aircraft. Fifteen ships were lost in the worst RCN disaster since SC 42, fourteen months before. Moreover, it was another manifestation of the declining success rate being experienced by Canadian groups in the mid-ocean since the renewal of the German U-boat wolfpack campaign in July. The earlier battles in defence of convoys ON 113 and ON 115 went well. Losses were slight, and the enemy paid in each case with the loss of an attacker. The same could be said of SC 94 in August, when losses to the convoy were admittedly high, but two U-boats were destroyed in exchange. However, with the battle of SC 97 later in August, the RCN's ability to make the enemy pay for his successes came to an end. The tragedy of ON 127 in early September was a portent of things to come, and with the passage of SC 107 the pressure for change—or for help—was overwhelming.[34]

The British always suspected that the Canadians were long on energy and zeal but rather short on the finer points of ASW and trade escort. The battle of SC 107 tended to confirm this point of view. So when the Chief of the Naval Staff, Vice-Admiral Percy W. Nelles, sought help from the RN through the "old boy" network in late November, the British were only too willing to give it—but on their terms.[35] By late 1942 the general situation in the North Atlantic was deteriorating rapidly. Mounting losses to shipping reduced imports into the United Kingdom at a time when Britain's reserves were being quickly eroded by the North African landings.[36] The war effort demanded that losses be cut, and, since quantitative improvements to the escort forces were out of the question, the one method available was to improve quality. Indeed, this had been one of the priorities of the new

Commander-in-Chief Western Approaches, Admiral Sir Max Horton, upon assuming his command in mid-November.[37] Thus it happened that the Canadians were, by their own admission, in some difficulty at the very time the British took up a new resolve to settle the matter of the North Atlantic.

The British proposed to handle the Canadian request for help, and their own need to move oil convoys directly from the Caribbean, by a reorganization of the escort system. Four long-range RN escort groups on the United Kingdom-Gibraltar route were to be withdrawn to move oil convoys direct from the West Indies, and their place on the North African run was taken over by the four "C" groups currently operating with MOEF. British-based Canadian escorts would have a greater opportunity to use the fine training facilities available at numerous RN bases. The fairer weather of this route, and the easier cycle, would guarantee ample time during lay-overs for training to be done. Finally, the British assured the Canadians that the availability of continuous air cover would help offset the "inexperience" of the RCN groups. These proposals were transmitted to Ottawa on 17 December 1942.[38]

The British proposals were received with disbelief, a response which soon changed to anger and resentment. Not only was the RCN being asked to abandon its primary and most prestigious commitment, but the blame for the recent rash of disastrous convoy battles was laid squarely at its door. This was not the type of help the RCN had in mind, nor was it a continuation of the load-sharing which was characteristic of the Allied cause. The Naval Staff, doubtless irked by the Admiralty's allegation that the Canadian escorts were inexperienced, was not prepared to let the British proposals go unchallenged. An investigation undertaken into the reasons for recent Canadian shortcomings concluded that the poor state of equipment in RCN escorts was primarily to blame. Canadian escorts lacked sufficient modern equipment to make them "competitive" with their British counterparts. In addition, Canadian groups were chronically under strength, both in overall numbers and in the allocation of destroyers.[39] The RCN did not skirt the fact that it needed more and better training, but it argued that this alone could not account for past failings.[40] However, the installation of modern equipment, particularly on the scale required by the RCN, would take time, and there was precious little of that. Modernization of the fleet was a long term project, but what the British could offer in terms of immediate assistance they extended to the Canadians.

As the Naval Staff marshalled its case, events at sea took a turn which robbed it of all legitimacy. Between Christmas 1942 and the new year, convoy ONS 154, escorted by group C.1, sailed into infamy. While luck and poor routing had a direct effect on the outcome of the battle, the terrible handling of ONS 154's defence and the heavy losses which ensued left the

RCN's challenge hopelessly undermined. The British proposals were accepted a few days after the beleaguered C. 1 pulled alongside in St. John's. The four Canadian groups of the MOEF, C.1-C.4, were handed over to the British, reducing FONF's command from an active strength of thirty-three escorts to two destroyers and nine corvettes, most of which were engaged in inshore duties.

It was several weeks before any of the "C" groups were actually transferred. In the meantime, steps were taken to ensure that the disasters associated with SC 107 or ONS 154 were not repeated. First, there was an infusion of RN destroyers and frigates into "C" groups. These fast and powerful escorts were much needed, and the Naval Staff had been trying for some time to obtain a large number of them from the British for commissioning into the Royal Canadian Navy. The British, however, were reluctant to hand over any destroyer or frigate, assuming that they were available, because that would further dilute the RCN's limited cadre of experienced personnel.[41] Nevertheless, in the end, RN escorts were assigned to fill the gaps in the "C" groups. Infusion of British escorts brought with it a subtle, but significant, change in the command of the groups. Whereas it was accepted practice for the most senior officer present to assume command, and since in three out of four instances the RN ships carried officers of greater rank or seniority than the RCN ones present, command of the groups passed to the Royal Navy.[42] Thus, it may well be that the British lack of faith in the Canadians extended to RCN officers as well. Certainly, Admiral Horton, upon assuming his post in November, had declared that poor leadership had contributed to the losses in the autumn battles of 1942 and that resourceful leadership was to be one of the goals of his qualitative improvements.[43]

One final and equally important step was taken to lessen losses in Canadian-escorted convoys. It was the Canadian lot during 1942 to escort the bulk of the slow trade, an unfortunate continuation of a previously established pattern. However, in the first two months of 1943 "C" groups escorted as many HX convoys (the medium to fast convoys now originating out of New York) as they had the previous six. While it has been argued that this was a mere coincidence, the change suggests that care was being taken to provide "C" groups with a speedy passage through the Greenland air gap.[44]

It is not yet clear when the official transfer of the groups took place. The appearance of "C" groups under commander-in-chief Western Approaches in the 1 March 1943 edition of the Admiralty's *Pink List* suggests that this was the date of the transfer.[45] In practice, groups were turned over to Admiral Horton's command throughout January and February as they arrived in Londonderry. The first "C" group to be affected secured alongside at 'Derry on 22 January having escorted HX 222 safely across. Not surprisingly, it was C.1 of ONS 154 fame, composed of the destroyer HMCS

St. Croix (recently assigned following refit), two British destroyers, HM Ships *Chesterfield* and *Vansittart*, which were attached for HX 222 only, and the Canadian corvettes *Battleford, Chilliwack, Kenogami, Napanee,* and *Shediac.* The destroyer *St. Laurent,* though still part of the group, had been diverted to Halifax with defects but later made an independent passage to the U.K. to rejoin.

Though for the next month or so the activities of individual escorts of C.1 varied considerably, the group set a pattern which the others would follow. The activities of the corvette *Kenogami,* for example, are indicative of the Canadians' experience.[46] Immediately upon arrival in 'Derry, a week's leave was granted to half the ship's company. Those remaining on board set about cleaning, scraping, painting, and doing minor repairs. *Kenogami* did not require dockyard work, but others did and were taken in hand as space allowed, with new equipment (notably modern radar and oerlikon guns) being added whenever possible. After the return of the liberty men, the crew spent the rest of the week finishing work already underway, and Sunday, 2 February, was observed as a day of rest. It was the last idle moment *Kenogami*'s crew would enjoy for quite some time. Starting Monday they began a week of feverish training ashore. Depth-charge crews, lookouts, machine gun and 2-pounder crews, boarding parties, 4-inch gun crew, ASDIC and radar crews, and the bridge personnel were all exercised. Officers and men were trained alike, and every warlike function of the ship was put through its paces under the direction of RN instructors. As the week drew to a close, *Kenogami* prepared for sea. She slipped on 11 February 1943 and proceeded to Moville where she refuelled from the duty oiler. There she was joined by at least one member of C.1, the destroyer *St. Croix.* The following day the two escorts went to sea and conducted ASW, towing, and fleet manoeuvres in company, after which they returned to their berths alongside the duty oiler. In the early hours of 13 February, *Kenogami* and her consort, being in all respects ready for sea, slipped and shaped a course to the northeast. Gloom and doom forecasters aboard the Canadian ships doubtless took comfort in the fact that the thirteenth had fallen one day short of Friday. But any smugness they may have felt evaporated as the ships came to anchor under the watchful gaze of Commodore G.O. Stephenson, RN, the "Terror of Tobermory." Tobermory, this otherwise peaceful haven on the Isle of Mull, was the home of the RN's escort work-up base, HMS *Western Isles.* Its notorious commander spared neither man nor ship, and he made no exception for Canadians. Their stay in Stephenson's lair began with his customary visit to the ships, one which, no doubt, instilled a desire to do well. The first full day at Tobermory was spent ashore covering the same ground that had been covered in 'Derry. The rest of the time alternated between training ashore and at sea, in the latter case with a tame submarine. Group exercises were conducted (and as far as can be determined all of C.1 was present) under the supervision of RN training officers from the depot ship, or from the recently commissioned training ship HMS *Philante*. *Philante* eventually eliminated the need for sailing the other "C" groups to Scotland as similar exercises could be conducted off Lough Foyle. The training period invariably ended with a night firing exercise, followed in C.1's case by a night passage to Northern Ireland.

C.1 secured alongside at 'Derry on 21 February and began a one-week stay during which the crews attended yet more training exercises ashore while the ships were prepared for an extended period at sea. Finally, on 27 February the group sailed as escort to convoy KMS 10, bound for North Africa. The passage of this convoy was the most spectacular of the six such convoys escorted by "C" groups and provided C.1 with ample opportunity to put its recent training into practice. Though attacking U-boats managed to sink one ship and torpedo another, the escort accounted for U-87. It was the only wholly Royal Canadian Navy U-boat kill in the Atlantic during this phase of the war, and perhaps the newly acquired expertise and equipment were responsible.

In February two other "C" groups arrived in Londonderry to follow C.1's lead. Both of these, C.2 and C.4, spent roughly a month in and around 'Derry, training, repairing, painting, and fitting new equipment. C.4, made up of the British destroyer *Churchill*, carrying the senior officer of the escort, the Canadian destroyer *Restigouche*, the corvettes *Amherst, Brandon, Collingwood, Sherbrooke*, and the British *Celandine*, sailed on 1 March to escort KMS 10B. Two weeks later, C.2, comprising the British destroyer *Sherwood*, the British frigate *Lagan*, the British corvettes *Polyanthus* and *Primrose*, and the RCN corvettes *Drumheller* and *Morden*, departed with KMS 11.[47] Neither of these operations, or the return trips, were noteworthy.

The last group to arrive in Londonderry under the terms of the transfer was C.3: the British destroyer *Burnham*, the British frigate *Jed*, and the Canadian corvettes *Eyebright, La Malbaie, Bittersweet*, and *Mayflower*. This was the famous "Barber Pole" group, and of all the Canadian escort groups, its record was the best. Perhaps this is why its training period was much reduced from that given the others. C.3 remained out of action for only two weeks. It then returned to the North Atlantic, bolstered by the addition of three RCN corvettes returning from the North African landings, to escort ON 172—the only Canadian-escorted convoy in the mid-ocean during the crucial month of March 1943.

The break in the pattern which C.3 represents is not yet fully understood. Perhaps it was felt that the "Barber Pole" group could hold its own with the British groups provided it received some assistance. But this seems unlikely. More likely, C.3 was recalled to duty with the MOEF because the

British were unable to maintain schedules with the reduced number of escort groups available to the MOEF, following the transfer. The Admiralty had hoped to manage the work of eleven groups with only nine by making them work a little harder.[48] It is conceivable that this proved to be too much. Indeed, it was the British who proposed at the Washington Conference in early March 1943 that the four "C" groups then doing coastal work be re-assigned to the MOEF, a suggestion which led to all the groups returning to duty with the MOEF by the end of the month.[49] However, the groups remained, for the time being, under commander-in-chief Western Approaches.

The situation in the mid-Atlantic by the end of March 1943 was not what it had been mere weeks before. The extension of land-based air cover from the U.K., Iceland, and later Newfoundland and the deployment of escort support groups changed the character of the battle for all time. From then on, the close escort which for so long had fought against mounting odds could count on reinforcements in very considerable strength. Thus, as the "C" groups returned to the MOEF, the scene was greatly changed, and since only the slow convoys increased sailings in April (the reason given by the British for the needed return of the four groups), the cycle for the Canadians remained relatively slack, and the training programme continued. The long weeks of intensive training were not repeated, but the lengthy layovers in 'Derry were used for training by HMS *Philante* and her officers.

Despite the fact that the Battle of the Atlantic was passing through its most important phase, the month of April was singularly unspectacular for the RCN. In large part this was a result of the cautious routing given Canadian-escorted convoys, a routing which kept them clear of the enemy.[50] Therefore, although very heavy losses were inflicted on the Germans over the next two months, few Royal Canadian Navy escorts gained sight of the enemy. Instead, the laurels went to British escort and support groups, aided by aircraft and excellent intelligence, which brought the mid-ocean campaign to an end. Only two Canadian-escorted convoys were remotely threatened in April: SC 127 and its escort C.1 were simply routed clear of danger, while HX 235, escorted by C.4, slipped unseen between two U-boat lines, screened from the nearest by a support group.[51]

With the increased sailings of fast convoys in May 1943, the tempo for the "C" groups returned to something nearer normal. However, though Canadians were now pulling their weight in the MOEF, they were merely the inner ring of a defence system which spanned the Atlantic. Nonetheless, it appears that May brought with it a renewed faith in the ability of Canadian escorts, since they were once again allowed to face the enemy. In the second week of May, C.2 with HMS *Biter*'s support group punched HX 237 through a U-boat line, the combined escort accounting for U-89. About a week later, HX 238, escorted by C.3, slipped gingerly through a pack sent to intercept it, while C.1 and the sixth support group safely escorted ON 184 through another concentration. The RCN was back in the fight, and by mid-month the "C" groups were all under RCN command, the terms of their transfer having expired.[52]

Thus, by the middle of May 1943, the RCN's effort in the Atlantic finally achieved the focus it had lacked for so long. Not only had the RCN's contribution to the MOEF been returned to Canadian command, but the reduction of support to the Allies—the return of the Operation Torch corvettes and those on loan to the USN—gave the RCN the leverage with which it set about putting its own house in order. The Battle of the Atlantic had reached its climax and found the RCN wanting. There was no shame in that, for Canada's contribution to the Battle was crucial, nonetheless, and would not be forgotten by those who understood its significance. As Admiral Sir Percy Noble observed, "The Canadian Navy solved the problem of the Atlantic convoys."[53]

It is now clear why the Royal Canadian Navy played so small a part in the final mid-ocean battle and why it has not received mention commensurate with the scale of Canada's contribution. What is not clear is why there is no mention of the transfer or its impact on operations in early 1943 in either of the official histories. Even though, in the final analysis, the Canadian component of the MOEF was only absent from the force for a brief period, the transfer of twenty RCN escorts to a British command was an event of major significance, if for no other reason that that it reduced FONF's command to little more than care and maintenance of a few coastal vessels. Moreover, the circumstances surrounding the transfer and the consequent minor role of the navy in the final defeat of the U-boat campaign are crucial to the history of the RCN. One is left to wonder what happened to the transfer in the writing of the Canadian histories.

While the period from January to May 1943 is the accepted crisis of the Battle of the Atlantic, the crisis of Canada's Atlantic war occurred in the period immediately before. Not only were Canadian escorts heavily engaged at that time, but the whole focus of wartime expansion was shaken and redirected in the process. The tendency has been to heap the blame for all the ills of hurried growth on the Canadian Naval Staff and Naval Service Headquarters. However, the choices which faced naval planners in the early years of the war were never enviable. The war and its insatiable demands for men and materials robbed the RCN of its opportunity to make expansion work. Even the RN had problems with operational efficiency during 1942 and was quite surprised to find that its wartime fleet had not lived up to prewar expectations.[54] Operational necessity was a curse which had to be accommodated.

Aid to the British in 1941 and 1942, and to the Americans after Pearl Harbor, directly affected the operational efficiency of the RCN—a fact its critics would do well to remember. Further, it is hardly surprising that Canadian historians have not focused on the defeat of the U-boats in May 1943. Whereas the British look upon the May victory as the crowning achievement of their naval war, for Canadians it was secondary to Canada's overall experience in the war. The crisis of 1943 was not an end in itself for the Royal Canadian Navy but merely one hurdle along the way to the final achievement of wartime competence.

Chapter II

OPERATIONAL INTELLIGENCE AND
THE BATTLE OF THE ATLANTIC: THE ROLE OF
THE ROYAL NAVY'S SUBMARINE TRACKING ROOM

Patrick Beesly

There is a story that when the news of the British disaster at the Battle of Coronel on 1 November 1914 reached Winston Churchill, then First Lord of the Admiralty, and he decided to withdraw two battle cruisers from the Grand Fleet to seek out and destroy Admiral Graf von Spee's squadron, the Naval Staff were aghast at the proposed depletion of Admiral Jellicoe's strength. In order to demonstrate that the chances of the two ships finding the Germans were infinitesimal, the staff officers produced the largest possible scale chart of the Pacific. Into this they inserted a small pin; withdrawing it, they explained that the small hole it made represented the range of vision on a clear day from the bridge of a battle cruiser. Reinserting it and pressing down, they then stated that the tiny extra area covered by its head showed the additional visibility from her masthead. Churchill is said to have been unimpressed. The two ships were duly despatched on their mission and, as is well known, by an extraordinary series of coincidences encountered von Spee at the Falkland Islands; there they carried out Churchill's orders and fully avenged Rear-Admiral Sir Christopher Cradock, admiral commanding the South American Station, and his men, who had been lost at Coronel.[1]

The story is no doubt entirely apocryphal, but it does demonstrate vividly the enormous difficulties, before the age of satellites, of finding the enemy in the vast spaces of the ocean. The actual course of events also shows how often sheer chance decides issues in wartime. The job of intelligence is to reduce that element of chance to a minimum, and to enable the commander of a weaker force to avoid battle or that of an equal or superior fleet to find and destroy his enemy under the circumstances most favourable to himself. To ask a sailor, or soldier or airman, for that matter, to fight without the benefit of good intelligence is like sending a boxer into the ring blindfolded—his chances of landing an effective blow are slight.

As in every other battle in every other war, the role of intelligence in the Battle of the Atlantic, surely one of the decisive battles in the history of the world, was vital to both sides. By this I do not mean that the struggle was won by the backroom boys sitting in comparative comfort and safety in London, Ottawa, and Washington or in Lorient or Berlin; the battle was fought and won at sea by the sailors and airmen of both sides who risked and all too often lost their lives in a bloody and bitter contest which started on 3 September 1939 and did not cease for a single moment, night or day, until 8 May 1945. But, if Allied intelligence had not eventually proved superior to German intelligence, the Battle of the Atlantic might have lasted much longer with incalculable results on the final outcome of World War II.

I concentrate largely on the British aspect of the intelligence scene in this chapter. In the first place, although Atlantic operational intelligence affected every participant of whatever nationality, and although, on the Allied side, it became truly international, it was basically a British success. Secondly, Rohwer and Douglas deal in greater detail with the German and Canadian aspects in the following chapter, and all I wish to do is to set the scene for them. Thirdly, because I served for virtually the whole war in the Admiralty's Operational Intelligence Centre (OIC) and was the deputy head of the Submarine Tracking Room (STR) from January 1942 I can speak from personal experience. I served under three or four brilliant individuals who made a quite disproportionate contribution to the Allied victory. I saw what they did; I knew the conditions and the immense pressures under which they worked—something that official files, no matter how comprehensive, can never reveal.

What, then, was the OIC, how did it work, and what was it supposed to do? It was a small section of the Naval Intelligence Division set up in 1937 and designed to receive, analyse, and then promulgate to the Naval Staff in the Admiralty, to naval and air force commands in Britain and overseas, and to the fleet information from every possible source which had a bearing on the movements and intentions of enemy forces on, over, and under the sea. It dealt in "hot" news in the same way that a daily newspaper does, although, increasingly, it also provided longer term appreciations upon which strategic as well as day-to-day tactical decisions could be taken. It had no executive powers, but as its expertise and knowledge increased, the centre came to influence all operational decisions in the Battle of the

Atlantic to a remarkable degree. Ships and aircraft were not deployed and convoys were not routed or diverted against its advice. The OIC had four main sections: one dealing with information about German surface ships, one handling Italian and Japanese intelligence, one, the STR, concerned with the movements of German U-boats (and also Italian and Japanese ones operating in the Atlantic and Indian Oceans), and one plotting the bearings received from direction-finding (DF) stations of enemy wireless telegraphy transmissions. Other sub-sections were set up to meet particular needs, such as mining, enemy air, disguised merchant raiders, and so on, but these four were the main departments. The OIC was always small, always working under great pressure and, often, in squalid and ill-equipped conditions. Nevertheless, its vital contribution to the Allied victory remains unquestioned.

A successful intelligence organization cannot be created overnight. British naval intelligence, which had been the best in the world in 1918, had, like the armed forces as a whole, been neglected between the wars. In 1939 the OIC, although well organized, suffered from the inability of its prime sources (cryptanalysis, direction finding, air reconnaissance, agents, and spies) to provide much worthwhile information. For the first twelve months of the war, German naval intelligence was distinctly superior to British. By early 1941, however, most of the OIC's sources and the OIC's own expertise had greatly improved. The pursuit and destruction of the German battleship *Bismarck* clearly demonstrated this fact. The Germans abandoned their attempts to use their few but immensely powerful capital ships for the *guerre de course* on the broad oceans. The Battle of the Atlantic, in the sense that it is generally understood as the U-boat war against merchant shipping which began with the torpedoing of the liner SS *Athenia*, became the dominant factor to which the intelligence of both countries devoted greater and greater effort.

Each side in this titanic struggle was driven to adopt a system of centralized control of its maritime operations by authorities ashore—the Germans with their submarine wolfpack tactics and the British and Canadians (and somewhat belatedly the Americans) with the convoy system and a tight and universal control of all shipping. This generated an enormous and largely unforeseen volume of signalling on both sides, something that was dealt with enthusiastically by the rival cryptanalysts—the British at Bletchley Park and the German x-B-Dienst. After thirty years of impenetrable silence the British have at last begun to disclose the triumphs of Bletchley Park. The revelation of this long concealed secret has had such an impact on the public on both sides of the Atlantic and in Germany that many people have asked why, if the British and their Allies knew so much, they did not win the war in 1943 or even earlier. It was not quite as simple as that. One, though not the only, reason was the less publicized success of the Germans in penetrating British cyphers, a success which preceded that of the British.

The German navy was determined, after World War I, that it should not again be placed at the disadvantage from which it had suffered as a result of the first-class decryption work of Admiral Reginald "Blinker" Hall's Room 40 at the British Admiralty.[2] Not only did the German Navy adopt, in common with their army and air force, the sophisticated and efficient Enigma machine cypher system (and the naval version was superior to that of the other two services), they retained under their own control a naval cryptanalysis department which made a brilliant attack on the Royal Navy's cyphers.[3] Aided by poor RN signal procedure during the Abyssinian crisis in 1935, and by the Admiralty's typically conservative refusal to adopt a machine cypher as the Royal Air Force and the United States Navy were doing, the Germans had, by the outbreak of war, made a partial penetration of a number of the RN operational codes and cyphers. This was of immense value to them in the Norwegian campaign in the spring of 1940. Then, in August of that same year, changes were made in those particular cyphers which rendered them secure for the rest of the war. Unfortunately, the same could not be said for the main cypher used for the control of the convoys. As the U-boat war spread further and further afield and the volume of traffic in Naval Cypher No. 3 grew, so the German successes increased. Although the British system was in many respects weak, it also had certain advantages: the Germans were never able to decrypt anything like 100 per cent of the traffic, and what they did decrypt was subject to such delays that even at the best only about 10 per cent could be processed in time to be of operational value. Nevertheless, starting late in 1940 and increasingly up to mid-1943, the x-B-Dienst was able, on many occasions, to supply Grand Admiral Karl Dönitz, admiral commanding U-boats, with timely information about routes and diversions of Allied convoys and to build up a generally accurate picture of their cycles and procedures. The British were not oblivious to the potential vulnerability of their convoy cypher and introduced frequent changes and modifications which caused the x-B-Dienst many difficulties. However, the sad fact is that the so-called "Long Subtractor" system, upon which all British cyphers were then based, was not capable of carrying the enormous load placed on it by the worldwide control of Allied shipping. It seems to have taken nearly two years for Bletchley Park to devise, test, produce, and distribute all over the world an entirely new cypher, the "Stencil Subtractor" system, but when this was finally introduced in June 1943 the x-B-Dienst became virtually a spent force.

Naval Cypher No. 3 was an Allied cypher, used by the Royal Canadian Navy and the USN as well as the Royal Navy. In so far as the Americans accepted it and continued to use it, rather than disclose to their Allies the secret of their own superior ECM (electrical cypher machine) cypher, they too must bear a share of responsibility for the losses which resulted from its

Plate 60. For many years, RCN officers trained on Royal Navy capital ships. Here, the battle cruiser HMS *Hood* on the day she was sunk by the *Bismarck*, 24 May 1941. (Imperial War Museum—Q 17879)

Plate 61. The battleship HMS *Duke of York* firing a broadside. (Imperial War Museum—A 7550)

Plate 62. U-Boat detection and destruction was helped immeasurably by radio intelligence from the Submarine Tracking Rooms in Ottawa, London, and Washington. HMCS *Chaudière* I approaching crippled U-744, 6 March 1944. (PAC—PA 115348)

Plate 63. RCN boarding party alongside U-744. (PAC—PA 112996)

Plate 64. Fairmile B-type motor launch HMCS Q121 escorting German submarine U-889 to harbour at Shelburne, Nova Scotia, May 1945. (PAC—PA 115375)

Plate 65. Captured German submarine, U-190, in St. John's harbour. (MCM)

Plate 66. A heavy price was paid when U-boats eluded convoy escorts. Crew of HMCS *Clayoquot*, sunk in approaches to Halifax by U-806 on Christmas Eve, 1944, being brought aboard HMCS *Fennel*. (DOH, NDHQ—GM-3001)

Plate 67. Burial at sea of Ordinary Seaman Kenneth Watson of HMCS *Assiniboine* I, who died in the action which resulted in the sinking of U-210 on 6 August 1942. (PAC—PA 115346)

weakness. OP-20-G, the American counterpart of OIC, estimated that in the eighteen months from January 1942 until June 1943 the equivalent of some sixty merchant ships were lost which might have been saved but for the work of the x-B-Dienst. It was not the Americans who proved early in 1943 that the convoy cypher was compromised and insisted on its replacement. The British, despite their concentration on the offensive task of breaking enemy's cyphers, had started on the task of producing a replacement long before this.

When I joined STR at the end of 1941, its head was that brilliant man, Rodger Winn. A barrister by profession, partially crippled by polio in his youth, now a temporary commander, Royal Naval Volunteer Reserve, Winn was a born intelligence officer. His staff consisted of four watchkeepers (three of them civilians), a male clerk, and a couple of young women. Located in the same room, but not directly responsible to Winn, were the DF plotting team of four and an observer from the Anti-Submarine Warfare Division. Over the next eighteen months we gained another four RNVR watchkeepers, a researcher, and some more clerical help, but numbers remained remarkably small throughout.

In the centre of the room was a large plotting table on which were displayed the current positions and routes of all British and Allied vessels and convoys in the North Atlantic and our estimate of the dispositions of the U-boats. On another chart table was a copy of the German Naval Grid (for they used a grid system for indicating latitude and longitude) and on the walls were other charts covering the South Atlantic, Indian Ocean, or Norwegian Sea. Graphs and charts showing the number and location of U-boats in port, training, or building, as well as Allied shipping losses and replacements occupied the rest of the wall space.

Next door to the STR was the Main Admiralty Plot, under the charge of Commander Richard A. "Dick" Hall, "Blinker" Hall's son. He and his two immediate subordinates had free access to our room and to all the information at our disposal, but not many other officers below the rank of post-captain enjoyed this privilege. Hall and his team were responsible for planning the routes of all convoys and independents (ships steaming on their own) and for devising and issuing all diversions. The object of the combined operation was to keep our merchant ships away from the U-boats or at least to give timely warning to those that appeared to be threatened and to ensure that they were provided with the strongest possible sea and air escort. The STR had direct communication by scrambler telephone or telex to the Commander-in-Chief Western Approaches, Admiral Sir Max Horton, the air officer commanding-in-chief Coastal Command, and indeed to all major maritime commands in the United Kingdom. There was similar direct communication with Bletchley Park and direct telephone and telex lines to the principal DF stations throughout the United Kingdom. If urgent signals had to be passed to authorities at sea or overseas, they received top priority. The OIC was the nerve centre of the Admiralty, and as the U-boat war became more and more desperate, an increasing number of top level operational decisions were taken in the STR, sometimes at the Hall/Winn level if speed was essential, sometimes at vice-chief or assistant chief of staff level if time permitted. Everything was first discussed and co-ordinated with Western Approaches and Coastal Command, and, so far as security permitted, all relevant information was passed without delay to those at sea.

Our day started about 0730 when Winn and I arrived and began to digest the information that had come in during the night and to adjust the plot accordingly. This was followed immediately by a three-way scrambler telephone conversation with Western Approaches and Coastal Command, when routes and diversions were discussed and sea and air escorts and patrols agreed. There then came a conference presided over by the assistant chief of staff (U-boats and Trade), repeated at 1800 most evenings. At noon each day a signal giving the STR's estimates in broad terms of the position of all U-boats in the Atlantic was despatched to all ships at sea and to all authorities concerned, and information and views were exchanged with our opposite numbers in Ottawa and Washington. Any fresh information coming in was dealt with immediately throughout the twenty-four hours either by Winn or myself or, at night, by the watchkeepers, who were relieved at 0900 and 1900 each day. Winn and I rarely departed much before 2000 and much later if some crisis arose. It was an exhausting but intensely exhilarating life, calling for a willingness to accept great responsibility. It also called for strong nerves because one could usually see the proof of the accuracy or the inaccuracy of one's judgment demonstrated within a matter of hours or at the most days. I found that the only way I could endure it was to try to treat it as sort of a game of chess: to have allowed oneself to picture too vividly tankers going up in flames or men drowning as a direct result of a faulty decision would have meant that one would never have been able to give a decision again. In this respect we did not differ from any officer in command of men in war, except that we did not command men. But if our appreciations were faulty, men paid with their lives. I am reminded of the man who said that he was looking for a one-armed lawyer. When asked why, he replied that any lawyer he had ever consulted had always said, "Well, on the one hand you could do so and so—but, on the other, you could do the opposite." We, like all good intelligence officers, had to be "one-armed lawyers." As Rodger Winn remarked, if we did no better than beat the law of averages our efforts were worthwhile, but I am glad to say that we achieved considerably more than that.

I have already referred to the fact that the German system of controlling their wolfpacks from U-boat Headquarters ashore resulted in a tremendous volume of signalling. As the number of operational U-boats increased, Dönitz's standard practice was to form them into patrols of between half a dozen to two dozen boats and to spread them out at right angles to the presumed line of advance of Allied convoys. They would then sweep forward on the surface during the day, usually reversing course at slower speed during the night so as not to overshoot their target, until one member of the pack sighted the convoy. The U-boat concerned would report immediately to headquarters but would not normally attack on its own. Instead it would shadow the convoy, reporting its position, course, speed, and any other relevant details until such time as the other members of the pack had also gained contact; headquarters would then give permission for all to attack together in an effort to swamp the defences. In order to deploy his boats to the best advantage, Dönitz required a great deal of information from them—position reports, fuel and torpedo state, weather conditions, action and damage summaries, and so on. He realized that all these transmissions would be intercepted by Allied direction-finding stations, but he seems to have failed to appreciate the continuing improvement in the Allied DF system which took place during the first two years of the war. We came to recognize the short signals used for sighting and shadowing reports and for weather reports, and even though we might not know the exact meaning of the various messages, their general purport was clear. Within minutes of any transmission being made, bearings had been obtained and passed to the Admiralty, or to Ottawa or Washington. The bearings did not always produce a neat "cocked hat" or fix,[4] but such was the skill which our plotters developed that it was usually possible to determine quickly the position of the U-boat involved, warn any convoy threatened, and divert others which appeared to be running into danger. All this was done quite often as quickly as the deciphered signal reached Dönitz and his staff in Lorient.

Moreover, once high-frequency direction-finding (HF/DF) sets were fitted in escort vessels, their operators could set watch on the appropriate frequency and obtain a bearing themselves of any subsequent signal made by the shadower. One of the escorts would then run down this bearing and, at the very least, cause the shadower to dive and lose contact even if it were not possible to attack it. None of this was possible in the early days, but in the second half of the war HF/DF afloat, which German intelligence failed to recognize until it was too late, was probably an even more important defensive and offensive weapon than ten-centimetre radar.

If DF afloat was a tactical killer, the great Allied network of shore DF stations, with their highly skilled operators and equally skilled and experienced plotting teams, came to represent one of the most useful weapons in the armoury of the Allied operational intelligence centres. It provided us at times with the best information we had about U-boat dispositions, and even when we were able to decrypt the actual contents of the German signals, DF was swifter and was almost always the first alarm bell to ring. Its value was naturally commensurate with the volume of signals made by the U-boats. With the virtual abandonment of wolfpack tactics at the end of 1943 and the introduction of renewed individual operations by U-boats in coastal waters in 1944, DF had less opportunity. Nevertheless, it remained one of our prime sources of information to the end of the war.

An intelligence officer's job is to build up a comprehensive picture from a mass of often seemingly unrelated scraps of information. Often we had to act before the picture could be completed, and of course we made many mistakes. Much of our work was a "guestimate," sometimes good, sometimes bad; we could only do our best. We relied heavily on the reports we received from our own warships and aircraft which had sighted or attacked U-boats and on the distress messages received from merchant ships which had themselves been attacked. Ship positions were usually accurate, but aerial navigation in those days (astral navigation without the help of electronics and satellites) was not nearly as precise as it is today, and aircraft positions were often many miles in error. One tried to check them by data from other sources, such as the established position of a convoy or even the DF fix of a U-boat attacked by the aircraft concerned.

Of course, incomparably our best source of information was crypt-analysis—Special Intelligence as it was then known, or "Ultra" as it is now generally although incorrectly called. Special Intelligence, derived from German Enigma, first became available during the Norwegian campaign when Allied cryptanalysts cracked the German air force cypher, which Bletchley Park codenamed "Yellow." However, the first naval version was not effectively broken until May 1941, when a series of carefully planned captures at last permitted a permanent penetration of the main German naval operational cypher, codenamed by them "Hydra."[5] This was used by all operational surface vessels and U-boats at that time, and it was decrypted continuously and completely, although with various delays in the process, until the end of hostilities. It provided us with a wealth of information, some up to date, some already overtaken by events. Even when the Germans introduced a special cypher, "Triton," on 1 February 1942 for their Atlantic U-boats, Hydra was still used by those boats operating in Norwegian waters and by all patrol craft which invariably escorted U-boats along the swept channels to and from their ports in Germany and the occupied countries. This provided the STR with precise knowledge of each U-boat as it left port and when or if it returned. We knew, therefore, which boats were at sea, and, albeit with some delay, which boats were overdue or lost. At any given moment we could be sure of the total strength of the operational U-boat fleet and, from cyphers used by boats training in the Baltic and from aerial reconnaissance, the numbers building and training, and so the threat for the future.

This was invaluable information, but with the introduction of Triton, the staff at Bletchley Park were temporarily defeated, and the STR lost priceless knowledge of the operational orders issued by Dönitz and the reports made by his commanders, which we had enjoyed for the previous eight months. No longer could we see the constantly shifting positions of the wolfpacks or the imminent danger in areas hitherto safe, as we had been able to do when we had learned in advance of Operation Pauckenschlag, the concentration on the northeastern seaboard of North America in mid-January 1942. We had been able to pass that factual information on to the Canadians and the Americans, but subsequent extensions of the campaign to Florida, the Caribbean and Gulf of Mexico, let alone to the Cape of Good Hope or the transfer of the main weight of attack back to the North Atlantic convoy routes in September 1942, could only be predicted by intelligent guesswork. Our guesswork was pretty good. When, in the middle of December 1942, Bletchley Park managed to crack Triton, our estimate of U-boat numbers and dispositions was still astonishingly accurate.

The break into Triton came just in time—the first five months of 1943 saw the climax of the Battle of the Atlantic.[6] Two years earlier Dönitz had found it difficult to maintain a dozen U-boats on patrol against convoys. Now his total fleet had grown to four hundred, of which half were operational, and sometimes one hundred were at sea in the Atlantic alone. On the Allied side escort groups, support groups, Woolworth carriers, and above all very-long-range aircraft were at long last becoming available in adequate numbers. The fatal Greenland gap in air cover in mid-Atlantic (known by RCN escort crews as the "Black Pit") was being closed slowly. The build-up for the Second Front was starting in earnest, but there could be no invasion of Europe if the men and supplies did not get through. Suddenly, the intelligence picture became clearer and firmer. Evasive routing of convoys and independents was more frequently successful: threats could more often be seen and encountered; and the scale of attack more accurately assessed. It certainly helped to tilt the scales in favour of the Allies.

The chief handicap remained the time taken to break the daily change in the Triton settings. Sometimes the delay was negligible, and we were able to read Dönitz's orders to his U-boats as quickly as his own commanders. But during those five critical months, we were often two, three, or even ten days adrift with our information. At the same time the x-B-Dienst was operating with peak efficiency and was often able to supply Dönitz with timely information about our routes and diversions so that he could take effective counter-measures. There were other difficulties: the Germans used a simple transposition code with their enciphered signals to disguise their grid references and this took further precious time to solve; convoys and U-boats were not always where their shore commands estimated them to be; chance encounters, unforeseen by either side, led to fierce battles; fog, gales, ice, or a calm sea and clear visibility produced unexpected results. The expression "the fog of war" took on a very real meaning which postwar historians, without the benefit of personal experience, find hard to understand.

Despite this the balance swung inexorably, and in the end suddenly, in favour of the Allies. By 24 May 1943, the U-boats had suffered such devastating losses that Dönitz withdrew his battered forces from the North Atlantic. The battle had been won, and intelligence had played a significant part in the victory.[7]

Dönitz, of course, did not give up. He sent his U-boats back again with fresh weapons and new equipment. But the Germans had also lost the scientific war, and the day of the conventional U-boat was over. They could only try to hold on in the desperate hope that entirely new types of U-boats would become operational in time to turn the tide. It was not to be, and from the autumn of 1943 the great superiority not only of Allied resources but also of Allied intelligence had a decisive effect in ensuring total Allied command of the sea routes and in preventing any real interference with the build-up and launching of the invasion of Normandy. Bletchley Park's mastery of Triton (and of almost every other version of Enigma) was such that delays in decrypting almost vanished, and as this was accompanied by a similar improvement in the supply of information from our other sources, the OIC's successes increased greatly.

Even at this stage the Allies could not be strong everywhere. But intelligence could now show precisely which areas, which convoys, and which ships were threatened, as well as which were clear of danger. Maximum available strength could be concentrated at the decisive points and other, safer targets almost stripped of their defences. With the failure of the x-B-Dienst it was now the U-boats which were being sent into the ring blindfolded. In the STR we knew at least as well as Dönitz what his U-boats were doing; we even knew the exact operational experience of each commanding officer and the state of morale both at sea and in U-boat Headquarters. It was complete intelligence mastery.

I do not think it unreasonable to claim that this was essentially a British triumph, not only at Bletchley Park but also in the OIC, where the results of cryptanalysis were studied and considered together with every other scrap of information and where the co-operation with the operational authorities had become so close and intimate. But, of course, the British were not the only operational authorities involved with the Battle of the Atlantic. Canada from the outset and America from before Pearl Harbor were equally responsible for hundreds of ships and convoys and for large areas of ocean, controlling warships, aircraft and convoys in those areas irrespective of nationality just as the British did in their zone. To do so effectively, they had to have the same benefit of the same intelligence as the British.

Central control of operations demanded centralized intelligence. By the middle of 1942 the British had persuaded their two Allies to follow their example and set up their own OIC's in Ottawa and Washington under Lieutenant-Commander John McDiarmid, RCNVR, and Commander Kenneth Knowles, USN. These two centres received and handled all non-Special Intelligence from their own areas exactly as we did, but cryptanalysis, because the fountainhead, Bletchley Park, was in England, had to be treated differently.

Although John McDiarmid's unit in Ottawa was a small one, RN and RCN relations were so close and amicable that we were able to provide him with Special Intelligence for his area in exactly the same way that we did with RN commands. By this I mean that we passed to him every scrap of information bearing on his area, but we did not bother him with extraneous information concerning events in North Norway, the Bay of Biscay, or the Baltic. McDiarmid visited London, and Rodger Winn and I spent some time in Ottawa. We knew and relied on each other. McDiarmid was free to run his own show and to form his own judgments about the area for which he was responsible. He did so magnificently. There was a constant two-way exchange of views and information, and, so far as I know, there was never any complaint that Ottawa was being denied any information it needed.

Commander Knowles in Washington received his Special Intelligence in raw form via the American cryptanalysis organization from Bletchley Park. Once again visits were exchanged, and such a good working relationship was established that the two centres might just as well have been part of a single organization. Signals and appreciations went back and forth daily with an agreement that they were seen by no one except Knowles and his deputy in Washington and Winn and myself in the Admiralty. We could thus be as outspoken as we liked, and indeed we were, without the risk of causing an international incident.

The result of all this was that the appreciations of the three centres, as presented to our respective authorities, became a joint affair and were identical. However, through no fault of McDiarmid or Knowles, relations between Ottawa and Washington were unnecessarily sour. The Americans distrusted Canadian security, and the Canadians resented the assumption of superiority of their neighbour, who had entered the war two years and three months after they had. I was sent to Ottawa and Washington in the autumn of 1943 to arrange for closer co-operation between the two centres. I spent three days persuading the Canadian director of Naval Intelligence and then the assistant chief of the Naval Staff to agree to McDiarmid accompanying me to Washington. I had no sooner managed to obtain their most reluctant approval when I received an urgent signal from the British Admiralty Delegation in Washington saying that, although I should personally be welcome in the Navy Department, under no circumstances was I to bring my Canadian colleague with me. I only hope that I managed to explain this away without making a bad situation worse.

Despite this bad feeling, the tri-partite intelligence organization worked excellently. The acceptance of the British concept of how to handle maritime operational intelligence, adopted willingly by the Canadians and, initially, with some reluctance by the Americans, did, at the very least, save many Allied lives and much shipping. It certainly did not win the Battle of the Atlantic, that was done at sea, but I do think that it hastened the Allied victory.

I started with one apocryphal story about Winston Churchill; let me conclude with another. As is well known, the great man constantly plagued and prodded his naval and military commanders with suggestions as to how they should conduct the war. Many of these were quite impracticable, but Churchill did not give up easily and he was a difficult man to argue with. On one such occasion, Admiral Sir Dudley Pound, the First Sea Lord, driven to desperation, protested vehemently that a certain proposal was "against all naval tradition." "And what," countered Churchill, "is naval tradition, but rum, sodomy and the lash?" As so often, he was unfair. The Royal Navy has many splendid traditions. I suggest that one of its lesser-known virtues is the ability, often displayed at the eleventh hour, to secure and handle good intelligence. The Operational Intelligence Centre and its Canadian and American counterparts were, in their way, war-winners.

Chapter 12

"THE MOST THANKLESS TASK" REVISITED: CONVOYS, ESCORTS, AND RADIO INTELLIGENCE IN THE WESTERN ATLANTIC, 1941-43

W.A.B. Douglas and Jürgen Rohwer

> In what proportions did the elements
> Combine to move those individual pawns
> Of power in their massed flesh-and-nerve formation
> Across the board? . . .

—E.J. Pratt, "Behind the Log" (a poem written in 1947 to describe Convoy SC 42)

I. CONVOY SC 42, SEPTEMBER 1941

Introduction

Patrick Beesly has described the organization and methods of intelligence on both the Allied and German sides in Chapter 11. Their estimates were the most important single element of operational decisions in the naval war. What this meant to Canadian forces in the Battle of the Atlantic can be illustrated by three convoys which were subject to heavy attack: SC 42 of September 1941, SC 107 of November 1942, and ONS 5 of May 1943. The Allies pitted their convoy routing system against German wolfpack tactics in each of these battles, and in each case the resultant communication methods presented certain problems to intelligence.

In the first place, the Admiralty in London transmitted a route recommendation to all commands concerned about eight days before a convoy was scheduled to leave port. The route depended upon the enemy situation and the availability of sea and air escort forces. The signal in 1941 always contained the following data:

1. the ocean route positions, designated by letters;
2. the position and the date of the mid-ocean meeting point (MOMP) where the ocean escort groups relieved each other in the area south of Iceland;
3. the standard route for the stragglers; and,
4. some secret reference points, designated by code words.

Approximately two or three days later, after co-ordination with the other commands concerned, the route was agreed upon, and the routing signal went out to the following commands:

a. port directors of the convoy assembly points;
b. naval commodores in command of bases of escort forces;
c. commander-in-chief Western Approaches (CinCWA);
d. air officer commanding-in-chief Coastal Command;
e. naval officer in charge, Iceland;
f. commanding officer Atlantic Coast (COAC), Halifax;
g. Naval Service Headquarters (NSHQ), Ottawa;
h. commodore commanding (later flag officer) Newfoundland Force (FONF), St. John's.

All pertinent information was sent to the Air Ministry and Headquarters, Fighter Command, and chief of Naval Operations (OPNAV), Washington, through the Special Naval Observer (SPENAVO), London.

These instructions could be transmitted by cable, landline, or telephone, but the port director's "sailing telegram" had to go by radio when the convoy sailed because some of the forces concerned were at sea. This signal contained the former points 1 to 3 inclusive, some information about the convoy commodore, vice-commodore, and rear-commodore and details of communications. In the second part of the telegram was a complete list of all ships, their nationality, position number, speed, cargo, and destination. Radio traffic was also indispensable for controlling feeder-convoys, for relieving local escort groups by the ocean escort group, and especially for signalling changes to the route, either because the oncoming convoy was going to pass too close, or because U-boats had been located near the given route. This unavoidable radio traffic opened up some important opportunities for German radio-intelligence (*Funkbeobachtungsdienst*, or x-B-Dienst).

Signal traffic analysis, the study of message characteristics, frequencies, and addresses, offered clues about traffic structure from which intelligence officers could deduce convoy schedules. This was more fruitful for the Germans than direction-finding, the Allies' great standby, because German receiving stations in occupied Europe were located relatively close to one another and thus offered only a very short base for German cross-bearings. The Luftwaffe tracking stations, on the other hand, often suggested convoy positions by locating signals of escorting aircraft in the eastern Atlantic.

Admiral Dönitz's most valuable source of information was cryptanalysis, carried out by the x-B-Dienst, from the enormous volume of signal traffic necessary for directing a great number of convoys at sea. The Royal Navy used three main crypto-systems based on a combination of codes and cyphers. Two systems had been in use since before World War II, and the third, Naval Cypher No. 3, came into force in 1941 for convoy control. Christened by the x-B-Dienst "Cologne," "Munich," and "Frankfurt," respectively, these crypto-systems had code groups that were super-enciphered by a long digit series known as the long subtractor system, changed at first every two months and later twice a month. Changes to the crypto-systems themselves involved a complicated logistical operation that made for infrequent alterations. The longer the period without change, the more opportunity the x-B-Dienst had to solve new code groups, although it was always one of the German cryptanalysts' greatest problems that they could tackle only one intercepted message at a time. Thus, even when one British system had been in force for a relatively long period (as in August 1940, December 1941, and February 1943), it was only possible to solve about 10 per cent of intercepted messages, and of these only one-tenth could be deciphered in time to be of operational use. It must be said that historians have only just begun the very necessary and formidable task of evaluating properly the decryption of radio traffic in World War II, and we must be careful not to overestimate the value of this source of intelligence.

The Germans produced their own generous quota of radio signals in order to implement group tactics by U-boats. The first test operations began in 1939, and the first real wolfpack operations began in the summer of 1940. The latter followed a regular pattern. Up to fifteen U-boats, after sailing from their French and Norwegian bases at intervals of several days, would report by radio when they passed the Iceland-Faröes gap or left the Bay of Biscay. They would in turn receive a "heading point" identified by a square on the German naval grid. When, after about five or seven days, most of the boats were in this area, the BdU (*Befehlshaber der U-boote* or U-boat headquarters) ordered a patrol line at right angles to an expected convoy in order to intercept the ships in daylight. If no convoy was picked up, the U-boats were given a line of advance and a day's run to sweep the assumed convoy course. The first U-boat to sight the convoy sent its contact signal; BdU ordered the others to concentrate, and the attack was then supposed to take place. One U-boat always acted as the shadower, sending off regular shadowing reports and transmitting beacon signals for other U-boats of the group. Once the operation was broken off BdU would signal a new heading-point for those U-boats having sufficient fuel and torpedoes and order the others home or to the U-tankers, or "milch cows."

From the earliest days of the war, and especially after the expansion of the Allied network of intercept stations around the Atlantic in 1940-41, intelligence was able to exploit this U-boat signalling by traffic analysis and land-based direction-finding. These provided fairly precise and up-to-date information about U-boat positions and even revealed when U-boats were establishing contact with convoys.

For sending off its contact report, a U-boat used short signals, based on a code book which reduced all the important terms, positions, and other necessary information to a few four-letter groups. The groups were super-enciphered by the daily key of the cypher machine "Schlüssel M" and could be sent off in a few seconds. To silence other stations on a given frequency, each short signal commenced with the Greek letters, "beta-beta" or, as it was called in British naval jargon, "b-bar."

When the British introduced the cathode-ray direction finder, proposed by Robert Watson-Watt, it became possible to get a fix, for instance, on a U-boat sending a contact signal after sighting a convoy. By comparing the fix of such a b-bar signal with the convoy situation on the trade plot, the Admiralty's Submarine Tracking Room (STR) could identify a threatened convoy and send a warning without knowing the contents of the signal itself. By this combined method of direction-finding and traffic analysis, the STR had an important intelligence source, independent from crypt-analysis and available throughout the war, especially during the greatest convoy battles.

Because German wolfpack tactics depended so much on radio messages, British, American, and Canadian naval authorities saved many convoys from heavy losses, routing them completely clear of U-boat wolfpacks, by the techniques developed in the STR. The increasing efficiency of these techniques can be seen in a comparison of the U-boat successes in two periods (see chart, p. 191).

From August to December 1940 an average of only eight U-boats were in the operational area of the Western Approaches, the Royal Navy's command west of England and Ireland to approximately 17°W. They reported 36 per cent of all convoys sailing on the England-America route. Sixteen per cent of all convoys sailed lost more than three ships. In the next period, from January to May 1941, notwithstanding the fact that the number of U-boats was increased to eleven on the average and that there was some assistance by air reconnaissance, only 23 per cent of the North Atlantic convoys were sighted and only 10 per cent of all convoys sailed lost more than three ships.

Up to this time cryptanalysis played a very marginal part on the British side. Patrick Beesly has explained how the British were first able to break the German "Enigma" naval cypher in May 1941. British boarding parties captured cypher machines, a short signal code book, the water-soluble

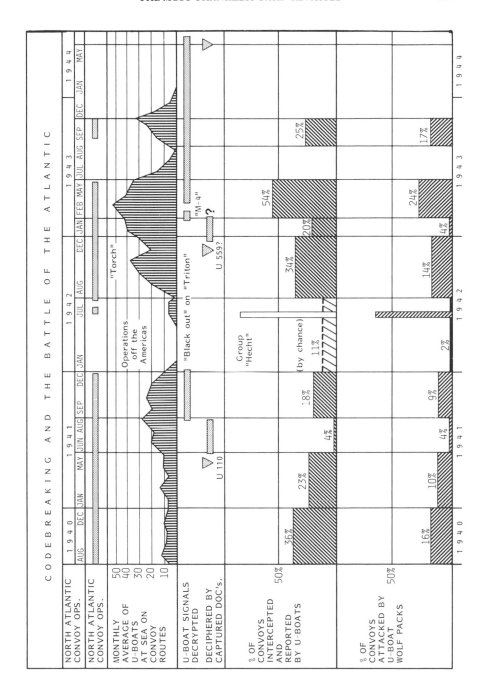

sheets of paper with the daily settings of the cypher machine, other procedure manuals and the wireless logs from the weather-reporting ship *München* and the U-boat, U-110. It took some time to evaluate this material and to make it operational, but, from the first part of June 1941, it was possible to decipher all intercepted German wireless messages and signals without great cryptanalytic effort by using the captured cypher settings and the captured machines. This had profound consequences for the Germans.

Although it is now clearly established that the interception and sinking of the German battleship *Bismarck* were based on radio-intelligence in the form of direction-finding and traffic analysis alone and had nothing to do with cryptanalysis or deciphering, the ability to read German wireless traffic almost immediately was largely responsible for the annihilation of the German surface-supply organization in the Atlantic in June 1941. This made further raids by big German surface ships on the convoys almost impossible. Less well known is the fact that U-boat operations suffered very heavily, so long as the captured cypher keys remained valid, after the capture of additional material from the weather-reporting ship *Lauenburg* at the end of June 1941. In fact, up to the beginning of August 1941, although more and more U-boats were at sea, the STR knew where they were and safely re-routed all except one of about fifty convoys on the North Atlantic route. Only on the England-Gibraltar route were U-boats able to make regular contact, thanks to the German agents at Algeciras and to the Focke-Wulf Condors whose aerial reconnaissance reports could not be evaded with the intelligence available to the Admiralty.

When the cypher keys ran out, the real work for the cryptanalysts began. They had had three months to prepare their methods and their machines to solve the daily settings of the "Schlüssel M" as quickly as possible. It was not to be an easy task. First the "bombes" (mathematical calculators), which were constructed to solve the 120 rotor-setting possibilities of German army and air force machines had to be adapted for the different combinations of rotor sequences in the naval machines. The German naval cypher machine had four different settings. Two interior settings had to be made every forty-eight hours by officers only, choosing three out of eight cypher rotors, which permitted 336 different combinations. Secondly, each rotor had a revolving ring with twenty-six positions to change the inside wire connections. This permitted 16,900 positions for three inset rotors. The two outer settings had to be changed every twenty-four hours by the cypher clerks. They had 1,547 possible plug connections on the plug board, and the operator could set each rotor to twenty-six different positions before beginning to encipher. This gave another 17,576 possibilities. By multiplying these factors one can get a theoretical total in the vicinity of 160 trillion.

With so many possible combinations, the Germans thought cryptanalytic successes would come too late to be of operational value, even if the enemy was able to capture a machine. But by using the bombe the British analysts could go through the combinations much faster than the Germans thought possible. Traffic analysis helped. Because the traffic analysts knew the normal format of contact signals, and could estimate from their own situation map the contents of such signals, they could feed the bombes with probable clear text as well as the enciphered text. By changing the data and terms of the probable text, it was sometimes possible for the bombe to solve the problem much faster than without this technique. When it was possible to decrypt such a message, a cryptanalyst had the solution of the daily key, and it was then possible to decrypt all intercepted signals of the same cypher circuit within hours. It is the very important, but painfully detailed, task of historians to establish the real time lags, without which one cannot evaluate the operational importance of this decrypting process that had so great an influence on convoy routing operations.

The Battle of Convoy SC 42, September 1941

Fast HX convoys were running every six days from Halifax during August 1941. They were escorted by an ocean escort group from the Western Rendezvous off St. John's, Newfoundland, to the Eastern Rendezvous south of Iceland, where the escorts were relieved by a British escort group, which brought the convoy to the North Channel, the passage leading past Northern Ireland to the Firth of Clyde and the Irish Sea. At the same time there was a cycle of slow SC convoys coming out, up to 20 August, every twelve days from Sydney, Nova Scotia, and after 20 August, every six days, also escorted by an ocean escort group to the Eastern Rendezvous. Two fast ON and one slow ONS convoy were sailing from Great Britain every twelve days. After 20 August there was an additional slow convoy, and the ON convoys thenceforth alternated between fast and slow convoys. Proceeding southwards from the North Channel, there were outbound OG convoys to Gibraltar and outbound OS convoys to Freetown, Sierra Leone; going in the other direction were the homeward-bound HG and SL convoys from Gibraltar and Freetown. They sailed every ten days and were escorted by British escort groups. During July and at the beginning of August BdU concentrated its operations on the Gibraltar route because it was possible here to use the assistance of the Focke-Wulf Condors. In August, however, there was a large build-up of new U-boats from homewaters in the Atlantic, so BdU decided to create an additional U-boat area in the north and try a new operational cycle on the North Atlantic convoy route. Nine boats coming out from Norway were given a heading-point southwest of Iceland. When, on 11 and 12 August, two of these U-boats reported the outbound convoys ON 4 and ON 5, BdU ordered eleven boats (which had searched without success for the convoy OS 2, after it had been located by x-B-Dienst) to go north to join the other nine. On 16 August these twenty boats had taken up their attack squares in the north, and three other boats, low on fuel, had taken up positions west of the North Channel. On the next day German air reconnaissance reported the outbound convoy OG 71, so the three U-boats west of the North Channel, and some outbound boats, were ordered to follow and attack this convoy. Only once, however, during the night of 19 August, were two very experienced commanders able to attack successfully. On 20 August the U-boats lost contact with OG 71.

Meanwhile, the British at Bletchley Park had decrypted the order by BdU to take up positions in the north, and all convoys were re-routed to the north of the German positions. Thus, three eastbound and four westbound convoys escaped detection. After waiting a week without success, BdU transferred eleven boats of this northern group to the area south of Iceland, to cover the evasive convoy routes passing to the north of the German positions. The other nine boats were transferred to the area west of the North Channel, in the hope of intercepting some outbound convoys. The last group had success; it intercepted OS 4 on 26 August, and the repeated attacks of U-557 resulted in the loss of four ships. The convoy was reported again the next day by air reconnaissance, but the established patrol line on the convoy course did not succeed because the U-boats reached their positions too late. In the north, two outbound boats were lost, the first to an air attack while the other, U-570, was captured after damage by an air attack. On the same day x-B-Dienst located the convoy HX 145 south of Iceland.

The northern group, ordered to deal with this convoy, failed to find it, so on 28 August the BdU ordered the northern boats to form two patrol lines, about one hundred miles apart, in the area where Dönitz assumed the convoy routes to be. Since the British had evaded all of the German U-boat positions, the Germans began to fear that their cypher had been compromised. Moreover, because it was possible that the British had captured the German grid-map, BdU decided to introduce lettered reference points. They were entrusted to the U-boat commanders in a sealed envelope before departure, and all positions were given by bearing and distance from one of these points. To identify the new reference letters, the naval analysis group in Hut 4, Bletchley Park, and the STR had to use more precious time, even after the text of the radio message had been completely decrypted. Thus, it was only after four days, on 1 September, that the STR had a correct picture of German U-boat positions.

In the north there were fourteen U-boats of the group "Markgraf," and the STR ordered the convoy ON 10 and the following ON 11, to evade the German group to the north. West of Ireland, a German aircraft reported the outbound convoy OG 73; the seven U-boats of group "Kürfurst" and the seven U-boats of group "Bosemüller" were ordered to intercept and attack.

On the next morning, one returning U-boat reported the homeward-bound SL 84 southeast of this position. BdU ordered group Bosemüller to close in on this convoy, but, on 3 September, contact with both convoys was lost, and BdU ordered the U-boats operating against them to concentrate on the outward-bound OG 73 as group "Seewolf." This was the general situation in the east, as SC 42 was beginning its passage from the Strait of Belle Isle (north of Newfoundland) in the western Atlantic.

The United States Navy was daily becoming more involved in the Atlantic war. In July a U.S. marine brigade had relieved the British occupation troops in Iceland, and U.S. convoys with American and Icelandic ships, escorted by U.S. destroyer groups, were now going back and forth between Newfoundland and Iceland on the same routes as the Allied convoys. (Not surprisingly, there were some incidents involving the enemy since the escorting destroyers were mostly old "four-stackers," similar to the fifty destroyers given to the British and the Canadians in the "Destroyer-Naval Base Deal" of September 1940.) During the Atlantic Conference of August 1941 in Argentia, Roosevelt and Churchill decided that the U.S. Atlantic Fleet should escort convoys as soon as possible. This would not happen until 15 September, but on 1 September Admiral Ernest King, the commander-in-chief of the U.S. Atlantic Fleet, issued his operational order No. 9 in which he ordered the USN to attack any suspicious contact which might endanger American-escorted ships. Thus, on 4 September, when a British plane from Iceland reported by signal lamp to the American destroyer USS *Greer* that there was a German U-boat in the neighbourhood, the *Greer* altered course and detected the U-boat with sonar. The British plane dropped several depth-charges before departing for Iceland. The German commander of U-652 assumed that the detonations came from depth-charges dropped by the destroyer and fired two torpedoes which missed the American ship. Thereupon, the *Greer* attacked the U-boat with depth-charges. This episode came to be known as the *Greer* incident.

On 6 September the German orders of 4 September were decrypted, and the STR learned of a well-calculated move 150 miles to the west by the German group Markgraf. The Admiralty re-routed all convoys around the new German disposition. HX 147, ON 11, ON 10, and ON 12 were ordered to assume a more northerly course. But on the same day, BdU decided, after waiting for sighting reports without success, to distribute Markgraf over a bigger area southeast of Greenland. It was instructed to go back and forth in this area to cover a greater part of the ocean in search of the convoys. Since the repositioning of the U-boats took some time, the delay in decrypting the German order had no immediate consequences, although the new dispositions were scheduled to cover the convoy routes.

When the German order of 6 September was decrypted two days later, it was difficult to identify the German reference points, and the U-boat estimate was not entirely correct. Nevertheless, re-routing was still success-ful. Convoy ON 12, near Iceland, was re-routed to the south. On the southwestern side of the new Markgraf area, the eastward-bound convoys HX 148 and SC 43 were also re-routed to the south, as was the American Task Force 15, a troop transport convoy escorted by a battleship, a cruiser, and fifteen destroyers, bringing an army brigade to Iceland to relieve the marines. In the northwest, convoy SC 42, fighting heavy seas and gale force winds, could not go back to the south because the escorts were short of fuel. The Admiralty re-routed it close to the Greenland coast to try an "end run," after which it was hoped that the escort group for ON 13, coming from Great Britain, could relieve the Canadian escorts between Greenland and Iceland. On 8 September the German U-boats had taken up their positions, and almost all Allied convoys were skirting the U-boat area estimated by the STR, but, in the northwest, U-81 intercepted and sank a straggler from convoy SC 42. The following day the most northwesterly boat, U-85, came upon SC 42 and sent out her contact signal. BdU ordered Markgraf to close and attack. Dönitz's instructions were uncompromising: "This convoy must not pass. At them—Attack them—Sink them!"

Since that spring, U-boats had developed some new techniques in the group system. Until mid-August, the shadower was not allowed to attack unless headquarters gave permission. By the time of SC 42's passage, however, the shadower was to attack at every opportunity. If necessary, the shadower transmitted homing signals on a medium-frequency beacon, and once attacks had begun, any U-boat, at this stage of the war, could issue subsequent shadowing reports. Furthermore, once the battle was under way the shadower was encouraged to carry out attacks as well as make sighting and shadowing reports. The low rate of success enjoyed hitherto encouraged U-boat commanders to fire from any attacking position avail-able. With sixteen U-boats of group Markgraf between Iceland and Green-land, the convoy approaching the danger zone would be a crucial test of new methods as well as of the recently adopted disposition of German submarines. At 1230 Greenwich Mean Time (all times will be given in GMT, which was about three hours ahead of local time), U-85's sighting report set in train the events which were to shatter the suspense that had been building for several days. The conditions were ideal for U-boats: the weather had moderated, visibility was at least thirty miles, and several ships in the convoy were making clouds of black smoke.

All that stood between the convoy and the U-boats closing in relentlessly for the kill (no mere hyperbole—the circumstances admit no other inter-pretation) were the ships of the escort. They were far beyond the range of the twelve Douglas Digby and five Catalina patrol aircraft based in New-foundland. Theoretically, air cover might have been available from Ice-land, but it would be another thirty hours before one of the nine Catalinas

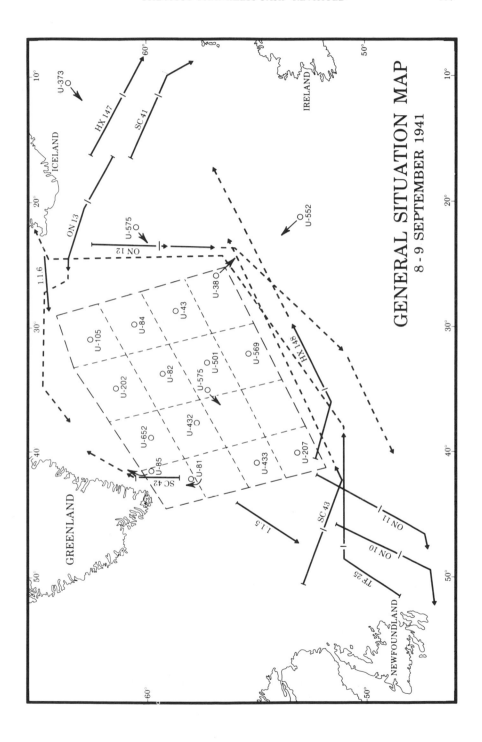

GENERAL SITUATION MAP
8 - 9 SEPTEMBER 1941

there was able to arrive on task. There was nothing to prevent U-boats from using their surface speed in daylight hours to acquire good attacking positions ahead of the convoy after dark on the first or second nights.

Disposed in twelve columns, the sixty-four merchant ships of SC 42 were under the escort of a group from the Newfoundland Escort Force (NEF). Until the United States Navy took over in the western Atlantic, the RCN's NEF served as a stop-gap measure that would eventually blossom into the Mid-Ocean Escort Force in 1942. In September 1941, however, it was just getting on its feet with ten escort groups, each consisting of one destroyer and three corvettes, one group of two destroyers and three corvettes, and one fast group of five destroyers for troop convoys. The groups had begun their escort duties in the early summer and were still in the formative stage. Escort Group 24 (HMCS *Skeena* and the corvettes *Alberni*, *Kenogami*, and *Orillia*) was allocated to SC 42.

Skeena was a River-class destroyer commanded by Lieutenant-Commander J.C. Hibbard, RCN. Like most Canadian destroyers throughout the war, she had a fair percentage of professional sailors on board: Lieutenants Erik Boak and William H. Willson, Sub-Lieutenant John W. "Jake" McDowall and Gunner (T) Frank Barlow. Among the other officers Sub-Lieutenant John A. Mitchell, RCNR, would later become a career naval officer as well. By any standards she was a well-officered ship, but like all destroyers of the time *Skeena* had little practical experience of U-boat attacks, and her equipment was rudimentary; she had no radar and no HF/DF equipment. Of the other escorts in the group, *Orillia* and *Alberni* had some experience of convoy operations. *Orillia*'s captain, Temporary Lieutenant W.E.S. "Ted" Briggs, RCNR, (later a well-known figure in the Canadian Broadcasting Corporation) had some formal naval training before the war. *Kenogami* was under the command of a volunteer reserve officer, Lieutenant-Commander Reginald "Cowboy" Jackson. As it was the ship's first ocean convoy after commissioning at Quebec in July, experience on board was minimal.

In addition to Group 24 there were two corvettes which would give unexpected depth to the Canadian surface escort. Captain Stephen Roskill, the official historian of RN operations during the war, states that HMC Ships *Chambly* and *Moose Jaw* joined the escort after they received orders from the Admiralty while on a training cruise. The facts are significantly different. These two ships combined the working-up of their neophyte ships' companies with the duties of the so-called Newfoundland local defence force. Acting Commander J.S.D. "Chummy" Prentice, RCN, a Canadian who had retired from the Royal Navy before the war, had the responsibility of running the work-ups programme at St. John's and was preparing to take the ships to sea for training on 8 September. Having access to the operations room, Prentice became aware of the situation

developing between Iceland and Greenland by 4 September and argued that
the commodore commanding the Newfoundland Force (CCNF) should
maintain a group at sea to give added support to whichever convoy was
threatened by U-boats. It was not clear then whether SC 42 or SC 43, about
to sail from Sydney, would need reinforcements, but captain (D[estroyers])
fell in with Prentice's suggestion. CCNF gave permission for *Chambly* and
Moose Jaw to sail three days early and maintain station between the Strait
of Belle Isle and Greenland until orders were issued to join either one
convoy or the other.

The ships sailed on 5 September (so hurriedly that *Moose Jaw* did not
have time to embark fresh provisions) and forged straight into the gale that
had slowed up SC 42 for three days. *Moose Jaw* was also commanded by a
regular officer, Lieutenant F. "Freddie" Grubb, RCN, and *Chambly* was
fortunate in having a very competent navigating officer (Mate A.F. Pickard, RCNR, later Captain "Tony" Pickard, RCN) and an experienced HSD
(Higher Submarine Detector: an ASDIC or sonar operator) rating on loan
for the training cruise. On the other hand, Lieutenant Grubb's report of
proceedings observed that almost the entire ship's company was seasick for
four days and that only a few of the hands on *Moose Jaw* were fit to carry out
their duties.

When CCNF ordered the ships to join SC 42, the transmission was
garbled, and for several precious hours they steamed towards the wrong
convoy, but in the early hours of 10 September they had sorted out the
confusion and were on their way to act as the first support group in RCN
history. By then, the convoy had come under attack. The poet, E.J. Pratt,
described the macabre beauty of the scene that lay ahead:

> When ships announced their wounds by rockets, wrote
> Their own obituaries in flame that soared
> Two hundred feet and stabbed the Arctic night
> Like some neurotic and untimely sunrise.
> Exploding tankers turned the sky to canvas,
> Soaked it in orange fire, kindled the sea,
> Then carpeted their graves with wreaths of soot.

U-85 had stalked the convoy for more than fifteen hours, unable to get in
a successful attack. A torpedo stuck in the tube, and four other torpedoes
were apparently set too deep or malfunctioned. Sighted by ships in the
convoy, these gave the alarm to the escort. *Skeena* and *Orillia* managed to
keep the U-boat down by active searching in the area astern of the convoy.
At 0037 on 10 September, however, U-432 caught up, gained a firing
position, and, with his first spread of torpedoes, sank the fourth ship in the
port wing column. Half an hour later U-81 acquired an attacking position,

fired and missed. By this time *Kenogami* was on the port quarter of the convoy, where she had sighted, and then lost contact with, U-85, which was trying to get into position, and *Skeena* was racing back in response to a submarine sighting on the port bow—probably U-81. An emergency turn of the convoy forty-five degrees to starboard at 0113 may well have foiled U-81's attack. Then a ship near the starboard quarter of the convoy reported another submarine, and the convoy promptly resumed its old course. As a result of this sighting everyone was in a thoroughly jittery state. A ship at the rear of the ninth column sighted U-652 at about 0248. The submarine charged up between columns seven and eight, with all hell breaking loose; merchant ships fired their limited armament, and the convoy made an emergency turn to port. *Skeena* steamed between columns seven and eight from the opposite direction at sixteen knots, frantically manoeuvring with full engine movements ahead and astern to avoid collision with the merchant ships wallowing in the darkness, while trying to get at her enemy. Hibbard sighted the U-boat, a ship in the seventh column called by megaphone that the submarine was on her starboard bow, and two ships about two hundred yards astern of *Skeena* blew up, all in a matter of a few moments. Hibbard attempted valiantly to ram the German submarine, but the U-boat was already crash-diving, and ASDIC contact was impossible amid the confusion of underwater sounds generated by the convoy. In spite of this, *Skeena* carried out an accurate depth-charge attack, although, unfortunately, with settings that were too shallow. The submarine surfaced when the convoy was safely past.

> . . . The triple task—
> To screen the convoy, counter-attack, and then,
> The humane third of rescuing the sailors,
> Seemed far beyond the escort's hope or effort.
> To save to kill, to kill to save, were means
> And ends closely and bloodily allied.

> . . . High strategy
> Demanded of the brain an execution
> Protested by the tactics of the heart.

In the wake of disaster *Orillia* went back to pick up survivors from the stricken ships and finding that one of them, the tanker *Tahchee*, could be salvaged, obtained permission to stay with her. *Skeena* did not hear from *Orillia* again, and the escort was now reduced to one destroyer and two corvettes. *Orillia*'s absence was not, however, significant when U-432 penetrated the screen from ahead and approached the convoy's port side on the surface at 0510. Her torpedoes struck the second ship in the port wing column, and the fifth ship in the second column, just as the third ship in the same column, *Regin*, sighted the U-boat on her port side and opened fire with her machine gun before the submarine withdrew on the surface. *Regin* then began rescue work.

In the meantime U-81 found *Skeena* and *Kenogami* barring the way to the port side of the convoy, so crossed over and, at 0528, fired from the starboard side. The torpedoes missed their targets, but a fifth, fired from the stern tube at 0553, sank the leading ship in the starboard column. After the convoy made an emergency turn to port, U-81 was sighted by the leading ship in the ninth column. U-81 successfully evaded the search immediately undertaken by HMCS *Alberni*. It may have been either this submarine or U-652 that *Regin* suddenly came upon at about 0700 as it returned from the rescue of survivors some miles astern. Had one of the escorts been in *Regin*'s position, it would have had a golden opportunity to counterattack. All the corvettes, however, were then standing by sinking ships, leaving only *Skeena* in her station when U-82 attacked at 0800 sinking *Empire Hudson*, the convoy's CAM ship (a merchant ship equipped with a catapult for launching fighter aircraft) that led the second column.

There was a pause in the action as daylight came. U-432 shadowed the convoy, making reports at 1151, 1256, and 1346, and the convoy was reorganized in eleven columns. The two corvettes were back in their stations ahead of the convoy when, at 1440, U-85 slipped by *Skeena* and *Alberni* at periscope depth and torpedoed the leading ship in the ninth column. All three escorts immediately formed a line of bearing and swept back toward, and through, the convoy. Sighting a periscope astern of the convoy at 1523 (U-85 was trying a second shot), *Skeena* closed at twenty-four knots and fired ten depth-charges at shallow settings on a position sighted by the captain and navigating officer. For the next two hours, having established ASDIC contact, *Skeena* and *Kenogami* hunted the submarine and damaged it enough to send it limping home the next day. While this hunt was underway, U-boat headquarters, perhaps buoyed by somewhat exaggerated claims from the submarine commanders, despatched an order that the convoy must not get through; U-boats were to sink every ship.

There were now at least five submarines in the vicinity of the convoy, and U-432 continued to make shadowing reports. There was also a Catalina aircraft on patrol, and about an hour after arrival, it forced a surfaced submarine (probably U-85) to dive. The presence of an aircraft may have inhibited U-boat movements, but at 2350 on 10 September U-82 attacked the starboard side of the convoy. She sank a tanker (the third ship in the tenth column) twelve minutes later (0002 on 11 September) and the leading

ship of the eighth column sixteen minutes after that. The U-boat used the
now familiar tactic of proceeding boldly on the surface among the ships of
the convoy for protection. The convoy made two successive emergency
turns, to port and to starboard, just as *Chambly* and *Moose Jaw* made a
providential and skilfully calculated appearance some miles ahead. *Chambly* obtained a firm ASDIC contact and attacked and surprised U-501 as she
was getting into position for the next onslaught. The German crew was
commanded by a captain who flouted the best traditions of the sea by being
the first rather than the last off his ship. When U-501 was forced to the
surface he made a flying leap from the conning tower to *Moose Jaw*'s upper
deck ("not being prepared to repel boarders," wrote Lieutenant Grubb, "I
sheered off"). The German crew handled the submarine poorly on their
first and last operational cruise. The U-boat sank, the first to be destroyed
by Canadian forces during the war, and the two corvettes took positions on
the screen.

   This episode served to blunt the first U-boat attack of the night, and it
was followed swiftly by U-433's unsuccessful attempt to get at the convoy
from the port bow. Within minutes of the submarine firing torpedoes that
missed their target, *Kenogami* sighted U-433, established ASDIC contact,
and dropped depth-charges before returning to her station. For the following hour all was quiet, the five escorts positioned at a range of about five
thousand yards from the convoy ahead, on the flanks and on the starboard
quarter. At about 0330 two more submarines, U-652 and probably U-207,
penetrated the screen on the starboard side. U-652 missed, but the other
U-boat scored hits on the leading and third ships of the starboard wing
column. *Skeena* immediately fired starshell to illuminate the scene and
searched the starboard side of the convoy without success. Unfortunately,
this attack resulted in the loss of three corvettes to the screen because
Kenogami, Moose Jaw, and *Alberni* fell back to pick up survivors and to
despatch one of the merchant ships by gunfire. Therefore, between 0445 and
0540 on 11 September U-202 and U-82 had no difficulty in attacking the
defenceless port side of the convoy. U-82 sank the third and fourth ships of
the fourth column, before seeking refuge within the convoy columns. All
Skeena could do was once again illuminate the starboard side of the
convoy, believing that *Kenogami, Alberni*, and *Chambly* were available to
protect the port side. Fortunately, the enterprising Norwegian captain of
the *Regin*, near the head of the second column, tackled one of the submarines as soon as he sighted it on the surface. "It can only be attributed to her
aggressive spirit," wrote a British analyst of these events, "that [*Regin*]
herself was not torpedoed." "It is to be deplored that this ship had nothing
better than machine guns with which to attack the U-boats." As this drama
was unfolding an unidentified submarine (probably U-207 again) torpedoed and sank the ship astern of *Regin*. Both *Skeena* and *Chambly*

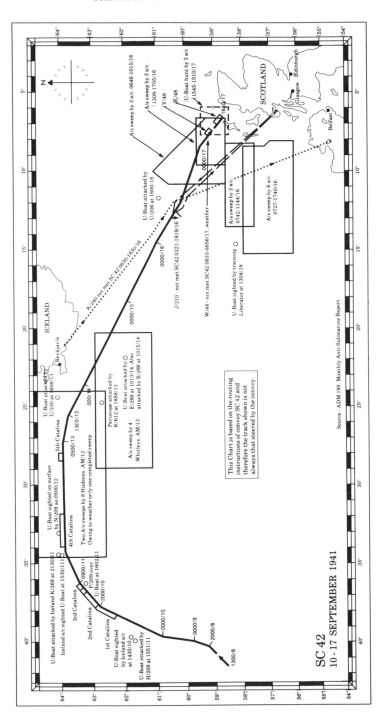

SC 42
10 - 17 SEPTEMBER 1941

Source - ADM 199 Monthly Anti-Submarine Report

remained unaware of this, mercifully the last successful attack on the convoy until 16 September.

It had been, in the words of captain (D) Newfoundland, an appalling tale of disaster. Commodore L.W. Murray, CCNF, wrote the following encomium:

> I consider that Lieutenant-Commander Hibbard RCN has acquitted himself in this action in a manner of which the Royal Canadian Navy may well be proud. Not only did he never lose hope which, with the meagre force at his disposal, a lesser man might well have done, but his mental and physical stamina was sufficient to keep him alert and active from the time of the first report of attack at 1004, 9th September, a period of 66 hours, much of which was a continuous battle. The strain of responsibility and command was not in any way made easier by the fact that his group had only recently been formed and that it was *Kenogami*'s first appearance in the NEF.

Captain Stevens (captain [D]) noted the lucidity of *Skeena*'s report, written during the only night in the month that the ship spent in harbour. It was new to him, as it was to Hibbard, that submarines appeared to be attacking on the surface from ahead and then diving into the convoy, and he suggested that in future two corvettes be detailed to proceed into the convoy when attacked from ahead.

After examining available Canadian, British and German sources, it is difficult not to agree generally with these observations, while differing in detail. In fact the Admiralty had been aware of submarine attacks from within the convoy since February 1941. It happened with convoy OB (an early designation for convoys westbound from Liverpool) 290 on 26 February, SC 26 between 2 and 4 April, and HX 133 in June. Indeed, at the convoy conference for SC 42, the convoy commodore had told ships not to hesitate to open fire on U-boats between the columns, whatever the risk to other ships.

The fortuitous arrival of *Chambly* and *Moose Jaw* received surprisingly little attention, then or afterwards. "Chummy" Prentice's claims of deliberately invoking the principle of support groups are borne out by contemporary written statements by Commodore Murray and Captain Stevens; it was an early and effective use of intelligence by the RCN that could not be exploited consistently because there were inadequate resources to do so. Both British and Canadian commentators glossed over another glaring circumstance—the misuse of escorts for rescue work. The fact that "the tactics of the heart" overcame the best interests of the convoy and that *Skeena* charitably assumed that merchant ship captains thought the naval vessels were relieving them of rescue work must be questioned. *Orillia* in particular, as the Admiralty report noted with a mild admonition, had no business salvaging *Tahchee* when one corvette formed 25 per cent of the entire escort force. It is a fair comment that the corvette captains still had too little experience of anti-submarine warfare to calculate the real consequences of following humane and essentially seamanlike instincts.

It is not certain how much attention the Admiralty and Coastal Command paid to the failure of the submarines to press home attacks after daylight on 11 September, in spite of constant shadowing reports and beacon signals by the five or more shadowing submarines for three more days until 14 September. U-boat headquarters blamed the onset of fog, but fog does not explain six unsuccessful attacks by U-202, U-652 and U-84 between 0540 on 11 September and 0245 on 12 September. The arrival of seven additional destroyers, three more corvettes, and a trawler permitted a much more vigilant watch by the escort force. The presence of aircraft from the dozen or so RAF squadrons now coming within range of the convoy from Iceland, Ireland, and Scotland, resulted in the sighting of U-207 on the afternoon of 11 September, the homing of two newly arrived destroyers onto the target, and the subsequent destruction of this aggressive and previously successful submarine. *Moose Jaw* made up for her earlier lapse by attacking a contact which could have been U-432, the shadowing boat, at 1230 on 11 September. U-433 reported a Q-ship (a merchant ship with disguised armament) after receiving, so it was said, five hours of depth-charging later that day. It is of interest that on 13 September, for the first time, three American destroyers, USS *Sims, Hughes,* and *Russell,* sailed from Iceland to assist another threatened convoy. This practice was followed again two weeks later for SC 44, and it led to the first torpedoing of an American destroyer, USS *Kearny,* in October.

Captain Roskill has recorded that seventeen boats attacked SC 42. In fact eleven U-boats attacked (including one on 16 September), and there is no evidence that more than six were close enough to attack at any given period. Twice on 10 September, three submarines attacked within a one or two-hour period, and the next day four attacked within ninety minutes, but at least eleven of the twenty-five recorded attacks on the convoy were made by single U-boats; co-ordination was minimal, something that perhaps Dönitz himself should be blamed for. He had always intended flotilla commanders to exercise tactical control of U-boat groups and only changed his mind when wartime experience seemed to show that this was not feasible. In 1939 and 1940 senior officers of submarine groups often found that they had lost the tactical picture after being forced to submerge, so control reverted to BdU, and each U-boat in a group was allowed to act independently according to the commanding officer's assessment of the situation. By late 1941, circumstances had changed to such an extent that BdU could have tried to reinstate local tactical control, but Dönitz had no way of making such a judgment because of basic weakness in his staff organization. All analysis of convoy operations depended on the study of U-boat signals received immediately after the end of each encounter. No staff officers were assigned to the task of reconstructing important convoy battles four to six weeks after the event (something that the Admiralty did frequently), with the result that no carefully considered tactical innovations could be introduced. All Dönitz could do was to bring his extraordinary personal leadership into play, and even this did not generate enough offensive spirit to suit his requirements in September 1941.

Of the sixteen submarines present in the group Markgraf (one turned back before the operation began), eleven can be shown to have fired their torpedoes. One of these, U-105, actually attacked an independent near the convoy on 11 September. This attack record represents the failure of Dönitz's attempts to encourage his U-boat commanders with a series of standing orders sent out by radio. The first of these orders on 2 September 1941 had urged submarines to attack and not to economize on torpedoes; Dönitz repeated this injunction on 11 September in connection with the attack on SC 42, telling his captains to seize every opportunity and to fire even when the firing data were poor; on 13 September, when it appeared that fog was hampering operations against SC 42, he sent out his sixth standing order of the month: cruise with torpedo tubes at the ready in fog and low visibility. On 11 September, having heard from U-652 that her torpedoes were expended and she was returning home, he ordered the U-boat back to the convoy and informed all commanders that they were to remain with a convoy so long as it was under attack. All of these instructions were read and analysed by the Admiralty's naval intelligence department. The analysis was made available to key Admiralty and Western Approaches personnel in November so that advances in U-boat warfare could be matched by appropriate responses in anti-submarine tactics. Combined with the practical experience of seamen and airmen, intelligence gave the Allies a priceless advantage at an early stage of the war.

From the purely Canadian point of view, the paucity of ships and aircraft and the inexperience of crews stands out more than anything else. These inadequacies were the result of calculated risks on the part of the British and Canadians. Because the British needed to be strong at home to counter possible invasion (still the first priority in Whitehall's calculations) and to drive the U-boats out of home waters, they were obliged to concentrate their forces in the eastern Atlantic. Temporary weakness in the west would soon, so the Admiralty reckoned, be remedied by American naval and air forces. Moreover, although the Canadian War Cabinet had attempted unsuccessfully to provide the RCN with more long-range aircraft and destroyers (and in their stead was relying on British naval assistance), Canada had actively sought responsibility for forming the major escort force in the western Atlantic. More was at stake than simply keeping open the sea lanes to Britain. What preoccupied Canadians, all the way from cabinet level to the service staffs, was national pride. Less self-reliance might have assured better balanced escort groups, combining, as the British naval historian Captain Donald Macintyre has suggested, more British and fewer Canadian ships. However, this was not the solution advocated by either country. The solution was to make do with slim pickings in the west, exercising the Admiralty's skills to outwit the enemy until the strength could be found to crush him. Thanks to the one-dimensional nature of Hitler's naval strategy, this policy secured victory at sea for the Allies.

II. CONVOY SC 107, NOVEMBER 1942

As a result of the Argentia meetings in Newfoundland in August 1941, the U.S. Navy not only supported Allied operations by sending task units to escort convoys under Admiralty control, but, as of 15 September, took over the operational direction of all Allied convoy operations west of 26°W. The procedure adopted was that, about ten days before an eastbound convoy left from Halifax (or, subsequently, from New York), the Admiralty would transmit a route recommendation to the chief of Naval Operations in Washington (OPNAV). Approximately two days later, after co-ordination with its own plans division, OPNAV would issue a preliminary route order to all commands concerned. Washington would also give the final route order when the convoy departed its harbour on the western side of the Atlantic. All later orders to the escort groups of British, Canadian and American convoys west of the change of operational control, or "CHOP" line, were to be sent by radio from Washington, sometimes following recommendations by the Admiralty or the commander-in-chief Western Approaches.

Thus, for example, on 6 October 1941, most of the German submarines at sea were chasing a Gibraltar convoy, and the North Atlantic convoy route was almost empty of U-boats. The Allied convoys east of the CHOP line at 26°W were escorted by British escort groups. West of the mid-ocean meeting point, the fast convoys were escorted by American task units, the slow convoys by Canadian escort groups. This system of direction and distribution of escort groups remained in use until April 1942.

There had been concern in German naval circles for some time that cypher equipment had fallen into enemy hands and that cypher security had been compromised following the loss of German supply ships in the Atlantic in June 1941. Accordingly, BdU introduced extra security measures. Dönitz gave the order to encode the two large letters of the German grid map by two other letters, chosen at random every forty-eight hours. This gave Hut 4 in Bletchley Park some problems in identifying the true German grid designations and positions.

Another difficulty stemmed from the increased number of ships and U-boats at sea and a resulting increase in the volume of German message traffic. Notwithstanding the fact that all messages that could be sent by telephone or teleprinter were relayed by these means, the proportion of wireless transmissions had grown from 12 per cent in 1940 to 29 per cent in 1943. In 1939 the daily average of 192 wireless messages needed only two cypher circuits, "home" and "foreign." But as the volume grew (319 in 1940, 473 in 1941, 1,200 in 1942 and 2,563 in 1943), it became necessary to establish, firstly, additional traffic circuits with separate frequencies and, secondly, new cypher circuits to reduce the number of signals enciphered with the same settings. Even though the experts had concluded that the cypher machine M-3, if correctly used, would continue to be secure, it was decided to prepare new code books, which formed the foundation of the individual telegram key. The most important innovation, however, was an exclusive new cypher network for U-boats in the Atlantic theatre, the first to be equipped with the new cypher machine M-4. In addition to this machine's three cypher rotors, with twenty-six letters each (to be chosen from a supply of eight), a fourth rotor "alpha," in the left position, increased the possible variations from 16,900 to 44,000.

When the cypher circuit "Triton" came into force 1 February 1942, Bletchley Park was suddenly struck blind with respect to all radio traffic with U-boats in the Atlantic Ocean area. Not being prepared for a cypher machine with four rotors, all decrypting attempts failed for the next eleven months. This was the first of several "blackouts," but, for several reasons, negative effects were limited. Since January 1942, the main field of the U-boat war had shifted to the American eastern coast and the Caribbean, where the U-boats cruised individually in a given field of operations trying to sink as much of the traffic sailing without escort as possible. In this form of operations, tactical operational radio traffic remained low. Radio intelligence in whatever form could do little to prevent shipping losses. With the introduction of the convoy system in American coastal waters in May to July 1942 BdU was forced to shift the main field of U-boat activity back to the North Atlantic convoy routes.

Now Allied convoy routing had to depend upon attack, sighting or tracking reports by Allied ships and aircraft, or fixes from direction-finding and traffic analysis. This information was only sufficient to pinpoint a small fraction of U-boats at sea, but the Operational Intelligence Centre (OIC) was quite well informed about the number of German submarines at sea. Transmissions by German patrol forces using the cypher network

"Hydra" could be deciphered regularly by the OIC. Intelligence officers could also deduce estimates based on the known operational rhythms of U-boats, but these were rarely precise enough to evade a U-boat, especially if BdU received a deciphered position report or routing signal of an expected convoy from x-B-Dienst in time for action. This is what happened in the case of convoy SC 107.

In the middle of October 1942, STR knew almost exactly the number of U-boats operating in the North Atlantic through "Hydra" decryptions. German escort vessels used this cypher to report their U-boat escorting operations off Norway and in the Bay of Biscay. But it was especially difficult to pinpoint the U-boat patrol lines correctly, because BdU moved such lines quickly, over great distances, in response to the latest information from x-B-Dienst about convoy positions or routes. The Germans were able to do this even though only a small fraction of the signals decrypted by x-B-Dienst were available in time for operational use.

From 16 to 19 October group "Panter" tried to concentrate on convoy ON 137 but failed in a heavy gale. Subsequently, several of the group went to a U-tanker nearby while the others were ordered to establish a new patrol line "Veilchen" northeast of Newfoundland, by 24 October, to intercept the next HX and SC convoys. Evaluating the decryptions available from the first part of October, Dönitz concluded that the next ON convoys would follow the route of ON 137, and he transferred the patrol line of group "Puma" to the south in two steps. His estimate was correct. On 22 October the southernmost boat of Puma contacted ON 139, but it was a very bad starting position. Only one of the boats would have been able to attack, and the group was called back the following day to a new patrol line. At the same time one of the boats returning from the supply group sighted convoy OS 42, and the submarines that had replenished followed as group "Südwärts."

On 25 October x-B-Dienst decrypted a three-day-old position of convoy ONS 140. Knowing the convoy course of 240 degrees and having a report about the position of two escorts on 25 October that coincided with that course, it seemed possible to intercept convoy ONS 140 by diverting Puma to the northwest.

Only three of all the German x-B-Dienst decryptions during October 1942 came early enough to base operations on them; the other decryptions gave only background information on routing methods and for the reconstruction of the convoy timetable. This was enough for BdU to establish the designation and the speed of an intercepted convoy. Sometimes, x-B-Dienst could find out not only the convoy designations but also the designations of escort groups and the names of some of the ships or escort vessels in these task units. However, this information almost always came too late to be used. We have found no indication in the German documents that BdU ever tried to operate against a convoy because its escort was a Canadian group which may have been weaker, less experienced, or not so well equipped as a British group.

Between 26 and 28 October, group Südwärts broke off from OS 42, west of the Azores. The first troop convoys for the Allied invasion of North Africa (Operation Torch) were on the Gibraltar run at this time. In the mid-Atlantic, ONS 140 evaded Puma, but the homeward-bound HX 212 was intercepted at the centre of the patrol line—the best possible situation for starting a convoy battle. With no information about the movements of group Puma available from decryption, owing to the Triton blackout, the STR could not evade the line. But, when the first contact signals were intercepted and plotted by direction-finding methods, it was possible to re-route convoy SC 106, then a day behind HX 212.

In the meantime, the Convoy and Routing Section of the commander-in-chief U.S. Fleet (COMINCH) had radioed the route of convoy SC 107 to all commands on 19 October. The route led from New York to the meeting points with feeder convoys from Halifax and Sydney, and to the Western Ocean Meeting Point where the Ocean Escort Group C.4 was to relieve the Western Local Escort. From there the route went north-northeast, so that the convoy would be in the "Black Pit" for the shortest possible time, coming to the CHOP line about 5 November and arriving at the North Channel about the tenth. A stragglers' route was promulgated to the south of the main convoy.

This signal was decrypted by x-B-Dienst almost completely, but the decryption was not complete until 2 November, after the convoy battle had already started, and the signal was out of date. COMINCH had changed the route to the south in the Newfoundland area on 20 October so that it ran northeast at forty-five degrees from the WOMP. X-B-Dienst decrypted this signal on 29 October, in time for BdU to rearrange the Veilchen patrol line. On the same day, the westbound convoy ONS 140 passed the southern end of the patrol line and was reported by U-437, the southernmost submarine of the thirteen boats of group Veilchen concentrated on SC 107's new course.

Convoy SC 107: The Opening Moves

There were five, big, type-IX German submarines off the coast of Newfoundland at this time. RCAF air patrols had reported two contacts on 29 October between Cape Sable and Cape Race. The following day two Hudson aircraft of No. 145 Squadron RCAF sighted a surfacing U-boat in the area of group Veilchen, a force which had not been identified by Allied intelligence. U-658 was sunk without being able to send off a report. On the same morning, one of the U-boats south of Newfoundland, U-522, was able

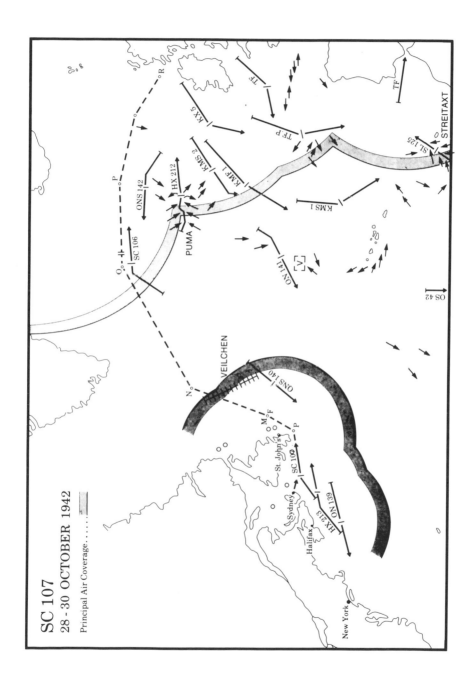

SC 107
28 - 30 OCTOBER 1942

Principal Air Coverage......

to establish contact with one of the feeder convoys and, after being put down by the Canadian destroyer, HMCS *Columbia*, of the Local Escort Group, to come up with the main convoy and send off a contact report: "Convoy in grid BB 6822, course 80°, speed 7 knots." BdU ordered U-522 to keep contact under all circumstances and report every two hours, and Admiral Dönitz ordered the two other submarines in the area, U-520 and U-521, to close at high speed.

The first contact report was intercepted by direction-finding stations, and the convoy was informed by radio that it was being shadowed. A short time later, the Ocean Escort Group C.4 took over, and the contact signals of U-522 were intercepted by the HF/DF sets of the destroyer HMCS *Restigouche* and the rescue ship *Stockport*. After the senior officer of the escort asked for and was granted air escort, a Digby of No. 10 Squadron RCAF, found, attacked, and sank U-520 east of the convoy. Behind the convoy, the *Columbia* was trying to put down the contact keeper, which tried, in turn, to fire two torpedoes at her but missed. Later in the evening, the convoy made a turn to the east to shake off the U-boats. By sheer chance the new course led through the patrol line Veilchen almost exactly at the gap caused by the loss of U-658. Convoy HX 213 was following some distance astern on a similar course. On the morning of 1 November, shortly after a Catalina flying boat of No. 116 Squadron RCAF had reported a U-boat behind the convoy, SC 107 was nearing the patrol line. There was a fifteen-knot westerly wind with moderate seas, and U-381 was about nine miles from the convoy.

When U-381 made a sighting report, BdU ordered Veilchen to close and attack. *Restigouche* and *Stockport* intercepted the U-boat's signal on HF/DF, and the senior officer ordered full speed to take his destroyer out along the bearing. At the same time he asked the convoy commodore to order an emergency turn to port. Some minutes later the blip of the U-boat appeared momentarily on the radar screen; the U-boat had spotted the oncoming destroyer and dived. Acting Lieutenant-Commander Desmond "Debbie" Piers slowed down to search for the U-boat by ASDIC and, after picking it up, attacked with depth charges. Many convoy battles were avoided by this tactic when the shadowing U-boat was driven deep and could not re-establish contact with its prey. This time the convoy had run out of luck.

To understand the significance of these opening events fully, three observations need to be made. In the first place, anti-submarine operations on the western side of the Atlantic were in a state of radical change. Goodwill and good intentions had gone a long way, but not far enough, to make American and Canadian airmen and sailors operating from Newfoundland work as a smoothly functioning team. Moreover, the RCAF was desperately short of long-range aircraft; one Canso squadron had only just arrived at Gander, and the Digby squadron was about to change over to Cansos—the amphibious version of Consolidated PBY Catalina flying boats. Secondly, Commander Brian Martineau, RN, of Coastal Command had visited Newfoundland a short while before, and, even as SC 107 was fighting for its life, he was completing a damning report about the inefficiency of the anti-submarine organization on the Atlantic coast.

His visit had visible results: on 30 October Eastern Air Command adopted RAF Coastal Command tactics for the escort of convoys. This meant that aircraft did not have to meet the convoy to succeed in their mission; they patrolled in parallel track sweeps fifty miles on either side of the convoy track and 100 miles ahead, as well as fifty miles astern. Such air coverage enabled No. 10 Squadron's Digbys to sink U-520, on the way to intercept the convoy. Similarly, anti-submarine sweeps were to be only over known areas of U-boat activity. The northeasterly sweeps by No. 145 Squadron RCAF out of Torbay, and the sinking of U-658, occurred because No. 1 Group RCAF at St. John's, having intelligence of some submarine activity in the path of the convoy, recognized it as a direct threat to SC 107. The source of 1 Group's intelligence was either the daily submarine estimate of the chief of Naval Operations, Washington, or Ottawa, and the location of U-boats northeast of Newfoundland may have resulted from radio transmissions by the southernmost submarines of group Veilchen when they spotted ONS 140 on 29 October.

The third important point is that the STR in Ottawa was then in full operation. Warnings were issued by Ottawa based on direction-finding information, an activity that Washington objected to because it interfered with the intelligence signals sent out from OPNAV. Ottawa argued vehemently (and ultimately successfully) that it was doing an essential job, and doing it better than OP-20-G (the United States Navy's operational intelligence centre in Washington) for that area north of 40°N and west of 40°W, an area agreed upon with the Admiralty.

Some remarks concerning Escort Group C.4 are also in order. The ships were formed in an *ad hoc* escort group because two regular members, the four-stack destroyer, HMCS *St. Croix*, and the corvette, HMCS *Sherbrooke*, had not been able to sail owing to technical defects. To make the escort up to six vessels, flag officer Newfoundland Force allocated the corvettes *Regina* and *Algoma* (previously earmarked for service in the Mediterranean in answer to an Admiralty request) to C.4. When *Regina* broke down outside St. John's and had to return to harbour, *Moose Jaw* sailed in her place but could not catch up with the convoy until late on 2 November.

HMS *Walker*, carrying the senior officer of the Western Local Escort Force group just relieved, stayed briefly to give added HF/DF capability. Unfortunately *Walker* had radio problems, could not communicate with anybody in C.4 except at very close range, and departed in a state of

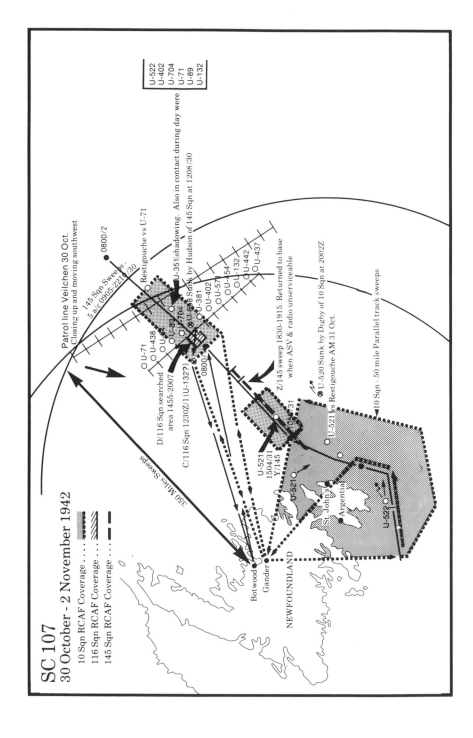

SC 107
30 October - 2 November 1942

10 Sqn RCAF Coverage . . . . .
116 Sqn RCAF Coverage . . . .
145 Sqn RCAF Coverage . . . .

U-522
U-402
U-704
U-71
U-89
U-132

Patrol line Veilchen 30 Oct.
Closing up and moving southwest

0800/2

145 Sqn Sweeps
5 a/c 0905-2210/30

Restigouche vs U-71

U-351 shadowing. Also in contact during day were

U-658 Sunk by Hudson of 145 Sqn at 1208/30

U-71
U-438
U-...
U-381
U-402
U-571
U-132
U-54
U-442
U-437

D/116 Sqn searched
area 1455-2007

C/116 Sqn 1230Z/1 (U-132?)

0800/...

330 Miles Sweeps

Z/145 sweep 1830-1915. Returned to base
when ASV & radio unserviceable

U-521
1504/31
Y/145

...31

U-520 Sunk by Digby of 10 Sqn at 2002Z

U-521 vs Restigouche AM 31 Oct.

10 Sqn - 50 mile Parallel track sweeps

U-521

St. John's
Argentia

U-52...

Botwood
Gander

NEWFOUNDLAND

frustration on the morning of 31 October. Only HMCS *Restigouche* had HF/DF because the captain had "scrounged" one earlier in the year at Londonderry. (NSHQ refused to authorize HF/DF in Canadian warships until full trials had proved it satisfactory, and *Restigouche* providentially became the testing platform.) The Canadian corvettes were fitted with the unreliable, short-range (four miles) Canadian radar SW 1C or SW 2C. *Restigouche* had the British type 286. The one British corvette in the group, HMS *Celandine*, had the far more satisfactory type 271, a ten-centimetre set with all-round coverage and about six-miles range in normal sea conditions. The ASDIC or sonar range of all the ships was no more than about 1,500 yards. When it is realized that surfaced U-boats could see the mast and funnel tops of ships in a convoy from about twelve miles by day and seven miles on a moonlit night, under normal conditions, it will be clear that they could shadow the convoy from well outside the normal radar range of surface vessels.

The Battle

With four corvettes and one destroyer, helped by HF/DF in the rescue vessel *Stockport*, Piers had to solve the problem of finding and driving off U-boats before they could attack. The convoy of forty-two ships, formed in ten columns, had a frontage of about three miles and a depth of about one; since radar was both unreliable and short-range, HF/DF was the key, and Piers showed a keen appreciation of this fact. Sad to say, the easy communications with ships, especially his megaphone conversations with *Stockport* and the convoy commodore, proclaimed the virtues of a simplicity that was of no avail to his RCAF compatriots. At 1505 on 1 November, a Hudson of No. 145 Squadron RCAF sighted and attacked U-521, six miles ahead of the convoy, forcing it down and probably averting an attack. None of the ships was aware of this.

Getting close to their maximum effective range, the Digbys of No. 10 Squadron RCAF failed to make any sightings on 1 November. One Catalina from No. 116 Squadron RCAF found the convoy before daylight but lost it when his radar broke down. He flew a square search without success and decided to go home. This suggests a failure to understand the new tactics, although, in fact, the Catalina's withdrawal resulted in a sighting to the northwest of the convoy. There is no German record of this incident, and it must remain a dubious claim, despite a faint possibility that it could have been U-132, lost later in the battle.

As soon as Piers knew he was being shadowed, he began to make vigorous sorties in the direction of the likely threat. He decided to use *Celandine* to investigate U-704's transmission and to stay for two hours after dusk in order to keep that submarine well clear. *Celandine*'s type 271 promptly broke down, and the corvette was without radar until 5 November. *Restigouche* turned toward U-402, after getting an intercept soon after dark, then picked up U-71 on radar. The starshell used to illuminate U-71 forced U-402 to dive and gave U-89 an indication of the convoy's bearing. The destroyer and one corvette were, therefore, well astern of the convoy, and only one corvette was protecting the starboard quarter when U-402 approached on the surface to within five hundred yards of the starboard side of the convoy. The ever-unreliable SW 1C radar had broken down in HMCS *Arvida*, but by sweeping the starboard side of the convoy and presumably firing starshell (there is no record of this in the log), *Arvida* prevented a second attack.

Having been forty degrees to port of the base course as an evasive measure, SC 107 now resumed its course. There was still a large hole in the screen and on the port quarter, but *Restigouche* was sticking close to the starboard quarter and stern positions. The destroyer detected U-381 on radar two miles astern, illuminated, and attacked. Twenty-five minutes later, U-381 fired a spread of torpedoes at *Restigouche* just as she reached a new leg of her zigzag, but the destroyer's bridge personnel remained blissfully unaware of their danger.

At 0315, while *Celandine* was still a long way out to port, U-402, having made an end run to get into a down-moon position, where her prey were silhouetted against the moonlight, closed to one thousand yards on the surface to sink the second and third ships in the port wing column. In the subsequent emergency turn to starboard and operation "Raspberry" (a standard tactic in which vesels steered preset courses while firing starshell), *Arvida* failed to see U-522 on the surface for its next attack at a range of three thousand yards at 0352. The torpedo hit but did not sink the third ship in the seventh column. Fortunately, HMCS *Amherst* saw U-402 trying to press home the advantage and attacked the U-boat with machine guns. Without good ASDIC contact the subsequent depth-charge attack was wide of the mark, but for the second time that night the escorts had at least frustrated an extremely aggressive submarine by timely and vigorous action.

While some of the group Veilchen were busy astern, finishing off victims and stumbling upon *Moose Jaw* looking for the convoy (U-521 fired torpedoes and mistakenly claimed a hit), U-402's captain, Baron von Forstner, was showing his genius for this type of warfare. A former executive officer to the great U-boat ace, Otto Kretschmer, in U-99, von Forstner was an apt pupil. He pressed home his attacks against SC 107 just as relentlessly as he had earlier attacked convoys SC 7 and HX 79. At 0700 he penetrated the screen between *Amherst* and *Moose Jaw* once again to sink the second and third ships in the second column. Almost simultaneously U-522 was evading *Arvida*. The absence of adequate radar was proving disastrous: this U-boat now sank the fourth ships in the seventh and starboard-wing columns before being driven under by illumination and furious fire from the merchant ships. In the meantime U-442 moved into firing position, but all of the torpedoes fired at 0747 missed.

By this stage the convoy had been reduced from forty-two to thirty-four ships, and the rescue vessel was crammed with more than two hundred survivors. Piers decided to protect the front of the convoy by using the newly joined *Moose Jaw* on the port bow, *Algoma* on the starboard bow, and *Celandine* in an extended screen five thousand yards ahead of *Restigouche* in the centre. *Amherst* and *Arvida* went back, both to screen the precious rescue vessel and to rescue more survivors. *Restigouche* forced off one submarine by steaming down U-132's HF/DF bearing while the STR in Ottawa warned the convoy at 1620 of danger ahead, stemming from U-522's three contact reports during the day. Air coverage was non-existent. The convoy was beyond the effective range of all aircraft except Catalinas, and the one available for this task had no radar. Under very marginal flying conditions this Catalina returned to the RCAF's flying boat base at Botwood, near Gander, Newfoundland, without making contact.

During the afternoon, U-522 lost sight of the convoy in mist and rain, but with *Amherst* and *Arvida* still astern screening *Stockport* and the straggler *Hatimura*, the U-boat was able to approach submerged to sink the fifth ship in the eighth column at 1643. *Arvida* rejoined immediately and on the way back to her station detected U-522. A five-charge pattern gave U-522 some trouble, but not enough to prevent it from surfacing at 1920 to report its success. *Restigouche* steamed out immediately on the bearing of the transmission and sent *Celandine* out to investigate another on the port bow. In the fog that settled over the area, *Celandine* lost the convoy and did not find it again for more than twenty-four hours.

Fog was, nevertheless, a welcome ally. During the night HMS *Vanessa*, a destroyer from Escort Group B.2 escorting the nearby convoy HX 213, joined to give the screen another escort with HF/DF and type 271 radar. On the other hand, several changes of course in the night led to extensive disorganization by daylight, and in spite of the convoy's evasive steering, U-438 made contact at about 0600. It was a lucky bonus that the submarine's attacks at 0716 and 0734 were unsuccessful.

At 1020 GMT, just after sunrise, the captain of *Amherst* received a report from his crowsnest lookout of a U-boat eight miles away, fine on the corvette's port bow. Lieutenant L. "Uncle Louis" Audette, promptly climbed the mast to see for himself and, politely refusing the lookout's offer to exchange places, proceeded to direct fire on the submarine (U-438) with one arm crooked around the mast and his free hand manipulating the binoculars. He received no answer to his ensuing report because within minutes U-521 had successfully torpedoed the second ship in the eighth column from the starboard side, and the senior officer was rather busy. When U-438 had dived and Audette felt it no longer posed a threat, he returned to his station on the screen; he was admonished by the escort commander for his spontaneous response to the situation.

There were no more attacks until dark. The implication in *Restigouche*'s report of proceedings that active pursuit of HF/DF bearings and attack of ASDIC contacts held off the U-boats is misleading. Of the four depth-charge attacks recorded by submarines, three were made by *Celandine*, who was lost and from fifteen to twenty miles astern all day. The only attack by *Restigouche* was on a doubtful contact ahead of the eighth column, and the ship steamed down between the convoy columns on receiving a report of a periscope. But no U-boat recorded firing at the convoy until nightfall. U-522 fired at *Celandine*, as the timing and description of the submarine and corvette reports reveal, at 1342, about twenty miles astern of the main body.

An evasive turn to port before sundown only helped U-89, which lay directly in the path of the convoy. With *Vanessa* on the port bow and *Moose Jaw* on the starboard, it is likely that these two strangers to C.4, and to each other, left more of a gap in the convoy's van than they should have done. U-89's first two salvoes missed, but its stern shot sank *Jeypore*, the convoy commodore's ship leading the fifth column. The ship caused mass confusion as it swung out of line wildly, barely missing the ships astern of her in nearby columns. One near-miss led the crew of the *Titus*, near the rear of the eighth column, to abandon ship, but half of the crew then re-boarded and brought her safely into harbour, thanks to unusual good luck, for, having fallen miles astern of the convoy, she was attacked by a U-boat whose torpedoes missed. Amid this ghastly scene the escort executed a half-hearted "Raspberry," in which only a few starshell and snowflake illumination devices were fired, and U-89 withdrew safely on the surface.

When the convoy made an evasive turn to starboard at 2130, *Moose Jaw* came across U-89 steering eastward and eventually, after receiving instructions from *Restigouche* to do so, dropped two charges even though not in contact, before rejoining the screen. U-89 promptly surfaced, and *Algoma*, coming up astern, saw the U-boat and attacked. At 2315 *Celandine* was astern screening the two American tugs that had taken over lifesaving duties from *Stockport*, crammed with over three hundred survivors. *Moose Jaw* and *Algoma* were also astern of station following their attack on U-89, and so U-132 took advantage of the yawning gap in the van of the convoy, between *Moose Jaw* and *Vanessa*, to sink the second ships in the seventh and ninth columns as well as a ship in the eighth column, the ammunition ship *Hobbema*. This time operation "Raspberry" resulted in no illumination at all, except for twelve rounds of starshell fired by *Restigouche*. However, at 2337 *Arvida* picked up a doubtful ASDIC contact near the torpedoed ships that became more solid as the corvette closed. Then an explosion of massive violence shook every ship in the convoy. The shock wave was such that *Arvida*'s stern appeared to lift out of the water. The rating recording events on the bridge of *Restigouche* noted in error that his ship had been torpedoed and inflated his lifebelt. *Algoma* suffered engine damage. The most likely explanation of this event is that U-132 fired a coup de grâce with its stern tube at *Hobbema* which touched off that ship's explosive cargo. U-132 was never heard from again. Then, apart from some inconclusive activities astern of the convoy, the U-boats, notwithstanding perfect visibility and the complete lack of air cover, lost contact with the convoy until dark.

In view of the large number of survivors, the rescue ships *Stockport*, *Pessacus*, *Uncas*, and *Gauger*, with *Celandine* (who had repaired her radar but was low on fuel and depth-charges) and *Arvida*, detached for Iceland at 1700. Once they were clear, SC 107 made a radical alteration to port, but this may simply have played into the enemy's hands. Some time after dark U-89 came up with the convoy and, at 2137, penetrated the port side of the screen just astern of *Moose Jaw* to sink the port wing ship. By morning the next day a reinforcement of three U.S. Navy and Coast Guard escorts from Iceland joined the screen, and Consolidated B-24 Liberators, long-range patrol aircraft of the RAF, based on Iceland made contact with the escort. Piers could talk to the airmen now, and he sent them out twice to put down U-boats detected by HF/DF. The result was decisive: U-boat headquarters ordered the group to attack only at night when in favourable positions and to halt operations at daybreak.

SC 107: Summary

In several respects this analysis breaks new ground. It enables us to establish the truth of some previously hazy events, and it permits reassessment of some judgments made at the time. All the sailors for instance, in their reports and reminiscences, complained that they had no air cover from Newfoundland worth speaking of. That was a myth. In the first two days of shadowing, two of the three U-boats available for the task were either sunk (U-520) or driven off by escorting Digbys and Hudsons (U-521). While flying sweeps over areas of known U-boat activity, Hudsons of No. 145 Squadron RCAF sank the one U-boat of group Veilchen (U-658) lying directly in the path of the convoy. At the same time, the sailors did have grounds for complaint: compared with the co-operation afforded by RAF Coastal Command, the procedures followed by Eastern Air Command were still primitive, something that resulted from circumstances beyond the control of RCAF aircrew. The long-range Catalinas did not give as much support as the shorter-range aircraft because No. 116 Squadron RCAF aircrew did not seem to fully appreciate their role—the Catalinas simply carried out a square search in the vicinity of the convoy when they could have carried out a parallel search just as effectively. In making this criticism, it is important to remember the hazards of flying in marginal weather conditions, at maximum endurance, when the prevailing winds were against the flying boats on their homeward leg. In a strong gale the Catalina had its work cut out to keep station on a fast ship. Proper tactical use of a weapon under such conditions demands determination and courage of the highest order, inspired by strong leadership at the squadron level. Owing to the absence of operational training units, the lack of adequate tactical training in the squadrons made it difficult to exercise such leadership. On the other hand, in spite of the service's shortcomings, the RCAF inflicted the only losses on the enemy. It would be a major triumph when six of the forty U-boats attacking ONS 5 in May 1943 were sunk. By comparison, the sinking of two of the sixteen U-boats attacking SC 107 was not bad at all, and since both of the submarines sunk on 30 October 1942 were victims of aircraft, RCAF air cover must, in the final analysis, be assessed as successful.

Admiral Sir Max Horton, commander-in-chief Western Approaches, said that Piers had done his best under trying circumstances, but that he was really too young and inexperienced to shoulder such an awesome responsibility. The director of the Admiralty's Anti-Submarine Division even deprecated the fact that the HF/DF bearings came from submarine transmissions. This, of course, was nonsense, and the complaint probably arose from the fact that C.4 did not always keep closed up to the convoy. It was an unfounded criticism, because the escort commander succeeded in holding off submarine attacks for the better part of twelve hours only by vigorous pursuit of HF/DF bearings; he might have done even better with close, well-co-ordinated air support. Moreover, as ONS 5 would reveal, the effectiveness of close screens depended on good radar, which Piers knew he did not have.

It is true that he did not always keep a tight rein on his captains. This should not have been a disadvantage unless they did not know what was on his mind. *Algoma*, *Moose Jaw*, and *Vanessa* had not had the opportunity to develop that rapport, and Piers kept these vessels close to him. But *Celandine*, *Arvida*, and *Amherst* had been part of the same group with *Restigouche* during at least three recent convoys. *Celandine*'s report of proceedings seems to doubt the merit of the search ordered on the evening of 2 November; *Amherst* was not sure of the correct action to take with U-438 when the senior officer did not acknowledge his report. The situation demanded fine judgment, and even though the senior officer disapproved, it was surely right for an escort to abstain from protracted ASDIC hunts that left a portion of the screen wide open during a wolfpack attack. Thus, even the veterans of the group were not working together as well as they should have been.

Where did the trouble lie? The staff answer was that it lay in training. Training was certainly part of the problem—as well it might be with the rapid expansion of the RCN. But the performance of the group would have been much better if *St. Croix* and *Sherbrooke* had sailed with it. Why didn't they? There is evidence that the ships simply did not have the technical staff to keep up with repairs, especially in an old ship like *St. Croix*. We must acknowledge the merit of a criticism made by the commander of Task Force 24, in Argentia, Newfoundland, Rear-Admiral R.M. Brainard, USN, that the Canadians were not doing enough to provide properly qualified engineering and technical personnel for their ships. Perhaps the RCN could have dealt with the situation more effectively. A nice historical question, and it bears upon the use of technology in all fighting services and leads to consideration of a most contentious issue: the state of equipment in Canadian ships.

The Naval Staff was reluctant to accept the new radar because it was not Canadian, and reluctant to fit HF/DF because the decision-makers in Ottawa were ignorant of its performance. Such ignorance was lamentable, though not altogether surprising. Canada, in many ways a poor relation in the Allied forces, had been denied the new aircraft and ships that it wanted so badly because Britain had more pressing needs elsewhere. Without up-to-date destroyers to replace aging vessels, the RCN found it difficult to keep up with other aspects of the anti-submarine war. Captain R.E.S. Bidwell, chief of staff to flag officer Newfoundland Force, reacted to Admiral Sir Max Horton's critique with a cry of anger, or anguish, or both: "How about giving us a few decent destroyers in the C Groups, Maxie? Instead of the discarded sweepings you're giving us now."

The one branch of the RCN that came out of this battle well was the Operational Intelligence Centre. Its warnings had been timely and accurate, if not complete, and without such essential expertise—even if the equipment and performance of the sea and air services had been without fault—the control of these forces would have remained in American or British hands.

III. CONVOY ONS 5, MAY 1943

General Developments from November 1942 to April 1943

Several vital changes occurred between November 1942 and the following April, when Canada assumed operational responsibility for the Canadian North West Atlantic theatre. It may be regarded as a direct result of SC 107, combined with the visit of Commander Martineau to Halifax and St. John's, that the RCN and RCAF began to concentrate on ways and means of improving efficiency. On 7 November Rear-Admiral L.W. Murray, now commanding officer Atlantic Coast, pointed out to the chief of the Naval Staff the need for a Canadian directorate of anti-submarine warfare similar to that in the Admiralty, for closer co-operation and a combined plot with the RCAF. He also urged the need for a separate coastal group in Eastern Air Command. On 26 November a document entitled "The Conduct of Anti-Submarine Warfare in the Royal Canadian Navy and Royal Canadian Air Force," produced by NSHQ, observed that the great strategic importance of the western Atlantic area was "now recognized by all Canadian authorities." Of foremost interest to those authorities were the needs of operational intelligence.

The STR in Ottawa was to be given every facility—enough officers were found to start watchkeeping around the clock in December—and was henceforth to be the only authority for U-boat fixes. This meant extensive improvements to communications between Ottawa, Halifax, and St. John's. But operational intelligence was going through its own crisis at this moment.

The STR had its origins in the Foreign Intelligence Section (FIS) formed under Commander J.M. "Jock" de Marbois, RCNR, and had begun plotting HF/DF bearings as early as 5 September 1939. In December 1940, after some discussion with the commander-in-chief of the Royal Navy's Atlantic and West Indies Station, it was agreed that Ottawa should promulgate the results of these plots. On 7 January 1942, after it had been passing information for some time to RCAF units on the East Coast, the FIS received advice from the Admiralty to promulgate fixes to all units in the western Atlantic. But near the end of February 1942, the United States Navy Department began to promulgate fixes to its own units, which resulted in duplication. The situation was further complicated by a delay in setting up the shipping diversion system in Washington. In January 1942 the Admiralty had also asked NSHQ to set up a Diversion Room to deal with all Allied merchant shipping in the area north of 40°N and west of 40°W. Captain Donald Farmer, RN (Ret'd.), director of Mercantile Movements in the Trade Division at Ottawa, aided by Naval Control Service officers from Quebec, Sydney, and Saint John, New Brunswick, and working on submarine estimates from Washington and London, took over this responsibility for about four months, whereupon it appears to have been assumed by OPNAV in Washington.

In April 1942 the radio intelligence or "Y" conference in Washington made NSHQ and OP-20-G the Atlantic plotting centres, while in May, Commander Rodger Winn of the Admiralty advised Ottawa to restrict U-boat tracking to north and west of 40°N and 40°W. On 2 May what was now the OIC promulgated its first fix to Halifax, St. John's, and to OP-20-G in Washington. Not until September did NSHQ decide to confine its fixes to the area described. All this time the duplication of fixes between Ottawa and Washington was creating friction between the two organizations, and it was during the battle for SC 107 that Ottawa suggested to commander-in-chief U.S. Fleet that fixes in the area be forwarded by Ottawa only, on Broadcast "L," to the units concerned.

The response in Washington, supported by the British Admiralty Delegation (BAD) there, was to demand control of all fixes in the western Atlantic; so on 1 December 1942 the Canadian Chief of the Naval Staff, Vice-Admiral Percy W. Nelles, wrote to Admiral Ernest J. King (COMINCH) proposing firstly, that there be a clear division of duties between Washington, Ottawa, and London in the promulgation of fixes and, secondly, that there be discussion on the question of general operational control. King replied on 17 December that he had ordered a drastic reduction in radio traffic and, more important, that "the same authority that controls the diversion of the convoy should be the one to send out warnings of enemy submarines in the vicinity of the convoys."

This direct relationship between operational intelligence and control has been noted by Gilbert Tucker in *The Naval Service of Canada*. The relationship assumes more significance in light of British and American reservations about the competence of Canadian sea and air forces during these crisis months of the Battle of the Atlantic. The air forces based on Newfoundland were able to resolve some of their difficulties at a conference in February 1943. Henceforth U.S. Army B17 squadrons could be employed in a rational system of air search in support of convoys, while Canadian and American controllers became more aware of each other's needs. The RCN had to live down the embarrassing fact that, instead of supplying the naval service with new destroyers, the Admiralty had withdrawn three of the four Canadian escort groups from the Mid-Ocean Escort Force from February to April. Their lordships had done so simply because disaster was foreseen if "inexperienced" forces were allowed to escort vital convoys while the U-boats were at the height of their activity. Admiral King did not consider this a critical issue. He appears to have decided early in 1943 that all of his efforts should be devoted to the southern routes and that the British and Canadians should take over in the north. Yet, when he proposed at the Atlantic Convoy Conference in March that Canada take over the theatre proposed by Vice-Admiral Nelles in December for Canadian promulgation of U-boat fixes, he still had doubts about Canada's ability to carry out her responsibilities. This is clear from his subsequent suggestion that the American naval commander in Newfoundland should remain in command until the Canadians had learned the ropes.

The other side of this coin is that, in spite of Nelles's letter, NSHQ does not appear to have grasped the full importance of operational intelligence. De Marbois was left out of the Canadian delegation to the Atlantic Convoy Conference initially, a decision, he observed later, that "would appear to have been in error." He and his deputy were sent for when it became clear that without a proper "Y" organization, neither the British nor the Americans were prepared to consider Canadian operational control. De Marbois may have had a prejudiced view, but his comments deserve to be heard:

> The conference demonstrated that the detail and efficiency of the RCN "Y" organization were better known in the U.S. and U.K. than in Canada. Since at this time the main concentration of the RCN was on the building of ships and the training of men, the authorities may perhaps be excused for having failed to study or attempt to understand the intricacies involved in operational intelligence work.

To make a Canadian commander-in-chief functional, several urgent measures were necessary. NSHQ would henceforth be responsible for all U-boat warnings and estimates in the North Atlantic eastward to 30°W and southward to 35°N. This information would go out on Broadcast "L," while the Admiralty would promulgate information westward to 47°W; COMINCH would use Broadcast "F," south of 35°N. Ottawa, therefore, had to appoint an authority for the diversion of shipping adjacent to operational authorities. In addition, the RCN had to install a high-power, low-frequency transmitter near Halifax (essential for communications with HX, ON, and SC convoys), while the RCAF had to seek means of improving communications between St. John's, Newfoundland, and Goose Bay, Labrador, besides establishing urgently required voice circuits between Halifax and St. John's. Within two weeks the Naval Board approved further measures to install direct scramble teletype between Halifax and Liverpool, and between NSHQ and the Admiralty.

Thus, although Ottawa did not engage in cryptanalysis, relying on constant exchanges with the Admiralty for information obtained by that means, Canada had taken over from the United States all of the functions associated with convoy routing and diversion in the Canadian North West Atlantic by the time of ONS 5 in May 1943. It would be Ottawa's warning about additional submarine frequencies early in May that would alert the escort in the battle for ONS 5 to the presence of more than one group of U-boats.

Timely decryption of "Enigma" traffic was still the best source of intelligence. In this respect, it was at the time of SC 107's battle that a very strange incident occurred in the eastern Mediterranean, an incident which was to have enormous consequences for the Battle of the Atlantic. On 30 October 1942, a British hunting group of destroyers forced U-559 to surface after heavy depth-charge attacks. One of this group, HMS *Petard*, had during work-ups—the operational training period—perfected a system of boarding a U-boat in case of an unsuccessful operation when the submarine broke surface. In a recent interview the officer who commanded this ship, then Commander Mark Thornton, RN, has explained how the first lieutenant with one other officer and a steward managed to board the boat before it went down. They retrieved from the wireless room a valuable collection of secret documents and transferred them in a dry state to the ship's whaler. The two officers then made another trip into the hull to get the new M-4 cypher machine, but at that moment the U-boat suddenly foundered. They drowned, but the steward managed to swim to safety. Bletchley Park used the papers to determine the general construction of the new machine, and by December this knowledge proved sufficient to begin decrypting messages sent in the Triton code. Several weeks passed, however, before the codebreakers could refine the process. It was not until after disastrous losses to the tanker convoy TM 1 in January 1943 that they were able to resume the rapid calculation of German daily settings which had characterized their previous success in penetrating naval Enigma. Then they were able to make significant contributions to the reduction of daily loss rates. Analysis of these rates and the numbers of U-boats at sea leads us to the conclusion that about 1.6 million tons of merchant shipping had been saved through "Ultra" in the second part of 1941, and more than six hundred and fifty thousand tons in the first five months of 1943, as a result of the breakthrough on "Triton."

After a slow start in the second half of December 1942 and early January 1943, during which time gaps and delays in decryption led to the convoy battles ONS 154 and TM 1 with heavy shipping losses, "Ultra" became so successful that it was possible to evade German U-boat patrol lines in the North Atlantic with six eastbound and eight westbound convoys in the next three weeks. But then, in February, the number of U-boats rose to more than forty, and BdU was able to form three long patrol lines which were difficult to circumvent. The movement of these groups owed much to x-B-Dienst, which was able to decrypt more and more convoy routing signals, or the daily Allied U-boat estimate, in time to counter evasive movements. The accuracy of the U-boat situation signals gave rise to a grave new concern about cypher security, but the investigation ordered by Admiral Dönitz concluded that all Allied information must have come from other sources such as direction-finding, radar location, and optical sightings by ships and aircraft. This conclusion was supported by the fact that two eastbound and three westbound convoys were intercepted in February, and two of them, SC 118 and ON 166, were attacked with success.

Nevertheless, BdU thought that it was time to introduce a new refinement to the M-4 cypher machine. On 1 March the second "Greek" rotor "beta" was put into service by a given code word. When this code word was decrypted by Bletchley Park, there was a new fear of total blackout. Rear-Admiral Edelsten, director of the Anti-Submarine Warfare Division of the Admiralty wrote on 9 March to the First Sea Lord, Admiral Sir Dudley Pound, "The foreseen has come to pass. The Director of Naval Intelligence reported on 8 March that the [Submarine] Tracking Room will be 'blinded' in regard to U-boat movements for some considerable period, perhaps extending to months!"

Without the customary reliable information on the enemy's dispositions, it appeared almost impossible to route the convoys clear of the German wolfpacks whose number was rising rapidly; convoy after convoy might be intercepted and lose up to 20 per cent of its ships, as had been the case with SC 121, HX 228, SC 122, and HX 229 in the first twenty days of March. Everything depended on how fast Bletchley Park could solve the new cryptological problem. By using all available sources at Bletchley Park, including machines from the army and air force, the experts were able to solve the new German puzzle. It was the cryptanalysts' greatest single wartime achievement. From 20 March onwards Triton was available to the STR with a time-lag of only one to three days. The convoys could be re-routed again. Furthermore, this intelligence lent itself to a new tactical development.

The Operations of April and May 1943

During the Casablanca Conference of January 1943, President Roosevelt and Prime Minister Churchill decided to put victory in the Battle of the Atlantic at the top of their list of priorities for Allied strategy in 1943. During the following Allied Convoy Conference in March 1943, a new command organization took shape. The U.S. Navy took over operational responsibility for all convoys on the U.S.-Mediterranean route and concentrated all its escort groups there. Operational control in the North Atlantic was divided between the RCN in the west and the RN in the east at 40°W. The seven British and five Canadian escort groups had to escort their convoys on both sides of this CHOP line, from the Western Ocean Meeting Point off Newfoundland to the Eastern Ocean Meeting Point off the North Channel.

In addition, it was decided to equip the North Atlantic route with six support groups, built around the first available escort carriers. It was necessary to cancel the North Russian convoys for several months in order to secure the vital escorts. The Home Fleet provided twelve fleet destroyers for support groups (identified by the prefix EG) 3, 4, and 5. As it happened only the last of these groups received its carrier (HMS *Biter*) in time. *Dasher*, designated for EG.3, was destroyed by an internal explosion in

Plate 68. Perhaps the RCN's greatest achievement was its wartime fleet expansion by shipbuilding and acquisition. Here, Flower-class corvette HMCS *Kenogami*, built 1940 by Port Arthur Shipbuilding Co. (MCM—NF 380)

Plate 69. HMCS *Vancouver* II, a Flower-class corvette built 1941 by Yarrows Ltd., Esquimalt, seen here with an extended fo'c's'le configuration, saw service in the Aleutian campaign and later in the Atlantic. (MCM—2-1500)

Plate 70. HMCS *Spikenard*, Flower-class corvette built 1940 by Davie Shipbuilding and Repairing Co., Lauzon, P.Q., was torpedoed and sunk south of Iceland, 10 February 1942. (MCM—NP 348)

Plate 71. HMC Ships *Haida* and *Athabaskan* I during evolutions off Plymouth, England, 1944. Both were Tribal-class destroyers built by Vickers-Armstrongs, Barrow, England (J. Boutilier collection)

Plate 72. Although not completed before the end of World War II, HMCS *Crusader*, a C-class destroyer, had two tours of duty during the Korean War. (PAC—PA 115360)

Plate 73. HMCS *Athabaskan* I, Tribal-class destroyer, was sunk off the coast of France, 29 April 1944, in a surface engagement with a German torpedo boat. (PAC—PA 115361)

Plate 74. Invasion craft on the way to the French coast, Canadian troops in foreground, 10 June 1944. RCN ships provided protection for cross-Channel flotillas. (PAC—PA 116339)

Plate 75. RCN ratings enjoy an enthusiastic welcome during the liberation of Greece, October 1944. (PAC—PA 116338)

March, and *Archer* only became available following repairs in mid-May. The sixth group was built around the American escort carrier USS *Bogue*, with three to four "flush-deck" destroyers. The first group was composed of two sloops and three new frigates; the second group, consisting of five new sloops, was ready only in the second half of May. That these few ships and aircraft could be used in such an efficient way was possibly the most decisive impact "Ultra" had on the Battle of the Atlantic.

A particularly dangerous situation developed around certain Allied convoys between 21 and 23 April. Up to the twentieth BdU had concentrated group "Meise" (twenty-one U-boats) in the area northeast of Newfoundland. On the same day x-B-Dienst decrypted a three-day-old routing signal to convoy HX 234 in time to place group Meise on a new patrol line covering the possible convoy courses on the twenty-first. Only a few hours later came a second decryption of the position of convoy SC 127 going east. Accordingly, BdU ordered a new patrol line "Specht" of seventeen boats on the possible convoy courses of the twenty-second. On 21 April, before Bletchley Park could decrypt these orders, three boats of group Meise, running for their new positions, intercepted HX 234 on its northeasterly leg and then the two southbound convoys ONS 3 and ON 178. Because of radio interference BdU did not receive these radio signals until many hours later, by which time Dönitz could only ask the U-boats to go after the nearest convoy and to report its positions. From the direction-finding fixes of these signals the STR obtained information about the position of "Meise" and was able to direct two of the support groups at sea, EG.3 and EG.1, to the assistance of the convoys in danger. From decrypts on 22 April, the STR received the impression that some of the U-boats had already contacted the westbound ONS 4, and EG.5 with the carrier *Biter* was instructed to stay with this convoy. However, BdU had ordered the U-boats in this area, which had not yet sighted the convoy, to go for HX 234. A group of outbound submarines from France received a new heading point in an area where BdU intended to form the next patrol line. Other decrypts of 22 April pinpointed the position of the new group Specht, farther to the south. The American 6th Support Group with the carrier *Bogue* therefore was ordered to cover convoy HX 235, escorted by the Canadian escort group C.4, which was now given a southern route.

Meanwhile, in the north, group Meise was trying to attack HX 234. The Germans enjoyed only limited success. Excellent defence by the British escort group B.4, (Commander E.C.L. Day, RN), efficient air escort by long-range Catalinas of the U.S. Navy No. 84 Squadron from Greenland and Iceland, and very bad weather combined to frustrate the submarines. The commander-in-chief Western Approaches had also ordered EG.4 to assist this convoy.

To the southwest, one of the U-boats following HX 234 had sighted

ONS 4. A short while later another U-boat reported the carrier group, so BdU ordered group Specht to proceed at high speed and form a new patrol line to intercept the convoy and carrier group. Bletchley Park decrypted this signal the following day, 24 April, and both convoys, ONS 4 and the fast ON 179 with the escort group B.5, were re-routed west of the German line. Very long-range Liberators of No. 120 Squadron RAF from Iceland and the carrier planes of HMS *Biter* gave effective support to both convoys and sank two enemy submarines. An attack on the carrier by U-404 failed because of malfunctioning torpedoes (Commander von Bülow misinterpreted the torpedo detonations at the time and claimed that he had sunk the carrier USS *Ranger*). Convoy SC 127, escorted by the Canadian group C.1, supported by EG.1, passed this dangerous area and avoided being sighted. Convoy HX 235, whose original route would have passed group Specht and the new concentration, codenamed "Amsel," sailed clear of the danger on the southern route accompanied by EG.6.

From 25 to 27 April, convoys ONS 4 and ON 179 steamed safely around group Specht. The remarkably exact Ultra-based U-boat plot enabled the STR to re-route the Canadian-escorted convoy SC 127 so that it would not pass through group "Star" in the north. EG.4 went to the support of this convoy, EG.1 having been required to go to the support of the southbound convoys.

From the weekly intelligence reports of the STR we know that there was a new blackout in "Special Intelligence," beginning on 26 April and lasting for about a week. This loss of information led rapidly to bigger and bigger differences between the real U-boat positions and the STR's estimates. So, on the twenty-eighth, groups Specht and Amsel, which were closing to form a long patrol line off Newfoundland, were thought to be more to the east than they were. Only group "Star" could be located, more or less accurately, by HF/DF bearings on U-boats' signalling during the operation that began when they sighted ONS 5 at the northern end of the patrol line.

From 29 April to 1 May, southeast of Cape Farewell (the southern tip of Greenland), group Star tried to come to grips with convoy ONS 5 escorted by the British group B.7 under Commander Peter Gretton, RN. Heavy gales blowing in this area, with snow and hail showers, scattered many of the ships in the convoy, but bad conditions also hampered U-boat operations. Thus, although there were stragglers and the escorts ran low on fuel because oiling was out of the question, only one ship was sunk. To help this convoy, the 3rd Support group (EG.3) was sent out from St. John's.

Far to the southeast, convoy HX 235 with its Canadian escort, covered by the American 6th Support Group with the carrier *Bogue*, passed the German transit area where the carrier planes drove down two U-boats. Instead of the long combined patrol line Specht and Amsel, the STR's in London and Ottawa placed group Specht in the area northeast of Newfoundland and Amsel much farther to the east. This estimate had already led to a re-routing signal that instructed convoy SC 128, escorted by EG.4, to go directly north on the thirtieth and move to the west on 1 May to evade Specht. Dönitz anticipated the move on the thirtieth after x-B-Dienst decrypted a position signal from SC 128; BdU ordered both groups Specht and Amsel to form a line that would cover all courses between north and east on 1 May.

During the night of 1 May EG.3, on the way to help ONS 5, passed through the new patrol line and was sighted by U-628, which took it for convoy SC 128. Group Specht was ordered to close and attack and so missed the convoy, coming up behind EG.3. In the north, where group Star had lost contact with the convoy ONS 5 in the heavy gales, EG.3 joined the depleted escort group B.7. Since group Specht could not now find SC 128, BdU ordered the twenty-nine submarines of Star and Specht to form a new concentrated patrol line, "Fink," on the projected course of the convoy, not realizing it had been rerouted clear to the west.

The Canadian authorities could not do the same for ONS 5, owing to the escorts' critical fuel situation; the convoy had to continue on the shortest possible route. Instead of SC 128, therefore, it was ONS 5 that ran into group Fink on the evening of 4 May. For the Germans it was the best possible starting position for a convoy battle: twenty-nine U-boats close to and on either side of the convoy; two other groups, "Amsel I" and "Amsel II" with eleven boats, lay in wait not far away and directly ahead.

The tactical phase of the convoy battle, the most decisive of the war, has been described in great detail in various books. It was not a battle with much Canadian participation; that is to say, no Canadian ships took part, although the corvette HMS *Sunflower* was under the command of Lieutenant J. Plomer, RCNVR, and some important contributions were made by RCAF as well as by U.S. Army aircraft. Not very much new can be said about ONS 5, but for our purposes it provides an interesting comparison with SC 42 and SC 107.

The convoy had sailed from Liverpool with forty-three ships in twelve columns, escorted by group B.7. Driving off all but one attack by group Star between 28 April and 1 May, Commander Peter Gretton had found himself by 4 May in charge of a force scattered into three main groups by the vicious gales. Thirty ships formed into ten columns, escorted by three destroyers (fitted with HF/DF and type 271 radar), one frigate, and two corvettes (all fitted with type 271), and two trawlers, comprised the main body of the convoy. Gretton did not have extra fuel tanks in his destroyer, HMS *Duncan*, so he had to detach to replenish her oil supplies. A separate group of six ships was escorted by the corvette HMS *Pink*, while six other merchant vessels were stragglers.

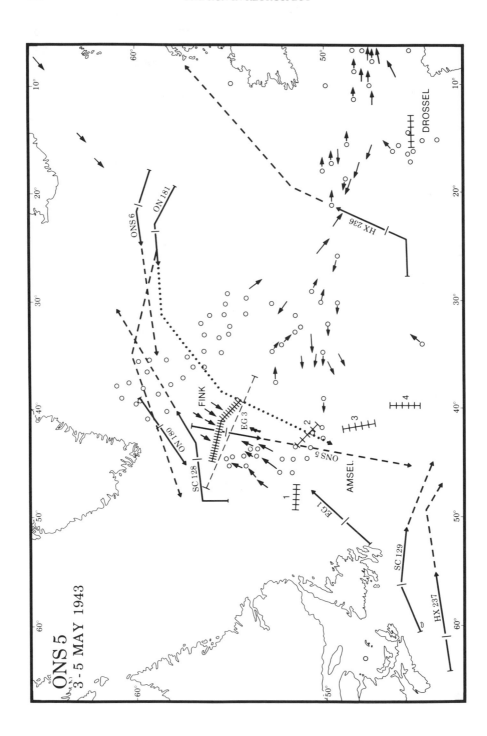

ONS 5
3 - 5 MAY 1943

BdU had formed group Amsel into four sections to mislead HF/DF operators, with the help of active radio deception, into believing that there was one long line of U-boats to the north and east of Newfoundland. When Specht and Star came together to form group Fink farther to the north, and Amsel changed its formation, OIC in Ottawa had good general intelligence but lacked details. Consequently, U.S. Army B17's from Gander made three sightings and attacks near group Amsel on 2 May. However, the fact that the search area allocated on 3 May was in the empty space between Amsel I and Amsel II suggests that the German deception plan worked.

On 4 May the air controller in Newfoundland sent out Canso's of No. 5 Squadron RCAF to support ONS 5 at maximum range. One of these sank U-630, thirty miles astern of the convoy, at 1800 and sighted a second U-boat about thirty miles to port. Another Canso on his way to join the convoy sighted a third boat near Amsel II. At this time, unlike the procedures followed in 1942, U.S. Army and RCAF aircraft were orchestrated into a general air plan, the result of the great efforts that had been made over the winter to improve air coverage. Yet sea-air co-operation was still poor. For example, the senior officer of the escort in HMS *Tay* heard the RCAF aircraft report of the latter's attack on a U-boat at 1800, but in spite of all efforts, he could not establish communications with the pilot.

The main battle took place between the afternoon of 4 May and the evening of 6 May. U-628 established the first firm contact at 1817 on 4 May, and the escorts (provided with listening frequencies by the OIC, Ottawa) were aware of intense radio activity among the U-boats before that. The convoy was steering south-southwest at seven knots, and the senior officer had stationed the four corvettes, the one remaining destroyer, and the frigate of B.7 group in a standard defensive pattern designed to give complete radar coverage. The two trawlers steamed close astern of the screen for rescue purposes, while two destroyers of EG.3, HM Ships *Offa* and *Oribi*, were stationed five miles on the convoy's port and starboard bows.

The first attack took place at 0028, six miles astern of the main body, when U-707 sank the *North Britain*. The corvette *Loosestrife* and trawler *Northern Spray* fell back to search the scene of the attack while the remainder of the escort executed operation "Raspberry," which produced three sightings and one attack on U-boats in the next half-hour. At the same time U-125 sank the straggler *Lorient*, unknown to the convoy or escort. At 0054 U-628 sank the leading ship in the eighth column. This time operation "Raspberry" resulted in two attacks on submarines, both of which had been detected by radar. At 0120 U-264 sank the first ship in the third column and the second ship in the second column, despite vigorous countermeasures, resulting from the previous attack, which were still taking place.

Nothing further happened for about four hours, but at 0506 HMS *Tay* suddenly detected a radio transmission close on the port bow, and U-358 torpedoed two ships in the port wing column. HMS *Loosestrife* sighted and attacked the U-boat before picking up survivors. At dawn the U-boats regrouped; four of them reported to BdU that they had been attacked and driven off during the night, three with heavy damage, although one of the damaged boats was still able to continue operations. BdU urged the submarine captains to make submerged attacks by day if they could, but to concentrate on getting ahead of the convoy for another night attack. Dönitz pointed out that there were forty U-boats present and that only those that acted swiftly were likely to gain success because the late arrivals might have nothing to shoot at. This battle could not last long because there was not enough sea room—the convoy was steadily approaching the Newfoundland shore.

At 1016 HMS *Offa* reported a transmission, and *Oribi*, investigating the HF/DF bearing, found three U-boats on the surface and attacked one. In the early afternoon, U-638 sank a ship near the head of the second column, and the escorts carried out the daytime countermeasure, operation "Artichoke," in which they steamed down the columns of the convoy. During this operation HMS *Sunflower* attacked an ASDIC contact. Almost simultaneously U-584 sank a ship in the detached group, just as HMS *Pink* was attacking—and destroying—U-192. At 1700 the escorts with the main body picked up more U-boat transmissions ahead but could do little about them since the destroyers were trying at every opportunity to take on fuel from the tanker in the convoy, a frustrating task, interrupted by breaks in the supply hose and the need to share time between the two destroyers.

At 1941 U-266 sank the lead ships in the two starboard columns and the third ship in the seventh column. The escorts immediately executed operations "Artichoke" and "Observant" (the latter a search around the torpedoed ships) and damaged U-266 in subsequent attacks. At 2039 *Offa* and *Oribi* pointed out, "Heavy WT activity indicated [that] the convoy was threatened with annihilation." But fog set in, and by 0100 on 6 May visibility was down to one hundred yards. The U-boats, lacking radar, were left sightless.

The U-boats had now sunk twelve ships since 4 May, nine of them in the main convoy, one in the detached group, and two stragglers. During daylight hours on 5 May eleven U-boats made contact, and nine more contact reports occurred during the evening. Two U-boats had been sunk, U-630 by RCAF aircraft on 4 May, U-192 by HMS *Pink* on 5 May. Four boats reported being depth-charged, three having to break off action as a result, one of these without having fired any torpedoes.

Defence of the convoy had been impressive against overwhelming odds; now the fog turned the tables. During the night the escorts, including reinforcements from EG.1, depth-charged fifteen U-boats, detected and rammed at least two on the surface, forced four boats to break off action, and sank four others. A grave loss, said Dönitz, who laid most of the blame on the fog. He later promulgated a message that British intercept stations managed to pick up:

> Our heavy U/B losses in the past month are attributable primarily to the present superiority of the enemy's location devices and the surprise from air which these have made possible. More than half our total losses have arisen as a result of this surprise. . . . Losses in actual combat with convoys have been small, *except in one case where particularly unfavourable conditions prevailed, and even of these losses, some were caused by air.* [Emphasis provided by director of Naval Intelligence.]

On analysing the results, commodore (D[estroyers]) Western Approaches, at Londonderry, made the pragmatic but important observation that depth-charge efficiency had been highly satisfactory (only 2 failures out of 340). He pointed as well to the effectiveness of a close radar ring created by well-trained escorts. Losses did not occur until the screen was reduced to five, then four. The screen really needed eight escorts and should not be weakened overall in order to put destroyers ahead—although "packing" on the threatened side was acceptable. *Offa* and *Oribi*, stationed five miles on each bow, had been little protection and were in danger of being torpedoed themselves; the ASDIC efficiency of escorts ahead was essential. One screen penetration had occurred when HMS *Tay* suffered a breakdown and was occupying a position in the van.

All the Allied observers pointed to combat efficiency as the main cause of success in defending the convoy and inflicting heavy damage, although several British commanders emphasized the terrible dangers of deliberately trying to fight a convoy through a patrol line. BdU emphasized the role of fog. Fog was indeed a decisive weapon for the escort, but without fog, which grounded aircraft, air cover could have made it more dangerous for submarines to carry out the daytime surface transits to their attacking positions. If conditions had been normal, BdU argued, the U-boats would have done better. It is an excuse that appears quite often in BdU's war diary, for instance in the case of SC 42 in 1941, but it is not a satisfactory explanation. Fog, after all, is normal—especially on the Grand Banks of Newfoundland; a weapon, to be effective, must be adaptable. ONS 5 established the adaptability of the surface escort and, by the same token, demonstrated the limitations of the standard submersible in warfare.

CONCLUSION

The three convoy battles described here illustrate the value of re-examining events of the past in the light of new knowledge. They tell us things about the naval and air forces of World War II that we did not know before; they confirm or, in some cases, correct previous accounts; moreover, they underline the essential relationship between men and technology in war. Intelligence played a critical part in both Allied and German strategy and tactics, and there is no doubt that the Allies won the intelligence battle by efforts that were almost superhuman. In the end, however, as in all warfare, we come down to simple basics. The astonishing battle for ONS 5 showed how important the human factor is in war. As the power and sophistication of weapons increase, it is a signal point to keep in mind.

Poets have often seen this more readily than others.

> Tirpitz and Fisher thirty years before
> Had scanned the riddles in each other's eyes.
> What was the argument about the belt
> That drained the sophistry of principle
> Inside a ring? *"Hit first, hit hard, hit fast!"*
> Tirpitz had trumped him with *"Hit anywhere."*
> And here today only one point was certain—
> Sailors above the sea, sailors below,
> Drew equally upon a fund of courage.

Chapter 13

THE LOWER DECK AND THE MAINGUY REPORT OF 1949

L.C. Audette

The Mainguy Report was made by Admiral Rollo Mainguy, RCN, Leonard Brockington, and L.C. Audette as a result of a naval inquiry into three mutinous incidents which occurred late in the winter of 1949.[1] Because of the findings of the Mainguy Report, we are concerned here primarily with certain lower deck attitudes and with the relationship between RCN officers and the lower deck. The world of the rating is, unfortunately, all too often the silent part of the "Silent Service." When the public does hear from it, it is usually over explosive events like Britain's Invergordon mutiny in 1931 or our own mutinies in 1949. There are probably two basic reasons for this situation. The first is that, with few exceptions, men from the lower deck are generally neither very articulate nor very skilled in the art of advocacy for whatever their case may be at any given time. The second reason is that the grievance procedure in the navy was extremely strained and cumbersome.

In mere numerical terms, ratings constitute some 90 per cent of the navy's complement. Policy may be determined for a navy at cabinet or ministerial level, strategy at flag officer level, and tactics at the level of ships' officers. But though the tactical decisions and orders are the responsibility of a ship's commanding officer, right or wrong, the final stress, the final effort, and the final courage in their execution comes largely from the ratings. If there is to be naval history, then it must be recognized that lower deck men stand side by side with admirals and officers in its making.

Even in the last half of the 1800's, men from the lower deck could be flogged around the fleet, keel-hauled, or put to death more mercifully for what would now be deemed minor transgressions. Because naval lore is usually expressed in terms of the Drakes and Nelsons of its history, rather than in terms of sailors, people too seldom remember the long struggle of the lower deck for recognition of any right but to obey, to toil, to be maimed and cast aside, or to die. The centuries before our own were not gentle; the situation has improved vastly, but it had not kept up with the times in 1949. The events of that year and the Mainguy Report itself show the perils of neglecting the lower deck and of not taking great pains to understand it. The whole tenor of the report revealed the extent to which the three commissioners were disturbed by what they learned and by the fact that those responsible for the lower deck had not acquitted themselves of their responsibilities.

The inquiry of 1949 was made necessary by three events markedly similar in nature which were euphemistically termed "incidents" at the time. In each case, a number of sailors in a ship gathered together, locked themselves in a mess deck, and did not take up duties which they knew to have been assigned to them. A comparable incident two years before in the cruiser HMCS *Ontario* had been described with equal attenuation, the events couched in periphrastic convolutions all of which sedulously eschewed the alarming word "mutiny." Moreover, there had been a similar occurrence in the destroyer HMCS *Iroquois* in July 1943. The pattern of behaviour was much the same. An officer, who had served in *Iroquois* at the time, wrote to me using the bland words "a locking of the fore lower mess deck doors," but the inquiry carried out in Britain by British naval officers called it "a refusal of duty by a large section of the ship's company." Lest the concept of five mutinies in a six-year period appear unduly distressing, I should point out that other navies are highly reluctant to publicize information of this nature unless the event is on the compelling scale of Britain's Invergordon mutiny.

Mutiny was defined by the National Defence Act as collective insubordination or a combination of two or more persons in resistance to lawful navy, army, or air force authority in any of His Majesty's forces or in any forces co-operating therewith. I can think of no definition more precisely descriptive of insubordinate sailors who have locked themselves in a mess deck and who do not carry out the work assigned to them.

The law at the time provided harsh punishment for mutiny: death for joining in a mutiny accompanied by violence, death for a ringleader in a mutiny with or without violence, and life imprisonment for joining in a mutiny not accompanied with violence and for such peripheral actors as those who cause, conspire, persuade, or fail to inform their superiors. Death or life imprisonment in the case of mutineers, and public reaction in the case of both the mutineers and those in charge, provided a strong incitement to euphemistic terminology. Even the press curbed itself so far as to call the events "incidents," always placed between inverted commas. We did likewise in the Mainguy Report; thirty years later I call them mutinies.

The geography and sequence of the mutinies in 1949 are important to an understanding of them in relation to one another and to prevailing circumstances. The mutiny in the destroyer HMCS *Athabaskan*, in which ninety crew members participated, took place at Manzanillo, on Mexico's Pacific coast, on 26 February; the one in the destroyer HMCS *Crescent*, involving eighty-three men, occurred in Nanking, China, on 15 March; and the one by thirty-two mutineers in the aircraft carrier HMCS *Magnificent* took place while she was under way in the Caribbean Sea on 20 March. The mutiny in *Athabaskan* became known in *Crescent* and *Magnificent* before the similar occurrences in those two ships. The mutiny of 1947 in HMCS *Ontario* was common knowledge as was the fact that several ratings who had been in *Iroquois* at the time of her ordeal in 1943 were serving in *Ontario* at the time of her troubles in 1947.

Thus, the Canadian government, the inquisitive populace, and that august caste known in hushed tones as "the senior officers" all became aware that three mutinies had broken out in the navy within three weeks. Each of these groups was sorely distressed. Fully as disturbed were the captains and the executive officers of the ships involved—the two traditional and sometimes justifiable targets for responsibility and reprisal in such situations—and the mutineers themselves, because of the dread peril in which they stood until immunity had been assured. The circumstances also produced the utmost anxiety among the senior officers responsible to a chief of the Naval Staff responsible to a minister of the crown responsible in turn to Parliament.

The very nature of the situation created difficulties for the inquiry. At the political level, there was serious concern that there might be undetected subversive of communist elements at work within our armed forces. Among the top ranks of the naval officers, there was a natural defensiveness about the fact that they had neither foreseen nor forestalled what had happened. Within the ships involved, the captains, executive officers, and other senior personnel on board had an uncomfortable feeling of involvement and of jeopardized careers. Among the mutineers themselves, there was generally a feeling of embarrassment and shame; yet there was also a defensiveness about what they had done. Fear and anxiety prevailed, and most people even remotely involved had some urges inimical to full disclosure, if not conducive to downright concealment.

The atmosphere in 1949 was far different from what it is today: concepts of "subversion" and "communism" sent shivers down the spines of most ordinary people, let alone those suspected of mutiny. The same sensation was experienced by the naval officers who had perhaps contributed to the mutinies and by the politicians who were held by the electorate to be responsible for everything unhappy. Three other events, apparently unrelated, suddenly gained new relevance and new connections with the three mutinies and the inquiry held into them.

The first of these was the defection from the Russian embassy in Ottawa three years earlier of the cypher clerk, Igor Gouzenko. As a result of Gouzenko's revelations, the Russian ambassador and a number of his staff were sent home in disgrace because of their espionage activities. Henceforth, it was not uncommon for Canadians to imagine Russian spies lurking under every bed.

The second event was the "Battle of Dow's Lake" in 1946, a "battle" which was a direct consequence of the serious postwar shortage of housing in Ottawa. Dow's Lake is a widening in the Rideau Canal on which is situated HMCS *Carleton*, the naval reserve division for the city of Ottawa. Late one afternoon, at the head of a mob of a few hundred people spearheaded by some large trucks, a misguided fellow named Hanratty wrested possession of some *Carleton* buildings and moved in with a number of homeless families to occupy them as lodgings. There was never the slightest doubt that the seizure was organized by the communists who had used a discouraged, ingenuous, and hapless Hanratty as their tool and the housing shortage as their cause. Although the mounted police and the government dealt most skilfully with the incident, the important thing from the point of view of the naval inquiry was that this unhappy and mildly ridiculous incident had occurred and that the government, the press, and the Canadian public were fully aware of the unconcealed communist influence behind it.

The third incident was the mutiny which had taken place in the cruiser HMCS *Ontario* in August 1947. I know of no communist influence in this event, but I do know that such a possibility had suggested itself to people at many levels.

One of the aspects of the mutiny in *Ontario* that was important to the 1949 inquiry was that many of the grievances which had been raised in *Ontario* were raised by the mutineers of 1949. One of these was dissatisfaction with the executive officer of the ship and a plea for his removal. In commenting on the treatment afforded to the executive officer of HMCS *Ontario*, we had this to say in the Mainguy Report:

> As a result, the Executive Officer was immediately transferred to another ship. In retrospect, the speed of his transfer, without a complete investigation, appears neither completely wise nor completely fair.

I should add an admiring tribute to Admiral Mainguy with respect to this issue. In the turmoil and pressures of the *Ontario* mutiny, the executive officer's transfer had been urged upon Mainguy, and he had agreed to it. Notwithstanding his involvement in the unduly hasty transfer, it was he who proposed the paragraph I have just quoted. His proposal is evidence of his wisdom and fairness, quite untainted by selfish considerations of vanity which would have stayed the hand of lesser men. This may explain, in part, why Mainguy was such an admirable chairman for the inquiry. The witnesses clearly trusted him; this I know because I was there to see and hear them giving their defence.

A second important aspect of the *Ontario* mutiny was that the prompt removal of the executive officer had received wide publicity within and without the navy (unfairly to his detriment because it was done without inquiry), and certainly it was generally known through the RCN. Men who were serving in *Ontario* at the time were subsequently transferred to HMC Ships *Athabaskan* and *Crescent* and were still serving in those ships when the mutinies occurred in them in 1949. There may also have been among such men some who had served in *Iroquois* at the time of her mutiny in 1943, a fact which did not come out in evidence before the inquiry.

The third aspect of the mutiny in *Ontario* that was important in all three ships in 1949 was the fact that no one was punished. Thus, the effectiveness and the impunity of mutiny as a successful method for attaining objectives was highlighted. There is a *mot juste* in French for the severed head and the bleeding back: "*pour encourager les autres.*" Had heads rolled in 1947, the spectacle might have discouraged the later mutinies.

Every effort was made in the *Ontario* and 1949 mutinies to have insubordinate behaviour look unlike mutiny. This was a universally attractive course, but the attempt was futile. The foul stench of mutiny was incapable of transforming itself into the healthy aroma of good behaviour. In the light of all four mutinies, there remains a dismal unanswered question— how much was error in judgement and how much was downright cravenness before an issue of such magnitude? The widely prevalent tendency to shade the mutinous nature of the "incidents" was only evidence of the instinctive fear found everywhere in life when men feel trapped by circumstances. At such times, we tend to view our contributory transgressions as trifling misdemeanors whereas similar ones on the part of others look like major outrages.

Thus it is clear that the atmosphere in which the commissioners undertook their inquiry was very different than it is today. Fear of communism and subversion existed in every quarter; there was a recent history of successful and unpunished mutiny; the war had come to an end four years earlier bringing about an unpleasant metamorphosis from sparkling hero to taxpayers' burden for the uniformed serviceman. The navy had declined in public esteem from its wartime peak because of the mutinies, and those who were destined to be our most important witnesses tended to show an instinctive disinclination towards full disclosure.

Mutiny is a manifestation of anarchy. Anarchy is feared and hated not only by those who wield power but also by the man in the street because it threatens his sense of security. Because mutiny is not only known but is also "felt" to be an extremely serious offence entailing severe punishment, men are driven to it only by serious, complex, and multiple causes. This fact, coupled with a reluctance to give evidence, makes inquiries into mutinies formidable undertakings.

Three mutinies in quick succession created an obvious need for a major inquiry. The Minister of National Defence, Brooke Claxton, had a hard task ahead of him in choosing persons to conduct the inquiry. There was, of course, an instinctive desire within the navy, from the chief of the Naval Staff right down to the lowliest of the mutineers, to cover matters up. Consequently, a purely naval group was out of the question—a matter of wisdom which had entirely escaped the Admiralty at the time of the Invergordon mutiny. Parliament and the Canadian public would have been outraged. In due course, and after a number of candidates had refused or declared themselves unable to act, the minister asked me to sit as one of the three members of the commission of inquiry.

The members of the naval inquiry finally constituted were Rear-Admiral E.R. Mainguy, RCN, as chairman, and Leonard W. Brockington and myself as commissioners. W.N. Wickwire, of Halifax was appointed inquiry counsel while Commander P.R. Hurcomb, RCN, judge advocate of the fleet, acted as assistant counsel.

I had first known Mainguy when he was captain (D[estroyers]) Newfoundland, during World War II. All who served in that command remember gratefully his kindness and consideration. He started the famous Crow's Nest Club for seagoing officers. Always a man to remember the lower deck, he also started the camp for ratings near St. John's. He it was who began the famous Friday "Captain (D)'s" cocktail parties at the Newfoundland Hotel. In the preparatory stages of the inquiry, I had objected to Mainguy being chairman. My objection had nothing to do with the man himself, whom I already knew and admired; I thought that the inquiry should be entirely civilian, or at the very least, have a civilian chairman. Mainguy's later acquittal of his role as chairman was so outstanding that I am sure that had I won my point it would have hindered the inquiry. Notwithstanding a cuff heavy with gold lace, he put men at ease in a manner which perhaps neither Brockington nor I could have done, and his quiet, reasonable manner with its gentle assurance of authority led men to speak frankly and freely.

Like Mainguy, Brockington had consideration for others— Cardinal Newman's definition of a gentleman. His humanity was evident from the start, and men responded to it. He was dreadfully handicapped by arthritis, but the beautiful voice which entranced the nation over the radio on important occasions remained the same. His mastery of the English language was as great as that of any man I have observed in this century, even including Winston Churchill; our report bears the imprint of his literary style. Under a sometimes gruff exterior, there was a warm heart and a cultured and deeply sensitive man. I am grateful for having had his friendship well beyond the limits of our joint task. A couple of years later, he and I became colleagues again for close to ten years, this time as members of the Court Martial Appeal Board.

Wickwire, the inquiry counsel, a Halifax lawyer of great ability, was a man with quick understanding for the problems of those less privileged than himself. Brockington and I, great lovers of classical music, discovered in Wickwire—a big, burly, former football player—a recent and fanatical convert to our cult. I spent many happy hours with each of these men. Wickwire helped us enormously in our task. Young as he was, he died only a few years after the inquiry.

Hurcomb, judge advocate of the fleet and assistant counsel to the inquiry, had a difficult role to play, but he played it to perfection. Being a naval officer, there might have been the appearance of a conflict of interest in acting for the inquiry. If there was such an appearance, I am in a position to say that he so acquitted himself of his duties that, if criticism is possible, it could only be for his appointment and not for his actions, which were always above reproach. No one could have asked for better colleagues than were given to me for such an exacting task.

The task of the commission was to investigate and report what had taken place. We were to ascertain if subversive elements had been involved in fomenting the mutinies and to make recommendations to prevent recurrences and to improve conditions of service in terms of relations between officers and men and the methods for ventilating grievances. The hearings were to be informal in order to encourage free and frank discussion. (Informality in matters of this nature was much less prevalent in 1949 than it may appear today.)

The procedure which we followed elicited a good deal of information, some of which may have been judged erroneously by our critics to be unimportant or even damaging to established opinion. We went on board each of the three ships and explained our role and operating procedure to the men. At our hearings, the witnesses were allowed to sit and even to smoke, on the grounds that the less anxiety a witness felt, the more he was apt to concentrate on the question before him rather than on his own personal predicament. In a reasonably favourable atmosphere, he even grows forgetful enough of the anxieties attached to his status as a witness to be truthful and open. This consideration was of great importance in our inquiry because nearly everyone had an axe to grind, an iniquity to conceal, or a state of affairs to preserve or destroy.

The witnesses were heard *in camera* and assured that they could speak in frankness without fear of punishment or prejudice to their careers. They had already received public assurance from the minister of National Defence that the evidence they gave would not be made known to anyone but the members of the inquiry and that the transcript of evidence would be destroyed after the report was written. Each of us sought and obtained many opportunities for private conversations with officers and men, with personnel of other navies, and with anyone who could contribute to the task at hand.

Because he discussed the matter with me, I know what moved Brooke Claxton to give the pledge that the evidence would not be seen or made known to anyone outside the inquiry. He sought to give subordinates confidence that they could speak freely and make full disclosure without fear of reprisals. However, I have a confession to make with respect to the evidence. While the other members of the inquiry destroyed their papers, I kept mine in my residence for twenty-five years, although no one had access to the thirty-six hundred pages of the transcript of evidence during that period. Because I deemed that the mutinies of 1949, the naval inquiry, and the Mainguy Report were sufficiently important that later researchers should have access to the documentation in order to assess the validity of our conclusions, I gave my files and my copy of the transcript of evidence to the Public Archives of Canada.

At sittings in Halifax, Esquimalt, Vancouver, and Ottawa, we heard 238 witnesses, of whom over 150 were petty officers and ratings. The witnesses ranged from the chief of the Naval Staff to the most recent of recruits. The greater number appeared at the inquiry's request, but over fifty testified at their own request. No one who sought to be heard was denied a hearing.

There were the truthful and mendacious, the shy and bold, those who enjoyed their moment in the limelight and those who hated it, the happy and the malcontent, the responsible and the irresponsible. There were remarkably few—if any—cold and deliberate liars. There were those of limited education who found themselves in difficulty when they sought to venture into the abstract field of policy or ideas, and it would be quite wrong to assume that all of these were from the lower deck. By and large, the witnesses contributed more to our task than I had foreseen that they would. Among the mutineers there was naturally a rather self-conscious prearranged pattern to their initial evidence about what had taken place. This pattern is clearly the easy one for a witness to pursue providing he remains within the limits of truth. It becomes exceedingly difficult for false evidence: prolonged lying requires such outstanding ability that almost no one can meet the supremely exacting test. However, as the interrogation of witnesses moved beyond questions of the "what happened" variety, they revealed more than they had planned and frequently a good deal more than they thought. We were impressed by the fact that most of the witnesses appeared frank, truthful, and free from fear. We also noticed that mutual confidence increased as the inquiry progressed.

In our report, we termed the postwar times to be full of restlessness, uncertainty, and change. Though we were unquestionably right, I now doubt that the full extent of the turmoil and ferment was appreciated at the time—by us or by anyone else. World War I had undermined much of our former social stability; World War II had done the same but to an even greater extent and at a faster rhythm because of the impetus for change already given by World War I. A touch of independence, a measure of iconoclasm, a clear contestation of any inherent right to be at the top all mingled with a new social heresy. That heresy held that the poor, the lower classes, and even the "lesser breeds" had rights to life, employment, adequate income, good health, a reasonable standard of living, and, where competence existed, to a place and status in the many varied hierarchies of the land.

If these new social views were mere heresy to some, they were positive anathema to others. There were still those in the navy in 1949, particularly among the higher ranks, whose social consciences and opinions came to them atavistically from remote generations. They faced some painful debates because Claxton, beyond being sensitive and immensely able, was also an advanced social thinker. The enormous value of men like Claxton is that they are the element in society which prevents mutinies and rebellions by sensing and lowering dangerous pressures. Less intelligent men are insensitive to injustice, unable to identify the necessary corrective measures and reluctant to implement them when identified by others. Change frightens the incompetent because they feel threatened by it.

Though we found criticism, unrest, and dissatisfaction throughout the RCN, we found no evidence of subversive or communist activities related to the mutinies. Nevertheless, we reminded the minister, and through him, Parliament and the public, of the restlessness ashore: strikes and labour unrest undoubtedly had some influence on the relations between "management" and "labour" within the navy.

There had been prior mutterings in the three ships which must have been known to some leading hands, petty officers, and even officers. We were told, however, that these signs of discord were not brought to the attention of the captains or executive officers. The mutineers spoke of many causes of complaint, and some of these were well founded. The multiplicity of complaints emanated in part from the seriousness of mutiny as an offence and from the severity of the punishment attributable to it: much appeared necessary to explain if not justify what had happened. Nearly all of the complaints bespoke a poor awareness among the officers of how to deal with men. However, before being too critical of the navy, it would be prudent to consider how many shore-based commercial "mutinies" called strikes occur in civilian life for well- or ill-founded reasons.

A salient cause which led to eventual insubordination was the unsuitability and irresponsibility of the executive officers and their apparent inability to engage either officers or men to follow them. There were many cases of the injudicious assignment of men to tasks which more enlightened superiors would have been reluctant to assign them: aircraft handlers were forced to clean up after officers' cocktail parties; stewards were unforgivably deprived of shore leave in order to suit the convenience of certain officers. During a "make and mend," or afternoon off-duty, just before sailing for Britain, a number of aircraft handlers (the future mutineers) in HMCS *Magnificent* were detailed to secure automobiles brought on board by ships' officers. This assignment was so deeply resented in the circumstances, even by some of the officers, that it had to be cancelled before completion of the task, making the initial error even more apparent to everyone.

In all three ships, the lack of an effective welfare committee was a contributory cause to the troubles. As far back as July 1947, Naval Service Headquarters had seen the need for such committees to provide machinery for the free discussion of items of welfare and general amenities between officers and men. On 28 July 1947, a year and a half before the mutinies, a message was issued from NSHQ to all ships ordering that "immediate steps" be taken to institute welfare committees and ensure that all classes of ratings were represented on them. There was no possible trace of ambiguity or equivocation in the message.

The executive officer in HMCS *Magnificent* was aware of this clear and unmistakable order, but because, in his own words, he "did not believe in the desirability" of welfare committees, there was no welfare committee in the ship. The only reason we could not classify this officer as a mutineer was that he lacked the co-operation of another insubordinate accomplice, although the passivity of the ship's captain might perhaps have been likened to complicity. A welfare committee existed in another ship, but no meeting was held during the cruise until after the mutiny—a classic case of "closing the barn door." In the third ship, the operation of the committee was completely frustrated by the captain and the executive officer who, through the fear born of ignorance, restricted the subjects for discussion. In all three ships, the men were aware of their officers' disobedience of orders on this score and resented having no forum in which to plead. It never seems to have occurred to the officers involved that their own defiance of orders led their men ineluctably down the path towards collective insubordination.

Officer non-compliance seems to have been widespread, flagrant in one ship, surreptitious in the other two. Here also there was impunity; the very early promotion of the most openly rebellious officer could be recognized as a gesture of defiance to the inquiry. The insubordination of the officers was all the more dangerous because the existing procedure for redress of grievances was cumbersome and impractical. Almost every witness testified that there was an opinion prevalent throughout the lower deck that anyone who made a complaint through proper service channels prejudiced his career—an opinion that was not without foundation.

There was a lamentable failure everywhere to share with the men knowledge of what was happening in the ships and of the reasons for it. Manoeuvres, for example, were often cancelled without explanation, leaving only perplexity, misunderstanding, and consequent annoyance among the ratings. Too little attention was paid to the welfare and entertainment of the ships' companies. Nor did the officers perceive just how much the resentment of certain tasks related to their social lives was a reflection of the constant levelling process in Canadian society.

We were dealing with two broad classes of officers at the time of the inquiry. The first was the wartime reservist turned permanent force after the war. The second was the prewar permanent force officer. Each group was secretly—and not always so secretly—hoping that the inquiry would lay the blame for events at the other's door. There was fault attributable to the reserve officer turned permanent force. He had definite shortcomings, and his most redeeming feature was his awareness of quite a few of his faults. Most of these officers were men of relatively modest academic achievement; many of them believed themselves suddenly to have attained a social eminence far in excess of what was theirs in reality. Few had any real experience in dealing with subordinates for the very good reason that hitherto they had never had any subordinates.

There was likewise fault attributable to the permanent force officer. He shared many shortcomings with the former reservist but possessed an ingenuous unawareness of them. His educational achievements were equally humble. Unlike the former reservist, he did not deem social eminence suddenly to have become his; on the contrary, he wrongly deemed it to have been his birthright. What most surprised the three commissioners was the curious abandon with which the permanent force officer could disobey orders which he deemed undesirable, an unexpected characteristic which was displayed right to the very top. This attitude made some of the permanent force officers fellow felons with the mutineers much more than either group realized, an aspect which never seems to have struck the insubordinate officers or the senior officers whose orders had been disobeyed.

The report mentioned "an artificial distance" between officers and men "not wholly connected with the necessity of maintaining the essential differences in rank." Then after noting the willing obedience given to superior character, skill, and education it acknowledged the survival of distinctions in speech and social status which were accepted in some other countries. There could be no doubt about what was implied in the words "survival" and "other countries." It was the survival of the Senior Service ethic as a result of the training of so many RCN officers with the Royal Navy, their so-called big ship time.

It was the view of the commission then and it is still my opinion today that the survival of distinctions in speech and social class—necessarily cultivated because of their very exoticism—was inimical to the interests of the Royal Canadian Navy because they were foreign to Canadian usage and custom.

During their training, many permanent force Canadian officers had had superimposed on them a type of life and a style of leadership alien to them and, far more importantly, alien to the men whom they were to command. This situation gave rise to another phrase in our report which was widely misinterpreted: "There is no form of artificial superiority which Canadians resent more than the variety imported from another land." This was true in 1949 and it is true today; the artificiality of the superiority arose exclusively from its importation.

This area of our report brought a good deal of uninformed criticism from those who found it hard to understand what they read; in 1949 these critics included some of the press and a number of the country's anglomaniacs and anglophiles. Our judgment, however, was purely analytical: it was not critical of English ways in England. Elsewhere in the report, we expressed our opinion on British traditions:

> We have sought to interpret the wishes of the great majority of men by stressing the need to "Canadianize" our Navy. In so doing, we wish to record that in common with most thoughtful Canadians, we have an abiding admiration and respect for the grand traditions and institutions of the Royal Navy for their continuing beneficent and steadying force wherever British and Canadian ships may sail. We hope that all that is good in these shared traditions will remain with us and that only what is inefficient and inconsistent with our national need, character, dignity and special conditions will disappear from the Navy of Canada.

Within the lower deck, we found an "almost universal opinion that the Canadian Navy was not sufficiently Canadian" and that there was "still too great an attempt to make the Canadian Navy a pallid imitation and reflection of the British Navy." In 1949, nothing distinguished Canadian ships or uniforms, and Canadian ships wore the White Ensign of Britain as their national flag. The lower deck and a number of officers in the less senior ranks resented this strange national anonymity of things naval in Canada and showed strong aspiration for change. However, at the very highest levels within the service there was unreasoned and fanatical resistance to such change. The extent of the dichotomy between the lower deck and the very senior officers became painfully apparent when the chief of the Naval Staff appeared before the inquiry. In an attempt to circumvent the issue, he pointed out the recent approval of a maple leaf as a distinguishing badge. When he objected that the much-sought-after "Canada" shoulder flashes or badges spoiled the appearance of the uniform, he was asked if the contribution to morale would not be worth the sacrifice in aesthetic value. This question was a mistake. He declared angrily that he had always refused to wear the flashes in the past and would never wear them in the future. It was almost as thought the choice were really his to make, another manifestation of the curiously insubordinate mentality that we found so often among the senior officers of the old school. The CNS even made a vulgar reference to putting "Canada" on the seat of the men's pants and an intriguingly irrelevant criticism of his own country: "I think that Canada makes enough damn noise in the world without doing anything about it." This may have been a regrettable moment in the inquiry, but it served two purposes. Firstly, it made clear the need for revised thinking at the top rather than in the lower deck. Secondly, it became clear advocacy for the views of the lower deck because only that fear which arises from feeling trapped by the correctness of an opposing view can provoke such wholly irrational anger.

Lack of sensitivity in human relations led to much dissatisfaction in the lower deck which consequently became fertile ground for mutinous behaviour. We found an absence of close confidence between officers and men in the three ships. Part of this unhappy situation arose from too frequent changes in personnel, a complaint as old as navies. The report quoted Nelson who, as a twenty-five-year-old post captain in 1783, complained that "the disgust of seamen to the Navy is all owing to the infernal plan of turning them over from ship to ship so that men cannot be attached to their officers or their officers care twopence for them." One hundred and sixty-six years later, we found the same condition prevailing in the Royal Canadian Navy.

A year or two after the inquiry, an amusing incident occurred that gave me encouragement for the work we had done. While I was driving to Montreal, I picked up a hitchhiking soldier in uniform. He was wearing an Atlantic Star ribbon. Intrigued, I asked him why he had left the navy. His arresting answer was that he had not liked naval life but that he understood that it had improved since "three sons of bitches" had made some sort of inquiry. I confessed to being one of the three.

We found in our report no causes sufficient to justify what had taken place. The cumulative weight of many major and minor suppressed grievances or complaints was great enough to explain if not to justify what had happened. Our role was one of inquiry after the fact, and it must be remembered that it is easier to determine afterwards what led to a mutiny than to perceive beforehand what is leading to it. We never sought out ringleaders for punishment or reproach; immunity had been assured before we began our inquiry. Beyond that, our search was for facts, for causes, for remedies and improvements, and not for guilty individuals. Had we sought to determine individual guilt, the guilty person would of necessity have been a man from the lower deck because only such men joined in the mutinies. The insubordination which we found among the officers was individual rather than collective. In any search for individual guilt, the strain on the collective loyalty of the lower deck would have been so intolerable that it would have defeated our more important objectives by compelling men to resort to deliberately unco-operative evidence.

The report stated that our conclusions were unanimous. However, there was an issue on which I dissented: the availability of alcoholic drink in the ships. There had been evidence which made me question the existing situation where alcoholic drink was available to both officers and men, though under different conditions of issue. My questioning of the practice was markedly unpopular in some quarters at the time, so much so that it led to some regrettably intemperate contestations. Because the naval inquiry dealt with matters of national importance and great public interest I thought that any supplementary views of my own, unendorsed by one or both of my colleagues, might be viewed as some form of dissent which would weaken the value of the remainder of the report. It also appeared to me that the subject matter lent itself to explosive misinterpretation for totally wrong reasons. To avoid all these undesirable impressions, I expressed my views to the minister of National Defence in a long letter dated 11 October 1949, which, quite properly, was not made public, although my colleagues saw it and it remains part of the record. In the same letter, I enlarged on the views we had expressed on the education of naval personnel. It is not without interest that the three mutinies involved men of the seamen's branch rather than men from other branches in which the men are generally better educated.

I would like to stress one observation made early in the Mainguy Report:

> Although this report in the very nature of things is bound to be critical, it must not be assumed that there are not many reasons for great national pride in the achievements of the Canadian Navy past and present, and in the men who inherit and guard its traditions. . . . We were asked to find out what was wrong with the Navy. If, therefore, we have stressed what is wrong it should not be forgotten that a great deal is also overwhelmingly right.

Unfortunately, many people failed to give to these words the importance that was due to them at the time.

Chapter 14

THE DESTROYERS' WAR IN KOREA, 1952-53

John Bovey

HMCS *Crusader* was under my command in the United Nations Special Force from May 1952 to July 1953. The other Royal Canadian Navy destroyers allocated to the Korean theatre during that period were HMC Ships *Nootka, Iroquois, Haida,* and *Athabaskan.* Because the nature of the naval blockade war in the Far East did not lend itself to ship allocation by squadron or division, destroyers of all navies were operated as individual units. Although the destroyers' operational tasks were, with a few exceptions, common to all, our extensive seatime (which amounted to some 68 per cent), combined with constant operations in company with different ships in different areas, limited our view of the war to our own experience. Thus, this chapter is concerned with only one aspect of the Korean conflict: the destroyers' war as seen from the bridge of one of HMC ships.

The so-called "Limited War" in Korea demanded almost unlimited versatility on the part of destroyers. During our thirteen-and-a-half-month commission abroad, we operated on the screen of a carrier, both on the way to and on the west coast of Korea, functioned as part of a major United States Navy hunter/killer group, steamed with the U.S. fast-strike carriers and heavies of Task Force 77, and, perhaps most importantly, operated actively in every individual task unit inshore from Haeju to the Yalu River on the west coast and from the "Bombline" patrol area to Chongjin on the east coast.

It was clearly not a single-purpose war for single-purpose ships. It was only a pity that the enemy had no warships for our guns to tackle and that we had to settle for shore batteries and trains. Trainbusting might seem to be a strange employment for a destroyer, but the ability to catch a train between tunnels, like snap shooting in a shooting gallery, is proof of the ability to fire quickly and accurately. The same ability was required for the suppression of enemy multi-gun batteries that had the temerity to open fire on our ships.

In order to place this glimpse of the destroyers' war in context, it is essential to examine the background to the Korean conflict and the dramatic naval events which occurred during the first year of hostilities. After V-E Day in May 1945, Russian armies overwhelmed the weakened Japanese forces in Manchuria and northern Korea and reoccupied the southern half of Sakhalin Island and the Kuril Islands. The supreme commanders' surrender document, known as "General Order, Number 1," stated, as a matter of convenience only, that Japanese forces north of the 38th parallel of north latitude (which bisects the Korean peninsula) would surrender to the Soviet commander and that forces south of that line would surrender to the American commander. The Russians soon transformed this "convenience line," brought about by the exigencies of war, into the Asian equivalent of the Iron Curtain.

By early December 1949, Allied intelligence estimates concluded that the North Korean government and its Allies were still completely dominated by the Russians and that the latter would resist the existence of any non-communist state on the Korean peninsula. It became apparent, shortly thereafter, that the North Koreans had established a timetable for the invasion of South Korea, and by May 1950, seven North Korean regular army divisions had been identified, backed by as many as one hundred to one hundred and fifty thousand conscripts.

The legendary repose of "the land of the morning calm" was shattered at 0400 on 25 June 1950 by an assault force of approximately one hundred thousand North Koreans. They marched south against the small, ill-equipped army of the Republic of Korea (ROK) and the five-hundred-man American provisional military advisory group, driving their opponents into a beleaguered beachhead at Pusan on the south coast of the peninsula. Meanwhile, on the eve of invasion, the Soviet delegation had walked out of the United Nations Security Council in a fit of pique, thereby forfeiting the veto power which they would almost certainly have used to block the U.N. resolution condemning North Korean aggression. That resolution empowered the Americans to initiate a remarkable scratch sea-lift to South Korea and the famed "Pusan Perimeter" held. Exploiting this foothold, the U.N. Commander-in-Chief, General Douglas MacArthur, began to prepare a daring amphibious outflanking strategy designed to land American troops half way up the west coast of Korea at Inchon.

There were only twenty United States Navy, Royal Navy, and Royal Australian Navy ships in Japanese waters at the time of the North Korean invasion, and ten of these were chance visitors. Thus, the naval war began with only a handful of vessels, plus eleven more that steamed into the battle zone a few days later from Hong Kong and Subic Bay in the Philippines. They were all placed under the United Nations command of the Commander Naval Forces Far East, Vice-Admiral C. Turner Joy, USN. The only naval action of the war took place on 1 July 1950, when the cruisers USS *Juno* and HMS *Jamaica* and the sloop HMS *Black Swan* annihilated four torpedo boats escorting ten trawlers along the east coast. The blockade was established two days later, and the first air strike from the USN-RN Task Force 77 was flown off at dawn that morning by HMS *Triumph* and USS *Valley Forge*.

At home, while the Canadian government vacillated and Parliament was prorogued, the three Esquimalt-based destroyers, which had been scheduled to sail for Europe, were made ready for service in the Far East. When the tremendous job of repairs, storing, ammunitioning, and bringing the vessels up to full war complement was completed, HMC Ships *Cayuga*, *Sioux*, and *Athabaskan* were sailed for Pearl Harbor on 5 July. However, it was not until two hours after their arrival in Pearl that Captain Jeffry V. Brock in *Cayuga* was ordered to place his ships under the operational control of the commander United Nations Forces Korea. Sailing via Kwajalein and Guam in the western Pacific, the group arrived in Sasebo, Japan, on 30 July. Twenty-four hours later, *Athabaskan* was off on her first operational patrol.

MacArthur's concept of landing in force at Inchon was brilliant, but the risks imposed by the restricted waters, the formidable sea walls, the lack of topographical intelligence, and the nature of the landing in the heart of an enemy city were daunting. Full credit must go to those who planned the operation, assembled the invasion fleet, and handled the ships with such boldness. Destroyers and then cruisers moved into the narrow tortuous channels and anchored under the enemy guns in order to eliminate them. By the evening of 15 September, the U.S. 1st Marine Division had stormed over the sea walls and dispersed the North Korean forces. Reinforcements were landed after the enemy had been routed, and within three days North Korean pressure on the Pusan Perimeter broke.

As the American 8th Army swept north, the commander-in-chief proposed to redeploy the 10th Corps and the 1st Marine Division by sea to the Wonsan/Hungnam sector on the east coast. However, the enemy had mined the principal harbours in that area, and so the landing at Wonsan was delayed until 25 October, while minesweepers tried to clear channels through an estimated three thousand mines. Meanwhile, the 1st ROK Corps had taken Wonsan itself and pressed on to Hungnam. Thus, when the 1st Marine Division landed, they were welcomed by rude signs from their friends in the Marine Air Group who had flown in without opposition.

At the same time, the Soviets intensified their efforts to salvage the North

Korean debacle and convinced the Chinese that American troops were intending to cross the Yalu. The Chinese responded by sending "volunteers" into battle on 25 November 1950.

Eleven days later, Captain Brock in HMCS *Cayuga*, with HMC Ships *Athabaskan* and *Sioux*, HMA Ships *Warramunga* and *Bataan*, and the USS *Forrest Royal*, was despatched to provide gunfire support and anti-aircraft fire during the evacuation of Chinnampo on the west coast. The reported urgency of the situation necessitated transit of serpentine channels at night with very few aids to navigation. Despite their Sperry high-definition warning surface (HDWS) radar, two ships became stuck in the mud and were forced to retire after freeing themselves. The remainder completed the hazardous passage only to find that the withdrawal was proceeding apace in a blaze of light, completely undisturbed by the enemy. The evacuation of Chinnampo was followed by similar retirements from Inchon, Wonsan, and Hungnam.

When attacked by a force of no less than seven Chinese divisions, the 1st Marines executed a classic fifty-mile withdrawal from Hungnam, removing not only their wounded but their weapons and equipment. The long rearguard march to the sea was closely supported by marine air groups and the fleet air wings of seven carriers. As the perimeter of the embarkation area contracted, withdrawal was further supported by the Naval Gunfire Group consisting of the battleship USS *Missouri*, two cruisers, eleven destroyers, and three rocket-launching landing ships. The operation was crowned with success as some 200,000 people, 17,500 vehicles, and 350,000 tons of cargo were removed from the beaches.

The retreat of the 8th Army on land, and the redeployment of the marines and 10th Corps by sea, enabled a stand to be made in the vicinity of the 38th parallel. The "stalemate war" began at this stage and protracted peace talks were initiated at Panmunjum. Throughout this period, the Soviet Union and Communist China had refused to acknowledge the existence or legality of the blockade, but neither nation tried to interfere with it. The threat of enemy submarine and torpedo boat activity was ever present, but fortunately none materialized. Enemy air efforts were also inconsequential because of the U.N. command of the sky by the RN and U.S. Marines on the west coast and by the USN on the east coast.

United Nations control of the sea was absolute. The tasks of blockade, defence of captured islands, support of army flanks, and interdiction of coastal communications were hampered only by the geography of the peninsula, enemy shore batteries, and by moored, bottom, and "drifter" mines. The west coast was a network of islands, estuaries, and mud banks swept by thirty-foot tides, while the targets and ports on the precipitous east coast were well defended. Throughout the war, the minesweepers—always in short supply—were constantly sweeping critical areas.

The blockade and interdiction of supply lines has never been a decisive weapon of war, and with the unlimited manpower available to the North Koreans and the Chinese, road and rail repair was rapid. Moreover, we knew that there were vast numbers of replacement trucks and trains in Manchuria. Nevertheless, the aggressive and persistent efforts of naval vessels and aircraft were of continuing importance, since we also knew that the more the navy could do to hurt the enemy, the better our chances would be at the peace table. For all its limitations, the effectiveness of the naval blockade and the enemy failure to oppose it actively opened up both Korean coasts to the application of a bombardment and an interdiction effort with few parallels in naval history. Thus, long after the truce talks began, ships of nine navies continued their bitter struggle along the coastlines of Korea. Ninety-five ships were hit, and an unlucky five were sunk. A blockade assignment could be either a monotonous patrol or an action-packed opportunity, depending on the initiative, ingenuity, and aggressiveness of the individual commanding officer.

I assumed command of *Crusader* on 3 April 1952 at Esquimalt while she was in the usual chaos of refit. Although the refit, storing, and dockyard trials were scheduled to be completed by the end of that month, work continued until we sailed, interspersed by only two four-day periods at sea for trials and work-ups. Eventually, ragged and worn, we sought rest by sailing to war at 1100 on Sunday, 25 May 1952. Internal drills and exercises helped pull the team together on our way out to Pearl Harbor, with the gooney birds providing aiming practice for the gunners. However, once at Pearl, we made up for our lack of expertise by undertaking three full days of sea exercises, including one day of direct and indirect shore spot bombardment.

As *Crusader* had long endurance, I intended to sail via Midway to Yokosuka in Japan, and we had the good fortune of being invited to join Destroyer Squadron 2 and to rendezvous with the commander of Carrier Division 6 in the USS *Bon Homme Richard*.

The commander had decreed that ATP1 (*Allied Tactical Publication 1*: a manoeuvring manual) would be used throughout, since it was to come into force on 1 July, and so we were doubly fortunate to be able to sail in company. The opportunity for intensive exercises on passage was particularly beneficial to the officers of the watch and to the communicators. Day and night shifts of formations were carried out, including exchanging stations on bentline screens, re-orienting bentline screens, acting as plane-guard, executing lifeboat drills, and carrying out highline transfers and fueling at sea from the carrier. Although we did not take on much fuel from her, we had two opportunities to exercise our speed in hooking up, while my piper greeted her with "Open the door, Richard" on his bagpipes.

Crusader was scheduled to top up with fuel from *Bon Homme Richard*, detach one day out of Yokosuka, and proceed directly to Sasebo. However, as the weather deteriorated and the winds climbed to storm force with miserably heavy seas and swells, I was ordered to remain with the group until it entered Yokosuka. There, we fueled, and the next day we sailed for Sasebo. After a quick briefing we sailed at 0700 on 24 June to rendezvous with HMCS *Iroquois* and USS *Bataan* prior to commencing our war operations.

Crusader was part of the United Nations blockading force commanded by the commander Task Force (CTF) 95, who flew his flag in a USN depot ship in Sasebo. He was responsible for both coasts of Korea. The inshore blockade required two to three cruisers, nine to twelve destroyers supported by carrier aircraft, numerous smaller ships, and, on the east coast, a battleship.

The west coast was commanded by commander Task Group (CTG) 95.1, the Royal Navy flag officer, second-in-command, Far East Station, who flew his flag in an RN depot ship in Sasebo or in a cruiser at sea or, on three occasions, in *Crusader*. The usual west coast ship requirement was for three to four destroyers, with the carrier Task Unit (TU) 95.1.1, to back up the Haeju Unit 95.1.5 and to support the three destroyers inshore in the Cho Do/Sok To Unit TU 95.1.2. In addition, one sloop was allocated to the Cho Do/Sok To area and one to the Haeju area as commander Task Unit (CTU), and USN rocket-launching landing ships and ROK anti-aircraft landing ships were allocated to TU 95.1.2 when available, while the cruiser supported all the inshore areas as required.

The east coast mantle of CTG 95.2 was worn by either a USN destroyer squadron commander or the captain of a USN cruiser. However, the policy and ship allocations came from CTF 95 who, for all practical purposes, wore the group command hat himself. The Wonsan Unit on that coast consisted of two destroyers plus a landing ship dock with her brood of minesweeping boats supported by a battleship or cruiser. The "Bombline Unit," stationed off Kosong, usually consisted of one cruiser and one destroyer or one battleship and one destroyer. The Yang-do Unit required four or five destroyers, although sometimes only three were available. In addition, ROK anti-aircraft landing ships patrolled the "Engine Block" and "Tail Light" areas between Chaho and Kosong.

For most of the time I was in the area I was fortunate in having Vice-Admiral R.P. Briscoe, USN, as the commander naval forces Far East (COMNAVFE); Rear-Admiral C.E. Olsen, USN, as CTF 95; Rear-Admiral E.G.A. Clifford, RN, as CTG 95.1; and Rear-Admiral R.F. Hickey, USN, as CTF 77. All of these flag officers were most helpful to *Crusader* and always receptive to my recommendations.

Crusader's main assets were her 4.5-inch guns, her sea-keeping qualities, her speed, and her long endurance. Her principal deficiencies were the lack of an efficient air warning radar and the lack of electronic counter-measures (ECM) equipment. Her operations (ops.) room was miniscule, but after a few minor modifications, it became far more efficient for radar navigation and bombardment gunnery than the relative ballrooms of later ships.

Our work-up had been hopelessly inadequate, and so our main preoccupation in the early days was in evolving and perfecting organizations and procedures to cope with operational situations. None of these situations were particularly difficult or, in isolation, unusual, but the composite requirements could not be appreciated while we were at home. All in all we forged a first-class team; while perhaps the heaviest loads fell on my First Lieutenant, John Husher, my Navigator, Bill Stuart, my Gunnery Officer, Freddie Copas, and my Engineer Officer, Terry Keohane, the load was shared by everyone and they all performed splendidly.

The ops. room was the command and navigation centre in every phase of the war, not only for tactical manoeuvring but also for bombardment and inshore navigation. I required that the radar ranges and bearings be taken by the officer of the watch (ops.) himself when we were inshore and that all navigational fixes be plotted on a chart. I knew that some ships used radar plotters for radar interpretation and bombardment maps for navigation, but I preferred to have the responsible officer do it himself, for he alone knew which part of a headland he had used for a fix. The officers of the watch alternated between the operations room and the bridge with the "con" (control) exercised by the officer of the watch (ops.) but always through the officer of the watch (bridge), who had the ultimate responsibility for using his "mark two eyeballs."

Our gunnery was awful when we first went inshore. Indeed, in one frustrated moment I recall turning to my principal control officer and saying, "Hold the bloody guns still on the beam and I'll swing the ship." But after some changes in personnel, and after a major design fault in the Mark 6 gunnery director had been overcome, we were suddenly able to hit first, hit hard, and keep hitting.

It soon became apparent that normal gunnery procedures were far too slow to meet the requirement for opening bombardment fire immediately. As a consequence, a modified "alarm" system was devised. The fire control room, known in destroyers as the "TS," and the director were closed up, and the guns were loaded with high explosive direct action shells, but the electrical firing circuits, known as "interceptors," remained open. The TS was kept up to date with target range by Sperry HDWS radar as well as the target's height and predicted movement, if applicable. It was then only necessary to give the order, for example, "Alarm train south," for the gun captains to close the interceptors and for the gunnery control officer in the director to open fire with instantaneous results. Modified versions of this procedure were arrived at for firing against aircraft and for cruising with only B and X mountings closed up. Experience also dictated that our original outfit of 4.5-inch ammunition was deficient by about 50 per cent. It was increased accordingly. We also painted the 4.5's with polished black engine enamel since prolonged firing caused the light grey paint to blister.

As fueling, ammunitioning, replenishing at sea, or transferring personnel, stores, or mail by jackstay occurred over one hundred and fifty times in just under three hundred days at sea, these evolutions (except for ammunitioning) were carried out by the watch on deck and ready-use gear storage was essential. One day, when we had had as many as eight transfers, I flew the flag hoist, "DESIG T-A-X-I," when closing the carrier. On another occasion, we ammunitioned from one ship on the starboard side while, at the same time, refueling from a second on the port side.

Special procedures were instituted for boarding parties for capturing small junks with a motor cutter constantly stocked with arms and supplies. We also kept portable automatic weapons and hand grenades stored on the high points of the ship for use by a "repel boarding" party, detailed to cover the vulnerable moment which occurred when larger craft were brought alongside.

Variety was the spice of life, and on one occasion when HMAS *Anzac* had relieved *Crusader* as CTU 95.1.2 in the Cho Do/Sok To area, the commander Task Group 95.1, who was flying his flag in HMS *Newcastle*, decided that the enemy and sea conditions were ideal for full-power trials, which he carried out with *Crusader* in company. Following this, he decreed that *Newcastle* and *Crusader* should replenish while underway. It was an interesting exercise during which the ships turned through 180 degrees while the Royal Fleet Auxiliary *Wave Chief* kept station on *Newcastle* and *Crusader* kept station on *Wave Chief*. On completing replenishment, *Crusader* joined the carrier, and the commander Task Group 95.1, who had flown from *Newcastle* to the USS *Badoeng Strait* by helicopter, transferred his flag almost immediately to HMCS *Crusader*, joining by jackstay, before we proceeded inshore.

Life in the "Corpen Club" (the carrier screen on the west coast which derived its name from an alteration of course pennant) was a bit prosaic even when I was screen commander, a task which rotated. We managed, however, to enliven our routine by daily transfers and efforts to ensure that the ship was second to none in manoeuvres, communications, and exercises. In spite of our lack of efficient air warning radar, our type 293 radar proved itself when *Crusader* took control of the combat air patrol for a full day while repairs were being carried out on the carrier's radar. This certainly gingered things up a good deal!

We kept a list of carriers, in order of merit, in the operations room, and we had a few amusing incidents, such as the one precipitated by USS

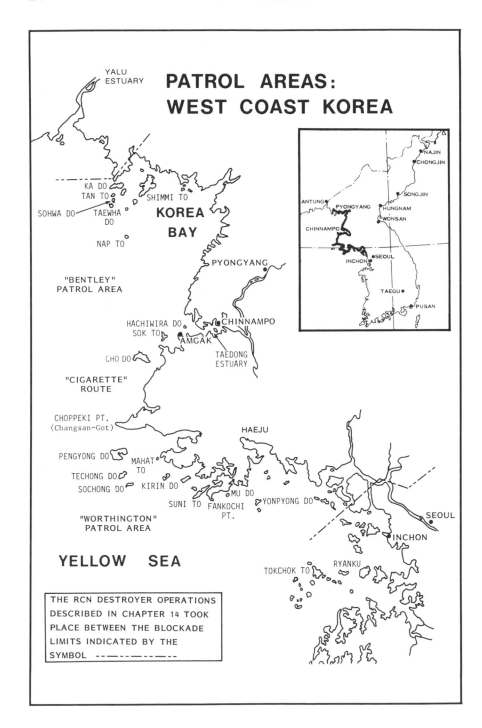

PATROL AREAS:
WEST COAST KOREA

YALU ESTUARY

KA DO
TAN TO
SOHWA DO
TAEWHA DO
SHIMMI TO
KOREA BAY
NAP TO

"BENTLEY" PATROL AREA

PYONGYANG

HACHIWIRA DO.
SOK TO
AMGAK
CHINNAMPO
TAEDONG ESTUARY

CHO DO

"CIGARETTE" ROUTE

CHOPPEKI PT.
(Changsan-Got)

HAEJU

PENGYONG DO
MAHAT TO
TECHONG DO
SOCHONG DO
KIRIN DO
SUNI TO
FANKOCHI PT.
MU DO
YONPYONG DO
SEOUL

"WORTHINGTON" PATROL AREA

INCHON

YELLOW SEA

TOKCHOK TO
RYANKU

THE RCN DESTROYER OPERATIONS
DESCRIBED IN CHAPTER 14 TOOK
PLACE BETWEEN THE BLOCKADE
LIMITS INDICATED BY THE
SYMBOL -- -- -- -- -- -- --

NAJIN
CHONGJIN
SONGJIN
ANTUNG
PYONGYANG
HUNGNAM
WONSAN
CHINNAMPO
INCHON
SEOUL
TAEGU
PUSAN

Bataan. Instead of using ATP 1 from the start of the patrol, *Bataan* decided to use the U.S. Fleet (USF) manoeuvring manual until the moment the latter became officially obsolete. At the magic hour, HMCS *Iroquois* (commanded by Captain W.M. "Bill" Landymore) was given a station using the USF method, and almost immediately thereafter, *Crusader* was given a station using ATP 1. We both wound up to stationing speed and found ourselves heading for the same spot!

Another incident, involving a set of teeth which was sent over from the aircraft carrier HMS *Glory* in the bottom of one of the large jackstay transfer bags, resulted in the following exchange of messages:

> To *Crusader* from *Glory*—
> We sent a bag with teeth intact,
> You sent it back still fully packed.
> By next event we'll try by chopper,
> Flown by our most expert dropper.
> Please place your Coxswain underneath,
> Mouth wide open to catch his teeth.
>
> To *Glory* from *Crusader*—
> We're sorry that the bag unpacked,
> Returned to *Glory* all intact.
> My Coxswain, poised as seems most proper,
> Mouth open wide will wait for your chopper.
> With many thanks your dentist's due,
> We'll try to stick them in with glue.

The inshore areas were all different and gave rise to different activities. However, they did have two common denominators: preventing the enemy from attacking the islands that we held offshore and enforcing the ban on any enemy movements whatsoever by water. Our Cho Do/Sok To blockade and island defence time was spent in shifting shallows, narrow channels, five-fathom tides, winter storms, and summer fogs. Owing to the strong tides, we were obliged to anchor much of the time when we were giving fire support to the islands, firing with shore spot on call. When we anchored, we broke our cable and attached a Dan buoy with the buoy wire stopped up to the guardrail, so that we could slip immediately if taken under fire.

Our prime task in the Cho Do/Sok To area was to provide suppression fire on the enemy guns on the Amgak peninsula, which used to bother Sok To and Hachiwira Do, the guerilla base in the Taedong estuary. As these were indirect bombardments, we took advantage of shore fire patrol parties, using the U.S. Marines whenever possible, or our own landing party if necessary. During the day, bombarding ships were distributed about the anchorage, but as the war progressed, this practice became increasingly hazardous because of enemy counterfire. Several of us were straddled, and once when an American rocket-launching landing ship was hit, there were five casualties. Between the islands and the enemy-held mainland, our ships spread out at night to gain the best possible protection. Some nights we would see a light and have a pot shot at it with one of our guns. Other nights we would lie still—silent sentinels.

Weeds and jellyfish were menacing when they got sucked into our condenser intakes. This happened to me just as I was passing an active battery, well before dawn. I took a short-cut through a very narrow channel, but before I realized it, I was down to about four knots and caught in a whirlpool. I had visions of going aground only three thousand yards from the enemy guns. By using full-speed engine orders (with slow-speed results), I managed to extricate myself. I am told that as my Chief Engine Room Artificer, "Spike" Ewald, came up to the bridge to inform me that four knots was the maximum, he took one look at the land under the forefoot and dove down the engine room hatch in one leap from the bridge. We christened the little beach where we almost came to rest, Crusader Bay.

The United States Air Force tactical command on Cho Do kept our anti-aircraft gunners on their toes with air raid warnings. We were usually plagued by MIG 15 fighters during the day. The Soviet planes were too high to bother us, but they were a nuisance for our carrier aircraft. The latter shot down two MIG's; an RN Sea Fury claiming one and a U.S. Marine Corsair the other. We had some strange raids which came into our area at night and orbited to the northwest without taking any offensive action. One was shot down by a U.S. Marine night-fighter. On another occasion we were able to open fire while stationed north of Sok To. A heavy overcast forced the enemy aircraft to come stooging in at low altitude. We engaged them with time-mechanical fuses when they were over friendly islands and with variable-time fuses when they were in the clear. If these aircraft were trying to attack Sok To, they failed because the only bombs that were released fell on the north end of the island where no one lived. At one moment during the raid, I ordered a shift of target and heard my gunnery direction officer (blind) order "Shift target left"; an instruction followed by the classic "The other left you bloody fool!" Although we did not clip any enemy wings, we did manage to drive them off.

All radar contacts were investigated, whether we were at anchor or underway—often without tangible results. One night we picked up an object on radar which, on closer inspection, looked as if it were a floating mine. A boarding party was sent away to investigate and discovered that it was a floating oil drum with no offensive attachments. On another night, shut in by fog, I closed a radar contact and manoeuvred *Crusader* alongside a junk which we illuminated with our twenty-inch signal lamp. Only two men were seen, waving frantically with white handkerchiefs; but a burst of bren-gun fire over their heads produced quite a crowd. The occupants were shepherded aboard, and a last-minute check of the junk was carried out by the officer in charge of the boarding party. Poking around with my dress sword (suitable only for wedding cakes but which he carried to impress the enemy as they were more afraid of naked steel than guns) he ran the blade through the deckboards only to hear a frightened "Ya ya ya" from a woman hidden in the bilge. She was chased aboard *Crusader*. Later, my first lieutenant reported to me, rather ambiguously I thought, that there were "eleven male prisoners under guard in the laundry and one woman in the duplex pistol room with one man on her."

Not infrequently junks were captured. Only one was in such bad condition that it could not be towed; but others could be towed up to eighteen knots. Some were unarmed, some were heavily armed, and a few had passes in consonance with our intelligence messages. Whenever identification was dubious, we turned the junk and its passengers over to the local guerrillas and let them deal with the problem. We ended up with a small arsenal of captured weapons and, on one occasion, a pound of heroin which we dumped overboard. Canadian destroyers captured a good many junks during the war, but the "junk gold prize" went to HMCS *Nootka*. She successfully engaged a hand-propelled mine-laying junk, captured its crew, and bagged a couple of Russian A-1 magnetic mines.

The result of this engagement was that the channel on the west coast had to be re-swept. The hard-working sweepers were always busy and required gunfire support. As sweepers like to make several passes back and forth over a mile or two of the channel at a time, I found that the best way of supporting them was to anchor in a swept area about half-way along the "patch" and give the shore batteries a few rounds to let them know we were there.

Patrols were carried out periodically to the Yalu River estuary to help our coastal blockade and to lend support to the South Korean-held island of Nap To. On our way there, we used to fire a few harassing rounds at the North Korean islands. In fact, we passed Sohwa Do and Taehwa Do so closely that we were able to bring our 40-mm and bren guns to bear. Once I decided to fire on the island of Tan To across from the southern tip of Shimmi To in the hope that the Chinese, thinking that their guns on Shimmi To had been captured, might fire back on their own batteries, starting a little internecine warfare.

As time went on, enemy activity increased, and it became routine for a "Whitbread" destroyer (named in honour of the British beer because RN warships had customarily patrolled the area) to be designated on a nightly, and often daily, basis. Enemy batteries became quite active, and HMNZS *Hawea*—a ship with no main armament aft—was straddled and followed out to about twelve thousand yards. On one of our runs inshore, we provided fire support for a large U.S.-led guerrilla raid landing near Mahat To. With aircraft spotting provided by HMS *Ocean*, we opened fire on a village containing North Korean troops and anti-aircraft guns. Later, we fired seventy-eight rounds in direct fire, with the CTU in HMNZS *Rotoiti* spotting from the flank. We ceased fire when *Rotoiti* reported the gunsites destroyed and the troops dispersed.

On another occasion, our Chief of the Naval Staff, Vice-Admiral Rollo Mainguy, RCN, arrived by helicopter from HMCS *Haida*. We showed him action immediately, as we were ordered to destroy a force of North Korean troops and two anti-aircraft guns on a small hillock on Suni To. As the approach was restricted, I anchored at fourteen thousand yards and opened fire with air-spotting from U.S. Marine Corsairs. The target was soon wreathed in smoke and large secondary explosions were observed. Our spotter aircraft reported that the gun emplacements had received direct hits and that the enemy troops had scattered.

Three times on the west coast we were fortunate enough to be in the right place at the right time to silence batteries that had engaged our ships. The first time was while supporting USS *Condor*, which was check-sweeping south of Cho Do. A single enemy gun opened fire on the American vessel just after dark. We opened fire immediately with our 4.5-inch main armament and 40-mm guns. The range was so close that our barrels were actually *depressed*, and the enemy area was completely obliterated. The second time was when HMAS *Anzac* was under fire by four guns and straddled repeatedly. *Anzac* returned the fire, slipped her cable, and tried to open the range. Being restricted by the channels and having no guns aft she was hard pressed. I increased to thirty knots, rounded the end of Cho Do a minute or two later, and opened fire at a range of eighteen thousand yards. Our first salvos silenced the enemy battery, but we kept on firing and closing the range until *Anzac* got clear. The third time was near Haeju. When passing south of Mu Do island, we received a "Help" message from an ROK minesweeper which was being attacked by four guns opposite the island. I altered course directly toward the guns, increased to thirty knots and opened fire with the forward mounts at eighteen thousand yards. Although our first rounds caused the battery to cease fire, we continued firing while closing the range. When the minesweeper was clear, I came about and continued fire with our after 4.5's, keeping the battery suppressed until I had opened to twelve thousand yards.

About midway through our tour of duty in Korean waters, it became evident that our anti-submarine skills were getting rusty. I knew that a U.S. hunter/killer group was in the area and requested that *Crusader* be allowed to take part in a major exercise. We joined USS *Epperson* (commander escort Destroyer Division 12) off Okinawa, and he allocated the submarine

USS *Sterlet* to *Crusader* for a two-hour session designed to help us hone our skills. In the afternoon we were joined by the submarine USS *Remora* and the remainder of the division, to practise single-ship and duet attacks.

Two days later Task Group 96.7, consisting of a carrier, five destroyers, and three destroyer escorts, did a full-scale defended sortie from Buckner Bay, Okinawa, with the screen augmented by local patrol craft, helicopters, and patrol aircraft, while the USAF Thunder Jets flew combat air patrol. After our sortie, we carried out various hunter/killer exercises for a further five days.

Crusader's polished gunnery warfare organization required rapid revision to cope with these anti-submarine exercises. The first few hours were rather hectic as the multiplicity of voice circuits in our small operations room resulted in considerable confusion. However, we soon settled down, and during the run to Yokosuka, we were fortunate enough to be included in extra exercises involving attacks by two submarines: one of the target submarines recorded a hit by our "Hedgehog" projectiles (the equivalent of a "probable" or perhaps a "kill").

The Korean operations provided a strange mixture: face-to-face fighting with enemy troops, guns, and aircraft; hunter/killer exercises; the (somewhat abbreviated) ceremony of receiving on board our chief of the Naval Staff from Ottawa and going into action with him; and the peacetime routine at Sasebo, Kure, and Yokosuka. When we were alongside in these ports, we fitted the Jack and Ensign staffs, replaced the rubber muzzle covers with ships badge tampions, champhered up the bright-work to a golden hue, and burnished the steel gun muzzles. In harbour, the hands shifted into night clothing: their blue uniforms minus the jumper (at sea, night clothing was clean dungarees). Both at sea and alongside the officers changed for dinner. Engaging the enemy throughout the night, sometimes led to the rather unusual sight of the first lieutenant taking "Hands Fall-In" at 0800 while still dressed for dinner. *Crusader*'s pentathlon team won the meet in Sasebo organized for Commonwealth ships in port—the depot ship, a cruiser, and four others. We provided one hundred men for the ship, a cruiser, and four others. We provided one hundred men for the coronation ceremonies for Queen Elizabeth II on board HMS *Ocean*. And in Yokohama we sent a funeral party to the Commonwealth cemetery for the one officer and five men killed in action off Songjin in HMCS *Iroquois*.

To return for a moment to the pomp and circumstance aspects of the war, Vice-Admiral Mainguy transferred his flag to HMCS *Haida* (Commander Dunn Lantier) after visiting the commander of the Canadian destroyers Far East (Captain J.C. Reed) in HMCS *Athabaskan*. Later he transferred his flag to *Crusader*, and as I have already described, *Crusader* wore his flag while we subdued the enemy guns—undoubtedly the first and only occasion on which a chief of the Naval Staff has personally engaged the enemy. After this, we took him on a tour of the island defence areas and entered Sasebo harbour with due ceremony—guard and bugle (though no band). After three days, we sailed on a fast patrol through the Inland Sea of Japan, passing HMS *Birmingham* (who paraded a royal marine guard and band for the CNS), and entered Kure with appropriate attention to ceremonial.

On another occasion, we were in Kure with an RN carrier and three RN destroyers during the visit of the First Sea Lord, Admiral of the Fleet Sir Rhoderick McGrigor, to his ships in Korea. He was accompanied by the Commander-in-Chief Far East Station, Admiral Sir Guy Russell, RN, and by the Flag Officer, Second in Command Far East Station, Rear-Admiral Clifford. The First Sea Lord also visited *Crusader*, being received on board by a guard and, after inspecting the ship and the ship's company, spoke to us at divisions. The following morning Rear-Admiral Clifford, as CTG 95.1, transferred his flag to *Crusader* and, with the First Sea Lord and the commander-in-chief, joined *Crusader* for passage down the Inland Sea.

We were always proud to wear the flag of CTG 95.1 and this time to be selected to have these Royal Navy flag officers on board as our guests— especially so as there were RN ships in Kure. As we sailed, with the Royal Marine Guard and Band paraded as a farewell to their First Sea Lord, I must admit I wondered whether this was not an occasion without precedent for one of Her Majesty's Canadian ships.

Most of *Crusader*'s three- and four-week patrols on Korea's east coast were in the Northern, "Windshield" and Yang Do Defence Unit areas. I was appointed in tactical command of these areas as CTU 95.2.2 for my last two patrols. The eastern coast of North Korea is generally steep-to and there is a southerly set of about one knot—just enough to ensure that "floater" mines drifted down upon us. We encountered three, blowing up one, sinking another, and breathlessly missing the third, which passed down the ship's side one night in the fog.

When I completed my first stint as commander of the task unit, I sent my report to CTF 95. The admiral and his staff seemed pleased with some of the revised orders for the task unit that I had submitted, along with recommendations for other changes. It was gratifying to learn later that each of my main recommendations was to be adopted. I suggested, among other things, that target identification at night or in fog could be improved by taking photographs of the coast with a telephoto lens and, at the same moment, taking pictures of the high-definition radar scan. These pictures could then be combined with forty-five degree oblique and vertical air-photographs in a target-identification atlas. This was agreed to, and a team from the Atsugi U.S. Naval Air Station arrived on board by helicopter. They brought with them an enormous aerial-photography outfit with a

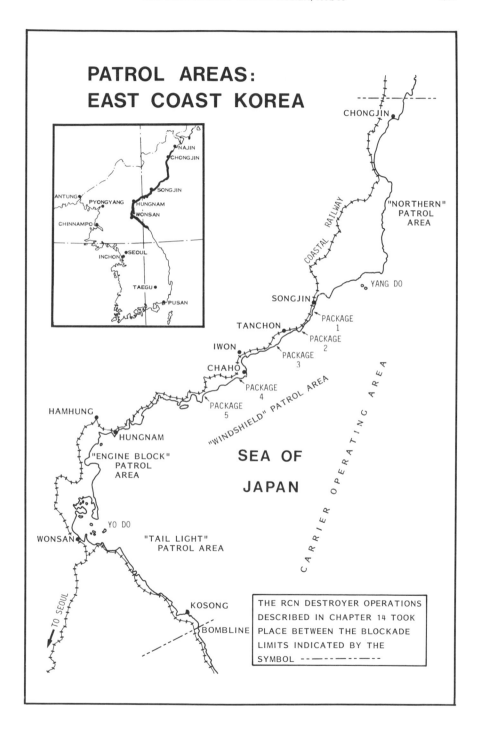

PATROL AREAS:
EAST COAST KOREA

NAJIN
CHONGJIN
SONGJIN
HUNGNAM
WONSAN
ANTUNG
PYONGYANG
CHINNAMPO
INCHON
SEOUL
TAEGU
PUSAN

CHONGJIN

COASTAL RAILWAY

"NORTHERN" PATROL AREA

YANG DO

SONGJIN

PACKAGE 1

TANCHON

PACKAGE 2

IWON

PACKAGE 3

CHAHO

PACKAGE 4

PACKAGE 5

"WINDSHIELD" PATROL AREA

CARRIER OPERATING AREA

HAMHUNG

HUNGNAM

"ENGINE BLOCK" PATROL AREA

SEA OF

JAPAN

YO DO

WONSAN

"TAIL LIGHT" PATROL AREA

TO SEOUL

KOSONG

BOMBLINE

THE RCN DESTROYER OPERATIONS
DESCRIBED IN CHAPTER 14 TOOK
PLACE BETWEEN THE BLOCKADE
LIMITS INDICATED BY THE
SYMBOL -- -- -- -- -- --

lens about one metre long. We proceeded up the coast via the "Tail Light," "Engine Block," and "Windshield" areas, taking pictures as we went. The result, when collated, proved extremely useful. The final *Target Identification Atlas*, with chart dimensions and four eight-inch by ten-inch photographs per page, was distributed to all task unit commanders.

On our way up the coast we covered Wonsan, and the commander Task Unit 95.2.1 requested that we have a go at a battery known as "Hairless Joe." This battery had been active the day before, shelling Yo Do (the U.S. controlled island known as "Brass Hat") as usual. Entering a crossfire zone like this seemed rather like putting one's neck in a noose, but we were lucky. Perhaps our accurate fire made the enemy keep his head down, or more likely he was taking the day off.

All these patrols were part of the Siege of Wonsan, and what was remarkable about this strategic victory was that a few marines and a handful of ships tied down an estimated sixty thousand enemy troops that might otherwise have been used as a counter-invasion force against the American, British, Canadian, Australian, and ROK soldiers of the Allied armies. This was the strategy; it remained for us to address the tactics.

Some tactics were timeless: for example, if your guns outrange those of the enemy, then engage the enemy outside his maximum range. Other tactics were as new as yesterday: for instance, "Alarm train southbound" must have shocked the ghosts of our gunnery ancestors long since departed.

"The Trainbusters Club" consisted of a select fraternity of American, British, Australian, and Dutch destroyers. *Crusader* joined the club in the autumn of 1952, as the first Canadian member, with a modest score of two freight cars (the locomotive having escaped into a tunnel). The two cars had been cut off cleanly enough by our 4.5's in local control, but I soon came to the conclusion that if we were going to excel in this activity we needed specialized teamwork. So, when the next opportunity arose a few days later, the whole gunnery action-team manned the armament. Within six minutes of *Crusader* closing to three thousand yards, the guns spoke. The first two broadsides raked the train and stopped it dead. Again, the locomotive unhooked itself and disappeared into a tunnel. But we still had fifteen cars left. We worked these over, car by car, with spectacular fires and explosions. I shifted fire then to the shore-battery sites at either end of "Package 2" (this particular target) and closed the range to give our 40-mm crews a chance to have a go. USS *De Haven* joined us to help complete the destruction. We withdrew to ten thousand yards at dawn, and CTF 77 sent in four Corsairs and four Skyraiders. The Skyraiders found our locomotive at the bottom of an embankment and reported the gun-sites abandoned. We fired a few farewell broadsides and departed.

Having four destroyers at my disposal during my last patrol as commander Task Unit 95.2.2, I turned over command and went off to train watch at "Package 3," just south of Tanchon. Lying quietly twenty-eight hundred yards off the track, we sighted our prey, another fifteen-car train. We opened fire, and it ground to a halt. But again, although I was certain the locomotive was hit, it uncoupled and ducked into the tunnel. We spent the remainder of the night smashing the cars sufficiently to prevent easy removal. Aircraft arrived at first light and demolished another four cars while we withdrew to ten thousand yards. The locomotive stuck its nose out of the tunnel at noon, whereupon I increased to thirty knots and opened fire, but it managed to retreat just in time.

That evening we sighted another train further inland. I closed again at thirty knots to skirt the inner edge of the swept channel—about three thousand yards off the coast. We opened fire at fourteen thousand yards— two cars were hit, and the train was stopped. Another train appeared, and fire was shifted to this one. It too was stopped. Our score: two more trains damaged and burning. As we were firing at the trains, the officer of the watch sighted a floating mine and we sank it with our close-range weapons. Simultaneously, another train was sighted close to Tanchon, and we turned to attack it. However, since it was at extreme range we obtained no hits, and so we returned to complete the destruction of our earlier prey. Four more cars were strewn across the track, two burning with brilliant orange flames, much to the delight of the ship's company. Morale was high. We had destroyed more trains than any other ship in any navy. *Haida* and *Athabaskan* joined the Trainbusters Club shortly thereafter, with scores of two trains each.

The enemy's guns were almost invariably sited at the mouth of a cave, and this fact necessitated immediate, accurate, and devastating fire on our part since they were withdrawn instantly when fired upon. There were about seven caves per gun, and so a battery had to be completely inundated with shellfire unless we observed the flash from a particular weapon. These emplacements were not only extremely resilient but easily repaired, and even the fire of eight-inch and sixteen-inch guns or airborne rockets and bombs failed to eliminate them permanently.

When we engaged targets such as power stations, storage sheds, or railyards in daylight and were likely to come under crossfire, my policy was: to keep outside ten thousand yards; to approach so that my guns would bear as long as possible; to have a second ship responsible for battery fire suppression while I tackled the main target; on completion to plot a course to alter to seaward with our ships turning together through less than ninety degrees (so as to be able to withdraw quickly if taken under fire); to exchange the roles of ships on the second run; and to carry out the second approach on a different course. We were flexible, of course, and if we sighted a worthwhile target in daylight we would force on, preferably at high speed regardless of enemy fire, while trying not to employ any specific tactic more than once.

One tactic, that of supporting our own troops in a landing, had to be brushed up from previous experience when *Sioux* and *Algonquin* had bombarded the Normandy beaches during the D-Day invasion. One night, we supported a combined U.S./ROK intelligence-gathering raid commanded by a U.S. marine major who looked like the late Hollywood actor, Wallace Beery. When the major was just off the beach, he discovered that the enemy had mustered a welcoming committee of about seven hundred, so he called for immediate fire within a hundred yards of his position. We were lying four thousand yards offshore, and as the first round (called the "warmer") is unreliable, we had visions of a rather messy scene when we opened fire with our main armament. However, the major reported that the closest enemy had been decimated and their remnants scattered.

Experience revealed that a light after dusk might indicate battery activity, since the enemy stored their ammunition underground. Consequently, when we were cruising at night, we loaded one of our forward 4.5's with starshell and an after 4.5 with high-explosive. The officer of the watch was given authority to open fire on any light. One evening, my gunner, Lieutenant R.E. "Dicky" Dorken, who was officer of the watch on the bridge, sighted a light, and inadvertently fired a starshell set to safe. Instead of rocketing skyward and illuminating the landscape with a blinding glare, the starshell did not detonate until it hit the enemy battery where ammunitioning must have been in progress. The result was a splendid secondary explosion which was still visible when I reached the bridge from my sea cabin.

Another occasion highlighted the age-old axiom of using sufficient force to achieve the objective. When I was CTU at Yang Do, I found myself, as the result of a serious shortage of ships, with three vessels instead of five—and one of my ships had only 3-inch guns. Accordingly, I asked CTF 95 for at least one more destroyer. He replied, "Regret no ships available." But the next night, to my delight and astonishment, a battleship escort hove into view. She was the enormous battlewagon USS *Missouri*: a vessel which we used to say fired Cadillacs since each of her sixteen-inch projectiles approximated a Cadillac in weight and cost. Never in my wildest dreams had I envisaged support from "The Mighty Mo" (CTF 77). I learned later that CTF 77 had heard of my request and had responded to it personally as he was heading north anyway.

We joined the "Windchasers Club" shortly after destroying the trains at Tanchon. In doing so we actually detached from U.N. Task Force 95 and joined U.S. Task Force 77 (whose aircraft had supported us in the Trainbusters Club). The Windchasers Club comprised three "Essex"-class carriers, one battleship, one cruiser, and twelve destroyers—USN ships under USN command supporting, but not under, the United Nations commander-in-chief. Our appetite for operating with fast carriers had been whetted by an incident that had occurred while cruising across the Sea of Japan on passage to Yang Do. My operations room had noted that CTF 77 had lost contact with his aircraft, although we could read both clearly. We offered to relay messages and for several hours acted as a radio-link between Task Force 77 and three major airborne strikes. All of the U.S. aircraft returned safely to their carriers, thanks to the sterling efforts of my Direction Officer, Lieutenant Eric Jones, and our full team of radar plotters. Thus, when we joined Task Force 77, it was gratifying to be welcomed by the commander himself, and to be congratulated on our trains. We all knew that *Crusader* was privileged to be recommended to this exclusive USN club.

As strikes were being flown off or landed on constantly from one or other of the carriers, the force steamed at twenty-seven knots most of the time. It was fortunate, therefore, that we were an experienced team since all of the destroyer manoeuvres had to be carried out instantaneously, precisely, and at thirty knots. Indeed, at one moment we even had to bulge the screen at full speed! The competition between destroyers was keen and we had to take on fuel every second day. We closed the tanker at twenty-eight knots, dropped to twelve with astern steam, and stayed put. There was certainly never a dull moment. The heavies replenished every four days in a smooth manoeuvre, combing the tracks of the service force, with the destroyers refueling and forming a bentline screen ahead.

We detached after a week with the fast carriers, and the ship's company was delighted when CTF 77 went out of his way once again to compliment us on our performance. This fact was highlighted by our designation as guide of the fleet for the twelve hours prior to our departure. On detaching from the task force, I was instructed to proceed to the "Bombline" patrol area on the east coast to relieve the USS *St. Paul*. Because she was an 8-inch heavy cruiser, I thought that there must be a mistake, but the message was correct, and off we sped at thirty knots in the general direction. While I had a full set of operation orders for the unit, I had no information available as to the actual location of the Bombline. Fortunately, I had been reading a *National Geographic* and remembered a little two-inch by four-inch map in the corner of one page. I sent for the magazine, and there was the Bombline and the nearby town of Kosong. The rest was easy.

The aim of the Bombline Unit was to give gunfire support to the 1st ROK Corps, and *Crusader* was manoeuvred to within two to three thousand yards off its right flank. It was, in fact, a most unreal sight, rather like looking at a sand table model of a war. As the land rose up from the sea to the hills inland, we could see quite clearly our own lines and the enemy lines, our own artillery and the enemy artillery, our own patrols and the enemy patrols. Fire missions were called for intermittently, and we demolished bunkers and cut trenches at ranges of from six to fourteen thousand yards and at heights of two to eight hundred feet with the aid of shore-spotting by the U.S. Marines.

In my effort to hit the enemy aggressively where it hurts most, I was fortunate to have a team which remained together for fifteen months and to have the right ship in the right place at the right time. We did our best to exploit HMCS *Crusader*'s superior speed, endurance, sea-keeping qualities, gun range, and weight of broadside to the full.

Korea was a gunnery war. Our ability to open fire instantly, accurately, and at long range was of paramount importance in that conflict as was our ability to close targets at high speed. The enemy knew which guns were effective, which ships had no guns, or no effective guns aft, and, above all, which ships fired accurately. Events proved that accurate counter-battery fire, commencing with the first salvo, almost always meant that the enemy pulled back and laid low. Conversely, inaccurate fire or guns that went out of sector, encouraged the enemy to fire for effect themselves.

While it seems relatively unlikely that Canada will be drawn into another war like the one in Korea, the possibility cannot be discounted. In the event, the speed, endurance and effective weaponry of Canadian warships would be of the utmost importance, and it might well be that future *Crusader*s would be called upon, once again, to demonstrate their worth by accurate, effective, and versatile firepower.

Chapter 15

CANADIAN NAVAL AVIATION, 1915-69

Stuart Soward

The RCN began recruiting aircrew for the Royal Naval Air Service (RNAS) in April 1915. More than six hundred Canadians joined the RNAS, and they became the potential nucleus of the future Canadian Naval Air Service (CNAS). Among these recruits were such men as L.S. Breadner, W.A. Curtis, R. Leckie, and H. Edwards, all of whom would later rise to the highest ranks of the Royal Canadian Air Force. Another, better-known, Canadian was Raymond Collishaw, a much-decorated World War I ace in the RNAS who rose to become an air vice-marshal in the RAF and retired toward the end of World War II following a distinguished career.

As the submarine war took on a fresh intensity in the spring of 1917, it became apparent that newly constructed U-boats would be able to take a heavy toll of shipping off the East Coast of Canada. Consequently, the RNAS proposed that two air stations, with a total of thirty-four seaplanes, be established at Halifax and Sydney, Nova Scotia. However, this proposal was turned down because of cost and a lack of manpower.

The RNAS suffered a major setback in April 1918, the effects of which lingered for nearly twenty years and had an almost disastrous impact on the Royal Navy. This reverse sprang from the amalgamation of the RNAS and the Royal Flying Corps (RFC) to form the Royal Air Force. While this amalgamation eliminated the private war being fought by the Admiralty and War Office, it left the Royal Navy without any authority to maintain an effective Fleet Air Arm (RNFAA). Instead, the RN was obliged to operate obsolescent and unsuitable RAF aircraft throughout much of the inter-war period. The only bright side in all of this was development in aircraft carrier design, particularly with regard to small seaplane carriers and catapult launching. It was not until 1937 that the Admiralty regained control of its Fleet Air Arm.

Unrestricted German U-boat warfare led the cabinet to approve measures in May for the creation of a Canadian Naval Air Service that was first proposed at an Allied naval conference in Washington on 20 April 1918. The CNAS became the Royal Canadian Naval Air Service (RCNAS) on 5 September, and it was responsible for operating air stations and squadrons of seaplanes on the East Coast.[1] It is ironic that the Canadian naval air service was suggested only three weeks after the demise, on 31 March, of the RNAS, which had been Canada's major source of support in naval aviation. Henceforth, the Admiralty played a reduced role in the development of the Canadian Naval Air Service, although an ex-RNAS officer, Lieutenant-Colonel J.T. Cull, RAF, provided the infant service with invaluable advice. Indeed the future looked promising, particularly in view of the large number of Canadians with wartime flying experience who might be expected to join the RCNAS. Conditions of service and pay details were established, including the payment of a risk allowance of a dollar a day, but with the signing of the armistice in November 1918, all plans for the development of the new air branch came to a halt.[2] The Minister of the Naval Service, C.C. Ballantyne, stated in a memorandum to his deputy that the RCNAS had not been abolished but merely discontinued until such time as the government decided on a policy with respect to a permanent air service.[3]

The following year Admiral of the Fleet Viscount Jellicoe of Scapa advised the Canadian government that he saw the future threat to Canada as coming from Japan. To meet this threat he proposed four Canadian fleet programmes to include aircraft torpedo squadrons, flying boat squadrons, and aircraft carriers. Nothing came of his proposals, but Jellicoe's vision later proved to be remarkably prophetic.

Finally, in 1924, the formation of a Canadian air service was approved and the RCAF created. During its first eight years, the RCAF was primarily employed as the government's civil airline. Gradually it developed a distinctive military character, and one of its responsibilities was to operate shore-based maritime aircraft in coastal patrol. However, naval aviation was given no place in the national defence scheme and was doomed to remain inactive.

Considerable interest was generated in Canadian naval circles in 1934 by the design of a small high speed aircraft carrier with a catapult launch system and a complement of seven seaplanes. Although Commodore Percy W. Nelles, the chief of the Naval Staff, expressed great interest in this design, nothing came of the idea. Nevertheless, it demonstrated that the RCN was capable of progressive thinking in aviation matters even if meagre budget allocations prevented the navy from acquiring such expensive equipment.

By 1943 the Canadian government could no longer ignore the fact that naval air forces were essential to the successful prosecution of the war at sea. The Admiralty had, as early as 1941, proposed that Royal Canadian Naval Volunteer Reserve personnel should become pilots and observers in the Royal Navy, while retaining their RCNVR status. In January 1943, Acting Captain H.N. Lay, the director of Operations, recommended that the Admiralty proposal be accepted and that two officers of senior rank be exchanged with the RN. Officers and men were also to be sent to the U.K. for service in Royal Navy carriers. An additional recommendation was made to build or purchase four escort carriers for service with mid-ocean escort groups. At the same time, the Director of Plans, Acting Captain H.G. DeWolf, emphasized the need for shipborne aircraft in the Atlantic air gap, together with the use of general aircraft for convoy protection. In keeping with these recommendations, a message was sent to the Admiralty in April 1943 proposing that Canadian personnel be trained and employed in the RNFAA. The Lay/DeWolf memorandum also urged the formation of a naval air division at Naval Service Headquarters and the despatch of a senior officer to the U.K. and the United States to study naval operations.[4] Thus, after twenty-five years, the first steps were taken to re-activate the Royal Canadian Naval Air Service.

Captain Lay was detached to Great Britain and the United States from April to August 1943 to study USN and RN naval air operations. On his return, he made the following recommendations for the formation of a RCNAS:

1. the naval air service should be modelled upon the RNFAA and established as soon as possible;
2. the service should concern itself with carrier operations, while the RCAF conducted coastal operations with shore-based aircraft;
3. the new service should commence with the manning of two escort carriers equipped with the necessary maintenance facilities.[5]

The ominous and puzzling aspect of these proposals was the restriction of the naval air service to carrier-based operations alone. Lay's recommendation is surprising in view of the fact that the RN and RAF had just fought a prolonged and acrimonious battle over coastal air reconaissance, and the Admiralty had assumed operational control of Coastal Command in 1941. In addition, the carrier-only decision appears highly dubious in light of the USN's success in operating a large, well-balanced force of land-based anti-submarine aircraft with full responsibility for maritime air patrols. Since all of the evidence pointed to the importance of placing the operational and administrative control of all maritime forces in the hands of one service, it is remarkable that no explanation was ever given to justify this decision. It was destined to remain a problem for the Maritime Command until 1959.

Following a Cabinet War Committee meeting in September 1943, an RCN/RCAF Committee suggested that the RCN undertake the operation of aircraft carriers, while shore-based facilities were left with the RN in the U.K. and with the RCAF in Canada. This recommendation was a significant one in terms of altering the RCN's small ship character. However, for reasons of expediency, the question of shore-based support facilities was not resolved satisfactorily.

Having settled upon the carrier concept, there was a good deal of discussion regarding the best ways for the RCN to acquire and man two light escort-carriers. Although Canadian naval personnel had been detailed to man one ship, it was not until mid-January 1944 that approval was given for the RCN to man the British escort-carriers *Nabob* and *Puncher*, with the RN providing the aircraft and air personnel.

Another step was taken in April 1944 when the Directorate of Naval Air Division (DNAD) was formed under Lieutenant-Commander (Pilot) J.S. Stead, RCN.[6] While the directorate was small, it established an identity and terms of reference for naval aviation which were essential in this formative period.

Just as it appeared that the last hurdles had been cleared, the RCNAS suffered two major setbacks. *Nabob* was damaged so severely in a torpedo attack on 22 August 1944 that it was not considered worthwhile to restore her to service. At the same time *Puncher* was allocated to an aircraft ferrying role. Despite these reverses, NSHQ, recognizing the need to involve RCN aircraft carriers in Pacific operations against the Japanese, proposed the acquisition of two light fleet-carriers. In February 1945, after the terms of their acquisition, their role in the Pacific campaign, and the specific ships in question were finally settled, the Canadian Cabinet War Committee agreed to the transfer of HM Ships *Warrior* and *Magnificent* from the RN. The British cabinet approved the terms of the proposal in April 1945 and allowed the Canadian government the option of buying the carriers at a later date. However, the government was not prepared to use the carriers to support the RN in the recapture of British possessions in the Indian Ocean area.[7] Instead, the cabinet intended to use Canadian warships in the Pacific against Japan and in operational theatres of war of direct interest to Canada. This view prevailed, and arrangements were made to transfer the two carriers and a flotilla of destroyers to the RCN.

In the summer of 1945, the Royal Navy began to form air squadrons with Canadian officers serving in the RNFAA. These recruits were augmented by 550 ex-RCAF pilots who had transferred to the RN in 1945 for flying duties in the Pacific.[8] The four squadrons designated for service in the RCN

Plate 76. HMCS *Ontario*, in which a 1947 mutiny resulted in the transfer of the executive officer. (MCM)

Plate 77. HMCS *Magnificent*, mutiny, Caribbean Sea, 20 March 1949. (PAC—PA 115371)

Plate 78. Vice-Admiral E. Rollo Mainguy, RCN, chairman of RCN inquiry into 1949 mutinies. (DOH, NDHQ)

Plate 79. HMCS *Crescent*, mutiny, Nanking, China, 15 March 1949. (PAC—PA 115389)

Plate 80. HMCS *Athabaskan* II, mutiny, Manzanillo, Mexico, 26 February 1949. (PAC—PA 115446)

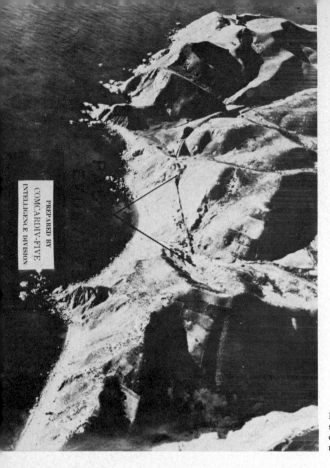

PREPARED BY
COMCARDIV-FIVE
INTELLIGENCE DIVISION

Plate 81. Aerial oblique view of the coast of Korea showing "Package 2" target area, an open stretch of railway track. Enemy trains took shelter from naval bombardment in tunnels. (DOH, NDHQ)

Plate 82. Destroyer firing at night. HMCS *Crusader* became a member of the Trainbusters Club for her destruction of enemy rolling stock. (PAC—Nk 1266)

Plate 83. Chief Petty Officer Joe Leary scanning for possible enemy targets, off North Korea, 5 June 1952. (PAC—PA 116333)

Plate 84. HMCS *Crusader*, C-class destroyer, returns to Esquimalt after distinguished action in the Korean War. (MCM)

Plate 85. Hawker Sea Fury of No. 871 Squadron being waved off for second approach to flight deck of HMCS *Magnificent*, 14 May 1952. (PAC—PA 115378)

Plate 86. View aft along the flight deck of HMCS *Magnificent* during Operation "Neverfail" off Halifax, 30 May 1950. Ship in background is HMCS *Micmac*. (PAC—PA 115445)

Plate 87. View from the bridge of HMCS *Magnificent* of the approach of HMS *Surprise* during the Coronation Naval Review, Spithead, England, 15 June 1953. (PAC—PA 115377)

Plate 88. HMCS *Bonaventure* (ex-HMS *Powerful*), "Hermes"-class aircraft carrier, decommissioned in 1969, two years after undergoing a $17 million refit. (MMBC)

Plate 89. HMCS *Labrador* conducted hydrographic surveys and helped supply remote Arctic weather stations between 1954 and 1957. (MCM—Lab 1016)

Plate 90. HMCS *Labrador* sailed the Northwest Passage from east to west in the summer of 1954. (MCM—Lab 217)

Plate 91. *Labrador's* helicopter flying oil barrels for electronic position indicator station. (M. Leeming collection)

Plate 92. Preassembled navigational beacon being airlifted from deck of *Labrador*. (M. Leeming)

Plate 93. Supplies being carried ashore from a landing barge equipped for Arctic duty. (M. Leeming)

Plate 94. Completed beacon, Craig Harbour, Ellesmere Island. (M. Leeming)

Plate 95. For years given low priority in federal defence budgets, Canada's naval reserves have dwindled to "a paper force preparing for a paper war." YMT 10 diving tender in simulated convoy exercise "Spring Thaw." (USN photo)

Plate 96. The aging gate vessel HMCS *Porte de la Reine* being "attacked" by the air reserve during a naval control of shipping exercise. (USN photo)

were the 803 and 883 fighter squadrons, to be equipped with Seafires, and the 825 and 826, to be equipped with Firefly aircraft as two-seater fighter reconnaissance squadrons. One of the pilots in 803 Squadron, R.H. Falls, was destined to become a chief of the Defence Staff.

As Canadian naval aviation developed and new squadrons were formed, a group of fifty ex-RCAF pilots and twenty ex-RNFAA aircrew became the core of expertise in the RCNAS. The training of Canadian ground crews and ship personnel proceeded quickly as some five hundred Canadians, qualified by the RN, joined the various squadrons and units.

On 19 December 1945, the government finally approved, in principle, the formation of a naval air branch.[9] It declared that an air branch would be formed within the authorized manpower of the RCN and would amount to approximately 11 per cent of the navy's peacetime strength of ten thousand men. This meant that the air branch was expected to man one aircraft carrier, two torpedo-bomber squadrons, two fighter squadrons, one shore-based air section, and an air staff at NSHQ with only eleven hundred officers and men. This was clearly impossible, and the branch's ability to plan orderly development was crippled for many years by its inadequate numbers.

As the formation of the air branch continued, a joint RCN/RCAF committee was directed by Vice-Admiral G.C. Jones, the chief of the Naval Staff, and Air Marshal R. Leckie, the chief of the Air Staff, to examine common requirements.[10] The outcome of these studies was that the RCN walked into a trap of dual control; the RCAF was granted the funding management of all naval air shore-based facilities and supporting air services, including such significant items as air stores and major aircraft repairs and maintenance. That RCN senior staff could have accepted such controls so naively after their exposure to the disastrous prewar Royal Navy Fleet Air Arm experience under RAF control is almost unbelievable. Air Marshal Leckie was originally a sub-lieutenant in the RNAS during World War I. He transferred to the RAF upon the disbandment of the RNAS and retransferred to the RCAF in 1940. One would have thought that, with his experience in the old RNAS, he would have been sympathetic to the formation of the Canadian naval air branch, but this was not the case. Remarks attributed to Leckie during his time as chief of the Air Staff reveal that he was prepared to do everything in his power to prevent the development of Canadian naval aviation.

Perhaps the Naval Staff were obsessed by the stringent restrictions on manpower and considered it more economical to allow the RCAF to support the naval air branch. Certainly, they do not appear to have argued strenuously enough for navy control of shore-based aviation. In the event, funds and manpower might have been reassigned from the RCAF budget and manpower allocation and the RCN might have achieved effective control of naval aviation. Under the new arrangement, the RCAF had the power to minimize naval air support facilities through its control of the purse strings. The run-down RCAF Station Dartmouth (Nova Scotia), where the naval air section was virtually a beggar tenant, illustrated this dismal state of affairs.

HMCS *Warrior* commissioned in January 1946 and embarked 803 (Seafires) and 825 (Fireflies) squadrons. The carrier sailed for Canada two months later. On its arrival the Seafires and Fireflies were transferred to the RCN air section at RCAF Station Dartmouth, where frantic efforts were being made to achieve some semblance of organization. At the same time 883 and 826 squadrons were temporarily de-activated. This was unavoidable since the manpower available to the RCN was insufficient to man these additional flying units.

The newly arrived squadrons began their working-up programme, but it soon became apparent that the problems of operating a naval air section, while under RCAF control, were considerable. There were shortages of flight crew clothing and stores, and the hangars and accommodations were substandard. In addition, the inadequate winterization of living spaces aboard *Warrior* necessitated her transfer to the milder West Coast for the winter of 1946.

In November of the following year, the chief of the Naval Staff, Vice-Admiral H.E. Reid observed that naval aircraft were merely weapons like torpedoes or guns.[11] In retrospect, this was a remarkable, not to say disturbing, viewpoint. It demonstrated not only a lack of appreciation for naval aviation but a profound ignorance of the importance of carrier operations as illustrated by such engagements as Midway and the Battle of the Coral Sea.

By the spring of 1948, it had become obvious that it was no longer possible to consider manning two light fleet-carriers in view of the manpower ceiling imposed upon the RCN. It was hoped that *Warrior* could be winterized and retained, but subsequently it was decided that she should be returned to the RN when HMCS *Magnificent* became available. *Magnificent* commissioned on 7 April, under the command of Commodore H.G. DeWolf, and *Warrior* returned to the U.K.

For more than two years the RCN had been attempting to change the RCN/RCAF agreement on the control of the naval air section at Dartmouth. Although the relinquishment of air stores and the transfer of search and rescue operations to RCAF Station Greenwood were accepted grudgingly by the RCAF, the air force remained singularly unresponsive to suggestions that they relinquish complete control of RCAF Station Dartmouth to the RCN. The RCN was occupying eleven of the fourteen hangars, operating fifty-six aircraft, and employing over nine hundred personnel. The RCAF, by comparison, was utilizing two aircraft and employing 250 personnel. A decision to transfer the air station to the RCN was at last made by the Cabinet Defence Committee in September 1948.[12] Thus, after twenty-eight years, the RCN assumed control of its own airfield, which it commissioned HMCS *Shearwater*. Although the station was badly run down and bereft of facilities, it was home to the air branch, and the expensive, time-consuming task of rebuilding it began.

Negotiations had gone on for some time with the United States Navy to replace the Fireflies in use by the RCN. These aircraft were difficult to maintain, few in number, and ill-suited to all-weather anti-submarine warfare (ASW) carrier flying. To enthusiasts, the Firefly V was one of the best two-seater fighters in the world, but to its detractors it was the worst. Both points of view were valid since it was the only single-engined, two-seater fighter in existence—a rather uncertain distinction. However, with the purchase of seventy-five used USN Avenger aircraft in April 1950, the RCN turned away from the RN and the Firefly and became oriented, operationally and logistically, toward the highly developed naval aviation of the United States. Not only was this a desirable step from the viewpoint of common operating techniques and logistic support, but the purchase gave Canadian naval aviation a well-proven, rugged, easily maintained aircraft. The Avenger was able to carry the latest ASW equipment and provide increased flying hours as well as operational capability. RCN aviation urgently required such an aircraft in order to develop pilot and crew training while utilizing the small number of ground personnel and limited facilities available. The Avenger filled these needs admirably.

The cabinet authorized the purchase and modernization of an aircraft carrier in April 1952.[13] The most suitable ship available at this time appeared to be the light fleet-carrier *Powerful*, which had been launched in November 1943 and had been laid up in Belfast since May 1946, when work on her had ceased. The decision to purchase her was significant: for the first time the RCN had the opportunity to own and operate a carrier that could be modified to meet Canadian requirements; however, it would be burdened with a ship that was already nine years old in terms of its hull and many of its fittings. Although conversion and completion of the ship were scheduled to take a further five years, the delays involved in negotiating an alternative were seen to be even less acceptable, and so purchase negotiations were commenced.

In 1951 and again in 1952 proposals were made for *Magnificent* to be used in Korea. Naval aviators were eager to see combat action in company with RN and Royal Australian Navy carriers, but the proposal was rejected on the grounds that *Magnificent* was primarily an ASW carrier and that her employment in a strike role could not be justified.[14] Moreover, it appears that her departure for Korea might have been interpreted in some quarters as a failure to meet Canada's NATO commitments.

Shortly thereafter, the RCN received a request from the Admiralty for a squadron of twelve Sea Furies and fourteen pilots to serve aboard HMS *Warrior* in Korea. The Cabinet Defence Committee approved the request, and special weapons training began for VF871 Squadron.[15] These preparations came to nought with the armistice on 27 July 1953. A number of the naval aviators were deeply disappointed since the Sea Furies were excellent fighters, and the pilots were anxious to engage in battle. Combat conditions, which few of the pilots had experienced, would have given them a chance to be "blooded." Moreover, they lost the opportunity to become more widely recognized by a public which barely knew that a naval aviation branch existed.

In 1955, the RCN's first anti-submarine helicopter squadron was formed. This squadron gave the navy a balanced ASW capability and proved—during operations aboard *Magnificent*—that a mixed complement of aircraft could operate with versatility in an ASW role. The obvious follow-up to this was helicopter operations aboard a small ship deck. Indeed, this idea had been suggested as early as 1943 in an inter-directorate memo at NSHQ.[16] Trials were carried out successfully in 1956 aboard the frigate HMCS *Buckingham*, and the decision was made in 1962 to fit the St. Laurent-class destroyers with a flight deck and hangar. This decision was the basis of later generations of RCN helicopter/ship combinations.

During November 1955, as *Shearwater* naval air station approached the seventh anniversary of commissioning, the first F2H3 Banshee all-weather jet fighters began to arrive. These aircraft had been purchased second-hand from the USN and brought up to the latest configuration. VF870 and VF871 squadrons, then equipped with Sea Fury aircraft, were reformed and re-equipped with Banshees. These jets, although destined for the new carrier (designated HMCS *Bonaventure*), had an important shore-based role as well, insofar as they were integrated into the North American Air Defence (NORAD) Command and became one of the most effective air units operating in the Canadian sector. The one aspect of Banshee operations that was never given much publicity was their excellent all-weather, shore-based intercept capability. There may have been good reason for this lack of acknowledgement. The RCAF was still equipped with the obsolescent CF100 aircraft, which had operational weapon limitations, and it was not the policy of the Department of National Defence to publicize the inadequacies of current operational equipment.

Although negotiations for building a replacement ASW aircraft in Canada for the Avenger had been completed for some time, the first Canadian-built anti-submarine aircraft was not delivered to the RCN until October 1956. Modifications, tailored for Canadian operations, had been incorporated in this aircraft, which was destined to play a large part in the development of Canadian naval aviation. The new aircraft, called the CS2F

Tracker, was not only an ideal carrier aircraft, but also had completely interchangeable parts with comparable USN aircraft. This strengthened the operational capability of the two navies' common ASW task and resulted in increased logistic support since Canadian-built Trackers could be serviced and supported at any USN base operating S2F aircraft.

As Trackers were being brought into squadron service in Canada, an interesting proposal came forward from the Royal Navy through the Canadian Joint Staff in London. It was an unofficial suggestion that the Admiralty would be sympathetic to the acquisition by the RCN of a Hermes-class aircraft carrier in lieu of HMCS *Bonaventure* (ex-HMS *Powerful*), which was still being converted to RCN specifications. This offer was difficult to assess; certainly it necessitated a close examination of cost, the implications of cancelling *Bonaventure*, and the date of availability. There was a feeling in some RN circles that the RCN was converting a ship which was being rescued from obsolescence only by the addition of new aircraft operating equipment, such as the steam catapult, mirror landing sight, and the angled deck, features which vastly improved the general operating capability of the light fleet-carriers. Some experts suggested privately that a slow, small, outdated carrier could never become more than marginally effective. The most disturbing fact was that the *Bonaventure* was felt to have almost no growth potential. If this was the case, what aircraft would be able to operate from her in the future? The Hermes/Centaur class, on the other hand, was designed to overcome many of the shortcomings of the light fleet-class ships such as *Bonaventure*. With double the horsepower, the Hermes had a speed of thirty knots, and with increased size and two steam catapults, greatly improved operational capability. Such vessels cost approximately £10 million, the price of the *Bonaventure*. One reason for the British proposal was cutbacks in the RN which had resulted in a surplus of warships. Some consideration was given to the proposal, but it was decided that progress on the *Bonaventure* had reached the point where changing ships would have been too difficult. No doubt there would have been political and financial repercussions as well. No one could say at the time that the decision to proceed with *Bonaventure* was a mistake, but the problem of replacement carrier aircraft had definite implications for the future.

At the beginning of 1957, the RCN received HMCS *Bonaventure*, the first Canadian-owned aircraft carrier to incorporate features designed to Canadian standards. Receipt marked a red letter day for Canadian naval aviation, and flying trials revealed that both Trackers and Banshees were compatible with the ship's equipment. *Magnificent* was returned to the RN. Although she was obsolete, her service and ready deck had done much to advance the cause of RCN aviation. The varied uses the carrier had been put to had established a degree of flexibility not often found in RCN ships.

In December 1957 Commodore A.H.G. Storrs, the assistant chief of the Naval Staff (Air and Warfare), initiated a thorough examination of the maritime air organization.[17] Over the years, the maritime forces had not effectively incorporated the best operational use of aviation. Maritime Air Command was controlled by the RCAF but was operated in a purely maritime environment. As a courtesy to the senior service, the air officer commanding made aircraft available for use on maritime patrols. Commodore Storrs's paper proposed that the Maritime Air Command be transferred to naval control in order to achieve a fully cohesive maritime force. There were valid reasons for this proposal, and it made little sense for the RCAF to operate a large, separate component on ocean operations in conjunction with the RCN. The reason the RCAF advanced for maintaining this role was that they had been doing it since World War II. The USN, on the other hand, considered the sea their exclusive area of jurisdiction and controlled and operated a highly developed maritime patrol network of short- and long-range, shore-based ASW aircraft. The RAF and RN had been forced to recognize the problem when the Royal Navy assumed control of RAF Coastal Command in 1941. Since the aircrew and aircraft remained an RAF responsibility while the Admiralty controlled operations, the problem had been only partially eliminated. The RCN was allowed only to operate aircraft from ships, while the Trackers at HMCS *Shearwater*, with their excellent ASW detection devices and range, were denied ocean surveillance.

The RCAF displayed little or no interest in maritime air operations in the years immediately after World War II since the bulk of the air force's experience had been with bombers or fighters, and there were no RCAF aircraft equipped for effective ASW operations. This would have been an opportune moment for the RCN to have assumed control of all operations concerned with ASW warfare. Commodore Storrs's paper recognized the need for a gradual turnover of maritime air forces to the RCN, with personnel and aircraft being transferred to the navy and absorbed into Maritime Command over a period of time. The paper also exposed the lavish build-up of personnel and facilities at RCAF maritime airfields. Support of thirty to forty aircraft involved three large, well-equipped air stations as well as support facilities and approximately four thousand personnel. This was a far more luxurious allocation of resources, proportionally, than the RCN was allowed to establish for naval aviation. Surprisingly, Commodore Storrs's paper for the Naval Board was set aside summarily; all of the copies were destroyed, and the subject was to be considered permanently closed. No explanation was given for the paper's rejection, and the background to the matter remains obscure.

Why was the reaction to a well-prepared proposal, submitted by a competent, highly qualified, senior board member, so negative? Certainly, over the years, senior naval officers had become aware of the problem, based on their own experience in Maritime Command. It may be that the pressures on the Naval Staff prevented them from analysing the paper properly. Quite possibly they could see nothing but trouble arising from such a controversial subject. It is well known that the services had to have mutual support in order to obtain approval for their new construction programmes and budgets. Perhaps the Naval Board felt that the RCN's position would be jeopardized if the RCAF was antagonized by debate on such a sensitive subject. In any event, the proposal was never presented to the Naval Board—a rejection which would have a serious impact on the future of the branch.

Negotiations for the reorganization of Maritime Command had been underway for some time when finally, in July 1959, it was agreed that the commander Maritime Forces would combine the operations of ships and aircraft in a joint headquarters, with the chief of the RCAF Maritime Command acting as his deputy. While this agreement placed command and control procedures under a single commander, it did not mean that the RCAF relinquished their control over the personnel, planning, aircraft availability, airfields, and support facilities. Nevertheless, in an operational sense, it was an improvement since the maritime commander could now utilize all operational naval aircraft at HMCS *Shearwater* as he saw fit without having to be concerned about any adverse reaction from the RCAF as had been the case previously.

An organizational change occurred in January 1960 which had a considerable effect on Canadian naval aviation. RCN aviation had been represented on the Naval Board since 1949 by a senior RN aviator on loan, followed later by a senior RCN officer with an understanding of naval aviation. There were occasional policy and personality clashes involving the RN officer and his non-aviation Canadian colleagues. There were times when senior Canadian naval officers resented an RN air officer who enjoyed access to the Naval Board. Consequently, the 1960 decision was made to abolish the Naval Board position. This loss of representation was unfortunate since all of the channels of communication now lay with the vice-chief of the Naval Staff, who might or might not have any interest or background in aviation. Not only was this link inadequate, but it contributed to ineffective representation with unfortunate results.

Between September 1962 and September 1963, there was another opportunity to obtain an aircraft carrier superior to *Bonaventure* and capable of operating the generation of fighter and ASW aircraft required to replace the Banshee/Tracker squadrons. The Banshee was nearing the end of its operational life in the RCN, and carrier operations involving these jets were becoming marginal in regard to current all-weather, day and night fleet air defence. What was needed was a larger carrier able to handle a mixed force of aircraft, encompassing fighters, ASW fixed-wing, and helicopter aircraft. The ideal ship for the job was a modified USN Essex-class carrier. Ships of this category were in good supply, and one could be made available to the RCN for a fraction of its value. A fully converted Essex, with the latest flight deck equipment, including steam catapults and mirror landing aid, could be made available for approximately $4 million. A considerable amount of information was available on this subject, but RCN senior staff displayed little interest in acquiring a U.S. carrier. Once again, the reluctance to update and improve the operational effectiveness of the air branch had an adverse effect upon the future of naval aviation.

At the same time a decision was made to retire the aging Banshees, which had performed so well ashore and afloat. Although the role played by the navy fighter squadrons in NORAD was generally downplayed, it is important to recognize that the Banshee, with its air-to-air Sidewinder heat-seeking missile, was the only fighter in Canada capable of the long-range destruction of incoming enemy aircraft (its RCAF counterpart was the CF100 which, although a good long-range fighter, had only conventional short-range rockets). As a result of the Banshee weapons system, naval squadrons demonstrated one of the highest intercept-kill ratios in the regular NORAD/Strategic Air Command exercises. Despite this, after sixteen years, RCN fighter operations were discontinued. The squadrons were disbanded and the pilots scattered or retired from the service. Air defence of the fleet no longer existed; yet the operational requirement for such defence was still in effect and formed part of the planning guide.

Canadian naval aviation suffered grievously from the decision to unify the forces in the mid-1960's. It had taken years to build a well-experienced staff of aviators at National Defence Headquarters. Almost overnight their lines of authority, communication, and support vanished. The RCN aviation staff was reduced to a small number of representatives reporting to an RCAF wing commander, who, in turn, was responsible to an RCAF group captain. In the space of a year, the naval aviation directorate was reorganized five times and given five different directors who spent most of their time writing terms of reference. The chaos resulting from unification adversely affected all branches of the services, but the effects on the naval aviation branch were particularly detrimental.

There is strong evidence that a self-preservation policy developed in the senior ranks of the RCN as the unification disease spread throughout the service. Two events support this belief. From 1965 to 1967 reports were heard repeatedly of a trade-off between the RCN and RCAF senior officers of Maritime Command.[18] The outcome of this trade-off was to be the assumption, by the RCAF in Maritime Command, of all fixed-wing maritime aircraft. In return, the maritime commander was to enjoy the backing of the RCAF in the conversion of the Maritime Command destroyer escorts so that they could carry ASW helicopters. These reports were strengthened when the maritime commander briefed senior aviators and squadron commanders at HMCS *Shearwater*. He stated quite clearly that the future development of Canadian naval aviation would be directed toward helicopter-equipped ships, a development which would be disastrous for naval aviation.

The mid-life refit of *Bonaventure* took place between April 1966 and August 1967. The cost of the overhaul soared from an initial $8 million estimate to over $17 million. At the same time, reports were circulated of expensive and unjustifiable repairs to cabins and fixtures. So much has been said on the subject that it is pointless to add more. However, one aspect of the refit which has not been generally revealed was that the ship's hull, main plumbing, and ring-main water systems were over twenty-three years old. These systems had never been replaced properly, and as the refit progressed, a large number of deteriorated and unsuitable fittings were exposed. In many cases these components had to be replaced or repaired at great expense. The cost of these extra, and urgent, repairs had to be accounted for as the refit progressed, and in many cases the work was disguised under other repairs. The most humiliating aspect of the debacle was not that there were $9 million spent in excess of the estimates on necessary repairs; the real tragedy was that no one attempted to justify the cost to the public. Bearing in mind the complete confusion at NDHQ, it is likely that no one really felt responsible at this point. When the damage was done, the fiasco of the *Bonaventure* refit was used as a political device for withdrawing the ship, a move which further diminished the fleet's capability.

Canadian naval aviation sustained its death blow in September 1969 when NDHQ announced *Bonaventure*'s retirement from service. Following her refit, the ship was in the finest operating condition she had ever achieved. Every aspect of her operational equipment and facilities was at an all-time high. Her Tracker and Sea King (helicopter) squadrons had proved to be an excellent ASW combination, and naval aviation's reputation was first class in Maritime Command. All of this was to be jeopardized now for the sake of $9 million that had already been spent. The decision to retire *Bonaventure* is incredible when one considers that the $9 million was only about one-quarter of the amount spent on the experimental RCN hydrofoil *Bras d'Or*, which had been mothballed. The irony was that although the funds were expended, the refit had provided employment to shipyards and subcontractors and produced an ASW carrier that would have been able to do an excellent job for years to come.

What was the purpose of scrapping the ship, and what was the true motive behind the decision? What was the position of the senior naval officers? Did the decision come from Maritime Command? We will probably never know the full answers to these questions. However, it is generally believed that the refit scandal gave the Trudeau government a chance to cut back on naval expenditures, even though, in doing so, it cut the heart out of the Canadian naval ASW capability assigned to NATO. Significantly, *Bonaventure*'s retirement eased the heavy manpower strain on Maritime Command and allowed the personnel from the carrier to be assigned to other vessels. This shift in resources also strengthened the future role of long-range maritime aviation, the preserve of RCAF Maritime Air Command. Furthermore, *Bonaventure*'s withdrawal from service cut the ground from underneath the ten-year-old Trackers and largely eliminated the possibility of fighter aircraft replacement for fleet defence. By reducing required personnel, it created a situation whereby the ASW helicopter programme had to be justified purely by assignment to the destroyer escorts.

It is generally safe to say that a number of the officers in the navy's Maritime Command welcomed the demise of *Bonaventure* and the diminished role of naval aviation, particularly as RCN aviation had consumed a large part of the operating budget. Their attitude is easier to understand when one considers the need for peacetime promotion and command at sea. The savings which resulted from *Bonaventure*'s withdrawal made it possible for the navy to maintain more small ships at sea, thereby guaranteeing an increased number of command positions. Similarly, it gave the destroyer escorts a new lease on life by marrying them to the Sea King helicopter to form a novel weapons system. It was generally conceded that without a helicopter the destroyer escorts' ability to track down and destroy enemy submarines was very marginal. This fact alone was sufficient to justify fitting helicopters to the small ships, and the helicopter/ship marriage was seen as a reasonable cost/benefit conversion. Significantly, these conversions led to the RCN's return to a small-ship-navy status with little aviation capability.

In 1982, nearly thirty-seven years after the establishment of the branch, it is perhaps worthwhile to consider the state of Canadian naval aviation today. At HMCS (now Canadian Forces Base [CFB]) *Shearwater*, there is one squadron of twenty-six-year-old Trackers, utilized on inshore, maritime surveillance duties. There are two Sea King ASW helicopter squadrons for detachment aboard destroyer escorts and one composite squadron, employing Trackers and helicopters for training and utility work. At CFB *Comox*, on Vancouver Island, there is a small detachment of Trackers and jet trainers for fleet support and utility work. As can be seen, the once healthy Canadian naval aviation branch has now been unified and reduced to a basic support role to the fleet, a far cry from the well-established, effective primary force of twenty years ago.

On the plus side, individual benefits have accrued from unification. A few naval aviators have realized healthy promotions and others have gained command of fighter and long-range maritime patrol squadrons. These achievements do little, however, to compensate for the loss of identity and sense of purpose that distinguished Canadian naval aviation previously. No doubt some critics would say this is merely a sign of changing times and that the demise of carrier aviation was the result of shifting requirements. This is an over-simplification of the situation. No doubt history will establish that Canadian naval aviation failed through neglect and misunderstanding on the one hand and RCAF hostility toward RCN aviation on the other. With the exception of a few enlightened and dedicated senior non-aviators, most RCN officers did not really understand the importance of carrier aviation or the degree of support required to sustain it. As a consequence, Maritime Command has no aircraft carrier and only a small supporting air component. The long-range Aurora patrol aircraft selected for Maritime Command is a naval patrol plane, and the replacement fighter for Air Defence Command is a naval-designed carrier aircraft. What is sadly lacking in the utilization of these aircraft is an effective, balanced Canadian naval aviation branch in an established operational role.

Chapter 16

HMCS LABRADOR AND THE CANADIAN ARCTIC

J.M. Leeming

Russia undertook Arctic exploration prior to World War II, and the United States, fearing Soviet aggression in that area, developed its own northern strategy, the "Polar Concept," in the later 1940's. Canada, however, displayed relatively little interest in the region, and it was not until 1948-49 that the Royal Canadian Navy carried out a series of operations in the Arctic: HMC Ships *Magnificent, Nootka,* and *Haida* visited Churchill, Manitoba, in 1948; the frigate HMCS *Swansea* conducted a training cruise to Frobisher Bay, on the south coast of Baffin Island, in 1949; and HMCS *Cedarwood* joined a U.S.-Canadian Aleutian scientific expedition to the Chukchi Sea (73° 15′ N) in the latter year.

At the same time, the RCN began to consider building a vessel specifically for northern operations, and in January 1949 a contract was let to Marine Industries Limited of Sorel, Quebec, to construct a modified United States Navy Wind-class icebreaker. The particulars of the new Arctic patrol vessel, HMCS *Labrador*, were:

length, overall	369 feet
breadth, extreme	63 feet, 6 inches
draught, full load	29 feet, 1 inch
displacement, maximum	6,490 tons
speed, maximum	16 knots

Labrador possessed a number of interesting and unusual features for a warship. Her twin screws were driven by six 2,000-horsepower diesel engines that delivered electrical energy to two 5,000-horsepower motors. A helicopter platform, capable of accommodating three helicopters, was fitted aft, while the hull was pierced by retractable Denny Brown stabilizers. In addition, she had three heeling tanks on the port and starboard sides connected by twenty-four-inch conduits through which reversible propeller pumps were capable of driving forty thousand gallons of water a minute, developing a ten-degree list from port to starboard in ninety seconds. The rocking motion produced in this way was invaluable in terms of working the vessel loose from pack ice. *Labrador*'s role was to carry out northern patrols to provide the RCN with the knowledge necessary for planning and conducting future operations; to perform ice-breaking duties; to assist in the logistic support of Arctic bases where ice-breaking was required; to carry out scientific surveys; and to perform rescue and salvage operations in the waters of the Canadian north.

Captain O.C.S. "Long Robbie" Robertson, RCN, was *Labrador*'s first commanding officer, and in anticipation of taking up his command, he spent several months gaining experience on board USN icebreakers. He was responsible for a number of important modifications to *Labrador*'s design during her construction. *Labrador* was launched on 15 December 1951, christened by Madame Jeanne St. Laurent, the wife of the Canadian prime minister, on 14 June 1952, and commissioned into the RCN on 8 July 1954. She sailed for Halifax on 10 July and arrived four days later. The next week and a half were taken up embarking hundreds of tons of stores, including a consignment of coal for the Royal Canadian Mounted Police outpost at Alexandra Fiord, on the east coast of Ellesmere Island. *Labrador* departed Halifax on 23 July with ten scientists and one RCMP officer on board and headed north.

The scientific party was headed by D.C. Rose of the National Research Council, whose principal interest was cosmic ray research. Commander E.M. Penton, RN (Ret'd.), conducted studies on the Admiralty's new gyromagnetic compass (AGM5), while T.E. Armstrong, on loan from the Scott Polar Research Institute, studied ice conditions. W.B. Bailey, J.G. Clark, and C.C. Cunningham dealt with oceanography. D.D. Lelievre and M. Bolton conducted meteorological studies, while Mr. E.I. Loomer investigated terrestrial magnetism. Inspector E.S.W. Batty of the RCMP sailed in *Labrador* in order to inspect RCMP posts in the eastern Arctic. *Labrador*'s own ship's company consisted of 21 officers and 204 men; I served as second-in-command.

The leader of each scientific group presented Dr. Rose and Captain Robertson with a weekly work plan that outlined where each group wanted to go, what they intended to do, the time involved, the gear that they needed transported ashore, and the help they required from the ship's company. Daily programmes were developed on the basis of these requests, though it goes without saying that the words "weather permitting" governed all activity.

The day before each "evolution" (naval or scientific undertaking), an operational order was distributed throughout the ship. It contained the object of the evolution and the way in which *Labrador* was to be employed; the names of the personnel involved; the materials required such as beacons, tools, and food; the communications involved; the responsibility of the engineering department; the duties of the electrical branch; the radar sets and the times that they were required; the employment of helicopters; and the utilization of *Labrador*'s boats.

A daily ship's tabloid called "Bergy Bits," after the little iceberg fragments (normally not more than fifteen feet high and thirty feet across) which dotted the seascape, was started. This newspaper was for the purpose of arousing the ship's company's interest in Arctic exploration as well as conveying local news. Thus when the ship entered Baffin Bay, the paper featured an article on Baffin's exploits. The wireless ratings provided national, international, and sports news, while the editor, Padre (P[rotestant]) Thomas Jackson, included a thought-for-the-day. It was not long before two of the crew members were discovered to be competent cartoonists. They developed a polar bear character, known affectionately as "Buzz Bear," and lampooned everyone from the captain to the cooks. Far from home in the endless days of Arctic summer, the crew found solace and amusement from the ship's little paper.

Labrador moved north through the Strait of Belle Isle, between Newfoundland and Labrador, and into Davis Strait, where she encountered fog banks that persisted all of the way to Lancaster Sound. Ominously, icebergs and bergy bits began to slide past in the gloom. Ice coverage is normally given in tenths, with ten-tenths constituting complete coverage, five-tenths, one-half ice and one-half open sea, and so forth. Fortunately, the first ice met was four-tenths and fairly rotten, having been weakened and undermined by the action of the sea and sun. Four-tenths to six-tenths ice is usually described as "open pack" while "polar ice" is more than one winter's growth and ten feet in thickness.

Labrador commenced her first ice-breaking mission when she entered Lancaster Sound, churning through fields of rotten pack ice. Not surprisingly, off-duty personnel poured out on deck to watch the ice floes crumple beneath her bows. Such sightseeing, whether occasioned by massive blue-white icebergs, seals, walruses, or lumbering polar bears, was known as "goofing" and "all hands to goofing stations" was a pipe heard repeatedly at the beginning of the voyage.

Open water lay beyond Lancaster Sound, and *Labrador* made her way easily to Resolute on the southern coast of Cornwallis Island, arriving there on 1 August. A weather station and an airstrip had been established at Resolute seven years earlier, and ionospheric, seismic, and magnetic stations had been set up sometime later. In the course of its development

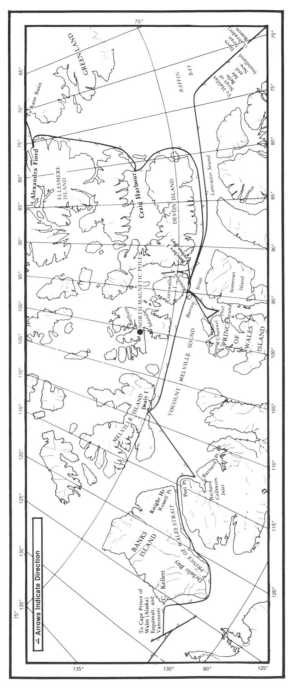

Northwest Passage Transit, HMCS *Labrador*: 23 July-20 September 1954

Resolute had become the principal centre in the central Arctic for resupply of Canadian vessels. But she had an even more important claim to fame. Located at roughly 75°N, Resolute boasted the most northerly flush toilets in the world.

When the weather conditions improved, *Labrador* landed a hydrographic party, consisting of two scientists and five sailors, equipped with a beacon, instruments, and provisions enough to last for three weeks. Beacons became *Labrador*'s motif during her journey across the Arctic. The eighteen-foot navigation markers consisted of a tripod constructed of four by fours, base planks that could be weighted down with boulders, and boards nailed to the tripod near the top to provide a target for visual sighting. The whole affair was painted orange and a flag of fluorescent red material was nailed to the top of a short mast. Packaged, a complete marker or beacon weighed 750 pounds and required a team of twelve men to transport it to remote sites. Once there, it could be erected in half an hour by a six-man team. During the later voyages, these beacons were prefabricated on *Labrador*'s flight deck and transported by Piasecki helicopter (HUP3) to appropriate spots.

While the hydrographic party was ashore, *Labrador* carried out her own scientific studies in Lancaster Sound and Barrow Strait. It was at this stage that it was discovered that it was possible to bring the Landing Craft Vehicle and Personnel (LCVP) back to the ship even in heavy fog. The LCVP was fitted with a radar reflector which produced a clear signal on the short-range radar, and using two-way radios, it could be guided accurately to a rendezvous point.

Just before *Labrador* reached Craig Harbour, Commander Penton completed his fourth trial of the Admiralty gyro-magnetic compass. The harbour was ice-bound, but a lead was found which enabled Special Constable Arreak, RCMP, his wife, four children, his worldly possessions and seventeen dogs to embark. The chief bosun's mate, Chief Petty Officer Reginald Player, was accustomed to somewhat less voracious crew members. The first time he went forward to give the dogs water, they fell upon his untended gloves in a frenzy, and the lead dog gulped them down in the midst of the snarling pack.

Unloading began the moment *Labrador* arrived at Alexandra Fiord on the east coast of Ellesmere Island on 8 August 1954. Owing to shallow waters and an unsuitable beach, rendered all the more treacherous by high winds and ice, the landing of supplies was confined to three hours on either side of high water, and resupply was not completed until midnight of the eleventh. The last fifteen tons of coal were landed in a race between the officers' and the chiefs and petty officers' teams. The chiefs won by less than a minute and were rewarded with an old porcelain mug and a battered tin plate, inscribed "Presented by the Ellesmere Island Jockey Club."

Despite difficulties, harbour soundings were completed and navigational beacons erected. In addition, a rendezvous was effected with the United States Coast Guard (USCG) vessel, *Eastwind*, and a probe was carried out into Kane Basin, where another AGM5 trial took place at 79°N.

Ice, fog, and gales dictated whether work was possible in the Arctic; we worked the daylight hours when conditions were good, and when they were adverse, we stopped. Consequently, Sunday was proclaimed whenever work was interrupted by inclement weather and the pipe was made, "Today will be considered Sunday." The padre held church service either on the flight deck or in the seamen's mess hall. In some cases Sundays and the weather did not match, and when *Labrador* returned to Halifax in 1955 the crew received two light-duty "make and mend" days to make up for two Sundays that were owing.

When *Labrador* returned to Resolute on 15 August, she found the resupply vessels *D'Iberville, C.D. Howe, H.B. Maclean, Gander Bay,* and *Maruba* at anchor in the approaches. The hydrographic party had completed their triangulation of the harbour and were taking soundings in the bay. By the nineteenth the survey of the harbour and approaches was completed. During that five-day period the ship carried out AGM5 trials, ran sounding lines, took oceanographic stations across Lancaster Sound and Wellington Channel, and visited Erebus Bay on Beechey Island. *Labrador*'s crew examined the graves of three of Sir John Franklin's sailors, which were marked with heavy oak headboards inscribed with their names and the name of their ship.

Using Resolute as a headquarters, *Labrador* continued her scientific studies but was defeated by heavy ice at the entrance to Peel Sound between Somerset and Prince of Wales Islands. As a result, she decided to return to Resolute, but received a message from *Monte Carlo*, a privately chartered Boston dragger engaged in terrestrial magnetism studies, that she was beset by ice in Baring Channel at the northern end of Prince of Wales Island. *Labrador* set course immediately to render aid, and when contact was made, *Monte Carlo* was taken in tow and her crew of eighteen came aboard *Labrador* to shower and use the canteen. Once the ships reached open water, *Monte Carlo* was supplied with fuel, water, and provisions and advised to return to Boston, as *Labrador* would no longer be available for rescue operations.

After landing mail and collecting stores at Resolute, *Labrador* steamed westward, carrying out studies en route before joining the Canadian-U.S. Beaufort Sea expedition consisting of the USS *Burton Island* and USCGS *Northwind*—both Wind-class icebreakers. Fog and heavy ice under pressure made progress slow but contact was made with *Burton Island* at Dealy Island, south of Melville Island, on 25 August.

Upon arrival at Dealy Island, a magnetic party was put ashore, and the captain of USS *Burton Island* and the chief scientist came aboard to discuss the work to be undertaken. A mess dinner was held that evening with the Americans to celebrate the first meeting of ships from the east and west. Fog kept the guests overnight, but when it cleared, the USN officers returned to their ship, the magnetic party was recovered, and a course was set for Prince of Wales Strait. However, owing to ice, fog, and pressure, the passage south across Viscount Melville Sound was an arduous and trying one.

Labrador reached Richard Collinson Inlet on 29 August. *Northwind* was already at anchor there and served as a fixed transmitting station for hydrographic survey work conducted by *Labrador* and *Burton Island*. The three captains and the three chief scientists utilized the occasion of the rendezvous to discuss future plans and a flexible scheme of co-operation.

Navigation beacons were erected at Bernard Point and Russell Point to mark the astro-stations previously taken by *Northwind*. The magnetic party was landed at Russell Point, and *Labrador* ran two lines of ocean-ographic stations across the northern entrance of Prince of Wales Strait. Then she proceeded for about twenty miles down the western side of the strait looking for Harvey Blandford of the Dominion Hydrographic Office and his party who had been marooned when their Weasel (a tracked vehicle for use in rough country) broke down. After rescuing this team and recovering the magnetic party, the survey continued along Banks Island.

At this juncture Captain Robertson decided to use *Labrador*'s helicopter to transport the scientists and their gear. Thus, forty-five miles of surveying were finished in four days compared to the ten miles of survey that Blandford had been able to accomplish in eighteen days with his Weasel. This was possibly the first time helicopters were used for survey work in the high Arctic.

At midnight on the last day of August, an "operation immediate" message was received from *Northwind* asking for assistance. *Labrador* and *Burton Island* set course at once for *Northwind* at Peel Point. At dawn, *Labrador*'s helicopter found her and led her out of the ice field in which she was trapped. When *Northwind* was clear of danger, course was set for Russell Point, where the helicopter departed for the area of Knight Harbour on Banks Island, where it recovered for the National Museum of Canada a large wooden sledge, a small anchor, and a magnetic compass from Vilhjalmur Stefansson's 1913-18 expedition.

Fog, rain, and sleet that promised to continue for several days forced an end to work on 5 September. Every morning, when the hands fell in for prayers, the padre proclaimed "This is the day which the Lord has made; we will rejoice and be glad in it." Huddled in the cold, with rain stinging their cheeks, the crew could only reflect on the irony of their situation.

After *Burton Island* had transferred an electronic position-indicator (EPI) to *Labrador* for later use, *Labrador* proceeded to De Salis Bay, on the south coast of Banks Island, carrying out oceanographic studies en route. It was clear by this time that *Labrador* would conquer the Northwest Passage, and a press release from NSHQ announced that she would attempt it.

On arrival at De Salis Bay, two microwave parties and a survival team (to test Arctic gear) were landed while *Labrador* ran sounding lines to seaward using microwave control. Upon completing these experiments, she returned and sent in the LCVP to pick up her personnel. The weather had started to deteriorate by this stage, and as the LCVP was backing off the beach, the surf swung her around and pounded her broadside, filling her rapidly with water. The personnel had to be recovered by helicopter, and it was not until three days later, when the weather moderated, that the LCVP could be brought off the beach.

Labrador then sailed to Cape Kellett at the southwestern end of Banks Island, where she acted as an EPI station for *Burton Island* and *Northwind*, which were operating along the west coast of the island. She worked with the two ships in the Beaufort Sea, north of Alaska and the Yukon, for eleven days, undertaking oceanographic and bathymetric studies and a final AGM5 trial, before heading south to Cape Prince of Wales, at the western extreme of Alaska. En route, she attempted current studies, but the weather was so bad that these exercises had to be cancelled. At the same time, on 22 September, the doctor reported that the chief stoker was seriously ill, and so the ship headed for Esquimalt at top speed.

The medical officer, Surgeon Lieutenant D.J. Kidd, RCN, and his staff, assisted by volunteers from the ship's company, worked night and day for almost a week to save the stoker's life. An amazingly complicated oxygen tent was devised by the engineer officer, Lieutenant-Commander (E) A.H. Kerley, RCN, from bits and pieces on board, that was capable of utilizing commercial oxygen supplies intended for use in oxyacetylene welding. The patient was kept alive with blood transfusions until we arrived at Esquimalt on 27 September, whereupon he was transferred to the RCN hospital, HMCS *Naden*. Sadly, he died ten days later.

The time spent in Esquimalt was hectic to say the least; reporters poured on board looking for stories, maintenance work had to be done, and the hull had to be painted. While all this was going on, Captain Robertson was fully engaged addressing various civilian organizations about *Labrador's* accomplishments.

Leave for the officers expired at midnight on 11 October in time for a "special operation." While the commanding officer kept *Naden's* duty officer suitably engaged, the wardroom officers manned the LCVP that had been loaded with one of our northern navigation beacons. They manoeuvred the landing craft silently shoreward and dragged the beacon up the steep bank to the parade square at *Naden*. There they assembled all 750 pounds of planking and ballast and chained it to the reviewing stand where the commodore of the barracks would hold divisions at 0800 the following morning. With *Labrador*'s calling card firmly in place, the LCVP was stowed on board by 0300 and the ship made ready to sail to Vancouver four hours later.

There was something very special about the journey to Vancouver; *Labrador* was to rendezvous off Point Atkinson with a great Arctic pioneer, the RCMP vessel *St. Roch*. Under the command of Sergeant Henry A. Larsen, RCMP, she had completed the Northwest Passage twice: from west to east in 1940-42 and from east to west in 1944. *Labrador*'s arrival was fortuitous since *St. Roch* had just completed a voyage from Halifax to Victoria via the Panama canal. The two Arctic veterans met as planned and, accompanied by *Labrador*'s helicopters, made their way into Vancouver harbour. *St. Roch* lay alongside *Labrador*, and Captain Robertson attended a ceremony at City Hall where the ownership of *St. Roch* was officially transferred to the City of Vancouver. That evening her blue ensign was laid up for the last time while buglers from *Labrador* played their sad refrain.

Labrador was the subject of tremendous publicity in Victoria and Vancouver, and sailors with her name on their cap tallies were swept off their feet with hospitality. Much to their delight there was no shortage of female companionship.

On 16 October, *Labrador* sailed for San Francisco for an operational visit. There had been relatively little publicity about her there, and this was a welcome change after the hectic pace of Victoria and Vancouver. While we were there, the City of San Francisco appealed for blood donors, and *Labrador* provided thirty-five volunteers (in accordance with the age-old naval custom: "Everyone from here to the left").

Labrador sailed for Balboa, Panama, on 21 October. The passage south was hot and humid, and hammocks were rigged on the upper deck. The sponson for the 3-inch 50-calibre gun (the gun had never been fitted) was flooded and used as a swimming pool. We arrived at Balboa on 2 November and transited the canal the following day. After reaching Colon, Panama, we shaped course for St. George's, Grenada, arriving there on the tenth.

While at anchor at Grenada we discovered that the starboard motor compartment had been flooded with salt water—a very serious matter indeed. We managed to pump the compartment dry and flush out the 5,000-horsepower motor in order to halt corrosion, but despite these measures we were obliged to sail for Halifax on the port engine alone.

HMCS *Labrador* arrived at Halifax on 21 November 1954; she was only the second ship to ever circumnavigate the North American continent. Her scientific accomplishments marked the beginning of Arctic exploration by Canadians, using one of the world's finest floating scientific platforms. *Labrador* had established that it was possible to take a large ship through the Northwest Passage. Moreover, the information gained was destined to enhance the RCN's ability to conduct high latitude operations with submarines, merchant ships, and naval vessels. Morale had been of the highest during the entire voyage, which in itself had been exciting and adventurous for a proud, well-led ship's company.

Labrador underwent refit in January 1955, defects, additions, and alterations numbering about three hundred. At the same time, NSHQ approved a request from Fleet Admiral Arleigh Burke, USN, the U.S. chief of Naval Operations, for *Labrador* to carry out survey work preparatory to the sea-lift of materials for the Distant Early Warning (DEW) lines in the eastern Canadian Arctic and to take charge of the sea-lift in Foxe Basin. The main efforts were to be focused on that basin, although Robertson had orders that scientific work was "not to interfere" with operational requirements.

As *Labrador* had never had first-of-class trials, she spent ten days in the middle of May completing them off the coast of Maine. Thereafter she took on stores and embarked eleven civilian scientists and two civilian technicians as well as a six-man diving team. On the first of June, she set sail again for that beautiful and unforgiving world of glinting ice-floes and polar sea-smoke.

Oceanographic and hydrographic studies were commenced at the western entrance to the Strait of Belle Isle. Captain Robertson was landed at Stephenville, Newfoundland, on the fifth, for a hurried trip to New York where he conferred for three days with the Commander, Task Force 6 (CTF6), Rear-Admiral R. Mason, USN. They discussed a vast range of problems concerning the sea-lift for the DEW line.

Fog—baffling and omnidirectional—enshrouded the ship as *Labrador* passed through the Strait of Belle Isle. A thousand feet off her bow the grey of the sea rose imperceptibly into a wall of fog. At one time fifty icebergs appeared as contacts on our radar screens. She crept forward through the maze, the fog lasting all of the way to Hudson Strait. Once there, on 15 June, *Labrador* transferred to CTF6's operational control.

When *Labrador* began making her way westward through Hudson Strait, she encountered 10/10 ice, approximately twelve feet thick. She broke through the floes that covered the bay at Coral Harbour and, shattered, they slid out to sea on the ebb tide. As soon as there was enough clear water in which to work, triangulation beacons were erected, beach clearance was commenced, and approaches were sounded for the supply ships that were due to arrive shortly.

Arrangements were also made for the civilian contractor to fill the beach and grade a hard-stand for the cargo, when landed. In addition, charts were made of the beach and of the approaches for the incoming U.S. ships.

At the beginning of July, *Labrador* set up EPI stations at Cape Donovan, on Southampton Island, and at Cape Enauolik, on Baffin Island. Ice prevented the use of boats at Cape Donovan, so *Labrador* lay four miles off and made ready to airlift a huge amount of equipment ashore. Everything had to be sorted so that materials to be used first had priority for the construction party that erected the station. This was the first time that the RCN had tackled a project of this sort, and the result was highly successful. The shore station was completed in less than two days during which time twenty flying hours and 290 man-hours had been expended in transportation and construction. This accomplishment compares favourably with the work undertaken at Banks Island in 1954 by *Northwind*, whose crew took 444 man-hours and thirty-six hours by boat to do the same job then.

Upon completion of the two stations, *Labrador* sailed north under EPI control, sounding a route for the supply ships to Hall Beach. She spent eight days at Hall Beach clearing beach-landing ramps, sounding anchorages, erecting navigational beacons, and preparing charts for the supply ships. There was time for a little play as well, and the ship's company won a softball game against a team from the civilian contractor, the Foundation Company of Canada.

Having completed her assignments, *Labrador* returned to the EPI stations to bring the personnel on board for a shower, pay, haircut, and break from their lonely existence. On 8 August she went to Coral Harbour, where the icebreaker USS *Edisto* was waiting with the first three ships. The cargo for Coral Harbour had already been off-loaded, stores were transported to *Labrador*, and she gave a spare EPI to the survey ship USS *Pursuit*. Adverse ice conditions in Foxe Channel delayed departure for the north, and so *Labrador* and *Pursuit* visited Chesterfield Inlet to begin soundings of the area. Shortly thereafter, *Edisto* arrived with a second group of cargo ships, and on 14 August, the convoy set sail for Hall Beach in two columns, led by *Labrador* and *Edisto*.

Good progress was made the first day, but, owing to darkness and ice, the columns were stopped until 0600 the next morning. The ships became locked in the ice during the night and had to be broken out and re-formed in their columns. A thirty-five mile advance was made during each of the next two days, then nine miles, then eight. Experience showed that more progress was made by keeping underway than by stopping at night, but for those in command, the passage was a nightmare. There was precious little sleep, and it was difficult to persuade merchant ship captains to risk damaging their ships by forcing them into the ice. The convoy reached open water after a week, and the ships anchored in their allotted berths off Site 1 at Hall Beach.

The ships had not emerged unscathed from their duel with the ice. *Pursuit* had ruptured a plate on her starboard bow near the keel; *Vermillion* had lost the tips of three of her four propeller blades; *Rushmore* had been holed in the forepeak; and *Dalton Victory* (a World War II Victory

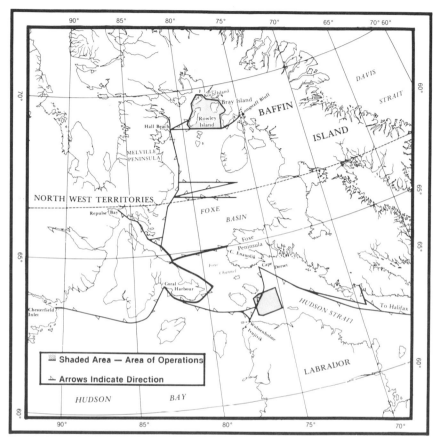

Eastern Arctic Operations, HMCS *Labrador*: 1 June-18 November 1955

ship) had ruptured a plate in her number one hold. As Captain Robertson was responsible for the operational control and safe conduct of the twenty-one ships in the task force, he was greatly relieved to learn that the damage was not more extensive.

Unloading commenced on a round-the-clock, weather-permitting basis for the next month. By 25 August, the *Monroe Victory* (the only civilian ship in the task force) had completed discharging her cargo, and *Edisto* escorted her out of the ice for her return voyage to the United States. *Labrador* and *Pursuit* sailed to Site 2 on Rowley Island in the northern sector of Foxe Basin to complete beach surveys. *Labrador* was back at Hall Beach on 31 August to welcome Vice-Admiral F.C. Denebrink, USN, commander Military Sea Transport Services (MSTS), Rear-Admiral R.

Mason, USN, CTF6, Brigadier-General F.T. Voorhees, U.S. Army, commander MSTS Atlantic Area, and Mr. Harry D. Lohman, vice-president of the Western Electric Company and their staffs, who came on board to hammer out operational plans.

The weather in the first half of September was very poor, and *Labrador* confined herself to surveying and charting Sites 2, 3 (Bray Island), and 4 (Longstaff Bluff). Returning by air after talks with the civilian contractor at Site 3, Captain Robertson spotted a polar bear stalking our geodetic party and was obliged to shoot it. (Civilian workers there had already boasted that they had the only red-headed polar bear in the Arctic; he had dipped his head into an open five-gallon can of red paint.) Cargo ships were now starting to unload construction materials for the early warning radar stations at Sites 2, 3, and 4; the icebreaker USS *Atka* had relieved *Edisto* and brought some of *Labrador*'s personnel back from Cape Donovan; and, at the same time, G. Robertson, deputy minister of Northern Affairs, and Captain T.C. Pullen, RCN, *Labrador*'s commanding-officer-designate, arrived for three days of familiarization.

On 16 September a distress signal was received from the Canadian Fisheries Research Board vessel *Calanus*. *Labrador* went to her assistance and then returned to Hall Beach where, by 27 September, operations were complete. She spent a further five days around Repulse before rendezvousing with the remaining ships in the area. Equipment and personnel were transferred, and for the first time since 7 July, *Labrador* enjoyed a full complement.

After several days of violent storms, she was back at the northern sites again. For the next fortnight, the crew extended surveys and erected beacons to assist with next year's re-supply. Gale after gale made these tasks tiresome and difficult. Of greater concern, though, was the fact that the captain had fallen seriously ill and needed to be evacuated by air. Course was laid for Coral Harbour and Captain Robertson was transferred to an RCAF Dakota aircraft to be taken to Montreal.

I took command of *Labrador* and commenced an intensive oceanographic and hydrographic programme in Hudson Strait, which, thanks to nine days of perfect weather, was completed. However, the weather took a turn for the worse on 9 November, and gales of up to sixty knots became daily occurrences. Bucking a storm *Labrador* made her way into the Atlantic and turned south for the long run to the Strait of Belle Isle. We began to establish a line of oceanographic stations at the western entrance to the strait on the fourteenth, but this work had to be suspended in order to take a seriously ill member of the crew to Stephenville, Newfoundland, for transfer to an RCAF aircraft for hospitalization in Halifax. The following day the Flag Officer Atlantic Coast, Rear-Admiral R.E.S. Bidwell, RCN, joined *Labrador* for the final leg of the journey. *Labrador* reached Halifax on 18 November 1955, after 170 days at sea.

The following messages summarized *Labrador's* remarkable five-and-one-half month accomplishment. From the Chief of Naval Operations, Admiral Burke:

> For Captain Robertson, RCN. With the Foxe Basin supply operation now successfully completed please accept my hearty congratulations for the most excellent performance by your task group. The undertaking was a stupendous effort with the accepted hazards of ice, weather, and unknown hydrography. The successful attainment of all objectives is a tribute to your professional ability and courage.

From the Commander, MSTS, Vice-Admiral Denebrink:

> Upon successful completion of your assigned tasks in MSTS Arctic operations in 1955, I wish to express my congratulations and my appreciation of the outstanding services you have rendered as a Task Group Commander of Combined U.S.-Canadian forces. Your leadership, courage, professional skills, and determination have been of the highest order throughout trying operations in uncharted waters and hazardous ice conditions and reflect the greatest credit upon you and your service. It has been a pleasure to have you serve with us in our mutual endeavors. Please convey to all your command my congratulations, best wishes, and appreciation for their substantial contribution. As a personal note may I say [that] when I saw you in Foxe Basin I knew at once you would deliver the goods. Well done.

Labrador's employment during 1956 included requests for her services from the U.S. commander, MSTS, to assist with the resupply of the DEW line; the Department of Transport, to assist with the resupply of Arctic weather stations; the Defence Research Board for oceanographic survey work in the Gulf of St. Lawrence during the winter of 1955-56 and scientific operations in the Arctic during the summer; the Department of Mines and Technical Surveys; and the Fisheries Research Board for her services during the summer months.

On 20 February 1956, *Labrador* sailed with Captain Pullen in command for a twelve-day scientific mission in the Gulf of St. Lawrence. Her next cruise was much more varied in character. On 15 March she sailed for Mayport, Florida, through gale winds of up to sixty-five knots. She painted ship there and sailed for New York, where a conference was held concerning summer operations for the resupply of the DEW line. Next, she was ordered to Greenland, three thousand miles away, to rescue nine Norwegian sailors trapped off Scoresby Sound on the east coast of Greenland due west of Iceland.

Just as she was passing Cape Race, the mission was cancelled. The

Norwegians had freed themselves, and *Labrador* returned to the Gulf of St. Lawrence via the Strait of Belle Isle. Her destination was Pictou, Nova Scotia, where she undertook to free HMCS *Wallaceburg*, an Algerine-class minesweeper trapped in the ice. She towed *Wallaceburg* to open water, detached, and returned to Halifax on 16 April.

On 5 July 1956, *Labrador* set off on her third summer cruise to the Arctic. A conference was held at St. John's, Newfoundland, with U.S. naval and military personnel concerning the projected northern operations. After embarking a U.S. army officer and a USN photographer, the course was set for Resolution Island.

Labrador conducted oceanographic work in Hudson Strait for two days before moving on to Brevoort Island, where she surveyed the approaches and cleared the beach preparatory to resupply activities. The inner harbour was sounded by *Labrador*'s "Pogo," a 35-foot, 10-inch, broad-beamed craft of welded aluminum construction, capable of accommodating seven men with stores for six weeks. Named after the cartoon character, she was a versatile little vessel, fitted with radio-telephone, gyro compass, echo sounder, and radar.

When the soundings were complete, *Labrador* returned to Resolution Island where the charts, photographs, and sailing directions for Brevoort Island were left for *Edisto*, which was expected shortly to escort a cargo vessel there. On the way to Coral Harbour, the medical officer revisited Lake Harbour and Ivujivik. Stores and mail were picked up at Coral Harbour before sailing to Cape Donovan and Cape Enauolik, where the EPI station equipment left behind in 1955 was recovered.

Labrador continued operations near Southampton Island until the end of July and then headed north for the main base area at Hall Beach. After erecting EPI stations at Hall Beach and on Bray Island, she sailed for Rowley Island and landed a party to survey Rowley and Koch Islands. She remained in the area for three weeks erecting navigational beacons, carrying out soundings, and conducting oceanographic studies.

Rear-Admiral H.S. Rayner, RCN, the chief of Naval Personnel and his secretary, Commander A.O. Soloman, flew to Hall in late August and visited *Labrador* for three days. *Labrador* met *Edisto* off Sea Horse Point towards the end of the month and distributed charts that the staff in *Labrador* had prepared. Then she took five ships and *Edisto* four for the passage to Hall Beach.

A top-level conference took place aboard *Labrador* on 7 September, when she was visited by Vice-Admiral J.M. Wells, USN, commander MSTS, Rear-Admiral R. Mason, USN, CTF6, Captain O.C.S. Robertson, RCN, Captain Alfred G. Ward, USN, and Commander Plummer, USN, the captain of *Edisto*. It was decided that *Labrador* would carry out surveys of the Gulf of Boothia, Prince Regent Inlet, and Bellot Strait. Six other areas

Eastern Arctic Operations, HMCS *Labrador*: 3 July-13 October 1956

would also be covered before she returned to Halifax about the middle of October.

Labrador occupied oceanographic stations and investigated shoals in central Foxe Basin. Then she discovered a channel between Prince Charles and Spicer Islands. On 16 September the two ships headed north, where oceanographic and current studies were carried out and radar beacons were erected at the eastern end of Fury and Hecla Strait. *Edisto* was having difficulty in transit but *Labrador* pressed on, and with the use of helicopters, set up a radar beacon on Crown Prince Frederik Island at the western end of the strait to assist *Edisto* with her passage. Shortly after entering the Gulf of Boothia, *Edisto* radioed that she had lost her starboard propeller and needed assistance. *Labrador* went to her rescue immediately and escorted her through heavy ice for about fifty miles until she was able to proceed on her own back to the United States.

Labrador returned to complete her third transit of Fury and Hecla Strait and on 20 September met difficult ice conditions before entering the Gulf of Boothia prior to surveying Bellot Strait with "Pogo." Fortunately, the conditions became intolerable and soundings had to be discontinued. Fortunately because the waters were treacherous, and Magpie Rock, lurking only three feet below the surface, was waiting to trap the unwary.

Course was then set for Erebus Bay on Beechey Island. HMS *North Star* had been stationed there 104 years before. She was the depot ship for Sir Edward Belcher's five-ship expedition in the 1852 search for Sir John Franklin. She alone survived two winters at Erebus to return to England. Her commanding officer had been Commander W.J.S. Pullen, RN, and his sailing master had been his brother T.C. Pullen, grand-uncles of Rear-Admiral H.F. Pullen, RCN, and his brother, Captain T.C. Pullen, RCN, *Labrador*'s commanding officer.

Having completed her oceanographic programme, *Labrador* turned southward on 5 October and proceeded through the Strait of Belle Isle. She anchored in the Bay of Islands to square away briefly before sailing to Stephenville where the Flag Officer Atlantic Coast, Rear-Admiral Bidwell, came on board. He sailed with her to Halifax, and at 1445 on 13 October 1956 *Labrador* secured alongside after 102 days in the Arctic.

Labrador had steamed 18,606 miles during that time, more than 12,000 of them in uncharted waters. She performed an immense amount of hydrographic work, running 12,000 miles of soundings, preparing numerous charts and sailing directions, taking panoramic and radar photographs, and otherwise contributing to the safety of navigation in the waters of Canada's northern archipelago. *Labrador*'s oceanographic work constituted the most extensive programme ever undertaken in the Canadian Arctic and included 200 oceanographic stations, 263 bathythermograph casts, 1,536 salinity samples, 923 oxygen analyses, 486 phosphate determinations, and 72 bottom samples. All of this work was accomplished on the understanding that it was not to interfere with our primary task of facilitating the resupply of the DEW line.

In March 1957 *Labrador* set sail on her first and only operational cruise to England, Norway, and Denmark. After a passage marred by stormy weather, she arrived at Portsmouth and moved on to Oslo on 1 April. The Norwegians displayed great interest in the ship while the crew enjoyed the opportunity to see Fridtjof Nansen's polar voyager, the *Fram*, Thor Heyerdahl's famous raft, the *Kon Tiki*, and ancient Viking ships. When *Labrador* visited Copenhagen she was involved in four hectic days of entertainment and welcomed over eight thousand visitors. Leaving Copenhagen, she sailed for home via the Kiel Canal, arriving in Halifax on 26 April.

Labrador commenced another ambitious programme on 25 June 1957. She headed for St. John's Newfoundland, having embarked seven scientists and their scientific equipment. Her stay in St. John's, however, was cut short since the USCGS *Eastwind* had been forced to return to Boston with damage to her main engines. Consequently, *Labrador* was called upon to take over *Eastwind*'s commitment and escort the tankers USS *Kankakee* and *Memphis* to Goose Bay, Labrador. *Edisto* arrived to help and took responsibility for *Memphis*. Having completed her assignment, *Labrador* turned south. As she approached St. Anthony, Newfoundland, on 1 July, an iceberg that had not appeared on radar suddenly loomed up in the thick fog. *Labrador*'s engines were thrown full astern; the ship shuddered and slowed and barely avoided a serious collision. St. Anthony harbour was ice-bound, so *Labrador* continued to La Scie and commenced a week's soundings of the beaches for future supply operations. Resolution Island was next, and work was undertaken in Gabriel and Hudson Straits. Hydrographic parties were landed but had to be recovered hastily when fog began to roll in. So, on to Frobisher Bay. Ice conditions were so difficult there that it was necessary to send the hydrographic party ashore by helicopter.

Labrador proceeded to Narssaq in Greenland. On 15 July she embarked some illustrious official passengers: Ambassador H.F. Feaver, the Canadian ambassador to Denmark, and Mrs. Feaver; Professor and Mrs. Niels Bohr; Ambassador Henrik Kaufman, Danish ambassador to the United States; Mr. Eske Brun, permanent undersecretary to Greenland; Miss Gunver Hirschsprung, secretary to Mr. Brun; Commander Norman Svend V. Rosenvinge, Danish consul, Boston; Mr. Christian L. Thomsen of the Danish atomic commission; and Major-General Erik Rasmussen, Danish air attaché to the United States and Canada.

Cabin space was at a premium and required considerable shuffling in order to ensure that the dignitaries were as comfortable as possible. *Labrador* sailed for Gronne Dal, receiving a tremendous reception there, and departed on the seventeenth for Godthaab, the capital of Greenland. The official party disembarked there, and *Labrador* returned to Resolution Island to recover the helicopter and the hydrographic teams.

During *Labrador*'s absence in Greenland, one of the helicopters had been instrumental in finding and recovering the body of a radar station employee who had gone mountain climbing contrary to orders. En route to Frobisher Bay *Labrador* landed stores by air for Dr. Ian A. McLaren and his wife, who were conducting studies for the Fisheries Research Board at Ney Harbour, while at Frobisher itself, Commodore H.L. Quinn, RCN, came on board to observe ice-breaking and scientific work for a few days.

Returning to the lower region of the bay, both helicopters were flown off with their hydrographic parties. Shortly after take-off one of the helicopters crashed; the second went to assist, only to meet the same fate. *Labrador* manoeuvred as close as she could, and the HUP3 was flown off (although it had only recently been classified as unserviceable). The wrecked machines were near the top of a 2,400-foot mountain swept by exceedingly dangerous turbulence. Conditions were no better the following day, so food and other necessary articles were dropped. A landing party was put ashore but recalled when the flying conditions improved. Fortunately, all of the crew were rescued, and Captain Pullen commended the pilot of the rescue aircraft, Lieutenant D.A. Oliphant, RCN, for his considerable skill.

Subsequently, *Labrador* rendezvoused with *Edisto*, and they sailed for Brevoort Harbour. *Labrador* remained in the area for three days, surveying, escorting cargo vessels, and generally assisting with the resupply. After seeing all ships out of the ice, she returned to York Sound and landed the executive officer, Commander C.A. Law, RCN, and a party of fourteen men in an attempt to rescue one of the disabled helicopters. The rescue operation was unsuccessful, and driving rain, fog, and leaky tents made their effort a most uncomfortable one. Several days later they were still not able to begin their climb, and all but three of them returned on board.

On 10 August *Labrador* provided ice escort for two U.S. tankers, USNS *Tamalpais* and *Tonti*, from Resolution Island to Frobisher. Owing to ice conditions, the three ships hove to twenty miles south of Cape Vanderbilt for the night. When convoying in ice, the breaker kept about a half-cable length ahead of the lead ship so that she could take advantage of the open water created by the breaker before the ice closed in and blocked her path. The USNS *Tamalpais* was a 22,000-tonner, loaded with aviation gasoline, and she made an awesome sight closing in from one hundred yards astern at ten knots when *Labrador* was halted temporarily by the ice. The following day *Labrador* discovered a new and much safer route into Frobisher, called Pike-Resor Channel.

After fuelling from *Tamalpais*, taking on stores and embarking thirty USAF personnel, *Labrador* sailed for York Sound to recover the men who had remained and as many of the items as possible from the wrecked helicopters. She put the USAF personnel ashore at Resolute Island on 15 August and sailed north into Davis Strait four days later. She engaged in oceanographic work while en route and continued it in Prince Regent Inlet while bound for Bellot Strait.

On 22 August *Labrador* occupied Fort Ross, an abandoned Hudson's Bay Company post on Somerset Island in Bellot Strait, as a base camp for her hydrographic parties. Five days later *Labrador* left the survey parties and proceeded up Prince Regent Inlet to carry out oceanographic studies and visit Fury Beach on the east coast of Somerset Island where a few relics of the 1825 wreck of HMS *Fury* were recovered for the Maritime Museum of Canada. *Labrador* continued her scientific studies after calling at Resolute for mail and returned to the western entrance of Bellot Strait via Peel Sound.

Eastern Arctic Operations, HMCS *Labrador*: 25 June-11 October 1957

Now that a deep-water passage had been established for Bellot Strait, *Labrador* turned south to meet three U.S. vessels (USCGS *Storis, Bramble,* and *Spar*) and continued oceanographic studies in Franklin Strait, which separates Boothia Peninsula on the east and Prince of Wales Island on the west. *Storis* radioed that she required medical assistance, and *Labrador* headed for her immediately, arriving 3 September. *Labrador* escorted the three ships through the ice to open water, and while they headed to the western entrance of Bellot Strait to conduct hydrographic studies, *Labrador* carried on with her own oceanographic work. The survey was completed by the tenth, Fort Ross was closed down, and all parties were brought back on board.

Labrador returned to Resolute to continue studies in Barrow Strait,

Wellington Channel, and Maury Channel, but meeting the polar pack twenty feet thick in Queen's Channel, she retreated to Erebus Bay. At one stage, in shoaling waters, there were only eighteen inches of water under her keel. The Franklin Memorial was visited by a recreational party of thirty which was almost joined by a polar bear, which, after smashing an oil drum with his paw, wandered off nonchalantly.

Leaving Erebus Bay, *Labrador* sailed for Arctic Bay. A full day was spent there rectifying electrical defects, Eskimo outboards, and wireless sets, etc., much to the relief of the Hudson's Bay Company manager. At Pond Inlet, the Roman Catholic priest, Father Jean Dufour, OMI, came on board, celebrated mass, and heard confessions. A shoal at the entrance to Navy Board Inlet was investigated and *Labrador* moved on to Grise Fiord.

It was while *Labrador* was at Grise Fiord, in a remote corner of the Canadian Arctic, that her days in the RCN became numbered. A message was received that she was to be transferred to Department of Transport control, but despite her change in fortunes there was still work to be done, work for which she was eminently suited. *Labrador* continued her oceanographic programme on the way to Thule, Greenland, and then through Baffin Bay and Davis Strait. She called at Cape Dyer, Exeter Bay, for mail and moved on to Pangnirtung, where the RCMP constable, who had been embarked earlier, issued a marriage licence and the ship's padre officiated at the marriage of the local minister.

One last effort was made to salvage the downed helicopters, but only a few pieces of equipment were recovered. Course was then shaped to Ney Harbour, where Dr. and Mrs. McLaren were embarked, and on to Frobisher Bay, where the RCMP constable and several civilians were put ashore. *Labrador* sailed through the Strait of Belle Isle to George Bay, Newfoundland, where the Flag Officer Atlantic Coast, Rear-Admiral H.F. Pullen boarded us from HMCS *Lauzon* for the passage to Halifax. *Labrador* secured alongside on 11 October 1957, her last major undertaking for the RCN at an end.

As an economic measure the Naval Staff recommended in October 1956 that *Labrador* be transferred to another government department. However, on 14 November 1956, the Naval Board declined to support this recommendation, preferring to put the decision in abeyance. The Minister of National Defence, G.R. Pearkes, was asked by the Minister of Transport, George Hees, to make *Labrador* available for winter operations in the Gulf of St. Lawrence and for summer resupply operations in the Arctic. But she was to remain in RCN hands, or, if that was not acceptable, the Department of Transport would be pleased to have her transferred to their department. After due consideration, the Chief of the Naval Staff, Vice-Admiral H.G. DeWolf, RCN, recommended the transfer, and it was approved, effective 1 April 1958.

The transfer elicited considerable comment in the press, and a number of parliamentarians expressed their concern about this move. The navy's attitude was that *Labrador* failed to support the RCN's role in the defence of Canada, particularly as it involved anti-submarine operations in the North Atlantic. Moreover, the transfer would release two hundred officers and men for duty in fighting ships and effect a considerable economy.

The executive officer, Commander C.A. Law, RCN, took over command on 4 November from Captain Pullen and on the eighteenth sailed for Saint John, New Brunswick, for refit. She was seen off at 0830 by a party of naval officers, led by Commodore E.W. Finch-Noyes, RCN, and the band from HMCS *Stadacona*. Six helicopters formed close escort, all of the ships in harbour manned the side and Rear-Admiral Pullen took the salute. A paying-off ceremony was held four days later at the Saint John drydock. The commanding officer delivered a final address to the remainder of the ship's company and read a message from the minister of National Defence to all who had served in her.

HMCS *Labrador* has become part of the history of the Arctic. Her achievements during a short and illustrious career in the Royal Canadian Navy were too many, too varied, and too important to be summarized so briefly. There is no doubt that she contributed more to man's knowledge of the Arctic during her four years with the RCN than any other ship. These accomplishments were due entirely to her two commanding officers, Captains Robertson and Pullen. Their professional skill, leadership, and determination to succeed were the keys to *Labrador*'s success as that hardy vessel moved through a polar world filled with challenges and dangers.

Chapter 17

THE IMPACT OF PUBLIC POLICY ON
A NAVAL RESERVE DIVISION

Michael Hadley

Victoria's HMCS *Malahat* is one of eighteen naval reserve units in key Canadian cities at present. It is typical in its training programmes, its relationship to the civilian community, and its integration into the regular force role. As elsewhere, its membership cuts across the civilian trades and professions. Despite the fact that it is closely allied with an operational naval base and thus has more immediate access to ships and facilities than most other units, *Malahat* serves as a useful example of the ways in which public policies have shaped the naval reserve. Public policy is defined here not only as official directives and statements, but also as that network of both tacit and explicit understandings which often influence major legislative or administrative decisions. *Malahat*'s relationship to the regular force, both in its expectations and its equipment, makes it a ready indicator of the changing priorities in defence thinking which will eventually affect all reserve units.[1]

The story of the postwar reserve begins where James Lamb's *The Corvette Navy* ends: "I turned and ran down the ladder into a waiting boat. And I left behind me a ship and a fleet, a host of friends and a way of life that I would never see again. The corvette navy was dead, and I walked away into the strange civilian world of peace."[2] It was the period of demobilization. The machinery of war was being disposed of; "war assets" were now considered liabilities; ships that had pulsed with life during World War II disintegrated into hulks; and vivid experience was rapidly becoming the stuff of memory. The government was turning its attention to new priorities, not least among them the formation of a peacetime navy. Historians have commonly accused the military of preparing to fight the last war, of lacking that foresight which hindsight alone can provide. Parliamentarians of the postwar years held similar views. Canada, it was charged, must learn the lesson of 1939. As Joseph Langlois, the Member of Parliament for Gaspé, proclaimed in the House of Commons in October 1945: "It was only when war broke out in 1939 that we woke up to the fact that Canada had for all practical purposes no navy at all. We must not forget that historical moment in the history of our navy."[3]

Yet despite the increased defence expenditures, prominent parliamentarians continued to voice concern about Canada's state of naval and military unpreparedness. Speaking on 3 April 1952, Major-General G.R. Pearkes, MP for Nanaimo, complained that the Canadian forces were still being organized along "time honoured [and] out-dated lines."[4] Shortly thereafter, Davie Fulton, MP for Kamloops, observed that the preparedness of Canada's reserve force was a "matter of shame and regret"; a reflection of the "state of unreality" in the nation's defence planning.[5] Eight years later the story was much the same. Addressing the House, Paul Hellyer, MP for Davenport, noted (on 4 April 1960) that since "real defence" would be "impossible" after the mid-1960's, continuance of the destroyer escort building and conversion programme seemed "quite unrealistic."[6] It was against this pessimistic and uncertain backdrop that much of the naval reserve policy was formulated.

Nine major concerns emerged during the immediate postwar debate in the House of Commons on the nature of the peacetime RCN. These were:

1. that as Canada could not afford a large navy, she must endeavour to secure quality instead of quantity; an argument which soom became a rationale for retrenchment;
2. that personnel with maritime experience should be retained in both the permanent and reserve forces in order to capitalize fully on the nation's investment in training,
3. that a united and strong peacetime navy was largely dependent on the continued integration of the RCN, RCN Reserve and RCN Volunteer Reserve;
4. that coastal security was a high priority which might be served by some type of coast guard force or fishermen's reserve;
5. that the elimination of irksome customs and traditions from the navy's life style and the modernization of the fleet would increase the RCN's effectiveness;
6. that trades pay should be comparable to that in civilian jobs;
7. that officers should constitute a smaller and less-privileged class;
8. that foreign training cruises would make the navy more popular and should be available to the reserves; and

9. that reserve divisions should be kept open even when bases were being closed and ships paid off.[7]

The debate on these issues was frequently caustic. As one MP remonstrated: "The Minister [of Defence] ought to remind the brass hats in the navy . . . that Nelson is dead and that the Canadian navy should be constructed along modern lines."[8] In announcing the fact that "the postwar Navy [would] consist of two light cruisers of the most modern design, up-to-date destroyers, and two large aircraft carriers" the minister rejoined that he would "bring the remarks about Nelson's death to the attention of the Staff."[9] This was not just jocular parliamentary banter. Rather it was a reflection of a deep dichotomy, a struggle between the proponents of progress and of tradition being fought out in naval circles and on the floor of the House.

Some of the points that the parliamentarians had debated became policy: pay was equalized, large classes of reservists went to sea in cruisers and destroyers in the late 1940's and early 1950's, and a number of reserve units remained open. But it was still an uphill struggle for the reserve. The Victoria *Colonist* for 29 August 1946 featured Major-General Pearkes's protests at the news that HMCS *Malahat* was scheduled to be paid off.[10] This was not the only time that *Malahat*'s future was to hang in the balance. Fortunately for local reservists, these protests prevailed. The decision was reversed, and *Malahat* was recommissioned in April 1947, in a ceremony attended by Rear-Admiral E.R. Mainguy, as the "Vancouver Island Royal Canadian Navy [sic] Reserve Division." That same month the Victoria *Times* reported that the division's establishment would be set at two hundred ratings and eighteen officers. It went on to add a curious phrase: "Of this establishment, 40 percent must be ratings and the remainder will probably be made up of former navy men." What the *Times* no doubt meant was that 40 per cent would be fresh recruits while 60 per cent would be sailors with wartime experience, a ratio reflecting parliamentary and Department of National Defence concerns that the wartime mariner remain the core of the reserve. But it was a ratio that could not be maintained for long, not even in the regular force.

By 1949 the navy's resources, despite postwar uncertainties, must have seemed, at risk of a pun, somewhat buoyant: wartime experience was still fresh, links with tradition and service life style were still strong, and ships were at hand. The "Marine News" section of the *Colonist* of 6 May reported with obvious pride: "Something unique among naval divisions of the British Commonwealth will be established Saturday afternoon with the commissioning of HMCS *Sault Ste. Marie* as the training and headquarters ship of Victoria's naval division HMCS *Malahat*." Thus "the first Algerine sweeper to be built for the Royal Canadian Navy [was to] make *Malahat* the first naval division in any of the navies of the British Commonwealth to have a sea-going major war vessel of its own for the purpose of training its personnel." A host of dignitaries, reflecting the importance of the occasion, attended the ceremony: the lieutenant-governor, the premier, Rear-Admiral Mainguy, flag officer Atlantic Coast, and Rear-Admiral H.G. DeWolf, flag officer Pacific Coast. A guard from the University Naval Training Division (UNTD) and the band from HMCS *Naden* were also in attendance. Articles and photographs in both the *Colonist* and *Times* during May recorded the events from commissioning to full-power trials. Winter cruises were to take reservists to the Gulf Islands and Puget Sound; summer training, like that in 1951, consisted of some ten cruises to such places as Bedwell Harbour and Santa Barbara.

The feeling of growth and purpose in these years was expressed in the headlines of a *Colonist* story of 10 June 1952, repeated a week later in the *Times*. In what may have been an unguarded comment, Captain A.G. Boulton, director of Naval Reserves, announced that "Victoria's naval reserve division may get one of Canada's new minesweepers as a training ship" to replace *Sault Ste. Marie*. He also noted the "RCN's objective of 20,000 officers and men, and 100 ships by 1954. By that time," he added, "the reserve force would number between 8,000 and 10,000 men." These objectives were never reached. There was always a serious gap between the War Establishment (7,500) and active-reserve strength, which stood at 3,769 on 30 April 1951.[11] The Boulton promise of a minesweeper was still being held out to *Malahat* in the 1970's, but by that time the promise and the ship were over twenty years old.

On 19 October 1951, R.O. Campney, the parliamentary assistant to the minister of National Defence, informed the House that the armed forces had more than doubled in size since April 1949. Consisting primarily of army personnel, they had "risen from . . . 41,500 to . . . over 84,000. Of these 84,000, over 35,000 have joined the services since the Korean War began in June 1950."[12] This growth had necessitated almost doubling the forces' payroll, providing new quarters and equipment, and reconditioning training establishments. Such reconditioning was to have a direct impact on *Malahat* somewhat later. Of equal significance was the altered ratio between hostilities-only personnel and new recruits. Though the RCN's growth in the period was proportional—from eight thousand with some fifteen ships in commission to approximately twelve thousand with twenty-eight operational vessels (and an equal number of harbour vessels and auxiliary tankers)—the commitment to further expansion was clear. As Mr. Campney observed:

> there are twenty-four other ships under construction at the present time, seven of which are escort vessels. Furthermore, the contracts for

another seven escort vessels and ten smaller craft have been let. A large program is already in progress looking to the rearmament and refitting of existing RCN ships in strategic reserve. In this connection more than thirty-four frigates and minesweepers have been brought out of reserve and at present are being reconditioned.[13]

He added that five destroyers had been employed in Korean waters since 30 July 1950, of which three had been on duty at all times.

On the same day, C.D. Howe, minister of Trade and Commerce and minister of Defence Production, reminded the House "that contracts had been allotted for one icebreaker, fourteen minesweepers, fourteen escort vessels and five gate vessels as well as a number of harbour craft."[14] "One of the limiting factors" in developing the reserve, Brooke Claxton, the minister of National Defence, informed the House, "is the number of ships [that the RCN can] put to sea each year to train both the active and reserve forces at sea."[15] Bearing in mind that there were only 2,850 naval reservists in 1980 (some 850 fewer than in 1951) and less than a quarter the number of ships, this policy statement is important: it distinguishes the navy's reserve from the army's. The militia was later to be drawn into supporting the Emergency Measures Organizations, Civil Defence, and Aid to the Civil Power while the naval reserve remained an integrated component of the regular force.[16] This has always been *Malahat*'s pride and a source of her achievement.

In the spring of 1953 the Flag Officer Pacific Coast, Rear-Admiral J.C. Hibbard, explained to the *Colonist* that "Canada's fast-growing navy [would] stand or fall on [its] ability to fight at sea with little or no notice."[17] Well-trained reservists were one of the keys to that preparedness. Even though a large navy could not be built, he conceded that it was "quality that [came] before quantity." Reservists had to be trained in the major tasks of the RCN, and units like *Malahat* had to prepare their officers and men for what amounted to a regular-force combat role in an essentially antisubmarine navy. *Malahat*'s training schedule for 24 February 1952, part of her ambitious weeknight winter training programme, reflected the division's concern about that role: 1900-2000 hours, astronomics for executive officers; 2000-2200, lectures on atomic warfare for shipwrights and constructors; 2000-2200, minesweeping problems for the electrical branch; 2000-2200, seamanship training; 2100-2200, navigation for junior officers, including a discussion of ship construction and stability.

The *Colonist* (3 July 1953) announced that in preparation for *Malahat*'s transfer to the historic Customs House, a diving survey of Victoria's Inner Harbour was to "include the possibility of building a jetty for sweepers of the reserve." The jetty was built, *Sault Ste. Marie* moved alongside, and the RCN renovated the interior of the Customs House at a cost of $50,000.[18]

Although no other minesweepers secured alongside, a new manning approach was articulated. Commodore K.F. Adams, commanding officer Naval Divisions—a new command in the RCN—announced a plan to develop each unit as a "completely balanced force" with every branch represented within every division. Mobilization was to be a matter of moving a division to ships of the reserve fleet. Minesweeping, escorting, and coastal patrol were the reserve's principal skills. For the period 1955-63 *Malahat* controlled, in addition to its internal programmes, two tenders, the naval reserve in air squadron VC 922 at Pat Bay (with three Expediters and eighteen pilots), and the Victoria College UNTD of thirty officer cadets.

However, a major shift in tactical thinking took place in the 1950's as a consequence of the programme of thermonuclear tests in Nevada. The "little or no notice" of attack which Hibbard's navy had prepared itself for in 1953 now seemed hopelessly short. As General Pearkes, the minister of National Defence, observed in an address to the House on 4 December 1957,

> a third world war would commence with a sudden ferocious thermo-nuclear attack of great intensity from several directions, by various means. Little or no warning could be expected... there will be no time for mobilization or reinforcement. ... Our reliance on forces in being ... will of necessity require some changes in the role of our reserve forces. The role of the naval reserve will remain reinforcement of the fleet-in-being in time of emergency. Reserve personnel will also replace regular personnel ashore and will be required to bring our ships to war complement. This rationalization will result in some reduction in strength, because [and here we have the ubiquitous phrase again] we are placing emphasis on quality rather than quantity.[19]

Shortly thereafter the Flag Officer Naval Divisions, Rear-Admiral K.F. Adams, was reported by the *Colonist* as demanding a reorganization of the RCNR which would "cut brass [and] add men."[20] Admiral Adams observed: "The potential threat of nuclear warfare has ordered us to reshape much of our military thinking."

During the next few years issues were raised in Parliament which threatened the existence not only of the naval reserve—though indeed five other divisions besides *Malahat* were eventually paid off—but the regular forces themselves. The apparent pointlessness of a defence policy in a nuclear age was reflected in the comments of various parliamentarians: "there is no defence against thermonuclear weapons and a war fought with such weapons would be suicide" (Harold Winch, MP for Vancouver East, 4 August 1960);[21] "we are stuck in this absurd situation of trying to find something that does not exist, that is a valid military role for Canada" (Colin

Cameron, MP for Nanaimo-Cowichan and the Islands, 5 December 1963);[22] "we should . . . work together towards reducing the amounts allocated for military purposes and the money taken from [the] military establishment should be . . . given to religious organizations" for use in underdeveloped countries (H. Lessard, MP for St. Henri, 5 December 1963).[23] If national defence was deemed militarily impossible and socially destructive, what was the point of the naval reserve? If the RCN could not kill a submarine or clear a mine, neither could the RCNR. The mood of strategical/tactical uncertainty and economic anxiety emerged in what the Victoria *Times* of 19 March 1960 decoratively reported as the "New Look" in maritime defence. As the Commanding Officer Naval Reserves, Commodore E.W. Finch-Noyes, was reported as saying: "the 'new look' is . . . general training in all departments . . . instead of the former system of advancement through specialist ratings." If technology, as it appeared, was outstripping reserve capabilities, the reserve must train for general duties with little opportunity for specialization.

But trades-training seems to have been a red herring. The real issue was that the government was not convinced that Canada had the money to fight the new kind of war and should therefore prepare to fight none. Defence cut-backs meant reductions in equipment and reductions in training establishments as well. Paul Hellyer, minister of National Defence, had undertaken a series of surveys of the three armed services in April 1963, shortly after having become minister. As Lucien Cardin, associate minister of National Defence, explained, there were two primary reasons for this: "the first one was that we are living in a new era, where scientific and technical progress controls our way of life,"[24] as an almost direct result of the atomic bomb. "Yet in spite of those changes . . . there did not seem to be any comparative transformation within the national defence department; we are still preparing to fight a war according to the standards of 1939, or 1914."[25] The second reason was just as crucial: despite the staggering escalation of the defence budget, which was expected to reach $2 billion by 1970, the government had no "assurance that the weapons and equipment available [would] be adequate to face conflicts which might arise in the next ten, fifteen or twenty years."[26] The cut-backs as reported in the *Times* meant the disbanding, for the second time, of HMCS *Malahat* with its complement of 180 and the University of Victoria UNTD with thirty officer cadets. Furthermore, it meant the closing of the naval reserve air squadron VC 922 and a reduction in the squadron VU 33.

As an aside to these statistics of disintegration, it is worth recalling the recruiting notice which first appeared in the Victoria newspapers in March 1953: an advertisement which reflected the attitude of serving personnel at that time. It showed a sailor standing on the quarterdeck in his traditional blue uniform with bell-bottom trousers, his duffle bag by his side, and his hammock with seven-seas lashings, tossed jauntily over his shoulder; the White Ensign fluttered in the background. The headlines read: "Conscious of his heritage/Proud of his skill/He serves in the Naval Reserve." The text followed: "He's a young man with every reason to be proud! He's playing an important part in Canada's defence forces as a member of the Royal Canadian Naval Reserve, and learning to accept adult responsibilities, preparing for his tomorrow." If the recruiter had been a student of social history, he would have realized how quaint and dated these sentiments were. And had he managed to attract such a lad, the promises could not have been kept. The sailor would have lost his tradition, his uniform, his defence role, and his ship before his skipper could have promoted him to leading seaman. And given the attrition rate of the day, the lad himself would have gone too. The mood of the times was captured in a comment to the House on 6 December 1963: "the government," it was noted, "had correctly focussed its attention on the department that offers the greatest opportunity for saving funds necessary for socially constructive pro- grammes."[27]

But loyalties were strong, and Victoria's naval reservists decided to remain in force as volunteers without facilities, at no cost to the taxpayer.[28] In Ottawa, David Groos, MP for Victoria, rose for his maiden speech to express regret at the closing of *Malahat* and to praise the commitment of her officers and men. The navy must be kept strong, he said, to counter the threat of the Soviet submarine. In a *Colonist* editorial of 7 December 1963 (the only editorial to have taken up the cause of the naval reserve), the newspaper reminded the government that the "abolition or reduction of reserve and auxiliary formations . . . has repercussions on the operations of the regular forces." Reserves, it was argued, provide not only the immediate back-up but "the base on which rapid expansion of manpower in a national emergency may be accomplished." These arguments had been heard before, yet they bore repeating. Equally important was the *Colonist*'s support of the role of *Malahat* and other reserve units, a role which Rear-Admiral Walter Hose had understood so clearly in the disheartening days of the 1920's. As the editorial explained, only a reserve force, that organization of citizen-sailors, can "sustain the willingness of the civilian element to undertake a share in the bulwark of national defence. Stringent curtailment of the means whereby they may do this dampens enthusiasm and deprives the country of a valuable asset. Nor is it easy to reactivate a unit once disbanded and its facilities removed."

HMCS *Malahat* was paid off and its assets sold; all personnel were released or placed on inactive reserve. The unit died hard. However, a turnabout occurred in April 1965, though the military reasons for it are not yet clear. Commodore P.D. Taylor, the commanding officer Naval Div- isions, praised the devotion of the reserves and "congratulated *Malahat* for having come through a period of adversity."²⁹ *Malahat* was alive again, though not particularly well. At the same time, the gate vessel *Porte de la Reine*, one of the five that had been announced thirteen years earlier and which had been laid up in reserve since 1957, was brought into service to "help recruiting in [the] reserves."³⁰ The Department of National Defence was trying to pull things together again. *Malahat's* commanding officer was delighted, for he noted that the unit's morale had never been higher than when it had had its own Algerine-class vessel. Over a year later, on 5 April 1966, the *Colonist* announced *"Porte de la Reine* Restored. . . . Gate Vessel Revived for Reserve Sailors." For the next fourteen years, and almost without change in equipment, such ships were to be the principal vessels for training the reserves. Indeed, since 1969, these ships have been manned almost entirely by reserves. The task remains the same: fleet augmentation and coastal patrol. But the reserve has not produced enough upper-deck watch-keeping certificates and diesel engine-room tickets to renew itself; nor has it trained enough officers for command. Virtually the same group of officers who ran the ships years ago as lieutenants take them to sea now as commanders and captains.

From 1975 to 1977 *Malahat's* initiative created, out of supposed weekend cruises, three annual convoy exercises. Naval control of shipping was now a primary task, and the unit provided a vivid scenario which involved the integrated training of five other Canadian reserve units, four USN Reserve units, the U.S. Coast Guard, Canadian Air Reserve and the Canadian minesweeping squadron. (The last mentioned, we are reminded, has had no minesweeping capability for years.) This was the first time that the reserves organized, though at first quite unofficially, an international scheme which provided training opportunities for the regular force. The convoy exercises demonstrated initiative, realism, and skill. Financial constraints since 1978 caused *Malahat* to shelve this plan, though it was reinstituted along modest lines in 1981.

Public policies on defence in the 1970's are common knowledge, but uneasiness prevails among concerned citizens about the state of the reserve which has been a vital part of the naval service for so long. Noting a lack of current equipment and the absence of any mobilization plan a detailed article in the *Financial Post* (19 February 1977) asked the central question, "Do Canada's reserves exist mostly on paper?" The naval reserve, with its slow-moving, thirty-year-old ships and simulated convoy exercises, appears to be a paper force preparing for a paper war. However, there is some hope of progress. A recent report of the Parliamentary Sub-Committee on Armed Forces Reserves has made firm recommendations to upgrade the status, capability, and role of reserves.³¹

Chapter 18

AN ENGINEER'S OUTLINE OF RCN HISTORY: PART II

J.H.W. Knox

The St. Laurent-class programme for the construction of seven anti-submarine escort vessels was announced in November 1948. This programme and the ones that grew out of it—involving the marriage of ship and helicopter—established the sea-going identity of the postwar RCN. What were required were small ships capable of twenty-five knots and having larger armament and more sophisticated action-information systems than the existing frigates. The proposed vessels were to be suited to rapid production in Canada in wartime and were to use equipment and material from North American, and preferably Canadian, suppliers. A new ship design of domestic origin was called for. The requirement for rapid wartime production also complemented the need for work in Canadian shipyards. Many of them were short of orders in 1948, and the St. Laurent programme, which eventually involved seven yards, promised to keep the nation's shipbuilding capacity alive.

A vast amount of work was involved in translating these naval and industrial priorities into reality; a new approach was needed since no Canadian shipyard possessed the experience of preparing a design of the type required. The conventional approach was for the naval authorities to prepare a specification and outline design. Then the contract-winning shipbuilder was expected to convert these into detailed designs, materiel orders, and construction schedules. However, not only did Canadian industry lack this conversion capability but the technical offices at Naval Service Headquarters were not staffed as a warship-design authority in the first place. Everything had to be created from scratch. Credit for this remarkable accomplishment must go to two officers: Commodore (E[ngin-eering]) (Rear-Admiral (E) from January 1949) J.G. Knowlton as chief of Naval Technical Services (CNTS) from December 1945 until January 1956; and Constructor Captain (Commodore from January 1953) R. Baker, RCNR, on loan from the Royal Corps of Naval Constructors, as director of Naval Construction/naval constructor-in-chief from July 1948 until June 1956.

The problem of naval technical staff was graphically illustrated by the growth of the engineer-in-chief's department. There were five officers in that department in 1948. By 1952, there were twenty-one, augmented by an even greater number of civilian engineers and technologists as well as dozens of overseers. The whole CNTS staff in 1948 numbered eighty-four. By 1956, with its outposts and agencies, it was in the region of four hundred. The early deficiency of numbers and expertise was overcome by steady recruitment, mainly from the United Kingdom, of a whole range of uniformed and civilian officers, many of them recognized experts in their fields.

No single shipyard maintained a drawing office capable of developing the types of systems required in naval ships or of integrating these systems into the close-knit assembly necessary in the St. Laurent design. Naval authorities suggested that various shipyards might unite their design drawing staffs in order to accomplish this work, but their suggestion was met by two serious objections. Firstly, the traditional competition between shipyards made this sort of co-operation difficult, and, secondly, the shipyards felt that they would lose the direct use of their draughtsmen for the commercial work upon which they relied. The problem was eventually resolved by establishing the Naval Central Drawing Office (NCDO) and its offshoot, the Naval Stores Central Procurement Agency (NSCPA).[1]

Setting up the NCDO under the direction of a consulting ship design firm was considered and might have been a reasonable solution, but Canadian Vickers made an offer to set up an office in conjunction with being designated Lead Yard. This solution was adopted. The recruits to this office, of whom there were large numbers, were almost all men from British shipyards versed in naval work. Under the guidance of the RCN overseeing team, they quickly developed new concepts in design and construction which contributed in large measure to the success of the new vessels. The NSCPA was established to assist in the work of identifying and developing Canadian sources of materiel of all kinds including boilers, turbines, gearing, pumps, motors, generators, winches, controllers, cable, and even guns and to ensure the standardization of equipment. This agency became a centre of knowledge for naval procurement and served the RCN well throughout three successive building programmes. When the time came later for the modernization and conversion of these ships, the NSCPA also ordered the replacement parts. The government disbanded the NSCPA in 1967 in order to hand this task over to industry. The NCDO, retitled, first, the Naval Ship Design Agency and, subsequently, the Marine Design Drawing Office, remains in existence, at least in vestigial form. The NCDO proved an essential element in the execution of the St. Laurent and subsequent destroyer escort (DE and DDE) programmes, and ensured similarity between ships of a class.

Another influential organization which came into its own in the era of the DDE programmes was the RCN Committee on Corrosion and Fouling (RCN/CCF). The RCN/CCF was founded in 1947 under the stimulus of work conducted by K.N. Barnard at the Naval Research Establishment (NRE) in Dartmouth, Nova Scotia. In this he demonstrated the benefits to be derived from his novel proposals for the "cathodic protection" of ships' underwater hulls and fittings. With the advent of the DDE and subsequent building programmes, the scope for the practice of corrosion engineering in Canada was expanded enormously. Much credit is due to Constructor Captain Baker that the RCN/CCF took the lead in this field. He reconstituted the committee in 1950, and its membership was enlarged to include industry and other government departments as well as all of the headquarters' technical directorates. The RCN/CCF can include among its successes the extensive adoption of both passive and active cathodic protection systems, plastic piping, and the use of aluminum in superstructures, fittings, and minesweeper framing. The committee continues an active life to this day and has been emulated by the Admiralty, the Royal Australian Navy, and the Royal New Zealand Navy.[2]

Constructor Captain Baker arrived in Naval Service Headquarters in the summer of 1948 as Commodore (E) Knowlton and his team were preparing proposals for the new escort vessels. The Naval Staff had placed major emphasis on seakeeping, maintaining seventeen knots in a seaway, noise reduction, nuclear biological and chemical defence and damage control (NBCD) features, a high standard of accommodation, air conditioning, weight saving, and mass producibility in Canada. Baker brought with him ideas for ocean escorts which challenged many accepted elements of design: removing redundant upper deck fittings which caused maintenance problems and spray; selecting a hull form for seakeeping ability rather than top speed; introducing acoustic insulation and mountings; equipping the hull with efficient thermal insulation; using aluminum alloys in the superstructure, funnel casing, masts and furniture to save weight; and designing a central galley and feeding area. The stability requirement selected by the designers called for avoidance of any capsizing moment as the result of damage, and a perspex model was prepared to demonstrate damaged stability characteristics. A flush-deck arrangement with a high swept-up turtle deck forecastle gave the cleanest possible lines for strength and ease of ship-handling and allowed the anchors to be stowed behind faired doors while the windlasses were located under the forecastle deck. Particular care was given to the provision of passageways and good access routes in order to facilitate rapid closing-down. The St. Laurent-class were the first NATO ships to provide such close-down arrangements together with NBCD filters. The resulting air-tight and pressurized "citadel," encompassing virtually all of the operations, living, and working spaces within the ship, allowed the ship to continue fighting during a nuclear attack.

Coincidental with the development of the staff requirement for the Canadian anti-submarine escort was the Admiralty's search for a power plant for a comparable class. Since Canada lacked a marine-propulsion plant design capability, the choice lay between United States Navy and Royal Navy machinery. The RN design, "Y.100," was selected with the proviso that the machinery, apart from the ship's set, should be produced in Canada. In the absence of existing facilities, this required the construction of a Naval Turbine Factory and a Main Reduction Gear Plant, both crown-owned but privately operated. In addition, three test plants were established at John Inglis for the main engines and at Canadian Westinghouse and Peacock Brothers for auxiliary machinery. The last is still in operation as the Naval Engineering Test Establishment.[3] Wherever possible, Canadian commercial standards were used for materiel, screw threads, pipes, valves, and so forth. This required conversion from the Admiralty standards used in the original British design and, since there were not always exact or satisfactory equivalents, many design adjustments. The development of a turbine rotor forging capability and the selection of suitable North American materiel for this critical element was a significant project in its own right. Success was not achieved without difficulty. The ingots, each weighing several tons, had to be shipped eight hundred miles at some 1600°F in a specially designed insulated box on a railway flat car from furnaces in Montreal to the specially purchased seven-thousand-ton rotor forging press in Trenton, Nova Scotia. A major machinery design change was made in the case of the main reduction gears.[4] It was decided that, in creating a new and complete gear manufacturing plant, the latest technology should be employed. This meant hardened and ground gearing to the Swiss MAAG design, and the effect was to place the St. Laurent gearing at the leading edge of known techniques.

Although the Admiralty had also selected the Y.100 machinery design, the RCN programme was ahead of the RN, and the Canadian authorities insisted on full-scale shore trials to demonstrate the prototype. These were carried out at the Pametrada test plant at Wallsend-on-Tyne, England. The most significant result was the identification and correction of a gear-scuffing problem which would have resulted in a serious setback if it had not been discovered before the sea trials of the lead ship.[5] In addition to the gearing, the Canadian propulsion plant differed from the British version in several respects. More extensive automatic controls were used. Other improvements included Maxim double effect evaporators, a 25 per cent larger generating capacity, and central air conditioning.

The electric power generation and distribution systems in the St. Laurent class (like those of HMCS *Labrador*) were designed to the United States Navy Bureau of Ships standards and were manufactured and tested to American military specifications. As a result, these systems proved one of the most satisfactory features of the ships.

Two twin 3-inch/50 calibre gun mountings were fitted in the St. Laurent-class ships. These were manufactured in the Sorel Industries gun factory which was set up specifically for the escort vessel programme but which provided guns as well to satisfy other RCN programmes and USN requirements arising from the Korean War. This factory was unique in that the complete gun and mounting were manufactured from raw materials in one plant. The American "Gunar" fire control system was selected for the St. Laurent class.[6]

The synchro tape gyro repeater and plotting table developed in conjunction with the St. Laurent programme were Canadian accomplishments of particular note. These developments were initiated by the electrical engineer-in-chief when the potential of a Sperry, Montreal, gyro retransmission unit, which gave multiple synchro outputs using a magnetic amplifier, was recognized. The specification for the table was written around the use of magnetic amplifiers. A target plot attachment was included as an integral portion of the projection head. The developer, Marsland, later requested the substitution of what was then a novel transistor amplifier. This became the first piece of transistorized equipment in the RCN and was probably the first such equipment available to any navy at that time (1955). The initial production run was for about 130 tables and ultimately some 500 tables were produced, including orders for the USN.

Not long after the commencement of the St. Laurent programme, additional building and conversion programmes were approved at an ever-increasing tempo. The warship programme included the construction of "Bay"-class minesweepers and the conversion of the Prestonian-class frigates and fleet-destroyers as well as the refit of a large number of Bangor-class minesweepers. Auxiliary vessels included "Glen" tugs and gate vessels in the 1950 programme, "Saint"-class tugs, conversion of the former HMS *Flamborough Head* (returned to Canada in 1950) to a technical apprentice training establishment, renamed HMCS *Cape Breton* in the 1951 programme, and diving tenders, crane lighters, ammunition lighters, harbour ferries, water boats, and numerous other small craft.

The first four Bay-class 152-foot wood and aluminum minesweepers were authorized in 1950. A further ten were authorized the following year, and, six having been transferred to France, a final six were ordered in 1955-56. This class was based on the British "-ton"-class design and encouraged the development in Canada of new techniques for wood, plastic, and, particularly, aluminum construction.

There was a steady succession of fleet-destroyer conversions: HMCS *Micmac* completed in November 1949 with a "Squid" anti-submarine mortar in lieu of A gun mounting, a quadruple 40-mm in lieu of B mounting, and two twin 4-inch guns in lieu of X and Y mountings; HMCS *Sioux* completed in January 1950 with two Squids in place of X and Y mountings, and, of particular note, bunks in lieu of hammocks—the first RCN warship to incorporate this modern touch. HMCS *Nootka* completed in November 1950 with two Squid in lieu of Y mounting and a twin 40-mm bofors mounting. HMCS *Iroquois* was the first Tribal to receive a full "DE" conversion in which twin 4-inch guns were fitted in A and B positions, a twin 3-inch/50 calibre in X, and two Squids in Y positions with an aluminum lattice mast carrying new American radar; *Iroquois* completed in October 1951, having been in hand for sixteen months in Halifax dockyard. She was followed over the next three years by all of her six sisters undergoing identical conversions. In February 1953 *Algonquin* was converted in Esquimalt dockyard to a configuration closely similar to the British "Type 15" anti-submarine frigate, a rearrangement which many of her RN sister Intermediate-class destroyers had undergone. This provided her with twin 3-inch and 4-inch gun mountings forward and aft, a Squid anti-submarine mortar, plus a new aluminum lattice mast and superstructure. HMCS *Crescent* completed a similar conversion in December 1955, also in Esquimalt. All the converted destroyers from *Iroquois* onward were fitted with the Mark 63 gunnery fire control system, which had to be especially adapted to the 4-inch mounting. This adaptation was the first independent Canadian initiative on a weapons-system basis. The Admiralty Fire Control Clock and range finder director remained in the ships with a number of modifications developed at the Dartmouth Naval Armament Depot.

In 1953 HMCS *Prestonian* was the first of twenty-one frigates to complete her conversion in a programme that was to continue until 1958. The forecastle deck was extended right aft enclosing the former quarterdeck and housing two Squid mountings. The bridge structure was rebuilt in aluminum, enlarged, and raised. The funnel height was increased in proportion. Improved habitability was provided, the electric generators were changed from three steam and one diesel to two of each type, and a new once-through Vapour-Clarkson auxiliary boiler was fitted.

All of the warship conversion and building programmes complemented the St. Laurent-class programme, since various features of the latter were developed and proven in the former. The NCDO was responsible for the

Plate 97. Commodore R. Baker, RCNR, director of Naval Construction/naval constructor-in-chief, 1948-56. (DOH, NDHQ—0-8755)

Plate 98. Rear-Admiral (E) J.G. Knowlton, chief of Naval Technical Services, 1945-56. (DOH, NDHQ—0874-2)

Plate 99. HMCS *Iroquois* I, first of the Canadian Tribal-class destroyers to commission (1942) underwent two postwar refits as a destroyer escort, in 1951 and 1958. (MCM—NF 1978)

Plate 100. HMCS *St. Laurent* II, the first of a class of destroyer escorts built in Canada and incorporating innovative Canadian naval technical advances. (MCM—DNS 19065)

Plate 101. Launching of HMCS *Ottawa* III, "St. Laurent"-class destroyer escort at Canadian Vickers Ltd., Montreal, 29 April 1953. (PAC—PA 116332)

Plate 102. HMCS *Skeena* II, "St. Laurent"-class destroyer commissioned in 1957. A 3-inch oblique 50-calibre gun mounting is located immediately forward of the bridge. (MCM—E 52088)

Plate 103. HMCS *Assiniboine* II in high speed turn with helicopter hovering. The "Beartrap" helicopter haul-down device, seen here in the centre of the flight deck, was a Canadian development later adopted by other Western navies. (MCM—DNS 33910)

Plate 104. Flag officer Atlantic Coast Rear-Admiral William Landymore and Mrs. Landymore departing from HMCS *Stadacona*. Having lost the fight to save the RCN, Landymore and many of his senior colleagues were relieved of their commands or felt obliged to resign. The hero's departure accorded Landymore illustrates the depth of feeling generated by the debate on Unification. (CFB Photo Unit, Ottawa [N])

Plate 105. White Paper on Defence, the Canadian government document which spelled the end of the Royal Canadian Navy. (DOH, NDHQ)

CANADA

WHITE PAPER
ON DEFENCE

HONOURABLE PAUL HELLYER
Minister of National Defence

HONOURABLE LUCIEN CARDIN
Associate Minister of National Defence

MARCH 1964

Prestonian conversion and Bangor refits, Canadian Vickers being the Prestonian Lead Yard as it was for the St. Laurent class.

A second group of seven DE's was decided on in 1952. These, to become the Restigouche class, differed from the St. Laurents principally in the substitution of a British-built 3-inch/70 calibre in place of the forward 3-inch/50 calibre gun. A Mark 69 director was added to the fire control system, and the air conditioning plant was enlarged by the addition of a steam turbine driven compressor. These ships were also to have been fitted with a Swedish L.70 40-mm bofors gun, but this was dropped from the final design.

Arrangements were made in the same year to purchase and complete to Canadian specifications the unfinished light fleet-carrier HMS *Powerful*. Renamed HMCS *Bonaventure*, she was to replace HMCS *Magnificent*. Work resumed on the ship at the Harland and Wolff yard in Belfast in July 1952. While the Admiralty overseer was responsible for the shipbuilder's work, under the contract between the Canadian and British governments, the RCN maintained a substantial staff in Bath and later in Belfast under the principal RCN technical representative. The specifications called for the incorporation of an angled flight deck, steam catapult, and mirror-landing aid. The armament was altered to include four twin 3-inch/50 calibre gun mountings while L.70 40-mm bofors with "Gunar" fire-control and USN pattern radar were fitted. At the last moment the 40-mm guns were omitted. The accommodation arrangements were reworked to approach new Canadian standards using RCN aluminum furniture, an electric galley, and central cafeteria. Closed circuit television was also installed. The Admiralty 3-drum main boilers were trunked and fitted with wide-range burners, while the main propulsion machinery was provided with remote controls located in a gas-tight compartment at the entrance to each main machinery space so that it could be operated safely under conditions of nuclear attack. The generating capacity was increased from the original design to provide 3,200 kw DC and 300 kw AC. A Lamont forced circulation auxiliary boiler and Junkers free-piston HP air compressors were incorporated. One each 3- and 4-bladed propellers were fitted to reduce vibration. Since *Bonaventure* was to operate Banshee jets, a "blend" fuel system was required to ensure properly constituted fuel. The arrangements specified by the engineer-in-chief provided two sets of equipment for the blending of kerosene and high octane aviation gasoline. There were fourteen fueling stations on the hangar and flight decks, each equipped with fuel filters, water separator, and power operated hose-reels with special tank filling nozzles capable of under- or over-wing fuelling. Tank capacity was increased from the original design to accommodate the kerosene. *Bonaventure* was completed on 17 January 1957.

In 1953 NSHQ began to consider the design of ships to follow the St.

Laurent and Restigouche programmes. The engineer-in-chief recognized the lack of a Canadian commercial organization capable of marine propulsion system design. His own department lacked the capacity to study the competing claims of all the foreign suppliers while at the same time conducting its day-to-day business. It was decided, therefore, to form a Canadian marine engineering projects agency similar to comparable agencies used by the USN and the Admiralty. These organizations, as well as the United States Coast Guard and the Yarrow-Admiralty Research Department (Y-ARD), were consulted. The arrangement finally selected consisted of a team of civilian engineers, which was to be known as the Naval Engineering Design Investigation Team (NEDIT). They were to be employees of a civilian firm but to be professionally responsible through the naval team leader to the engineer-in-chief. The Admiralty agreed to supply an RN officer as interim team leader, and Peacock Brothers accepted the contract to staff the team, which was then co-located with the Naval Engineering Test Establishment, also staffed by that firm. NEDIT was formed in January 1953 by Commander (E) (later Vice-Admiral and chief naval engineer officer of the Royal Navy) R.G. Raper, RN. The NEDIT staff was transferred to the federal civil service in 1957 and disbanded in 1966, being partially absorbed into the Maritime Engineering Division at NDHQ.[7]

One of the first NEDIT projects involved preliminary design work on a less expensive escort vessel to succeed the Restigouche class. This was to be smaller, slower, and less capable than its predecessors. The proposed vessels were designated the Vancouver class and were to be fitted with a single shaft and a steam turbine main engine of the Y.100 type. The Admiralty designation for this plant was Y.101 and it was fitted, in due course, in the Royal Navy's Blackwood-class frigates. However, the Canadian single shaft design was dropped in 1955-56 in favour of a Repeat Restigouche design.

The Repeat Restigouche was a six-ship programme approved in 1957. Later, the lead ship was named *Mackenzie*. The last two ships were completed to a revised design as Annapolis-class helicopter-carrying destroyer escorts or DDH's, of which more will be said below. Changes from the Restigouche design in the first four ships which became the Mackenzie class were deliberately minimized. In the engineering realm these changes included the substitution of motor driven air conditioning compressors for the turbine driven compressor, a Vapour-Clarkson for the B&W "D" type auxiliary boiler, and a 500 kw Fairbanks-Morse for the 200 kw GM diesel generator in the boiler room. Spares purchased for the earlier programmes were, in certain cases, used in the construction of these ships. There was no 3-inch/70 calibre gun available for the fourth and last ship, HMCS *Qu'Appelle*, so a 3-inch/50 calibre weapon was substituted.

Some consideration appears to have been given as early as 1943 to completing the frigates then under construction as anti-submarine helicopter carriers.[8] A dozen years were to elapse, however, before this suggestion was taken up seriously. In 1955 the RCN had acquired Sikorsky HO4S anti-submarine warfare helicopters for operation from HMCS *Bonaventure*, but it was recognized that even light fleet-carriers were enormously expensive platforms and that, if maximum potential was to be obtained from the helicopters, several smaller and therefore cheaper platforms were needed. In an effort to explore this alternative, a temporary flight deck was built over the quarterdeck of the frigate HMCS *Buckingham*. In October 1956, *Buckingham* began a three-month rough-weather flying trial using the smaller Sikorsky S58 helicopter. Promising results prompted further trials in the destroyer escort *Ottawa* a year later. From these it was evident that the limitation was not the pilot's ability to land on a moving deck, but the deck crew's inability to secure and reposition the helicopter on deck. A key requirement therefore was a means of instantly securing the helicopter on deck and of providing a controlled traverse between the landing position and the hangar. A development contract was let to Fairey Aviation of Dartmouth, Nova Scotia, in 1959. This resulted in the Helicopter Hauldown and Rapid Securing Device (HHRSD), known popularly as the "Beartrap."

In August 1957, in response to a naval staff requirement for a tanker supply vessel able to increase the effective endurance of the escort vessel fleet by replenishment at sea, the preliminary design of HMCS *Provider* was begun. She was an adaptation of the U.S. Maritime Administration "Mariner" class using standard commercial shipbuilding practice to Lloyd's Rules. The lines aft were altered to provide greater breadth in the machinery spaces so that a second and third ship of the class might have room to accommodate a nuclear propulsion plant.[9] A Westinghouse main engine of the T5 tanker type was selected. The boilers were "boxed" and automatic and remote controls in a machinery control room were provided in order to permit steaming "closed down" for up to six hours under nuclear attack. A Rover 40 kw emergency gas turbine generator was also provided—the first marine gas turbine used by the RCN. The contract was awarded to Davie Shipbuilding, who began construction in September 1960 and delivered her in September 1963. Subsequently it proved necessary to make structural alterations to *Provider*'s stern to overcome vibration problems which derived, in part at least, from her altered lines.

The RCN gave serious consideration for the first time in 1957 to acquiring nuclear submarines, potentially the most effective anti-submarine vessels available. A number of naval engineers of all disciplines were given nuclear power training in the United Kingdom, and in 1958 a Nuclear Submarine Survey Team was formed to examine the feasibility and cost of

nuclear submarine acquisition. Consideration was also given at this time
to nuclear propulsion plants for future tanker supply vessels. RCN engineers were associated with a study of nuclear propulsion for icebreakers
conducted by Y-ARD in Britain in the early 1960's, and the 1964 Canadian
White Paper on Defence stated that "careful study [was] being given to the
possibility of constructing two or three nuclear powered submarines with
powerful anti-submarine weapons." But, the paper noted, a firm decision
could not be taken on the project immediately because of its magnitude.

From the early 1950's the RN had provided the RCN with the continuous services of HM submarines based on Halifax so that the RCN could
gain experience in "live" ASW training. In exchange, the RCN provided
volunteers to the RN submarine service in sufficient numbers to offset the
manpower drain which the Halifax-based 6th Submarine Squadron
entailed. The RCN also provided docking and running maintenance for
the Halifax Squadron. Similar facilities were needed on the Pacific coast,
and in 1960 the USS *Burrfish* was obtained from the USN and, manned by
an RCN crew, was commissioned as HMCS *Grilse* in May 1961. This ship
was wholly supported from Esquimalt dockyard and received two major
and two minor refits before being replaced by HMCS *Rainbow* (ex-USS
Argonaut), purchased in 1968. *Rainbow* was paid-off to disposal in 1976.

Following the completion of the nuclear submarine survey, a conventional submarine survey was begun in 1961. This group examined possible
means of acquisition and alternative types of diesel-electric submarines.
Prime contenders for Canadian service were the U.S. Barbel type which
adopted the hydrodynamically efficient Albacore hull form, and the RN
Oberon type. The scales were tipped away from the American design and
from building in Canada by the substantial savings to be obtained by
purchasing British-built Oberons then in production. This was particularly so in view of the requirement for only three boats. In April 1962, the
purchase arrangement was announced and HMC Submarines *Ojibwa*,
Onondaga, and *Okanagan* were commissioned in Chatham in 1965, 1967,
and 1968. Their construction and the incorporation of a number of Canadian modifications was overseen by a team of RCN engineers resident in
Chatham.

The sea trials of helicopters operating from escorts and the identification of engineering solutions to the handling, securing, and stowage problems (coupled with recognition of the powerful advantages of ASW helicopters) prompted two warship conversion programmes. The last two
Mackenzie-class ships were completed as DDH's, while the whole of the St.
Laurent class of seven ships, starting with HMCS *Assiniboine*, was converted to the DDH configuration. These conversions were referred to as the
Improved St. Laurent or "ISL" class. It was fortunate that there was just
enough room between the after end of the St. Laurent bridge structure and

the arcs of the after mortar to fit a hangar and flight deck; well, just enough, if one tinkered around with the funnel. In fact, the funnel and uptakes had to be split in two, one on either side of the hangar, in order to prevent them from being blown away! A variable depth sonar (VDS) and fin stabilizers were also fitted, while one AS mortar was removed. The flight deck equipment developed for the DDH's, in addition to the Beartrap, included a constant tension winch, a traverse track between flight deck and hangar, a tail guide and winch to straighten the newly landed helicopter, fuelling equipment, and a landing signals officer's console. Later trials added two stabilized horizon references or "horizon bars," approach radar, TACAN (a tactical air navigation device), "traffic lights," and additional fire fighting equipment. By November 1962, it had been decided that the Sikorsky HSS-2, to be built in Canada and designated CHSS-2, was the helicopter best suited to the task. This was a twin-engined 19,000-lb. machine capable of carrying both submersible "dunking" sonar and anti-submarine torpedoes, It was a slightly larger aircraft than the HU2K originally proposed, and this meant that the hangars had to be widened. HMCS *Assiniboine* entered a fourteen-month conversion in early 1962 and, having recommissioned in June 1963, began her helicopter trials programme in late 1964. During the next three years many changes and additions were made as techniques were developed for helicopter operations from destroyers. In 1967 HMCS *Saguenay* embarked the first operational air detachment, and by 1969 all nine DDH's were operational in their new role. As finally arranged, the DDH had a most impressive capability which permitted the all-weather day and night operation of a large helicopter on deck with up to thirty-one degrees of roll and nine degrees of pitch, heaving at twenty feet per second in winds up to fifty knots. Others agreed. The Japanese, Indian, and U.S. navies have all purchased equipment based on the RCN system and manufactured by Dafindal of Toronto. A twin HHRSD system has been installed in the four DDH 280 Tribal-class ships.

The VDS fitted in the ISL and Annapolis-class DDH's was the culmination of another long development programme. After World War II scientists from the NRE, concerned about the limitations imposed on sonar by ship noise and variations in water temperature (or thermal gradients), began to think about separating the transducer, which broadcast and received the sound signals which bounced or "pinged" off enemy submarines, from the ship. The plan was to tow the sonar over the stern of the ship. The first problem was to develop a satisfactory means of towing and handling a large device at considerable depth and speed. Extensive hydrodynamic and mechanical trials were conducted for some years using NRE craft and auxiliary vessels. A workable pilot system was developed eventually, including a winch and drum, cable and fairings, and a body containing a rudimentary sonar. This system was tried first in HMCS *Crusader* and then, in 1959, in HMCS *Crescent*. Cable "kiting" and "tow-off" problems were persistent until a segmental rather than a continuous fairing, developed by NRE, was adopted. Many mechanical failures occurred, but as the weaknesses were found, they were corrected and the handling system and techniques were improved. The VDS system offered sufficient promise that an operational installation was decided upon for incorporation in the ISL class. The prototype, designated AN/SQA-501 handling gear using the AN/SQS-504 sonar, was fitted and tried in HMCS *St. Laurent* in 1963 prior to her conversion. Production equipment was fitted in the remainder of the class during their conversions as well as in the Annapolis class during construction. In addition, VDS equipment was sold to the Dutch and British navies, and these sales helped offset the cost of development.

In 1961 work was begun in NSHQ on a more advanced and capable sonar system, using integrated solid-state hull mounted and variable depth transducers. The system, including AN/SQS-505 sonar and the AN/SQA-502 handling gear, was designated "Diana One"; the VDS portion was designed for deep towing with shock absorbing (boom bobbing) incorporated in the handling gear. The towed body and hence the handling gear were substantially larger. The prototype was tried in HMCS *Terra Nova* as part of the first phase of her conversion to the Improved Restigouche or "IRE" configuration. The production version of the system was installed in the remaining three IRE conversions, retro-fitted in *Terra Nova*, and installed in the four DDH 280 Tribal-class destroyers. The SQS-505 sonar was the first major piece of equipment in the RCN to have completely solid state electronics. Systems engineering and specifications for the whole Diana One system were developed by the Naval Technical Services organization. The National Research Council Ship Division developed the towed body in its hydrodynamics laboratory. Its form was a blimp-shaped "body of revolution" having particularly good hydrodynamic characteristics. EDO Canada, Canadian Westinghouse, Hollandse Signaalapparaten (HSA), Fleet Industries, and Standard Telephone and Cable were the principal contractors.

In the early 1960's NSHQ examined the possibility of constructing a general purpose (GP) frigate.[10] The frigate hull form was derived from, but larger than, that of the St. Laurent and succeeding classes. Gas turbine boost, like that which was then being adopted for propulsion in the RN Tribal-class frigates, was considered but rejected as too complex and not supported by an established marine gas turbine manufacturing facility in Canada. A steam plant, essentially similar to the Mackenzie-class Y.100 development, with steam conditions of 550 lb./sq. in. and 850°F, was selected by NEDIT and designated "N613." An integrated automatic digital information display system for command and control as well as automatic conbustion and machinery control were among measures intended to reduce the complement from that required by the St. Laurent class. This reduction, coupled with the increased space available in the larger hull, which was dictated by the deck space requirements of topside equipment, was to allow significantly improved standards of habitability. Considerable empasis was placed on "human engineering," and to this end the Defence Research Medical Laboratory prepared detailed mock-ups of the bridge, operations room, and machinery control room.

It should be noted that the command and display system which was to have been fitted in the GP frigates, code-named DATAR, was to have been the culmination of a Canadian initiative in the field of digital information display and control systems.[11] Had the GP frigate gone ahead, the RCN would have had in place a system substantially ahead of its time. As it was, the technology came to fruition somewhat later: first in the action information system for the hydrofoil, HMCS *Bras d'Or*, where it was identified as the "AIS 400," and second in the DDH 280-class command and control system, where it was identified as the "CCS 280."

Canadian naval interest in hydrofoils had its beginnings in 1943 when General George Pearkes, then general officer commanding Pacific, stated a requirement for a high speed smoke maker to be used in amphibious operations. A hydrofoil seemed the only satisfactory solution, and by the end of the war four prototype vehicles had been delivered. The NRE, aware of the attractions of high speed vessels and of the potential offered by hydrofoils, pursued the subject over more than a decade and through a succession of test craft all of which used the "surface piercing" form of foil. In 1959, the NRE tabled a report proposing a 200-ton all-weather hydrofoil for ASW application.[12] This proposal was discussed the following January at a meeting of American, British, and Canadian scientists. It was agreed that each nation would concentrate its high speed ship research: the British on hovercraft, the Americans on submerged-foil hydrofoils and the Canadians on surface-piercing foils. The conference recommended an extension of NRE hydrofoil work to a prototype craft. De Havilland Aircraft of Canada (DHC) was given a feasibility study in 1961, and by the end of the following year sufficient work had been done that the Naval Board was able to authorize construction of a prototype ASW hydrofoil ship for which DHC was the prime contractor. The name *Bras d'Or*, and the designation, "FHE 400," were adopted later. Parallel studies examined questions of materials, fighting equipment, and foilborne stability. Canadian Westinghouse was awarded a contract to design and develop the fighting equipment suite. Tests and trials of structural members and foils, protective coatings, supercavitating propeller models, hydraulic steering and stabilizer actuators, the action information system, and the full-scale foilborne propulsion system were progressively completed permitting identification and correction of problems as they arose. Assembly of the ship took place at the Sorel Shipyard of Marine Industries. On 5 November 1966, ironically "Guy Fawkes Day," a disastrous fire occurred in the nearly completed ship. In April of the following year, after the programme had been reappraised, it was decided to repair the fire damage, make a number of modifications to the design, complete the ship, and take delivery of the fighting equipment but to defer fitting it until completion of the initial foilborne sea trials.

In September 1968 the ship, having been delivered to Halifax from Sorel on its specially constructed "slave dock," commenced hullborne sea trials without the foilborne transmission system. On 9 April 1969, with the foilborne transmission satisfactorily through its shore trials and now installed in the ship, Bras d'Or became foilborne for the first time. That summer a foilborne speed of sixty-three knots was recorded in the full load condition in three- to four-foot waves. Foilborne trials were interrupted for a year when the main foil centre span was found to have developed cracks from a seawater leak. This required the span to be replaced. When a full trials programme including rough water trials was resumed, it included operation hullborne in seas up to state six (twelve-foot waves) and foilborne at speeds up to forty-five knots in sea state five (ten-foot waves). The feasibility of a 200-ton all-weather open-ocean hydrofoil had certainly been established. Unfortunately, the costs of a refit, including further foil repairs, fitting the fighting equipment, and carrying out trials of the ship as an ASW vehicle, were felt to be unwarranted. Even if the trials were successful, the RCN was not certain that the construction of a squadron of such ships, at the expense of a similar investment in conventional vessels, would be justified. In 1971 the Bras d'Or was laid up in a state of preservation pending a final decision on its disposal.[13]

The 1964 White Paper on Defence had generated three ship programmes: the construction of operational support ships (OSS) to extend the endurance and effectiveness of the destroyer escort fleet; the continued modernization of the fleet with the improvement of the Restigouche class (IRE); and the construction of new destroyer escorts to replace the wartime units due for retirement.

The two OSS were improvements on HMCS Provider with enhanced facilities for helicopter maintenance, for sea lift, and for replenishment at sea, including new and simplified deck gear. Accommodation was increased, and a 3-inch/50 calibre gun mounting was provided. These vessels incorporated many lessons learned from the earlier ship in a hull of nearly identical dimensions. The tank top deck was enclosed. Dual purpose solids/liquids replenishment stations were adopted. Improved handling facilities—elevators, forklifts, conveyors, and cranes—were incorporated. A contract for both ships was let to Saint John Shipbuilding and Drydock. The first OSS, HMCS Protecteur, was laid down in October 1967 and commissioned in July 1970; HMCS *Preserver* followed one year later.[14]

The IRE class was originally planned to include all seven Restigouche-class ships, but economy measures forced three to be dropped in 1968. The improvements included the AN/SQS 505 hull mounted and variable depth sonars already described, the anti-submarine rocket-delivered torpedo system (ASROC), and major communications and electronic warfare advances that required a taller mast of lattice construction. The lead ship, HMCS *Terra Nova*, was converted in Halifax dockyard in two phases. The first, from May 1965 to February 1966, was followed by prototype sea trials of the new AN/SQS 505 sonar lasting seven months. The second phase was completed in August 1968. Two ships, *Kootenay* and *Restigouche*, were converted by Halifax Shipyards between 1970 and 1973 while *Gatineau* was converted in Esquimalt dockyard.

The new destroyer escorts stemming from the 1964 White Paper were initially identified as the "Repeat Nipigon" class. Eventually, they were designated the "DDH 280" class. By the time they had been revised to carry two CHSS-2 helicopters, a surface-to-air missile system, the SQS 505 VDS, and a gun, they had grown considerably. At this point the NEDIT engineers, stimulated by industry and recognizing the power, maintenance, and manning limitations offered by the most advanced Y.100 steam plant, made strong representations favouring a gas turbine power plant. Their arguments were accepted, industry was invited to make proposals for a comprehensive "machinery package," and the United Aircraft of Canada, Ltd. (Canadian Pratt and Whitney [P&W]) proposal was accepted.[15] This provided a raft-mounted all-gas turbine propulsion plant, consisting of two P&W (USA) FT-4 main and two P&W (USA) FT-12 cruise engines, driving Lips variable pitch propellers through MAAG (Switzerland) reduction gears. A Bailey remote machinery control system was included which provided full bridge control of the engines. The propulsion system was proven in the shore test of one shaft line of machinery at the U.S. Naval Boiler and Turbine Laboratory in Philadelphia where a suitable brake and other facilities were available. A "total-energy" auxiliary package was supplied by Garrett Marine comprising Solar (USA) gas turbine generators, waste heat and oil-fired boilers and evaporators.[16] A major effort was made toward reduction of radiated noise. The Italian manufactured Oto Melara 5-inch/54 calibre gun, the Dutch HSA M22 fire control system, and the Raytheon Canada guided-missile launching system for the Sea Sparrow missiles comprised the surface and air weapons system. Litton Canada developed the automated CCS 280 command and control system.[17]

A marked change was evident in the procurement arrangements for the DDH 280 class compared with those for the St. Laurent class. The insistence on Canadian or, at a minimum, North American manufacture was gone. "Target-incentive" contracts replaced "cost plus fixed-fee." The shipbuilders and prime equipment contractors were made responsible for the performance of their products. The lead shipyard, Marine Industries, was to be made responsible for the detailed design and the production drawings developed under contract at the NCDO (renamed the Naval Ship Design Agency). United Aircraft of Canada, Garrett Marine, Raytheon, Litton, and other suppliers were to be similarly responsible.

No account of naval engineering would be complete without some discussion of the engineers themselves and their organization. The structure of the RCN prior to World War II was essentially identical to the RN in terms of its personnel divisions, although less extensive in its development. During the three decades from 1910 the Engineering Branch was the sole RCN technical body, and its development paralleled its parent branch in the RN. The proliferation of things technical was so dramatic during World War II that a multitude of new specialties was introduced, some by building on the strengths of serving personnel, some by the direct entry of suitably qualified civilians. These specialists supplemented naval personnel in a branch structure which continued to adhere to the prewar RN mold in which the users of equipment were also the maintainers. The specialists were attached to the user branches as technical experts with the consequence that electrical engineering specialists, for example, were found in each of the torpedo, signals, navigation, and engineering branches, but they were unable to share their common expertise.

Initially, the Special Branch, created on 7 December 1941, was the catch-all for many of the new specialists, both technical and otherwise. However, toward the end of the war, two new engineering branches began to coalesce: Electrical and Ordnance. Shortly after the war, a fourth, the Constructor branch, completed the naval engineering picture, although it should be noted that shipwright officers and, before them, carpenters had been included as part of the Engineering Branch from the outset. The wartime and immediate postwar developments represented Canadian initiatives which often diverged from or anticipated RN practices.

Structural changes continued after World War II, the first comprehensive change being the introduction of the "General List" scheme in 1960, as a result of the deliberations of the Tisdall Committee.[18] This was an emotional occasion since it brought to an end the coloured stripe or distinguishing cloth by which an officer's branch could be recognized. The committee began by examining the benefits of amalgamating all the existing technical branches and concluded that, while every naval officer should be a seaman first, he should have the basic knowledge of a practical engineer. Four years later, the Landymore Personnel Structure Review Team relaxed the General List approach to the extent that the engineer and seaman officers were recognized as having separate and distinct career paths with little prospect of the downstream interchange envisaged by

Tisdall. The structure was changed again in January 1969 with the advent of the unified Canadian Forces organization. The naval engineers formed a distinct and separate grouping (the maritime engineer, or MARE classification) while the seamen formed the maritime surface and sub-surface, or MARS classification.

This outline describes a continuing process: the evolution of naval engineering. It is still developing and is, for that reason, inconclusive. However, I hope that before too many memories are dimmed and all of the pioneers have passed on to the engineers' Valhalla, a more complete work will do justice to the significant accomplishments of Canadian naval engineers. Naval engineering in Canada has moved from an era of dreams and bare survival in the first three decades as a miniscule Canadian adjunct to the Royal Navy, through the hectic and explosive activity of World War II, including massive programmes for the building in Canada of warships to British designs, to maturity in the postwar years. This was when ships and equipment of Canadian design, built to meet specific Canadian requirements, appeared in substantial numbers, drawing their share of recognition in the international forum of naval engineering and establishing a distinctive sea-going character for the RCN.

Chapter 19

THE ROYAL CANADIAN NAVY AND
THE UNIFICATION CRISIS

A. Keith Cameron

In 1964 the government of Lester B. Pearson tabled its White Paper on
Defence, a document that stands as a milestone in the life of Canada's
armed forces. The paper's sponsor, if not its architect, was Paul Hellyer,
appointed as minister of National Defence when the Liberals came to
power in April 1963. Hellyer was no stranger to the Department of
National Defence: he served as parliamentary assistant to the minister in
1956 and as associate minister in 1957, a position he held until the government resigned that same year. From 1957 to 1963 he sat in the front ranks of
the Liberal opposition as the defence critic.

In its simplest form, the 1964 White Paper argued that contemporary
and future defence tasks required a reorganization of Canada's armed forces
and a reshaping of the force structure. Canada was still committed to a
policy of collective security through the North Atlantic Treaty Organization (NATO), the North American Air Defence Command (NORAD), and
the United Nations Charter. However, the government maintained that the
traditional organization of a navy, army, and air force, each with its own
operational command structure, each with its own chief having access to
the minister on individual service matters and acting in concert through a
Chiefs of Staff Committee where common or overlapping functions were
concerned, would not meet the challenges of the future adequately. As an
alternative, the government proposed the integration of the armed forces
under a single chief of Defence Staff and a single Defence Staff. This would
be the first step toward a single unified defence force for Canada.

This was not the first time that Canada's armed forces had been faced with reorganization. In 1918 Prime Minister R.L. Borden had instructed General Sir Arthur Currie to study and plan for the amalgamation of the armed forces, then consisting of a navy of 5,123 officers and men and a sizeable army. But before Currie could do much, both he and Borden were retired from office.

In 1922, to "promote economy and increase efficiency," Parliament approved a reorganization which saw the Department of the Naval Service, the Department of Militia and Defence, and the Air Board (which administered the Canadian Air Force) replaced by a single Department of National Defence under one minister and one chief of staff.[1] The Defence Council of the day consisted of the minister, the deputy minister, the chief of staff, and the director of the Naval Service. Associate members were the adjutant general, the quartermaster general, and the director, Canadian Air Force. This arrangement, under which a single chief of staff exercised control over the three services and advised the minister on all service matters, proved unworkable from the outset. The position of chief of staff was abolished by order-in-council in June 1927. Eight months later, on 7 March 1928, the director of the Naval Service was renamed chief of the Naval Staff, a position equal to that of the chief of the General Staff.[2] The Royal Canadian Air Force in the meantime was beginning its transition to permanent force and single service status, and in November 1938, Air Vice-Marshall G. M. Croil was named to the new position of chief of the Air Staff.

At the end of World War II, the government took up the cause of reorganizing the armed forces once again. The wartime expedient of the three separate departments, each with its own minister, was abandoned on 12 December 1946 in favour of a single Department of National Defence under one minister, Brooke Claxton. He initiated a programme four months later which introduced a common pay scale, amalgamated legal services on a tri-service basis, organized cadet colleges along tri-service lines, provided cadets with a common uniform, introduced a standard code of service discipline, organized the deputy minister's office along functional lines, and established a Chiefs of Staff Committee to foster and achieve inter-service co-operation and co-ordination. Later, during the years of the Diefenbaker government, medical services were consolidated under a single surgeon-general, and the postal services as well as the chaplain services were amalgamated.

However, there was evidence to suggest that these efforts neither promoted economy nor increased efficiency, at least to the degree desired by the government. The 1964 White Paper drew heavily upon the 1963 Report of the Royal Commission on Government Organization (the Glassco Commission), which cited two examples of the inability of the existing structure to produce satisfactory results. When the medical services were amalgamated in 1953, the surgeon-general had been made responsible to the Personnel Members Committee, one of more than two hundred standing tri-service committees operating under the Chiefs of Staff Committee. The "Personnel Members Committee had all the defects of its parent committee in aggravated form," the commissioners observed. "Procrastination and inter-service disagreements, amounting to a virtual refusal to accept direction, [had] proved formidable obstacles to progress." The second example the commissioners referred to was the unsuccessful attempt in 1950 to develop an integrated teletype relay system under tri-service committee direction. "The lack of an effective executive authority in that case led to an abandonment of the attempt at consolidation and the development of three wasteful and increasingly inadequate networks," the commissioners reported.[3]

The commissioners also attacked the size of the forces' growing "administrative tail." They contended that budgeting, accounting, supply, construction, and general administration had elements common to all three services and that the maintenance of "three separate organizations for such functions was uneconomic."[4] But the support functions were not the only areas the commissioners criticized. They remarked on the fact that the RCAF's maritime air component had less in common with the air division in Europe and the air defence forces in NORAD than it did with the RCN, since both the RCN and maritime air operated in the same area under the control of the Supreme Allied Commander, Atlantic (SACLANT). And, again, with respect to operations, they reported that "in finding signallers for the Congo at short notice, the Canadian Army could look only to its own resources in the Royal Canadian Corps of Signals, having no access to the large reservoir of communications personnel in the other two services."[5]

These criticisms, while they may have appeared to serving personnel as over-simplifications of complex problems, gave a good indication of the direction in which the commissioners, and perhaps the public, thought the services should have been moving, and they evoked a sympathetic response in Hellyer and his colleagues. The White Paper agreed with the Glassco Commission's assessment of the problem. But it disagreed with the recommended solution, which was to transfer executive control of common requirements gradually to one individual, the chairman, Chiefs of Staff. This solution, the White Paper maintained, would not resolve the weaknesses inherent in the committee structure. Nor would it lead to improved operational control and effectiveness, the streamlining of decision-making processes, or the reduction of overhead. It was considered essential to establish a single command structure at National Defence Headquarters to convert the three services into one single unified force in order to achieve these goals.

The White Paper was tabled in the House on 26 March 1964 and was well covered by the press and other media in subsequent days. On 3 April 1964 the Chief of the Naval Staff, Vice-Admiral H.S. Rayner, repeated the text of a letter from the minister, outlining the steps that would be taken to achieve the single unified defence force. The first step would be the establishment of the single defence staff at NDHQ for which the target date, including the passage of enabling legislation, was July 1964, only four months away. The second step was to be the reorganization and integration of the field command structure, a sequence likely to take about a year. The third and final step would be the unification of the three services, probably requiring three or four years. In the process, personnel reductions would have to be made, through normal retirement where possible and compulsory release where necessary, with special benefits provided for in the latter case. The minister went on to say that the process outlined "was not immutable. As the lessons of the reorganization are learned, changes in plan or in the timing may result. However, the end objective of a single service is firm."[6]

Despite the controversy that ensued, especially over unification, the minister was able to adhere remarkably well to his timetable. Bill C-90 was passed by parliament as scheduled in July 1964. It abolished the positions of the chairman, Chiefs of Staff, and the three services chiefs, establishing in their place a single chief of Defence Staff who was made responsible for the control and administration of the three armed services. With the changeover on 1 August 1964, Admiral Rayner, the RCN's eighth chief of the Naval Staff, became its last. The Naval Board of Canada, which met for the first time on 9 February 1942, ceased to exist under Bill C-90. The navy's senior representative at NDHQ became Vice-Admiral K.L. Dyer, chief of Personnel in the new integrated headquarters organization. Two other senior naval officers, Rear-Admiral R.P. Welland and Rear-Admiral C.J. Dillon, became deputy chiefs at NDHQ, Admiral Welland as deputy chief of Operational Readiness and Admiral Dillon as deputy Comptroller General.

Other changes were also in the making at the command level. Rear-Admiral J.V. Brock, flag officer Atlantic Coast, maritime commander Atlantic and commander Atlantic Sub-Area since July 1963, was summoned to Ottawa in September 1964 and informed by the minister that his services were no longer required. It was no secret that Brock had reservations about some aspects of integration and unification and that he had expressed his concern through service channels and to his colleagues. He felt strongly, for example, about the traditional right of access by the senior naval officer to the minister and, if necessary, to the prime minister, on important naval matters, a right he saw being denied under the reorganization. The news of his firing was received with surprise and great regret by those serving in the Atlantic Command, who, when the day came for his departure, saw him off in a manner befitting a distinguished officer.

Brock was succeeded in November 1964 by Rear-Admiral W.M. Landymore, who had been succeeded, in turn, as flag officer Pacific Coast and maritime commander Pacific by Rear-Admiral M.G. Stirling on 26 October 1964. Shortly after his arrival in Halifax, Admiral Landymore was called to Ottawa, along with a number of other commanders, for a briefing on unification. Landymore had talked with Hellyer about the reorganization of the forces during the latter's visit to the West Coast, shortly after the tabling of the White Paper in the House. The minister had assured the admiral on that occasion that there would be "no ramming [of] the system down the throats" of service personnel and that the system would be allowed to evolve gradually with changing times and conditions. Now, eight months later, the minister's message was quite different. "Unification was a fact. It was coming and coming soon. Commanders could either accept it or get out." Admiral Landymore's response to the minister was that he could not go along with a plan that would appear, in principle, to wipe out the navy completely.[7]

Despite the apparent acceleration of the integration/unification process, Admiral Landymore was convinced, upon returning to his command, that the government's objectives of reduced overhead and more effective command and control could be achieved through integration alone, without entering into those further measures which he saw as destroying the identity and the effectiveness of the RCN. It was his understanding, since unification had not been clearly defined, that discussion was still possible and that the concept of a single chief supported by a single Defence Staff, a single defence programme financed through a single budget, and single administrative procedures were as far as unification need and should go. It seems that as late as August 1964 Admiral Landymore was supported by Canada's new Chief of the Defence Staff, Air Chief Marshal F.R. Miller, who, in describing the reorganization plan to an audience at the Canadian National Exhibition said,

> I would like to stress that the integration that I speak of has to do with the management or command rather than with the fighting elements themselves. We do not comtemplate attempting to make a fighting soldier into a fighting airman or into a fighting sailor. The complexity of training necessary for dealing with modern warfare on land, sea or air is such that in a relatively short period of engagement in the Armed Services it is impossible for any one individual at the fighting level to master the skills involved in the three environments. We do, however, expect that at a certain rank level the staff of the Canadian Defence Force can be made up of officers of any of the three Services and that it will be a single effective staff.[8]

Two events of special significance to the RCN occurred in the subsequent lull before the storm. The first was the announcement by the minister on 22 December 1964 of the government's five-year equipment programme for the Canadian armed forces, forecast to cost in the area of $1.5 billion. This was the programme designed to reshape the Canadian force structure in accordance with White Paper priorities. These called for re-equipping the army as a mobile force, providing an adequate air- and sea-lift for the army's immediate deployment in an emergency, acquiring tactical aircraft, and maintaining a relatively constant improvement of maritime anti-submarine capability. The cost of re-equipping the forces was to be assisted greatly by personnel reductions; the prediction was that unification would permit 25 per cent of the budget to be devoted to capital equipment in the years ahead, while at the same time giving more for less in terms of force effectiveness.

The programme promised the RCN four helicopter-equipped destroyers (DDH), two operational support ships, one conventional submarine to replace HMCS *Grilse* on the West Coast, conversion of seven Restigouche-class destroyers to carry anti-submarine rockets, twelve additional Sea King (CHSS-2) helicopters, a major refit of HMCS *Bonaventure*, and installation of the latest anti-submarine warfare detection systems in CS2F Tracker aircraft; Argus and Neptune aircraft were also to receive the latest ASW detection systems.[9]

The second event of special significance occurred at noon on 15 February 1965 when HMC ships in mid-Pacific and North Pacific waters, off the coast of South America, in the Caribbean and in the North Atlantic joined shore establishments in Canada in the lowering of the White Ensign and the hoisting of the new Canadian flag in its place. In special ceremonies held at HMCS *Naden* and HMCS *Stadacona*, the latter watched by thousands of Canadians over the Canadian Broadcasting Corporation's television network, the RCN laid aside the only ensigns it had worn since its birth more than half a century earlier. If there was a sense of loss, and for most there was, there was at the same time a sense of pride in a trust well discharged and in a new obligation happily undertaken.

Hellyer called senior officers to Ottawa again in the late spring of 1965 and announced that he intended to implement a single walking-out dress and a common rank structure by 1 July 1967. The news was received with anything but enthusiasm in the Atlantic Command. Over the next year, as Admiral Landymore carried out his regular, frequent visits to units of his command, he was often hard pressed to provide details on these and other unification issues, since he had little information to give. The normal chain of command was not being used for communication purposes. Usually, information would be "leaked" through the media by a defence spokesman. One question which was put to Admiral Landymore repeatedly, at both naval and air force bases in his command, was "why do we hear about these things in the newspapers?"[10]

On 6 June 1966 Admiral Landymore received instructions to be prepared to brief the Parliamentary Defence Committee in Ottawa on 23 June, to be preceded by a private briefing of the minister and associate minister the previous day. Following the latter briefing, the section on personnel (in which the admiral described the actual state of affairs in his command) was censored and rewritten by the minister's staff. The excuse given was that the minister wanted a more positive approach taken at the Parliamentary Defence Committee briefings at which, incidentally, no member of the Defence Staff was present. The paper subsequently tabled in the House of Commons by the minister was not the paper delivered originally in the minister's conference room by Admiral Landymore.

At a meeting on 24 June 1966, Admiral Landymore told the minister that the policies being proposed could lead to disaster, that the question of identity was very important to the RCN, and that unification was not being accepted by the navy in his command. (This was not an idle statement: a few months earlier, at a meeting of all lieutenant-commanders and above in the Halifax area, called by Admiral Landymore to clear the air of rumours and to help him decide his future course of action, all but three of the 367 officers present had enthusiastically supported his position.) This particular meeting with the minister was inconclusive, and the minister asked Admiral Landymore to return to Ottawa in approximately two weeks time.

Ten days later, on 4 July 1966, it was announced that Air Chief Marshal F.R. Miller, chief of the Defence Staff, Lieutenant-General R.W. Moncel, vice-chief of the Defence Staff, Vice-Admiral K.L. Dyer, chief of Personnel, and Lieutenant-General F. Fleury, the comptroller general, would retire shortly. The reasons for these early retirements were not known to Admiral Landymore, although it was rumoured later that Admiral Dyer, General Moncel, and General Fleury had gone together to the minister to inform him that studies carried out by their staffs had failed to show that unification would achieve significant economies.

When Admiral Landymore returned to Ottawa on 12 July for his scheduled meeting with the minister, it was not without hope that something might still be done about the question of naval identity. A few days earlier, the minister had announced that the highland regiments would be permitted to keep their traditional dress. But when the admiral raised the subject of naval identity, again the minister refused to make any concessions. The admiral then asked that each serviceman be given the opportunity to retire honourably without financial penalty, if he felt he could not continue under the new system. At this point the minister asked him to resign. When the admiral refused, the minister told him he would be retired involuntarily, on a date to be determined later. On leaving the minister's office Admiral Landymore met Admiral M.G. Stirling, maritime commander Pacific, who said that he was there to inform the minister that he intended to resign since he could not support the unification policy. These were not the only changes that would occur. Within a month, of the thirteen most senior officers in the armed forces, only two had held their present appointments for more than a month: Lieutenant-General R.P. Rothschild, chief of Materiel Command, and Air Commodore G.G. Diamond, chief of Transport Command.

On the evening of 16 July, a message from Canadian Forces Headquarters relieved Admiral Landymore of his command and appointed Air Commodore Ralph Gordon, his deputy, in temporary command. A few days later, on 19 July 1966, the command said its good-byes to Admiral and Mrs. Landymore. The roadways were lined with groups of officers and men of every rank and from all three services while civilian personnel from the dockyard spilled out from every building to join the spontaneous demonstration, and every ship in the harbour displayed the same flag hoist, "Bravo Zulu [well done] Landymore."

Meanwhile, Commodore J.C. O'Brien, the senior Canadian officer afloat, had been called to Ottawa to speak to General J.V. Allard, the new chief of the Defence Staff, and the minister. When asked to take over the command, Commodore O'Brien sought assurances that the projected shipbuilding and aircraft replacement plans would not be delayed and that there would be no reductions in the size of the fleet. I believe he made reference as well to the press announcement by "a defence spokesman" that consideration was being given to "trying" Admiral Landymore by court-martial. Most importantly, O'Brien (now promoted to the rank of admiral) was assured that, henceforth, all functional commanders would report directly to the chief of the Defence Staff rather than through the branch chiefs.[11]

A few weeks later Hellyer visited the Atlantic Command, for the first time since early in Admiral J.V. Brock's day as flag officer, and addressed an overflow gathering of all ranks in the gymnasium at HMCS *Stadacona*. During the question period that followed his talk, the minister was booed openly over the unification issue until Rear-Admiral O'Brien restored order.

Later in the year, the Parliamentary Defence Committee heard further testimony from Admiral Landymore, Generals Fleury, Moncel and C. Foulkes, and Air Chief Marshal Miller, but by this time Bill C-243, the Canadian Forces Reorganization Act, had received second reading in the House and had therefore been approved in principle. The bill was given final passage on 8 May 1967. And on 1 February 1968 amendments were proclaimed to the National Defence Act which brought the Royal Canadian Navy to an end as a legal entity. Canada's sailors, soldiers, and airmen became members of a single service, the Canadian Armed Forces, which continues to serve our country today.

Perhaps it is too early to attempt to draw conclusions about the process of unification that included the RCN amongst its casualties, but an attempt must be made. This chapter has shown that the so-called "Admirals' Revolt" was a misnomer. There was no collusion amongst the commanding admirals, all of whom were genuinely concerned with the preservation of the fleet and the integrity of the navy. In their commitment, they were expressing the mood of the large majority of the officers and men under their command. There were generals and senior airmen as well who refused to cross over the line toward unification, but it was the admirals who drew the headlines.

It is also untrue that the navy was unprepared to accept change; the concept of a single chief of Staff and a single headquarters staff was readily accepted, and even welcomed, by the navy's senior officers. Changes at the operational command level were also encouraged. The problem was with unification, which was never properly explained and which remains a controversial issue even today.

It is my opinion that most senior officers felt that the minister could be reached before the final step of unification was taken. Many of them, like Admiral Landymore, tried but without success.

Finally, what about the public perception of the unification crisis? There was certainly plenty of publicity given to the unification events and many political barbs were tossed across the floor of the House, but there is little evidence of informed debate over the essentials of the unification proposal. Perhaps it was because few people understood what was intended that Hellyer was able to steer the bill through its second reading before the Parliamentary Defence Committee heard the views of those who were opposed. Even then, there was a feeling, I believe, expressed almost sadly in the press, that the services had failed to make their points.

This suggests to me, in retrospect, that over the long haul of the postwar years, and especially during the late 1950's and early 1960's, when Canada was already embarked on a voyage of great social change, we in the navy had somehow failed to keep in touch with the public mood or to explain adequately our relevancy in changing times. Consequently, our admirals were left in a time of crisis to plead for the retention of symbols, traditions, and a system to which the mass of the public could not relate. While there is no question that the RCN left its successor a proud history and a more meaningful heritage than it had received at birth, this same question of relevancy must occupy the minds of all those who serve Canada now.

APPENDIX

APPENDIX: THE PRINCIPAL VESSELS IN THE MARINE AND FISHERIES FLEET IN 1906

1. *Fisheries Protection Cruisers and Ice-Breakers*[1]

Vessel	Length (feet) and Construction	Year Bought	Builder and Year	Purchase Cost ($)	Annual Maintenance ($)
Constance	116, composite	1891	Polson, Owen Sound, Ont., 1891	41,900	21,992
Curlew	116	1892	Polson, Owen Sound, Ont., 1892	41,900	12,990
Petrel	116, steel	1893	Polson, Owen Sound, Ont., 1893	41,900	25,590
Osprey	127, wood (schooner)	1896	Shelburne, N.S., 1896	9,992	8,911
Kestrel	126, wood	1903	Al Wallace, Vancouver, B.C., 1903	63,920	33,962
Vigilant[2]	175, steel	1904	Polson Iron Works, Toronto, Ont., 1904	143,900	31,595
Falcon		1904		9,000	7,981
Canada[3]	200, steel	1904	Vickers, Barrow, England, 1904	215,600	51,457
Princess	165, steel	1906	Grangemouth, Dkyd., England, 1896	45,000	23,678
Stanley	207, steel	1888	Fairfield, Glasgow, Scotland, 1888	141,133	36,397
Minto	225, steel	1899	Gourlay, Dundee, Scotland, 1899	185,317	69,249
Champlain	132, steel	1904	Fleming and Ferguson, Paisley, Scotland, 1904	90,033	36,445
Montcalm	252, steel	1904	Fleming and Ferguson, 1904	265,333	89,091
Lady Grey[4]	183, steel	1906	Vickers, Barrow, England, 1906	215,000	(a new ship)

2. *Lighthouse Supply/Buoy Tenders, Hydrographic, Arctic Patrol*[5]

Vessel	Length (feet) and Construction	Year Bought	Builder and Year	Use
Aberdeen	180	1894	Fleming and Ferguson, 1894	Lighthouse and supply and buoy
Arctic	165, wood	1904	Howaldtwerke, Kiel, 1901	Arctic exploration
Brant	100, wood	1899	John White, Charlottetown, P.E.I., 1899	Lighthouse supply
Frontenac	113, composite	1901	Canadian Govt. Shipyard, Sorel, P.Q.	St. Lawrence Channel tug
G.T.D.	123, wood (schooner)	1890	Wilson, Bridgewater, N.S., 1890	Wreck vessel
James Howden	100, wood	1903	Canadian Govt. Shipyard, Sorel, P.Q., 1903	St. Lawrence Channel tug
La Canadienne (2)[6]	154, iron	1881	R. Duncan, Port Glasgow, Scotland, 1880	Fisheries
Lac St. Pierre	100, wood	1901	Canadian Govt. Shipyard, Sorel, P.Q., 1901	St. Lawrence Channel tug
Lansdowne	189, wood	1883	O'Brien, Maccan, N.S., 1883	Lighthouse supply and buoy
Lord Strathcona	160, steel	1902	Rennoldson, South Shields, England	Salvage steamer
Quadra	174, steel	1891	Fleming and Ferguson, 1890	Lighthouse supply and buoy
Reserve	80, wood	1903	Notter, Buffalo, U.S.A., 1884	Lighthouse supply and buoy
Rouville	130, wood	1906	Canadian Govt. Shipyard, Sorel, P.Q., 1906	Lighthouse supply and buoy
Scout	104, wood	1900	J.R. Miller, Cardinal, Ont., 1900	Buoy tender

Shamrock	117, wood	J.C. Kaine, Quebec, 1898	1898	Buoy tender
Stadacona	168, iron	Gromp and Sons, Philadelphia, U.S.A., 1893	Not Known	Hydrographic
Verchères	100, wood	Canadian Govt. Shipyard, Sorel, P.Q.	1906	Lighthouse and construction
Verchères	104	Polson Iron Works, Toronto, Ont., 1901	1901	St. Lawrence Channel tug

[1] Data obtained from L.P. Brodeur papers and from Thomas E. Appleton, *Usque ad Mare: A History of the Canadian Coast Guard and Naval Services* (Ottawa: Queen's Printer, 1969).

[2] CGS *Vigilant* was the first "modern" warship built in Canada.

[3] CGS *Canada* was used also as a naval training vessel commencing 1905. An earlier training warship, the corvette *Charybdis*, donated by the British Admiralty in 1880, proved too expensive to maintain and was sold at Halifax in 1884.

[4] The next icebreaker to be built for Canada was CGS *Hazen*, which was also the first ship of any kind ordered from Canadian Vickers Ltd. Sold to Russia and renamed *Mikula Seleaninovich*, she fell into French hands in 1919, was bought back by Canada in 1923, renamed CGS *Mikula*, and remained in service until 1937 (*Usque ad Mare*, p. 178).

[5] Data obtained from *Usque ad Mare*.

[6] *La Canadienne* was the second government vessel to bear the name.

NOTES

CHAPTER ONE: THE ROYAL NAVY'S LEGACY TO THE ROYAL CANADIAN NAVY IN THE PACIFIC, 1880-1914

1. *British Columbian*, 9 November 1910, p. 1. The interview was appropriately entitled "Naval Base is Now Canada's."
2. Printed in Gilbert N. Tucker, *The Naval Service of Canada: Its Official History*, vol. 1, *Origins and Early Years*, (Ottawa: King's Printer, 1952), p. 376.
3. *British Columbian*, 9 November 1910, p. 1.
4. Gilbert N. Tucker, "The Career of H.M.C.S. *Rainbow*," *British Columbia Historical Quarterly* 8 (1943): 1-30. Her displacement was 3,600 tons; length, 300 feet; beam, 43½ feet; draught, 17½ feet; designed speed, 19.75 knots; armament, 2 x 6-inch and 4 x 12-pounder guns, and 2 x 14-inch torpedo tubes.
5. *Colonist*, 8 November 1910.
6. *Times*, 7 November 1910.
7. *Colonist*, 8 November 1910.
8. *British Columbian*, 9 November 1910, p. 4.
9. The classic statement of this theme in relation to Canada is Charles P. Stacey, *Canada and the British Army, 1846-* *1871*, rev. ed. (Toronto: University of Toronto Press, 1963). British Columbia was a variant of the Canadian experience. Her Majesty's Government did not view British Columbia as a self-supporting, self-governing territory and thus did not expect it to be self-defending.
10. John S. Galbraith, "Myths of the 'Little England' Era," *American Historical Review* 67 (1961): 34-48.
11. See, generally, John S. Galbraith, "The 'Turbulent Frontier' as a Factor in British Expansion," *Comparative Studies in Society and History* 2 (1960): 150-68; John Gallager and Ronald Robinson, "The Imperialism of Free Trade," *Economic History Review*, 2d ser., 6 (1953): 1-15; and, in particular reference to British Columbia, Barry M. Gough, " 'Turbulent Frontiers' and British Expansion: Governor James Douglas, the Royal Navy, and the British Columbia Gold Rushes,"*Pacific Historical Review* 41 (1972): 15-32; and "The Character of

the British Columbia Frontier," *BC Studies* 32 (1976-77): 28-40.

12. On this point and the details which follow concerning the Royal Navy's role in B.C. history, see Barry M. Gough, *The Royal Navy and the Northwest Coast of North America, 1810-1914: A Study of British Maritime Ascendancy* (Vancouver: University of British Columbia Press, 1971).

13. Barry M. Gough, "Official Uses of Violence against Northwest Coast Indians in Colonial British Columbia," in *Pacific Northwest Themes: Historical Essays in Honor of Keith A. Murray*, ed. James W. Scott (Bellingham, WA: Center for Pacific Northwest Studies, 1978), pp. 43-69, this being a preliminary statement of a forthcoming book *Gunboat Frontier: British Maritime Authority and Northwest Coast Indians, 1846-1890*.

14. Barry M. Gough, "Canada and the North Pacific, 1871-1914: Problems of a Lion's Cub in an Open Den," *South Atlantic Quarterly* 76 (1977): 348-65; W.J. Illerbrun, "A Selective Survey of Canadian-Hawaiian Relations," *Pacific Northwest Quarterly* 63 (1972): 87-103; Merze Tate, "Canada's Interest in the Trade and Sovereignty of Hawaii," *Canadian Historical Review* 44 (1963): 20-42, and "British Opposition to the Cession of Pearl Harbor," *Pacific Historical Review* 29 (1960): 555-75.

15. Ian H. Nish, *The Anglo-Japanese Alliance: The Diplomacy of Two Island Empires, 1894-1907* (London: Athlone Press, 1966), pp. 353-58; Arthur J. Marder, *From the Dreadnought to Scapa Flow: The Royal Navy in the Fisher Era, 1904-1919*, vol. 1, *The Road to War, 1904-1914* (London: Oxford University Press, 1961): pp. 236-37; Arthur J. Marder, *British Naval Policy, 1880-1905: The Anatomy of British Sea Power* (London: Putnam, 1940), pp. 425-34; and Max Beloff, *Imperial Sunset*, vol. 1, *Britain's Liberal Empire, 1897-1921* (New York: Alfred A. Knopf, 1970), pp. 100-103. Canada's relations with Japan in this period are reviewed by Arthur R.M. Lower in *Canada and the Far East, 1940* (New York: Institute of Pacific Relations, 1940), pp. 7-13.

16. Admiralty (Adm.) 1/7513, Y101 (also in

Admiralty Pacific Station Records, RG8, 3B, vol. 15, PAC), Bickford to secretary of the Admiralty, confidential, 17 September 1901. See also Tucker, *Naval Service of Canada*, 1:84.

17. Adm. 1/7513, Bickford to secretary of the Admiralty, 17 September 1901.

18. Ibid., Kerr minute, 14 October 1901.

19. Marder, *Dreadnought to Scapa Flow*, 1:40.

20. P.K. Kemp, *The Papers of Admiral Sir John Fisher* (London: Navy Records Society, 1960), 1:100, 161, 193. See also "Naval Necessities," *Selborne Papers, 1904-1905*, Navy Library, London, pp. 10-11, 169-73.

21. Great Britain, *Parliamentary Papers*, vol. 48 (1905), (Command [Cmd.] 2335).

22. "Financial Effect on Fleet Re-organization," confidential, *Selborne Papers*, pp. 2-3.

23. Colonial Defence Committee, "Canada: Strategic Conditions at Esquimalt, 26 May 1905," Cabinet 11/27, 347 M, Public Record Office (PRO), London, England.

24. Adm. 116/933, "Statement Showing Where Savings Could be Effected," November 1904.

25. See "Correspondence relating to the Garrison of Halifax and Esquimalt," *Parliamentary Papers*, vol. 54 (1905), (Cmd. 2565).

26. Adm. 1/7806, Y4. Goodrich to secretary of the Admiralty, 1 March 1905.

27. Tucker, *Naval Service of Canada*, 1:124.

28. Ibid., p. 125.

29. Ibid.

30. An Act Respecting the Naval Service of Canada: 9-10 Edw. 7, c.43, ibid., pp. 377-85.

31. Ibid.

32. See Tucker, *Naval Service of Canada*, 1:170-211; Donald C. Gordon, *Dominion Partnership in Imperial Defense, 1870-1914* (Baltimore: Johns Hopkins Press, 1965), passim; and Richard A. Preston, *Canada and "Imperial Defense"* (Durham, NC: Duke University Press, 1967), passim.

33. PAC, Borden Papers, MG 26H 1(a), 123:66804, *British Naval Expenditure in Aid of the Dominion of Canada during the Nineteenth Century* (Secret), printed at the Foreign Office, 26 October 1912.

CHAPTER TWO: L.P. BRODEUR AND THE ORIGINS
OF THE ROYAL CANADIAN NAVY

1. L.P. Brodeur papers (hereafter cited as LPBP), Brodeur to Bostock, 25 May 1921. Originals of the Brodeur correspondence are held in the Public Archives of Canada (PAC), Ottawa.
2. PAC, LPBP, Brodeur to Desbarats, 10 June 1921.
3. Gilbert N. Tucker, *The Naval Service of Canada, Its Official History*, vol. 1, *Origins and Early Years* (Ottawa: King's Printer, 1952), p. 84.
4. PAC, LPBP, L.P. Brodeur, "Proceedings of the 1909 Imperial Conference on Naval and Military Defence," Fourth day, 5 August 1909, p. 43.
5. Winston Churchill (at a meeting in the City of London on the final day of fighting in Operation Torch, the Allied invasion of North Africa in November 1942): "Now this is not the end. It is not even the beginning of the end. But it is, perhaps, the end of the beginning."
6. Thomas E. Appleton, *Usque ad Mare: A History of the Canadian Coast Guard and Marine Services* (Ottawa: Queen's Printer, 1969), p. 31.
7. PAC, LPBP, Spain to Goudreau, 28 January 1907.
8. PAC, LPBP, "Proposals for Canadian Naval Reserve: Summary of Memorial Presented to the Governor General of Canada in Council by the Navy League, Toronto Branch, 14 October 1898," Crutchley (secretary of the Navy League, London, England) to Brodeur, 31 January 1907.
9. PAC, LPBP, Wickham to Prefontaine, 30 November 1905.
10. PAC, LPBP, "An Address Delivered by Clive Phillipps-Wolley on Behalf of the Victoria-Esquimalt Branch of the Navy League to an Audience in the City Hall, Victoria, British Columbia, Tuesday 14 May 1907."
11. PAC, LPBP, "The Navy League (Toronto Branch) Annual Report of the Executive Committee for the Year 1907: To be submitted to the Members at General Meeting, held in the Canadian Military Institute, 10 February 1908, at 8 p.m."
12. PAC, LPBP, W. Hewes Oliphant, "Shall Canada Have a Navy of Her Own?" *The Standard of Empire*, 16 April 1909.
13. PAC, LPBP, "Confidential Papers laid before the Imperial Defence Conference, 1909 (Secret)," Colonial Office, 1909, p. 6.
14. Ibid.
15. PAC, LPBP, "Proceedings of Colonial Conference on Military and Naval Defence," Fifth day, 23 April 1907, pp. 128-32.
16. Ibid., pp. 139-41.
17. Ibid., p. 470.
18. Ibid., pp. 480-81.
19. PAC, LPBP, Brodeur to Wickham, 5 February 1908.
20. PAC, LPBP, Wickham to Brodeur, 22 May 1909.
21. It is unfortunate that the record of the day, the *Canadian Annual Review*, devoted relatively little attention to the Wickham position. See *Canadian Annual Review*, 1907, p. 347.
22. PAC, LPBP, Secretary, the Navy League, to Brodeur, 17 August 1909. See also Brodeur response, 20 August 1909.
23. PAC, LPBP, Grey to Brodeur, 29 April 1909. Much of this correspondence has not been revealed previously and sheds new light on the origins of the RCN.
24. PAC, LPBP, Jayne to Brodeur, 9 June 1909.
25. PAC, LPBP, Browne to Brodeur, 12 July 1909. The final paragraph is believed to be an afterthought by Browne but may have been an observation by Brodeur or Kingsmill. Even today many of Browne's observations have a familiar ring to them.
26. PAC, LPBP, "Proceedings of the 1909 Imperial Conference on Naval and Military Defence," Sixth day, 19 August 1909, p. 86.
27. PAC, LPBP, Crewe to Grey, 16 September 1909.
28. PAC, LPBP, Brodeur to Laurier, 26 August 1909. This letter is a marked-up typewritten draft. Sir Wilfrid Laurier's letter of 4 September 1909 correlates with it and suggests that the letter of 26 August or one very similar to it was in fact sent.
29. PAC, LPBP, Laurier to Brodeur, 4 September 1909.
30. Tucker, *Naval Service of Canada*, 1:165.

Vickers and Sons and Maxim also made a written proposal relating to ship construction to Brodeur in May 1909, PAC, LPBP.

31. *Canadian Annual Review*, 1909, p. 88.
32. PAC, LPBP, Grey to Brodeur, 14 March 1911.
33. PAC, LPBP, Brodeur to Grey, 16 March 1911.
34. PAC, LPBP, Smith to Brodeur, 31 March 1911. The Pacific Station was subsequently extended to 180°W but, lacking a fleet to handle such responsibilities,

Canada lost these stations in later years.
35. Tucker, *Naval Service of Canada*, 1:165-68.
36. PAC, LPBP, Roper and Ling to Desbarats, 25 July 1910.
37. PAC, LPBP, Brodeur minute, 6 August 1910.
38. PAC, LPBP, Brodeur to Desbarats, 7 August 1910.
39. PAC, LPBP, Roper and Ling to Desbarats, 11 August 1910.
40. PAC, LPBP, Brodeur to Desbarats, 19 August 1910.

CHAPTER THREE: COMMANDER E.A.E. NIXON AND THE ROYAL NAVAL COLLEGE OF CANADA, 1910-22

1. Sections 32 to 36 of An Act Respecting the Naval Service of Canada: 9-10 Edw. 7, c. 43, as quoted in Gilbert N. Tucker, *The Naval Service of Canada: Its Official History*, vol 1, *Origins and Early Years*, (Ottawa: King's Printer: 1952), p. 155.

CHAPTER FOUR: THE ROAD TO WASHINGTON: CANADA AND EMPIRE NAVAL DEFENCE, 1918-21

1. For example, R. MacGregor Dawson, *The Development of Dominion Status* (Toronto: Oxford University Press, 1935), pp. 36-54. See also, J. Bartlett Brebner, "Canada, the Anglo-Japanese Alliance and the Washington Conference," *Political Science Quarterly* 50 (1935): 45-57; R. Graham, *Arthur Meighen* (Toronto: Clarke, Irwin, 1965), 84; J.S. Galbraith, "The Imperial Conference of 1921 and the Washington Conference," *Canadian Historical Review* 29 (1948): 143-52; M. Tate and F. Foy, "More Light on the Abrogation of the Anglo-Japanese Alliance," *Political Science Quarterly* 74 (1959): 532-53; J.C. Vinson, "The Imperial Conference of 1921 and the Anglo-Japanese Alliance," *Pacific Historical Review* 31 (1962): 257-66.
2. M.G. Fry, *Illusions of Security: North Atlantic Diplomacy 1918-22* (Toronto: University of Toronto Press, 1972).
3. C.S. Gray, *Canadian Defence Priorities: A Question of Relevance* (Toronto: Clarke, Irwin, 1972), p. 21.
4. CAB 4/7, CID Papers 255-B, "General Staff Paper on the Military Liabilities of the Empire," 27 July 1920.

5. By 11 November 1918, 1,005 new ships had been ordered for the Royal Navy or were building. By December 1919, 611 had been cancelled, 319 were completed, and 95 were nearing completion. 122 *House of Commons Debates*, 5s., 1377. By March 1920, ships still under construction were: 1 battle cruiser (HMS *Hood*, laid down in 1916), 9 light cruisers, 2 flotilla leaders, 8 destroyers, 13 submarines, 2 aircraft carriers, and 5 auxiliary vessels (126 *HC Debates*, 5s., 414). For 1921, ships in service included: 38 battleships, 2 battle cruisers, 87 light cruisers, 300 destroyers, and 106 submarines. By March 1928, a total of 1,538 ships had been scrapped (2,139,515 tons). New construction since 1918 was 56 ships (332,515 tons) (214 *HC Debates*, 5s., 2145).
6. Cmd. 8566, Imperial War Conference, 1917. Extracts from Minutes of Proceedings and Papers . . . ; and Minutes of Proceedings and Papers (other than those published in Cmd. 8566) (Confidential, HMSO, 1917), Meetings 28 and 30 March 1917.
7. CAB 24/51, "Naval Defence of the Brit-

ish Empire," 17 May 1918; also Adm. 1/8520, Board Minutes no. 260 (18 April), 286 (16 May), and 291 (23 May).

8. R.A. Preston, *Canada and "Imperial Defense"* (Durham: Duke University Press, 1967), p. 502.

9. Adm. 116/1815, Admiralty to Jellicoe, 23 December 1918. Also, Jellicoe Papers, British Museum Add. MSS 49045, pp. 54-55, Borden to Geddes, 15 August 1918.

10. Jellicoe Papers, pp. 43-44. See also, Jellicoe, "Naval Policy of the Empire," *Brassey's Naval and Shipping Annual* (London: William Clowes, 1926), p. 63.

11. Adm. 116/1815, Geddes to War Cabinet, 17 December 1918.

12. Adm. 116/1745-62, established early in 1918 to study the naval aspects of winding down the war.

13. Adm. 1/8571; and Adm. 167/56, Board Minutes no. 958.

14. A complete set of the Jellicoe Reports is included in the Jellicoe Papers, Add. MSS 49045-57. See also Adm. 116/1831, Jellicoe to Admiralty, 3 February 1920, Enclosure 1.

15. Adm. 116/1815, Wemyss to First Lord, 31 October 1919.

16. Adm. 116/1677, chief of Naval Staff to Admiralty Board, 1 January 1920; Adm. 167/61, Memo to Admiralty Board, 14 January 1920; CAB 4/7, CID Paper 257-3, 27 September 1920, and CID Paper 131-C, February 1921.

17. Adm. 116/3610, CID Paper N-11, 2 March 1921; also B.D. Hunt, "Smaller Navies and Disarmament," in *Dreadnought to Polaris* ed. A.M.J. Hyatt (Toronto: Copp Clark, 1973), pp. 50-52.

18. PAC, RG24, vol. 3833, Ballantyne to N.W. Rowell, n.d.

19. Ibid., RG24, vol. 4044, Naval Committee Meeting, 13 March 1919.

20. Ibid., MG26, Borden Papers, Borden to Milner, 31 January 1919.

21. Adm. 1/8587, Adm. Memo "Canadian Naval Forces" (n.d.).

22. DND Directorate of History (DOH), 4000-100/4, "The Early Days of the Royal Canadian Navy."

23. PAC, RG26, Borden Papers, "Naval Defence of the British Empire," note by L.C. Christie, 30 September 1918.

24. DOH, Occasional Paper no. 2, 3 July 1919.

25. PAC, RG24, Desbarats to Kingsmill, 30 October 1919.

26. R. Bacon, *Life of John Rushworth, Earl Jellicoe* (London: Cassell, 1936), p. 419; also, Jellicoe Papers, Add. MSS 49045, vol. 57, 3 December 1919.

27. DOH, Report of Admiral of the Fleet Viscount Jellicoe, etc. . . . on Naval Mission to the Dominion of Canada (November-December, 1919) (3 vols.): vol. 1 published as Sessional Paper, no. 61 (1920); vols. 2 & 3 marked "Secret." This report is discussed again in Chapter 5.

28. PAC, MG26, Borden Papers, Foster to Borden, 25 March 1920.

29. PAC, RG24, vol. 3964, Commander Stephens's note.

30. PAC, MG26, Borden Papers, Foster to Borden, 25 March 1920.

31. Adm. 1/8587, "Canada Naval Forces," Jellicoe to Ballantyne, 24 March 1920.

32. Canada, *HC Debates* (1920), 1:707.

33. PAC, MG26, Borden Papers, Ballantyne to Borden, 12 April 1920.

34. DOH, Occasional Paper no. 32, 4 June 1921.

35. C.P. Stacey, *Canada and the Age of Conflict* (Toronto: Macmillan of Canada, 1977), p. 334.

36. PAC, MG26, Meighen Papers, speech at London, Ontario, 1 September 1921.

37. *Documents on Canadian External Relations (DCER)*, vol. 3, doc. 209, Governor General to Colonial Secretary, 15 February 1921; also A.R.M. Lower, "Loring Christie and the Genesis of the Washington Conference of 1921-22," *Canadian Historical Review* 47 (March 1966): 38-48.

38. Stacey, *Canada and the Age of Conflict*, p. 342.

39. Fry, *Illusions of Security*, pp. 151-52.

40. *DCER*, vol. 3, doc. 218, Imperial Conference Resolutions.

41. CAB 32/3, Imperial Conference Meetings, 22, 27 July 1921.

42. PAC, RG26-H, Borden Papers, Borden to King, 10 January 1922.

43. Fry, *Illusions of Security*, pp. 177-81; also Adm. 1/8630, contains Minutes of Meetings of the British Empire Delegation.

44. Adm. 116/1776, CID Paper 176-C, 28 July 1922; Adm. 167/66, Memo on Fleet Reductions, 20 January 1922; also Admiralty submissions to the Churchill Com-

mittee on Service Estimates in January-
February 1922, contained in CAB, CP
3692A, 4 February 1922.
45.   PAC, MG26-H, Borden Papers, Borden
to King, 10 January 1922; Canada, Sessional Papers, 58, no. 9 (1922), Paper

no. 47.
46.   PAC, MG26-H, King Diaries, 28 December 1921.
47.   PAC, MG30, Desbarats Diaries, 22 February 1922.

CHAPTER FIVE: THE ROYAL CANADIAN NAVY BETWEEN THE WARS, 1922-39

1.   Gilbert N. Tucker, The Naval Service of
Canada: Its Official History, vol. 1,
Origins and Early Years (Ottawa: King's
Printer, 1952), p. 327.
2.   James Eayrs, In Defence of Canada, vol.
1, From the Great War to the Great
Depression (Toronto: University of Tor-
onto Press, 1964), p. 171.
3.   Fraser M. McKee, Volunteers for Sea
Service: A Brief History of the Royal
Canadian Naval Reserve, Its Predeces-

sors and Successors (Toronto: Houston's Standard Publications, 1973), p.
34.
4.   Ibid., p. 36.
5.   Vernon W. Howland, "Recollections of
the RCNVR," manuscript in Rear-Admiral Pullen's possession.
6.   Frank L. Houghton, "A Sailor's Life
for Me," manuscript in J. Boutilier's
possession, pp. 115-21.
7.   Tucker, Naval Service of Canada, 2:6-7.

CHAPTER SIX: "BIG SHIP TIME": THE FORMATIVE YEARS
OF RCN OFFICERS SERVING IN RN CAPITAL SHIPS

1.   The author, Rear-Admiral R.H. Leir,
was the last official RCN midshipman
casualty of World War II. He was posted
dead from HMS Exeter on 12 March
1942 but had the temerity to resurrect in
1945 and write this chapter.
2.   Gilbert N. Tucker, The Naval Service of
Canada: Its Official History, vol. 1,
Origins and Early Years (Ottawa: King's
Printer, 1952), p. 122.
3.   Ibid., pp. 188-211.
4.   Based on the author's recollections.
5.   A "pier head jump" is a last minute
posting where an officer or man figura-

tively—if not literally—jumps on board
his ship while it is drawing away from
the jetty.
6.   When the author was discharged "dead"
in 1942, his account with Gieves stood
in the red to the extent of £8.9.0. The
debt was cancelled in a neat note of con-
dolence to his parents. It was quietly
re-instated on his account when he was
re-equipped in December 1945.
7.   "RPC Dinner 1900 WSB" Request the
pleasure of your company for dinner at
seven o'clock in the evening. Will send
boat.

CHAPTER SEVEN: AN ENGINEER'S OUTLINE OF RCN HISTORY: PART I

1.   The background material for this chapter was taken largely from Gilbert N.
Tucker, The Naval Service of Canada,
Its Official History, vol. 1, Origins and
Early Years (Ottawa: King's Printer,
1952).
2.   For a further account see Tucker, The
Naval Service of Canada, 1:238 ff.
3.   K.C. Barnaby, 100 Years of Specialized
Shipbuilding and Engineering (London: Hutchinson, 1964), pp. 96-97.

4.   For a detailed account of the activities of
the new department see, J. de N. Kennedy,
History of the Department of Munitions and Supply, Canada in the Second
World War (Ottawa: King's Printer,
1950).
5.   F.N. Smith, "History of the British
Admiralty Technical Mission in Canada," manuscript prepared ca. 1946 when
the mission was closed.
6.   D.J. Goodspeed, A History of the Defence

Research Board of Canada (Ottawa: Queen's Printer, 1958).

7. Prime Minister, United Kingdom, to Prime Minister, Canada (telegram), 18 December, 1940, ARO, M.014391/41.

8. P.R. Elliot, *Allied Escort Ships of World War II* (Annapolis: United States Naval Institute Press, 1977), p. 23.

9. Ibid., p. 357.

10. "Shipbuilding in Canada during the Second World War," *Journal of Naval Engineering* 1, no. 3 (1947): 6-10.

CHAPTER EIGHT: PRINCES THREE: CANADA'S USE OF ARMED MERCHANT CRUISERS DURING WORLD WAR II

1. G.R. Stevens, "Working notes on the history of the Canadian National Railway" (prepared in 1968), in Commander F.M. McKee's possession.

2. J. Dosie to F.M. McKee, personal communication, March 1971.

3. V.S. Godfrey to F.M. McKee, personal communication, July 1967.

4. A.C. Wurtele to F.M. McKee, personal communication, March 1968.

5. J.C.I. Edwards to F.M. McKee, personal communication, June 1968.

6. J.C.I. Edwards to F.M. McKee, personal communication, June 1968.

7. Report of proceedings of HMCS *Prince Robert* by Captain W.B. Creery, RCN, September 1945. Much of the material related to *Prince Robert*'s activities in Hong Kong is drawn from this report of proceedings.

8. V.S. Godfrey to F.M. McKee, personal communication, July 1967.

CHAPTER NINE: THE ROYAL CANADIAN NAVY'S QUEST FOR AUTONOMY IN THE NORTH ATLANTIC, 1941-43

1. External Affairs to CNS, letter of 30 June 1941: File NSS 1550-157/1. The files cited are normally RCN files deposited at the Directorate of History (DOH), Department of National Defence Headquarters, Ottawa.

2. PAC, RG24, vol. 3840, File NS 1017-10-18, "The Naval Defence Policy of Canada," dated 30 October 1935.

3. PAC, RG2, 7-C, vol. 1, Cabinet War Committee (CWC), Minutes, 17 May 1940.

4. File NSS 1700-193/96, High Commission for United Kingdom to External Affairs, telegram #672 of 23 May 1940.

5. See Prime Minister Mackenzie King's remarks in CWC, Minutes, 25 May 1940.

6. The flag officer commanding Canadian naval forces based on Halifax.

7. CWC, Minutes, 25 May 1940.

8. SS *Athenia* was torpedoed on 4 September 1939 with a loss of 128 people, including many women and children.

9. DOH, recorded interview with Rear-Admiral L.W. Murray, RCN (Ret'd.).

10. Admiralty file M. 03538/1940 copy in 1650-1. Report of interview by Commodore Sir F. Dreyer, RN, with Rear-Admiral P.W. Nelles dated 28 January 1940.

11. File NS 1048-48-31, Admiralty to NSHQ signal 0016B/20 May 1941.

12. CWC, Minutes, 27 May 1941.

13. File NS 1048-48-31, NSHQ to Admiralty signal 2108Z/21 May 1941.

14. This matter was dealt with at length by the CWC during May 1941. For a resumé see C.P. Stacey, *Arms, Men and Governments* (Ottawa: Department of National Defence, 1970), chapter 4. Commander B. German, RCN, was sent as a "camouflaged observer" for Canada with the British Mission.

15. ABC-1 was forwarded by Britain to the Dominions for comments.

16. ABC-1 is reproduced in U.S. Congress, *Pearl Harbor Attack*, 79th Congress, 1st Session (1946), part 15, pp. 1485-1541.

17. See CWC, Minutes, 3 June 1941, and especially the prime minister's comments.

18. *Pearl Harbor Attack*, part 15, p. 1488.

19. Ibid., p. 1493 and Annex II. Canada was an "Associated Power" under the terms of ABC-1.

20. CWC, Minutes, 3 June 1941 and 7 June

1941.

21. Interview with Rear-Admiral H.N. Lay, RCN (Ret'd.).

22. PAC, RG24, vol. 8081, File NNS 1272-2, Chiefs of Staff Committee (CSC) to minister, memorandum of 22 April 1941 on subject of ABC-22. CSC, Minutes, 20 April 1941.

23. PDB 124 in Permanent Joint Board on Defence (PJBD) journal included in Cabinet War Committee, documents (PAC appended to Minutes).

24. S.W. Dzuiban, *Military Relations Between the United States and Canada: 1939-1945* (Washington: U.S. Government Printing Office, 1959), p. 74.

25. Lay interview.

26. CSC to minister, memoranda of 24 May 1941 and 28 May 1941, CSC, Minutes. Reply of minister to chief of the General Staff in Minutes.

27. As early as April 1941, USN ships were using Shelburne, Nova Scotia, as a base in accordance with the terms of "The Joint Canadian-United States Basic Defence Plan" (Basic Plan-1) dated 10 October 1940. A copy of this plan is in the army files in DOH. All provisions of Basic Plan-1 were embodied in an RCN Operational Plan dated 17 December 1940 in File NS 1078-13-2.

28. File NS 1048-43-31, Naval Service Headquarters (NSHQ), "History of North Atlantic Convoy Escort Organization and Canadian Participation Therein: September, 1939 to April, 1943" (August 1943). This manuscript was written by personnel in the Department of Plans. ABC-22 was included as paragraph 12D of WPL-51.

29. Samuel E. Morison, *The History of United States Naval Operations in the Second World War*, 15 vols. (Boston: Little, Brown, 1947-62), 1:60-61.

30. File NS 1550-157/1, U.S. naval attaché to CNS, letter of 23 August 1941.

31. File NSS 1550-157/1, CNS to Canadian naval attaché, Washington, memorandum of 25 August 1941.

32. File NS 1048-48-31, CNS to CCNF signal 2011Z/27 August 1941.

33. File NS 1700-193/96, British Admiralty Delegation (BAD), Washington to Admiralty and NSHQ signal 1825R/5 September 1941.

34. See CWC, Minutes, 9 October 1941. The RCAF would not accept strategic control by COMINCH of its anti-submarine aircraft based on Newfoundland although the RCN would of its ships.

35. ABC-1, paragraph 14(a) and Annex II and V.

36. NSHQ, "History of Canadian Participation."

37. File NSS 1550-157/1, secretary of the Navy to COAC and CCNF signal 1930Z/7 December 1941; CCNF to naval secretary, letter of 18 December 1941; naval secretary to FONF, letter of 6 January 1942. After the U.S. entered the war, FONF and CTF 24 prepared a combined operational plan based on ABC-22 on the authority of the 22nd recommendation of the PJBD: PAC, RG24, vol. 2844, File NS 1017-10-35.

38. ABC-1, Annex II; WPL-51; WPL-51, paragraph 12d and ABC-22, Annex I.

39. PAC, RG24, vol. 4044, File NS 1078-3-4, Naval Council, Minutes, 5 August 1941.

40. NSHQ, "History of Canadian Participation."

41. Commodore Murray found himself in the peculiar position of having to teach Admiral Bristol and his staff the method of control and protection of shipping and having to turn over his operational responsibilities to a foreign admiral whose country was providing no resources for the job in hand.

42. File NS 1048-48-31, Admiralty to COMINCH signal 0026A/29 January 1942; COMINCH to Admiralty signal 2335Z/2 February 1942; Admiralty to COMINCH signal 0123A/4 February 1942.

43. File NS 1048-48-31, NSHQ to Admiralty and COMINCH signal 1934Z/4 February 1942. Murray, promoted to rear-admiral in December 1941 to put him on equal terms with Rear-Admiral Bristol, was now flag officer Newfoundland Force (FONF).

44. The "air gap" was the term for an ocean area outside the range of anti-submarine aircraft flying from Canada and Iceland.

45. Lay interview.

46. CWC, Minutes, 21 October 1941. See U.S. State Department memorandum of 20 October 1941.

47. CSC, Minutes, 20 June 1942.

48. Lay interview. Admiral Lay explained

that Admiral Brodeur had been the butt of jokes by the British because of his difficulty with English.

49. Admiral Brodeur was selected to be naval attaché, Washington, from a list of three officers put forward by CNS to the Cabinet War Committee in August 1940. Brodeur had close connections in the cabinet, in particular with Ernest LaPointe. Throughout his tenure as naval attaché and then as NMCS, he kept in contact with his political acquaintances. Interview with Captain (N) N.D. Brodeur, Canadian Forces.

50. File NSS 1550-157/1, Canadian Joint Staff (CJS) to CSC, memorandum of 11 July 1942. The memorandum reported on the Portal-Towers (U.K.-U.S.) agreement on long-range aircraft, which was reached without consulting the CJS.

51. File NSS 1550-157/1, NMCS to CNS signal 1508Z/17 July 1942.

52. Admiral Bristol died of a heart attack while duck hunting.

53. Murray interview.

54. PAC, RG24, vol. 3844, File NS 1017-10-35, CTF 24 to COAC and FONF, letter of 21 September 1942. Also CTF to COMINCH signal 0145Z/10 October 1942: File NSS 155-157/1.

55. PAC, RG24, vol. 3844, File NS 1017-10-35. Both FONF and COAC thanked CTF 24 for his "helpful suggestions" by letter.

56. File NS 8280B, Naval Control Service Officer, Sydney to Captain E. Brand, letter of 1 September 1942.

57. Lay to Reid (FONF), letter of 26 October 1942. This is the first mention by the author could find on the topic. However, the letter states that Lay had "been thinking for some time" about the question of command relationships.

58. File NSS 1550-157/1, NMCS to CNS, letter of 26 October 1942.

59. The Americans were considerably more helpful than the British. In September 1942, Admiral Leahy appointed officers to effect liaison between JCS and CJS.

60. File NSS 1550-157/1, NMCS to CNS, letter of 6 November 1942.

61. HF/DF was also known popularly as Huff Duff.

62. BAD (Washington) to NSHQ signal 2209Z/7 November 1942.

63. File NSS 1550-157/1, BAD to NSHQ

signal 1909Z/19 November 1942; NSHQ to BAD signal 2043Z/20 November 1942; BAD to NSHQ signal 0245Z/26 November 1942.

64. Lay interview.

65. File NSS 1550-157/1, Nelles to King, letter of 1 December 1942.

66. Lay papers. Director of Operations Division (DOD) to CNS, memorandum of 2 December 1942.

67. File NSS 1550-157/1, NMCS to NSHQ signal 1621Z/2 December 1942. NSHQ was not included in CTF 24's message.

68. FONF file, Report of proceedings to November 1942, of FONF dated 16 December 1942.

69. File NSS 1550-157/1, King to Nelles, letter of 12 December 1942.

70. Lay papers. DOD to CNS, memorandum of 26 December 1942 re. projected conference.

71. File NS 8280A, DOD to CNS and VCNS, memorandum of 28 December 1942 regarding Captain Lay's visit to COAC.

72. File NSS 1550-157/1, CTF 24 to FONF signal 2033Z/5 January 1943 ordered the transfers of HMCS *Leamington* and *Columbia*; NSHQ to CTF 24 signal 1634Z/7 January 1943; CTF 24 to NSHQ signal 2037Z/8 January 1943.

73. Ibid., CNS to COMINCH signal 1920Z/12 January 1943; Nelles to King, letter of 15 January 1943.

74. Ibid., Nelles to Brodeur, Murray, Reid; letters all of 19 January 1943.

75. Authorities directly involved in the command structure numbered eight; COMINCH, CINCLANT, CTF 24, NSHQ, COAC, FONF, USAAF (Nfld.), and air officer commanding Eastern Atlantic Command (AOC, EAC).

76. All correspondence to this point had been of a personal nature between COMINCH and CNS. King, however, was very busy directing a "Two Ocean War" and might have instructed Edwards to write Nelles so as not to delay the reply.

77. File NSS 1550-157/1, Edwards to Nelles, letter of 17 January 1943; CTF 24 to COAC signal 1815Z/20 January 1943; Nelles to Edwards, letter of 21 January 1943.

78. File NSS 8280B, NSHQ to Admiralty signal 1645Z/22 January 1943.

79. File NSS 1550-157/1, Murray to Nelles,

letter of 24 January 1943.

80. Ibid., NMCS to CNS, letter of 23 January 1943.

81. Ibid., COMINCH to CTF 24 signal 2331Z/1 February 1943; King to Nelles, letter 31 January 1943; Nelles to King, letter of 6 February 1943.

82. Ibid., COMINCH signal 2013Z/2 February 1943.

83. Lay papers. Captain Lay prepared various proposals during February including "Proposed Plan for Organization of Anti-Submarine Forces" (15 February 1943) and "Commander-in-Chief N.W. Atlantic" (17 February 1943).

84. Lay interview.

85. PAC, RG24, vol. 8073, File NSS 1270-128, Atlantic Convoy Conference, Minutes, 1 March 1943.

86. Noble avoided the issue of command relationships in his remarks. The Royal Navy did, however, work behind the scenes at the conference to make the Royal Canadian Navy's course smooth. Interview by author with Captain E. Brand, RCN (Ret'd.).

87. Atlantic Convoy Conference, Minutes, 1 March 1943.

88. Ibid.

89. Admiral Brodeur's remark obviously upset Admiral Edwards and ruffled a few feathers in the USN. Vice-Admiral Mears, RN, worked behind the scenes to smooth the rough water between the RCN and USN. Brand interview.

90. File NSS 1550-157/1, NMCS to CNS signal 2003Z/6 March 1943.

91. Atlantic Convoy Conference, Minutes, "Report of the Sub-Committee on Command Relations."

92. Lay papers. Lay to Bidwell, letter of 19 March 1943.

93. Lay interview.

94. Murray, Lay, Brand, Rear-Admiral J.C. Hibbard, and Rear-Admiral E.W. Finch-Noyes interviews.

95. CWC, Minutes, 11 March 1943.

96. P.C. 485. The Naval Council became the Naval Board on 22 January 1942; the problem of command relationships and the Nelles/King confrontation was never discussed in the CWC although it may have been unofficially. Nelles announced to the CWC on 4 February 1943 that there would be a conference on command relationships in Washington.

97. "Canadian North West Atlantic Command" 0021 file in NSS 1550-157/1. This is indicated by a series of messages during April 1943, between COAC and NSHQ.

98. File NSS 8280A, Admiralty to NSHQ signal 2153Z/8 April 1943.

99. File NS 1048-48-31, COMINCH to CNS signal 2216Z/12 March 1943. This signal was amplified by NMCS to CNS 1637Z/13 March 1943. Murray papers.

100. Ibid., NMCS signal. It was at this time that Grand Admiral Karl Dönitz, admiral commanding U-boats, had just opened what proved to be his last offensive to smash the convoy system and reports of heavy losses caused alarm in Washington and elsewhere.

101. Murray papers. Murray to Nelles teletype 1508Z/14 March 1943.

102. File NS 1048-48-31, CNS to COMINCH signals 1702Z/14 March 1943 and 2125Z/15 March 1943.

103. King to Nelles, letter. A teletyped undated copy of this letter is in the Murray papers. It was obviously sent by CNS to COAC presumably on 15 March 1943.

104. Murray papers. Murray to Nelles teletype undated. This was probably part of a teletyped conversation between CNS and COAC with both dictating directly to the operator. This material was considered very sensitive.

105. The agitation Murray showed in the reply that he suggested be sent to King was quite uncharacteristic of him. King's slight at his professional ability obviously offended Murray deeply.

106. File NS 1048-48-31, CNS to First Sea Lord signal 1401Z/23 March 1943; First Sea Lord to CNS signal 2005Z/26 March 1943; CNS to COMINCH signal 1631Z/27 March 1943; COMINCH to CNS and Admiralty signal 1251Z/30 March 1943.

107. File NSS 1550-157/1, DNI to OPNAV, letter of 16 April 1943.

108. Ibid., OPNAV to NHSQ signal 1855Z/24 April 1943.

109. COAC file, Report of proceedings for April 1943, of CinC, CNA dated 16 May 1943.

110. File 1550-157/1, CinCCNA to CTF 24 signal 2116Z/29 March 1943.

CHAPTER TEN: ROYAL CANADIAN NAVY PARTICIPATION
IN THE BATTLE OF THE ATLANTIC CRISIS OF 1943

1. See Lund, Chapter 9. See also Gilbert N. Tucker, *The Naval Service of Canada: Its Official History*, vol. 2, *Activities on Shore During the Second World War* (Ottawa: King's Printer, 1952), p. 405, where he credits the Commonwealth with having 98 per cent of the escorts.
2. Tucker, *Naval Service of Canada*, and Joseph Schull, *The Far Distant Ships* (Ottawa: Queen's Printer, 1952).
3. Stephen W. Roskill, *The War at Sea*, 3 vols. (London: HMSO, 1960), 2 (appendix 0): 485.
4. Tucker, *Naval Service of Canada*, 2:457.
5. Ibid., p. 412.
6. Schull, pp. 161-76.
7. J. Marc Milner, "Canadian Escorts and the Mid-Atlantic 1942-1943," Master's thesis, University of New Brunswick, 1979, appendices 2 and 3, pp. 172-74.
8. Donald Macintyre, *The Battle of the Atlantic* (London: B.T. Batsford, 1961), *The Naval War Against Hitler* (New York: Charles Scribners' Sons, 1974), and *U-Boat Killer* (London: Weidenfeld & Nicolson, 1956).
9. Macintyre, *U-Boat Killer*, pp. 78-82.
10. W. Chalmers, *Max Horton and the Western Approaches* (London: Hodder and Stoughton, 1958), p. 157.
11. PAC, RG24, vol. 11, 595, MS 1-2-6. Report of proceedings, HMCS *Veteran*, SC 45, 17 October 1941.
12. PAC, RG24, vol. 3892, NSS 1033-6-1. Commanding officer, HMCS *Chambly*, to captain (D[estroyers]) Newfoundland, 4 November 1941.
13. Ibid., captain (D) Newfoundland to commodore commanding Newfoundland Force, 2 September 1941.
14. Terry Hughes and John Costello, *The Battle of the Atlantic* (New York: Dial Press, 1977), p. 233.
15. Patrick Abbazia, *Mr. Roosevelt's Navy* (Annapolis, MD: U.S. Naval Institute Press, 1975), p. 262.
16. Roskill, *The War at Sea*, and *White Ensign: The British Navy at War 1939-45* (Annapolis, MD: United States Naval Institute, 1960).
17. Samuel E. Morison, *History of United States Naval Operations in the Second World War*, 15 vols. (Boston: Little, Brown, 1947-62), 1:12-13.
18. J.M. Waters, Jr., *Bloody Winter* (Princeton, NJ: Van Nostrand, 1967), pp 23-24.
19. See also Morison, *History of United States Naval Operations*, 1:117. One of the reasons why the eastern terminus of escorts operating from Newfoundland was switched to Londonderry was because the USN wanted access to proper training facilities.
20. Abbazia, *Mr. Roosevelt's Navy*, p. 426.
21. Alan Easton, *50 North* (Toronto: Ryerson, 1963). Easton's book contains perhaps the best appreciation of Canada's corvette fleet in the fall of 1941. See especially p. 49.
22. James B. Lamb, *The Corvette Navy* (Toronto: Macmillan, 1979), pp. 134-35.
23. DOH, NDHQ, NS1033-7-2. J.O. Cossette, naval secretary to the commanding officer Atlantic Coast, commanding officer Pacific Coast, commodore commanding Newfoundland Force and other senior RCN commands, statement on "Training and Manning Policy," 24 December 1941.
24. Tucker, *Naval Service of Canada*, 2:457.
25. Ibid., 2:436-67.
26. C.P. Stacey, *Arms, Men and Governments* (Ottawa: Department of National Defence, 1970), pp. 315-19.
27. W.A.B. Douglas and B. Greenhous, *Out of the Shadows* (Toronto: Oxford University Press, 1977), pp. 59-70.
28. PAC, RG2, 7-C, C-4875, Minutes of the Cabinet War Committee, 7 January 1943.
29. In the autumn of 1942 the MOEF comprised eleven escort groups: six British, B.1, B.2, B.3, B.4, B.6 and B.7; four Canadian, C.1, C.2, C.3, C.4; and one American, A.3. The designations indicated the nationality of the groups, but in practice the groups were seldom composed of escorts from a single service. The corvettes of B.6, for example, were Norwegian, while the four "C" groups contained within their number one wholly British escort group. The lone American group contained only a token American force of destroyers or cutters, the

bulk of its numbers being made up of RCN or RN corvettes.

30. DOH, NSH 1000-973, H.G. DeWolf, director of Plans, to the chief of the Naval Staff (CNS), 29 December 1942.

31. The new commissions included the corvettes which would play prominent roles in the 1942 battles, such as HMC Ships *Amherst* and *Battleford*. By early December 1941, forty-four of the fifty-seven corvettes, and ten of the twelve RCN destroyers then in commission were assigned to the NEF—78 per cent of the RCN's ocean going escort forces. See Milner, p. 39.

32. PAC, RG24, vol. 11, 929 MS-00220-3-6, "it is essential that groups sail from St. John's at full strength if we are to avoid [a] repetition of SC 42 losses." Flag officer Newfoundland Force to NSHQ, 30 May 1942.

33. Milner, pp. 73-93.

34. Ibid., chapter 3.

35. Nelles wrote to Vice-Admiral E.L.S. King, RN, an old friend who was just stepping down as assistant CNS (Trade). King's reply can be found in DOH, NS 8440.

36. See C.B. Behrens, *Merchant Shipping and the Demands of War* (HMSO: London, 1955), Chapter 14, "The Effects of the North African Campaign and the Beginnings of the World Shipping Crisis."

37. Chalmers, *Max Horton and the Western Approaches*, pp. 162-63.

38. PRO (London), PREM 3, 331/8, A.V. Alexander to W.S. Churchill, 15 December 1942.

39. In fact destroyers were crucial to the defence of a convoy, and the RCN was in such need of these ships that Prime Minister W.L. Mackenzie King sent a personal plea to Winston Churchill in early December 1942, asking that fourteen be made available to the Canadian navy.

40. For an account of this affair see Milner, pp. 107-24. The various memos which formed the RCN's case were submitted to the CNS in late December 1942, and can be found in the following DOH files, M-11, NS 8780, NS 8440-60.

41. Milner, "Canadian Escorts and the Mid-Atlantic," appendix 15. The relationship between the British position on the apparent poor showing of the RCN and

the request for destroyers emerges in a letter from an official in the British prime minister's office to an Admiralty colleague. The former, who was engaged in drafting an interim reply to Mackenzie King's request, wrote: "we feel it would be difficult to send an interim reply without the risk of prejudicing the Canadian reply on the tanker escorts or explaining the relation of the two questions." Boyd-Shannon to Chapman, 22 December 1942. PRO, Adm. 1, 12564.

42. The fact that Canadian groups had fallen under the command of RN officers became a bone of contention between the two navies, for Naval Service Headquarters clearly wanted "C" groups operating with RCN commanding officers. See commander-in-chief Western Approaches to NSHQ, 29 March 1943. PAC, RG24, vol. 3995, NSS 1057-1-27.

43. Chalmers, *Max Horton and the Western Approaches*, p. 163.

44. Milner, "Canadian Escorts and the Mid-Atlantic," appendix 15.

45. PRO, Adm. 187, vol. 24, Admiralty *Pink List*, 1 March 1943.

46. This section is based on a study of all the available deck logs of HMC Ships in the "C" groups, PAC, NS 7000-7999, the Admiralty's *Pink Lists*, PRO, Adm. 187, vols. 23-25, and the RCN "Daily States," DOH, NS 1650-DS.

47. Milner, "Canadian Escorts and the Mid-Atlantic," appendix 15.

48. DOH, M-11, H.G. DeWolf, to CNS, 21 December 1942.

49. Tucker, *Naval Service of Canada*, 2:412.

50. Milner, "Canadian Escorts and the Mid-Atlantic," p. 143.

51. J. Rohwer and G. Hümmelchen, *Chronology of the War at Sea 1939-1945* (New York: Arco, 1972), pp. 319-20.

52. DOH, NS 8440-60, Nelles to First Sea Lord, 7 January 1943. Under the terms of the agreement the "C" groups were to remain under the commander-in-chief Western Approaches until they were deemed operationally efficient, or in any event no later than mid-May 1943.

53. Schull, *Far Distant Ships*, p. 122.

54. PRO, Adm. 1, 12062. The director anti-submarine warfare, RN, conceded in his "Battle of the Atlantic Summary" of May 1942: "what was not sufficiently

foreseen was the enormous expansion of our A/S effort that [the] war would demand and what a decrease in killing efficiency this would entail as a result of the inevitable decrease in initial training and the curtailing of A/S practises caused by operational requirements." The British had just come through a period when their own training programmes had been greatly reduced in order to man new construction quickly, and they were obviously dissatisfied with the poor level of competence of hurriedly trained crews—the price of expansion. A further indication of their stretched resources at this time is the recall, without replacement, of the RN anti-submarine warfare liaison officers at St. John's and Halifax in July. See naval historian's notes, DOH, NS 1700-193/96.

CHAPTER ELEVEN: OPERATIONAL INTELLIGENCE AND THE BATTLE OF THE ATLANTIC: THE ROLE OF THE ROYAL NAVY'S SUBMARINE TRACKING ROOM

1. Four young Canadian midshipmen—Palmer, Hatheway, Cann, and Silver—also lost their lives when the British flagship, HMS *Good Hope*, went down.
2. For details of Admiral Hall's activities, see W. James, *The Eyes of the Navy* (London: Methuen, 1955), and Barbara W. Tuchman, *The Zimmerman Telegram* (Toronto: Collier-Macmillan Canada, 1970).
3. The Enigma machine cypher system is described in detail by Douglas and Rohwer in Chapter 12.
4. Ideally, three bearing lines on a target should intersect perfectly to form a neat asterisk, showing the target's location. However, in practice, tiny errors often creep into the calculations with the result that the three lines intersect to form a small triangle, known as a "cocked hat."

5. Naval traffic for a few days was decrypted with some delay in 1940, but changes in the Enigma settings then defeated BP for another twelve months.
6. Details of this period are to be found in Chapters 9 and 10.
7. U-boat losses in all areas and from all causes during the spring of 1943 were as follows:

January-March	40
April-June	73
Total	113

Although 139 new U-boats commissioned during this period (actually increasing the total of operational and non-operational boats from just under to just over four hundred), this was a loss rate that no service in the world could sustain and from which very few other navies could have recovered.

CHAPTER TWELVE: "THE MOST THANKLESS TASK" REVISITED: CONVOYS, ESCORTS, AND RADIO INTELLIGENCE IN THE WESTERN ATLANTIC, 1941-43

1. The authors have not provided specific documentation for this chapter but offer instead a general description of sources. A number of published studies are particularly relevent: Jürgen Rohwer, "The U-boat War Against Allied Supply Lines," in J. Rohwer and H.A. Jacobson, eds., *Decisive Battles of World War II* (London: Andre Deutsch, 1965); J. Rohwer, *Die U-Boote-erfolge der Achsenmächte, 1939-1945 (The U-Boat Successes of the Axis Powers, 1939-1945)* (Munich: J.F. Lehmanns Verlag, 1968); J. Rohwer and G. Hümmelchen, *Chronology of the War at Sea 1939-1945* (New York: Arco Publishing, 1972); J. Rohwer, *The Critical Convoy Battles of March 1943* (London: Ian Allan, 1977); P. Beesley, " 'Special Intelligence' und die Konvoisteverung" (" 'Special Intelligence' and Convoy Control"), *Marine Rundschau* 74 (April 1977): 169-82; W.A.B. Douglas, "Kanadas Marine und Luftwaffe in der Atlantikschlacht" ("Canada's Navy and Air Force in the Battle of the Atlantic"), *Marine Rund-*

schau 77 (March 1980): 151-64. (Another article on this subject will be appearing in English in Sidney Aster, ed., *The Second World War as a National Experience* [Ottawa: DND, 1981]). See also, J. Rohwer, " 'Special Intelligence' und die Geleitzugteverung in Herbst 1941" (" 'Special Intelligence' and Convoy Control in the Autumn of 1941"), *Marine Rundschau* 75 (November 1978): 711-19.

The British and American official histories remain indispensable: S.W. Roskill, *The War at Sea*, 3 vols. (London: HMSO, 1960) and S.E. Morison, *The History of United States Naval Operations in the Second World War*, vol. 1 (Boston: Little, Brown, 1947), vol. 10, (1956). The Canadian official history by Gilbert N. Tucker, *The Naval Service of Canada, Its Official History*, vol. 2, *Activities on Shore during the Second World War* (Ottawa: King's Printer), is important. Joseph Schull, *The Far Distant Ships* (Ottawa: Queen's Printer, 1952) is less useful for operational detail. The official history of British Intelligence, F.H. Hinsley et al., *British Intelligence in the Second World War: Its Influence on Strategy and Operations*, vol. 1 (New York: Cambridge University Press, 1979) is another essential source. Also relevant is W.F. Craven and J.L. Cate, eds., *The Army Air Forces in World War II*, vol. 2 (Chicago: University of Chicago Press, 1949).

Of the enormous literature concerning the Battle of the Atlantic specific use is made of the following: Patrick Beesly, *Very Special Intelligence* (London: Hamish Hamilton Ltd., 1977); Peter Gretton, *Crisis Convoy: The Story of the Atlantic Convoy HX 231* (London: P. Davies, 1974); Erich Gröner, *Die deutschen Kriegsschiffe 1815-1945 (German Warships 1815-1945)* vol. 1 (Munich: J.F. Lehmanns Verlag, 1945); Ronald Lewin, *Ultra Goes to War* (New York: McGraw-Hill, 1978); Philip Lundeberg, "La Réplique des Etats-Unis à la Guerre au Tonnage," *Revue d'histoire de la Deuxième Guerre Mondiale* 18 (1968): 67-96; Donald G. Macintyre, *The Battle of the Atlantic* (London: B.T. Batsford, 1961), *U-Boat Killer* (London: Weidenfeld and Nicolson, 1956); S.W. Roskill, *The Secret Capture* (Lon-

don: Collins, 1959); J.C. Slessor, *The Central Blue* (London: Cassell, 1956); Ronald Seth, *The Fiercest Battle: The Story of North Atlantic Convoy ONS-5, 22nd April-7th May 1943* (London: Hutchinson, 1961); John Waters, Jr., *Bloody Winter* (Princeton, NJ: Van Nostrand, 1967).

Two Master's theses were used: W.G. Lund, "Command Relationships in the North West Atlantic, 1939-1945" (Queen's University, Kingston, Ont., 1972), and M. Milner, "Canadian Escorts and the Mid-Atlantic 1942-1943" (University of New Brunswick, 1979).

Primary sources include the BdU War Diary; (an English translation of the original is available at the Directorate of History at National Defence Headquarters, Ottawa), U-boat torpedo firing records, and U-boat logs. The German originals are at the Bundesarchiv-Militärarchiv, Freiburg, and the Bibliothek für Zeitgeschichte, Stuttgart, which hold a great collection of evaluations from primary sources. We should especially like to acknowledge the help given by Robert Coppock of the Ministry of Defence, Navy, in London, in analysing U-boat operations from U-boat logs, microfilms of which are in the naval historical section naval at MOD, London. British Admiralty papers at the Public Record Office, London, especially the monthly antisubmarine reports (1939-45) and the various reports of proceedings (all in the Admiralty 199 series), were used extensively. Most important among Admiralty papers are the records of naval intelligence (Admiralty 223 series). Used in conjunction with the Enigma decrypts from Bletchley Park now becoming available at the PRO (DEFE series), they provide the basis of our understanding as to how intelligence was used in the Battle of the Atlantic. The Air Ministry papers also contain a great deal of material that is useful. The authors are in the debt of Mary Paine and Fred Lambert for their research assistance at the PRO.

The Operational Archives of the United States Navy in Washington provided us freely with its great collection of convoy papers especially its signal folders and the daily situation maps and other relevant sources. For this we are greatly indebted to Dean Allard and Bernard Cavalcante. William Cunliffe gave us access to the just-released "Ultra" Papers in the National Archives, especially the United States Navy's World War II OP-20-G Final Report Series on the Battle of the Atlantic.

In Canada, the Directorate of History at National Defence Headquarters and the PAC, both in Ottawa, contain large amounts of relatively untapped material about Canadian naval and air operations during the Second World War. The authors have relied particularly on ships' logs and reports of proceedings, RCAF squadron diaries and operations record books, other RCN and RCAF papers in RG24, Department of National Defence records. Private correspondence and interviews with C.L. Annis, L.C. Audette, Peter Gretton, F. Grubb, D. Hanington, Vernon Heakes, J.C. Hibbard, G.O. Johnson, L.W. Murray, D. Piers, Brian B. Schofield, Patrick Beesly, John M. Waters, Jr., Kenneth Knowles, John McDiarmid, Eric Brand, and M. Thornton were also of direct use. We would especially like to thank William Constable who prepared the convoy battle maps which accompany this chapter.

CHAPTER THIRTEEN: THE LOWER DECK AND THE MAINGUY REPORT OF 1949

1. *Report on Certain "Incidents" Which Occurred on Board HMC Ships* Athabaskan, Crescent, *and* Magnificent *and on Other Matters Concerning the Royal* *Canadian Navy* (Ottawa: Department of National Defence, 1949). All quotations used in the chapter are from this report.

CHAPTER FIFTEEN: CANADIAN NAVAL AVIATION, 1915-69

1. The establishment of the RCNAS was confirmed by order-in-council PC 2154 on 5 September 1918. The detailed scale of pay, allowances and pensions for the RCNAS was laid down, subsequently, by order-in-council PC 2707 on 6 November 1916. See, J.D. Kealy and E.C. Russell, *A history of Canadian Naval Aviation 1918-1962* (Ottawa: Naval Historical Section, Canadian Forces Headquarters, Department of National Defence, 1965), p. 5ff.

2. The RCNAS was disbanded in early December. See PC 3009, 5 Dec. 1918, quoted in Gilbert N. Tucker, *The Naval Service of Canada: Its Official History*, vol. 1, *Origins and Early Years* (Ottawa: King's Printer, 1952), pp. 258, 258n.

3. Ballantyne to Desbarats, 5 Dec. 1918, NS 63-9-1, Directorate of History, (DOH), NDHQ, DHist 77/58.

4. MacDonald, memorandum to Lay, 29 April 1943, in "Report on the formation of a Royal Canadian Naval Air Service with covering submission by A/Captain H.N. Lay, RCN, 27 August 1943," Copy no. 7, NS 1700-913, vol. 1, Public

Archives Record Centre (PARC).

5. Ibid.

6. The terms of reference for DNAD were approved at this time, Stead having previously held the appointment of Staff Officer (Air) since Sept. 1943. See Minutes 235-12, 24 April 1944, Naval Staff minutes, DOH, NDHQ.

7. Cabinet War Committee Minutes, 13 Sept. 1944, quoted in Tucker, *Naval Service of Canada*, 2:100, 100n.

8. The total number of pilots transferred from the RCAF to the Royal Naval Volunteer Reserve (Air) in 1945 was 550. Naval Member Canadian Joint Staff (London) (Commodore P.D. Taylor, RCN) to Naval Secretary [Captain (S.) S.A. Clemens, RCN], 12 June 1958, DOH, NDHQ, DHist, 1700-219.

9. Cabinet Minutes, 19 Dec. 1945, quoted in Abbott memorandum to Cabinet, 16 Feb. 1946, NS 8020-500 RRSM, vol. 1, PARC.

10. "Agreement governing the relationship between the Royal Canadian Air Force and the Royal Canadian Navy and the use of the Royal Canadian Air Force

facilities by the Royal Canadian Navy," 9 March 1946, NS 1550-12, vol. 1, PARC.

11. Conversation between the author and chief of the Naval Staff, Vice-Admiral H.E. Reid.

12. Minutes of the 46th Cabinet Defence Committee meeting, 14 Sept. 1948, NS 1700-223/224, vol. 2, PARC.

13. Minutes of the 85th Cabinet Defence Committee meeting, 23 April 1952, quoted in Minister of National Defence [Brooke Claxton]memorandum to Cabinet Defence Committee, 11 June 1952, NS 8000-CVL 22, vol. 1, PARC.

14. DNPO (Captain A.H.G. Storrs, RCN), memorandum to VCNS [Rear-Admiral H.G. DeWolf, RCN] 22 Oct. 1951, NS 1650-40, vol. 3, PARC; Naval Secretary [Commander (S) H.A. McCandless,

RCN] to CANFLAGLANT [Rear-Admiral E.S. Bidwell, RCN], 7 April 1952, NS 1650-26, vol. 6, PARC.

15. Minutes of the 92nd Cabinet Defence Committee meeting, 17 March 1952, NS 1650-40, vol. 5, PARC.

16. SO (Fuel) [Staff Officer (Fuel), Lieutenant D.W.J. Overend, RCNVR (SB)], memorandum to DOD [Director of Operations Division, A/Captain H.N. Lay, RCN], 23 Jan. 1943, NS 1700-913, vol. 1, PARC.

17. Conversation between author and Rear-Admiral A.H.G. Storrs, RCN (Ret'd.), Oct. 1979.

18. Conversation between author and Lieutenant-Commander R. Heath, RCN (Ret'd.), Oct. 1979.

CHAPTER SEVENTEEN: THE IMPACT OF PUBLIC POLICY ON A NAVAL RESERVE DIVISION

1. Dominion of Canada, *Official Report of Debates, House of Commons* (hereinafter cited as *Hansard*), the official records of the Directorate of History (DOH) at National Defence Headquarters, Ottawa, and the records of the various public archives are obvious sources of material on the naval reserve. Moreover, most reserve units have maintained "scrap books" (usually unprofessionally collated compendia of newspaper clippings, photographs, and memorabilia) which are important sources of historical data. Oral history remains a largely untapped source. Some units have prepared sketches of their principal events. See, for example, J.M. Thornton, *HMCS Discovery and Deadman's Island: A Brief History* (Vancouver: n.p., n.d.); E. Corbet, *Calgary's Stone Frigate: HMCS Tecumseh, 1923-1973* (Calgary: Century Calgary Publications, 1975); Fraser M. McKee, *Volunteers for Sea Service: A Brief History of the Royal Canadian Naval Volunteer Reserve, its Predecessors and Successors* (Toronto: Houston's Standard Publications, 1973); and Hector Swain, *Cabot: History of the Naval Reserves in Newfoundland* (St. John's: n.p., 1975).

2. James B. Lamb, *The Corvette Navy: True Stories from Canada's Atlantic War* (Toronto: Macmillan, 1979), p. 174.

3. *Hansard*, 1945, vol. 2, p. 1500. For background details see James Eayrs, *In Defence of Canada: From the Great War to the Depression* (Toronto: University of Toronto Press, 1964); *In Defence of Canada: Appeasement and Rearmament* (Toronto: University of Toronto Press, 1965); *In Defence of Canada: Peacemaking and Deterrence* (Toronto: University of Toronto Press, 1972).

4. *Hansard*, 1952, vol. 1, p. 1092. Later he argued: "Our naval forces have been given no offensive role" (p. 1093).

5. *Hansard*, 1952, vol. 2, p. 1230.

6. *Hansard*, 1960, vol. 7, p. 1569.

7. *Hansard*, 1945, vol. 2, pp. 1500, 1501, 1507, 1527 and 1536.

8. *Hansard*, 1945, vol. 2, p. 1509.

9. Ibid.

10. I am indebted to Leading Wren Bonnie Pearse for her archival work in updating the "Malahat Scrap-Book" to cover the period under review. References to the local press are from her sources.

11. *Hansard*, 1951, vol. 5, p. 4778. Brooke Claxton, minister of National Defence, reported this figure during a debate on the Defence Estimates on 27 June 1951.

12. *Hansard*, 1951, vol. 1, p. 200.

13. *Hansard*, 1951, vol. 5, p. 4775. Claxton

reported: "The present strength of the Navy as of June 25, 1951 . . . is officers 1,593, and men, 10,115, for a total of 11,708."

14. *Hansard*, 1951, vol. 5, p. 214.
15. *Hansard*, 1951, vol. 5, p. 4778.
16. *Hansard*, Session 1957-1958, vol. 2, p. 1921. W.M. Johnson, MP for Kindersley, for example, argued that in the light of sophisticated nuclear weaponry and the swiftness of any future war, "a second look should be given to the role of the militia in Canada. . . . They can throw away all [their] old British 303 Enfields and sten guns because they will never have an opportunity to use them. . . . A more useful role connected with civil defence makes more sense. They should be trained to fight fires and to deal with similar local emergencies."
17. *Colonist*, 5 March 1953.
18. *Colonist*, 5 February 1954. The *Colonist* for 15 June 1956 quoted the actual renovation costs as $66,000.
19. *Hansard*, 1957, vol. 2, p. 1902. The cost of the armed forces for the fiscal year 1956-57 was navy ($326,699,000), army ($459,452,000), and air force ($863,100,000).
20. *Colonist*, 21 January 1958.
21. *Hansard*, Session 1957-58, vol. 3, p. 7574.
22. *Hansard*, 1963, vol. 6, p. 5496.
23. *Hansard*, 1963, vol. 6, p. 5499.
24. *Hansard*, 1963, vol. 6, p. 5521.
25. *Hansard*, 1963, vol. 6, p. 5522.

26. It actually reached $1.8 billion. For commentary, see John Saywell, ed., *Canadian Annual Review for 1970* (Toronto: University of Toronto Press, 1971), p. 359. Canada's tendency to respond to short-term needs is reflected in *Canadian News Facts: The Indexed Digest of Canadian Current Events* (Toronto: n.p., 1970), vol. 4, no. 18, p. 531: "Defence Minister Donald S. Macdonald said October 22 [1970] his department is reconsidering plans to cut Canada's armed forces to a strength of 82,000 by 1973. He also held out the possibility that the current Quebec crisis [FLQ, War Measures Act] will lead to an unfreezing of the national defence budget, pegged at its current level of 1.8 billion until the 1973-1974 fiscal year." By 1974 it had reached $2.42 billion (2.2 per cent of the gross national product).
27. *Hansard*, 1963, vol. 6, p. 5571. Speech by H.W. Herridge, MP for Kootenay West.
28. During discussion of this point at the "Conference on the History of the Royal Canadian Navy: 1910-1965," Rear-Admiral M.G. Stirling, RCN (Ret'd.), explained that while many politicians wanted to close *Malahat*, senior naval officers quietly urged the reservists to "hang on."
29. *Colonist*, 14 April 1965.
30. *Colonist*, 19 March 1965.
31. *Action for Reserves*, Canada, Commons, issue no. 49, 15 Dec. 1981.

CHAPTER EIGHTEEN: AN ENGINEER'S OUTLINE OF RCN HISTORY: PART II

1. "B.J.G.," "The Birthplace of a Ship," *The Crowsnest* 4 (August 1952) 1:30.
2. R. Judge, "The RCN Committee on Corrosion and Fouling," *Naval Technical Review*, 3, no. 1 (1960): 8-12.
3. I.G. Wilkie, "Design and Functions of a Naval Engineering Plant" (Paper presented at the Annual Convention of the Institute of Power Engineers, Montreal, 8 November 1955).
4. E.B. Good, "Canadian Y. 100." *Journal of Naval Engineering* 9 (1956): 164-77.
5. D.K. Nicholson, "Experience with Hardened and Ground Gearing in the Royal Canadian Navy" (Paper presented at the Institute of Marine Engineering,

London, 11 April 1961).
6. "First of the Sub-Killers," *Canadian Shipping and Marine Engineering News*, 27, no. 2 (1955): 28.
7. D.J.I. Garstin, "Naval Engineering Design Investigation Team (Royal Canadian Navy)," *Journal of Naval Engineering* 10 (1957): 314.
8. R.A. Douglas, "Helicopter/Ship Interface," *Journal of Naval Engineering* 24, (1978): 212.
9. B.R. Spencer, "Some Recent Developments in the Marine Propulsion of Naval Vessels" (Paper presented at the Annual Meeting of the Canadian Shipbuilding and Ship Repair Association Technical Section, Montreal, 4 March

1958).

10. A.A. Purvis, "The General Purpose Frigate," *Naval Technical Review*, 1, no. 3 (1962): 20-30.

11. C.R. Nixon, "Shipboard Digital Data Processing," *Naval Technical Review*, 2, no. 2 (1963): 24-27.

12. "All Weather 200-ton Hydrofoil Craft and Their Application in ASW (Anti-Submarine Warfare)," NRE Report, September 1959.

13. M.C. Eames and E.A. Jones, "HMCS *Bras d'Or*—An Open Ocean Hydrofoil Ship," *Transactions of the Royal Institute of Naval Architects* 113: 111; and M.C. Eames and T.G. Drummond, "HMCS *Bras d'Or*—Sea Trials and Future Prospects" (Paper presented at a meeting of the Royal Institute of Naval Architects, London, 13 April 1972).

14. H.A. Shenker, R.K. Odell, C.D. Roushorn, and A.C. Husband, "Operational Support Ship for the Royal Canadian Navy" (Paper presented at a meeting of the Eastern Canadian Section of the Society of Naval Architects and Marine Engineers, 1966).

15. R.H. Dillon, "DDH 280: Why the Navy Chose Gas Turbines," *Canadian Shipping and Marine Engineering News* 44, no. 6 (1973): 20.

16. D.H. Benn, "The Propulsion Plant for the DDH 280," *Canadian Shipping and Marine Engineering News* 40, no. 6 (1969): 56.

17. K.P. Farrell, R.E. MacLaren, C.L. Bennett, J.D.S. Reilley, K.L. Redman and A.E. Partridge, "The DDH 280 Class Design," *Marine Technology* 9, no. 1 (1972): 1-41.

18. E.P. Tisdall, B.R. Spencer, A.H.G. Storrs, H.G. Burchell, J. Plommer and F.D. Elcock, *Report of the Ad Hoc Committee on RCN Personnel Structure*, Ottawa, National Defence Headquarters, 9 November 1959.

CHAPTER NINETEEN: THE ROYAL CANADIAN NAVY AND THE UNIFICATION CRISIS

1. National Defence Act (1922), in D.J. Goodspeed, *The Armed Forces of Canada 1867-1967* (Ottawa: Queen's Printer, 1967), p. 91.

2. Gilbert N. Tucker, *The Naval Service of Canada*, vol. 1, *Origins and Early Years* (Ottawa: King's Printer, 1952), pp. 340-41.

3. *White Paper on Defence* (Ottawa: Queen's Printer, March 1964), p. 18.

4. Ibid., p. 17.

5. Ibid.

6. *The Crowsnest* 16 (March-April 1964): 3.

7. Toronto *Daily Star*, 23 July 1966, p. 1.

8. Goodspeed, *Armed Forces of Canada*, p. 268.

9. *The Crowsnest* 17 (January 1965): 5.

10. Halifax *Chronicle-Herald*, 20 July 1966.

11. Personal communication, Captain Christopher Pratt, RCN (Ret'd.), to the author, January 1980.

NOTES ON CONTRIBUTORS

Commander (R) Louis de la Chesnaye Audette, OC, QC, was born in Ottawa in 1907. He practiced law in Montreal 1931-39, before serving in the RCN from 1939 to 1945. He was mentioned in despatches and retired from the Naval Service as a commander, Royal Canadian Naval Reserve. After the war he served as first secretary, Department of External Affairs, 1945-47; a director, Export Development Corporation, 1946-71; member 1947-53 and chairman 1954-59, Canadian Maritime Commission; member, Northwest Territories Council, 1947-1959; a director 1948-59 and president 1954-59, Park Steamship Co. Ltd; Canadian delegate, Planning Board for Ocean Shipping (NATO), 1950-59; member, Court Martial Appeal Board, 1951-59; a director, Crown Asssets Disposal Corporation, 1953-60; chairman, Preparatory Committee, Intergovernmental Maritime Consultative Organization (UN), 1954-59 and president of its First Assembly (London 1959); chairman, The Tariff Board, 1959-72; and administrator, Maritime Pollution Claims Fund, 1973-78.

Lieutenant-Commander Patrick Beesly was born in 1913 and educated at Oundle School and Trinity College, Cambridge, where he read history and captained First Trinity Boat Club. In June 1939 he joined the Royal Naval Volunteer Reserve as a sub-lieutenant (Special Branch). He served throughout World War II in the Naval Intelligence Division, firstly in its French Section but from mid-1940 onwards in its Operational Intelligence Centre.

Until the end of 1941 he was assistant to Paymaster-Commander (later Vice-Admiral) Sir Norman "Ned" Denning and specialized on armed merchant raiders. He was then transferred to the Submarine Tracking Room as deputy to its head, Commander (later Captain) Rodger Winn RNVR (Sp), occupying this position with the rank of Lieutenant-Commander until the end of the war when he was appointed staff officer (Intelligence) to the commander-in-chief, Germany. Demobilized in December 1945 he joined the well known firm of Henry Hope & Sons Ltd., Metal Window Manufacturers, finally retiring as managing director in 1974. Since then he has devoted himself to writing on naval intelligence matters. His publications include: *Very Special Intelligence, The Story of the Admiralty's Operational Intelligence Centre, 1939-1945*, (1977), *Very Special Admiral, The Life of Admiral J.H. Godfrey, CB*, (1980), and articles for *The Naval Review, Navy International, The Royal United Services Journal*, the *Marine Rundschau* and the USN Institute's *Proceedings*. He is currently writing an account of the famous Room 40 OB (the Royal Navy's WWI cryptographic bureau) and the renowned Director of Naval Intelligence, Admiral Sir Reginald Hall.

James A. Boutilier is an historian who has specialized in naval history and British colonial policy with particular reference to the Pacific Islands. He was born in Halifax, Nova Scotia, in 1939 and attended Dalhousie University (BA: 1960), McMaster University (MA: 1962), and the University of London (PhD: 1969). He joined the University Naval Training Divisions in 1956 and was commissioned as a sub-lieutenant in the Royal Canadian Naval Reserve (RCNR) in 1959. Two years later he was promoted to the rank of lieutenant while serving as a navigating instructor in the UNTD programme. His RCNR time included service afloat in HMC Ships *Swansea, Lauzon, Beacon Hill*, and *Athabaskan* and ashore in HMC Shore Establishments *Stadacona, Naden, Cornwallis, Star*, and *Scotian*. He moved to London, England, in 1962 to continue his graduate work and was attached to the Royal Naval Reserve (RNR) London Division, HMS *President*. In 1964 he transferred to the RNR and served in minesweepers in the Baltic, North Sea, and Channel areas. In 1969 he was appointed as the first history lecturer on the staff of the University of the South Pacific in Suva, Fiji. In 1971 he took up his current appointment in the history department at Royal Roads Military College, Victoria, British Columbia, where he teaches twentieth century naval history. He also holds an adjunct professorship in Pacific history at the Centre for Pacific and Oriental Studies, University of Victoria. He is the author of over two dozen articles and the editor of a major volume on missionary activity in the Pacific Islands, *Mission, Church and Sect in Oceania*.

Captain John H.G. Bovey, DSC, CD, US Bronze Star with Combat "V," spent the major part of World War II at sea in HMC and HM ships, including service as group signals officer while in HMS *Caldwell* and in command of HMCS *Wallaceburg* as senior officer W7 Group. In the postwar period he served in HMS *Argonaut* and in command of HMC destroyers *Qu'Appelle*, *Crusader*, *Saguenay*, and *Athabaskan*. While in *Athabaskan* he was also commander, Third Canadian Escort Squadron. His appointments ashore included: director Service Conditions and Welfare at Naval Service Headquarters; deputy director and acting director of Naval Intelligence; Naval Commander, Newfoundland; and Naval Attaché, Moscow and Helsinki. After retiring he was appointed to HMCS *Malahat* as supernumerary captain for duties as a convoy commodore from 1967 to 1977. Pursuing a subsequent career in real estate with Pemberton, Holmes Ltd., he obtained his licence as an agent and became president of Plyad Investment Corporation as well as a director of several other companies. In addition, he has served on many service organization boards. He was provincial president of the SPCA, director of economic development, Greater Victoria Chamber of Commerce, and chairman of Conservative and Social Credit Constituency Associations.

Rear-Admiral Nigel David Brodeur, CD, was born in 1932 of a naval family. He entered Royal Roads Military College in Victoria, British Columbia, in 1950 and subseqently served in an aircraft carrier, a cruiser, and several destroyers and frigates. He commanded the destroyer HMCS *Terra Nova*, the Canadian Forces Maritime Warfare School, and the Fifth Canadian Destroyer Squadron and attended the Canadian Forces Staff College as well as the National Defence College. He was a contributor to *Soviet Naval Policy: Objectives and Constraints* (1975). Promoted to rear-admiral in 1980 he is currently chief of Maritime Doctrine and Operations in National Defence Headquarters.

Rear-Admiral Patrick Willet Brock, CB, DSO, began his naval career with cadet training in the Royal Naval College of Canada in Halifax, Kingston, and Esquimalt in 1917-20. He transferred to the Royal Navy as a midshipman in 1921. Specializing in torpedo warfare, he served mainly in cruisers and destroyers. His service in World War II was divided between the Admiralty and the Indian Ocean, Mediterranean, and Normandy in HMS *Mauritius*. Command of HMS *Kenya* in the Korean War brought him a DSO, the US Bronze Star, and appointment as director of Operations Division. He became flag officer Middle East in 1954 and served in the Canal Zone and Cyprus. Since retirement in 1957 he has been a trustee of the National Maritime Museum (1960-74), a vice-president of the Society for

Nautical Research, chairman of *The Naval Review*, and has done research for the Maritime Museum of British Columbia. He was co-author of *Steam and Sail* (1973) on ships of the transition period.

Captain A. Keith Cameron, CD, was born in Prince Edward Island in 1925. He entered the Royal Canadian Naval College, *Royal Roads*, in 1942. After graduation, he served in the battleship HMS *Duke of York* before joining the cruiser HMCS *Ontario* in Belfast for her World War II deployment in the Pacific theatre. A career officer, Captain Cameron held peacetime appointments on both coasts and in National Defence Headquarters, Ottawa. From 1963 to 1966 he served as secretary to the flag officer Atlantic Coast under Rear-Admirals K.L. Dyer, J.V. Brock, and W.M. Landymore, respectively. He resigned from the Canadian Armed Forces in 1974, while chief of Staff (Logistics and Administration) to the maritime commander, Pacific. In 1975, Captain Cameron became curator, Maritime Museum of British Columbia, Victoria, a position he still holds. His curatorial exhibitions include "The Navy on the British Columbia Coast (1778-1968)." He is also vice-president of the British Columbia Museums Association and a director of the RCN Benevolent Fund.

Commander William A.B. Douglas, the official historian for the Canadian Armed Forces, served in the RCN from 1950 to 1973. He was born in Southern Rhodesia (Zimbabwe) in 1929 and divided his formative years between England and Canada. After receiving his undergraduate training in history at the University of Toronto he transferred from the University Naval Training Division to the permanent force and eventually specialized as a navigating officer. He was naval staff officer at the Royal Military College, Kingston, Ontario, from 1964 to 1967 before joining the Directorate of History at National Defence Headquarters. He received his MA from Dalhousie University and his PhD from Queen's University before retiring to take up the position of director at the Directorate of History. Author of a wide range of articles in naval, aviation and Canadian service history, he has written in collaboration with Brereton Greenhous *Out of the Shadows: Canada in the Second World War* (1977), and is now preparing volume II of the official history of the Royal Canadian Air Force. His association with Jürgen Rohwer in this book had its origins in two international conferences in 1978, one in Ottawa and one on radio intelligence during World War II which Dr. Rohwer hosted in Bonn-Bad-Godesburg and Stuttgart.

Barry Morton Gough, FR Hist S, was born in 1938 in Victoria, British Columbia, and attended the University of British Columbia (BEd: 1962), the University of Montana (MA: 1966), and Kings College, University of

London (PhD: 1969). His life-long interest in the sea and those who use the sea has led him to write many articles, which have been published in historical journals, and a number of books on naval and maritime subjects, including *The Royal Navy and the Northwest Coast of North America, 1810-1914: A Study of British Maritime Ascendancy* and its companion volume, *Distant Dominion: Britain and the Northwest Coast of North America, 1579-1809*, both published by the University of British Columbia Press. The latter volume won the 1980 John Lyman Award for the best book in Canadian Maritime History, presented by the North American Society for Oceanic History. His work in progress includes a study of British "gunboat diplomacy" directed towards the native Indians of British Columbia. He now teaches at Wilfrid Laurier University, where he is a professor of history.

Captain (NR) Michael Hadley, CD, PhD, entered the RCNR in 1954 through the University Naval Training Division training sheme. He served first in the cruiser HMCS *Quebec* (ex-HMS *Uganda*), then in frigates and Algerine-class minesweepers. When commissioned in 1957 he was posted to the West Coast Minesweeping Squadron. He has since held various posts in Naval Reserve Divisions in Vancouver, Winnipeg, and Victoria; served in the Great Lakes Training Centre in Hamilton; and subsequently held command of HMC Ships *Porte Quebec*, *Porte de la Reine*, and *Porte Dauphine*. In 1974 he served briefly as liaison officer aboard the German training ship *Deutschland* during her visit to the West Coast. From 1974-78 he was commanding officer of Victoria's reserve division HMCS *Malahat*, where he was instrumental in developing the combined RCNR-USNR annual live convoy exercise "Spring Thaw." In civilian life he teaches in the Department of Germanic Studies, University of Victoria, and has published books, articles, and reviews on German literature and thought. He is president of the Maritime Defense Association of Canada.

Barry Hunt was educated at the Royal Military College, Kingston, Ontario, the University of Western Ontario, and Queen's Univeristy. From 1960 to 1967 he served with the Royal Canadian Regiment. Since 1967, he has been a member of the Royal Military College faculty lecturing in Commonwealth and naval history. In 1974-75, he was visiting professor of Strategic Studies at the University of Western Ontario, and in 1980-81 visiting professor at the US Navy Postgraduate School, Monterey, California. In addition to publishing several articles on British naval history and co-editing *War Aims and Strategic Policy in the Great War* (1977), Dr. Hunt is the author of the biography *Sailor-Scholar: Admiral Sir Herbert Richmond, 1871-1946* (1981).

Captain (N) James Henry Woodman Knox, CD, PEng, entered the RCN as a midshipman (E[ngineering]) in 1948. Until taking up his current appointment as Naval Advisor, Canadian Defence Liaison Staff, London, England, in 1980, Captain(N) Knox had served continuously in naval engineering appointments in the RCN and Canadian Forces. These appointments included: command of the Ship Repair Unit (Pacific); director of Marine and Electrical Engineering in National Defence Headquarters, Ottawa; and project engineer, and subsequently, project manager of the FHE 400 hydrofoil programme. Sea appointments included HM Ships *Victorious* and *Liverpool*, HMC Ships *Quebec, Huron,* and *Bonaventure,* and the Third Canadian Escort Squadron. From 1958 to 1962, Captain(N) Knox undertook graduate studies and field work in nuclear engineering at Queen's University, Atomic Energy of Canada Ltd., Chalk River, Naval Service Headquarters, Ottawa, and the Yarrows-Admiralty Research Department, Glasgow. Captain(N) Knox was educated at Upper Canada College; the Royal Canadian Naval College, *Royal Roads*; the RN Engineering College, Plymouth; the RN College, Greenwich; Queen's University; and the Royal College of Defence Studies, London.

Commander John McWhannell Leeming, CD, was born and educated in Victoria, British Columbia. He was a member of the Shanghai Municipal Police from 1933 to 1940. He served from 1941 to 1946 in the RCNVR and from 1946 to 1961 in the RCN, in Bangor and Algerine-class minesweepers, a frigate, HMCS *Strathadam,* a cruiser, HMCS *Ontario,* and an arctic patrol vessel, HMCS *Labrador.* He was mentioned in despatches following a Hedgehog explosion aboard HMCS *Strathadam* in April 1945. His last sea appointment, from 1954 to 1955, was on board HMCS *Labrador* during the first year-and-a-half of her commission with the RCN. From 1961 to 1964, he assumed the position of secretary-manager of the Victoria Automobile Club and the Victoria Branch of the British Columbia Automobile Association. Commencing in 1965, he worked at the Canadian Armed Forces Rocky Point Ammunition Depot, retiring as administrator in 1973. He held a part-time position from 1973 to 1976 at the Legislative Buildings in Victoria, on the staff of the Sergeant of Arms before taking up full retirement in 1976.

Rear-Admiral Richard Leir, CD, was born and educated in British Columbia. He joined the RCN in 1940. A survivor of the sinking of the battleship HMS *Prince of Wales* and, four months later, the cruiser HMS *Exeter,* he was listed as "lost in action" for three years while a Japanese prisoner-of-war. During his thirty-five years in the RCN he served in the Korean War, commanded the Canadian destroyers *Skeena* and *Crusader,* the Prestonian-class frigate *Sussexvale*, and the First Canadian Escort Squadron. He flew his flag as commander of the Atlantic Fleet, flag officer Pacific Command, and chief of Maritime Operations in Ottawa. An amateur carpenter and stonemason he now renovates old houses.

Commander Wilfred Lund, CD, was born in Victoria, British Columbia. He joined the RCN through HMCS *Venture* from University School in 1959. He entered the submarine service in 1965 and after basic training in the United States Navy served in various submarines on both coasts and in the United Kingdom. He passed the Royal Navy's Commanding Officers Qualifying Course, "The Perisher," in 1976 and subsequently attended the Senior NATO Tactical Course at HMS *Dryad*. He commanded HMCS *Onondaga* from 1976 to 1978 and then served on the staffs of CANCOM-SUBRON ONE and COMSUBLANT. He was a member of the Class of 1980 of the Naval Command College at the United States Naval War College and currently is a member of the directing staff at the Canadian Forces Command and Staff College. Commander Lund holds degrees from the University of Victoria and Queen's University at Kingston. He has contributed to various naval journals and presented a paper to the annual meeting of the Canadian Historical Association.

Commander(R) Fraser Murray McKee, CD, was born and educated in Toronto. He joined the RCNVR in early 1943 as a seaman and was commissioned a year later. He served in armed yachts, the Algerine-class minesweeper, HMCS *Wallaceburg*, and the frigate, HMCS *Royalmount*, and remained on active service until 1946. After the war he took a degree in forestry, and now works for a directory publishing company. He remained in the Naval Reserve after the war, in Montreal and Toronto, becoming an anti-submarine specialist. He is still involved in Naval Control of Merchant Shipping operations. He has published a book on the history of the Naval Reserves, *Volunteers for Sea Service* (1973), and has contributed articles on naval subjects and book reviews to several magazines. He is the editor of the Naval Officers' Associations' newsletter *Starshell*, is a vice-president of the Navy League of Canada, and lives in Toronto.

Joseph Marc Milner is a native of the maritimes with an abiding interest in the sea. He received his MA with Distinction from the University of New Brunswick in 1979. His thesis, "Canadian Escorts and the Mid-Atlantic, 1942-43," dealt with the problems faced by RCN escort groups operating in the infamous Air Gap during the crisis of the Battle of the Atlantic. He is presently completing his doctoral research in this field at the University of New Brunswick. He is married, with two children.

Rear-Admiral Hugh Francis Pullen, OBE, CD, joined the Royal Naval College of Canada in 1920. When the college was closed in 1922 he spent two years as a cadet with the Canadian Pacific Steamships Ltd., joining the RCN as a cadet in 1924. He served in the North Atlantic and Pacific during World War II. His last three appointments were as chief of Naval Personnel and a member of the Naval Board (1953-1955); flag officer Pacific Coast and maritime commander Pacific (1955-1957); and flag officer Atlantic Coast, maritime commander Atlantic, and commander Atlantic Sub-Area (NATO) (1957-60). He was the deputy commissioner for the Atlantic Provinces at Expo '67. As a member of the Society for Nautical Research and the Navy Records Society, he has a keen interest in naval and nautical history. His publications include: *Atlantic Schooner* (1967), *The Shannon and the Chesapeake* (1970), *The Pullen Expedition* (1979), and *The Sea Road to Halifax* (1980), as well as articles in the *Canadian Geographical Journal* and the *Nova Scotia Historical Quarterly*.

Jürgen Rohwer was born in 1924. He joined the German navy in 1942, serving as an officer successively on a destroyer, a blockade runner, and a minesweeper. After the war he studied history and geography at the University of Hamburg. After completion of his university career in 1954 he was active in defence studies, and in 1959 he was appointed director of the Library of Contemporary History at Stuttgart, becoming an associate lecturer at Stuttgart University in 1971. He holds important positions in several German organizations for the study of defence and weapons, has since 1958 been editor of the influential German naval magazine *Marine Rundschau* and is recognised throughout the world as one of Western Europe's outstanding naval historians. His many studies of naval history published in German include: *Seemacht heute* (1957), *Entscheidungsschlachten des Zweiten Weltkriegs* (1960), *U-Boote, eine Chronik in Bildern* (1962), *66 Tage unter Wasser, Atom-U-Schiffe und Raketen* (1965), *Die U-Boot-Erfolge der Achsenmächte, 1939-1945* (1967), *Chronik des Seekrieges 1939-1945* (1968), *Seemacht: Von der Antike bis zur Gegenwart* (1974). The penultimate of these books has been published in the English language in two volumes under the title *Chronology of the War at Sea 1939-1945*. In addition, he published *The Critical Convoy Battles of March 1943* (1977) in English. Dr. Rohwer has also contributed to many international magazines and collected works on contemporary history, naval history, World War II, and librarianship.

Lieutenant-Commander Stuart Soward, CD, served in the Royal Canadian Air Force, the Royal Naval Volunteer Reserve, and the RCN as a pilot for twenty-six years. One of the first Canadian pilots to join the Canadian naval aviation branch, he was a member of 825 Squadron aboard HMCS

Warrior in 1946. He was an active aviator in several operational squadrons serving extensively aboard the aircraft carriers, HMCS *Magnificent* and HMCS *Bonaventure*. In 1955 he was commended by the chief of the Naval Staff for the invention of an aircraft carrier night landing aid. He assumed command of a naval aircraft squadron in 1961. He was technical advisor on the research and preparation of the official *History of Canadian Naval Aviation* (1965). He retired from the Canadian Armed Forces in 1970 and is currently a member of the RN Fleet Air Arm Officers Association and the Naval Officers' Associations of Canada.